Mechanisms of Cell-Mediated Immunity

BASIC AND CLINICAL IMMUNOLOGY

SERIES EDITORS: Stanley Cohen, State University of New York at Buffalo. Robert T. McCluskey, The Children's Hospital Medical Center, Harvard Medical School

Mechanisms of Cell-Mediated Immunity

ROBERT T. McCLUSKEY AND STANLEY COHEN, *Editors*

Mechanisms of
Cell-Mediated Immunity

EDITED BY

ROBERT T. McCLUSKEY

The Children's Hospital Medical Center
Harvard Medical School

STANLEY COHEN

State University of New York at Buffalo

A WILEY BIOMEDICAL-HEALTH PUBLICATION

JOHN WILEY & SONS, New York ● **London** ● **Sydney** ● **Toronto**

Library of Congress Cataloging in Publication Data

McCluskey, Robert T.
   Mechanisms of cell-mediated immunity.

   (Basic and clinical immunology) (A Wiley biomedical-health publication)
   Includes bibliographical references.
   1.   Cellular immunity.   I.   Cohen, Stanley,
1937-   joint author.   II.   Title.   [DNLM: 1. Immunity, Cellular.   QW541 M486   1974]
QR185.5.M3   574.2'9   73-22188
ISBN 0-471-58168-2

Printed in the United States of America

10 9 8 7 6 5 4 3 2 1

Preface

Although delayed hypersensitivity was recognized as a distinctive form of allergic reaction early in the century, little progress was made in unraveling the responsible mechanisms until the classical studies of Landsteiner and Chase, who demonstrated in 1942 that tuberculin reactivity could be transferred to normal recipients with peritoneal cells from sensitized donors, but not with antibody-containing serum. These experiments clearly indicated that the reactivity was cell mediated; yet for many years thereafter, the possibility that certain antibodies with unusual properties (such as high affinity) were responsible remained alive. Probably this problem could not have been solved as long as the delayed reaction could be defined only in terms of a characteristic type of inflammatory reaction in the skin (or with even less precision in certain autoimmune lesions or allograft reactions). Early reports of *in vitro* systems of tuberculin sensitivity by Rich remained controversial. However, beginning with the experiments of George and Vaughan, which were soon extended by David, Bloom, and their respective collaborators, *in vitro* correlates of delayed hypersensitivity became firmly established. This opened the way for the discovery during the past decade of a series of lymphocyte-derived mediator substances that have been defined collectively as "lymphokines." The *in vitro* properties of some of the lymphokines suggested that they were involved in the mechanisms which lead to the accumulation of mononuclear cells in delayed hypersensitivity reactions. At about the same time, methods for tracing cell populations by autoradiography in transfer experiments became available, and this resulted in an increased understanding of the nature of the infiltrating mononuclear cells. In particular, it was shown that the vast majority are not specifically sensitized cells. In addition, it was found by a number of investigators in several laboratories that the small percentage of cells that were specifically

v

sensitized did not specifically or preferentially accumulate at the reaction site. Rather, the reaction seemed to be triggered by sensitized cells which had randomly arrived at the site. These two lines of investigation, one relating to *in vitro* properties of lymphocyte products and the other relating to the cellular populations involved in delayed hypersensitivity reactions, provided much of the impetus for the modern work in this field. The delayed hypersensitivity reaction was shown to be only one of a general class of immune responses, now defined as cell-mediated immunity. In the past decade, there has been an explosion of knowledge relating to cell-mediated immunity, and investigations have gone far beyond the local delayed reaction and its direct *in vitro* correlates. Major advances have included the recognition of the T and B lymphocyte subpopulations, the exploration of surface markers and receptors on these cells, mechanisms of lymphocyte stimulation, interaction between T and B cells in various immune responses, and increasing knowledge of the properties and actions of the elusive transfer factor. This knowledge has led to an understanding of the role of T cells not only in the classic delayed hypersensitivity reaction, but in all of the various manifestations of cell-mediated immunity as well. This immune system has been shown to play an important role in the response to certain kinds of infection, in certain transplantation reactions, and is becoming increasingly important in our understanding of tumor immunology. Although these subjects have been covered in reviews or workshops, there has been no comprehensive text covering these major advances. The present volume has been designed to provide such a treatise. We believe that knowledge in this field, while not having reached a plateau, has consolidated to an extent that would make such a text of value to immunologists, students, and clinicians for some years to come.

ROBERT T. MCCLUSKEY
STANLEY COHEN

September 1973
Boston, Massachusetts
Buffalo, New York

Contents

Mechanisms of Cell-Mediated Immunity

Chapter One

Cell-Mediated Reactions
in vivo

ROBERT T. MCCLUSKEY AND PAUL D. LEBER

Department of Pathology, Harvard Medical School and the Children's Hospital Medical Center, Boston, Massachusetts

In the following chapters of this volume, most of the major recent advances in our understanding of cell-mediated immune reactions are reviewed, including the nature of antigen receptors on lymphocytes, T and B cell interaction in the immune response, cytotoxic effects of lymphocytes, transfer factor and *in vitro* forms of cell-mediated reactions. In this chapter we consider the area in which the study of cell-mediated immunity began—the local delayed hypersensitivity reaction in the intact animal.*

The delayed hypersensitivity reaction may be defined on the basis of several features. It is an immunologically specific response occurring in appropriately sensitized individuals upon local (usually intracutaneous) injection of antigen. The reaction becomes apparent grossly only after several hours and then exhibits gradually increasing erythema and induration. The histologic picture is characteristic, with a predominantly mononuclear cell infiltrate. A fundamental feature of delayed reactivity

---

*The terms cell-mediated immune reaction and delayed hypersensitivity reaction are often used interchangeably, although the latter term is sometimes used in a more restricted sense, to refer only to the local inflammatory reactions elicited by antigen.

was discovered by Landsteiner and Chase in 1942 (1), who showed that reactivity can be transferred to unsensitized hosts by lymphoid cells, but not by serum. The reaction may occur in the absence of demonstrable serum antibody. Another basic aspect of delayed sensitivity, which also serves to distinguish it from antibody-mediated reactions, is the nature of the antigenic determinant required for elicitation, as discussed by Jones and Schlossman in Chapter 5.

Although these characteristics define delayed reactions fairly satisfactorily, it is not always possible to be sure that an inflammatory response is due to delayed sensitivity, especially where all criteria cannot be examined. The histologic picture, although characteristic, is not pathognomonic. Certain antibody-mediated reactions may be characterized by a predominantly mononuclear cell infiltrate, as discussed later. Moreover, mononuclear cell accumulation may be seen in situations where it is not certain that immunologic mechanisms are involved at all. Even transfer with lymphoid cells is not conclusive, since some of the transferred cells can produce antibodies in the recipient. However, when coupled with the failure to transfer with serum, the demonstration that cell transfer results in the capacity of the recipient to develop typical lesions is compelling evidence for a cell-mediated mechanism. Such evidence can be strengthened by showing *in vitro* correlates of delayed sensitivity, employing the antigen in question. Based principally on this type of evidence, it is now recognized that cell-mediated mechanisms are responsible for certain responses to a wide variety of antigens, including microbial, viral, and heterologous protein antigens, simple reactive chemicals (contact sensitivity), tumor-specific antigens, transplantation antigens, and autologous antigens (which accounts for some forms of autoimmune disease). Obviously, in many instances, especially in actively immunized hosts, humoral antibody is present as well, resulting in a mixed type of reaction.

A number of factors are known to be important in the induction of delayed sensitivity. Administration of antigen in adjuvant facilitates such reactivity. Intradermal injections of antigen are generally most effective and intravenous injections least effective. In fact, under appropriate experimental conditions, intravenous administration of antigen can lead to tolerance as measured by delayed sensitivity, sometimes in the face of continued antibody production; this phenomenon has been called immune deviation (2). The nature of the antigen is important; microbial antigens are particularly effective. Indeed, for some time it was believed that delayed hypersensitivity was a type of reactivity restricted to such antigens. In order to produce a prolonged state of "pure" delayed sensitivity (i.e., without accompanying demonstrable antibody) against purified plasma proteins such as BSA or BGG, it is necessary to follow a carefully defined immunization procedure, which generally consists of the use of extremely small doses of antigen, antigens modified by chemical means, or very weak antigens (3). Delayed sensitivity has not been convincingly produced with pure polyssaccharides, although such material is capable of stimulating antibody formation. Delayed sensitivity is exhibited to varying degrees in different species and is especially pronounced in man and the guinea pig. The mouse shows relatively poor delayed responses in the skin, but readily exhibits other kinds of cell-mediated reactions, such as allograft rejection or cellular immunity to infectious agents.

CLASSIFICATION AND LIFE HISTORY OF MONONUCLEAR CELLS

Until fairly recently, almost nothing beyond the descriptive level was known of the mononuclear cells participating in cell-mediated reactions. As long as such knowledge was based on histologic observations, relatively few definite conclusions could be reached, since the morphologic distinction between various types of mononuclear cells is often impossible and since most of the important properties of these cells cannot be deduced from their appearance. In the past decade considerable progress has been made in unraveling the origin, nature, and immunological specificity of the cells comprising the infiltrate in delayed reactions, in large part as a result of autoradiographic studies in which more or less clearly defined populations of cells have been traced, and also through electron-microscopic studies. In this discussion, which is based on evidence obtained by such techniques, major emphasis is placed on two kinds of cell-mediated reactions—the delayed hypersensitivity reaction elicited by intradermal injection of protein antigens, and certain tissue-specific autoimmune lesions characterized by mononuclear cell infiltration (encephalitis, adrenalitis, thyroiditis). In addition, a few comments are made about the cells in allograft reactions, a subject that is more fully covered in Chapter 10.

CLASSIFICATION OF MONONUCLEAR CELLS IN DELAYED REACTIONS

The two most important types of mononuclear cells in delayed reactions are lymphocytes and mononuclear phagocytes (monocytes and macrophages); and it will be useful to describe certain aspects of the morphology, classification, and "life history" of these cells separately.

Lymphocytes

Lymphocytes have traditionally been defined in morphologic terms, but it is clear that even structurally identical lymphocytes may have different origins, life spans, and functions. The recognition that there are two major classes, the T lymphocyte and the B lymphocyte, represents a major advance, but has certainly not resolved all problems related to lymphocyte classification. T lymphocytes are derived from stem cells in the bone marrow, whose progeny migrate to the thymus, where they acquire the capacity to perform certain immunologic functions. The T lymphocytes that leave the thymus form a major part of the recirculating pool, traveling from lymph nodes and other lymphoid tissue via lymphatic ducts to the circulation and back to lymphoid tissue, where they localize principally in certain regions, designated thymus-dependent zones (in lymph nodes, the deep or paracortical areas; in the spleen, the periarteriolar areas). Two major functions are ascribed to T lymphocytes: (1) they are basically responsible for cell-mediated reactions, and (2) they somehow facilitate the production of antibody by B cells against certain antigens (helper cells). There is evidence that these and other functions may reside in different subpopulations of T cells (4–6).

The B cells (the thymus-independent lymphocytes) also derive from stem cells in the bone marrow. In birds, they migrate to the bursa of Fabricius, where they undergo further maturation before seeding peripheral lymphoid tissue. A mammalian analog for the bursa has not been convincingly demonstrated and it seems unlikely that a single corresponding central lymphoid organ will be found. B lymphocytes typically occupy certain areas of lymphoid tissue (predominantly follicular regions in lymph nodes). They form a part of the recirculating pool. B lymphocytes lack certain receptors present on T cells (Lya, Lyb, and Lyc in the mouse); conversely, they have readily demonstrable Ig on their surface and receptors for C3, in contrast to T lymphocytes. The possibility that the antigen receptor on T cells is immunoglobulin in nature is discussed in detail by Schlossman in Chapter 5. B cells also appear to constitute the antigen-reactive cells that can be identified by autoradiography using labeled antigen. The main function so far attributed to B lymphocytes is their capacity to differentiate into antibody-producing cells.*

Although there are clear differences between T and B lymphocytes,

---

*Until recently, antibody production was thought to be the only function of B cells. However, it has now been shown (6a) that B cells can produce migration inhibition factor (MIF). Previously, the production of MIF and other lymphokines was thought to be a property confined to T cells.

they are quite similar or identical in certain respects, so that their identification within an inflammatory site is generally not possible. For the most part, they are indistinguishable on structural grounds. Only when B cells undergo differentiation into antibody-producing cells do they acquire distinctive features, and these are at first recognizable only by electron microscopy, in the form of a well-developed endoplasmic reticulum and later by acquisition of characteristic features of plasma cells. Moreover, T and B lymphocytes cannot be clearly separated on the basis of life span, or ability to recirculate (7,8), even though the T lymphocytes constitute the bulk of the long-lived recirculating population. There is evidence that there are subpopulations of T and B lymphocytes with different migration pathways. Thus, Lance and Taub (9) have shown that lymphocytes home to some extent selectively to either spleen or lymph nodes and Tigilaar and Asofsky have demonstrated that lymph-node-seeking and spleen-seeking lymphocytes collaborate in graft-versus-host (GVH) reactions (6). Both subpopulations were shown to be sensitive to *in vitro* treatment with antitheta antibody and complement, so they appear to be T cells. In other types of experiments, Griscelli et al have found that large lymphocytes taken from rat mesenteric nodes home preferentially to the intestine and adjacent nodes; in contrast, lymphocytes from peripheral nodes migrate preferentially to peripheral nodes (10). Moreover, Craig and Cebra have shown that numerous plasma cells appear in the intestinal mucosa of irradiated rabbits following injections of Peyer's patch cells; almost all of these cells were shown to contain IgA, indicating that at least some of the gut-seeking lymphocytes are B cells (11).

T and B lymphocytes cannot be distinguished on the basis of size, at least not by ordinary morphologic means. Lymphocytes have long been classified as small and large, or small, medium, and large, but since there is continuous variation in size, this does not result in separation into two (or three) distinct populations. Both T and B lymphocytes can exist as large or small lymphocytes. Large lymphocytes are dividing cells, as evidenced by their capacity to incorporate ^{3}H-thymidine. Small lymphocytes as such do not divide, but following appropriate stimulation can transform into large, dividing cells. This type of cell is variously referred to as a blast cell, activated lymphocyte, or large pyroninophilic cell. It is characterized by a large nucleus, prominent nucleoli, and numerous cytoplasmic constituents, including free and aggregated ribosomes, a Golgi apparatus, a varying amount of endoplasmic reticulum, and mitochondria. Both T and B cells can exist in this form and distinction between the two cannot be made on structural grounds unless, as noted above, differentiation of B cells into the plasma cell series has begun. In the case of T cells there is clear evidence that small T lymphocytes can be transformed into blasts, which after several days of division gradually become smaller, assuming the appearance of large and then small lymphocytes (12). This probably also occurs with B cells, although in this case differentiation into plasma cells, which are end-stage cells, may be the usual pathway. Unfortunately, there appears to be at present no reliable way of identifying surface markers on single cells in tissue sections. It is obvious therefore that T and B lymphocytes cannot be recognized directly within inflammatory infiltrates.*

Mononuclear Phagocytic Cells (Monocytes, Macrophages)

Mononuclear phagocytes are normally found in many sites throughout the body, including bone marrow, blood, lymphoid tissue, liver, lungs, and serous cavities. In addition, they are present to some extent in all types of inflammatory reactions and are the predominant cell in some kinds of inflammation. Although the cells found in various locations differ in certain respects, such as size, staining properties, or enzyme composition, recent evidence (summarized in ref. 13) indicates that all highly phagocytic mononuclear cells and their precursors belong to one system. The precursor cells are found in the bone marrow, and are first recognizable as promonocytes. This is a population of continuously, rapidly dividing cells, which gives rise to blood monocytes, constituting a pool of incompletely differentiated cells with a relatively short half-life (22 hours in the mouse). They localize in various tissues and inflammatory sites, where they differentiate further into macrophages. Recent studies have shown that the macrophages in several kinds of acute inflammatory reactions are derived from circulating monocytes and not, as had previously been held likely, from proliferation of histiocytes already present in the tissue, or from circulating lymphocytes (14,15). However, in certain forms of chronic inflammation, local multiplication of macrophages also occurs, accounting for some of the macrophages in the infiltrate. Macrophages do not produce antibodies and do not appear to recognize specific antigens, or to discriminate between immunogens and nonimmunogens. They can, however, bind many kinds of antigen, either because of its physicochemical properties or because of

---

*While surface antigens on individual lymphoid cells cannot readily be identified in tissue sections, Shevach and Green (12a) have recently developed techniques to identify large collections of B cells, as for example in the follicles of lymph nodes. Under appropriate conditions, when a frozen section is overlayed with a suspension of complement coated red cells, specific adherence of RBC's is observed in areas containing a preponderance of B cells, presumably due to the presence of C3 receptors on those cells.

opsonization. Following this, antigen can be ingested and more or less completely degraded. However, small amounts may be retained on the plasma membrane (16). There is considerable evidence, from *in vitro* and *in vivo* observations, that macrophages may enhance antibody formation; based on evidence obtained by Unanue and associates (16), it seems probable that this results from small amounts of antigen bound to the surface of macrophages, in which form they may be presented to lymphocytes. There is less direct evidence concerning the question of whether macrophages also participate in the induction of delayed hypersensitivity, but it seems probable that they do (17).

Although the distinction on morphologic grounds between fully differentiated macrophages and lymphocytes presents no problem, differentiation between monocytes and medium or large lymphocytes is not always possible. When the cells can be obtained in suspension, additional criteria can be employed to characterize them, especially their ability to phagocytose particles and to adhere to glass. However, even these properties do not always allow distinction between monocytes and lymphocytes.

In addition to lymphocytes and mononuclear cell phagocytes, neutrophils, basophils, and eosinophils accumulate to varying degrees in cell-mediated reactions, as is discussed here and in Chapters 3 and 12.

PATHOGENESIS OF DELAYED REACTIONS

In order to facilitate understanding of the following discussion it is convenient to summarize briefly the present understanding of the pathogenesis of the delayed reaction. The immunizing injection of antigen stimulates the proliferation of T lymphocytes, principally in the draining nodes, some of which are specifically sensitized to the antigen. These newly formed lymphocytes enter the circulation. Following the challenging injection, a few of these circulating T cells come in contact with the antigen, which stimulates them and causes them to produce and release a group of mediators designated lymphokines, which bring about an inflammatory reaction characterized chiefly by accumulation of monocytes and other lymphocytes, and to a lesser extent of granulocytes.

LYMPH NODE CHANGES IN DELAYED SENSITIVITY

If immunization is carried out with immunogen known to favor the development of delayed sensitivity rather than antibody formation, such as a contact-sensitizing material, a skin allograft, or certain tissue-specific antigens, characteristic changes are seen in the draining lymph nodes (18). Within the first 2 days, enlargement of the node occurs, resulting chiefly from trapping of circulating lymphocytes and possibly decreased migration of cells from the node (19). However, within 2 to 3 days, numerous large proliferating cells (called blasts, large pyroninophilic cells, or large lymphocytes) appear, principally in the thymus-dependent areas. Ultrastructurally these cells have been described as containing numerous clusters of ribosomes, but little or no endoplasmic reticulum (20). Because of this, and because of their location, and because on other grounds cell-mediated reactions are known to depend on T cells, they are presumed to be proliferating T cells. The proliferation lasts only a short time and generally by 7 to 9 days the paracortical areas are occupied mainly by small and large lymphocytes. In animals given ³H-thymidine on days 3 to 4, so as to label the proliferating cells, it has been found that most of these lymphocytes are labeled, indicating that they are derived from the large dividing cells. It is not known what percentage of these newly formed lymphocytes represents cells specifically sensitized to the immunizing antigens, although it is clear that there is a large increase in the number of such cells. Although proliferation is presumed to be initiated by interaction between antigen and specific receptors for antigen on certain T cells, it seems likely that lymphocytes with other specificities are secondarily stimulated to proliferate. In any case, some of these newly formed lymphocytes leave the node via efferent lymphatics to enter the circulation, which gives them an opportunity to come in contact with antigen anywhere throughout the body.

In contrast to the changes just described, when an immunogen that preferentially stimulates antibody formation and not delayed sensitivity is used, proliferation of paracortical cells is not found and the most conspicuous features are development of germinal centers and appearance of plasma cells in the medullary cords (18). Obviously, in many instances both delayed sensitivity and antibody formation are stimulated, and the nodes exhibit features of both types of response. In addition, when the antigen is administered in Freund's adjuvant, accumulation of macrophages with granuloma formation is generally seen.

Aside from the development of sensitization within draining lymph nodes, there is evidence that sensitization may also occur peripherally; i.e., circulating lymphocytes may come in contact with antigen in extranodal sites and be stimulated to proliferate. The relative importance of the two forms of sensitization undoubtedly varies from one situation to another, depending on factors such as the nature of the antigen, the lymphatic drainage, and the accessibility of the antigen to circulating cells. In certain types of allografts, peripheral sensitization is probably of major importance (21).

MORPHOLOGIC FEATURES OF CELL-MEDIATED REACTIONS

Although all forms of cell-mediated reactions are characterized by infiltrates in which mononuclear cells predominate, there are notable (and not generally emphasized) differences between delayed reactions, contact reactions, allograft reactions, and presumed cell-mediated autoimmune lesions. No attempt will be made to describe these reactions in detail (for an extensive discussion of morphologic features, see ref. 22). Since information concerning the origin, nature, and extent of specific sensitization of the infiltrating lymphocytes is derived from studies of all these types of reactions, and since much of the evidence concerning the nature of these cells is derived from autoradiographic studies rather than from morphologic observations, these questions are examined in a later section.

Delayed Sensitivity Reactions

The fully developed delayed reaction elicited by intradermal injection is characterized by a predominantly mononuclear cell infiltrate, which is most intense just beneath the dermis, and which shows some tendency to surround nerves and venules. In the dermis, the cells are more widely scattered. A few cells may be found invading the epidermis. In severe reactions, necrosis may be seen. In contact reactions, the infiltrate is much more intense in the upper dermis and epidermis. Contact reactions may also differ from the usual type of delayed reaction by containing numerous basophils (see the section on cutaneous basophil hypersensitivity). Delayed reactions elicited by protein antigens generally fade within a few days. In the later stages a small number of plasma cells may be found.

There is disagreement about certain morphologic features of delayed reactions. One question concerns the extent to which neutrophils are an intrinsic part of the response. There is no doubt that neutrophils are always present in the infiltrate, and are often seen in large numbers, especially early in the reaction. To some degree their presence may be attributable to the use of irritating antigens, endotoxin contamination, antibody-mediated components of the reaction, or a response to necrosis. However, they cannot all be explained away in this fashion and it must be concluded that neutrophils are really *bona fide* components of delayed hypersensitivity reactions.

As indicated earlier, it has not been possible to determine with precision the composition of the mononuclear cell infiltrate on the basis of structural studies alone. However, it is clear that both lymphocytes and mononuclear phagocytes are present in large numbers. On the basis of histologic (23,24) and electron-microscopic studies, it has been concluded that the predominant cell in the fully developed lesion in guinea pigs is the monocyte or macrophage. In a careful electron-microscopic study of the tuberculin reaction in the rat, it was estimated that 20% of the mononuclear cells were lymphocytes, and the rest mononuclear cell phagocytes (25). Most of the lymphocytes were classified as small or medium, although "activated" lymphocytes were also present. None of the cells is unique for delayed reactivity, and they can all be found in other kinds of inflammation. The percentage of lymphocytes may vary in different species; in man they may appear to be present in greater numbers than in the guinea pig.

It is worth noting that ordinary delayed reactions to protein antigens do not exhibit typical features of granulomatous reactions, i.e., lesions with nodular accumulation of macrophages, usually with epithelioid cells and giant cell formation. Evidence has recently been obtained that delayed sensitivity can express itself in the form of a granulomatous response if the antigen used for challenge is coupled to sepharose beads and injected intravenously, following which granulomatous lesions appear in the lung (26,27). These observations suggest that a delayed response to an antigen that is not readily diffusible or digestable may include features of a granulomatous reaction.

The sites of leukocyte emigration have been examined by light and electron microscopy (22). Emigration occurs principally from venules, as in other types of inflammatory reactions. Monocytes and granulocytes have been clearly shown to leave the vessels by passing between endothelial cells. The precise pathway of lymphocyte emigration has not been clearly determined, but it has been suggested that they may migrate directly through endothelial cells. A similar pathway has been described for the emigration of lymphocytes in experimental autoimmune neuritis (28) and for the homing of lymphocytes into lymph nodes through the postcapillary venule (29). However, this latter interpretation has recently been questioned by Schoefle (30), who concluded that the lymphocytes pass between endothelial cells. Accordingly, it seems prudent at present to regard the route taken by lymphocytes leaving vessels under any circumstances as not established.

Cutaneous Basophil Hypersensitivity (Jones-Mote Reactivity)

Reactions elicited in animals immunized with a variety of protein antigens in saline or in incomplete Freund's adjuvant exhibit certain differences from the usual type of delayed reaction. In particular, they are characterized by accumulation of large numbers of basophils and for this reason have been designated cutaneous basophil hypersensitivity (CBH) reactions (31,32). When purified proteins are used, this type of reactivity develops shortly after immunization, and is transient, waning within a few weeks. The gross appearance of the lesion and its time of development after challenge are similar to the usual delayed reaction. In some lesions, basophils may account for more than 50% of the infiltrate. It should be noted that basophils cannot be identified in ordinary histologic sections, so they can be overlooked easily. Degranulation is sometimes seen, with granules being found free in the interstitial tissues. The other cells in the infiltrate are similar to those found in the usual type of delayed reaction (in which a very small number of basophils may be found). Cutaneous basophil reactivity can be transferred with lymph node cells, but not with serum (33). Furthermore, induction of this type of reactivity is associated with proliferation of cells in paracortical regions in draining lymph nodes (34), suggesting that the process depends on T cells, like classical delayed sensitivity. The function of the basophils in the reaction is not clear, but may be related to their content of pharmacologic mediators such as histamine and heparin.

Aside from being seen in animals immunized with protein antigens in saline or incomplete adjuvant, numerous basophils may be found in certain other reactions that are known or presumed to be cell mediated, notably in some skin allografts, delayed reactions to vaccinia virus, and certain contact reactions (32). In summary, cutaneous basophil reactivity shares many of the basic features of delayed reactivity; whether the basophils accumulate because different lymphokines are involved in such reactions and if so, whether this happens because different populations of T cells are involved, is not known.

Retest Reaction

When antigen is injected into a site where a delayed reaction of the same specificity had been previously elicited, a distinctive type of response is sometimes seen (35). The reaction appears about 2 hours after injection, becomes maximal at 6 to 8 hours, and is characterized histologically by a striking accumulation of eosinophils. Although characteristic, the eosinophilic component of the retest reaction is not essential to its pathogenesis. Indeed, if care is taken to avoid antibody production, a reaction with the same accelerated temporal evolution may be elicited, although few or no eosinophils participate (35a). The explanation for this observation apparently lies in the requirement for specific antibody for the production of an eosinophilic chemotactic factor by the sensitized lymphocyte, as is discussed at greater length in Chapter 12 by Cohen et al.

Allografts

Experimental skin or renal first-set allografts (in immunologically unmodified hosts) generally develop, after several days, an infiltrate in which lymphocytes (large or small) predominate, as judged morphologically. In some grafts, 80 to 90% of the cells appear to be lymphocytes. The reactions differ therefore from ordinary delayed reaction, in which mononuclear phagocytes predominate. In some allografts, especially late ones, numerous plasma cells may also be present. Basophils may be present in large numbers in some skin allografts (32). However, electron-microscopic studies of skin allografts have not always revealed basophils, indicating that they are not an invariable component (22). After the onset of necrosis, an additional inflammatory reaction appears, in which numerous granulocytes and macrophages are seen.

Autoimmune Lesions

Certain tissue-specific autoimmune diseases (adrenalitis, thyroiditis, encephalitis) are characterized by a predominantly mononuclear cell infiltrate. Since in some instances these diseases can be transferred with lymph node cells but not with serum, they are presumed to represent cell-mediated reactions. However, it also appears that at least in some cases humoral antibody is responsible for such lesions since they can be transferred with serum, if it is collected at the appropriate time after immunization, and sometimes after removal of the target organ (36–38). Furthermore, in certain tissue-specific autoimmune lesions, plasma cells and germinal centers are conspicuous, especially in the later stages (39), providing evidence for an antibody-mediated component. Moreover, in some lesions eosinophils are numerous. Accordingly, the conclusion that a given tissue-specific autoimmune lesion results principally or entirely from cell-mediated mechanisms can be considered fairly secure only if transfer can be accomplished with cells and not with serum. These criteria are met in certain models, including autoimmune encephalitis and adrenalitis induced in rats by immunization with tissue-specific antigen in Freund's adjuvant plus pertussis (40). The infiltrates in these lesions typically contain very high percentages (up to 80%) of lymphocytes, as judged morphologically, and thus differ from ordinary delayed reactions. Information concerning the nature of the lymphocytes in these lesions is discussed in the next section.

NATURE AND SPECIFICITY OF MONONUCLEAR CELLS IN CELL-MEDIATED REACTIONS

Until about 10 years ago it seemed possible that the majority of mononuclear cells in delayed reactions were specifically sensitized to the eliciting antigen, and that they were either attracted to the site or arrested there by the antigen. This conclusion appeared attractive especially because of the results of transfer experiments: Following injection of a population of mononuclear cells from an immunized donor, local challenge of the recipient by antigen brings about an accumulation of mononuclear cells resembling the donor population. However, several studies have clearly shown that this interpretation is wrong. Thus, when prospective recipient guinea pigs were given repeated injections of ^{3}H-thymidine for 3 days prior to transfer of unlabeled lymph node cells from sensitized donors, the great majority (80 to 90%) of the mononuclear cells in the test site were found to be labeled (41). The labeled cells were clearly of recipient origin and could not therefore have been specifically sensitized. Further, they must have been derived from circulating cells, since no labeled mononuclear cells were found in normal skin. Moreover, they must have been derived from precursors that were rapidly and continuously dividing in the absence of specific antigenic stimulation. All these characteristics are possessed by monocytes. Subsequent studies by Lubaroff and Waksman provided direct evidence that the majority of mononuclear cells in tuberculin reactions in rats are derived from bone marrow precursors (42,43). In one of these studies (43), thymectomized, irradiated Lewis rats were restored with bone marrow from allogeneic donors. They were then passively sensitized to tuberculin by transfer of lymph node cells from a sensitized Lewis donor. Among cells teased from the reaction site at 24 hours, the majority (about 75%) were shown by immunofluorescence to be derived from the transferred allogeneic marrow. They concluded that the marrow provided a source of monocytes.* Liden showed that the majority of cells in contact reactions in the guinea pig were marrow derived (44). The results of these studies are in agreement with estimates of the percentage of macrophages in delayed reactions based on morphologic observations, cited in an earlier section.

These findings appear to correspond nicely to certain *in vitro* studies on the mechanisms of delayed hypersensitivity using the migration inhibition techniques (see Chapter 2). It was found that a few cells from sensitized guinea pigs, when mixed with normal peritoneal exudate cells, rendered the entire population inhibitable by specific antigen (45). Subsequent studies showed that it was the lymphocyte that reacted with antigen, leading to production of a factor which resulted in macrophage immobilization (MIF). Later it was found that lymphocytes from sensitized animals also produce a factor chemotactic for macrophages (46). Thus, there is a mechanism that might account for emigration of monocytes and a mechanism that could lead to their immobilization at the reaction site. Although there is no reason to doubt that these factors function *in vivo*, it seems likely that additional mechanisms affecting monocytes come into play, as in other types of inflammation.

Moreover, the elucidation of mechanisms responsible for monocyte accumulation in delayed reactions has tended to obscure the fact that there are numerous lymphocytes in the infiltrate. As mentioned earlier, their number, judged on morphologic grounds, varies in different forms of cell-mediated reactions, but they often appear to constitute the majority cell, especially in allograft reactions and certain autoimmune lesions. Several questions may be asked about these lymphocytes. To what extent are they specifically sensitized? Are they predominantly T or B cells? What is known of their life span and capacity to recirculate?

With respect to the question of specificity, it seems clear that the great majority of the lymphocytes appearing in cell-mediated reactions are not sensitized to the eliciting antigen.† Some evidence for this conclusion was obtained in transfer studies of delayed sensitivity, employing labeled donor cells (41). Thus, in experiments in which recipients were injected with labeled lymph node cells from donors sensitized to one antigen

---

*The possibility that some of the marrow-derived cells may have been B lymphocytes was not considered at that time; this question is discussed in a later section.

†It should be emphasized that this is different from asking the question of whether the majority of *mononuclear cells* in the infiltrate are specifically sensitized. Monocytes cannot be specifically sensitized in the sense that lymphocytes are presumed to be, but only through binding of cytophilic antibody.

and unlabeled cells from donors sensitized to an unrelated antigen, approximately equal numbers of labeled cells (about 5%) were found in each of two skin sites injected with either antigen. These studies were carried out before the evidence described above concerning the bone marrow derivation of the majority of mononuclear cells was obtained, and it must be admitted that no critical attempt was made to distinguish between monocytes and lymphocytes in the donor inoculum. However, from other studies it seems probable that the majority of the labeled donor cells employed in these experiments were lymphocytes. Similar findings were made by others (47,48). Only one series of experiments based on cell transfer showed an increased number of labeled cells in a reaction elicited by the antigen against which the donor of the labeled cells had been immunized, and the differences from control sites were only slight (49). Cohen et al (50) used a different design in an attempt to detect preferential accumulation of specifically sensitized cells. Guinea pigs were immunized with two unrelated antigens and given ^{3}H-thymidine in a schedule so as to label cells proliferating in response to the first, but not the second antigen. No difference was detected in the percentage of labeled mononuclear cells at skin reactions elicited simultaneously with each antigen at separate sites.

The question of preferential accumulation of specifically sensitized lymphocytes has been more critically examined in a study of autoimmune adrenalitis and encephalitis (40). These models offer a more suitable system in which to study this question, since the lesions contain a considerably higher proportion of lymphocytes than do delayed reactions. The experiments were performed using a technique described by Levine and Hoenig (51). Small heat lesions were produced in the brain and adrenal of prospective recipient rats. The lesions at 5 days were characterized by necrosis and usually showed a surprisingly mild adjacent inflammatory reaction, with a few macrophages and neutrophils and virtually no lymphocytes. If the animal was then given lymph node cells from donors immunized with adrenal tissue, an intense lymphocytic infiltrate developed within 24 hours around the adrenal lesion, but not around the brain lesion. The reverse occurred if the donors had been immunized with central nervous system tissue. Thus, the initiation of the infiltrate was entirely organ specific. If a rat received cells from both kinds of donors, infiltrates developed around both lesions. One experiment designed to detect preferential accumulation of specifically sensitized lymphocytes was carried out as follows. Rats with 5-day-old heat lesions in the brain and adrenal received lymph node cells from both adrenal- and brain-sensitized donors, with cells from one type of donor labeled and cells from the other type unlabeled. Careful examination of autoradiographs of smears of donor cell showed almost all of the labeled cells to be lymphocytes or blasts; labeled cells that could be identified as monocytes or macrophages were extremely rare. Examination of the infiltrates around the heat lesions at 24 or 48 hours after transfer showed significant numbers of labeled cells, almost all of which appeared to be lymphocytes. Furthermore, they were found in approximately equal numbers in each site, indicating that specifically sensitized lymphocytes did not preferentially accumulate at the appropriate site.

In all experiments employing suspensions of cells disrupted from lymphoid tissue, the possibility must be considered that the results are misleading, because a large number of cells not destined or ready to enter the circulation are suddenly injected intravenously. Evidence that the results found in the transfer studies did in fact parallel what happens in the actively immunized host was obtained in other experiments (52), in which it was shown that lymphocytes labeled *in situ* by an intralymph-node injection of ^{3}H-thymidine were found 24 and 48 hours later in autoimmune lesions in the brain and adrenal. A technique was used that ensured that labeling of cells occurred only within the injected node, so that any labeled cells later found outside the node must have migrated there (53). Furthermore, the injection did not result in morphologically apparent damage to the node, suggesting that cells were not artificially dislodged from the node.

There is evidence that a similar type of nonspecific accumulation of lymphocytes occurs in allografts. In one study, attempts to find significant numbers of donor cells in skin allografts in transfer experiments using labeled lymph node cells from animals sensitized to antigens in the graft have failed (54). Although interpretation of these results is complicated, they suggest that the great majority of lymphocytes in the graft were of recipient origin and because of the timing in these experiments probably were not sensitized. Experiments of a different design have also been employed (55). ^{3}H-Thymidine was injected twice daily in small amounts into the base of a skin allograft on a rabbit's ear; a second allograft from the same donor and an allograft from a different donor were placed on the opposite ear. Most of the label was incorporated into cells at the site of injection and in the draining node; therefore, heavily labeled cells found in sites remote from the injection were presumed to have migrated there. At the time of rejection, it was found that each graft on the uninjected side contained approximately equal numbers of labeled cells (up to 11%). It was concluded that proliferating lymph node cells do enter grafts in significant numbers, but they do not accumulate preferentially in the specific graft responsible for the stimulation of the node. One potential flaw in these experiments is that there may have been cross-reactions between transplantation antigens in the two grafts.

In contrast to these results, Lance and Cooper have recently reported significant preferential accumulation of lymphocytes in skin allografts of the same donor type as was used to stimulate lymphocyte proliferation (56). In these experiments, CBA mice were immunized to the transplantation antigens of C57 Bl/6 mice by skin grafts. During the first 4 days after skin grafting, the animals were given repeated injections of ^{125}I UDR. At 11 days, suspensions of lymph node and spleen cells were obtained, aliquots of which were labeled *in vitro* with ^{51}Cr and injected into syngeneic recipients that had been skin grafted 3 days earlier with C57 Bl/6 donors or A strain donors. The recipients were killed 24 hours later and radioactivity in the skin sites counted. It was found that the ^{125}I UDR-labeled cells, but not the ^{51}Cr-labeled cells, accumulated to a significantly greater extent (5 to 10X) in the C57 than in the A allograft. These results appear quite impressive. However, since they are at variance with other studies in which attempts have been made to demonstrate preferential accumulation of specifically sensitized lymphocytes in cell-mediated reactions, it would be important to have them confirmed. Further, the results would have been more convincing if they had been based on experiments, in which alternate recipients bearing both C57 and A allografts were each given labeled cells of one specificity and unlabeled cells of the other specificity.

In experiments of a different design, Emeson and Thursh have demonstrated a slight preferential accumulation of transfused long-lived lymphocytes from donors immunized with a graft in syngeneic recipient nodes draining that type of histocompatibility antigen (57). Subsequently, they obtained similar results employing two different red cell antigens (58). These experiments appear to be particularly well controlled, and although the differences between the nodes draining the relevant antigen and the contralateral nodes draining the other antigen were slight, they were consistent. A difference between these experiments and most of those described earlier is that long-lived lymphocytes were employed. Further, the effect was demonstrated within lymph nodes, rather than in a cell-mediated inflammatory reaction.

Thus, a number of studies have failed to provide evidence for preferential trapping of lymphocytes in cell-mediated reactions elicited by the particular antigen used to stimulate the lymph nodes, and even where this effect has been claimed, the differences from control reactions have been small. In any case, it is clear from these studies that there is a population of lymphocytes with the propensity to emigrate into all kinds of cell-mediated reactions. These observations do not mean of course that there are no specifically sensitized lymphocytes in the lesions, but only that they enter the infiltrate roughly in proportion to the extent that they are represented in the circulation among the kinds of lymphocytes prone to emigrate into cell-mediated inflammatory foci. For many reasons it must be presumed that the reaction is initiated by contact between a few specifically sensitized T cells and antigen. The mechanism responsible for this contact is unknown. It is possible that a few lymphocytes migrate into an area of slight inflammation, as is found at the site of injection of antigen. As the inflammatory reaction develops, more cells enter the lesion and provide an increasing chance for contact between specifically sensitized cells and antigen.

Although we have been discussing cell-mediated reactions, it may be that the kind of lymphocyte that enters such reactions may also emigrate in certain other types of inflammation as well.* For example, Koster and McGregor (59) have described the influx of lymphocytes, with properties similar to those we are describing, into the peritoneal cavity following injection of casein (to which the animals were not sensitized). Similarly, Asherson and Allwood have shown that labeled lymph node cells accumulate in inflammatory sites induced by croton oil (60). However, as is well known, in most forms of acute inflammation lymphocytes are not present in significant numbers and this suggests that the mechanisms responsible for their accumulation in cell-mediated reactions are relatively distinctive.

What is known of the properties of the lymphocytes that accumulate in cell-mediated reactions? First, they appear to be predominantly or entirely newly formed cells. Evidence for this comes from several sources. In the passive transfer experiments in rats with autoimmune adrenalitis or encephalitis discussed above, it was found that cells labeled *in vitro* with ^{3}H-thymidine showed a considerably greater tendency to appear in the lesions than did cells labeled with ^{3}H-adenosine (40). Also, when lymphocytes were labeled *in situ* in lymph nodes (55,52) with ^{3}H-thymidine, significant numbers of labeled lymphocytes were found in lesions shortly thereafter. Asherson and Allwood (60) found that cells taken from nodes of immunized mice showed a greater tendency to enter inflammatory sites than did cells taken from nonimmunized donors. Furthermore, this tendency was maximal at 4 days. In addition, in rats injected with Listeria monocytogenese (which is associated with the development of cell-mediated immunity) there appear many newly formed lymphocytes in the thoracic duct lymph, and these cells are capa-

---

*For this reason Asherson and Allwood have referred to the type of cell under discussion as inflammatory lymphoid cells (60).

ble of entering inflammatory foci (61). Similarly, in mice infected with tubercle bacilli there is seen marked proliferation of lymphoid cells in the periarteriolar regions of the spleen (62). The cells range from blast cell to small lymphocytes; however, most of the cells are large lymphocytes with pyroninophilic cytoplasm. Following transfer of such cells, they are found to enter into the formation of developing tubercles. (For further discussion see Chapter 8 by North.)

Although it is not possible to identify which of the T cells in a donor inoculum is responsible for initiating a cell-mediated reaction in the recipient, it must be concluded that these are included among the newly formed lymphocytes. Although several lines of evidence point in this direction, the mere fact that transfer can be achieved with lymph node or thoracic cells obtained within a few days after immunization must mean that the responsible cells have recently proliferated. Conversely, some evidence against the possibility that long-lived lymphocytes are very effective was obtained by Coe et al (63), who showed that cells capable of transferring delayed hypersensitivity in rats persist in the thoracic duct lymph despite prolonged drainage, a procedure known to result in depletion of long-lived recirculating lymphocytes (64). Aside from this, there is evidence that once formed, at least many of these cells do not become part of the pool of long-lived recirculating cells, which until recently has been considered to include all T lymphocytes. Thus, McGregor et al have found that following transfer, the newly formed lymphocytes appearing in the thoracic lymph of rats infected with Listeria monocytogenes, which include cells capable of transferring protection against infection with this organism, are not recoverable from the thoracic duct of the recipients (65). However, in experiments in which the fate of large dividing lymphocytes obtained from lymph nodes was studied following intravenous injection into syngeneic recipient rats, it was found that some could be found in the thoracic duct lymph of the recipients (10). These findings indicate that some newly formed lymphocytes can recirculate, whereas others cannot. The exact nature of either type remains to be determined; however, the evidence obtained so far suggests that those that enter inflammatory foci in general do not recirculate. Further, such cells appear to have a short life span (65). Aside from entering inflammatory foci, it is not known what the fate of these cells is.

In contrast to these findings, long-lived recirculating lymphocytes have been shown to be excluded from nonspecifically induced acute inflammatory sites (15). However, they apparently have not been specifically looked for in delayed reactions or in long-standing forms of inflammation, in which lymphocytes often predominate.

not known if cells can migrate directly from the mammalian thymus to inflammatory foci. In one study, transfused labeled thymus cells were not found in delayed reactions in recipient rats (73).

Little is known of the mechanisms that are responsible for the emigration of lymphocytes in inflamed tissue. Until recently it was thought that lymphocytes could not respond to chemotactic stimuli, but Ward has presented evidence in preliminary form that products released from antigen-stimulated lymphocytes could attract lymphocytes across micropore filters (74). The kind of lymphocyte responding in this system remains to be determined. Some evidence has been obtained *in vivo* that monocytes or macrophages are necessary for the accumulation of lymphocytes in autoimmune encephalitis and adrenalitis (40). Prospective recipient rats with heat lesions were irradiated with 800 R and some were reconstituted with bone marrow cells prior to transfer of lymph node cells from appropriately sensitized donors. The lesions were studied 48 hours after transfer. The point of interest is that although both lymphocytes and macrophages were found in the reconstituted animals, neither type of cell was found in the nonreconstituted animals even though they had received large numbers of lymphocytes. These findings suggest that monocytes or other bone-marrow-derived cells must be in the infiltrate before lymphocytes can be attracted.

Finally, it may be that in certain very long-standing inflammatory reactions the factors that bring about lymphocyte emigration may be similar to those causing physiological homing to lymph nodes. This is suggested by the fact that in many instances such reactions are characterized by the formation of rather well-organized lymphoid tissue. Further, Smith et al (75) have shown that there is considerable traffic of lymphocytes through chronically inflamed tissue, resembling that through a lymph node.

REFERENCES

1. Landsteiner, K. and Chase, M. W., *Proc. Soc. Exp. Biol. Med.* **9**, 688 (1942).

2. Asherson, G. L. and Stone, S. H., *Immunology* **9**, 205 (1965).

3. Gell, P. G. H. and Benacerraf, B., *Adv. Immunol.* **1**, 319 (1961).

4. Segal, S., Cohen, I. R., and Feldman, M., *Science* **175**, 1126 (1972).

5. Cantor, H. and Asofsky, R., *J. Exp. Med.* **131**, 235 (1970).

6. Tigelaar, R. E. and Asofsky, R., *J. Exp. Med.* **137**, 239 (1973).

6a. Yoshida, T., Sonozaki, H., and Cohen, S., *J. Exp. Med.* **138**, 784 (1973).

7. Howard, J. C., *J. Exp. Med.* **135**, 185 (1972).

8. Howard, J. C., Hunt, S. V., and Gowans, J. L., *J. Exp. Med.* **135**, 200 (1972).

9. Lance, E. M. and Taub, R. N., *Nature* **221**, 841 (1969).

10. Griscelli, C., Vassalli, P., and McCluskey, R. T., *J. Exp. Med.* **130,** 1427 (1969).

11. Craig, S. and Cebra, J., *J. Exp. Med.* **134,** 188 (1971).

12. Gowans, J. L., *Ann. N. Y. Acad. Sci.* **99,** 432 (1962).

12a. Shevach, E. M. and Green, I., *Transpl. Rev.,* in press.

13. Van Furth, R., Ed., *Mononuclear Phagocytes,* Blackwell Scientific Publications, Oxford and Edinburgh, 1970.

14. Spector, W. G., Walters, M. N., and Willoughby, D. A., *J. Pathol. Bacteriol.* **90,** 181 (1965).

15. Volkman, A. and Gowans, J. L., *Brit. J. Exp. Pathol* **46,** 62 (1965).

16. Unanue, E. R., Schmidtke, J., Cruchand, A., and Grey, H. M., Interactions among antigen, macrophages and lymphocytes, *VIth International Symposium in Immunopathology* (P. A. Miescher, Ed.), Grune and Stratton, New York, 1970.

17. Unanue, E. R., and Feldman, J. D., *Cell. Immunol.* **2,** 269 (1971).

18. Oort, J. and Turk, J. L., *Brit. J. Exp. Pathol.* **46,** 147 (1965).

19. Werdelin, O., Foley, P. S., Rose, N. R., and McCluskey, R. T., *Immunology* **21,** 1059 (1971).

20. de Petris, S., Karlsbad, G., Permis, B., and Turk, J. L., *Int. Arch. Allergy* **29,** 112 (1966).

21. Strober, S. and Gowans, J. L., *J. Exp. Med.* **122,** 347 (1965).

22. Wiener, J., Ultrastructural aspects of delayed hypersensitivity, in *Current Topics* in *Pathology,* Vol. 52, Springer-Verlag, Berlin, Heidelberg, and New York, 1970.

23. Waksman, B. H., *Immunity* (G. E. W. Wolstenholme and M. O'Connor, Eds.), Little, Brown, Boston, Massachusetts, 1959, p. 280.

24. Flax, M. H. and Caulfield, J. B., *Am. J. Pathol.* **43,** 1031 (1963).

25. Wiener, J., Spiro, D., and Zunker, H. O., *Am. J. Pathol.* **47,** 723 (1965).

26. Kasdon, E. J. and Schlossman, S. F., *Am. J. Pathol.* **71,** 365, 1973.

27. Unanue, E. and Benacerraf, B., *Am. J. Pathol.* **71,** 349 (1973).

28. Astrom, K. E., Webster, H., and Armason, B. G., *J. Exp. Med.* **128,** 469 (1968).

29. Marchesi, V. T. and Gowans, J. L., *Proc. Roy. Soc.* **159,** 283 (1964).

30. Schoefle, G. I., *J. Exp. Med.* **136,** 568 (1972).

31. Dvorak, H. F., Dvorak, A. M., Simpson, B. A., Richerson, H. B., Leskowitz, S., and Karnovsky, M. J., *J. Exp. Med.* **132,** 558 (1970).

32. Dvorak, H., Delayed hypersensitivity, in *The Inflammatory Process,* 2nd ed. (B. W. Zweifach, L. Grant, and R. T. McCluskey, Eds.), Academic Press, New York, 1973.

33. Richerson, H. B., Dvorak, H. F., and Leskowitz, S., *J. Exp. Med.* **132,** 546 (1970).

34. Dvorak, A. M., Bast, R. C., and Dvorak, H. F., *J. Immunol.* **107,** 442 (1971).

35. Arsason, B. G. and Waksman, R. H., *Lab. Invest.* **12,** 737 (1963).

35a. Leber, P., Milgrom, M. and Cohen, S., *Immunol. Comm.,* in press.

36. Rose, N. R. and Kite, J. H., in *1st International Convocation on Immunology* (N. R. Rose and F. Milgrom, Eds.), S. Karger, Basel, Switzerland, 1969, p. 247.

37. Nakamura, R. M. and Weigle, W. O., *J. Exp. Med.* **130,** 263 (1969).

38. Vladutui, A. and Rose, N. R., *Science* **174,** 1137 (1971).

39. Flax, M. H., Cell-mediated hypersensitivity in the pathogenesis of experimental allergic thyroiditis and its role in extralymphoid plasmacytosis, in *Cellular Interactions in the Immune Response* (S. Cohen, G. Cudkowicz, and R. T. McCluskey, Eds.), S. Karger, Basel, Switzerland, 1970.

40. Werdelin, O. and McCluskey, R. T., *J. Exp. Med.* **133,** 1242 (1971).

41. McCluskey, R. T., Benacerraf, B., and McCluskey, J. W., *J. Immunol.* **90,** 466 (1963).

42. Lubaroff, D. M. and Waksman, B. H., *J. Exp. Med.* **128,** 1425 (1968).

43. Lubaroff, D. M. and Waksman, B. H., *J. Exp. Med.* **128,** 1437 (1968).

44. Liden, S., *Acta Pathol. Microbiol. Scand.* **70,** 58 (1967).

45. David, J. R., Lawrence, H. S., and Thomas, L., *J. Immunol.* **93,** 274 (1964).

46. Ward, P. A., Remold, H. G., and David, J. R., *Cell. Immunol.* **1,** 162 (1970).

47. Turk, J. L. and Oort, J., *Immunology* **6,** 140 (1963).

48. Kay, K. and Rieke, W. O., *Science* **139,** 497 (1963).

49. Najarian, J. S. and Feldman, J. D., *J. Exp. Med.* **118,** 341 (1963).

50. Cohen, S., McCluskey, R. T., and Benacerraf, B., *J. Immunol.* **98,** 269 (1967).

51. Levine, S. and Hoenig, E. M., *J. Immunol.* **100,** 1310 (1968).

52. Werdelin, O., Wick, G., and McCluskey, R. T., *Lab. Invest.* **25,** 279 (1971).

53. Werdelin, O., McCluskey, R. T., and Witebsky, E., *Lab. Invest.* **23,** 144 (1970).

54. Najarian, J. S. and Feldman, J. D., *J. Exp. Med.* **115,** 1083 (1962).

55. Prendergast, R. A., *J. Exp. Med.* **119,** 377 (1964).

56. Lance, E. M. and Cooper, S., *Cell. Immunol.* **5,** 66 (1972).

57. Emeson, E. E. and Thursh, D. R., *J. Immunol.* **106,** 635 (1971).

58. Thursh, D. R. and Emeson, E. E., *J. Exp. Med.* **135,** 754 (1972).

59. Koster, F. T. and McGregor, D. D., *Science* **167,** 1137 (1970).

60. Asherson, G. L. and Allwood, G. G., *Immunology* **22,** 493 (1972).

61. McGregor, D. D. and Mackaness, G. B., Lymphocytes, in *The Inflammatory Process,* 2nd ed. (B. W. Zweifach, L. Grant, and R. T. McCluskey, Eds.), Academic Press, New York, (1974).

62. North, R. J., Mackaness, G. B., and Elliott, R. W., *Cell. Immunol.* **3,** 680 (1972).

63. Coe, J. E., Feldman, J. D., and Lee, S., *J. Exp. Med.* **123,** 267 (1966).

64. McGregor, D. D., *Fed. Proc.* **25,** 1713 (1966).

65. McGregor, D. D., Koster, F. T., and Mackaness, G. B., *J. Exp. Med.* **133,** 389 (1971).

66. Koster, F. D., McGregor, D. D., and Mackaness, G. B., *J. Exp. Med.* **133,** 400 (1971).

67. Williams, R. M. and Waksman, B. H., *J. Immunol.* **103,** 1435 (1969).

68. Volkman, A., *J. Exp. Med.* **124,** 241 (1966).

69. Brahim, F. and Osmond, D. G., *Anat. Rec.* **168,** 139 (1970).

70. Moorhead, J. W., Kite, J. H., McCluskey, R. T., Werdelin, O., and Wick, G., *Clin. Immunol. Immunopathol.,* in press.

71. Rose, N. R., Kite, J. H., Flanagan, T. D., and Witebsky, E., Humoral and cellular immune factors in spontaneous autoimmune disease, in *2nd International Convocation on Immunology* (S. Cohen, G. Cudkowicz, and R. T. McCluskey, Eds.), (1971), p. 268. S. Karger, Basel (Switzerland) and New York.

72. Welch, P., Rose, N. R., and Kite, J. H., *J. Immunol.* **110,** 575 (1973).

73. Kosunen, T. U., *Immunology* **19,** 117 (1970).

74. Ward, P. A., Offer, C. D., and Montgomery, J. R., *Fed. Proc.* **30,** 1721 (1971).

75. Smith J. B., McIntosh, G. H., and Morris, B., *J. Pathol.* **100,** 21 (1970).

Chapter Two

Migration Inhibition Factor and Other Mediators in Cell-Mediated Immunity

HEINZ G. REMOLD AND JOHN R. DAVID

Departments of Medicine and Biological Chemistry, Robert B. Brigham Hospital and Harvard Medical School, Boston, Massachusetts

In vitro techniques applied to the study of delayed hypersensitivity have enhanced our knowledge of the mechanism of this reaction, aided in delineating the cell types involved, and, most important, demonstrated the presence of soluble mediators. This chapter focuses on the macrophage migration inhibition technique and briefly reviews the biologically active soluble substances produced by stimulated lymphocytes.

MIGRATION INHIBITION

Inhibition of Migration of Cells from Tissue Explants

In vitro studies on delayed hypersensitivity were initiated by Rich and Lewis in 1932 (1). These workers made tissue culture preparations of spleen fragments and buffy coat cells from guinea pigs sensitized to human tubercle bacillus. Old tuberculin (OT) consistently inhibited the migration of wandering cells from these explants, while the same concentration of OT had no effect on explants from normal animals. Mononuclear macrophages and polymorphonuclear cells were the types most affected, while lymphocytes appeared to migrate normally. Quantitation of this phenomenon was introduced by Moen and Swift, who measured the area of migration with antigen and compared it directly to the area of migration from explants without antigen (2). The reaction demonstrated immunologic specificity (2). Considerable work was carried out in this system over the next few years by other investigators (3–5) and in the past 10 years by Johanovsky and coworkers (6,7).

Capillary Tube Migration

The technique of placing cells in capillary tubes and observing the effect of antigen on their migration out of the tube onto glass, introduced by George and Vaughan (8), has proved to be a useful method for the detection of cellular or delayed hypersensitivity and for the study of the mechanism of this immune reaction. Considerable information has been accumulated with this method relating to the types of cells involved in the interaction of antigen with sensitive cells and the biologic results of the interaction. The numerous parallel findings from *in vitro* experiments and *in vivo* observations strongly suggest that the *in vitro* phenomenon is a measure of delayed hypersensitivity, at least in the initial phase of what appears to be a complex reaction.

The technique is described in detail in Appendix 2. It has certain advantages over the use of explants. The capillaries are uniform in size, which simplifies quantification. The cells can easily be washed free of unbound serum, or, conversely, they can be incubated with serum which contains antibody. Purified cell populations can be used, and the contributions of various cell types, i.e., macrophages, lymphocytes, or neutrophils, can be readily assessed. Cells other than peritoneal exudates have also been used. Further, mixtures of cells from sensitized and nonsensitized populations can be made, and the interaction of different cell types investigated.

Specificity of Inhibition of Migration by Antigen

The immunologic specificity of inhibition of migration has been demonstrated with numerous antigens (2,9,10). For example, cells from guinea pigs sensitized to ovalbumin were consistently inhibited from migrating when incubated with ovalbumin while the same cells were not inhibited by diphtheria toxoid.

Specificity was further explored using as antigens hapten-protein conjugates which Benacerraf and Gell (11) and Benacerraf and Levine (12) had used in studying the specificity of delayed reactions *in vivo*. For these experiments, guinea pigs were sensitized with 2,4-dinitrophenyl-conjugated guinea pig albumin (DNP-GPA) (13). Cells from these animals were readily inhibited from migrating by DNP-GPA but not by DNP-BGG.

These experiments indicate the importance of the carrier protein in delayed hypersensitivity reactions *in vitro,* as had been shown to be the case *in vivo* (11,12), in contrast to the predominant hapten specificity of reactions mediated by humoral antibodies. Studies by Carpenter and Brandriss using the explant technique demonstrated similar specificity using hapten-protein conjugates (14).

Studies relating the specificity of the *in vitro* reaction to delayed hypersensitivity *in vivo* and to the immunogenicity of a molecule were carried out with DNP coupled to oligopeptides of L-lysine (10). Schlossman et al (15) had previously reported experiments using these synthetic chemically defined antigens in which they found that hapten-oligopeptides must have 7 or more lysyl residues in order to act as immunogens or to be capable of eliciting delayed hypersensitivity *in vivo*. However, hapten-oligopeptides containing 3 to 6 lysines could react readily with preformed antibody but were neither immunogenic nor capable of eliciting delayed hypersensitivity. Experiments showed that only DNP oligolysines which were immunogenic and could elicit delayed hypersensitivity *in vivo* could inhibit macrophage migration *in vitro*.

Further, Stulbarg and Schlossman showed that lymphocyte reactivity to DNP oligolysines in the antigen-induced incorporation of ^{3}H-thymidine assay exhibits the same type of specificity as that found with these antigens in the inhibition of migration assay (16). Such hapten-carrier specificity has been seen in other reactions in which antigen probably reacts directly with cells rather than with humoral antibody, such as the secondary immune response (17,18) and desensitization (19). The results from the two *in vitro* assays and the *in vivo* studies suggest that the receptor site for antigens on the sensitive cells is different from the receptor site for circulating antibody.

The Sensitive Cell in Inhibition of Migration

Studies on mixed populations of normal and sensitive cells had revealed that the presence of as few as 2.5% cells from a sensitized guinea pig would cause a population of 97.5% normal peritoneal exudate cells to be inhibited by antigen (20). As the peritoneal exudate cells contain a predominance of macrophages and approximately 10 to 20% lymphocytes, it was of interest to determine which of these cells carried the specific immunologic information. When sensitive lymph node lymphocytes were added to normal peritoneal cells, the population was inhibited by antigen. Experiments showed that the sensitive lymph node cells alone or the normal peritoneal cells alone were not inhibited by antigen, but mixtures of the two containing 15 to 35% sensitive lymph node cells were inhibited by antigen (21).

The reaction observed was immunologically specific. Additional studies showed that the sensitive cells had to be living to produce inhibition (20). Puromycin, an inhibitor of protein synthesis, prevented the inhibition of migration by antigen, further demonstrating that the reaction was not a simple agglutination by antigen (22).

The data suggested that in this system the lymphocyte was the sensitive cell but that a large number of peritoneal nonsensitive cells (presumably macrophages) need be present, as the indicator cells, for the phenomenon of inhibition of migration to be observed.

In an elegant series of experiments, Bloom and Bennett demonstrated directly that the lymphocyte and not the macrophage was the sensitive cell (23). When the purified peritoneal lymphocytes from PPD-sensitive guinea pigs were added to peritoneal exudate cells from normal animals, the mixture was inhibited from migrating by PPD. Significant inhibition was present when the lymphocytes constituted as few as 0.6% of the total cells. This is approximately the same number of lymphocytes as would be present in the lowest concentration (2.5%) of unpurified sensitive peritoneal cells which will cause normal cells to be inhibited (20). The experiments marking the lymphocyte as the sensitive cell with macrophages secondarily affected by their reaction with antigen have been confirmed by Dumonde (24) and by Bartfeld and Atoynatan (25).

THE MEDIATORS

By what means can a few sensitive lymphocytes, after contact with the sensitizing antigen, attract and involve large numbers of nonsensitive cells? This may come about through the release of soluble mediators or factors with various biologic effects. Since the discovery of migration inhibition factor (MIF), soluble factors with numerous different biologic activities have been reported. These are listed in Table 1. These substances are discussed here, beginning with those which involve reactions with macrophages.

Table 1   Soluble Mediators from Antigen-Stimulated Lymphocytes

1. Migration inhibition factor
2. Chemotactic factor for macrophages
3. Chemotactic factor for neutrophils
4. Chemotactic factor for eosinophils
5. Macrophage activating factor
6. Cytotoxic factors
7. Proliferation inhibitory factor
8. Skin reactive factor
9. Blastogenic factor for lymphocytes
10. Interferon
11. Immunoglobulin
12. Transfer factor

Migration Inhibitory Factor (MIF)

The isolation of a soluble substance elaborated by sensitive lymphocytes in response to antigen that inhibited normal macrophage migration was reported independently by Bloom and Bennett (23) and by David (27).

Properties of Guinea Pig MIF

MIF activity is first detectable in lymphocyte culture supernatants at 6 or 8 hours and can still be found after 4 days (26). Thus, MIF production occurs earlier than blast transformation. The production of MIF can be suppressed by puromycin. MIF is heat stable at 60°C for 30 minutes and is nondialyzable. It elutes from Sephadex G-100 or G-75 with molecules of molecular weights ranging from 35,000 to 50,000 (29). In studying MIF from PPD-stimulated lymphocytes (tuberculin-purified protein derivative) Bloom and Jimenez have found peak activity in fractions containing molecules of 25,000 MW (30). MIF migrates on acrylamide gels as a prealbumin at pH 9.1 (29). This step results in an approximate 1600-fold purification of MIF. In collaborative experiments with Bloom, we have found that MIF produced by PPD-sensitized lymphocytes also migrates as a prealbumin on acrylamide gels (Remold, David, and Bloom, unpublished results). The activity of MIF is destroyed by chymotrypsin but not by RNAse or DNAse, suggesting that it is a protein (31). It is particularly interesting that MIF activity is completely destroyed by treatment with neuraminidase (31). This indicates that it is a glycoprotein and that sialic acid is necessary for its function. When subjected to isopycnic centrifugation in cesium chloride density gradients, MIF behaves as a glycoprotein in that activity is recoverable in a portion of the gradient containing material more dense than the reference pure protein (31). Recently Dumonde et al (32) described a method of purifying MIF 1300-fold using rabbit antiserum to guinea pig serum. By this method, removal of accompanying serum proteins from the lymphocyte supernatants was obtained.

The results of fractionation studies indicate that MIF is smaller than the immunoglobulins and that high levels of activity are still present when antigen has been separated from it. These data are clearly in favor of MIF being immunologically nonspecific in its activity, acting as a pharmacologic agent.

Production of MIF in Response to Mitogen Stimulation

There have been several reports that concanavalin A (Con A) can stimulate lymphocytes to produce a migration inhibitory factor (33,34). In studies comparing antigen-stimulated MIF and Con A-stimulated MIF by means of physicochemical methods, we found that MIF produced by Con A has properties similar to antigen-stimulated MIF when tested by Sephadex filtration in CsCl gradients and digestion by chymotrypsin and neuraminidase (34). Using the same methods, it was found that the characteristics of another lymphocyte mediator, lymphotoxin, were similar whether produced by Con A or antigen stimulation (35). Further, in preliminary experiments with Dr. Peter Ward, Con A-stimulated cells produced an active chemotactic factor for macrophages.

The results reported here demonstrate that no major differences between MIF (and LT) from antigen and from concanavalin A-stimulated cells are discernible with methods employed. However, more sophisticated methods are necessary to prove their true identity.

The Macrophage Migration Inhibitory Factor from Humans

Recently, Rocklin et al (36) compared the properties of human MIF with guinea pig MIF.

When MIF from antigen-stimulated human lymphocytes obtained from the blood, tonsil, or spleen was subjected to Sephadex G-100 and G-75 gel filtration, MIF activity was recovered only from the fraction containing molecules of the size of chymotrypsinogen (MW 23,000). The specific antigen used to produce the human MIF, SK-SD (streptokinase-streptodornase), eluted in fractions containing molecules with a molecular weight greater than 25,000.

Fractionation of human MIF on disc electrophoresis at pH 9.1 revealed that peak human MIF activity occurred in a fraction corresponding to albumin and not in the prealbumin region. Fractionation by CsCl density gradient centrifugation showed peak activity in fractions that contain material isopycnic to albumin. No MIF activity was found in fractions denser than protein.

These results, taken together, lead us to conclude that human MIF is a protein with a molecular weight smaller than that of guinea pig MIF and lacking a polysaccharide moiety detectable with the methods presently employed.

This conclusion was supported by the results of digestion experiments using neuraminidase. When human MIF was incubated with neuraminidase from *Clostridium perfringens* at pH 5.1, MIF activity was not abolished, showing that sialic acid residues are not important for its biological activity. Incubation with water-insoluble chymotrypsin, however, destroyed activity completely, indicating the protein nature of human MIF.

The Chemotactic Factor for Macrophages

Studies on the cells found *in vivo* at the sites of delayed hypersensitivity reactions have shown that the majority are rapidly dividing nonsensitive mononuclear cells, and that only a few are specifically sensitive cells (37). This finding made reasonable the hypothesis that lymphocytes interacting with antigen could produce a chemotactic factor that would attract monocytes (capable of becoming macrophages) to the site. In collaboration with Dr. Peter Ward, we detected chemotactic substances in supernatants from antigen-stimulated lymphocyte cultures (38). These studies were carried out *in vitro* using Boyden chambers containing an upper and a lower compartment separated by a micropore filter. The cell suspension was placed in the upper compartment, and the lower compartment contained the test material. Chemotactic activity was assessed by counting the number of cells that migrate through the micropore filter toward the lower compartment. The production of chemotactic factor was found to be immunologically specific. The chemotactic factor was relatively heat stable after incubation at 56°C for 30 minutes. On Sephadex G-100 columns, peak activity was found in fractions where MIF peak activity was found.

This chemotactic factor was differentiated from MIF by gel electrophoresis. Peak chemotactic activity was found in the fraction containing albumin. In contrast, MIF peak activity was found in the prealbumin region in all of the experiments (29). These experiments indicate that the mononuclear cell chemotactic factor can be dissociated from MIF by the slower electrophoretic migration of the chemotactic factor in disc electophoresis.

Furthermore, preliminary experiments employing isopycnic centrifugation in CsCl gradients as described in the section on MIF suggest that chemotactic factor bands in the protein region and not in fractions denser than protein as does MIF (Remold and Ward, unpublished observations). This agrees with experiments employing neuraminidase digestion which does not abolish chemotactic activity.

Chemotactic Factors for Other Cells

When acrylamide gel fractions from Sephadex G-100 filtered, stimulated lymphocyte supernatants were tested for chemotactic activity for neutrophils, it was found in the fraction closest to the gel origin containing materials that migrate slowly (38). It was also separated from the chemotactic factor for macrophages by sucrose gradients.

The finding that a neutrophil chemotactic factor is readily distinguishable from the mononuclear chemotactic factor by differences in electrophoretic behavior implies that the two factors are different molecular entities.

Using unfractionated lymphocyte supernatants, Cohen and Ward have reported the presence of a factor chemotactic for eosinophils (39). However, this activity is present only when antigen-antibody complexes are added to the lymphocyte supernatants. Ward has also reported a factor chemotactic for lymphocytes (40).

Macrophage Aggregation Factor

Lolekha et al reported that they observed clumping of macrophages when they incubated peritoneal exudate cells obtained from sensitive animals with antigen (41). This macrophage aggregation reached a maximum at 24 hours. Further, they showed that supernatants from sensitive lymphocytes which had been incubated with specific antigen caused peritoneal exudate cells from normal animals to clump at 3 to 4 hours. The have referred to the active material as macrophage aggregation factor or MAF.

In all likelihood MAF is another manifestation of MIF. The assay for MAF has an advantage in that it can be done in a test tube and thus requires little in the way of equipment. However, it has the disadvantages that quantification is limited and controls for toxicity are not simple to include.

Macrophage Activating Factor

Mackaness has shown that the enhancement of macrophage function during infection has an immunologic basis (42) and involves the lymphocyte (43). Besides being more spread out on glass and being more phagocytic than their normal counterparts (44), the stimulated macrophages show enhanced bactericidal capacity which is effective even against organisms antigenically unrelated to those infecting the host (42). It seems reasonable that the mediators which are at least part of the link between the two cell components in hypersensitivity might also be involved in the activation of macrophages so dramatically evident in cellular immunity.

Mooney and Waksman studied the effect of whole supernatants from stimulated lymphocyte cultures on macrophages (45). More cells were observed in dishes incubated with supernatants from antigen-stimulated lymphocytes than in the control dishes, and the number of "amoeboid" macrophages was considerably increased in those dishes.

Nathan et al (46) used MIF-rich fractions from Sephadex-chromatographed supernatants to study the effect of mediators on monolayer cultures of macrophages. After 72 hours of incubation twice as many macrophages were adherent to the bottom of the culture dish in MIF-treated cultures than in control cultures (46). This was not due to macrophage multiplication. If radioactive starch was added to these macrophage monolayers, the amount of starch phagocytized in the MIF-treated cultures was increased. While most of this enhancement could be accounted for by the increased number of macrophages in stimulated dishes, phagocytosis per cell was still increased about 20%. If dead tubercle bacilli were substituted for starch, the increased phagocytosis per cell was even more marked, approximately 50% (46).

In another series of experiments, Nathan compared the oxidation of glucose in macrophages treated with MIF-rich fractions with glucose oxidation in control cultures. He found that, under the influence of MIF, the treated macrophages showed an increase in glucose carbon-1 oxidation per cell from four- to eightfold (46).

To determine how much of the observed glucose oxidation represented metabolism through the hexose monophosphate shunt (HMPS),

CO_2 production after 3 days in supernatant fractions was compared using glucose labeled either on carbon-1 or carbon-6. The amount of oxidation of glucose-6-^{14}C was quite small, so that nearly all the observed oxidation of glucose-1-^{14}C could be attributed to HMPS. The reason for the increased HMPS activity is as yet unknown.

If the MIF-treated macrophages are observed by time-lapse cinematography, the cells appear more spread out than macrophages in control supernatants, and there is more ruffled membrane activity. In fact, the filmed cells appear to resemble closely the activated macrophages described by Mackaness (43) and by Cohn and Benson (47,48).

In more recent studies, Nathan carried out the characterization of this activating factor by neuraminidase digestion, Sephadex G-100 fractionation, and CsCl density gradient centrifugation (49). The activating factor could not be distinguished from MIF by these means, suggesting that, in fact, it is MIF. The kinetics of activation were further studied. The 3-day activation period can be divided into two stages. In the first, requiring 1 to 2 days, the macrophages are refractory to the influence of activating factor, but undergo changes which render them receptive. In the second stage, they respond to activating factor. Once the macrophages have been activated, the effect persists in the absence of activating factor for 24 hours.

Cytotoxic Factors

The production of a soluble cytotoxic material by sensitized lymphocytes stimulated with specific antigen was first described by Ruddle and Waksman (50,51). These workers showed that supernatants from sensitized rat lymph node cells, stimulated by soluble antigen, killed normal rat embryo fibroblasts. Later, others described the production of a cytotoxic factor from lymph node, spleen, and peritoneal cells obtained from guinea pigs with delayed hypersensitivity to a number of antigens using mouse cells as targets (52,53).

Granger and Williams (54) were the first to report the release of soluble toxic factors by sensitized lymphocytes incubated with their specific target cells as well as by normal lymphocytes stimulated nonspecifically by PHA. Further studies by Williams and Granger showed that lymphocytes from several species produced lymphotoxin (55). For example, mouse lymphotoxin produced morphological changes in L cells after 12 hours of incubation, and its effect was reversible up to 25 hours. Furthermore, it resists heating to 100°C for 20 minutes, has a molecular weight 85,000 to 95,000 and is stable at pH 2 to 12. It has a buoyant density like protein and is sensitive to phenol extraction and resistant to RNAse, DNAse, and trypsin. At pH 8.6 it migrates with albumin in electophoresis (56).

The production of lymphotoxic factor from lymphocytes obtained from human adenoid tissue was described by Williams and Granger (57). Human lymphotoxin (HLT) activity eluted from Sephadex G-100 fraction was estimated to contain molecules of molecular weight 80,000 to 90,000. HLT was stable between pH 5 and 8 and when heated to 56° for 1 hour, but lost activity after heating to 100°C for 2 minutes. It was resistant to RNAse, DNAse, and trypsin. It lost its activity when extracted with phenol and had a buoyant density on CsCl of ρ_{25} = 1.33, which is similar to protein. HLT at pH 8.6 is weakly charged and behaves as a slow moving beta or fast gamma globulin in electrophoresis (58). Its activity was not affected by rabbit antihuman serum but was neutralized by rabbit anti-HLT (58). Thus, the human cytotoxic factors are also clearly different from human MIF.

Coyne et al (59) found that peak activity of guinea pig lymphotoxin on Sephadex G-100 columns coincided with peak MIF activity. Sephadex G-75 fractionation revealed a major peak of activity in the fraction with molecules slightly smaller than albumin (MW 35,000 to 55,000). It is heat-sensitive at 60° for 30 minutes. Experiments using disc electrophoresis showed lymphotoxic activity in the fraction corresponding to albumin. Subjection of prepurifed lymphotoxin to isopycnic centrifugation in a CsCl gradient showed that lymphotoxin activity could be recovered from fractions containing the albumin marker. Further, incubation with neuraminidase did not abolish lymphotoxin activity; however, treatment with chymotrypsin abolishes lymphotoxin activity. According to these findings guinea pig lymphotoxin seems to be protein, and sialic acid does not appear to be required for its action. It is readily distinguishable from MIF.

Cloning Inhibitory Factor

Lebowitz and Lawrence have described a factor that prevented the growth of HeLa cells in culture (60). The factor was found in the supernatants from cultures of human tuberculin-sensitive blood lymphocytes incubated for 36 hours with PPD. A 98% reduction in HeLa cell clones was found in flasks containing supernatants from PPD-stimulated lymphocytes. Essentially, no reduction in cloning was found in cultures containing supernatants from controls. The cloning inhibitory factor is nondialyzable. Its activity was destroyed by heating to 56°C for 30 minutes, differing from the heat stability at this temperature of human lymphotoxin (58) and human MIF (36). Thus far the cloning inhibitory factor differs from human lymphotoxin in that it has not killed cells, and it is sensitive to heating at 56°C for 30 minutes. It is considered as separate from the cytotoxic factors unless it is shown to kill cells when concentrated. A material with similar biological activity, called proliferation inhibitory factor (PIF), was described by Green et al (61). Of special interest is the finding that PIF only affected proliferation of human cells in culture. It inhibited proliferation of HeLa cells, human amnion, HEp 2, and KB cells; it had no activity on chick embryo fibroblasts and none on mouse L cells, the cell line so exquisitely susceptible to human lymphotoxin. Preliminary data suggest that PIF is stable to 85°C for 30 minutes, nondialyzable, nonsedimentable at 90,000 × g, and destroyed by trypsin.

Although at first these findings stand in contrast to the results of the work on lymphotoxin, it is of interest that PIF is found when leukocyte culture supernatants are diluted. When tested at a dilution of 1–5, the supernatants were toxic to cells (61). These factors might have *in vivo* importance in inhibiting the growth of grafts or tumors.

Skin Reactive Factor

Evidence that soluble substances produced by stimulated lymphocytes might be playing a part in delayed hypersensitivity reactions *in vivo* was first obtained by Bennett and Bloom (28). They stimulated tuberculin-sensitive guinea pig lymph node lymphocytes with PPD in serum-free medium and found that the supernatants, in addition to demonstrating MIF activity, produced reactions following intradermal injection characterized by induration, erythema, and mononuclear cell infiltration. This skin reactive activity was found in the same Sephadex fraction as MIF eluting from Sephadex G-100 in the fraction containing molecules the size of serum albumin and a little smaller.

The production of skin reactive factor (SRF) by antigen-stimulated lymphocytes was also reported by Dumonde et al (62) and by Krejci et al (63). Pick et al (64) carried out studies on the characterization of SRF-containing supernatants from stimulated cell cultures. Peak skin reactivity on Sephadex G-200 was found by these workers in a fraction that contained molecules the size of albumin. Some activity was also found in the smaller adjacent fraction. Further purification of active Sephadex fractions on DEAE-cellulose was carried out, and an active fraction was obtained which eluted before albumin. The skin reactive activity was completely destroyed by pepsin digestion and partially destroyed by trypsin or papain digestion; it was insensitive to DNAse and RNAse.

More recently Pick et al (64,65) and Schwarz et al (66) independently reported that concanavalin A stimulated the production of SRF; PHA was also used as a stimulant in similar studies (67).

There are several questions about skin reactive factor which are as yet unresolved. It is quite likely that the skin lesions are the effect of a combination of at least some of the lymphocyte factors. It would be of interest to know where skin activity is found after electrophoresis on acrylamide gels, and whether, like MIF, skin reactive factor is destroyed by neuraminidase.

Mitogenic or Blastogenic Factors

Gordon and MacLean (68) and Kasakura and Lowenstein (69) simultaneously reported that supernatants from mixed human leukocyte cultures (MLC) contained materials that were mitogenic for unrelated lymphocytes. Subsequently several investigators have reported that nonsensitive lymphocytes undergo transformation when cultured in supernatants obtained from sensitized lymphocytes that had been incubated with specific antigen.

Valentine and Lawrence (70) found that supernatants from tuberculin-sensitive cells with PPD caused an increase in thymidine incorporation by nonsensitive cells. This blastogenic factor was nondialyzable, did not sediment at $100,000 \times g$, and was destroyed by heating at $56°C$ for 30 minutes. Maini et al (71) have also described a mitogenic factor produced by human tuberculin-sensitive lymphocytes during stimulation with PPD. Studies by Janis and Bach (72) also indicate that mitogenic capability is present in supernatants from MLC. They have stated that maximum blastogenic activity from MLC is found at about 4 days and that it is present in the $105,000 \times g$ supernatant. The factor is excluded on Sephadex G-25 and is unaffected by treatment with RNAse or DNAse.

The production of a mitogenic factor by guinea-pig-sensitized lymphocytes in response to specific antigen has been reported from several laboratories (53,62,73–75). The possibility raised by the existence of mitogenic factors, that of a substance which can turn on or recruit nonsensitive cells, could provide a mechanism for expanding a cellular reaction and enlarging the production of other mediators.

Factors Mediating the Cooperation of T and B cells

Interaction between T and B lymphocytes *in vitro* is now well established (76,77). Recently Feldman and Basten demonstrated that T–B lymphocyte cooperation as measured by antibody response is as effective when the cell populations were separated by cell-impermeable membranes as when they were mixed together (78). This finding suggests the existence of a mediator produced by T lymphocytes which is capable of activating B lymphocytes. Using lymphocyte supernatants, Sjöberg et al demonstrated the existence of a similar factor (79).

Interferon

Leukocytes or lymphocytes have been shown to produce interferon when stimulated by various viral interferon inducers or by some nonviral inducers (80–83). Glasgow demonstrated that peritoneal exudate cells from mice immunized against Chikungunya virus (CV) incubated *in vitro* with CV produced 2 to 10 times more interferon than cells from nonimmunized controls (84). He found the reaction to be immunologically specific.

Green et al (61) described the production of interferon-like material by tuberculin-sensitive human lymphocytes when incubated with PPD.

Interferon after PHA stimulation was maximum during the first 4 days of culture and with antigen between days 4 and 7, which correlates with the appearance of blastoid cells in the culture. The antigen-induced viral inhibitor also showed certain characteristics associated with interferon: It is stable at pH 4 to 10 at 4°C for 24 hours, nonsedimentable at 100,000 g for 2 hours, resistant to DNAse and RNAse, but destroyed by trypsin. Its effect was species specific for cells of human origin; it did not protect mouse L cells, chick embryo fibroblasts, and rabbit kidney cells against the viruses tested. Recently Epstein et al (85) could demonstrate that interferon production of stimulated lymphocytes is increased threefold in the presence of macrophages. No interferon was detected in cultures of macrophages alone.

It is rather surprising that lymphocytes, which produce interferon upon challenge by antigen, apparently simultaneously allow viral replication in the stimulated cells. This was first described in lymphocytes stimulated by PHA (86). Recently Bloom et al have used this phenomenon in an ingenious assay for the detection of specifically sensitive cells (87). Lymphocytes are stimulated by antigen, and then later, virus is added. The virus multiplies in the stimulated cells and can be detected in a plaque assay.

The production of interferon during or following a specific immunologic reaction is potentially very meaningful. Since persons who are unable to mount an adequate delayed hypersensitivity response are plagued by viral infections it will be especially interesting to learn whether antigen-induced interferon produced by lymphocytes could be significant in immunity to these organisms.

Antibody Production

Lymphoid tissue and lymphoid cells taken from sensitized animals or persons are known to produce immunoglobulins under various culture conditions. Meyers et al (88) showed that under conditions used to produce MIF specific antibody is produced. Although the amount of antibody is small and difficult to detect, its presence should be considered when other biological activities of unfractionated fluids from lymphocyte cultures are assessed, as some systems may be sensitive to low levels of antigen-antibody complexes.

SUMMARY AND CONCLUSIONS

In conclusion, it is apparent that a number of biologically active mediators produced by appropriately stimulated lymphocytes may contribute significantly to the mediation of cellular hypersensitivity *in vivo*. The biological activities of these mediators *in vitro* suggest that they may be capable *in vivo* of attracting other cells, notably macrophages, of keeping them at the site, and of activating them, as is discussed in detail in the next chapter. This is quite consistent with the data available from *in vivo* experiments on the contribution of specifically sensitive and non-sensitive cells to the delayed hypersensitivity response. However, it is also clear that the situation *in vivo* is complex and that factors other than sensitive lymphocytes, antigen, and macrophages may influence the delayed reaction. Thus, the number of cells involved, local tissue factors, and lysosomal enzyme levels might be of importance for the manifestation of *in vivo* delayed hypersensitivity.

After adding up all the new information, it becomes increasingly evident how little we know about cellular immune reactions. Not only does the question of the nature of the mediators, their *in vivo* distribution, and their exact conditions of release remain to be determined, but also their effect on receptor cells is not understood. We barely start at this time to notice certain changes in the macrophage, without yet being able to see the correlations. Without a doubt, this will be one of the major areas to require attention in the near future. The further characterization of the mediators and their interaction with the target cells is of no less importance.

Further studies might well reveal a sequence of reactions taking place between the mediator and the target cell, as is the case in the clotting, kinin, and complement systems, rather than a single reaction step (89,90).

Eventually all those efforts should be crowned by the understanding of the *in vivo* events that culminate in the manifestation of cellular immunity. Significant progress in defining cellular reactions may be important in maintaining man's health and ameliorating some of his serious diseases. Even apart from this aspect, cellular immunity is a most interesting phenomenon to investigate as it is one of the fascinating examples in cell biology where various reaction mechanisms of a cell can be modulated by chemical substances.

REFERENCES

1. Rich, A. R. and Lewis, M. R., *Bull. Johns Hopkins Hosp.* **50,** 115 (1932).
2. Moen, J. K. and Swift, H. F., *J. Exp. Med.* **64,** 339 (1936).
3. Heilman, D. H., Feldman, W. H., and Mann, F. C., *Am. Rev. Tuberc.* **50,** 344 (1944).
4. Marks, J., *J. Pathol. Bacteriol.* **75,** 39 (1958).
5. Fabrizio, A. M., *Am. Rev. Tuberc.* **65,** 250 (1952).
6. Svejcar, J. and Johanovsky, J., *Z. Immunitaetsforsch.* **122,** 420 (1961).
7. Svejcar, J., Pekarek, J., and Johanovsky, J., *Immunology* **15,** 1 (1968).
8. George, M. and Vaughan, J. H., *Proc. Soc. Exp. Biol. Med.* **111,** 154 (1962).
9. David, J. R., Al-Askari, S., Lawrence, H. S., and Thomas, L., *J. Immunol.* **93,** 264 (1964).
10. David, J. R. and Schlossman, S. F., *J. Exp. Med.* **128,** 1451 (1968).
11. Benacerraf, B. and Gell, P. G. H., *Immunology* **2,** 53 (1959).
12. Benacerraf, B. and Levine, B. B., *J. Exp. Med.* **115,** 1023 (1962).
13. David, J. R., Lawrence, H. S., and Thomas, L., *J. Immunol.* **93,** 279 (1964).
14. Carpenter, R. R. and Brandriss, M. W., *J. Exp. Med.* **120,** 1231 (1964).
15. Schlossman, S. F., Ben-Efraim, S., Yaron, A., and Sober, H. A., *J. Exp. Med.* **123,** 1083 (1966).
16. Stulbarg, M. and Schlossman, S. F., *J. Immunol.* **101,** 764 (1968).
17. Ovary, Z. and Benacerraf, B., *Proc. Soc. Exp. Biol. Med.* **114,** 72 (1963).
18. Schlossman, S. F. and Levine, H., *Cell. Immunol.* **1,** 419 (1970).
19. Schlossman, S. F., and Levine, H., *J. Immunol.* **96,** 111 (1967).
20. David, J. R., Lawrence, H. S., and Thomas, L., *J. Immunol.* **93,** 274 (1964).

21. David, J. R., *Immunopharmacology, Proceedings of the 3rd International Pharmacological Meeting 1966,* Pergamon Press, London, 1966, p. 11.

22. David, J. R., *J. Exp. Med.* **122,** 1115 (1965).

23. Bloom, B. R. and Bennett, B., *Science* **153,** 80 (1966).

24. Dumonde, D. C., *Brit. Med. Bull.* **23,** 9 (1967).

25. Bartfeld, H. and Atoynatan, T., *Proc. Soc. Exp. Biol. Med.* **130,** 497 (1969).

26. Bennett, B. and Bloom, B. R., *Transplantation* **5,** 996 (1967).

27. David, J. R., *Proc. Natl. Acad. Sci.* **56,** 72 (1966).

28. Bennett, B. and Bloom, B. R., *Proc. Natl. Acad. Sci.* **59,** 756 (1968).

29. Remold, H. G., Katz, A. B., Haber, E., and David, J. R., *Cell. Immunol.* **1,** 133 (1970).

30. Bloom, B. R. and Jimenez, L., *Am. J. Pathol.* **60,** 453 (1970).

31. Remold, H. G. and David, J. R., *J. Immunol.* **107,** 1090 (1971).

32. Dumonde, D. C., Page, D. A., Matthew, M., and Wolstencroft, R. A., *Clin. Exp. Immunol.* **10,** 25 (1972).

33. Schwartz, H. J., Pelley, R. P., and Leon, M. A., *Fed. Proc.* **29,** 360 abstr. (1970).

34. Remold, H. G., David, R. A., and David, J. R., *J. Immunol.* **109,** 578 (1972).

35. Coyne, J. A., Remold, H. G., and David, J. R., *Fed. Proc.* **30,** 647 abstr. (1971).

36. Rocklin, R. E., Remold, H. G., and David, J. R., *Cell. Immunol.,* in press.

37. McCluskey, R. T., Benacerraf, B., and McCluskey, J. R., *J. Immunol.* **90,** 466 (1963).

38. Ward, P. A., Remold, H. G., and David, J. R., *Cell. Immunol.* **1,** 162 (1970).

39. Cohen, S. and Ward, P. A., *J. Exp. Med.* **133,** 133 (1971).

40. Ward, P. A., *Biochemistry of the Acute Allergic Reactions,* Blackwell Scientific Publications, Oxford, 1971, p. 229.

41. Lolekha, S., Dray, S., and Gotoff, S. P., *J. Immunol.* **104,** 296 (1970).

42. Mackaness, G. B., *J. Exp. Med.* **120,** 105 (1964).

43. Mackaness, G. B., *J. Exp. Med.* **129,** 973 (1969).

44. Mackaness, G. B., *Infectious Agents and Host Reactions,* W. B. Saunders Company, Philadelphia, 1970, p. 62.

45. Mooney, J. J. and Waksman, B. H., *J. Immunol.* **105,** 1138 (1970).

46. Nathan, C. F., Karnovsky, M. L., and David, J. R., *J. Exp. Med.* **133,** 1356 (1971).

47. Cohn, Z. A. and Benson, B., *J. Exp. Med.* **121,** 835 (1965).

48. Cohn, Z. A. and Benson, B., *J. Exp. Med.* **122,** 455 (1965).

49. Nathan, C. F., Remold, H. G., and David, J. R., *J. Exp. Med.* in press.

50. Ruddle, N. H. and Waksman, B. H., *Science* **157,** 1060 (1967).

51. Ruddle, N. H. and Waksman, B. H., *J. Exp. Med.* **128,** 1237 (1968).

52. Heise, E. R. and Weiser, R. S., *J. Immunol.* **103,** 570 (1969).

53. Dumonde, D. C., Wolstencroft, R. A., Panayi, G. S., Matthew, M., Morely, J., and Howson, W. T., *Nature* **224,** 38 (1969).

54. Granger, G. A. and Williams, T. W., *Nature* **218,** 1253 (1968).

55. Williams, T. W. and Granger, G. A., *Nature* **219,** 1076 (1968).

56. Williams, T. W. and Granger, G. A., *J. Immunol.* **102,** 911 (1969).

57. Williams, T. W. and Granger, G. A., *J. Immunol.* **103,** 170 (1969).

58. Kolb, W. P. and Granger, G. A., *Proc. Natl. Acad. Sci.* **61,** 1250 (1968).

59. Coyne, J. A., Remold, H. G., and David, J. R., *Fed. Proc.*, **30**, 647 abstr. (1971).

60. Lebowitz, A. and Lawrence, H. S., *Fed. Proc.* **28**, 630 (1970).

61. Green, J. A., Cooperband, S. R., Rutstein, J. A., and Kibrick, S., *J. Immunol.* **105**, 48 (1970).

62. Dumonde, D. C., Howson, W. T., and Wolstencroft, R. A., *Immunopathology, 5th International Symposium,* Schwabe and Company, Basel, Switzerland, 1968, p. 263.

63. Krejci, J., Pecareck, J., Johanovsky, J., and Svejcar, J., *Immunology* **16**, 677 (1969).

64. Pick, E., Krejci, J., Cech, K., and Turk, J. L., *Immunology* **17**, 741 (1969).

65. Pick, E., Krejci, J., and Turk, J. L., *Nature* **225**, 236 (1970).

66. Schwarz, H. J., Leon, M. E. A., and Pelley, R. P., *J. Immunol* **104**, 265 (1970).

67. Pick, E., Brostoff, J. J., Krejci, J., and Turk, J. L., *Cell. Immunol.* **1**, 92 (1970).

68. Gordon, J. and MacLean, L. D., *Nature* **208**, 795 (1965).

69. Kasakura, S. and Lowenstein, L., *Nature* **208**, 794 (1965).

70. Valentine, F. T. and Lawrence, H. S., *Science* **165**, 1014 (1969).

71. Maini, R. N., Bryceson, A. D. M., Wolstencroft, R. A., and Dumonde, D. C., *Nature* **224**, 43 (1969).

72. Janis, M. and Bach, F. H., *Nature* **225**, 238 (1970).

73. Bloom, B. R. and Bennett, B., *Fed. Proc.* **27**, 13 (1968).

74. Spitler, L. E. and Lawrence, H. S., *J. Immunol.* **103**, 1072 (1969).

75. Wolstencroft, R. A. and Dumonde, D. C., *Immunology* **18**, 559 (1970).

76. Cheers, C., Breitner, J. C. S., Little, M., and Miller, J. F. A. P., *Nat. New Biol.* **232**, 248 (1971).

77. Chan, E. L., Mishell, R. I., and Mishell, G. F., *Science* **170**, 1225 (1970).

78. Feldman, M. and Basten, A., *J. Exp. Med.* **136**, 49 (1972).

79. Sjöberg, O., Andersson, J., and Moller, G., *J. Immunol.* in press.

80. Friedman, R. M. and Cooper, H. L., *Proc. Soc. Exp. Biol. Med.* **125**, 901 (1967).

81. Wheelock, E. F., *Science* **149**, 310 (1965).

82. Gresser, I., *Proc. Soc. Exp. Biol. Med.* **108**, 799 (1961).

83. Kono, Y., *Proc. Soc. Exp. Biol. Med.* **124**, 155 (1967).

84. Glasgow, L. A., *J. Bacteriol.* **91**, 2185 (1966).

85. Epstein, L. B., Cline, M. J., and Merigan, T. C., *Cell. Immunol.* **2**, 602 (1971).

86. Edelman, R. and Wheelock, E. F., *Science* **154**, 1053 (1966).

87. Bloom, B. R., Jimenez, L., and Marcus, P. I., *J. Exp. Med.* **132**, 16 (1970).

88. Meyers, O. L., Shoji, M., Remold, H. G., and David, J. R., *Cell. Immunol.* **3**, 442 (1972).

89. Ratnoff, O. D., *Adv. Immunol.* **10**, 145 (1969).

90. Wuepper, K. D., Tucker, E. S., and Cochrane, C. C., *J. Immunol.* **105**, 1307 (1970).

Chapter Three

In Vivo Manifestations of Lymphokine and Lymphokine-Like Activity

TAKESHI YOSHIDA AND STANLEY COHEN

Department of Pathology, State University of New York at Buffalo

In the preceding chapter attention was focused on a class of soluble mediator substances that can be produced by lymphocytes under certain experimental conditions. These substances have been defined collectively as "lymphokines" by Dumonde et al (1), and, for convenience, this term is used throughout the present discussion. When the triggering event for lymphokine production is the stimulation of sensitized lymphocytes by specific antigen, the lymphocytes must be obtained from donors that exhibit delayed hypersensitivity, or cellular immunity (2–4). Moreover, at least one of the lymphokines has been shown directly to be produced by T cells, which are generally accepted as the mediator cells for the various biologic reactions dependent on cellular immunity (5). Thus,

Some of the work reported here was supported by N.I.H. Grant No. AI-09114 and funds from a Dr. Henry C. and Bertha H. Buswell Fellowship.

although lymphokine production has been observed predominantly in *in vitro* situations, various lymphokines have been suggested as the putative mediators of the reactions of cellular immunity *in vivo*. The best known example is MIF, which is discussed in detail in the preceding chapter. In this chapter we explore evidence in support of this contention. Such evidence falls into several broad categories. The simplest focuses on the effects produced when lymphokines obtained under the usual *in vitro* conditions are injected directly into experimental animals. Closely related are experiments in which attempts are made to transfer one or another of the reactions dependent on cellular immunity to normal recipients by using living lymphocytes within chambers permeable to soluble factors but not intact cells. Another broad category is related to those studies in which extracts of tissues that are the sites of reactions of cellular immunity are examined for lymphokine or lymphokine-like activity. Finally, it is possible to manipulate certain *in vivo* model systems that are simple correlates of the usual, rather complex manifestations of delayed hypersensitivity.

MACROPHAGE DISAPPEARANCE REACTIONS

Willoughby et al have found that rats immunized with complete Freund's adjuvant have increased numbers of monocytes in their peripheral blood for several weeks following immunization (6). This is of some importance, since, as was pointed out in Chapter 1, the blood monocytes are the precursors of the macrophages that are found in reactions of cellular immunity and in inflammatory exudates as well. Yoshida et al (7) have confirmed and extended these studies. They found that rats or guinea pigs immunized with various antigens in complete Freund's adjuvant showed increases in peripheral blood monocytes for at least 2 weeks following immunization, in agreement with previous studies. However, when specific antigen was injected intravenously into such immunized animals, there was a prompt reduction in the number of circulating monocytes. The maximal disappearance of monocytes from the circulation occurred at 6 hours following antigen administration. Following this drop, there was a slow return to normal or slightly elevated levels over the next 20 to 24 hours. Labeling experiments with ^{3}H-thymidine showed that this was not due to the reappearance of the "lost" monocytes, but rather was caused by a rapid release of new cells from the bone marrow. It was shown in these studies that the effect of antigen on blood monocytes was a function of the state of delayed hypersensitivity of the animals, and that this reaction was therefore a manifestation of cellular immunity. It was postulated that these alterations of the monocyte content of peripheral blood were caused by the systemic release of MIF. Attempts to detect the release of MIF or MIF-like substances into the circulation in this experimental setting are discussed in a subsequent section.

A similar reaction of macrophages in peritoneal exudates has been described by Nelson and Boyden (8). They induced nonspecific peritoneal inflammatory exudates in delayed hypersensitive guinea pigs by the intraperitoneal injection of glycogen. Three or four days after the injection of this irritant, these exudates consist mainly of mononuclear cells, and of these, macrophages predominate. The intraperitoneal injection of specific antigen at this time causes a prompt reduction in the macrophage content of such exudates; 5 hours following antigen administration there is a drop of approximately 90% in the absolute number of these cells recoverable in the peritoneal fluid. There is a slow recovery of macrophage content over the next 24 to 48 hours. This reaction, which is known as the macrophage disappearance reaction, or MDR, clearly has features in common with the effect of antigen on circulating monocytes described by Yoshida et al (7). Several lines of evidence have been presented to show that the MDR is a manifestation of cell-mediated immunity (8–10). Perhaps most convincing is the recent demonstration that the MDR can be transferred to unimmunized animals by T, but not by B lymphocytes (5). This was accomplished by separating lymphocytes from sensitized guinea pigs on the basis of the presence or absence of a receptor for the third component of complement on the lymphocyte surface. There is good evidence that lymphocytes with such receptors (complement receptor lymphocytes, or CRL) correspond to B cells and that lymphocytes which lack such receptors (NCRL) correspond to T cells (11–13). Such evidence includes the location of CRL in thymus-independent areas of lymphoid tissue and NCRL in thymus-dependent areas of such tissue, and in mice, a dissociation between Θ-bearing and CRL lymphocyte populations. It was found by Sonozaki and Cohen (5) that NCRL, but not CRL, is capable of transferring the MDR.

Nelson and North (10) have reported that the MDR is a consequence of increased macrophage adhesiveness induced by specific antigen. This leads to clumping and sticking of macrophages to peritoneal surfaces, with a subsequent drop in the number recoverable from the peritoneal fluid (10). The bulk of the experimental evidence favors the view that the MDR is an *in vivo* analog of the migration inhibition reaction *in vitro*. It provides an especially suitable model system with which to explore lymphokine activity *in vivo*.

Previously, Najarian and Feldman (14) had attempted to transfer tu-

berculin or contact sensitivity passively by implanting sensitized lymphocytes and antigen in micropore chambers in guinea pigs. As stated in
Chapter 1, these reactions could be transferred by living cells, but not
by antiserum. Najarian and Feldman attempted to demonstrate that the
reaction was produced by a soluble factor released from the lymphocytes,
rather than by local proliferation of donor cells or direct interaction
of donor cells with host cells. This attempt proved unsuccessful. The
failure may have been in part related to barriers to free diffusion of
soluble mediator and/or antigen in their system, which involved the
subcutaneous implantation of chambers containing cells, but no antigen.
Also, there was no attempt made to purify the cell populations used
for transfer. Donor macrophages were thus present with the lymphocytes
in the chambers, and they may have absorbed sufficient amounts of
lymphocyte-derived mediator substance to prevent the reaction outside
the chamber, where the test antigen was placed. For these reasons, Sonozaki and Cohen (15) performed analogous experiments using the MDR
as the model system. It was found that as few as 2×10^6 lymphocytes
from sensitized donors, when implanted with specific antigen in micropore chambers within the peritoneal cavity of normal animals with
preexisting inflammatory peritoneal exudates, were capable of inducing
an 84% reduction in the macrophage content of those exudates. As was
the case when lymphocytes were transferred directly, populations of cells
corresponding to T, but not B cells were capable of mediating the reaction. In the same report (15), it was shown that supernatant fluids from
cultures of sensitized lymphocytes incubated in the presence of specific
antigen could substitute for intact lymphocytes. The injection of such
fluids into unimmunized animals with peritoneal exudates reduced macrophage content by approximately 70%. These results all provided evidence that the MDR is mediated by a soluble factor, or lymphokine.
Moreover, they showed that at least one lymphokine was produced by
T cells.

RECOVERY OF LYMPHOKINE-LIKE ACTIVITY FROM TISSUES

If lymphokine activity is involved in the pathogenesis of the various
forms of cell-mediated immunity, it should be possible to demonstrate
the presence of such substances in extracts of tissues that are the sites
of these reactions. Since none of the currently known lymphokines is
available in pure form for absolute characterization or identification,
and it has not yet proved feasible to prepare monospecific antisera
against these factors, it is not possible to identify the substances directly.

Rather, one must look for lymphokine or for lymphokine-like activity in the extracts by the various biologic assays currently available. In this regard, many investigators have attempted to detect MIF activity in extracts of delayed hypersensitivity skin reaction sites. These attempts have been uniformly unsuccessful. There are several possible explanations for this failure, the most obvious one being that MIF might not play a role in the evolution of the delayed hypersensitivity reaction in the skin. Another and less heretical possibility is that only small amounts of MIF are produced and released at these sites, and that this material is rapidly adsorbed to cells or other tissue constituents. The adsorbed MIF might not be released into the medium by the relatively crude extraction procedures currently in use. Even under *in vitro* conditions, MIF-rich supernatant fluids lose activity on standing in the unfrozen state, not only by denaturation, but also because the MIF adsorbs to the surface of the container (16). Results of experiments designed to show adsorption of MIF to macrophages are not entirely consistent. It seems as if peritoneal exudate macrophages are more effective than alveolar macrophages in this regard (17,18), although some reports indicate that alveolar cells can be inhibited in their migration, and thus probably adsorb MIF (19,20). Even if MIF is not completely adsorbed *in vivo,* it may be that local enzymatic activity degrades any remaining free material rapidly. There is also a technical difficulty in these experiments. The controls for these kinds of experiments make use of extracts of normal skin or skin undergoing a nonimmunological inflammatory reaction. The migration of macrophages in the presence of the experimental extract fluid is compared to the migration of these cells in the presence of extract fluids from these control sites. Pick et al (21) and Okuyama et al (22) have shown that normal macrophages can spontaneously release an MIF-like substance when cultured *in vitro.* It is possible that the presence of such activity in extract fluids, as well as sublethal concentrations of nonspecific toxic products of metabolism, might lead to a "base line" migration inhibition that would mask the presence of true MIF.

Chemotactic Factors in Skin Extracts

Cohen et al (23) studied extracts of skin sites of classic delayed hypersensitivity as well as contact reactions to simple skin-sensitizing compounds in an attempt to detect various lymphokine activities in these extracts. Contact reactions are especially suitable for such study because they are manifestations of pure cell-mediated immunity without an Arthus component, and because they do not require intradermal injection, thus eliminating the effect of mechanical trauma on the tissues studied. In agreement with the results of others, they were unable to detect MIF activity. However, when the extracts were injected in the peritoneal cavity of unimmunized guinea pigs bearing glycogen-induced exudates, a two- to threefold increase in macrophage content was consistently observed. This result should be contrasted to that observed when MIF-rich lymphocyte culture supernatants are injected into similarly prepared guinea pigs and a reduction rather than increase in macrophage content occurs. This result suggested that macrophage chemotactic factors might be present in the extract fluids. Accordingly, extracts of sites of delayed reactions to various protein antigens or of sites of contact reactions to *o*-chlorobenzoyl chloride, a potent sensitizing agent, were examined by means of the Boyden double-chamber assay system (24) for the presence of *in vitro* chemotactic activity. Chemotactic activity toward macrophages and lymphocytes, but not neutrophils, could be detected in these extract fluids. Extracts prepared from normal skin or from skin sites of nonspecific inflammatory reactions did not show such activity. Ultracentrifugation analysis in sucrose density gradients of these chemotactic factors demonstrated them to be similar to the respective factors previously obtained from supernatant fluids from lymphocytes cultured with specific antigen (see Chapter 2). Thus, at least 2 lymphokines, or at least lymphokine-like activities, could be recovered from sites of cell-mediated reactions.

Lymphokine Activity in Serum

As was discussed previously, circulating monocytes "disappear" rapidly when delayed hypersensitive animals are challenged intravenously with specific antigen. Attempts were made to detect MIF activity in the sera of such animals. Preliminary studies, using soluble protein antigens, were unsuccessful (7). Recent studies along these lines have made use of guinea pigs immunized by intramuscular injection of 0.5 mg of the BCG strain of tubercle bacilli, and subsequently challenged intravenously with 0.5 mg of BCG. This procedure induces an intense state of delayed hypersensitivity, and this state is associated with massive splenomegaly as well as peripheral lymphadenopathy. Sera were obtained from these animals at various times following intravenous challenge. MIF activity was detectable in the sera of these animals, but never in unimmunized animals or those controls which were immunized but unchallenged. Activity was maximal at 6 to 12 hours, corresponding to the times of greatest reduction in the numbers of circulating monocytes. Similar observations have been made by Salvin and Youngner (25) using mice immunized and challenged with BCG.

In addition to the theoretical implications of such studies, they raise the possibility of detecting MIF activity in the sera of patients with various diseases thought to involve cell-mediated immunity. This provides a convenient alternative to studies in which peripheral white blood cells from such patients are utilized for migration inhibition assays.

Lymphokine Activity in Peritoneal Exudates

The macrophage disappearance reaction (MDR) has been described in detail in a previous section. As stated there, this reaction seems to be an *in vivo* analog of the *in vitro* migration inhibition assay. Accordingly, peritoneal exudate fluids from animals undergoing the MDR have been examined for the presence of detectable MIF (26). Guinea pigs with delayed hypersensitivity to ovalbumin and bearing 4-day-old glycogen-induced peritoneal exudates were challenged by an intraperitoneal injection of specific antigen. Animals were sacrificed at various intervals after this injection, and peritoneal exudates were collected, using a total of 100 ml of buffered saline. Cells were removed by centrifugation, and fluids concentrated 20-fold by pressure dialysis. Fluids obtained from similar animals challenged with saline, or from unimmunized, exudate-bearing animals challenged with egg albumin, were used as controls. The experimental fluids prepared had detectable MIF activity at dilutions of up to 1:6. Maximal activity was recovered between 4 and 6 hours following antigenic challenge, slightly earlier than is the case for serum MIF. Preliminary attempts to assay for chemotactic activity in these preparations have led to the detection of small but definite amounts of macrophage chemotactic factor, as well as MIF. Lymphocyte chemotactic factor could not be demonstrated, which is consistent with the observation that the number of these cells remains relatively constant during the MDR.

Leu et al (18) have recently reported that peritoneal exudate macrophages have receptors for MIF and can adsorb that substance. Since cells were removed by centrifugation in the studies described above, it is clear that the MIF activity detected represented MIF produced in excess of that required to saturate the macrophages present. Such excess MIF makes its appearance at the same time, or shortly before the MDR reaches a maximum.

Lymphokine Activity in Joint Fluid

Stastny and Ziff (27) have reported both cytotoxic and migration inhibitory activity in fluid from arthritic joints. The former was detected by the inhibition of ^{14}C-labeled amino acid incorporation, the latter by the classic MIF assay. Two fractions were obtained with these activities; one was dialyzable, the other was not. The dialyzable macrophage migration inhibitor was characterized by low molecular weight (4000), and was produced *in vivo* by polymorphonuclear leukocytes in association with acute synovitis. In contrast, the nondialyzable migration inhibition factor was found mainly in effusions from chronic synovitis, and especially in cases of rheumatoid arthritis. Moreover, *in vitro* cultures of rheumatoid synovial membranes, containing intense mononuclear cell inflammatory infiltrates, could be shown to release similar substances into the culture medium. The factor involved has a molecular weight of approximately 70,000, higher than the reported value for human MIF. It is possible that the cytotoxic factor which may be present at low concentrations during the migration inhibition assay damages the macrophage membranes and makes them less motile, and that the substance does not represent true MIF. Studies on the viability of the cells in this system, and on the reversibility of the migration inhibition effect, would be of interest. In any case, these studies point out that substances with biologic activity similar to lymphokine activity are present at certain inflammatory sites, and it is quite likely that these substances play a role in the pathogenesis of the reaction at these sites.

REACTIONS INDUCED BY LYMPHOKINE INJECTION

As stated in the preceding chapter, Bennett and Bloom (28) first reported that MIF-rich lymphocyte culture supernatants could induce an inflammatory reaction when injected into normal guinea pig skin. The reaction was predominantly mononuclear, and was histologically similar to a typical tuberculin reaction. SRF does not produce a pure mononuclear infiltrate; variable numbers of neutrophils are also found. However, as pointed out in Chapter 1, neutrophilic infiltration is frequently present in classic reactions of delayed hypersensitivity as well. Bennett and Bloom could not separate the responsible agent, which was named skin reactive factor, or SRF, from MIF by Sephadex chromatography. Since then, a number of other reports of SRF activity in cultures of lymphocytes stimulated by specific antigen have appeared (16,21,29), and in addition, it has been shown that lymphocytes from nonimmune animals can be triggered by various mitogens to produce SRF (30–32). The conditions of culture which are necessary are similar to those used for the production of MIF by mitogen-stimulated lymphocytes.

Skin reactions induced by SRF start to appear within 2 hours following injection, and reach maximum size in under 12 hours. The reaction fades slowly but is definitely present at 24 hours. The rapidity of evolution, as compared to a delayed reaction elicited by antigen in a sensitized animal, probably reflects the fact that preformed material is being presented to the animal in large amounts in the former situation. In any case, the term "delayed hypersensitivity" is something of a misnomer; as we have seen, certain manifestations of cellular immunity such as the MDR attain peak intensity relatively shortly after elicitation.

As was already discussed, extracts of skins that are the sites of cell-mediated reactions contain detectable lymphokine activity as assayed by their effect on mononuclear cells *in vitro* and *in vivo*. In addition, it has been found that these extracts, when injected into normal guinea pig skin, produce inflammatory reactions which are in every way identical to those produced by SRF obtained from lymphocyte cultures (Figures 1a–c) (23). This is of some interest for two reasons. First, the observation demonstrates yet another lymphokine or lymphokine-like activity in these extracts. More important, it shows the presence of skin reactive activity in a situation where chemotactic activity is demonstrable but MIF activity is not. In this regard, it is relatively difficult to demonstrate an effect of MIF made in one species upon macrophages of another, although it is possible to do so (33,34). In contrast, SRF seems to show little species specificity (35). It is widely acknowledged that SRF probably represents the combined actions of several lymphokines. All these observations raise the possibility that chemotactic factors may be of more importance in this regard than MIF. Another point that emerges is that different lymphokines may play different roles in different reactions of cellular immunity. It may well be that chemotactic factor activity predominates in the mechanism of evolution of the skin reaction of delayed hypersensitivity. As we have seen, MIF may be of importance in reactions occurring either in the circulatory system or in the peritoneal cavity. Lymphotoxic factors almost certainly play a role in certain autoimmune states, and so on. Thus, although any given manifestation of cell-mediated immunity probably represents an interaction of many lymphokines, the specific "blend" probably varies with the particular reaction under study. This concept may explain the pleomorphic histologic manifestations of cell-mediated reactions described in Chapter 1 by McCluskey and Leber. This point was discussed in detail; a single example will serve here. There are a number of situations in which eosinophils

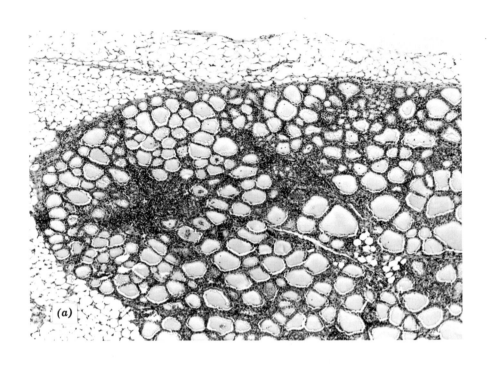

(a)

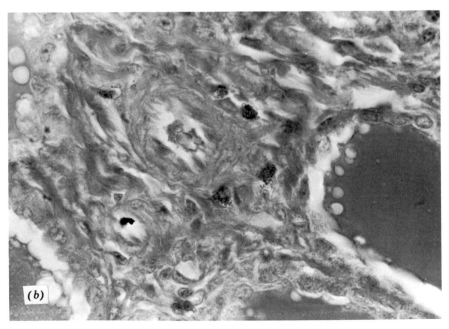

(b)

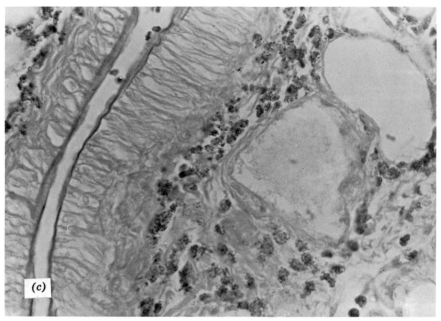

Figure 2. Eosinophils in experimental autoimmune thyroiditis. (a). Low-power view of thyroid showing moderate lymphocytic infiltration. (b). High-power view showing several eosinophils near a thyroid follicle. (c) Inflammatory infiltrate near a vessel in the thyroid. The bulk of the inflammatory cells in this field are eosinophils.

is similar to that of lesions produced by SRF. It should be emphasized that in these and other studies involving the detection of eosinophils in guinea pigs, special histologic fixation and stains are necessary, as granules are poorly preserved and the cells are weakly stained by routine procedures in this species.

These *in vivo* studies suggested that certain experimental autoimmune reactions which were manifestations of cellular immunity should be associated with eosinophil infiltration, provided that appropriate antibody was also present. A study designed to test this possibility was undertaken. Guinea pigs were immunized with thyroglobulin in complete Freund's adjuvant. Thyroids were excised at suitable intervals and stained for eosinophils (Figures 2a–c). Every animal with lymphocytic infiltration of the thyroid and circulating antibody had eosinophils within the thyroid gland as well. Animals with thyroiditis but no antibody did not have eosinophil infiltration, nor did animals given antibody passively in amounts equal to those found in the positive experimental animals (38). Interestingly, the eosinophils were not found predominantly within the areas of greatest lymphocytic infiltration, but rather were found between these areas and connective tissue trabeculae containing vessels. The pattern suggested that the eosinophils were appearing in an interface area where antibody was entering from the general circulation and lymphokine was diffusing following local production by the lymphocytic infiltrates.

LYMPHOKINE-LIKE ACTIVITY FROM NONLYMPHOID CELLS

As has been indicated previously, it is possible to obtain a migration inhibitory factor from lymphocytes in the absence of an immune reaction; this can be accomplished by stimulating normal lymphocytes with mitogenic substances such as concanavalin A (39,40). Recent reports have also described MIF or MIF-like activity in supernatants of proliferating lymphocyte cultures in the absence of mitogenic stimulation and similar activity in supernatants from cultures of various nonlymphoid cells such as fibroblasts or cells derived from lung and brain (41,42). There is a great deal of controversy as to whether or not these substances represent "true" MIF. This controversy is in part related to the nature of the assay system involved. Anything that is toxic to a macrophage may prevent its migration by nonspecifically damaging it. As a *reducto ad absurdum,* a dead cell cannot wander. Not all of the reported studies have focused on the important questions of cell viability and reversibility of effect. In any case, what these studies do demonstrate is that substances which can modify the behavior of macrophages in a manner similar to the effect of certain lymphokines are ubiquitous in nature.

Lymphokine-Like Activity Induced by Viral Infection

In a recent study, MIF-like activity was demonstrated in the supernatant fluids from virus-infected cultures of the BGM line of African green monkey cells (43). Both Newcastle disease and mumps virus were effective. This activity in virus-infected cultures was in addition to the spontaneously occurring inhibitory activity that is sometimes found in noninfected replicating cell cultures, as described above. The virus-induced activity was not due to nonspecific cytotoxic material released by dead or dying cells, and did not require cell proliferation for its production. Continued incubation of macrophages with the material for several days allowed for an escape from migration inhibition, demonstrating the reversibility of the reaction. The macrophages remained viable as demonstrated by trypan blue exclusion studies. Sephadex G-100 chromatography revealed activity peaks in fractions corresponding to molecular weights of 11,000 and 65,000, which are similar to values obtained for molecules with MIF-like activity from other sources (28,44), although different from the value obtained for human MIF by Rocklin et al (45). The MIF or MIF-like material produced by virus-infected cultures appeared to be distinct from interferon.

In another study it was shown that infection of BGM cell cultures with mumps virus leads also to the production and release of factors with chemotactic activity for neutrophils and macrophages (46). Infection of chick embryos with either mumps or Newcastle disease virus leads to the production of factors with the same biologic activity. These factors appear to be produced by the infected cells and do not represent viral components. They are distinct from both interferon and the MIF-like substances described above, but have some features in common with lymphokine chemotactic factors.

SUMMARY AND IMPLICATIONS

Although lymphokines are the putative mediators of reactions of cellular immunity, it is only recently that investigators have addressed themselves to the questions of (1) the nature of the lymphocyte populations that are involved in production and release of lymphokines, and (2) whether or not there is evidence for the direct participation of any or all of the known lymphokines in various reactions of cellular immunity *in vivo*. This chapter has focused mainly on the second problem. As we have seen, it is possible to detect biological activity similar to the activities recoverable from activated lymphocyte cultures in various fluids or extracts obtained from tissue sites of *in vivo* reactions. In these experiments, MIF, the various chemotactic factors, and on occasion, cytotoxic factors have been described. A brief summary is presented in Table 1. The major uncertainty which exists to a greater or lesser degree in all such studies is whether the activity detected is caused by a true lymphokine or a mimicking substance. In absolute terms, this is semantically equivalent to asking whether the substance present *in vivo* was produced by an appropriately stimulated lymphocyte. In practical terms, what we are asking is the degree of similarity of the responsible factors to the previously described materials found in lymphocyte culture supernatants. Such characterization is based on physicochemical studies, enzyme degradation, heat stability, biologic spectrum of activity, etc. Thus, at the present state of knowledge, no absolute answer is possible. Neverthe-

Table 1   Lymphokine and Lymphokine-Like Activity in Various Sources

	MIF [a]	Chemotactic Factors [b]	Cytotoxic Factors	SRF [c]
Lymphocyte culture supernatant	+ [d]	+	+	+
Delayed skin reaction sites	−	+	?	+
Peritoneal Fluid	+	+	?	?
Joint fluid	+	?	+	?
Serum	+	+	?	?
Virus-infected culture	+	+	?	+
Mumps-infected parotid gland	+	+	?	?

[a] Migration inhibition factor.
[b] Chemotactic factors for macrophages, neutrophils, or lymphocytes.
[c] Skin reactive factor.
[d] +, Detected; − not detected, ?, not studied.

less, the various experiments described here demonstrate that various lymphokine-like activities are ubiquitous in nature, and thus, lymphokine production may be one aspect of a far more general phenomenon that represents a major nonimmunologic as well as immunologic form of host defense. The experiments on the induction of chemotactic and MIF activity by virus infection, for example, show that infection leads to the release *in vitro* of substances that affect the behavior of inflammatory cells. Unpublished observations in our laboratory, using the mumps-infected monkey parotid gland as a model, have shown that these factors may be produced *in vivo* as well. The factors, when injected into normal animals, are biologically effective. Thus, they might well serve to limit a viral infection by a mechanism that involves neither interferon nor the immune system.

Experiments in which the soluble products of lymphocyte activation are injected into animals are somewhat easier to interpret. The major pitfall here is that almost anything foreign to an animal will serve as an irritant and produce an inflammatory response. Since the biologic repertoire is limited, a nonspecific inflammatory reaction might by pure coincidence look very much like a specific immunologic one. In this regard, factors that lead to the appearance of an infiltrate with a single kind of cell predominating, especially one which is ordinarily not present in great numbers, are most convincing. One example of a factor that behaves in this manner is ECF, which is specifically chemotactic for eosinophils, both *in vitro* and *in vivo,* and therefore produces a specific inflammatory reaction in which those cells predominate.

Perhaps the most unambiguous kind of evidence for an *in vivo* role for a given lymphokine is the induction of a specific cell-mediated response *in vivo* by lymphocyte culture supernatants containing that agent, or by the induction of the response by lymphocytes enclosed in micropore chambers which allow interaction with host cells only through the production of such soluble factors. This has proved possible in the case of the MDR, but not in the case of the classic tuberculin reaction in the skin. It is clear that further work is needed along these lines.

In summary, there is little doubt that at least some of the lymphokines play a role *in vivo.* Moreover, it is possible that similar substances, induced by nonimmunologic means, play a corresponding role. As was seen in the preceding chapter, there is a long list of lymphokines such as PIF, MAF, and blastogenic factor that have not been studied in *in vivo* situations. It would be surprising if these did not also have an important biological function.

REFERENCES

1. Dumonde, D. D., Wolstencroft, R. A., Panayi, G. S., Matthew, M., Morley, J., and Howson, W. T., *Nature (London)* **224,** 38 (1969).
2. Bloom, B. R. and Bennett, B., *Science* **153,** 80 (1966).
3. Watanuki, M., Yoshida, T., and Hashimoto, T., *Med. Biol.* **78,** 129 (1969).
4. Bloom, B. R., *Adv. Immunol.* **13,** 101 (1971).
5. Sonozaki, H. and Cohen, S., *Cell. Immunol.* **3,** 644 (1972).
6. Willoughby, D. A., Coote, E., and Spector, W. G., *Immunology* **12,** 165 (1967).
7. Yoshida, T., Benacerraf, B., McCluskey, R. T., and Vassalli, P., *J. Immunol.* **102,** 804 (1969).
8. Nelson, D. S. and Boyden, S. V., *Immunology* **6,** 264 (1963).
9. Nelson, D. S., *Immunology* **9,** 219 (1965).
10. Nelson, D. S. and North, R. J., *Lab. Invest.* **14,** 89 (1965).

11. Bianco, C., Patrick, R., and Nussenzweig, V., *J. Exp. Med.* **132,** 702 (1970).

12. Dukor, P., Bianco, C., and Nussenzweig, V., *Proc. Natl. Acad. Sci. U.S.A.* **67,** 991 (1970).

13. Bianco, C. and Nussenzweig, V., *Science* **173,** 154 (1971).

14. Najarian, J. S. and Feldman, J. D., *Transplantation* **1,** 495 (1963).

15. Sonozaki, H. and Cohen, S., *Cell. Immunol.* **2,** 341 (1972).

16. Hashimoto, T., Watanuki, M., and Yoshida, T., Proc. Jap. Immunol. Soc. **3,** 69 (1969).

17. Thrasher, S., Yoshida, T., van Oss, C. J., Cohen, S., and Rose, N. R., *J. Immunol.* **110,** 321 (1973).

18. Leu, R., Eadleston, A. L. W. F., Hadden, J. W., and Good, R. A., *J. Exp. Med.* **136,** 589 (1972).

19. Galindo, B. and Myrvik, Q. W., *J. Immunol.* **105,** 227 (1970).

20. Bartfeld, H. and Atoynatan, T., *Proc. Soc. Exp. Biol. Med.* **130,** 497 (1969).

21. Pick, E., Krejci, J., Cech, K., and Turk, J. L., *Immunology* **17,** 741 (1969).

22. Okuyama, H., Kikuchi, Y., and Morikawa, K., Fifth Joint Meeting, Japan-U.S.A. Co-op. Med. Sci. Program, Tokyo, 1970, p. 303.

23. Cohen, S., Ward, P. A., Yoshida, T., and Burek, C. L., *Cell. Immunol.,* in press.

24. Ward, P. A., *In Vitro Methods in Cell-Mediated Immunity* (B. R. Bloom and P. R. Glade, Eds.), Academic Press, New York, 1970, p. 481.

25. Salvin, S. B. and Youngner, J. S., *Fed. Proc.* **31,** 754 (1972).

26. Sonozaki, H., Yoshida, T., and Cohen, S., in preparation.

27. Stastny, P. and Ziff, M., *Immunopathology of Inflammation,* Int. Congr. Series 229, 1971, p. 66.

28. Bennett, B. and Bloom, B. R., *Proc. Natl. Acad. Sci. U.S.A.* **59,** 756 (1968).

29. Krejci, J., Pekarek, J., Johanovsky, J., and Svejcar, J., *Immunology* **16,** 677 (1969).

30. Pick, E., Krejci, J., and Turk, J. L., *Nature (London)* **225,** 236 (1970).

31. Pick, E., Brostoff, J., Krejci, J., and Turk, J. L., *Cell. Immunol.* **1,** 92 (1970).

32. Schwartz, H. J., Leon, M. A., and Pelley, R. P., *J. Immunol.* **104,** 265 (1970).

33. Rocklin, R. E., Meyers, O. L., and David, J. R., *J. Immunol.* **104,** 95 (1970).

34. Thor, D. E., Jureziz, R. S., Veach, S. R., Miller, E., and Dray, S., *Nature (London)* **219,** 755 (1968).

36. Yoshida, T., Nagai, R., and Hashimoto, T., in preparation.

36. Cohen, S. and Ward, P. A., *J. Exp. Med.* **133,** 133 (1971).

37. Torisu, M., Yoshida, T., Ward, P. A., and Cohen, S., in preparation.

38. Cohen, S., Rose, N. R., and Brown, R. C., *Fed. Proc.* **30,** 454 (1971).

39. Schwartz, H. J., Pelley, R. P., and Leon, M. A., *Fed. Proc.* **29,** 360 (1970).

40. Remold, H. G., David, R. A., and David, J. R., *J. Immunol.* **109,** 578 (1972).

41. Papageogiou, P. S., Henley, W. L., and Glade, P. R., *J. Immunol.* **108,** 494 (1972).

42. Tubergen, D. G., Feldman, J. D., Pollack, E. M., and Lerner, R. A., *J. Exp. Med.* **135,** 255 (1972).

43. Flanagan, T. D., Yoshida, T., and Cohen, S., in preparation.

44. Yoshida, T. and Reisfeld, R. A., *Nature (London)* **226,** 856 (1970).

45. Rocklin, R. E., Remold, H. G., and David, J. R., *Cell. Immunol.* **5,** 463 (1972).

46. Ward, P. A., Cohen, S., and Flanagan, T. D., *J. Exp. Med.* **135,** 1095 (1972).

Chapter Four

Antigen Recognition

WILLIAM E. PAUL AND BARUJ BENACERRAF

Laboratory of Immunology, National Institute of Allergy and Infectious Diseases, National Institutes of Health, Bethesda, Maryland and Department of Pathology, Harvard Medical School, Boston, Massachusetts

Perhaps the most striking feature of the immune response is the vast number of foreign substances that induce the production of highly specific antibody molecules and the development of a state of *specific* cellular hypersensitivity in an immunocompetent host. Indeed, antigenic specificity may be regarded as the touchstone of immunology, and the analysis of the molecular and cellular basis of this specificity has been a major endeavor of immunologists since the first recognition of immune phenomena in the late nineteenth century.

An attempt to explicitly formulate a theoretical basis for immunologic specificity was first made by Ehrlich (1). Ehrlich's theory, although prescient in many respects, lacked a crucial element provided through the clonal selection theory of Burnet (2). Burnet proposed that individual immunocompetent cells possessed unique surface receptor molecules; only a limited panel of antigens, capable of interacting with that particular receptor, could activate that cell. The vast potentiality of the organism was explained through the existence of large numbers of clones of individual cells, each bearing different receptor molecules. The immune response involved the selective activation, proliferation, and differentiation of a limited set of specific clones. The introduction of this theory by Burnet coincided with a great resurgence of research in immunology. A substantial portion of this research has been aimed at testing the clonal theory. In broad terms, the Burnetian view of immunology appears to be correct (3), although it has been most fully tested for humoral rather than cellular immune responses.

In this chapter, we review the cellular and molecular basis of antigen recognition, particularly as it pertains to cellular immune responses. As with so many other segments of immunology, this topic is in great flux and that flux primarily involves movement from indirect evaluation of the system through whole-animal studies to more direct studies at the cellular level. Our understanding of the crucial aspects of this topic is thus based on both animal and cellular studies, and we devote considerable attention to both approaches.

CELLULAR BASIS OF THE IMMUNE RESPONSE

Prior to a consideration of the specific recognition mechanisms of immunocompetent cells, a brief review of the origin and function of the various types of cells involved is required. The principal cells involved in immune responses are macrophages and lymphocytes. Each of these cells originates from stem cells found in hematopoietic tissue.

Macrophages have an important and complex role in both the induction and expression of immune responses. Upon introduction of antigen into an animal, some of this antigen is found in association with macrophages. In lymph nodes, macrophages in the peripheral sinuses and dendritic cells in follicles can be demonstrated to contain antigen, some of which is on their surfaces (4). The nature of the bond between macrophage surface and antigen is not clear. It has been established that macrophages possess surface receptors for γ G immunoglobulin (5) and for complement (6) and that antigen-antibody and antigen-antibody-complement complexes are bound to macrophage surfaces. In addition, macrophages of nonimmunized animals bind antigen to their surfaces. The kinds of forces involved in this interaction are not known. This surface-bound antigen appears to be especially potent in the induction of specific immune responses (7). Indeed, one test of the immunogenicity of an antigen may well be its ability to bind to macrophage surfaces.

Other roles have also been proposed for macrophages in the induction of specific immune responses. RNA extracts of peritoneal exudate cells treated with antigen are, in some instances, capable of initiating immune responses under conditions in which free antigen is apparently ineffective (8). In several systems, RNA-antigen complexes formed in such cells have been demonstrated to be especially potent antigens, and it has been proposed that a principal role of the macrophage is to produce highly immunogenic complexes which are very efficient in specifically activating lymphocytes (9). Roelants and Goodman (10), however, have demonstrated that macrophages may complex RNA to a variety of substances that are nonimmunogenic or only weakly immunogenic, thus casting some doubt as to the general physiologic significance of these complexes. Fishman and Adler (11) have reported that lymphocytes cultured with antigen-free RNA-rich extracts derived from peritoneal exudate cells that have been incubated with T2 phage produce modest T2 antibody responses. Moreover, from studies performed with peritoneal exudate cells and lymphocytes derived from rabbits differing in their light-chain allotypes, they indicated that the antibody produced bore light-chain allotypic markers characteristic of the donor of the RNA rather than of the donor of the lymphocytes (12). This implies that genetic information concerning immunoglobulin structure was transferred from the peritoneal exudate cell to a lymphocyte. Nonetheless, these effects are of very small magnitude and are difficult to obtain regularly.

Of these several possible roles for macrophages in the immune response, it seems likely to us that surface presentation of antigen is the one of greatest general import for immune responses. Very recently, evidence has been presented which suggests that macrophages and their products have important antigen-independent effects on the maturation and immunological function of thymus-derived cells (13,14).

In addition to their role in the induction of immune responses, macrophages are important in the expression of immunity. It is well known, for example, that macrophages congregate at the site of delayed hypersensitivity reactions and that the migratory behavior of macrophages is inhibited by a factor secreted by activated lymphocytes. A detailed discussion of these aspects of macrophage participation in the immune response can be found in other chapters of this book.

The lymphocytes participating in specific immune responses can be subdivided into two general classes, the thymus-dependent lymphocytes, and the thymus-independent, or bone-marrow-derived lymphocytes (Table 1). The thymus-dependent (T) lymphocyte originates from stem cells in the hematopoietic tissue (15,16). Descendants of these stem cells migrate into the thymus where they undergo a complex set of differentiation events leading to a relatively mature cell which then emigrates into the peripheral lymphoid tissue. The T lymphocytes, and their thymocyte precursors, bear characteristic surface antigens which allow their identification. In the mouse, several such T-specific antigens are known (17,18). They include ϕ, Lya, Lyb, and Lyc; genetic polymorphism exists

Table 1   Lymphocyte Classes

Class	Thymus-Dependent	Thymus-Independent
Abbreviation	T	B
Origin of stem cells	Bone marrow (yolk sac and liver in embryonic and fetal life)	Bone marrow (yolk sac and liver in embryonic and fetal life)
Site of differentiation	Thymus	Unknown in mammals; Bursa of Fabricius in birds
Location in periphery	Recirculating pool Paracortical regions of lymph nodes Periarteriolar areas of spleen	Superficial cortex; follicles of lymph node and spleen
Surface markers	θ	Immunoglobulin; complement receptor
Functions	Delayed hypersensitivity Specific "killer" activity Helper effects in activation of B cells	Precursors of antibody secreting cells Antibody-dependent, lymphocyte-mediated cytotoxicity

for each of these markers, so that isoantisera have been prepared and the specificity of such sera have been determined quite precisely. T-specific antigens have, in addition, been recognized in the guinea pig (19), chicken (20), and rat (21). These antigens have been of prime importance in the characterization of T cell function.

The T lymphocytes are responsible for delayed hypersensitivity (22) and its *in vitro* counterparts (19), for destruction of target cells by sensitized lymphocytes (23), and for the "helper" effect (24,25). The latter refers to the fact that the activation of precursors of antibody-producing cells, which themselves are members of the other major lymphocyte class, is, in many instances, markedly augmented by the action of specific T lymphocytes. This capacity of T lymphocytes to aid the activation of precursor cells has led to the T cells, in this instance, being referred to as "helper" cells. It is not yet clearly established whether the same T cells are (1) responsible for delayed hypersensitivity, (2) act as "killer" cells, and (3) mediate the helper effect, or whether subclasses of T lymphocytes exist which mediate only one or two of these functions. Similarly, although it is clear that the T lymphocytes are primarily responsible for each of these effects, it is by no means certain that the other major lymphocyte class plays no role whatever in these responses. These matters are considered further in chapter 12.

The thymus-independent (B) lymphocyte also originates from stem cells in hematopoietic tissue. In the chicken, the bursa of Fabricius acts as the anatomic site in which maturation of this cell type occurs (26,27). In mammals, the organ in which stem cells differentiate into mature B lymphocytes has not been ascertained. It has been suggested that the gut-associated lymphoid tissue acts as a bursal analog (28), but the evidence on this point is not yet persuasive. The B lymphocyte lacks the characteristic T markers, such as Θ, but it bears other cell surface molecules that aid in its detection. Thus, as is discussed in some detail, these cells possess relatively large amounts of surface immunoglobulin (29); many B cells possess a surface receptor for the third component of complement (30) and recent reports suggest a receptor for aggregated Fc fragments (31,32). B lymphocytes function primarily as precursors of antibody-synthesizing cells. Recently, evidence has been adduced that B lymphocytes, or a subset of B lymphocytes, from nonsensitized animals may cause the destruction of antibody-coated target cells (33).

ANTIBODY STRUCTURE AND SPECIFICITY: A BRIEF REVIEW

The current approach to the study of antigen recognition molecules is to evaluate the surface-binding properties of lymphocytes from immune and nonimmune animals and to determine the character of molecules required for specific activation of cells as well as to ask what agents interfere with such activation. The results obtained are usually compared to the structural, antigenic, and binding characteristics of serum antibody molecules, as the latter constitute a well-established immunologic recognition system and are the prime candidates to act as cellular receptor molecules. Thus, the specific activation of precursors of antibody-forming cells (B cells) can be explained most simply if the receptors on precursor cells are similar or identical in specificity to the antibody to be secreted by the descendant of the precursor cell. If the receptor differed from antibody in this respect, the specificity of the antibody response would be very difficult to account for. Moreover, invoking the concept of the "parsimony of nature," immunoglobulin has been postulated to act as the receptor for T lymphocytes as well, despite the fact that these cells cannot be demonstrated to secrete such molecules and that substantial numbers of immunoglobulin molecules cannot be found on T cells. This contention is discussed more fully later, and in Chapter 5 as well.

A brief review of some of the structural and binding properties of antibody molecules is useful in the evaluation of studies of cellular antigen recognition mechanisms. Antibody molecules are immunoglobulins, of which several classes exist. All consist of a basic unit containing 2 heavy (H) polypeptide chains and 2 light (L) polypeptide chains. In man, 5 major H chain classes have been described, γ, μ, α, δ, and ϵ, and subclasses of γ, μ, and α exist. There are 2 major light-chain classes— κ and λ. An immunoglobulin may be described on the basis of its constituent chains—thus $\gamma_2\kappa_2$ for κ-type IgG molecules or $(\mu_2\lambda_2)_5$ for λ-type IgM molecules. The latter is a pentamer of the basic unit described above. It has been proposed that a gene coding for a polypeptide approximately half the size of an L chain is ancestral for the genes coding for immunoglobulin molecules in contemporary animals and that the modern genes arose through reduplication of the ancestral gene. Moreover, analysis of the primary amino acid sequence of H and L chains has led to the thesis that H and L chains can be divided into domains of approximately 110 amino acids, yielding 2 domains per L chain and 4 per H chain. L chains consist of a variable domain and a constant domain. Thus, the carboxyl terminal halves of all κ chains are identical, save for small differences associated with polymorphic or allelic forms, while the amino terminal half varies considerably between individual κ chains. The situation for γ chains is somewhat more complex. The N terminal domain is variable and the remaining 3 domains are constant, again except for genetic polymorphism. The variable domains of the H and L chains appear to contain the antigen-binding sites while the constant domains are critical to the biological function of antibodies (for review, see ref. 34 and 35).

Immunoglobulin molecules can also be separated into fragments by enzymatic cleavage (36). Papain digestion generally leads to the production of two types of fragments—Fc and Fab pieces. The Fc piece can be regarded as essentially a dimer of the 3rd and 4th (or C terminal) domains of H chains; the Fab fragments consist of a portion of the H chain (the Fd fragment) which is essentially the 1st and 2nd domains plus an intact L chain. Antisera specific for H chains, L chains, Fc fragments, and Fab fragments have all been produced. In addition, antibodies specific for the unique or idiotypic determinants of individual immunoglobulin molecules have been obtained. Sera of each of these types have been utilized as reagents in the evaluation of the chemical nature of antigen-binding receptors, and the specificity of such sera is often crucial to the interpretations of such experiments.

The second major feature of antibodies which is useful in the comparative studies of cellular receptors is their specificity. Antibody molecules will bind to the antigen used in their elicitation and will do so with great specificity (37). For example, antibodies induced by immunization with tartaric acid derivatives of proteins can distinguish D and L isomeric forms of tartaric acid (38). Perhaps the most detailed studies of antigen-binding characteristics have been carried out with hapten derivatives of proteins and polypeptides.

Thus, small defined chemical groups such as the 2,4-dinitrophenyl (DNP) radical can be introduced into proteins or polypeptides. Upon immunization, antibody molecules will be produced which bind not only to the immunizing antigen but also to DNP derivatives of unrelated proteins and, indeed, to univalent DNP-amino acids. Because the bulk of DNP groups are substituted on the ϵ-amino group of lysyl side chains in proteins, the binding of antibody to ϵ-DNP-L-lysine is generally studied. Antibodies induced against DNP proteins bind ϵ-DNP-L-lysine with moderate to relatively high standard free energies $\Delta F° = 6.5$ to 12 kcal/mole) (39). Moreover, the DNP group tends to be an "immunodominant" determinant in that the antibody which binds to it generally has the great bulk of its binding energy directed at the DNP group. Other haptens have not received the detailed attention that the DNP group has, but the situation appears generally similar for antibodies specific for several, including 4-hydroxy-3-iodo-5 nitrophenacetyl (NIP), azophenylarsonic acid, and azophenylsulfonic acid. Moreover, studies of antibodies to polyalanyl and polylysyl derivatives of protein reveal that a very high percentage of the binding energy is directed at tetra- and pentapeptides (40). Thus, an important feature of the antibody population produced as a result of immunization with hapten-protein conjugates is that they contain a considerable proportion of molecules with a high degree of specificity for the haptenic group. These antibodies are especially valuable because precise analyses of their fine specificity is possible, and, consequently, they may be compared to the fine specificity of antigen-binding receptors on immunocompetent cells. Finally, the recent description of myeloma proteins with the capacity to bind ligands specifically, such as the DNP group (41) and phosphoryl choline (42), represents a major advance in the study of antibody specificity, aι.J preliminary attempts to explore receptor specificity on this basis have been made (43,44).

Specificity of Cellular Immune Responses

As is discussed in the subsequent section, direct antigen-binding by T lymphocytes has been much more difficult to demonstrate and to study than has been the case for B lymphocytes. Consequently, the evaluation of T cell receptors requires considerable attention to the study of initiation and elicitation of cellular immune responses, both *in vivo* and *in vitro*.

Studies of delayed hypersensitivity (DH) *in vivo* have revealed a very precise character of specificity and one which would not have been anticipated from the studies of the specificity of serum antibody molecules. Guinea pigs immunized by appropriate routes with a DNP derivative of the isologous protein guinea pig albumin (GPA) develop a state of delayed hypersensitivity to DNP-GPA and produce antibodies which bind to DNP-GPA. As discussed in the preceding section, a considerable fraction (indeed, the great majority) of these antibody molecules bind to DNP derivatives of unrelated proteins as well as to ϵ-DNP-L-lysine. The elicitation of the delayed hypersensitivity skin reaction, on the other hand, shows a high degree of conjugate specificity. The immunizing antigen elicits marked reactions while DNP derivatives of unrelated proteins produce, at best, very meager responses. This phenomenon of conjugate specificity in delayed hypersensitivity has been observed for a variety of haptenic groups including, in addition to DNP, trinitrophenyl (TNP), *p*-nitrobenzoyl, *p*-chlorobenzoyl, *o*-, *m*-, and *p*-azobenzenesulfonate, *p*-azobenzoate, acetyl and benzyl penicilloyl (45). Moreover, the specificity requirement for induction of DH reactions is even more demanding. Thus, the relevant recognition system can distinguish between conjugates of a given hapten to a given protein through different bonds. Gell and Silverstein (46) prepared *p*-thiocarbamidobenzenesulfonate guinea pig albumin and *p*-azobenzenesulfonate guinea pig albumin. The first derivative possesses benzenesulfonate groups linked primarily to ϵ-amino groups of lysine, whereas in the second derivative, the benzenesulfonate group is linked to GPA through azo bonds with tyrosines, tryptophans, and histidines. An animal immunized with the *p*-thiocarbomido derivative makes little or no response to the *p*-azo derivative and animals sensitized to the *p*-azo derivative do not demonstrate delayed hypersensitivity to the

p-thiocarbomido derivative (Table 2). A similar situation was demonstrated for two other pairs of GPA conjugates: p-thiocarbamidobenzoate and p-azobenzoate; and p-nitrobenzoyl and $p$nitrobenzeneazo. An alternate demonstration of this highly sophisticated type of conjugate specificity involves the interposition of spacer molecules between hapten and carrier (47). Thus, animals immunized with trinitrophenylated GPA (TNP-GPA) make little or no response to TNP-aminocaproyl-GPA although the only difference between the two conjugates is the interposition of an aminocaproyl group between the TNP group and the ϵ-amino group on lysyl side chains of GPA (Table 2).

In addition to the capacity of the recognition mechanism to distinguish the carrier molecule and the nature of the bond between the hapten and the carrier, a precise discrimination between haptenic groups is also noted in the elicitation of DH reactions. Thus, Gell and Silverstein (48) have demonstrated that guinea pigs sensitized to p-azobenzoate-GPA display the largest DH reactions to p-azobenzoate-GPA, intermediate reactions to m-azobenzoate-GPA, and small reactions to o-azobenzoate-GPA. Indeed, in a quantitative comparison of cross-reactivity in terms of ligand binding by antibody and of activation of lymphoid cells in $vitro$ to incorporate ^{3}H-thymidine into DNA, the cells appeared to be equivalent to antibody in their capacity to distinguish between related haptenic groups (49) (Table 3).

To summarize this segment, then, the recognition system for DH distinguishes hapten, carrier, and nature of linkage. Only relatively small changes in any of these components can be made without considerable or complete loss of the capacity of the conjugate to elicit the reaction. On the other hand, antibody molecules produced by such animals may bind, with high energies of interaction, to the haptenic group coupled to a wide variety of carriers. Some antibody molecules exist, however, which do have specificity characteristics like that of the DH recognition system. For example, some antibodies produced in response to hapten-carrier immunization are conjugate specific and can be precipitated only by the hapten-carrier complex used for immunization (50,51). What appears to be lacking is an appreciable component of delayed hypersensitivity with specificity characteristics similar to anti-DNP antibody. This may overdraw the case to some extent as in an exceptional system—the p-azophenylarsonate system—evidence for some hapten-specific delayed hypersensitivity has been obtained (52). On balance, however, one finds a marked dissociation in the specificity of elicitation of delayed hypersensitivity reactions and in the specificity of serum antibody molecules produced by immunized animals. This

Table 2 Conjugate Specificity of Elicitation of Delayed Hypersensitivity Reactions [a]

A. Nature of Carrier

Immunogen	Test Antigens		
TNP-GPA [b]	TNP-GPA $+++$ [b]	TNP-OVA 0	TNP-RSA $+$
Tosyl-GPA [b] Tosyl-OVA	Tosyl-GPA 18^{b} Neg.	Tosyl-OVA Neg. 14	
p-Nitrobenzoyl-GPA $_c$ (PNB-GPA)	PNB-GPA 16	PNB-BSA 4	PNB-OVA 0

B. Mode of Linkage

Immunogen	Test Antigens GPA conjugate:					
GPA conjugate:	p-Thiocarbamidobenzenesulfonate	p-Azobenzenesulfonate	TNP-GPA	TNP-aminocaproyl-GPA	Tosyl-GPA	Tosyl-aminocaproyl-GPA
p-Thiocarbamidobenzenesulfonate [c]	15	0				
p-Azobenzenesulfonate	0	15				
TNP-GPA [b]			16	8		
TNP-aminocaproyl-GPA			8	16		
Tosyl-GPA [b]					18	0
Tosyl-aminocaproyl-GPA					0	17

[a] Delayed hypersensitivity reactions are reported as mean diameter in millimeters, or, in one case, on a 0 to 4+ scale.
[b] Benacerraf and Levine, (47).
[c] Gell and Silverstein, (48).

suggests that few, if any, functional T cells exist with highly hapten-specific receptors.

The stimulation of cellular immune responses, *in vitro,* displays specificity requirements similar to those for the elicitation of delayed hypersensitivity skin reactions. The model that has received the most attention is the stimulation by antigen of DNA synthesis by lymphoid cells from immune animals. The involvement of T lymphocytes in this response appears quite clear. Antigen-stimulated DNA synthesis in guinea pigs tends to correlate with a state of DH in the donor animal (53); no response *in vitro* is obtained if the cells are derived from an animal that has circulating antibody but no delayed hypersensitivity (54). Removal of T lymphocytes by lysis with an antiserum specific for T cells largely removes the capacity of the cell population to manifest this response (19). On the other hand, removal of the B cells and enrichment of T cells by passage over glass bead columns increases the responsiveness of the recovered cells (55).

The study of the specificity of stimulation of DNA synthesis clearly demonstrates the main elements described above for DH. Lymph node cells from guinea pigs immunized with DNP-GPA are stimulated by as little as 10^{-3} μg/ml of this conjugate, whereas DNP-ovalbumin and DNP-hemocyanin cause very modest responses and do so only at 10^{+2} μg/ml (56); DNP-bovine serum albumin does not cause any detectable response (57). Moreover, change of the structure of the haptenic substituent changes the degree of the response. Thus, trinitrophenyl (TNP) GPA causes a significantly smaller response in cell cultures derived from guinea pigs immunized with DNP-GPA than does DNP-GPA. *O*-nitrophenyl-GPA causes no measurable response whatever (58). Similarly, when guinea pigs have been immunized with *p*-iodophenylsulfonyl-GPA (pipsyl-GPA), the immunogen and the serologically cross-reacting hapten-GPA conjugate, toluenesulfonyl-GPA, stimulate *in vitro* lymph node cell DNA synthesis, whereas the GPA conjugates of poorly cross-reacting haptens such as pentachlorobenzoyl-GPA and DNP-GPA do not stimulate the cells (49) (Table 3). Thus, the recognition system involved in interaction with hapten-carrier conjugates precisely detects elements of both carrier and hapten structure. The energy of interaction with the haptenic group alone is apparently very low as shown in the enormous difference between DNP-GPA and DNP-BSA in their capacity to elicit cellular responses in cells from a DNP-GPA immune animal.

Similar, although less detailed and quantitative, data have been gathered from studies of the specificity of elicitation of migration inhibitory factor (MIF) production and of *in vitro* destruction by sensitized lymphocytes of erythrocytes coated with hapten-protein conjugates.

Table 3   Relative Capacity of Cellular Immune Responses and of Antibody Molecules to Detect Differences in Haptenic Structure

| Haptenic Group | Relative Capacity of Guinea Pig Albumin Conjugate to Stimulate In Vitro DNA Synthesis | | Relative Affinity of Antibody for Hapten-Aminocaproate | |
	Concentration of Antigen Required for 50% Maximum Stimulation by Homologous Antigen (μg/ml)	Relative Stimulation Capacity [a]	Equilibrium Constant (L/M)	Relative Binding Capacity [b]
p-Iodophenylsulfonyl	0.17	1.0	$3.2 < 10^5$	1.0
Toluene sulfonyl	0.91	0.19	0.75×10^5	0.23
2,4-dinitrophenyl	>100	<0.002	$<0.06 \times 10^5$	<0.01
Pentachlorobenzoyl	>100	<0.002	n.d. [c]	—

Lymph node cells from guinea pigs immunized to P-iodophenylsulfonyl-GPA were exposed to the immunizing antigen and to related GPA conjugates and stimulation of DNA synthesis measured. The capacity of antibody from these animals to bind various hapten-aminocaproates was also measured.

[a] Relative stimulatory capacity is concentration of p-iodophenylsulfonyl-guinea pig albumin required for 50% maximal stimulation divided by concentration of the given hapten-guinea pig albumin conjugate required for 50% maximal stimulation.
[b] Relative binding capacity is equilibrium constant for binding of a given ligand divided by that for binding of pipsyl-aminocaproic acid.
[c] No detectable binding.

A striking *in vitro* example of differences in the specificity of cellular immune phenomena and of serum antibody can be drawn from studies of target cell destruction. Brunner et al (59,60) have demonstrated that the lymphocytes of C3H mice that had been immunized with mastocytoma cells derived from DBA/2 mice efficiently destroy, *in vitro,* the mastocytoma cells. These two mouse strains differ at the H-2 locus, the C3H mouse being $H-2^k$ and the DBA/2 mouse, $H-2^d$. Serologically the H-2 type can be distinguished from $H-2^d$ by at least 12 antigenic determinants. C57BL/6 mice, of the $H-2^b$ histocompatibility type, bear 6 of the specificities that DBA/2 ($H-2^d$) mice possess and C3H ($H-2^k$) mice lack. Moreover, sera produced by C3H mice immunized with DBA/2 cells are capable of interacting with the determinants shared by C57BL/6 mice. Consequently, if the specificity of serologic and cellular responses were similar, immunization of C3H mice with DBA/2 mastocytoma should cause the C3H lymphocytes to have at least some cytotoxic activity for C57BL/6 cells. Nonetheless, no such activity of cells from immunized C3H mice could be detected. This work, which parallels that of Brondz (61,62), establishes, in a system quite different from conventional hapten-protein conjugates, that the specificity of cellular immune responses and that of serum antibody molecules are not identical. An analysis of the data reported by Mauel et al and by Brondz indicates that immune lymphocytes are able to lyse target cells which share an entire *D* or *K* sublocus of the H-2 complex with the cells used for immunization. This suggests that, in specificity terms, a similarity exists between the gene product of a sublocus of the H-2 region and a protein carrier whereas the individual H-2 specificities resemble haptenic groups. Thus, antibody molecules interact with individual determinants or haptens quite well, whereas sensitized T cells can be activated only by a structure very similar to the immunogen.

The final aspect of T cell function to be discussed in specificity terms is the one that has received perhaps the greatest attention in recent years—that is, the helper or carrier effect which T cells exert in the activation of precursors of antibody-producing cells. Through studies of the immune response to sheep erythrocytes and related antigens, it has become clear that the bone-marrow-derived or B lymphocytes act as precursors of antibody-synthesizing cells (63,64). Nonetheless, in the absence of T lymphocytes these precursor cells make a limited response, or none at all, depending on specific conditions. It now appears that two general classes of antigens exist—the T dependent and the T independent. The former includes erythrocytes, most serum proteins, and haptenic derivatives of such materials. The thymus-independent antigens, in the mouse, are type III pneumococcal polysaccharide (65), polymerized flagellin of salmonella (66), lipopolysaccharides (67), and poly-vinylpyrollidone (67,68). The analysis of secondary antihapten antibody responses in terms of this cellular interaction also leads to the general conclusion that "helper" T cells are carrier or conjugate specific and not hapten specific in the sense that serum antibody molecules are hapten specific. Thus, guinea pigs primed with DNP-bovine γ-globulin (BGG) demonstrate a secondary anti-DNP response when challenged with DNP-BGG but little or no response to DNP conjugated to an unrelated carrier such as ovalbumin (OVA) (69). If guinea pigs or rabbits are independently immunized with a hapten-protein conjugate and with a second unrelated protein, an anamnestic antihapten antibody response may be elicited by a haptenic derivative of the second protein (70,71). Such a response would not be obtained if the immunization with the second protein had been omitted. Through transfer studies it has been demonstrated that the augmented response is based on cells specifically sensitized to the carrier (25,72). These carrier-specific cells have been termed "helpers" in view of their function in augmenting the responses of B cells. Raff has demonstrated that, in the mouse, helper cells bear the isoantigen Θ which is a marker of thymocytes and thymus-derived lymphocytes (24). The hapten-specific precursor cells, on the other hand, lack this isoantigen.

The original observations that secondary responses are best achieved by the use of the same hapten-carrier conjugate for both primary and secondary challenge immediately suggest that the T cells are not highly specific for hapten; if they were, one would hardly have expected that the phenomenon of conjugate specificity of antihapten anamnestic antibody responses would exist. Granting, then, that the bulk of the helper effect is mediated by carrier- or conjugate-specific T cells, is there evidence for the existence of any functional T cells with a high degree of hapten specificity? On the one hand, there are a series of guinea pig and rabbit experiments in which no evidence for hapten-specific helper cells was obtained (72). For example, guinea pigs which have been primed with DNP-BGG when challenged with DNP-OVA do not make an augmented primary anti-OVA response, whereas if they are challenged with sulfanilazo-BGG, an augmented primary antisulfanilazo response ensues. Thus, immunization with DNP-BGG generates BGG-specific helper cells but no functional DNP-specific helpers. Similarly, guinea pigs immunized with DNP-OVA followed by sulfanilazo-BGG in complete Freund's adjuvant do not produce anti-DNP antibody in response to secondary challenge with sulfanilazo-DNP-glucose oxidase although an anamnestic anti-DNP response to DNP-BGG occurs.

Two recent experiments have been reported as evidence for the existence of a significant number of functional DNP-specific helper cells. The first is based on Potter and Lieberman's demonstration that inbred mice fail to produce antiidiotype-specific antibodies to a given myeloma protein if the immunoglobulin of the immunized animal possesses the same allotypic markers as does the myeloma protein (73). Iverson (74) confirmed this finding by showing that C3H myeloma protein MP5563 failed to immunize CBA mice; moreover, he found that immunization of CBA mice with a DNP derivative of MP5563 also failed to elicit the production of antiidiotype antibodies. However, if the CBA mice had been skin painted with 1-fluoro-2,4-dinitrobenzene (DNFB) prior to immunization with DNP-MP5563, then, indeed, a small antiidiotype response ensued upon challenge with the DNP-myeloma protein. This experiment may be interpreted as demonstrating a hapten-specific helper effect in that presensitization with DNFB prepared the recipient for an augmented antiidiotype response to DNP linked to a protein apparently unrelated to that involved in primary immunization. Iverson concluded that this result was likely due to hapten-specific T cells but no direct proof that T cells mediated the effect was offered. Janeway (75) has recently attempted to repeat this experiment in a closely related system: the immunization of BALB/c mice with a DNP derivative of the BALB/c γG myeloma LPC-1. BALB/c mice make no antiidiotype response to LPC-1 or to DNP-LPC-1. Although skin painting with DNFB does not prepare these animals for an antiidiotype response to DNP-LPC-1, preimmunization with DNP-OVA does, indeed, permit the recipients to make an antiidiotype response to DNP-LPC-1. However, analysis of this finding reveals that anti-DNP antibody and not DNP-specific T cells is responsible for the helper effect in this instance.

The second major report of functional, hapten-specific T cells is that of Mitchison (76). Mice were immunized with bovine serum albumin, and, some time later, were treated with antilymphocyte serum, which has its primary effect on recirculating T cells. The spleen cells from the ALS-treated mice when transferred into an irradiated syngeneic animal did not manifest a secondary anti-BSA response upon challenge with DNP–BSA. However, if spleen cells from mice immunized with DNP-chicken γ-globulin were transferred together with the cells from the ALS-treated BSA-immunized animal, the recipient did produce anti-BSA antibody after DNP-BSA challenge. This experiment has been interpreted as showing that DNP-specific helper cells act to augment the response of BSA-specific B cells in a case in which BSA-specific T cells have been largely eliminated by ALS. The magnitude of this effect is small and it has not been formally demonstrated that it is due to the action of DNP-specific T cells derived from the DNP-chicken γ-globulin immune donor.

Finally, as in the case of delayed hypersensitivity, there is an apparently unique situation in which a hapten (*p*-azophenylarsonic acid) is recognized by T cells. Utilizing *p*-azophenylarsonic acid derivatives of a non-immunogenic carrier, Alkan and Goodman (77) have demonstrated a hapten-specific helper effect.

It would be prudent to conclude that small numbers of functional hapten-specific T cells may indeed exist. However, these cells are obviously rare, whereas both hapten-specific B cells and hapten-specific antibody molecules are quite common. The obvious question is why are there so few hapten-specific T cells, or, if present, why do such hapten-specific T cells fail to function?

RECEPTORS ON T AND B LYMPHOCYTES

Chemical Nature

The most direct method for evaluating an antigen-binding cellular receptor is to add the antigen to a cell suspension and to observe the characteristics of its binding to cells. The use of this approach was first reported by Naor and Sulitzeanu (78), who studied the binding of small amounts of BSA, radiolabeled with ^{125}I, to lymphocytes of nonimmune mice. They observed that a few lymphocytes ($\sim 1/1000$) had bound sufficient label so that they could be detected by radioautography. This observation has been confirmed and extended in several laboratories. The antigens that have been studied thus far include hemocyanin, flagellin, a branched chain polypeptide consisting of iodotyrosine, glutamic acid, D-L alanine and lysine (TIGAL), DNP-GPA, ferritin, and chicken γ-globulin (CGG). The conditions utilized for binding involve incubation of cells with low concentrations of antigen at $O°C$, in the presence of sodium azide. Under these conditions, pinocytosis and phagocytosis should be markedly diminished. Morphologically, the cells that bind the antigen in nonimmune animals resemble small lymphocytes. Indeed, in nonimmune animals, few, if any, large cells bind antigen.

The binding of antigen to these cells may be inhibited by prior addition of antiimmunoglobulin antibodies to the cell suspension (79–81). This strongly suggests that the antigen-binding receptor on these cells is immunoglobulin in nature. In general, antilight-chain sera are effective inhibitors of antigen binding and, of the antiheavy-chain sera, anti-μ has been the most effective inhibitor for mouse and human antigen-binding cells, whereas antigen-binding cells of adult guinea pigs are primarily blocked from binding antigen by anti-γ_2 antibody.

Concomitant with the discovery of antigen-binding receptors on lymphocytes was the demonstration that some lymphocytes possessed easily detectable surface immunoglobulin. This had been anticipated from the *in vitro* stimulation of DNA synthesis in lymphocytes by antiimmunoglobulin sera (82) and was initially shown by Coombs et al utilizing a mixed agglutination procedure (83). Raff, and coworkers (29) subsequently demonstrated that ^{125}I-labeled or fluorescent antiimmunoglobulin bound to some but not all lymphocytes. Thus, 10 to 15% of mouse peripheral blood lymphocytes bound antiimmunoglobulin while 40 to 50% of mouse spleen lymphocytes did. These frequencies complemented those of Θ-bearing cells, suggesting that immunoglobulin-bearing cells were Θ negative and thus not thymus derived. In support of this concept is the lack of detectable binding of antiimmunoglobulin reagents to mouse thymus cells and the increased frequency of immunoglobulin-bearing cells in the lymphoid organs of thymus-deprived mice (84). An estimate that immunoglobulin-bearing cells possess, on the average, approximately 80,000 molecules of immunoglobulin, has been provided by the studies of Rabellino et al (85) in which the capacity of cell-associated immunoglobulin to inhibit the binding of radiolabeled soluble immunoglobulin by antiimmunoglobulin was tested. Similarly, studies of the maximum number of antiimmunoglobulin molecules which may bind to an immunoglobulin-bearing cell yield a value of 70,000 to 80,000 molecules/cell (86). Very recently, it has been proposed that these cell surface immunoglobulin molecules are in a state of vigorous flux. Vitetta and Uhr (87) and Marchalonis et al (88) have labeled lymphocyte surface proteins with ^{125}I through the use of lactoperoxidase. Radioactivity associated with immunoglobulin is rapidly lost from the cell surface and appears in the culture medium. On the other hand, cross-linking these surface immunoglobulin molecules on the cell surface with antiimmunoglobulin antibody causes them to migrate to one pole of the cell ("cap formation") and to be endocytosed (89). The importance of the dynamic state of surface immunoglobulin in the activation and regulation of immunocompetent cells is not yet certain but these phenomena are now under very active study in several laboratories.

The Θ-negative, immunoglobulin-bearing lymphocytes have been considered to be members of the B lymphocyte class. Indeed, the possession of easily detectable amounts of surface immunoglobulin is now regarded as a marker of B lymphocytes. Applying this criterion to antigen-binding cells, Davie and Paul have demonstrated that virtually all of the DNP-GPA-binding lymphocytes of guinea pigs possess large amounts of surface immunoglobulin (81). This was done by initially incubating the lymphocytes with small amounts of ^{125}I-DNP-GPA and then, after washing, adding fluoresceinated antiimmunoglobulin. All cells classed as antigen binding by autoradiography were fluorescent when exposed to an ultraviolet light source.

It thus appears that the direct antigen-binding procedure used by most investigators primarily detects cells of the B lymphocyte pool. The specificity characteristics of B lymphocyte receptors have been relatively straightforward to study and are discussed below.

It has been estimated that if thymocytes possessed 1000 immunoglobulin molecules/cell, the techniques utilized would have detected them. However, one cannot be as certain that peripheral T lymphocytes would be scored as positive if they possessed 1000 or even 5000 immunoglobulin molecules, because they are usually evaluated in the presence of B lymphocytes possessing many more such surface immunoglobulin molecules. Recently, Nossal et al (90) have utilized a very sensitive indirect autoradiographic procedure to demonstrate surface immunoglobulin on T lymphocytes. Their results indicate that immunoglobulin exists on these cells but in very small amounts, perhaps no greater than the amount found on the surface of erythrocytes. The biological significance of this observation appears, therefore, somewhat in doubt. As described above, the direct antigen-binding procedure is difficult to apply to T lymphocytes. Nonetheless, several investigators have reported some antigen binding by thymus cells (91–93). In one such experiment, antiimmunoglobulin did not have an inhibitory effect on antigen binding (94).

The paucity or absence of surface immunoglobulin on T cells, as determined by the procedures used thus far, is compatible with one of the following possibilities: (1) T cells have very few surface immunoglobulin receptor molecules; (2) the surface immunoglobulin of T cells is not available for detection by these methods; (3) the T cell receptor is immunoglobulin of a class not detectable by the reagents employed; (4) the receptor molecules of T cells are not immunoglobulin.

Another approach to the evaluation of antigen-binding receptors has been to study the aggregation of sheep erythrocytes around lymphocytes to form rosettes. Rosette formation involves a small fraction of lymphocytes and appears to be immunologically relevant in that the number of rosette-forming cells (RFC) increases after immunization with sheep erythrocytes (95,96) and the specific removal of rosette-forming cells from a population diminishes the ability of that population to transfer the capacity to respond to sheep erythrocytes to irradiated syngeneic animals (97). Greaves et al (95,96) have reported that approximately 45% of RFC in unimmunized mice may be lysed by anti-Θ and complement and thus appear to be T lymphocytes. The fraction of RFC which can be lysed by anti-Θ remains the same in the first 3 to 5 days after immunization and falls thereafter. Greaves and Hogg (98) have observed that rosette formation by Θ-positive cells can be inhibited by anti-L chain sera and in some cases, by anti-μ sera but not by sera directed at the γ class of H chains. However, Takahashi et al (99) have recently reported that anti-Θ sera prepared in mice congenic for the Θ gene, although considerably more potent than conventional anti-Θ, failed to lyse any RFC. These authors were able to lyse some RFC with conventional anti-Θ. They suggest that antibodies other than anti-Θ in the conventional preparations were responsible for the lysis of RFC; their study thus casts some doubt on the reports that specific T lymphocytes do form rosettes with sheep erythrocytes. Nonetheless, some of the differences in various reports could be resolved by differences in technique. Thus, one would anticipate that T cell rosettes might be less stable than B cell rosettes and thus more dependent on precise details of procedure.

The most convincing evidence of the immunoglobulin nature of T cell receptors derives from functional studies. It has been shown by Ada and Byrt (100) that incubation of spleen cells from nonimmune mice with ^{125}I-labeled antigens of exceedingly high specific activity results in the specific loss of the capacity of that cell population to mount an immune response. This is presumably due to the destruction of the antigen-binding cell by radiation from the labeled antigen. It has recently been shown that the function of both B and T lymphocytes can be specifically inhibited in this way. Basten et al (101) transferred thymocytes and B lymphocytes, which were obtained from the spleens of irradiated mice reconstituted only with bone marrow, into syngeneic irradiated animals. The recipients were immunized with chicken γ-globulin (CGG). An antibody response, as judged by specific plaque-forming cells in the spleen, ensued. If either the thymocytes or B lymphocytes were omitted, no response was obtained, demonstrating the requirement for both cell types in this system. Incubation *in vitro* of either the B lymphocytes or the thymocytes with CGG-^{125}I, of high specific activity, resulted in the failure of the recipients to mount an anti-CGG response, although their response to sheep erythrocytes was unaffected. Moreover, the substitution of a similar amount of nonradioactive CGG had no effect on the subsequent response of the recipient. Thus, both T and B cells appear to be capable of directly interacting with antigen. For both cell types, the inhibitory effect of incubation with CGG-^{125}I could be entirely prevented by the prior addition of anti-L chain sera to the cell preparation. This strongly implies that both the T and B cells bear receptors containing, at least, L chains of immunoglobulin.

This conclusion has also been reached by Mason and Warner (102) on the basis of the finding that an anti-L antiserum inhibited the capacity of mouse lymphocytes to induce a graft-versus-host reaction, which is clearly a T cell phenomenon. In addition, Greaves et al (103) have reported that the *in vitro* stimulation by antigen of blast transformation and DNA synthesis in human peripheral blood lymphocytes can be partially inhibited by Fab fragments of anti-L chain antibodies.

These functional studies, as noted above, constitute the most convincing evidence that T cells bear immunoglobulin molecules which act as cell surface receptors. It must be pointed out, however, that other investigators have not been able to duplicate these findings and the antiimmunoglobulin sera involved may possess certain special qualities. In particular, natural antibody to mouse lymphocytes, which exists in most rabbit sera, must be scrupulously removed or it may complicate interpretation of such experiments.

At our present state of knowledge, in spite of the principle of biologic economy, which would lead us to assume that Ig is the surface receptor of the T cell, the problem of the chemical nature of the T cell receptor must still be regarded as unresolved.

Specificity of Receptors

The specificity of B cell receptors has recently been studied directly utilizing the binding of ^{125}I antigen to cell receptors and the capacity of specific immunoadsorbents to bind cells. The hapten-carrier system has provided the most useful data on this point because the same structural moiety can be presented to the cell on different protein carriers in order to assess the relative contribution of hapten and carrier to the binding reaction.

Davie and Paul (81) have shown that guinea pig B lymphocytes which bind DNP-GPA-^{125}I to their surface have highly hapten-specific receptors. ϵ-DNP-L-lysine can inhibit the binding of DNP-GPA-^{125}I to the cell. Moreover, DNP-BSA and DNP-GPA are precisely equivalent as inhibitors of the binding of DNP-GPA-^{125}I. This last point is particularly important as lymphocytes from animals immunized to DNP-GPA respond, *in vitro*, with DNA synthesis to very low concentrations of DNP-GPA but do not make a detectable response to DNP-BSA even at a 4 log higher concentration (Table 4).

The other major approach to the evaluation of the specificity of cell surface receptors has been the use of cellular immunoadsorbents. Wigzell and Andersson (104) first demonstrated that specific immunocompetent cells would bind to glass bead columns to which antigen had been previously adsorbed. Subsequently, urethane foam (105), polyacrylamide beads (106), agarose beads (58), and nylon fibers (107) have been em-

Table 4   Relative Specificity of T and B Cells[a]

B Inhibition of Antigen Binding			T Stimulation of *In Vitro* DNA Synthesis		
Concentration of Inhibitor (μg/ml)	% Inhibition		Concentration of Stimulant (μg/ml)	E/C	
	DNP-GPA	DNP-BSA		DNP-GPA	DNP-BSA
1	71%	78%	0.01	3.4	1.2
10	92%	94%	1.0	5.5	1.2
			100	9.8	1.4

[a] Lymph node cells from guinea pigs immunized to DNP-GPA were divided into two portions. With one aliquot, the capacity of either 1 μg or 10 μg/ml of DNP-GPA or DNP-BSA to inhibit the binding of ^{125}I-DNP-GPA (o.2 μg/ml) was measured. This binding largely reflects receptors on specific B cells. The other portion of cells was placed in culture with varying concentrations of DNP-GPA or DNP-BSA. Stimulation of DNA synthesis is reported as E/C, which is counts per minute in presence of antigen/counts per minute in absence of antigen. This assay largely reflects the activity of specific T cells.

ployed as solid supports for antigen. Using these procedures, antigen-binding B lymphocytes may be specifically removed from a cell population. In experiments involving DNP-GPA-^{125}I-binding lymphocytes (81,57), the removal of the cells is hapten specific as shown by the fact that adsorbents bearing DNP-GPA, DNP-BSA, and DNP-hemocyanin are equivalent in their capacity to deplete these cells.

Moreover, in the transfer of primary immune responses to irradiated syngeneic mice or guinea pigs, hapten-protein adsorbent treatment of the cells is effective in diminishing the antihapten antibody synthesis of the recipient in response to immunization with the same hapten on a protein unrelated to that on the adsorbent (81,108). This experiment provides biological support for the conclusions as to hapten specificity of B cell receptors which had been reached by binding studies.

Upon immunization, the number of cells capable of binding antigen increases markedly (57). The cells also appear to be B lymphocytes by virtue of their possession of large amounts of surface immunoglobulin. These antigen-binding cells resemble those of unprimed animals in most respects. In one interesting way, however, they demonstrate a quantitative difference. The affinity for antigen of their receptors is markedly greater (109–111). This may be shown by determining the concentration of the univalent ligand ϵ-DNP-L-lysine required to inhibit the binding of DNP-GPA-^{125}I by 50% of the antigen-binding cells. Approximately

$10^{-3}M$ ε-DNP-L-lysine is required to inhibit 50% of cells from a nonimmune animal from binding DNP-GPA, whereas 30 days after immunization 10^{-8} to $10\ M^{-9}$ ε-DNP-L-lysine suffices. This increase in the affinity of cell surface receptors on precursors of antibody-synthesizing cells has its parallel in the increase in affinity of antibody secreted by plaque-forming cells and in the affinity of serum antibody molecules (110).

The direct evaluation of T cell receptors has, thus far, been based solely on cellular depletion studies utilizing specific adsorbents. Davie and Paul (58) have shown that incubation of DNP-protein-agarose bead conjugates with lymph node cells from immune guinea pigs specifically diminishes the capacity of that cell population to respond, *in vitro,* with DNA synthesis when exposed to antigen. This response, as described earlier, is largely a T-cell-dependent phenomenon. Cell suspensions were prepared from the lymph nodes of guinea pigs that had been immunized with DNP-GPA and with keyhole limpet hemocyanin (KLH). These cells were gently mixed with agarose beads to which DNP-GPA had been conjugated and the cells which did not adhere to the beads had a diminution in their capacity to respond to DNP-GPA, although their response to KLH was normal. DNP-BSA-agarose and ε-DNP-L-lysine-agarose bead conjugates were both ineffective in removing DNP-GPA-reactive T cells, although independent experiments demonstrated that ^{125}I-DNP-GPA-binding cells (B cells) and anti-DNP antibody secreting cells were bound to the same extent by these DNP adsorbents. Thus, the conjugate specificity characteristic of the activation of T lymphocytes appears to be a direct function of cell surface antigen-binding receptors on these cells. These receptors, in addition, discriminate between related forms of the haptenic group. TNP-GPA-agarose partially diminishes the antigen responsiveness of a cell population from an animal immune to DNP-GPA. Moreover, the response of this population to TNP-GPA is diminished, in relative terms, to a greater degree than is the response to DNP-GPA. O-nitrophenyl-GPA, which cross-reacts serologically to a very slight degree with DNP-GPA, neither stimulates cells from a DNP-GPA-immune animal, nor, when conjugated to agarose, does it diminish the responsiveness of a cell population to DNP-GPA.

Thus, antigen depletion studies in this system strongly reinforce the concept that differences in specificity exist between receptors on T and B cells. T cell depletion studies utilizing cellular immunoadsorbents have not yet been reported in other systems, with one exception. Both Brondz (61) and Golstein et al (112) have recently shown that spleen cells from mice immune to histocompatibility antigens borne by cells of other inbred strains, specifically adhere to a monolayer culture of cells derived from the second strain. Golstein et at (112) have recovered these adherent lymphocytes by trypsinization; the recovered cells demonstrate an enrichment in their *in vitro* cytotoxicity for the monolayer cells. The procedures utilized for adherence of allospecific T cells resemble those of Davie and Paul (58) for the removal of DNP-GPA-immune cells in that both are exceedingly gentle procedures compared to the more usual column chromatography in which rapid flow should tend to remove cells held only by relatively few bonds. This may explain the lack of other reports of specific depletion of T cell function by antigens conjugated to solid particles.

In sum, then, the available data on specificity of antigen-binding receptors of T cells indicate that prime specificity is directed at conjugate- or carrier-specific determinants and that few, if any, functional T cells have receptors with a high degree of hapten specificity.

Immune Response Genes

One further, and critical, factor in antigen recognition is a series of autosomal dominant genes that exert control over the immune response of animals to certain sets of antigens. These immune response (Ir) genes were first described by Kantor et al (113) in the study of the immune response of guinea pigs to the DNP conjugate of poly-L-lysine (PLL). Subsequently, a considerable body of work has been accumulated on the Ir genes of guinea pigs and mice (114,115). Two prototype examples are discussed: DNP-PLL in guinea pigs and, in mice, a series of branched-chain polymers including tyrosine, glutamic acid, D-L alanine, and lysine [(T,G)-A-L]; histidine, glutamic acid, D-L alanine, and lysine [(H,G)-A-L]; and phenylalanine, glutamic acid, D-L alanine, and lysine [(Phe,G)-A-L].

The immune response of guinea pigs to DNP-PLL and to a series of other compounds including the copolymer of L-glutamic acid and L-lysine (GL), polyarginine, and protamine is controlled by a single autosomal dominant gene (or a series of linked genes) termed the PLL gene (116,117). This gene is possessed by some random-bred Hartley guinea pigs and by all strain 2 inbred guinea pigs; strain 13 guinea pigs lack the PLL gene. Animals possessing the PLL gene produce large amounts of anti-DNP antibody when immunized with DNP-PLL and develop a considerable degree of delayed hypersensitivity to DNP-PLL. Animals lacking the PLL gene make either no or a very small amount of anti-DNP antibody and do not develop detectable delayed hypersensitivity in response to DNP-PLL immunization. The gene product appears to function primarily in T cells, on the basis of the following evidence:

1. Animals lacking the PLL gene cannot be induced to demonstrate PLL-specific T cell functions such as delayed hypersensitivity (116) and helper effects (72) in the activation of antibody-forming cell precursors.

2. No defect is present in the capacity of PLL-negative animals to secrete anti-DNP antibody when the DNP group is presented on another carrier. Moreover, guinea pigs immunized with electrostatic complexes of DNP-PLL and bovine serum albumin produce anti-DNP antibodies indistinguishable from those produced by similarly immunized animals that possess the PLL gene (118). Importantly, the PLL-negative animals immunized with DNP-PLL-BSA do not manifest delayed hypersensitivity to DNP-PLL, although they secrete anti-DNP antibody.

3. No difference exists in the frequency of DNP-specific antigen-binding B cells in DNP-PLL responder and nonresponder guinea pigs (119).

Thus, in PLL-negative animals, PLL and DNP-PLL do not function as carrier molecules. DNP-PLL can behave as a macromolecular hapten in such PLL-negative animals. The defect in PLL-negative animals does not appear to be in precursors of antibody-synthesizing cells (B cells). The data do not unambiguously establish that the T cell is the site of action of the PLL gene, but when taken together with data from the mouse Ir genes, the findings strongly suggest the importance of gene function in T cells.

The branched polymer (T,G)-A-L causes C57BL/6 mice to produce significant amounts of antibody, whereas CBA mice make a meager antibody response to this antigen (120). The response is controlled by a single autosomal gene which has been termed Ir-1 (immune response-1). Mice homozygous for the responder allele make considerable amounts of antibody, whereas mice homozygous for the nonresponder allele produce very limited responses. It has been estimated that the latter mice produce less than 10% as much antibody as the former mice. Heterozygotes produce intermediate quantities of antibody.

As in the PLL system, T-derived lymphocytes play an important role in the expression of Ir-1 gene function (121,122). Thus, C3H mice [poor responders to (T,G)-A-L] produce mainly γM antibody upon immunization with (T,G)-A-L and neonatally thymectomized mice produce essentially the same amount of antibody as their normal controls. This suggests that the response of the "low responders" is essentially independent of the function of thymus-derived lymphocytes. C3H.SW mice, which are "high responders" to (T,G)-A-L, produce principally γG antibody. Neonatal thymectomy of these animals results in a markedly diminished immune response to (T,G)-A-L. The response of the thymus-deprived C3H.SW mice, indeed, resembles that of the "low-responder" C3H mice and is principally γM in class.

Another approach to the evaluation of the cellular defect in low-responder mice has been reported by Shearer and coworkers (123). They have attempted to estimate the frequency of T cells reactive to (Phe,G)-A-L in high- and low-responder strains by transferring limiting numbers of thymus cells together with a large excess of bone marrow cells to irradiated syngeneic recipients. The recipients were then immunized with (Phe,G)-A-L and the fraction of animals manifesting a measurable immune response determined. By plotting the fraction of responding animals against the number of transferred cells and assuming a simple Poisson distribution, they were able to estimate the frequency of an immunocompetent cell unit among the T cells. Their value for "low-responder" mice was 1 in 6×10^7 thymocytes, while "high-responder" mice had an approximately tenfold greater frequency of (Phe,G)-A-L-sensitive cells. These studies in the guinea pig and in the mouse indicate, then, that Ir genes function in T cells.

Although the data from the DNP-PLL system in guinea pigs suggest that B cell function is not impaired, there is some evidence suggesting that specific B cell defects may exist in animals lacking certain Ir genes. Thus, mice immunized with the branched-chain polymer of phenylalanine, glutamic acid, proline, and lysine [(Phe,G)-Pro-L] produce antibodies directed against "Phe,G" specificities or "Pro-L" specificities. That is, some antibodies bind to (Phe,G)-A-L while others bind to the polymer of tyrosine, glutamic acid, proline, and lysine [(T,G)-Pro-L]. Mice that are low responders to (Phe,G)-A-L make little or no "Phe,G"-specific antibody upon immunization with (Phe,G)-Pro-L, suggesting that the Ir gene plays some role in the generation or activation of "Phe,G"-specific B cells (124,125). A similar observation has recently been made in guinea pigs. The immune response to the copolymer of glutamic acid and alanine (GA) is controlled by a gene closely linked to the PLL gene. When GA-unresponsive animals are immunized with the terpolymer of glutamic acid, alanine, and tyrosine (GAT), they produce significant amounts of antibody to GAT. However, very little of this antibody binds to GA, although GA-responder guinea pigs produce considerable anti-GA antibody in response to immunization with GAT (126). Finally, Shearer et al (123) have studied the frequency of precursors of anti-(T,G)-A-L antibody secreting cells by an approach similar to that previously described for the evaluation of antigen-sensitive T cells. They find that low-responder mice possess fewer precursor cells than do high-responder mice.

In summary, then, Ir genes appear to function in T lymphocytes. They may also function in B lymphocytes, although the evidence on that point is still controversial.

One crucial and unexpected finding concerning the Ir genes is their close linkage to the genes controlling histocompatibility antigens. This linkage was first described in the Ir-1 system by McDevitt and Chinitz (127). They observed that different strains of inbred mice of the same H-2 type made similar responses to (T,G)-A-L and that congenic mice differing only at the H-2 locus differed in their response. Moreover, when F1 mice of high- and low-responder parents were crossed back to one or the other parent, a close genetic linkage between the Ir gene and the H-2 type was noted. A similar linkage was subsequently established between the PLL gene and the major strain 2 histocompatibility gene complex of guinea pigs (128).

The intimacy of the genetic linkage between Ir and histocompatibility genes is best revealed by the observation that in random-bred guinea pigs, such as the Hartley strain, PLL responsiveness is always associated with the presence of the strain 2 histocompatibility serological specificities (129). The presence of this linkage in both a random-bred and an inbred strain, which presumably diverged from a common ancestor long ago, and the maintenance of close association in all tested members of the random-bred strain is convincing evidence for the very close genetic association of these traits.

The precise mapping of the relation of the Ir gene to histocompatibility genes has been undertaken in the mouse. The existence of mice whose H-2 complex is derived by genetic recombination from two other H-2 types has provided a system in which such mapping is feasible. An analysis of the responsiveness of "recombinant" mice indicates that Ir-1 is within the H-2 complex and is located in a region to the "right" of the K ("left side") determinants and to the "left" of the genes for serum substance (114). It is not currently certain how large this region is. However, the substantial recombination frequency between K end ("left side") determinants and D end ("right side") determinants implies that considerable genetic material may be potentially available in the "middle" of the H-2 complex. This, in turn, raises the possibility of the existence of multiple Ir loci within this area. Lieberman and her colleagues (130) have recently obtained data establishing the existence of at least two H-2-linked loci. Her experiments are as follows: The immune response of mice to the idiotypic determinants of both IgA and IgG (γ_2a) myeloma proteins depends, in part, on H-2-linked Ir genes (131,132). In the response to both proteins, little or no antibody is produced by mice whose immunoglobulins possess the same H chain allotypic determinants as the myeloma protein. Among inbred mice that have different allotypic markers on their H chains, the immune response to both proteins is controlled by autosomal dominant H-2-linked Ir genes. Mice of the H-2^a and H-2^k histocompatibility types are good responders to the IgA protein, while mice of the H-2^b and H-2^d genotypes are poor responders. The control of the response to IgG proteins is quite different. H-2^b mice are good responders, whereas H-2^a, H-2^d, and H-2^k mice are poor responders. The H-2 linkage has been best shown on the basis of the immune response of mice congenic to the C57BL/10 but bearing H-2 complexes of other types. In particular, the B10.A mouse (essentially a C57BL/10 of H-2^a histocompatibility) responds well to IgA myeloma proteins and poorly to IgG. The C57BL/10 (H-2^b) itself responds well to IgG myeloma proteins and poorly to IgA. A small series of mice exist which are congenic to the C57BL/10 and in which the H-2 complex is derived from genetic recombination between H-2^a and H-2^b types. Of 5 different recombinant strains which have been tested, 4 are good responders to one class of myeloma protein and poor to the other and in each case the Ir gene appeared linked to determinants associated with the "K end" of the H-2 complex. However, one strain, referred to as the B.10A 4R, is a good responder to both the IgG and IgA myeloma proteins. This suggests that the crossover event involved in the formation of this recombinant H-2 complex occurred somewhere between the Ir genes controlling the immune response to IgA and IgG myeloma proteins. Evidence from other laboratories studying other responses of the B10.A 4R suggests that the result observed by Lieberman is not due to another genetic mechanism such as unequal crossover. This experiment thus indicates that at least two H-2-linked Ir loci exist. Moreover, as the number of strains studied to establish the distinctness of the Ir genes for IgA and IgG myeloma proteins was small, Lieberman's experiments imply that many Ir loci exist.

It is very clear that the Ir genes play an important role in antigen recognition, but the mechanism through which they exert their function is quite unknown. Two general possibilities exist. Ir genes may be structural genes for antigen receptor molecules or they may code for molecules that act in an auxiliary fashion with receptors. Let us first consider the possibility that the Ir genes code for the surface receptor. In the most straightforward version of this hypothesis, the Ir gene would be the structural gene for the variable domain of H and/or L polypeptide chains of immunoglobulin. As discussed earlier, immunoglobulin is clearly the receptor molecule on B cells and is a major candidate for the T cell receptor. A role for Ir genes as structural genes for the variable domain of *conventional* immunoglobulin H chains is clearly ruled out by genetic evidence. In the mouse, genes controlling idiotypic specificities are linked to the gene complex controlling H chain constant region allotypes (133). As the former appear to be markers of the H chain variable region and the latter to be markers of H chain constant regions, it is reasonable to conclude that genes controlling H chain variable regions are linked to those controlling H chain constant regions. These genes are clearly not linked to the H-2 complex (134), thus excluding the possibility that the Ir genes are variable region genes for conventional H chains. An alternate possibility is that the Ir genes code for a set of variable region genes quite distinct from those expressed in conventional immunoglobulin molecules and that these genes are at a locus distinct from the variable region genes associated with either H, κ or λ chain constant region genes. The possibility that Ir genes might code for receptors which are entirely distinct, both genetically and chemically, from immunoglobulin must also be considered.

A principal objection to the concept that the Ir gene product is the T cell receptor is the discrepancy in apparent specificity of Ir gene products and the specificity of cellular immune responses. Thus, Ir genes control the immune response to a series of antigens that often cross-react little or not at all, even by tests of the specificity of DH and of *in vitro* stimulation of DNA synthesis (117). It may be argued, of course, that the Ir genes thus far described are, in fact, complexes of large numbers of genes, one for each controlled antigen. In view of the heterogeneity of the cellular immune response even to a single well-defined antigen, this view would require a very large number of Ir genes and presents definite complexities. Another possibility is that the Ir gene controls a primordial structural gene for receptor and that somatic changes in this gene generate sufficient numbers of new receptor genes to account for a large number of substances being controlled by a single inherited genetic factor. This possibility requires a precisely regulated somatic mechanism to generate reproducibly the genes controlling the immune responses to several antigens. Jerne (135) has suggested that Ir genes may not code for receptors at all, but may, indirectly, control the generation of receptor molecules of given specificity. The hypothesis he has proposed is that individual members of a species inherit a set of genes for immunoglobulin variable domains which bind to the major histocompatibility antigens of that species. All the other immunoglobulin variable domains produced by the mature animal are derived by mutations occuring in those lymphoid cells which originally bore receptors capable of interacting with the histocompatibility antigens that the individual possessed. Jerne proposes a mechanism affording high survival value to cells mutating away from surface immunoglobulin specific for host histocompatibility antigens. Thus, if one antihistocompatibility antibody gene would more likely mutate to yield immunoglobulins specific for one type of antigen, whereas another antihistocompatibility gene regularly mutated to yield immunoglobulin of another specificity, this theory might explain Ir genes.

The other general possibility is that the Ir gene product aids in an auxiliary way in the activation of T lymphocytes. Among the possibilities to be considered is that the Ir gene codes for surface molecules which, although not specific receptors, act to increase the energy binding of certain molecules to the cell surface. An example might be that the PLL gene coded for a surface molecule which bound PLL, or indeed any compound with repeating positive charges, with a modest degree of energy. If the equilibrium constant were of the order of 10^{+3} L/M, it would be very difficult to detect any direct binding, but the increment in binding energy in a situation in which the antigen was simultaneously bound by a specific receptor and Ir gene product would be substantial. If the T cell has very few receptors, as appears likely, then a very high energy of binding per receptor might be crucial to activate the cell. This possibility would also serve to explain the rather broad range of specificity of the Ir genes. Other types of auxiliary mechanisms could be proposed, but direct evidence to test them is not yet available.

The identification of the Ir gene products and the determination of their mode of action constitute one of the major unsolved problems of immunology. An approach to the analysis of the Ir gene product is that recently described by Shevach et al (136). This experiment takes advantage of the finding that Ir genes associated with both the strain 2 and the strain 13 histocompatibility complex have been described in guinea pigs. The response to the DNP conjugate of the copolymer of L-glutamic acid and L-lysine (DNP-GL) is associated with the strain 2 complex, while the immune response to the copolymer of L-glutamic acid and L-tyrosine (GT) is associated with the strain 13 complex; (2 × 13) F_1 animals are responsive to both antigens and, thus, peritoneal exudate lymphocytes from F_1 animals immunized to both DNP-GL and GT may be stimulated by either antigen to incorporate tritiated thymidine into DNA. If the lymphocytes are cultured in the presence of strain 2 alloantisera to strain 13 histocompatibility antigens, they respond normally to DNP-GL but their response to GT is virtually eliminated. Similarly, the use of an anti-2 serum suppresses the response to DNP-GL without affecting the response to GT. This indicates that alloantisera prevent the action of Ir gene products, presumably by blocking the product on the surface of the cell either through steric hindrance or through the existence in the alloantisera of antibodies to Ir gene products. Experiments of this type may lead to an identification of the precise nature of the Ir gene product.

CONCLUSION

In the development of this chapter, we have reviewed experiments establishing three major levels of antigenic recognition involved in initiating and regulating immune responses.

For many antigens, an optimal antibody response can be mounted in the animal only if recognition occurs at each level. It will also be clear from the data that a definitive picture of the antigen-recognition, cell-activation schema cannot yet be presented. In closing this chapter, however, we suggest one version of the complex events involved.

The initial contact of antigen with the system involves an interaction with macrophages, or possibly another type of adherent lymphoid cell. We suggest that of the many functions proposed for macrophages the most likely is that macrophages bind antigen to their surface and this surface antigen is crucial to the activation of specific T lymphocytes. The T lymphocyte recognizes such macrophage-bound antigens through specific receptors. As reviewed, it appears that few surface copies of this receptor are present, but it is by no means ruled out that receptors exist which are accessible to macrophage-associated surface antigens but not to soluble antigens. At this writing, the chemical nature of the T cell receptor remains in doubt as does the precise role of Ir gene products in antigen recognition.

Upon activation, T lymphocytes appear to differentiate and divide. This population of cells produces a series of lymphokines and some of these lymphocytes develop into cells which mediate direct cytotoxicity. One important problem which requires resolution is the degree of functional heterogeneity among the T lymphocytes and the relative importance of regulatory interaction between T cell types.

In regard to B lymphocyte activation, we postulate that the key event is the simultaneous interaction of a T cell product and antigen. This T cell product would be a lymphokine capable of activating B cells. Preliminary evidence suggests that such a substance may exist and may be the mechanism of T–B cell interaction (see ref. 137). When antigen binds to B cells in the absence of this postulated lymphokine, activation of the B cell is achieved only within very limited concentration ranges. Concentrations of antigen lower than that critical for activation may have essentially no effect on the B cell, whereas concentrations higher than that required for activation cause tolerance. In the presence of "B cell lymphokine," antigen can activate specific B cells over a much wider range of concentrations and the response will involve both IgM and IgG components.

One difficulty with this theory is that it does not adequately explain the requirement that T and B cells both be specific for determinants on the same molecule for optimal results and the recent demonstration that efficient cellular interaction between T and B cells requires sharing of some major histocompatibility genes (138). These considerations suggest that T and B cells simultaneously interact with antigen and that this effectively brings the B cell into areas of high lymphokine concentration. One possible site for such interaction would be at the macrophage surface. Alternatively, the postulated "B cell lymphokine" may bear antigen or an antigen fragment.

In either case the outcome of this interaction is the activation of specific B cells. In some instances, at least, it appears that such activation may lead to a switch in surface immunoglobulin from μ class to γ class and may result in the synthesis of IgG antibodies by the progeny of precursor cells bearing IgM receptors (139).

Finally, specific T cells may cause inactivation of B cells, as well as activation. The clearest example of that is provided by the work of Okumura and Tada (140) on the IgE response of rats, but several other instances of such suppressive effects of T cell have been reported. Indeed, antigenic competition may well be due to suppressor activities of T cells (141–144).

In summary, then, the T cell seems to exert a central role in antigen recognition. It is directly involved in cellular immune responses, which are T cell mediated; it has a crucial regulatory role in B cell responses; and it seems to be the cell in which Ir gene function is predominantly exerted. Major efforts to delineate the nature of T cell receptors, to verify the postulate of lymphokines active on B cells, and to identify Ir gene products are therefore indicated if our understanding of and ability to manipulate this central aspect of the immune response is to progress.

REFERENCES

1. Ehrlich, P., *Proc. Roy. Soc.* **66**, 424 (1900).
2. Burnet, F. M., *The Clonal Selection Theory of Acquired Immunity*, Cambridge University Press, London and New York, 1959.
3. Siskind, G. W. and Benacerraf, B., *Adv. Immunol.* **10**, 1 (1969).
4. Ada, G. L., Parish, C. R., Nossal, G. J. V., and Abbot, A. *Cold Spring Harbor Symp. Quant. Biol.* **32**, 381 (1967).
5. Huber, H., Douglas, S. D., and Fudenberg, H. H., *Immunology* **17**, 7 (1969).
6. Lay, W. and Nussenzweig, V., *J. Exp. Med.* **128**, 991 (1968).
7. Unanue, E. R. and Askonas, B. A., *J. Exp. Med.* **127**, 915 (1968).
8. Fishman, M., *J. Exp. Med.* **114**, 837 (1961).
9. Gottlieb, A. A., *Biochemistry* **8**, 2111 (1969).
10. Roelants, G. E. and Goodman, J. W., *J. Exp. Med.* **130**, 557 (1969).
11. Fishman, M. and Adler, F. L., *Cold Spring Harbor Symp. Quant. Biol.* **32**, 343 (1967).
12. Adler, F. L., Fishman, M., and Dray, S., *J. Immunol.* **97**, 544 (1966).
13. Gery, I. and Waksman, B., *J. Exp. Med.* **136**, 143 (1972).
14. Mosier, D. E. and Pierce, C. W., *Fed. Proc.* **31**, 776 (1972).

15. Ford, C. E., in *The Thymus: Experimental and Clinical Studies* (C. E. Wolstenholme and R. Porter, Eds.), Little, Brown, Boston, Massachusetts, 1966, p. 153.

16. Moore, M. A. and Owen, J. J. T., *J. Exp. Med.* **126**, 715 (1967).

17. Raff, M. D. and Wortis, H., *Immunology* **18**, 931 (1970).

18. Schlesinger, M. and Yron, I., *Science* **164**, 1412 (1969).

19. Shevach, E., Green, I., Ellman, L., and Maillard, J., *Nat. New Biol.* **235**, 19 (1972).

20. McArthur, W. P., Chapman, J., and Thorbecke, G. J., *J. Exp. Med.* **134**, 1036 (1971).

21. Goldschneider, I. and McGregor, D. D., *Fed. Proc.* **31**, 776 (1972).

22. Cooper, M. D., Peterson, R. D. A., South, M. A., and Good, R. A., *J. Exp. Med.* **123**, 75 (1966).

23. Cerottini, J. C., Nordin, A. A., and Brunner, K. T., *Nature* **228**, 1308 (1970).

24. Raff, M. C., *Nature* **226**, 1257 (1970).

25. Mitchison, N. A., *Eur. J. Immunol.* **1**, 18 (1971).

26. Glick, B., Chang, T. S., and Jaap, R. G., *Poultry Sci.* **35**, 224 (1956).

27. Warner, N. L., Szenberg, A., and Burnet, F. M., *Aust. J. Exp. Biol. Med. Sci.* **40**, 373 (1962).

28. Perey, D. Y. E., Finstad, J., Pollara, B., and Good, R. A., *Lab. Invest.* **19**, 591 (1968).

29. Raff, M. C., Sternberg, M., and Taylor, R. B., *Nature* **225**, 553 (1970).

30. Bianco, C., Patrick, R., and Nussenzweig, V., *J. Exp. Med.* **132**, 702 (1970).

31. Basten, A., Sprent, J., and Miller, J. F. A. P., *Nat. New Biol.* **235**, 178 (1972).

32. Paraskevas, F., Lee, S.-T., Orr, K. B., and Israels, L. G., *J. Immunol. Methods* **1**, 1 (1971).

33. van Boxel, J. A., Paul, W. E., Frank, M. M., and Green, I., *Fed. Proc.* **31**, 786 (1972).

34. Cunningham, B. A., Gottlieb, P. D., Pflumm, M. N., and Edelman, G. M., *Prog. Immunol.* **1**, 3 (1971).

35. Hood, L. and Prahl, J., *Adv. Immunol.* **14**, 291 (1971).

36. Porter, R. R. and Press, E. M., *Ann. Rev. Biochem.* **31**, 625 (1962).

37. Landsteiner, K., *The Specificity of Serological Reactions*, Dover, New York, 1962.

38. Landsteiner, K. and van der Scheer, J., *J. Exp. Med.* **50**, 407 (1929).

39. Eisen, H. N. and Siskind, G. W., *Biochemistry* **3**, 996 (1964).

40. Arnon, R., Sela, M., Yaron, A., and Sober, M., *Biochemistry* **4**, 948 (1965).

41. Eisen, H. N., Simms, E. S., and Potter, M., *Biochemistry* **7**, 4126 (1968).

42. Potter, M. and Leon, M. A., *Science* **163**, 369 (1968).

43. Köhler, H., *Fed. Proc.* **31**, 751 (1972).

44. Cosenza, H., *Fed. Proc.* **31**, 752 (1972).

45. Paul, W. E., *Transplant. Rev.* **5**, 130 (1970).

46. Gell, P. G. H. and Silverstein, A. M., *J. Exp. Med.* **115**, 1037 (1962).

47. Benacerraf, B. and Levine, B. B., *J. Exp. Med.* **115**, 1023 (1962).

48. Silverstein, A. M. and Gell, P. G. H., *J. Exp. Med.* **115**, 1053 (1962).

49. Paul, W. E. and Siskind, G. W., *Immunology* **18**, 919 (1970).

50. Haurowitz, F., *J. Immunol.* **43**, 331 (1942).

51. Eisen, H. N., Carsten, M. E., and Belman, S., *J. Immunol.* **73**, 296 (1954).

52. Leskowitz, S., *J. Exp. Med.* **117,** 909 (1963).

53. Stulbarg, M. and Schlossman, S. F., *J. Immunol.* **101,** 764 (1968).

54. Mills, J. A., *J. Immunol.* **97,** 239 (1966).

55. Rosenthal, A. S., Davie, J. M., Rosenstreich, D. L., and Blake, J. T., *J. Immunol.* **108,** 279 (1972).

56. Paul, W. E., Siskind, G. W., and Benacerraf, B., *J. Exp. Med.* **127,** 25 (1968).

57. Davie, J. M., Rosenthal, A. S., and Paul, W. E., *J. Exp. Med.* **134,** 517 (1971).

58. Davie, J. M. and Paul, W. E., *Cell. Immunol.* **1,** 404 (1970).

59. Brunner, K. T., Mauel, J., Rudolf, H., and Chapuis, B., *Immunology* **18,** 501 (1970).

60. Mauel, J., Rudolf, H., Chapuis, B., and Brunner, K. T., *Immunology* **18,** 517 (1970).

61. Brondz, B. D., *Folia Biol.* **14,** 115 (1968).

62. Brondz, B. D. and Goldberg, N. E., *Folia Biol.* **16,** 20 (1970).

63. Davies, A. J. S., *Transplant. Rev.* **1,** 43 (1969).

64. Miller, J. F. A. P. and Mitchell, G. F., *Transplant. Rev.* **1,** 3 (1969).

65. Howard, J. G., Christie, G. H., Courtenay, B. M., Leuchars, E., and Davies, A. J. S., *Cell. Immunol.* **2,** 614 (1971).

66. Feldmann, M. and Basten, A., *J. Exp. Med.* **134,** 103 (1971).

67. Andersson, B. and Blomgren, H., in *Cellular Interactions and Receptor Antibodies in Immune Responses* (O. Mäkelä, A. Cross, and T. U. Kosunen, Eds.), Academic Press, New York, 1971, p. 345.

68. Andersson, B. and Blomgren, H., *Cell. Immunol.* **2,** 411 (1971).

69. Ovary, Z. and Benacerraf, B., *Proc. Soc. Exp. Biol.* **114,** 72 (1963).

70. Rajewsky, K., Schirrmacher, V., Nase, S., and Jerne, N. K., *J. Exp. Med.* **129,** 1131 (1969).

71. Katz, D. H., Paul, W. E., Goidl, E. A., and Benacerraf, B., *J. Exp. Med.* **132,** 261 (1970).

72. Paul, W. E., Katz, D. H., Goidl, E. A., and Benacerraf, B., *J. Exp. Med.* **132,** 283 (1970).

73. Potter, M. and Lieberman, R., *Adv. Immunol.* **7,** 91 (1967).

74. Iverson, G. M., *Nature* **227,** 273 (1970).

75. Janeway, C. A., Jr. and Paul, W. E., *Eur. J. Immunol.* **3,** 340 (1973).

76. Mitchison, N. A., *Eur. J. Immunol.* **1,** 68 (1971).

77. Alkan, S. and Goodman, J. W., *Fed. Proc.* **30,** 532 (1971).

78. Naor, D. and Sulitzeanu, D., *Nature* **214,** 687 (1967).

79. Warner, N. L., Byrt, P., and Ada, G. L., *Nature* **226,** 942 (1970).

80. Dwyer, J. M. and Mackay, I. R., *Lancet* **1,** 164 (1970).

81. Davie, J. M. and Paul, W. E., *J. Exp. Med.* **134,** 495 (1971).

82. Sell, S. and Gell, P. G. H., *J. Exp. Med.* **122,** 423 (1965).

83. Coombs, R. A., Gurner, B. W., Janeway, C. A., Jr., Wilson, A. B., Gell, P. G. H., and Kelus, A. S., *Immunology* **18,** 417 (1970).

84. Unanue, E. R., Grey, H. M., Rabellino, E., Campbell, P., and Schmidtke, J., *J. Exp. Med.* **133,** 1188 (1971).

85. Rabellino, E., Colon, S., Grey H. M., and Unanue, E. R., *J. Exp. Med.* **133,** 156 (1971).

86. Stobo, J. D., Talal, N., and Paul, W. E., *J. Immunol.* **109**, 701 (1972).

87. Vitetta, E. S. and Uhr, J. W., J. Immunol. **108**, 577 (1972).

88. Marchalonis, J. J., Cone, R. E., and Atwell, J. L., *J. Exp. Med.* **135**, 956 (1972).

89. Taylor, R. B., Duffus, W. P. H., Raff, M. C., and de Petris, S., *Nat. New Biol.* **233**, 225 (1971).

90. Nossal, G. J. V., Warner, N. L., Lewis, H., and Sprent, J., *J. Exp. Med.* **135**, 405 (1972).

91. Ada, G. L., *Transplant. Rev.* **5**, 105 (1970).

92. Sercarz, E., Decker, J., De Luca, D., Evans, R., Miller, A., and Modabber, F., in *Cellular Interactions and Receptor Antibodies in Immune Responses* (O. Mäkelä, A. Cross, and T. U. Kosunen, Eds.), Academic Press, New York, 1971, p. 157.

93. Dwyer, J. M., Warner, N. L., and Mackay, I. R., *J. Immunol.*, **108**, 1439 (1972).

94. Engers, H. D., *Fed. Proc.* **31**, 735 (1972).

95. Greaves, M. F. and Möller, E., *Cell. Immunol.* **1**, 372 (1970).

96. Greaves, M. F., Möller, E., and Möller, G. *Cell. Immunol.* **1**, 368 (1970).

97. Bach, J.-F., Muller, J.-Y., and Dardenne, M., *Nature* **227**, 1251 (1970).

98. Greaves, M. F. and Hogg, N. M., *Prog. Immunol.* **1**, 111 (1971).

99. Takahashi, T., Old, L. J., McIntire, K. R., and Boyse, E. A., *J. Exp. Med.* **134**, 815 (1971).

100. Ada, G. L. and Byrt, P., *Nature* **222**, 1291 (1969).

101. Basten, A., Miller, J. F. A. P., Warner, N. L., and Pye, J., *Nat. New Biol.* **231**, 104 (1971).

102. Mason, S. and Werner, N. L., *J. Immunol.* **104**, 762 (1970).

103. Greaves, M. F., Torrigiani, G., and Roitt, I. M., *Nature* **222**, 885 (1969).

104. Wigzell, H. and Andersson, B., *J. Exp. Med.* **129**, 23 (1969).

105. Mage, M. G., Evans, W. H., and Peterson, E. A., *J. Immunol.* **102**, 908 (1969).

106. Truffa-Bachi, P. and Wofsy, L., *Proc. Natl. Acad. Sci.* **66**, 685 (1970).

107. Rutishauser, U., Millette, C. F., and Edelman, G. M., *Proc. Natl. Acad. Sci.*, **69**, 1596 (1972).

108. Wigzell, H. and Mäkelä, O., *J. Exp. Med.* **132**, 110 (1970).

109. Davie, J. M. and Paul, W. E., *J. Exp. Med.* **135**, 643 (1972).

110. Davie, J. M. and Paul, W. E., *J. Exp. Med.* **135**, 660 (1972).

111. Möller, E. and Mäkelä, O., personal communpcation.

112. Golstein, P., Svedmyr, E. A. J., and Wigzell, H., *J. Exp. Med.* **134**, 1385 (1971).

113. Kantor, F. S., Ojeda, A., and Benacerraf, B., *J. Exp. Med.* **117**, 55 (1963).

114. McDevitt, H. O. and Benacerraf, B., *Adv. Immunol.* **11**, 31 (1969).

115. Benacerraf, B. and McDevitt, H. O., *Science* **175**, 273 (1972).

116. Benacerraf, B., Green, I., and Paul, W. E., Cold Spring Harbor Symp. Quant. Biol. **32**, 567 (1967).

117. Green, I., Paul, W. E., and Benacerraf, B., *Proc. Natl. Acad. Sci.* **64**, 1095 (1969).

118. Green, I., Paul, W. E., and Benacerraf, B., *J. Exp. Med.* **123**, 859 (1966).

119. Davie, J. M., Paul, W. E., and Green, I., *J. Immunol.* **109**, 193 (1972).

120. McDevitt, H. O. and Sela, M., J. Exp. Med. **122**, 517 (1965).

121. Grumet, F. C., *J. Exp. Med.* **135**, 110 (1972).

122.   Mitchell, G. F., Grumet, F. C., and McDevitt, H. O., *J. Exp. Med.* **135,** 126 (1972).

123.   Shearer, G. M., Mozes, E., and Sela, M., *Prog. Immunol.* **1,** 509 (1971).

124.   Mozes, E., McDevitt, H. O., Jaton, J.-C., and Sela, M., *J. Exp. Med.* **130,** 493 (1969).

125.   Mozes, E., McDevitt, H. O., Jaton, J.-C., and Sela, M., *J. Exp. Med.* **130,** 1263 (1969).

126.   Bluestein, H. G., Green, I., Maurer, P. H., and Benacerraf, B., *J. Exp. Med.* **135,** 98 (1972).

127.   McDevitt, H. O. and Chinitz, A., *Science* **163,** 1207 (1969).

128.   Ellman, L., Green, I., Martin, W. J., and Benacerraf, B., *Proc. Natl. Acad. Sci.* **66,** 322 (1970).

129.   Martin, W. J., Ellman, L., Green, I., and Benacerraf, B., *J. Exp. Med.* **132,** 1259 (1970).

130.   Lieberman, R., Paul, W. E., Humphrey, W., and Stimpfling, J., *J. Exp. Med.* **136,** 1231 (1972).

131.   Lieberman, R. and Humphrey, W., *Proc. Natl. Acad. Sci.* **68,** 2510 (1971).

132.   Lieberman, R. and Humphrey, W., *J. Exp. Med.* **136,** 1222 (1972).

133.   Pawlak, L. L., Mushinski, E. B., Nisonoff, A., and Potter, M., *J. Exp. Med.,* **137,** 22 (1973).

134.   Herzenberg, L. A., Warner, N. L., and Herzenberg, L. A., *J. Exp. Med.* **121,** 415 (1965).

135.   Jerne, N. K., *Eur. J. Immunol.* **1,** 1 (1971).

136.   Shevach, E., Paul, W. E., and Green, I., *J. Exp. Med.* **136,** 1207 (1972).

137.   Katz, D. H. and Benacerraf, B., *Adv. Immunol.* **15,** 1 (1972).

138.   Katz, D. H., Hamaoka, T., Dorf, M. E., and Benacerraf, B., *Proc. Natl. Acad. Sci.* **70,** 2124 (1973).

139.   Pierce, C. W., Solliday, S. M., and Asofsky, R., *J. Exp. Med.* **135,** 675 (1972).

140.   Okumura, K. and Tada, T., *J. Immunol.* **107,** 1682 (1971).

141.   Radovich, J. and Talmage, D. W., *Science* **158,** 512 (1967).

142.   Möller, G. and Sjoberg, O., *Cell. Immunol.* **1,** 110 (1970).

143.   Gershon, R. K. and Kondo, K., *J. Immunol.* **106,** 1524 (1971).

144.   Katz, D. H., Paul, W. E., and Benacerraf, B., *J. Immunol.* **110,** 107 (1973).

Chapter Five

Cellular Receptors: Their Nature and Specificity

GERALD JONES AND STUART F. SCHLOSSMAN

Department of Medicine, Harvard Medical School and Division of Tumor Immunology, Children's Cancer Research Foundation, Boston, Massachusetts

It is now well recognized that the immune response consists of cellular and humoral reactions, each of which is subserved by different types of lymphocytes. Thymus-derived, or thymus-dependent, lymphocytes (T cells) are responsible for the reactions of cellular immunity, and thymus-independent or bursa-dependent lymphocytes (B cells) are responsible for humoral immunity. Since the elucidation of the role of the thymus in 1962 (1) a great deal of experimental evidence has accumulated in support of the basic dichotomy in immune reactions delineated above. This simple scheme, however, needs to be qualified in that T cells are indirectly involved in many humoral responses via an incompletely understood mechanism of cell cooperation (2,3).

One of the major outstanding problems in immunology is the extent to which humoral and cellular immune reactions share common mechanisms, in particular whether the induction of the response in both instances involves identical recognition structures with similar discriminatory powers. There is a great deal of evidence that the antibody produced in response to a given antigen does not cross-react with unrelated

*Supported by MRC Traveling Fellowship (to G. Jones) and Grants NSF GB25474 and USPHS AI09003 (to S. Schlossman).

97

antigens. This specificity of the product of B lymphocytes implies that activation of the cell by antigen involves an identical and equally specific cell surface receptor, viz., antibody. If this were not so, cells would require surface receptors of another molecular species with a recognition specificity identical to that of antibody—an unlikely event. This argument, and other considerations, has led to the postulate that all antigenic recognition by lymphocytes is mediated by antibody molecules incorporated into the structure of the lymphocyte surface (4). One can clearly see the need for such an hypothesis in the case of B lymphocytes, and at the moment there is no viable alternative. In the case of T lymphocytes, however, there is no compelling reason to assume that antibody mediates recognition since these cells do not produce antibody, although they may secrete other products (5,6). It would of course be simpler to envisage a common recognition mechanism for both subpopulations of lymphocytes, but this view may be too restrictive.

This review discusses the induction by antigen of cellular and humoral immunity in an attempt to define the discriminatory ability of the two lymphocyte populations and the nature of the receptors involved. Most of the evidence reviewed consists of studies with hapten-carrier conjugates with particular reference to the DNP-oligolysine system in guinea pigs.

The terms "specificity" and "affinity" are often used loosely. We define the specificity of an antibody toward an antigen as the degree of closeness-of-fit or complementarity between the antibody and that antigen. By affinity we imply that, using a given technique at appropriate antigen and antibody concentrations, the energy of binding between a univalent antigenic determinant and antibody has a certain numerical value. Affinity and specificity are therefore two terms of differing precision used to describe the same phenomenon and in this review they are used interchangeably.

Similarly, one can describe the specificity of a cellular immune reaction in terms of the complementarity of cell surface receptors and the homologous antigen compared with unrelated antigens. Since T lymphocytes do not secrete a readily identifiable product that binds antigen nor bind antigen themselves (by most techniques) all measurements of T cell specificity depend on indirect approaches such as antigen-induced proliferation or MIF production. In the case of B lymphocytes, cellular specificity is often assumed to be identical to that of the secreted antibody. Although it is valid to compare the specificities of different cell populations toward one or more antigens it is difficult to compare the specificity of cells with that of antibody in solution. This point is elaborated further below.

THE OLIGOLYSINE SYSTEM

A series of DNP-oligolysines may be prepared by block polymerization techniques or by stepwise solid-phase synthesis. The stepwise technique has the advantage that one may introduce predetermined modifications of the molecule such as alterations in the optical configuration of the amino acids or the substitution of other amino acids for lysine. Methods of preparing DNP-lysines and separating the various components are described elsewhere (7,8). These antigens have proved useful in the analysis of cellular and humoral specificities. DNP-oligolysines containing 7 or more L-lysine residues induce all strain 2 and most Hartley guinea pigs to synthesize anti-DNP antibody and develop cellular immunity (7,9). Responder guinea pigs, i.e., polylysine gene-positive animals (PLL+), all develop skin reactivity, and lymphocytes from such animals can be activated *in vitro* by antigen to proliferate or produce migration inhibitory factor. Nonresponder animals (PLL−) do not respond to immunogenic DNP-oligolsines in saline or with ordinary doses of adjuvants. Such nonresponder animals can be made to produce anti-DNP antibody by immunization in adjuvants containing large amounts of *M. tuberculosis* or in association with foreign proteins (10), although they still do not develop skin reactivity or the capacity to respond *in vitro* to immunogenic DNP-oligolysines. Further experiments using DNP-oligolysines with D-lysine in the place of L-lysine have shown that in PLL+ guinea pigs the essential requirement for immunogenicity is a spatial relationship involving L-lysines (8).

Cellular Receptors: Nature and Specificity

Previous studies with a variety of antigens have shown the specificity of cellular immune reactions (11–14). In hapten-protein conjugate systems, delayed hypersensitivity skin reactions or *in vitro* cell activations are maximally elicited by the homologous antigen. The same hapten on a different protein either produces no effect or weak cross-reactions. Similar degrees of carrier specificity are observed in secondary antibody formation.

In the DNP-lysine system the same features of carrier specificity are shown in the elicitation of cellular immune reactions *in vivo* and *in vitro*. In animals sensitized to immunogenic α,DNP-oligolysines, nonimmunogenic α,DNP-oligolysines containing fewer than 7 L-lysine residues do not elicit a delayed skin reaction nor can they induce secondary antibody formation *in vivo* or cell activation *in vitro*. But these small nonimmunogenic peptides can provoke passive cutaneous anaphylaxis and Arthus-type skin reactions. Thus small peptides are not entirely without effect *in vivo*. The mechanism is still unclear but it points out the difference between the passive interactions of an antibody with its antigenic determinant to produce PCA or Arthus reactions and the activation of cellular receptors.

Immunogenic molecules are required not only to elicit a delayed response but are needed also *in vivo* to desensitize. Injection of large doses of antigen into an animal with delayed hypersensitivity can make the animal specifically unresponsive to subsequent intradermal challenge with that antigen. The unresponsiveness is short-lived, lasting 3 to 10 days depending on the dose of antigen given. Animals sensitized to α,DNP-Lys$_{7-10}$ could be readily desensitized to this compound or larger immunogenic α,DNP-oligolysines. Nonimmunogenic α,DNP-Lys$_{3-6}$, or oligolysines without the DNP group or DNP proteins could not produce specific desensitization as assessed from delayed skin reactions (15).

In vitro models of cellular immunity have allowed a more detailed examination of the mechanism and specificity of cell activation. Lymph node cells or peritoneal exudate cells from animals sensitized to α,DNP-lysines can discriminate between various DNP-oligolysines when assayed by antigen-induced proliferation *in vitro* or production of MIF (16,17). Nonimmunogenic peptides, however, cannot themselves activate lymphocytes nor can they inhibit immunogenic peptides from activating cells. For example, a 100-fold molar excess of α,DNP-Lys$_5$ does not inhibit α,DNP-Lys$_9$ from triggering cells *in vitro* nor does α,DNP-Lys$_5$ by itself initiate cell proliferation. Similar findings occurred with other peptides. In general inhibition of cell activation by nonimmunogenic peptides or by haptens has not been demonstrated except to a minor degree at very high concentrations of the hapten and at suboptimal concentrations of the stimulating antigen (18). The difficulty in inhibition of the DNA synthetic response by hapten contrasts with the relative ease of inhibiting antigen-antibody combination with free hapten and the ease of blocking the binding of DNP conjugates to lymphocytes by heterologous conjugates (19). This contrast is discussed later. In other systems inhibition of antigenic interaction with T cells by hapten has been described (20,21). One report has described significant inhibition (50%) of cell activation *in vitro* by hapten at a tenfold molar excess (22).

Further studies in the oligolysine system have shown the remarkable discriminatory ability of cells mediating cellular immune reactions. The immunological reactivity of a series of α,DNP-lysines was studied, mainly in an attempt to determine whether the carrier specificity of cellular recognition could be accounted for by the interaction of oligolysine-specific cells and hapten-specific cells (23,24). The various peptides differed in hapten position and by substitution of D-lysine for L-lysine residues. Lymph node cells from strain 2 guinea pigs immunized with α,DNP-Lys$_9$, α,DNP-Lys$_9$(L$_7$DL), α,DNP-Lys$_9$(LDL$_7$), 14ϵ,DNP-Lys$_{14}$, 5ϵ,DNP-Lys$_9$, 9ϵ,DNP-Lys$_9$, 10ϵ,DNP-Lys$_9$, ϵ,DNP-Lys-Ala$_3$-Lys$_7$, and Lys$_9$ could readily discriminate between these peptides and were maximally stimulated to proliferate *in vitro* by the homologous antigen. The specificity of delayed skin reactions *in vivo* and MIF production *in vitro*, when tested, precisely matched the specificity of the proliferation response. For example, in lymph node cultures from animals sensitized to 14ϵ,DNP-Lys$_{14}$ only this compound and 9ϵ,DNP-Lys$_9$ (a homologous member of the series) produced significant stimulation. Despite the similarity in lysine and hapten content and the demonstrated capacity of 5ϵ,DNP-Lys$_9$, α,DNP-nonalysines, and Lys$_{8-10}$ to stimulate their respective cell cultures, virtually no stimulation was produced by these antigens in 14, ϵ, DNP-Lys$_{14}$ cultures. Similarly, in cultures obtained from animals sensitized to 5ϵ,DNP-Lys$_9$ practically no cross-reactions were seen with immunogenic peptides when the haptenic group was placed on a different lysyl residue or where D-lysine residues were substituted for L residues. When cross-reactions do occur they can be attributed to the common oligolysine determinant. For example, in cultures obtained from animals sensitized to α,DNP-Lys$_9$(LDL$_7$), α,DNP-Lys$_9$(L$_7$DL) and α,DNP-Lys$_9$ cross-react extensively, but so does Lys$_9$ without the DNP group. These results suggest that two populations of cells occur as a consequence of sensitization with DNP-oligolysines. Most of the cells have specific receptors for the DNP-oligolysines used to induce the response and a smaller population of cells is specific for the immunogenic oligolysine portion of the molecule. Thus cells bearing DNP-oligolysine receptors are activated efficiently only by the homologous immunizing antigen, whereas oligolysine-specific cells, which account for the cross-reactions, may be activated by oligolysines and oligolysine components of heterologous DNP-oligolysines. Similar demonstrations of specificity have been shown with another series of monosubstituted DNP-oligolysines, hapten-protein conjugates, and other antigens (14,25,26).

Davie and Paul (27) have demonstrated a high degree of specificity of cells mediating cellular immune reactions by a different technique. They showed that DNP-GPA-agarose beads could specifically remove the cells responsive to DNP-GPA *in vitro*, but no such depletion could be achieved with DNP-BSA or DNP-lysine. Antihapten antibody-forming cells were depleted by a variety of immunoabsorbents containing hapten, unlike the behavior of cells involved in *in vitro* proliferation.

These data on cellular specificities in the oligolysine system clearly indicate a high degree of discriminatory ability by the lymphocytes concerned. Similar results have been found in other hapten-carrier systems. Although the origin of the reactive cells in this system with regard to delayed skin reactions or MIF production has not been definitely established, T lymphocytes are clearly involved in the proliferative response to antigen *in vitro* (17,28–30) although some of the dividing cells are B cells (31). Whether pure T cells display the same discriminatory ability as mixed populations of T and B cells has not been determined.

Humoral Specificity

In the DNP-lysine system, as in other hapten-carrier systems, most of the antibody produced in guinea pigs is directed against the immunodominant DNP group. Antibody raised by immunizing animals with immunogenic peptides, such as α, DNP-Lys$_9$ cross-reacts extensively with non-immunogenic peptides, such as α, DNP-Lys$_{3-6}$ (32,33). Similar conclusions have been reached in other studies with a series of ϵ, DNP-oligolysines (25). Anti-DNP-oligolysine antibody as determined *in vitro* by hapten inhibition, equilibrium dialysis, or fluorescence quenching assays can discriminate only with difficulty between immunogenic and nonimmunogenic DNP-oligolysines. Serum antibody to α,DNP-Lys$_{10}$ or α,DNP-Lys$_{7-10}$ cannot easily differentiate α,DNP-Lys$_{5-6}$ from α,DNP-Lys$_7$. The largest estimates put the increment in affinity of α,DNP-Lys$_7$ over α,DNP-Lys$_{5-6}$ at 1 to 11% of the total.

Despite the extensive cross-reactions of anti-DNP antibody with various DNP conjugates, however, secondary production of anti-DNP antibody *in vivo* displays the same degree of carrier specificity as cellular activation *in vivo* (33a).

Further studies utilizing improved techniques for antibody purification and measures of specificity in responder and nonresponder animals have shown higher discriminatory ability of antihapten antibody. Analysis of anti-DNP antibody raised in PLL+ Hartley or strain 2 animals has shown that antibody can recognize the precise chain length of DNP-oligolysine used to induce the immune response. For example, analysis of antibodies raised to α,DNP-Lys$_{7-10}$, α,DNP-Lys$_{12}$, or α,DNP-Lys$_{10}$ shows that all responder antibody can recognize the precise DNP-oligolysine used to induce the immune response as reflected by stronger binding of the homologous immunizing peptide than of heterologous peptides (34).

When nonresponder animals (PLL-) are made to respond to DNP-oligolysine in the presence of high doses of adjuvants containing myco-bacteria, they do not develop cell-mediated immunity. Furthermore, antibody raised in nonresponders does not peak in binding energy with the precise chain length of the DNP-oligolysine used to induce the immune response, whereas antibody raised in responders with the same adjuvant mixture does. A small fraction of the total antibody produced may be responsible for this difference. Preliminary analysis of clonal patterns of antibody by isoelectric focusing has shown that most of the clones in responder and nonresponder animals are identical (35). These findings emphasize that the major difference between responder and nonresponder guinea pigs must reside at the T cell level.

One can therefore summarize the immune responsiveness of PLL+ guinea pigs to immunogenic DNP-oligolysine as follows. Secreted antibody, and presumably B cell receptors, are directed predominantly against the DNP group, while T cells recognize some spatial configuration involving 7 L-lysines and a portion of the hapten. This interpretation explains the extensive cross-reaction of antibody with DNP compounds and the lack of cross-reaction with T cells under similar circumstances. It also explains why hapten has little effect on cellular reactions. The failure to activate B cells *in vivo* by heterologous DNP conjugates, despite the extensive cross-reactions between anti-DNP antibody and heterologous DNP conjugates, indicates that B cell activation requires more than antigen-antibody combination at the cell surface. Cellular cooperation between oligolysine-specific T cells and DNP-specific B cells can account for this carrier specificity in anti-DNP production (36–38), although it should be noted that antibody itself can discriminate between different carriers (34).

Can we compare the specificities or discriminatory abilities of T cells, B cells, and secreted antibody? In our present state of knowledge the answer must be no. We can give precise figures for degrees of cross-reaction between antihapten antibodies and different hapten conjugates or between cell populations and different hapten-carrier conjugates, but since the majority of T cells are not hapten specific the failure to elicit cellular cross-reactions with heterologous hapten conjugates is not surprising. Even if T cells were hapten specific, it would be difficult to compare cross-reactions at the T and B cell level since T cells do not have an identifiable product to compare with antibody. Estimates of specificity involving cellular activation introduce a host of complicating factors such as the binding of antigen to cell surfaces and the all-or-nothing nature of DNA replication. As mentioned earlier the *in vivo* activation of B cells via surface antibodies cannot be explained by standard thermodynamic principles applied to the behavior of antibodies in solution.

Further information is required on the behavior of immunoglobulin molecules incorporated into cell membranes compared with their behavior in solution and the effect of activated T cells on the stimulation of hapten-specific B cells. Also, we need more information on the nature of the stimulating signal to the cell—whether a conformational or permeability change in the cell membrane is required, for how long, and over what fraction of the cell surface.

These considerations make it difficult to compare the specificities of T and B cells. All we can say is that T and B cells recognize different aspects of antigenic structures and that there is no indication that T cell recognition is of a crude or limited nature compared with antibody or B cell recognition.

THE NATURE OF ANTIGEN-SPECIFIC RECEPTORS

Receptors on B Cells

Numerous studies in different laboratories using a variety of techniques have shown that subpopulations of lymphocytes carry surface immunoglobulin (39–46) and that only cells of the marrow-derived population (B cells) appear to stain (47–51). There are still disagreements regarding the problem of allelic exclusion (41,52–54) or the existence of more than one subclass of immunoglobulin on the same cell (46,48,55–57).

The demonstrations that the binding of antigen to lymphocyte can be blocked by antiimmunoglobulin (anti-Ig) and that anti-Ig can produce lymphocyte activation are strong evidence in favor of a recognition role for this surface Ig (19,58–62).

There is in fact no good evidence against the view that Ig is the receptor for antigen on B cells.

Receptors on T Cells

The lack of easily demonstrable Ig on T cells has provoked a controversy regarding the recognition of antigen by such cells. There are two main points of view:

a. Ig is the receptor for antigen on all lymphocytes and the inability to demonstrate its presence on T cells is due to low concentration, the existence of a new class of immunoglobulin, or some peculiarity of the T cell surface.

b.   T cell recognition is subserved by a completely different molecular species.

Before discussing the implications of the latter view we review the evidence, mainly of an indirect nature, suggesting the presence of receptor Ig on T cells.

1.   *Inhibition of the mixed leukocyte reaction by anti-Ig.*   Several independent studies have shown that the mixed leukocyte reaction is thymus dependent and that virtually all the responding cells are thymus derived (63–65). Thus the demonstration by Greaves et al that mixed leukocyte reactions in the human are inhibited by various preparations of antilight-chain sera provides evidence for the existence of Ig determinants on T lymphocytes (66,67). Although negative results are not usually given much prominence it should be noted that this inhibition has not been demonstrated in mouse cultures (68,69) nor has it been confirmed in the human system (70).

2.   *Inhibition of graft-versus-host reactions by anti-Ig.*   The reactions produced in F_1 hosts by injection of parental lymphoid cells are known to be thymus dependent (71) although other cells play a role (72,73). Several investigators have found that pretreatment of donor cells with anti-Ig preparations blocks their ability to produce graft-versus-host reactions (74–77). One investigator has extensively qualified his original data in that only a few antilight-chain preparations are effective (78). In the chicken Lydyard and Ivanyi (79) have shown by the use of anti-T cell, anti-B cell, and anti-Ig sera that only the anti-T cell serum blocks graft-versus-host reactions. They also noted that the concentration of serum used was critical since high concentrations had nonspecific cytotoxic effects. Other investigators, working with graft-versus-host reactions, have confirmed that anti-T cell serum, but not anti-B cell or anti-Ig, blocks the activity of donor cells (80). The latter results are in agreement with the effects of thymectomy and bursectomy on anti-Ig-induced lymphocyte transformation (81,82).

3.   *Inhibition of rosette formation by anti-Ig.*   The formation of rosettes by mixing sheep erythrocytes and mouse lymphoid cells has been extensively studied by Greaves and others (83). There is no doubt that the inhibitions produced by antilight-chain serum in this system are extremely consistent and cannot be explained by passively absorbed antibody (54). The crucial point is the origin of the rosette-forming cells—all are agreed that B cells may form rosettes, but the existence of T cell rosettes is still disputed. Most of the evidence for the T cell origin of rosettes depends on the use of anti-Θ serum or anti-H-2 serum as markers of T cells (84–86). While anti-Θ serum certainly has activity against

thymus-derived lymphocytes there have been two reports of contaminating anti-B cell activity in anti-Θ serum (87,88). The use of an anti-Θ serum raised between congenic mice should help to clear up this problem. Preliminary results (89) indicate that congenically raised anti-Θ serum does not affect sheep red cell rosettes in the mouse. Similar considerations apply to possible contamination of anti-H-2 antisera. In the chicken the situation is much clearer (80). Rosette formation is abolished by prior bursectomy, by pretreatment of the cells with anti-Ig or antibursa cell serum, or by passage of the cells through columns of insoluble antilight chain, but not by treatment with anti-T cell serum. Precisely the converse findings occur with graft-versus-host reactions (see above). These results have been confirmed in the chicken (90).

4. *Demonstration of Ig on activated T cells.*   There have been two reports, utilizing indirect immunofluorescent and immunoferritin techniques, of Ig determinants on human lymphoblasts of presumed thymic origin (91,92). These results were not confirmed in studies on mouse lymphocytes (93).

5. *Inhibition of helper activity by anti-Ig.*   Lesley et al have developed an *in vitro* culture system of humoral immunity, similar to the Mishell-Dutton system, utilizing TNP as hapten and sheep erythrocytes as carrier (94). Cooperation can be demonstrated between B cells recognizing TNP and T cells recognizing sheep erythrocytes in this system. The synergistic effect of T cells can be blocked by prior treatment with antilight-chain serum and complement. Such treatment had no effect on the TNP-specific B cells, which is odd in view of the data demonstrating Ig on B cells and the ability of anti-Ig and complement to kill such cells (95). Despite this objection the data do suggest the presence of Ig on helper T cells. This finding needs confirmation in other cooperating systems.

6. *Blocking of antigenic suicide of T cells by anti-Ig.*   Radiolabeled antigen of high specific activity may abrogate the immune response to that antigen, presumably by binding to the appropriate antigen-sensitive cells and producing radiation damage (96). Basten et al have exploited this technique for two different purposes—first, to show that specific recognition by T and B cells occurs, and, second, to show that antigenic suicide could be blocked by pretreatment of the cells with antilight-chain serum (97). One objection to this experiment is the unfortunate use of chicken gamma globulin as an antigen and the failure to determine if rabbit antimouse light chain binds to chicken globulin. Since the latter is quite possible the observed block might be due to residual antimouse light-chain binding to the radiolabeled antigen and thereby protecting the cells. Another objection is the lack of absorption controls with light chains to determine if the activity present was in fact due to anti-Ig.

7. *Direct labeling or isolation of Ig from T cells.*   Using very sensitive autoradiographic methods two groups have reported the presence of Ig on T cells (98,99). Bankhurst et al used prolonged exposure times to obtain positive autoradiographs, but it is difficult to determine whether the Ig demonstrated was produced by the cells or passively absorbed from the serum. Indeed, Nossal et al, using the extremely sensitive technique of indirect autoradiography, admit that red cells show surface Ig by this method. This clearly raises the issue of passive absorption and emphasizes the need for experiments utilizing genetic markers to determine the source of the detected immunoglobulin.

A completely different approach has been used by Marchalonis et al (100). They have applied the lactoperoxidase technique of iodination to living thymocytes and analyzed by coprecipitation and fractionation the nature of the labeled molecules. Immunoglobulin (monomeric IgM) was detected in lysates produced by $9M$ urea but the quantity found was sufficient to provide only 400 molecules/cell. This again forcibly presents the issue of passive absorption for which no controls were performed. Furthermore, a 1% contamination of thymocytes by B lymphocytes, carrying 40,000 Ig molecules/cell, would be sufficient to account for all the data. Later experiments suggested a higher density of Ig molecules on T cells (101), but these results have not been confirmed by other investigators using the same technique (102).

The foregoing discussion describes some of the evidence in favor of the Ig nature of the T cell receptor. There are many inconsistencies in the data and often contradictory reports in different laboratories. This contrasts with the experimental evidence for Ig on B cells. Passive absorption of immunoglobulin to T cells or the existence of nonspecific toxic components in certain antisera could explain many of the positive findings. Although the issue is still open the results suggest that some other molecular species may subserve recognition on T cells.

What sort of recognition mechanism and what type of molecule might be expected on T lymphocytes? It has been suggested that T cell recognition may belong to a cruder, more archaic process that predates the evolutionary arrival of immunoglobulin (80). Such recognition processes are presumed to be responsible for the "sorting out" phenomena that occur with embryonic tissue mixtures and with dissociated sponge cells (103–105). The cellular specificities described above in the oligolysine system and other hapten-carrier systems are against any such general view of crude recognition mechanisms in T cells. But there are unusual features of T cell recognition, particularly with respect to the recognition of histocompatibility antigens. Several authors have reported very high numbers (1 to 3%) of antigen-reactive cells in graft-versus-host reactions and mixed leukocyte reactions (106–111). In mixed leukocyte cultures of parental and F_1 cells it has been shown by chromosomal and surface antigenic markers that no recruitment of F_1 cells occurs; i.e., the response is unidirectional (65,112). Nor does the mixed leukocyte reaction depend on prior exposure to cross-reacting environmental antigens since normal reactivity is found in germ-free animals (113). In graft-versus-host reactions the possibility of recruitment does not arise since 30 to 50 grafted cells can produce a lesion on the chorioallantoic membrane of the chick embryo (106). Since recruitment does not occur the large size of clones recognizing histocompatibility antigens must imply some degree of antigenic cross-reaction or overlap in recognition. This might occur either because of the existence of similar determinants on different complex antigens or because there are lymphocytes capable of responding to more than one antigenic determinant, i.e., multipotential cells. It is difficult to exclude the possibility that complex antigens such as H-2 or AgB share with other antigens many determinants to each of which only a very small percentage of cells responds. Nor can the existence of multipotential cells be excluded by the demonstration that there is no overlap in the recognition of two distinct antigens since a far greater number of antigens needs to be studied. There is also evidence that T cells in the mouse display considerable difficulty in distinguishing various red cells in the absence of humoral cross-reaction (114–116). Since T cell recognition was assessed indirectly by helper activity in cooperating systems it is difficult to compare cross-reactions at the T and B cell level in these systems.

If these findings, as well as the data on the recognition of alloantigens, are indicative of overlap in cellular recognition, how can they be reconciled with the refined specificity of cellular reactions in hapten-carrier systems? There are two major possibilities. First, the recognition of cellular antigens may involve special mechanisms such as the optimal presentation of antigenic determinants on cell surfaces or some special significance of histocompatibility antigens in the generation of immune diversity (117); these considerations would not apply to soluble antigens such as DNP-oligolysine. Second, the specificity of antigenic recognition by T cells may vary with different antigenic systems, being of a poor discriminatory nature for H-2 and red cells and of a much higher order for oligolysines. It is possible that all antigens may be arranged along a spectrum with high degrees of B or T cell discrimination at either end.

Other unusual features of T cell recognition are shown in studies of cell-mediated cytotoxicity (118–121). First, in these systems there is evidence that T cells recognize whole H-2 configurations and not individual alloantigenic specificities, unlike humoral antibody. The recognition of H-2 in these instances is reminiscent of the recognition of hapten-carrier conjugates in that antibody may recognize immunodominant alloantigenic specificities (cf. DNP) while T cells may recognize and be directed against the whole H-2 complex (cf. DNP-oligolysine). Second, some form of binding of lymphocytes to target cells occurs, at least in the Brondz model, but this requires incubation at 37° for 2 to 3 hours rather than 30 minutes at 4°, the latter being the conditions for most antigen-binding studies. Third, anti-Ig has no effect on cytotoxicity in the Brunner system (122).

If these data are indicative of a different form of receptor on T cells, then the obvious question arises: What type of surface structure could subserve this function? Some have suggested that the histocompatibility antigens themselves might function as receptors. Since the structure of these molecules has not been resolved and there is no knowledge of their heterogeneity at the cellular level it is not possible to say whether they could function as antigen receptors. It is tempting to see analogies between T cell recognition and allogeneic inhibition (123), particularly since in the PHA-mediated model of allogeneic inhibition antibodies to the foreign antigen can block cytotoxicity (124). However, the two specificities displayed in this phenomenon (self and nonself) are too restricted to account for cellular immune reactions and there is evidence that PHA-activated cells are nonspecifically toxic to syngeneic as well as allogeneic cells (125). Ceppellini has suggested a recognition role for HLA antigens on the basis of the inhibition by anti-HLA antibodies of the mixed leukocyte reaction (126). Of course, since all lymphocytes carry histocompatibility antigens any effect of such antisera could be due to steric block of the true receptor. Any experiments involving the use of such antisera need to circumvent this problem. An attractive feature of the view that histocompatibility antigens function as receptors is that this provides a ready explanation for the observed linkage between H-2 status and immune responsiveness (127) although another explanation has been offered (117). One ingenious attempt to determine the role of histocompatibility antigens in immune responsiveness is the report that antisera to strain 2 antigens in F_1 guinea pigs (strain 2 × strain 13) block the cellular response to strain-2-linked antigens, while antisera to strain 13 antigens have a minimal effect (128). Although no specific absorption controls were performed, the data clearly exclude simple steric block as the mechanism of inhibition. These findings suggest that the Ir gene product is in fact histocompatibility antigen but they do not imply that these surface antigens function as antigen receptors. Taken in conjunction with the observation that F_1 animals, of high-responder and low-responder parentage, usually display intermediate immune responsiveness, all the current evidence is consistent with the idea that histocompatibility antigens play an auxiliary role in antigen recognition; i.e., the presence of certain histocompatibility surface antigens nonspecifically boosts the interaction between cell surface receptors and foreign antigens. While Ir genes function mainly in T lymphocytes there is no reason why such an auxiliary mechanism might not also play a role in antigenic recognition by B cells, although the latter possibility has not been unequivocally established (129–132).

SUMMARY

In conclusion, we have provided evidence for receptors of varying discriminatory properties on T and B cells. The available evidence favors Ig as the receptor on B cells but not on T cells. The recognition of antigen by T cells involves several unusual features but the nature of the antigen receptor remains completely obscure. There is no good evidence that histocompatibility antigens subserve such a role. Since there are many biological recognition mechanisms, e.g., the receptors for drugs and hormones, that do not depend on immunoglobulin this view need not imply that T lymphocytes are unusual in their recognition properties. It suggests that B lymphocytes are exceptional in that they utilize a highly specialized recognition molecule while T lymphocytes use other structures common to many other cells. Further approaches to characterization of T cell receptors may involve either attempts to block T cell functions with various reagents or to isolate the receptor in soluble form and then determine its properties.

REFERENCES

1. Miller, J. F. A. P., *Proc. Roy. Soc. B.* **156,** 415 (1962).
2. Claman, H. N., Chaperon, E. A., and Triplett, R. F., *Proc. Soc. Exp. Biol. Med.* **122,** 1167 (1966).
3. Playfair, J. H. L., *Clin. Exp. Immunol.* **8,** 839 (1971).
4. Mitchison, N. A., *Cold Spring Harbor Symp. Quant. Biol.* **32,** 431 (1967).
5. Bloom, B. R., in *Mediators of Cellular Immunity* (H. S. Lawrence and M. Landy, Eds.), Academic Press, New York, 1969, p. 247.
6. Dumonde, D. C., Wolstencroft, R. A., Panayi, G. S., Matthew, M., Morley, J., and Howson, W. T., *Nature* **224,** 38 (1969).
7. Schlossman, S. F., Yaron, A., Ben-Efraim, S., and Sober, H. A., *Biochemistry* **4,** 1638 (1965).

8. Yaron, A. and Schlossman, S. F., *Biochemistry* **7**, 2673 (1968).

9. Schlossman, S. F., Ben-Efraim, S., Yaron, A., and Sober, H. A., *J. Exp. Med.* **123**, 1083 (1966).

10. Green, I., Paul, W. E., and Benacerraf, B., *J. Exp. Med.* **123**, 859 (1966).

11. Salvin, S. B. and Smith, R. F., *J. Exp. Med.* **111**, 465 (1960).

12. Gell, P. G. H. and Benacerraf, B., *Adv. Immunol.* **1**, 319 (1961).

13. Benacerraf, B. and Levine, B. B., *J. Exp. Med.* **115**, 1023 (1962).

14. Gell, P. G. H. and Silverstein, A. M., *J. Exp. Med.* **115**, 1037 (1962).

15. Schlossman, S. F. and Levine, H., *J. Immunol.* **99**, 111 (1967).

16. David, J. R. and Schlossman, S. F., *J. Exp. Med.* **128**, 1451 (1968).

17. Stulbarg, M. and Schlossman, S. F., *J. Immunol.* **101**, 764 (1968).

18. Paul, W. E., *Transplant Rev.* **5**, 130 (1970).

19. Davie, J. M. and Paul, W. E., *J. Exp. Med.* **134**, 495 (1971).

20. Möller, E. and Mäkelä, O., in *Cell Interactions,* 3rd Lepetit Colloquium, London, 1972.

21. Mitchison, N. A., in *Cell Interactions,* 3rd Lepetit Colloquium, London, 1972.

22. Walters, C. S., Moorhead, J. W., and Claman, H. N., *J. Exp. Med.* **136**, 546 (1972).

23. Schlossman, S. F., Herman, J., and Yaron, A., *J. Exp. Med.* **130**, 1031 (1969).

24. Dunham, E. K., Yaron, A., and Schlossman, S. F., in preparation (1973).

25. Paul, W. E., Stupp, Y., Siskind, G. W., and Benacerraf, B., *Immunology* **21**, 605 (1971).

26. Stupp, Y., Paul, W. E., and Benacerraf, B., *Immunology* **21**, 595 (1971).

27. Davie, J. M. and Paul, W. E., *Cell. Immunol.* **1**, 404 (1970).

28. Mills, J. A., *J. Immunol.* **97**, 239 (1966).

29. Shevach, E., Green, I., Ellman, L., and Maillard, J., *Nat. New Biol.* **235**, 19 (1972).

30. Rosenthal, A. S., Davie, J. M., Rosenstreich, D. L., and Blake, J. T., *J. Immunol.* **108**, 279 (1972).

31. Elfenbeim, G. J., Shevach, E. M., and Green, I., *J. Immunol.* **109**, 870 (1972).

32. Schlossman, S. F. and Levine, H., *J. Immunol.* **98**, 211 (1967).

33. Levin, H. A., Levine, H., and Schlossman, S. F., *J. Immunol.* **104**, 1377 (1970).

33a. Schlossman, S. F. and Levine, H., *Cell. Immunol.* **1**, 419 (1970).

34. Levin, H. A., Levine, H., and Schlossman, S. F., *J. Exp. Med.* **133**, 1199 (1971).

35. Williamson, A. R. and Schlossman, S. F., in preparation (1973).

36. Rajewsky, K., Shirrmacher, V., Nase, S., and Jerne, N. K., *J. Exp. Med.* **129**, 1131 (1969).

37. Mitchison, N. A., Rajewsky, K., and Taylor, R. B., in *Developmental Aspects of Antibody Formation and Structure,* Academic Press, New York, 1970.

38. Katz, D. H., Paul, W. E., Goidl, E. A., and Benacerraf, B., *J. Exp. Med.* **132**, 261 (1970).

39. Raff, M. C., Sternberg, M., and Taylor, R. B., *Nature* **225**, 553 (1970).

40. Jones, G., Marcuson, E. C., and Roitt, I. M., *Nature* **227**, 1051 (1970).

41. Pernis, B., Forni, L., and Amante, L., *J. Exp. Med.* **132**, 1001 (1970).

42. Coombs, R. R. A., Gurner, B. W., Janeway, C. A., Wilson, A. B., Gell, P. G. H., and Kelus, A. S., *Immunology* **18**, 417 (1970).

43. Coombs, R. R. A., Gurner, B. W., McConnell, I., and Munro, A., *Int. Arch. Allergy* **39,** 280 (1970).

44. Wolf, B., Coombs, R. R. A., Gell, P. G. H., and Kelus, A. S., *Immunology* **19,** 921 (1970).

45. Paraskevas, F., Lee, S.-T., and Israels, L. G., *J. immunol.* **106,** 160 (1971).

46. Rabellino, E., Colon, S., Grey, H. M., and Unanue, E. R., *J. Exp. Med.* **133,** 156 (1971).

47. Raff, M. C., *Immunology* **19,** 637 (1970).

48. Jones, G., Torrigiani, G., and Roitt, I. M., *J. Immunol.* **106,** 1425 (1971).

49. Unanue, E. R., Grey, H. M., Rabellino, E., Campbell, P., and Schmidtke, J., *J. Exp. Med.* **133,** 1188 (1971).

50. Rabellino, E. and Grey, H. M., *J. Immunol.* **106,** 1418 (1971).

51. Kincade, P. W., Lawton, A. R., and Cooper, M. D., *J. Immunol.* **106,** 1421 (1971).

52. Wolf, B., Janeway, C. A., Coombs, R. R. A., Catty, D., Gell, P. G. H., and Kelus, A. S., *Immunology* **20,** 931 (1971).

53. Sell, S. and Gell, P. G. H., *J. Immunol.* **104,** 114 (1970).

54. Greaves, M. F., *Eur. J. Immunol.* **1,** 195 (1971).

55. Abdou, N. I., *J. Immunol.* **107,** 1637 (1971).

56. Bankhurst, A. D. and Warner, N. L., *J. Immunol.* **107,** 368 (1971).

57. Lee, S.-T., Paraskevas, F., and Israels, L. G., *J. Immunol.* **107,** 1583 (1971).

58. McConnell, I., Munro, A., Gurner, B. W., and Coombs, R. R. A., *Int. Arch. Allergy* **35,** 228 (1969).

59. Byrt, P. and Ada, G. L., *Immunology* **17,** 503 (1969).

60. Dwyer, J. M. and Mackay, I. R., *Lancet* **i,** 164 (1970).

61. Warner, N. L., Byrt, P., and Ada, G. L., *Nature* **226,** 942 (1970).

62. Sell, S. and Gell, P. G. H., *J. Exp. Med.* **122,** 423 (1965).

63. Takiguchi, T., Adler, W. H., and Smith, R. T., *J. Exp. Med.* **133,** 63 (1971).

64. Johnston, J. M. and Wilson, D. B., *Cell. Immunol.* **1,** 430 (1970).

65. Jones, G., *Clin. Exp. Immunol.,* in press.

66. Greaves, M. F., Torrigiani, G., and Roitt, I. M., *Nature* **222,** 885 (1969).

67. Greaves, M. F., Torrigiani, G., and Roitt, I. M., *Clin. Exp. Immunol.* **9,** 313 (1971).

68. Roitt, I. M. and Festenstein, H., unpublished observations.

69. Vischer, T. L. and Jaquet, C., *Immunology* **22,** 259 (1971).

70. Fröland, S. S. and Natvig, J. B., *Int. Arch. Allergy* **41,** 248 (1971).

71. Gowans, J. L. and McGregor, D. D., *Prog. Allergy* **9,** 1 (1965).

72. Simonsen, M., *Prog. Allergy* **6,** 349 (1962).

73. Hilgard, H. R., *J. Exp. Med.* **132,** 317 (1970).

74. Mason, S. and Warner, N. L., *J. Immunol.* **104,** 762 (1970).

75. Cole, L. J. and Maki, S. E., *Nat. New Biol.* **230,** 244 (1971).

76. Riethmüller, G., Rieber, E.-P., and Seeger, I., *Nat. New Biol.* **230,** 248 (1971).

77. Tyan, M. L., *J. Immunol.* **106,** 586 (1971).

78. Rouse, B. T. and Warner, N. L., *Cell. Immunol.* **3,** 470 (1972).

79. Lydyard, P. and Ivanyi, J., *Transplantation* **12,** 493 (1971).

80. Crone, M., Koch, C., and Simonsen, M., *Transplant. Rev.* **10,** 36 (1972).

81. Ivanyi, J., Marvanova, H., and Skamene, E., *Immunology* **17,** 325 (1969).

82. Alm, G. V. and Peterson, R. D. A., *J. Exp. Med.* **129,** 1247 (1969).

83. Greaves, M. F. and Hogg, N. M., in *Cell Interaction in Immune Responses* (O. Mäkelä, A. Cross, and T. U. Kosunen, Eds.), Academic Press, New York, 1971.

84. Schlesinger, M., *Nature* **226,** 1254 (1970).

85. Greaves, M. F. and Möller, E., *Cell. Immunol.* **1,** 372 (1970).

86. Möller, E. and Greaves, M. F., in *Cell Interaction in Immune Responses* O. Mäkelä, A. Cross and T. U. Kosunen, Eds.), Academic Press, New York, 1971.

87. Baird, S., Santa, J., and Weissman, I., *Nat. New Biol.* **232,** 56 (1971).

88. Greaves, M. F. and Raff, M. C., *Nat. New Biol.* **233,** 239 (1971).

89. Takahashi, T., Old, L. J., McIntyre, K. R., and Boyse, E. A., *J. Exp. Med.* **134,** 815 (1971).

90. Kiszkiss, D. F., Choi, Y. S., and Good, R. A., *J. Immunol.* **109,** 1405 (1972).

91. Hellström, U., Zeromski, J., and Perlman, P., *Immunology* **20,** 1099 (1971).

92. Biberfeld, P., Biberfeld, G., and Perlmann, P., *Exp. Cell Res.* **66,** 177 (1971).

93. Jones, G. and Roitt, I. M., *Cell. Immunol.* **3,** 478 (1972).

94. Lesley, J. F., Kettman, J. R., and Dutton, R. W., *J. Exp. Med.* **134,** 618 (1971).

95. Bianco, C., Patrick, R., and Nussenzweig, V., *J. Exp. Med.* **132,** 702 (1970).

96. Ada, G. L. and Byrt, P., *Nature* **222,** 1291 (1969).

97. Basten, A., Miller, J. F. A. P., Warner, N. L., and Pye, J., *Nat. New Biol.* **231,** 104 (1971).

98. Bankhurst, A. D., Warner, N. L., and Sprent, J., *J. Exp. Med.* **134,** 1005 (1971).

99. Nossal, G. J. V., Warner, N. L., Lewis, H., and Sprent, J., *J. Exp. Med.* **135,** 405 (1972).

100. Marchalonis, J. J., Atwell, J. L., and Cone, R. E., *Nat. New Biol.* **235,** 240 (1972).

101. Marchalonis, J. J., Cone, R. E., and Atwell, J. L., *J. Exp. Med.* **135,** 956 (1972).

102. Vitetta, E., Bianco, C., Nussenzweig, V., and Uhr, J. W., *J. Exp. Med.* **136,** 81 (1972).

103. Moscona, A., *Exp. Cell Res.* **3,** 535 (1952).

104. Moscona, A., *Proc. Natl. Acad. Sci. U.S.A.* **43,** 184 (1957).

105. Spiegel, M., *Biol. Bull.* **107,** 130 (1954).

106. Simmons, M. J. and Fowler, R., *Nature* **209,** 588 (1966).

107. Simonsen, M., *Cold Spring Harbor Symp. Quant. Biol.* **32,** 517 (1967).

108. Wilson, D. B., Blyth, J. L., and Nowell, P. C., *J. Exp. Med.* **128,** 1157 (1968).

109. Bach, F. H., Bock, H., Graupner, K., Day, E., and Klostermann, B., *Proc. Natl. Acad. Sci. U.S.A.* **62,** 377 (1969).

110. Nisbet, N. W., Simonsen, M., and Zaleski, M., *J. Exp. Med.* **129,** 459 (1969).

111. Wilson, D. B. and Nowell, P. C., *J. Exp. Med.* **133,** 442 (1971).

112. Wilson, D. B., Silvers, W. K., and Nowell, P. C., *J. Exp. Med.* **126,** 655 (1967).

113. Wilson, D. B. and Fox, D. H., *J. Exp. Med.* **134,** 857 (1971).

114. Playfair, J. H. L., *Nat. New Biol.* **235,** 115 (1972).

115. Falkoff, R. and Kettman, J., *J. Immunol.* **108,** 54 (1972).

116. Hoffman, M. and Kappler, J. W., *J. Immunol.* **108,** 261 (1972).

117. Jerne, N. K., *Eur. J. Immunol.* **1,** 1 (1971).

118. Mauel, J., Rudolf, H., Chapuis, B., and Brunner, K. T., *Immunology* **18,** 517 (1970).

119. Brondz, B. D. and Snegiröva, A. E., *Immunology* **20.** 457 (1971).

120. Ax, W., Koren, H. S., and Fisher, H., *Exp. Cell Res.* **64,** 439 (1971).

121. Golstein, P., Svedmyr, E. A., and Wigzell, H., *J. Exp. Med.* **134,** 1385 (1971).

122. Chapuis, B. and Brunner, K. T., *Int. Arch. Allergy* **40,** 321 (1971).

123. Hellström, I. and Hellström, K. E., *Ann. N. Y. Acad. Sci.* **129,** 724 (1966).

124. Möller, E., *J. Exp. Med.* **126,** 395 (1967).

125. Perlmann, P., Perlmann, H., and Holm, G., *Science* **160,** 306 (1968).

126. Ceppellini, R., Miggiano, M., Curtoni, E. S., and Pellegrino, M., *Transplant. Proc.* **3,** 63 (1971).

127. McDevitt, H. O. and Benacerraf, B., *Adv. Immunol.* **11,** 31 (1969).

128. Shevach, E. M., Paul, W. E., and Green, I., *J. Exp. Med.* **136,** 1207 (1972).

129. Mozes, E., McDevitt, H. O., Jaton, J.-C., and Sela, M., *J. Exp. Med.* **130,** 493 (1969).

130. Mozes, E., McDevitt, H. O., Jaton, J.-C., and Sela, M., *J. Exp. Med.* **130,** 1263 (1969).

131. Shearer, G. M., Mozes, E., and Sela, M., *Prog. Immunol.* **1,** 509 (1971).

132. Bluestein, H. G., Green, I., Maurer, P. H., and Benacerraf, B., *J. Exp. Med.* **135,** 98 (1972).

Chapter Six

Mechanisms of Lymphocyte Activation

KURT HIRSCHHORN AND ROCHELLE HIRSCHHORN

Arthur J. and Nellie Z. Cohen Professor of Genetics and Pediatrics, Mt. Sinai School of Medicine of the City University of New York, and Assistant Professor of Medicine, New York University School of Medicine.

Since the discovery by Nowell in 1960 (1) that phytohemagglutinin (PHA), an extract of the kidney bean, can stimulate peripheral blood leucocytes to enlarge and divide, and the demonstration in 1961 (2,3) that the stimulated cells are lymphocytes, this cell culture system has been the basis for numerous experimental studies in immunology, cell biology, and genetics. The present chapter mentions these earlier reports only as they are relevant to the discussion, but they are reviewed in detail in several publications (4–8).

It is our intention in this chapter to examine in detail the early events following exposure of lymphocytes to nonspecific and immunologically specific stimulants, and to review briefly the subsequent activities and the fate of these cells. We restrict our discussion primarily to human material, since our own experience has been with human cells, and since the majority of the *in vitro* studies have used human material.

*The original work reported was supported in part by U.S.P.H.S. Grants #HD 02552 and A1 10343 and Genetics Center Grant GM 19443. Rochelle Hirschhorn is the recipient of an N.I.H. Research Career Development Award A1 70254. Kurt Hirschhorn is a Career Scientist of the New York City Health Research Council (I-513).

MITOGENS AND BINDING SITES

Lymphocyte stimulation can be achieved by a variety of stimulants. They include plant extracts, the principal ones being PHA (1), pokeweed mitogen (PWM) (9,10), concanavalin A from the jackbean (Con A) (11,12) and those derived from numerous other, less well-studied species (11,13); antilymphocyte sera (14,15); a streptococcal mitogen associated with but different from streptolysin S (SLSM) (16,17); staphylococcal extracts, such as the exotoxin (18); Hg++ (19) and Zn++ (20); periodate (21); enzymes (22); antigen-antibody complexes (23,24); cyclic AMP (cAMP) (25,26); and various mitogenic factors derived from cultured cells (27). These represent the majority of the currently known class of stimulants referred to as nonspecific, due to their ability to stimulate lymphocytes from any normal individual, including newborns of numerous species (28). Another stimulant in this category is antigamma globulin (29). However, if this is directed against a specific allotype, it will only stimulate lymphocytes possessing that allotype (30), making these antiallotypic antibodies difficult to classify.

Another class of stimulants are called specific, because they act only on lymphocytes derived from individuals who demonstrate an immune response against the substance used. In most cases, this response is one of delayed hypersensitivity (31). There are occasional exceptions to this rule (32). The specific agents include antigens from bacteria, such as tuberculin (PPD) (33,34), viruses, such as smallpox vaccine (35), fungi, such as coccidiodin (36), pollens, such as ragweed (37), and drugs, such as penicillin (32).

Along with the antiallotypic antibodies, another type of stimulant not fitting the definition of specific or nonspecific is the allogeneic lymphocyte (38,39). Cocultivation of lymphocytes, referred to as mixed lymphocyte culture (MLC), from genetically unrelated individuals results in cross-stimulation, referred to as the mixed lymphocyte response (MLR). Since the response is observed even in fetal lymphocytes (28) and does not require presensitization (40,41), it partly fits the nonspecific category, but the requirement of the ability to recognize the genetic differences between the cell donors necessary for the response gives specificity to the reaction. Some laboratories have reported such a response with purified HLA antigens (42), lymphocyte extracts (38), and nonlymphocytic cultured cells (43).

It may safely be assumed that activation by any of these agents must follow interaction of the agent with the lymphocyte cell membrane as a first step. This implies a receptor for each of these agents. It is clear that specific receptors for specific stimulators are only detectable in individuals presensitized to the antigen, and that only a minority of circulating cells carry a specific receptor in an active form. Similarly, the receptor for the MLR is specified by the individual's histocompatibility genes (44), or the product of a highly polymorphic gene closely linked to these (45), and therefore varies from person to person. The receptors for the nonspecific stimulators, on the other hand, appear to be universal, but even these may vary from cell to cell. There is evidence (46) that there is a differential response, at least in the mouse, between B and T cells, in that the former are more responsive to PWM and the latter to PHA and Con A, although B cells can be activated by PHA bound to sepharose and PWM is certainly able to stimulate T cells (47). Since PHA stimulation can be enhanced by the presence of red blood cells in the culture (48), presumably by their action as a concentrating agent producing a matrix of PHA, it is possible that the relative sensitivities of different classes of lymphocytes to different nonspecific stimulators are simply due to a difference in the number or distribution of the various binding sites on the membrane.

The exact nature of the receptors for the nonspecific stimulators is at present unknown. Some studies indicate that PHA binding is mediated by cell surface sugars. N-Acetylgalactosamine has been shown to inhibit both agglutination (49) and mitogenesis (50) by PHA, although in quite high concentrations. Kornfeld (51) has isolated a glycoprotein receptor for PHA from red cells, whose determinant sugar, galactose, appears also to inhibit the action of the PHA used. However, this PHA was a purified hemagglutinating fraction, which also has mitogenic activity. It is not clear whether the nonhemagglutinating mitogen in PHA attaches to the same receptor site or is similarly inhibited. A red cell surface glycoprotein recently isolated by Marchesi (52) contains both a PHA receptor and several blood group antigens.

Although nothing definite is known about receptors for PWM, the fact that this molecule has 26 internal disulfide bridges (10), along with the finding that the mitogenic action of mercuric ions can be inhibited by sulfhydryl chelating agents (53), indicates the possibility that free sulfhydryl groups may represent one of the classes of receptors whose binding leads to lymphocyte activation.

Much work has been done (54) attempting to identify receptors for Con A on a variety of cell types, including lymphoid cells, and it appears to be yet another class of glycoproteins.

While the binding sites for antilymphocyte antibodies may be multiple, those for the antigamma globulins and antiallotypic antibodies are clearly surface immunoglobulins, most likely synthesized by the cells carrying them, since there exists cellular specificity within an individual

(55). Such surface immunoglobulins also appear to be involved in the binding of stimulating specific antigens, since light chains have been found to block (55,56) reactions primarily associated with cellular immunity and both μ-type heavy chains and light chains to block reactions primarily involving antibody synthesis (57). Light chains may also be the receptors responsible for recognition in the MLR (56).

Stimulation by antigen-antibody complexes in the presence of complement (23) may be due to binding to the complement receptors which have recently been found to be characteristic of B lymphocytes (58).

There is evidence that the presence of macrophages is essential for or at least enhances the response to antigens (59) and in MLC (60). While it is possible that the macrophages act simply as a concentrating focus allowing cell-antigen or cell-cell interactions, the recent finding of a supernatant factor derived from cultured macrophages, capable of producing a complete response to antigens by pure lymphocytes, indicates a more active role for these cells (61).

While it is tempting to postulate that the binding of a stimulator to a receptor results in the primary events of activation directly at the membrane, it is equally possible that these receptors act simply to concentrate stimulators on appropriate cells. This could then be followed by internalization of the stimulator to its site of action inside the cell, as is the case with some hormones. In support of this, it has been found that addition of PHA directly to isolated nuclei results in an increase in synthesis of RNA, acetylation of histones, and actinomycin D binding, all of which alterations have also been found in the intact cell following stimulation by PHA (62).

MEMBRANE CHANGES

However, some of the early changes reported in activated lymphocytes are those relating to the cell membrane. An alteration of charge has been reported (63,64), although this may only represent attachment of the stimulator or blocking of a surface charge, such as on sialic acid.

Several studies (65,66) have demonstrated changes in phospholipid metabolism early in the 1st hour after exposure to PHA, and possibly to other agents (67). The major change after PHA appears to be increased incorporation of phosphate into phosphatidyl inositol (65), and much of this represents increased turnover and interconversion of the phospholipids as well as synthesis (68,69). Later there is also an increased synthesis and accumulation of all the phospholipid fractions (70). The increased turnover, while demonstrating involvement of the membrane,

may be due to the process of internalization already mentioned. A two-
to threefold increase in the turnover of the fatty acid moiety of lecithin
is seen within 1 hour of PHA stimulation and is initially restricted to
plasma membrane (71). Similar evidence derives from the report of increased incorporation of glucosamine into membrane glycoproteins (72).

The strongest evidence for the role of the membrane in actual initiation of activation derives from the studies of the role of cyclic adenosine-
3', 5'- monophosphate (cAMP) and adenyl cyclase early in lymphocyte
stimulation. Addition of low doses of cAMP or possibly its derivative,
dibutyryl-cAMP, to unstimulated lymphocytes produces a small degree
of activation as measured by RNA, protein, and DNA synthesis (25,26,
73). Similar stimulation and/or doubling in cell divisions has been reported for rat thymocytes (74). Addition of these materials at higher
doses inhibits the stimulation of the cells by PHA. This inhibition can
also be produced by the addition of theophylline, an agent known to
inhibit phosphodiesterase, the enzyme responsible for the degradation
of cAMP (75). Measurement of cAMP levels in PHA-stimulated cells
shows an increase very early, within 1 to 2 minutes of addition of the
mitogen, followed by a gradual decrease to below control levels by 6
hours after PHA. Measurement of adenyl cyclase, the enzyme responsible for the production of cAMP, shows a rise in activity within the first
few minutes of culture with PHA (76).

Phytohemagglutinin and antilymphocyte sera have also been reported
to stimulate directly adenyl cyclase activity of lymphocyte lysates (77).
Utilizing cytochemical techniques, adenyl cyclase activity has been found
on the nuclear membrane of the lymphocyte (78), suggesting that cAMP-
dependent enzymes in the nucleus as well as the protein kinases of the
cytoplasm might be affected (73). Alpha and beta adrenergic agents,
such as norepinephrine, and isoproterenol and their inhibitors have been
shown (79) to influence lymphocyte activation. Several of these agents
also have a rapid effect on cAMP levels. The activity of adenyl cyclase
is markedly affected by calcium ions which are essential for lymphocyte
activation (80). There is also a significant increase in calcium ion uptake
within minutes after addition of PHA (81).

Similar findings have been observed in thymus cells (74). However,
it is not clear if the population of cells that respond mitotically within
hours in thymus suspensions is at all related to or identical with those
cells in the peripheral blood which respond after days.

All of these observations indicate a likely role for cAMP in the initiation of lymphocyte stimulation, perhaps similar to that found with hormonal activation of target cells. In such hormonally activated cells, increase in the intracellular level of cAMP follows immediately upon at-

tachment of the hormone to its receptor sites at the cell membrane. This increase results from the activation of the enzyme adenyl cyclase at the membrane, catalyzing the formation of cAMP from adenosine triphosphate. The action of the increased cAMP, termed "second messenger," results in the activation of the target cells (82). The mechanism of this activation appears to be due to the ability of cAMP to activate a series of intracellular enzymes, particularly the kinases (83), which are capable of phosphorylating various substances including histones. In addition to mediating hormonal effects upon their respective target cells, there is evidence that alterations in the intracellular level of cAMP play a fundamental role in controlling rates of cellular growth in mammalian as well as bacterial cells (82). One possible route for these activities is by way of controlling the action of RNA polymerase in gene transcription (84). Finally, changes in cAMP levels have been shown to affect membrane lipids and transport (82). Recently, a role for cyclic AMP in the early activation of lymphocytes has been postulated (84a), which may be even more important than that of cAMP.

Increase of molecular transport across lymphocyte membranes by many different mechanisms has been demonstrated to occur within minutes after exposure to PHA. For example, α-aminoisobutyric acid (85,86), 3-O-methyl glucose (87), uridine (88), and other molecules (89) are taken up in greater amounts. Sodium and potassium ion exchanges increase probably by means of increased activity of ouabain-sensitive ATP-ase (90,91). Calcium influx increases (81,92), probably mediated by its ATP-ase. Perhaps most important is the immediate increase in respiration-dependent pinocytosis (89,93), originally demonstrated with neutral red. The increased formation of pinocytotic vacuoles has been seen in electron micrographs (94).

It therefore appears clear that there are numerous and important changes at the membrane very early in lymphocyte stimulation which could potentially be responsible for the intracellular changes associated with activation.

MORPHOLOGICAL CHANGES

The major morphological changes observed in PHA-stimulated cells, consisting of enlargement, basophilia, and pyroninophilia, first led to the recognition that these cells resemble the immunologically competent cells observed by Gowans during the graft-versus-host response (95). Since then, numerous morphological alterations have been observed, a number of which may be relevant to the activation and action of lymphoid cells. Early after exposure to the mitogen, there is marked increase in motility, associated with the formation of processes, termed "uropods," and evidence of endocytosis. The uropods have been shown to contain the Golgi apparatus and to have a high concentration of lysosomes (96). Structural changes in membranes, including an increase in intramembranous particles and in nuclear pores, have been described but these could not be detected very early after stimulation (97). Insulin receptors also appear on the membrane following transformation (98), as well increases in ouabain binding sites (99). While many organelles, including ribosomes, mitochondria, lysosomes, and centrioles, can be seen in the resting cells, there is marked increase in lysosomes and polyribosomes within the first 48 hours of culture. Particularly in a proportion of cells cultured with PWM, a marked increase is seen of rough endoplasmic reticulum (100). The most dramatic change is in the nucleus, which develops from heterochromatic clumped chromatin to diffuse euchromatin with prominent nucleoli (101). By 72 hours, many cells are in mitosis.

LYSOSOMES

When comparing intracellular lysosomal enzyme distribution between unstimulated cells and lymphocytes cultured in the presence of PHA for 2 hours, a significant shift can be observed from the granular or lysosome-rich fraction to the free cell sap. Nonlysosomal organellar enzymes do not show this alteration. While it is likely that there is a true shift of these enzymes from the lysosomes, it is possible that the observation represents leakage of enzyme during the handling of more fragile lysosomes. That these organelles are more fragile after culture with PHA can be independently demonstrated by the induction of leakage with lower doses of membranolytic substances, such as filipin and streptolysin S, than are required for lysosomes from control cells. It is likely that these more fragile organelles represent secondary lysosomes, formed by a merger of pinocytotic vacuoles with primary lysosomes (93). Lysosomes contain a variety of hydrolytic enzymes, including DNAse, RNAse, and acid proteases, which may play a role in the intracellular reorganization associated with activation. Among these are cathepsins known to be active on nuclear proteins. They also contain substances, such as phospholipases, which may have the capacity for killing other cells with which the activated lymphocyte comes in contact (102). In fact, it has been shown that acid phosphatase activity exists on the outer surface of the uropod, which is the process by which the lymphocytes attach to other cells (96).

Later in culture, by 48 hours, there is a net increase in intracellular lysosomal enzyme activity (103), associated with the increased number of lysosomes observed (104). Their possible role in the processes involved in cell division is beyond the scope of this chapter.

NUCLEAR CHANGES

Among the earliest changes reported in stimulated lymphocytes are the acetylation of histones (105) and the increased phosphorylation of nuclear proteins (106), including histones. These changes may be related to the observed increase of binding to the nucleus of acridine orange (107) and actinomycin D (108).

It is of interest that similar changes have been described during gene activation in several other cell systems, such as the fertilized sea urchin egg and in regenerating liver. It is believed that the state of association of histones and other nuclear proteins with DNA plays a major regulatory role in the sites and rates of new RNA synthesis. There is also correlation between the extended state of nuclear chromatin ("euchromatin"), high template activity for RNA synthesis, and high acetylation of histones, as compared with condensed chromatin ("heterochromatin"), which has low template activity and low acetylation. This general topic is discussed fully elsewhere (109). The increased phosphorylation of nuclear proteins, also correlated with increased template activity, may be mediated by a variety of protein kinases, whose activity is known to be dependent on the level of cAMP.

It has been reported that there is an increase in the activity of endogenous RNA polymerase I and II (110,111) possibly dependent on the level of cAMP (84), in the nuclei of lymphocytes, within a few hours after exposure to PHA. This may account in part for the increased DNA-dependent synthesis of RNA. However, there is also evidence that these nuclei possess increased template activity under experimental conditions dependent on the use of exogenous (bacterial) RNA polymerase (111,112). This implies that there is a true increase in the amount of DNA available for the transcription of new RNA.

There are several possible mechanisms by which this template capacity can be increased, any or all of which may be operating in the stimulated lymphocyte. We have already mentioned the increased acetylation of histones and the increased phosphorylation of nuclear proteins, the latter possibly related to higher levels of cAMP. In addition, it is possible that the free lysosomal cathepsins mentioned earlier may directly alter nuclear proteins, thereby exposing new DNA sites for new RNA transcription. It had previously been shown that exposure of isolated liver nuclei to trypsin results in an increase of the template activity of these nuclei (113). Similarly, exposure of the nuclei of unstimulated lymphocytes to trypsin results in a marked increase in template activity, while similar exposure of nuclei from stimulated lymphocytes, which already have higher template activity, brings about a lesser relative increase (112). This can be interpreted to mean that the stimulated nuclei already have uncovered many previously covered sites of DNA. In addition, exposure of lymphocytes to known inhibitors of proteolytic enzymes results in inhibition of their stimulation by PHA (114).

RNA SYNTHESIS

Within 30 minutes after PHA stimulation, there is a detectable increase in the rate of RNA synthesis. This continues to increase over the first few hours, and is maintained for a long period of time. Several newly synthesized species of RNA have been described. These include a labile heterogeneous nuclear fraction (possibly messenger RNA precursor), a small molecular weight RNA transported from the nucleus to the cytoplasm (possibly transfer RNA precursor), and the precursor for ribosomal RNA. While the latter represents only 15 to 20% of the new RNA in the cytoplasm, changes in its metabolism have been studied in the greatest detail and are thoroughly reviewed elsewhere (115). In brief, it has been shown that in the resting lymphocyte, following the breakdown of the 45S precursor for ribosomal RNA into the 18S and 28S fractions required for ribosomal assembly, there is almost total rapid degradation of the 18S fraction. This results in a very slow development of new ribosomes. Within 2 hours after PHA stimulation, the rate of 18S degradation or wastage falls markedly and there is rapid increase in ribosomal assembly. Thus, there is both an increase in true synthesis of ribosomal RNA and an increase in ribosomes on the basis of salvage of one of their components. This results in a large increase in cytoplasmic ribosome content, which may represent the component responsible for the amplification of protein synthesis by providing the machinery on which it occurs. The probable increases in transfer RNA and messenger RNA synthesis provide the other components necessary for increased protein synthesis. It is not clear at the present time whether any new species of messenger RNA are synthesized or whether there is only an increase in the synthesis of preexisting types, since hybridization experiments have not revealed such new species (116). However, an increase in a rapidly labeled polyribosomal RNA rich in poly (A) which acts as a messenger RNA in a cell-free preparation has been reported. This increase is seen within 2 hours only after addition of PHA but also after addition of low levels of dibutyryl cyclic AMP (117). In addition, there may be salvage and increased transport into the cytoplasm of molecules previously destroyed in the nucleus. Enzymes required for providing the building blocks for RNA synthesis, such as uridine kinase (118) and ornithine decarboxylase (119), are also increased during culture.

A potential mechanism for the amplification of RNA synthesis is the induction of RNA-dependent DNA polymerase (reverse transcriptase), which has recently been demonstrated in stimulated lymphocytes (120,121). This enzyme could make new copies of DNA, which would in turn allow for increased RNA transcription. The finding of membrane-associated DNA in stimulated lymphocytes lends some credence to this possible mechanism (122).

LIPID AND CARBOHYDRATE METABOLISM

Most studies of lipid metabolism in stimulated lymphocytes relate to the shifts in phospholipid turnover early in culture as discussed previously. Similar alterations in phospholipid metabolism continue to occur later in culture (70), and may represent additional membrane synthesis and activity. Little is known about other aspects of lipid metabolism of stimulated lymphocytes at this time.

Several studies (123,125), designed to elucidate carbohydrate metabolism in these cells, have demonstrated a marked increase in lactate production within the first hours of culture. This has been interpreted to represent increased glycolysis. There is evidence that the hexose monophosphate shunt, which can also serve indirectly as a source for the increased lactate production, is also increased, in that there is a preferential conversion of radioactive carbon into CO_2 when glucose labeled in the C1 position rather than in the C6 position is used (126). Additionally, activities of G_6PD and $_6PGD$ are increased preferentially (127). However, studies during the first 4 hours of culture indicate a more minor role for the shunt pathway (128). Krebs cycle activity is also increased and thus acetate and aspartate can partially substitute for glucose as sources of energy metabolism (129). However, increased glucose utilization appears to be required for full activation (129,130). Shifts in the pattern of lactate dehydrogenase isozymes indicate that conditions in stimulated lymphocytes resemble those found in other cell types during more anaerobic metabolism involving lactate production. Not only is there an increase in total lactate dehydrogenase, but there is a preferential synthesis of the muscle type of subunits (131,132).

PROTEIN SYNTHESIS

Increase in the rate of protein synthesis in stimulated lymphocytes can be detected easily by 4 hours, and this continues to increase linearly for at least 48 hours. This new synthesis is puromycin sensitive and actinomycin D sensitive. The measurement of protein synthesis provides an easy, early, and reproducible technique for evaluating lymphocyte response, for titrating stimulators, and for determining nutritional requirements of these cells. It is easier than the measurement of RNA synthesis, less time-consuming than morphological evaluation, and more reproducible than the measurement of DNA synthesis, due to the asynchrony of the latter in these cultures. It also is probably more relevant to the functional response of lymphocytes during their immunologic activity. With the use of this technique, it has been possible to compare the efficacy of various culture media, to begin to characterize the serum fractions necessary for the response, and to show that these cells probably require fewer "essential" amino acids than do other cultured cells. A requirement for asparagine has, however, been demonstrated, accounting for the inhibition of lymphocyte responses by asparaginase (133). There are recent reports that activation can be detected within 1 hour of culture by measuring protein synthesized in nuclei isolated from activated cells (134).

Among the many proteins synthesized, only a few have been identified, and even among these, some, rather than showing an increase in synthesis, may only be altered in such a way as to improve their detection. The latter possibility is particularly true of the increased activity of some of the various enzymes studied.

Among the enzymes showing increased activity after stimulation are most of the lysosomal enzymes studied (103). This was to be expected in view of the increase in the number of these organelles (104,135). These include, among others, acid phosphatase, aryl sulfatase, and acid α-glucosidase (103,136,137). A number of nonlysosomal enzymes also show an increase in activity when measured in cell extracts. Among these are glucose-6-phosphate dehydrogenase (136), lactate dehydrogenase (131,138), cystathionine synthase (139), uridine kinase (118), DNA polymerase (140), and carbamyl P-synthetase (141) as well as polynucleotide ligase and DNAse (142). Some, including lactate dehydrogenase (131) and adenosine deaminase (143), show shifts in isozyme patterns with preferential increase in the activity of certain isozymes. Mitogen stimulation also induces a drug metabolizing enzyme system (aryl carbon benzpyrene hydroxylase) in lymphocytes (144). A number of nonenzymatic proteins can also be detected after stimulation. These include interferon (145) and a factor from cells of patients with cystic fibrosis and obligate heterozygotes which inhibits rabbit tracheal cilia (146). An increase in insulin receptors on the membrane has also been detected as well as an increase in ouabain binding sites (98,99).

These changes indicate a general increase in many metabolic pathways in stimulated lymphocytes. How many of these are primary to the response, and how many are simply a reflection of increased metabolic activity as a result of stimulation, such as is likely for the increase in carbohydrate metabolism, is not understood at this time. It is also not clear if the appearance of, for example, cystathionine synthase and interferon represents transcription of previously repressed portions of the genome.

It is, of course, possible that some of these activities play an important role in the effector function of stimulated lymphocytes. Among the increased activities found in the first 2 days of culture are those of the mediators of cellular immunity, which may, in part, represent lysosomal enzymes or other products. These include, among others, migration inhibitory factor, cytotoxic factors, chemotactic factors, and blastogenic factors (147,147a). It is not clear whether these factors are immunologically specific products, or whether some may be synthesized by all metabolically active cells, as was suggested in Chapter 3. For example, a migration inhibitory factor is produced by fibroblasts (147b), and its biologic role may include wound healing and organ organization. It is clear, however, that specific immunologic stimulation of sensitized lymphocytes results in the production of these factors. An effector role is also possible for interferon, another substance found to increase with stimulation (145). Since many of these enzymes and factors are increased before cell division occurs, and may be present even in the unstimulated cell, although in low concentration, it is possible that even increased true synthesis may represent simply amplification of the production of products of genes already active in the resting cell. However, it must be remembered that template activity for new RNA synthesis has been shown to increase early in stimulation (112). Although much of this increase could be for new ribosomal RNA synthesis (115), there is evidence to suggest early increases in messenger-like RNA (117).

One of the factors thought to be synthesized in lymphocytes does appear to have a specific immunologic role. This is transfer factor (147), which is discussed in detail in Chapter 11. Transfer factor is a small molecule capable of inducing delayed hypersensitivity in nonsensitive individuals, when prepared from the lymphocytes of persons sensitized to a particular antigen. It now appears that this factor may contain double-stranded RNA and may be a portion of an informational molecule. While its mode of action *in vivo* is not understood, its role may be in recruitment of uncommitted cells for a cellular immune response. In addition it is possible to postulate another role for this puzzling molecule, that is, in the development of memory cells. We would propose that the early embryo contains lymphoid precursor cells, which have no antigen receptors, but are capable of a mixed lymphocyte response when meeting cell surfaces differing from their own. It has been shown that the MLR is present quite early in fetal life (28), and that HLA differences *per se* are not sufficient to induce this response (45). [The latter finding puts an obstacle to acceptance of the mechanisms for the development of memory cells proposed by Jerne (148).] The stimulant for the MLR could be maternal, or the appearance of tissue-specific cell surfaces containing embryonic antigens. The responding cell, containing the genetic information required for all, or at least many antigen receptors (gamma globulins?), produces these and becomes a multipotential recognition cell. Each specific membrane receptor is physicochemically associated with a specific RNA informational molecule in the cytoplasm (transfer factor?). Later in fetal life, and particularly after birth, numerous antigens enter the individual, and there is chance meeting between an antigen and a cell carrying the relevant receptor among many others. Interaction between the antigen and its receptor results in a signal to its specific cytoplasmic RNA, which in turn induces the cell to produce only the one type of receptor, resulting in a monoclonal memory cell. The action of the RNA molecule could be by at least two mechanisms. One would be by specifically derepressing the genes necessary for the production of the specific receptor. The other could operate via the reverse transcriptase mentioned, so that additional copies of the appropriate DNA are made and carried to the offspring of the activated cell. The various processes could of course occur over numerous cell generations during which differentiation progresses. It may even be a requirement that, before a new genetic product is made, that is before derepression can occur, at least one cell division is required. This has been demonstrated, for example, in the induction of casein synthesis in mammary gland cells by insulin, cortisone, and prolactin (149) and for the induction of a primary antibody response under certain conditions (150).

The most important immunologic proteins produced by lymphocytes are the gamma globulins. While it is clear that lymphocytes synthesize gamma globulins, there is disagreement as to whether there is an increase in synthesis following stimulation. We believe that there is an increase, but that the degree is porportional to the total increase in protein synthesis, that is, there is no relative increase after PHA stimulation (151). It has been shown that PWM does produce a relative increase, at least of IgM, especially in B cells, but even in that study calculations of the data given show a similar absolute increase of IgM production after PHA as that seen with PWM (152). The amounts synthesized are much less than those produced by mature plasma cells. There is some evidence that a portion of the immunoglobulin produced may be specific antibody, but more work remains to be done before this issue can be clarified.

DNA SYNTHESIS AND MITOSIS

DNA synthesis begins by 24 hours after PHA exposure and reaches a peak between 48 and 72 hours. Antigen stimulation of sensitized cell causes a peak between the 3rd and 4th day, while maximal DNA synthesis in MLC develops by 5 to 6 days. The peak of mitotic activity occurs about 1 day later. Direct cinemicrographic observations of antigen-stimulated cultures beginning on the 3rd day of culture, that is, after some divisions may already have occurred, have demonstrated a generation time ranging from 8 to 14 hours (153). In these studies there appeared to be clonal proliferation, while earlier studies of PHA-stimulated cells, using radioactive DNA labeling and autoradiography, as well as chromosome aberrations, showed that different cells observed in division at one point in time could be in their 1st, 2nd, or 3rd mitosis (154,155). This asynchrony in DNA synthesis and mitosis could be due to continuous stimulation of successive groups of cells by the mitogen or to recruitment by blastogenic factors produced in culture.

Among the enzymes involved in DNA synthesis, DNA polymerase (140) has been reported to increase in activity on the 2nd day of culture with PHA. One of the DNA polymerases, that concerned with DNA repair, has specifically been shown to be present and, as would be expected, to be deficient in lymphocytes from patients with xeroderma pigmentosum (156), a genetic disease due to the lack of this repair enzyme.

Under the usual conditions of culture, the lymphocytes continue to divide up to 5 times and then die.

LONG-TERM LYMPHOID CELL LINES

Small aliquots of peripheral blood leucocytes from 20 to 30% of normal individuals, when cultured with suboptimal amounts of highly purified PHA, go on to become established as essentially permanent suspension cultures, doubling every 12 to 24 hours (157). Such lines can also be established spontaneously from patients with infectious mononucleosis, sarcoidosis, and a variety of viral diseases, as well as from large quantities of white cells from normals (158). The yield from small quantities can be improved to virtually 100% by the combined use of PHA and herpes-like virus (Epstein-Barr virus, HLV) (159).

The established cells are lymphoid in character, resembling stimulated lymphocytes morphologically. They synthesize and secrete immunoglobulins of the IgG, IgM, and IgA varieties. Single cells from these cultures, when cloned, give rise to populations which again produce the various types of gamma globulin in the same culture, indicating that these cells are relatively undifferentiated lymphoid cells, capable of further differentiation in culture. This is further confirmed by their ability to produce many of the mediators of cellular immunity, including migration inhibitory, cytotoxic, blastogenic, and chemotactic factors, thereby demonstrating properties attributed to T as well as B cells. They also produce interferon, some components of complement, and about 20% of the cells are capable of phagocytosis. This implies that they may even be able to differentiate toward the direction of reticuloendothelial cells. They show remarkable genetic stability, as measured by inherited polymorphisms of enzymes, chromosomal normality (especially from those lines established from normals), and histocompatibility antigens. The latter are made by these cells in such large amounts that the medium in which they are cultured has been used as a source for the purification and chemical analysis of HL-A antigens.

It is clear that these cultured lymphoid cells will be of quite general use in studies of immunology, cell biology, and genetics.

CONCLUSION

It is clear that *in vitro* studies of peripheral blood lymphocytes have already contributed a great deal of basic information to the fields of cellular immunity, cell biology, and human genetics. The recent addition of long-term lymphoid lines to the tissue culture armamentarium promises to extend these basic studies at an even more rapid pace.

A good beginning has been made on the utilization of at least short-term lymphocyte culture in the study of clinical defects in the immune response (160). While some of this work relates to problems involving the humoral antibody response, most of the studies deal with problems in cellular immunity. This is true both for inherited diseases, such as thymic alymphoplasia and Wiskott-Aldrich syndrome, as well as acquired defects in delayed hypersensitivity, such as those associated with sarcoidosis and lymphoid neoplasia. With the increasing fund of knowledge about the behavior of lymphocytes and their subclasses from normal individuals, one can predict with reasonable certainty that continued studies of these cells from abnormal individuals will increase in importance in solving the basic defects.

REFERENCES

1. Nowell, P. C., *Cancer Res.* **20,** 462 (1960).
2. Hastings, J., Freedman, S., Rendon, O., Cooper, H. L., and Hirschhorn, K., *Nature* **192,** 1214 (1961).
3. Carstairs, K., *Lancet* **11,** 984 (1961).
4. Ling, N. R., *Lymphocyte Stimulation,* North-Holland Publishing, Amsterdam, 1968.
5. Elves, M. W., *The Lymphocyte,* J. B. Lippincott Company, Philadelphia, 1966.
6. Naspitz, C. K. and Richter, M., *Prog. Allergy* **12,** 1 (1968).
7. Valentine, F. T., The transformation and proliferation of lymphocytes *in vitro,* in *In Vitro Correlates of Cell-Mediated Immunity* (J. P. Revillard, Ed.), S. Karger, Basel, Switzerland, 1971.
8. Douglas, S. D., *Transplant. Rev.* **11,** 39 (1972).
9. Farnes, P., Barker, B. E., Brownhill, L. E., and Fanger, H., *Lancet* **2,** 1100 (1964).
10. Börjeson, J., Reisfeld, R., Chessin, L. N., Welsh, P. D., and Douglas, S. D., *J. Exp. Med.* **124,** 859 (1966).
11. Douglas, S. D., Kamin, R., and Fudenberg, H. H., *J. Immunol.* **103,** 1185 (1969).
12. Powell, A. E. and Leon, M. A., *Exp. Cell Res.* **62,** 315 (1970).
13. Barker, B. E. and Farnes, P., *Nature* **215,** 659 (1967).
14. Grasbeck, R., Nordman, C. T., and DeLaChapelle, A., *Lancet* **2,** 385 (1963).
15. Holt, L. J., Ling, M. R., and Stanworth, D. S., *Immunochemistry* **3,** 359 (1966).
16. Hirschhorn, K., Schreibman, R. R., Verbo, S., and Gruskin, R. H., *Proc. Natl. Sci.* **52,** 1151 (1964).
17. Taranta, A., Cuppari, G., and Quagliata, F., *J. Exp. Med.* **129,** 605 (1969).
18. Ling, N. R. and Husband, E. M., *Lancet* **1,** 363 (1964).
19. Schoepf, E., Schultz, K. H., and Gromm, M., *Naturwiss.* **5,** 568 (1967).
20. Ruhl, H., Kirchner, H., and Bochert, G., *Proc. Soc. Exp. Biol. Med.* **137,** 1089 (1971).
21. Novogrodsky, A. and Katchalski, E., *FEBS Letters* **12,** 297 (1971).
22. Mazzei, D., Novi, C., and Bazzi, C., *Lancet* **2,** 802 (1966).
23. Bloch-Shtacher, N., Hirschhorn, K., and Uhr, J. W., *Clin. Exp. Immunol.* **3,** 889 (1968).

24. Moller, G., *Clin. Exp. Immunol.* **4,** 65 (1969).

25. Hirschhorn, R., Grossman, J., and Weissmann, G., *Proc. Soc. Exp. Biol. Med.* **133,** 1361 (1970).

26. Smith, J. W., Steiner, A. L., and Parker, C. W., *J. Clin. Invest.* **50,** 442 (1971).

27. Dumonde, D. C., Wolstencroft, R. A., Panayi, G. S., Matthew, M., Morley, J., and Howson, W. T., *Nature* **224,** 38 (1969).

28. Jones, W. R., *Am, J. Obstet. Gynecol.* **104,** 586 (1969).

29. Adinolfi, M., Gardner, B., Gianelli, F., and McGuire, M., *Experientia* **23,** 271 (1967).

30. Sell, S., *J. Exp. Med.* **127,** 1139 (1968).

31. Oppenheim, J. J., *Fed. Proc.* **27,** 21 (1968).

32. Fellner, M. J., Baer, R. L., Ripps, C. S., and Hirschhorn, K., *Nature* **216,** 803 (1967).

33. Hirschhorn, K., Bach, F., Kolodny, R. L., Firschein, I. L., and Hashem, N., *Science* **142,** 1185 (1963).

34. Pearmain, G., Lycette, R. R., and Fitzgerald, P. H., *Lancet* **1,** 637 (1963).

35. Elves, M. W., Roath, S., and Israels, M. C. G., *Lancet* **1,** 806 (1963).

36. Kelley, J. B., Stanfield, A. B., and Dukes, C. D., *Am. Rev. Resp. Dis.* **97,** 1131 (1968).

37. Richter, M. and Naspitz, C. K., *J. Allergy* **41,** 140 (1968).

38. Bach, F. H. and Hirschhorn, K., *Science* **143,** 813 (1964).

39. Bain, B., Vas, M. R., and Lowenstein, L., *Blood* **23,** 108 (1964).

40. Lamvik, J. O., *Scand. J. Hematol.* **3,** 325 (1966).

41. Wilson, D. B., Silvers, W. K., and Nowell, P. C., *J. Exp. Med.* **126,** 655 (1967).

42. Viza, D. C., Degani, O., Dausset, J., and Davies, D. A. L., *Nature* **219,** 704 (1968).

43. Hashem, N. and Rosen, F. S., *Lancet* **1,** 210 (1964).

44. Amos, D. B. and Bach, F. H., *J. Exp. Med.* **128,** 623 (1968).

45. Eijsvoogel, V. P., vanRood, J. J., duToit, E. D., and Schellekens, P. Th. A., *Eur. J. Immunol.,* **2,** 413 (1972).

46. Douglas, S. D., *Transplant. Rev.* **11,** 39 (1972).

47. Greaves, M. F. and Bauminger, S., *Nature* **235,** 67 (1972).

48. Yachnin, S., *Clin. Exp. Immunol.* **11,** 109 (1972).

49. Borberg, H., Woodruff, J., Hirschhorn, R., Gesner, B. M., Miescher, P., and Silber, R., *Science* **154,** 1019 (1966).

50. Borberg, H., Yesner, I., Gesner, B., and Silber, R., *Blood* **31,** 747 (1968).

51. Kornfeld, S. and Kornfeld, R., *Proc. Natl. Acad. Sci.* **63,** 1439 (1969).

52. Marchesi, V. T. and Andrews, E. P., *Science* **174,** 1248 (1971).

53. Schöpf, E., in *Leukozyten Kulturen,* 29 (G. Brittinger, H. J. Roggenbach, and K. Havemann, Eds.), F. K. Schattauer Verlag, Stuttgart, 1971.

54. Allan, D., Auger, J., and Crumpton, M. J., *Nature* **236,** 23 (1972).

55. Litwin, S., *J. Immunol.* **108,** 1129 (1972).

56. Greaves, M. F., Torrigiani, G., and Roitt, I. M., *Nature* **222,** 885 (1969).

57. Warner, N. L., Byrt, P., and Ada, G. L., *Nature* **226,** 942 (1970).

58. Bianco, C. and Nussenzweig, V., *Science* **173,** 154 (1971).

59. Oppenheim, J. J., Leventhal, B. G., and Hersh, E. M., *J. Immunol.* **101,** 262 (1968).

60. Gordon, J., *Proc. Soc. Exp. Biol. Med.* **127,** 30 (1968).

61. Bach, F. H., Alter, B. J., and Soloday, S., *Cell. Immunol.* **1,** 219 (1970).
62. Rubin, A. D., Davis, S., and Schultz, E., *B.B.R.C.* **46,** 2067 (1972).
63. Sundaram, K., Phondke, G. P., and Ambrose, E. J., *Immunology* **12,** 21 (1967).
64. Currie, G. A., *Nature* **216,** 694 (1967).
65. Fisher, D. B. and Mueller, G. C. *Proc. Natl. Acad. Sci.* **60,** 1396 (1968).
66. Kay, J. E., *Nature* **219,** 172 (1968).
67. Lucas, D. O., Shohet, S. B., and Merler, E., *J. Immunol.* **106,** 768 (1971).
68. Pasternak, C. A. and Friedericks, B., *Biochem. J.* **119,** 481 (1970).
69. Fisher, D. B. and Mueller, G. C., *Biochem. Biophys. Acta* **248,** 434 (1971).
70. Fisher, D. B. and Mueller, G. C., *Biochem. Biophys. Acta* **176,** 316 (1969).
71. Resch, K., Ferber, E., and Gelfand, E. W., 7th Leukocyte Culture Conference, 1972.
72. Hayden, G. A., Crowley, G. M., and Jamieson, G. A., *J. Biol. Chem.* **245,** 5827 (1970).
73. Cross, M. G. and Ord, M. G., *Biochem. J.* **124,** 241 (1971).
74. MacManus, J. P., Whitfield, J. F., and Youdale, T., *J. Cell. Physiol.* **77,** 103 (1971).
75. Robison, G. A., Butcher, R. W., and Sutherland, E. W., *Ann. Rev. Biochem.* **37,** 149 (1968).
76. Smith, J. W., Steiner, A. L., Newberry, W. M., Jr., and Parker, C. W., *J. Clin. Invest.* **50,** 432 (1971).
77. Colobert, L. and Lagarde, A., *C. R. Acad. Sci. Paris* **271,** Ser. D, 726 (1970).
78. Coulson, A. L., *Blood* **38,** 485 (1971).
79. Hadden, J. W., Hadden, E. M., and Middleton, E., Jr., *Cell. Immunol.* **1,** 583 (1970).
80. Alford, R. H., *J. Immunol.* **104,** 698 (1970).
81. Allwood, G., Asherson, G. L., Davey, M. J., and Goodlord, P. J. *Immunology* **21,** 509 (1971).
82. Robison, G. A., Butcher, R. W., and Sutherland, E. W., in *Cyclic AMP,* Academic Press, New York, 1971.
83. Kuo, J. F. and Greengard, P., *Proc. Natl. Acad. Sci.* **64,** 1349 (1969).
84. DeCrombrugghe, B., Chen, B., Anderson, W. B., Gottesman, M. E., Perlman, R. L., and Pastan, I., *J. Biol. Chem.* **246,** 7343 (1971).
84a. Haddeu, J. W., Haddeu, E. M., Haddox, M. K., and Goldberg, N.D., *Proc. Natl. Acad. Sci.* **69,** 3024 (1972).
85. Mendelsohn, J., Skinner, A. S., and Kornfeld, S., *J. Clin. Invest.* **50,** 818 (1971).
86. vandenBerg, K. J. and Betel, I., *Exp. Cell Res.* **66,** 257 (1971).
87. Peters, J. H. and Hausen, P., *Eur. J. Biochem.* **19,** 509 (1971).
88. Peters, J. H. and Hausen, P., *Eur. J. Biochem.* **19,** 502 (1971).
89. Robineaux, R., Buna, C., Anteunis, A., and Orme-Roselli, L., *Ann. Inst. Pasteur* **117,** 790 (1969).
90. Quastel, M. R. and Kaplan, J. G., *Nature* **219,** 200 (1968).
91. Quastel, M. R. and Kaplan, J. G., *Exp. Cell Res.* **63,** 230 (1971).
92. Whitney, R. B. and Sutherland, R. M., 7th Leukocyte Culture Conference, 1972.
93. Hirschhorn, R., Brittinger, G., Weissmann, G., and Hirschhorn, K., *J. Cell Biol.* **37,** 412 (1968).
94. Inman, D. R. and Cooper, E. H., *J. Cell Biol.* **19,** 441 (1963).

95. Gowans, J. L. and McGregor, D. D., *Prog. Allergy* **9,** 1 (1965).

96. Biberfeld, P., *Exp. Cell Res.* **66,** 433 (1971).

97. Scott, R. E. and Marchesi, V. T., *Cell. Immunol.* **3,** 301 (1972).

98. Krug, V., Krug, F., and Cuatrecasas, P., *Proc. Natl. Acad. Sci.* **69,** 2604 (1972).

99. Wright, P., Quastel, M. R., and Kaplan, J. G., 7th Leukocyte Culture Conference, 1972.

100. Chessin, L. N., Borjeson, J., Welsh, P. P., Douglas, S. D., and Cooper, H. L., *J. Exp. Med.* **124,** 873 (1966).

101. Tokuyasu, K., Madden, S. C., and Zeldis, L. J., *J. Cell Biol.* **39,** 630 (1968).

102. Hirschhorn, R., Lysosomes and Inflammation, in *The Inflammatory Process* (B. W. Zweifach, L. Grant, and R. T. McCluskey, Eds.), Academic Press, New York, 1974.

103. Hirschhorn, R., Hirschhorn, K., and Weissmann, G., *Blood* **30,** 84 (1967).

104. Parker, J. W., Wasaka, M., and Lukes, R. J., *Lab. Invest.* **14,** 1736 (1965).

105. Pogo, B. G. T., Allfrey, V. G., and Mirsky, A. E., *Proc. Natl. Acad. Sci.* **55,** 805 (1966).

106. Kleinsmith, L. J., Allfrey, V. G., and Mirsky, A. E., *Science* **154,** 780 (1966).

107. Killander, D. and Rigler, R., *Exp. Cell Res.* **39,** 701 (1965).

108. Darzynkiewicz, Z., Bolund, L., and Ringertz, N. R., *Exp. Cell Res.* **56,** 418 (1969).

109. Allfrey, V. G., *Fed. Proc.* **29,** 1447 (1970).

110. Handmaker, S. E. and Gratt, J. W., *Biochem. Biophys. Acta* **199,** 95 (1970).

111. Pogo, B. G. T., *J. Cell Biol.* **53,** 635 (1972).

112. Hirschhorn, R., Troll, W., Brittinger, G., and Weissmann, G., *Nature* **222,** 1247 (1969).

113. Frenster, J. H., *Nature* **206,** 680 (1965).

114. Hirschhorn, R., Grossmann, J., Troll, W., and Weissmann, G., *J. Clin. Invest.* **50,** 1206 (1971).

115. Cooper, H. L., in *The Cell Cycle and Cancer* (R. Baserga, Ed.), Marcel Dekker, New York, 1971.

116. Torelli, U. L., Henry, P. H., and Weissman, S. M., *J. Clin. Invest.* **47,** 1083 (1968).

117. Rosenfeld, M. G., Abrass, I. B., Mendelsohn, J., Roos, B. A., Boone, R. F., and Garren, L. D., *Proc. Natl. Acad. Sci.* **69,** 2306 (1972).

118. Lucas, Z. L., *Science* **156,** 1237 (1967).

119. Kay, J. E. and Cooke, A., *FEBS Letters* **16,** 9 (1971).

120. Penner, P. E., Cohen, L. H., and Loeb, A. L., *Nat. New Biol.* **232,** 58 (1971).

121. Gallo, R. C. and Whang-Peng, J., in *Biological Effects of Polynucleotides* (R. F. Beers and W. Braun, Eds.), Springer, New York, 1971, p. 303.

122. Hall, M. R., Meinke, W., Goldstein, D. A., and Lerner, R., *Nat. New Biol.* **234,** 227 (1971).

123. Roos, D. and Loos, J. A., *Biochem. Biophys. Acta* **222,** 565 (1970).

124. Pachman, L. M., *Blood* **30,** 691 (1967).

125. Hedeskov, C. J., *Biochem. J.* **110,** 373 (1968).

126. Machaffie, R. A. and Wang, C. H., *Blood* **29,** 640 (1967).

127. Hirschhorn, R., unpublished observations.

128. Stjernholm, R. L. and Falor, W., *J. Ret.* **7,** 471 (1970).

129. Roos, D. and Loos, J. A., *Exp. Cell Res.,* **77,** 121 (1972).

130. Polgar, P. R., Foster, J. M., and Cooperband, S. R., *Exp. Cell Res.* **49,** 231 (1968).

131. Rabinowitz, Y. and Dietz, A. A., *Biochem. Biophys. Acta* **139,** 254 (1967).

132. Hellung-Larsen, P. and Andersen, V., *Exp. Cell Res.* **54,** 201 (1969).

133. Waithe, W., Hathaway, P., and Hirschhorn, K., *Clin. Exp. Immunol.* **9,** 903 (1971).

134. Rosenberg, S. A. and Levy, R., *J. Immunol.* **108,** 1080 (1972).

135. Biberfeld, P., *J. Ultrastruct. Res.* **37,** 41 (1971).

136. Nadler, H. L., Dowben, R. M., and Hsia, D. Y. Y., *Blood* **34,** 52 (1969).

137. Hirschhorn, K., Nadler, H. L., Waithe, W., Brown, B. I., and Hirschhorn, R., *Science* **166,** 1632 (1969).

138. Bloom, A. D., Tsuchioka, M., and Wajima, T., *Science* **156,** 979 (1967).

139. Goldstein, J. L., Campbell, B. K., and Gartler, S. M., *J. Clin. Invest.* **51,** 1034 (1972).

140. Loeb, L. A. and Agaruwal, S. S., *Exp. Cell Res.* **66,** 299 (1971).

141. Ito, K. and Uchini, H., *J. Biol. Chem.* **246,** 4060 (1971).

142. Pedrini, A. M., Nuzzo, F., Carrocchi, G., Dalpra, L., and Falaschi, A., *B.B.R.C.* **47,** 5 (1972).

143. Hirschhorn, R. and Levytska, V., *Cell. Immunol.,* in press.

144. Whitlock, J. P., Jr., Cooper, H. L., and Gelboin, H. V., *Science* **177,** 618 (1972).

145. Friedman, R. M. and Cooper, H. L., *Proc. Soc. Exp. Biol. Med.* **125,** 901 (1967).

146. Conover, J. H., Beratis, N. A., Conod, E. J., Ainbender, E., and Hirschhorn, K., *Ped. Res.* **7,** 224 (1973).

147. Lawrence, H. S., *Adv. Immunol.* **11,** 195 (1969).

147a. Papageorgiou, P. S. and Glade, P. R., *Lymphology* **5,** 80 (1972).

147b. Papageorgiou, P. S., Henley, W., and Glade, P. R., *J. Immunol.* **108,** 494 (1972).

148. Jerne, N. K., *Eur. J. Immunol.* **1,** 1 (1971).

149. Turkington, R. W., *Curr. Top. Dev. Biol.* **3,** 199 (1968).

150. Nakamura, I., Segal, S., Globerson, A., and Feldman, M., *Cell. Immunol.* **4,** 351 (1972).

151. Ripps, C. S. and Hirschhorn, K., *Clin. Exp. Immunol.* **2,** 377 (1967).

152. Parkhouse, R. M. E., Janossy, G., and Greaves, M. F., *Nat. New Biol.* **235,** 21 (1972).

153. Marshall, W. H., Valentine, F. T., and Lawrence, H. S., *J. Exp. Med.* **130,** 327 (1969).

154. Buckton, K. E. and Pike, M. C., *Nature* **202,** 714 (1964).

155. Bender, M. A. and Prescott, D. M., *Exp. Cell Res.* **27,** 221 (1962).

156. Burk, P. G., Lutzner, M. A., and Robbins, J. H., *Clin. Res.* **17,** 614 (1969).

157. Broder, S. W., Glade, P. R., and Hirschhorn, K., *Blood* **35,** 539 (1970).

158. Glade, P. R. and Broder, S. W., in *In Vitro Methods in Cell-Mediated Immunity* (B. R. Bloom and P. R. Glade, Eds.), Academic Press, New York, 1971.

159. Beratis, N. and Hirschhorn, K., in *Long-Term Lymphocyte Cultures in Human Genetics* (D. Bergsma, Ed.), Birth Defects Original Article Series National Foundation, New York, **9**(1), 247 (1973).

160. Fudenberg, H., Good, R. A., Goodman, H. C., Hitzig, W., Kunkel, H. G., Roitt, I. M., Rosen, F. S., Rowe, D. S., Seligman, M., and Soothill, J. R., *Pediatrics* **47,** 927 (1971).

Chapter Seven

Cytotoxic Reactions of Lymphocytes

BYRON H. WAKSMAN, M.D.

*Professor, and Chairman, Department of Microbiology, Yale University,
New Haven, Connecticut*

The cytotoxic effect of lymphocytes on adjacent cells was first clearly seen in tumors undergoing immunological rejection (1) and was subsequently recognized in allografts of normal tissues, in contact allergy, and in a variety of experimental autoallergic lesions (2). This observation led to the demonstration that immune lymphoid cells mixed with tumor cells of donor type could prevent takes of the tumor when the mixture was transplanted to a suitable host (3). Such cell transfers provided, for a number of years, the simplest means of studying lymphocyte cytotoxicity. The use of newborn, embryonic, or irradiated adult recipients, or of privileged sites such as the anterior chamber of the eye, facilitated study by restricting host cell participation (4). The use of diffusion chambers constructed with micropore filters for "*in vivo* culture" (5,6) was the extreme development of this type of investigation.

In the last decade, *in vitro* cell culture has replaced other techniques as the principal setting for similar investigations. There has been a rapid proliferation of new studies that make use of more or less well-defined populations of lymphocytes, e.g., from animals subjected to thymectomy, thoracic duct drainage, irradiation, or treatment with antilymphocyte

Supported by U.S. Public Health Service Grants AI-06112 and AI-06455.

sera (ALS), frequently combined with repopulation with thymocytes or bone marrow. Agents such as anti- Θ or antibody against specific light and heavy chains are used to distinguish thymus-processed T lymphocytes from thymus-independent B lymphocytes. Finally, lymphocytes bearing receptors of a particular specificity are purified by making use of their ability to adhere to monolayers of specific target cells or by passage through columns of antigen-bearing immunosorbents (Wigzell). Recent reviews dealing with various aspects of the field can be found in refs. 7 to 15.

IN VIVO OBSERVATIONS

It is more than a decade since the recognition that cell-mediated immunologic reactions as a group possess certain fundamental features in common (2). These lesions uniformly begin with a perivenous infiltration of hematogenous lymphocytes and monocytes. In the zone of infiltration, an "invasive-destructive" lesion, i.e., parenchymal damage of varying degree, depending on the cellular makeup of the involved tissue, is observed. There may also be vascular damage, varying from slight permeability changes to complete vascular necrosis. This description was based on the pioneering morphologic studies of Medawar and Simonsen on allograft rejection and the graft-versus-host (GVH) reaction, as well as on those of Gell on "delayed" reactions to soluble antigens. With the introduction of electron microscopy, it became possible to attempt a distinction between cytopathogenic effects produced by lymphocytes as such and those of the more numerous monocytes or macrophages. The morphologic and other findings are reviewed here briefly.

Tumor Rejection*

The study of cellular immunity to tumors may be said to have started with the morphologic observation of Kidd and Toolan in 1950 (1) that transplanted tumors show a "lymphocytic" infiltrate at 5 to 7 days with what appears to be direct killing of the tumor cells by the lymphocytes. This finding was supported by the systemic transfer of tumor immunity with recipient lymphocytes (17), the development of neutralization techniques in which the killing of tumor cells by admixed immune lymphocytes is tested by transferring them to a susceptible recipient (1,3,18), and finally the evaluation of this killing *in vitro* (see ref. 19). Antibody

*See refs. 8, 11, and 16.

against tumor antigens was shown to block the cytotoxic effect (19–22). The role of macrophages, possibly coated with specific cytophilic antibody, in killing at least certain types of tumors was strongly suggested both on morphologic grounds and on the basis of transfer studies (18,23), as well as in later studies with cultures (24,25). Gorer (26) made a distinction between biologic types of tumors subject to different rejection mechanisms (complement-mediated lysis by antibody, lymphocyte cytotoxicity, and destruction by macrophages) which may well account for some of the conflicting results of recent *in vitro* work, described below. A distinction has also been recently made (27) between rejection of tumor cells injected into the site of a delayed reaction against an antigenically unrelated tumor and the failure of the same cells to be rejected at the site of rejection of a second tumor. This difference appears to correspond to the recently recognized distinction between cytotoxicity mediated *in vitro* by soluble cytotoxic factors released from sensitized lymphocytes that have reacted with specific antigens and the direct killing of target cells by immune lymphocytes in the absence of obvious mediators.

Transplanted Normal Tissues*

Full-thickness skin allografts (in rabbits) during rejection show a massive invasion of mononuclear cells, especially into the epidermis, closely correlated with rapid and progressive necrosis of the involved epidermis (28). The invading cells are described as intermediate in morphology between lymphocytes and monocytes. Frequent discontinuities are seen in the opposed plasma membranes of these and the adjacent epidermal cells, possibly related to the rejection process. Vascular labeling shows that the permeability change observed is closely correlated with passage of the infiltrating mononuclear cells through the vascular endothelium (29).

The same mononuclear cell infiltration is seen in kidneys undergoing rejection (30–34). Here, however, the first lymphocytes are seen leaving the vessels within a few hours after grafting. These undergo transformation into large, replicating pyroninophilic cells (blast transformation) by the 2nd or 3rd day. The appearance and spread of these cells are associated closely with vascular damage and focal tubular necrosis. At 5 to 7 days, a massive infiltration of mononuclears begins, derived apparently from stimulated blasts in the draining lymph nodes and spleen,

---

*See ref. 7.

and there is now widespread cortical necrosis resulting, at least in part, from second-order events such as ischaemia.

In the grafted lung, a similar early involvement of the walls of veins by mononuclear cells results in disruption of the endothelial and muscular layers, with narrowing of the vascular lumen and sometimes obliteration of the vessel and infarction (35). In the liver, the early (1 to 3 days) perivenous infiltration of mononuclears takes place in the portal areas (36). The later and more extensive wave of infiltrating lymphocytes and/or monocytes occurs in the sinusoids and is associated with local hepatocellular damage and finally progressive fulminant necrosis.

In none of these cases is it clear whether the two waves of lymphocytes, those appearing and undergoing transformation at the site in the first day or two and those arriving at 5 to 7 days, i.e., following the immune response stimulated by antigen in the draining lymphoid organs, are comparable in potential and exert the same type of cytotoxic effect on adjacent parenchymal elements. The apparent heterogeneity of T lymphocytes, mentioned below, justifies further examination of this question.

Contact Allergy

The electron-microscopic study of the contact lesion elicited in sensitized guinea pigs by 2,4-dinitrochlorobenzene by Flax and Caulfield (37) was the first careful morphologic description of any of the lesions under consideration and provided a model for the studies of allografts, autoallergies, etc. The characteristic infiltration of lymphocytes and monocytes into the upper dermis and epidermis begins within 5 hours after application of the allergen. By 8 to 10 hours there is extracellular edema in the epidermis, with disruption of tonofibrils in the epidermal cells and damage of their desmosomes. Focal cytoplasmic degeneration and osmiophillic aggregates of mitochondria and other organelles become obvious at 24 hours. Closely correlated with the mononuclear cell migration is leakage of the superficial veins and venules, starting as early as 2 hours and maximal by 12 to 18 hours (38). However, other mechanisms than injury by lymphocytes may play a role in this vascular alteration, since perfusion of the reaction site (39) shows the local release of histamine, kinins, and esterase.

Delayed Reactions to Soluble Antigens

Gell described the classical delayed reaction as a "perivascular island" of mononuclear cells (40,41). The cells appearing first were subsequently shown to be T lymphocytes (42). The secondary invaders, which make up 70 to 80% or more of the cells at peak response (12 to 24 hours), are typical marrow-derived monocytes (43,44). The former emigrate from small veins and the latter both from these and from venules (45). As in the other lesions described, cellular diapedesis is accompanied by permeability changes in the corresponding vessels (38,45–47). An unusually rapid clearance of the specific eliciting antigen as well as of other antigens at the reaction site is not observed (48,49). At the same time hydrolytic enzymes, such as aminopeptidase and acid and alkaline phosphatases, presumably released from the infiltrating monocytes, accumulate locally (50). A similar enzyme release has been thought to account for the liquefaction in caseating pulmonary tubercles (51,52).

Experimental Autoallergic Disease

In this group of processes, as in tumors and grafts undergoing rejection, the earliest lesion is mononuclear cell infiltration about small vessels, appearing at 5 to 7 days, and followed by damage of parenchymal elements in close relation to the infiltrating cells (53). The prototype is autoallergic encephalomyelitis, produced in response to immunization with central nervous system myelin. This lesion begins with passage of mononuclear cells and plasma proteins through the walls of venules (54,55). These cells penetrate between myelin lamellae at the node of Ranvier or via the outer mesaxon and strip off the myelin, phagocytizing it and adjacent oligodendroglia cells. In intense lesions, focal dissolution and vesicular disintegration of myelin are also seen. The initial lesion of autoallergic neuritis is described in similar terms (56). In autoallergic thyroiditis (57), the invasion of thyroid follicles by infiltrating lymphocytes and histiocytes leads to progressive destruction of these, beginning with alterations of the thyroid acinar epithelium closely comparable to the epidermal changes in the early lesion of contact allergy.

Lesions Produced by Transferred Lymphoid Cells

Lesions identical with those described in actively immunized animals are elicited in tumors or normal tissues transplanted to recipients of suitably sensitized lymphoid cells (17,58). These are lymphocytes appearing first in draining lymph nodes of immunized donors, then in thoracic duct lymph and peripheral blood, and finally in remote nodes and spleen (58,59). They are derived from thymus-processed or T lymphocyte precursors (60). The findings have been duplicated in several experimental species and with each of the categories of lesions described above (contact allergy, delayed reactions to soluble antigens, autoallergies). The claim that transfer can be achieved with peritoneal macrophages (61) remains open to question, because of contamination of the latter by lymphocytes. Several studies have purported to show that transferred lymphocytes act by the manufacture of soluble factors or indeed antibody (62,63). A γ-globulin extracted from sonicates of sensitized lymph node cells, if given daily in massive doses to graft recipients, could produce a type of graft rejection similar to the so-called white graft. This mechanism is considered distinct from the usual form of lymphocyte-mediated rejection and is perhaps comparable to that produced by serum antibody. We do not review this problem here and also omit discussion of transfer factor, derived from transferred lymphoid cells (reviewed in ref. 64, see also Chapter 11), of the use of RNA from sensitized donor cells to render normal lymphocytes reactive, and of RNA to alter the antigenicity of target tissues.

The transfer of lymphoid cells to recipients which differ genetically from the donor and which for any reason fail to reject the donor cells results in a GVH reaction (runt disease, secondary disease) (7,65,66). The effector cells are T lymphocytes (67) which, after homing to the thymus-dependent areas of spleen and lymph nodes, react against histocompatibility antigens of the host by blast transformation and the stimulation of a secondary proliferation of reticuloendothelial cells of host as well as donor origin. Widespread invasive-destructive lesions follow, comparable to the lesions described in grafted organs, and localized in particular to the liver, gastrointestinal tract, skin, heart, and joints (see, e.g., refs. 68 to 70). Histochemical and electron-microscopic examination of GVH lesions has emphasized the role in tissue destruction of activated reticuloendothelial cells containing numerous large lysosomes full of hydrolytic enzymes (71). Also, Weiser and his colleagues (72) have noted the production of an unusually acute type of GVH following transfer of immune peritoneal exudate cells, i.e., a mixture of sensitized lymphocytes and macrophages coated with cytophilic antibody. Runt disease can be largely inhibited by antibody against target cell antigens (73), an effect comparable to "enhancement" in actively sensitized animals (20–22) and one that is duplicated quite precisely *in vitro*. Some of the GVH lesions, notably the epidermolytic skin lesion, are secondary to the interaction of transferred lymphocytes with host leukocytes, appear to depend in part on released soluble factors (70,74), and may be qualitatively different from the more usual invasive-destructive lesion. Parabiosis intoxication, seen in pairs of animals with a permanent vascular anastomosis (75), duplicates essentially all the features of the systemic GVH, including liver and gastrointestinal necrosis, vascular damage, and dermatitis (76,77).

An unsolved problem is the pathogenesis of the early immunosuppression accompanying the GVH (78,79) and the widespread lymphopenia, atrophy of lymphoid organs, and runting seen after the inflammatory lesions described above subside (65,80,81). Thymus and other lymphoid atrophy, bone marrow atrophy, lymphopenia, and anemia are also characteristic of parabiotic disease (76,77). These are not due to infection, as in some of the other runting syndromes (82), but may be due to massive release of soluble factors that damage host cells, inhibit DNA synthesis, or otherwise interfere with cell proliferation. Gershon has found evidence for "suppressor T cell" activity in a variety of systems, including the GVH, in which DNA synthesis (^{125}I UDR incorporation) is the usual parameter measured (82a,b). He relates these observations closely to the findings in systems involving tolerance and antigenic competition (see below).

The local transfer of cells capable of a primary reaction against host histocompatibility antigens (as with parental cells transferred to an F$_1$ host; reviewed in ref. 83) in the skin gives rise to large islands of activated host reticuloendothelial cells and coextensive parenchymal destruction (84), the "transfer reaction." If injected beneath the kidney capsule, they produce a striking invasive-destructive lesion (83,85). Both unimmunized and immunized lymphocytes produce this lesion while tolerant cells do not, and lymphoma cells invade but do not destroy. Transfer of cells from an active lesion to the kidney of a new F$_1$ host, which provides continuing antigenic stimulation, results in continued parenchymal destruction (86). Curiously, the adequate stimulus is provided by host leukocytes rather than histocompatibility antigen in the kidney itself, and is eliminated by whole-body irradiation of the host.

The transfer of mixtures of lymphocytes and the target cells (usually tumor) to which they will respond (1) developed into a quantitative technique in the hands of Winn and his collaborators (3) and was employed to show the sequence of appearance of specifically cytotoxic lymphocytes in the draining lymph nodes starting at 4 days and then in the various other peripheral lymphoid organs (87). When antigenically distinct tumor cells were injected as a mixture with cells preimmunized against one of them, only the corresponding tumor cells were killed while the other tumor grew freely (88). As noted earlier, such a result implies direct lymphocyte cytotoxicity rather than cytotoxicity effected via soluble mediators. The lymphocytes themselves have been said to be damaged in this process (89; see ref. 4). When sensitized peritoneal macrophages, freed largely or entirely of lymphocytes, are used in similar transfers it has been possible to observe apparently specific tumor rejection (88,90). Again, however, the possibility of lymphocyte contamination of the cell suspensions employed has proved difficult to rule out.

The use of privileged sites to study the behavior of grafted tissues is somewhat peripheral to our subject and is mentioned here only for the sake of completeness (see review 4 by Amos). In general, grafts to organs lacking a suitable lymphatic drainage fail to sensitize but are rejected in a normal manner if sensitization is carried out elsewhere. Examples are the brain and the hamster cheek pouch. Organs possessing a lymphatic drainage but little or no vascular supply may permit sensitization but not rejection, since sensitized host lymphocytes cannot gain access to the donor cells. Examples here are the cornea or anterior chamber of the eye, cartilage, and bone. A particularly interesting case is provided by the trophoblastic barrier between mother and fetus, which prevents rejection of the fetus as a graft even when the mother has been sensitized to paternal antigens (reviewed in ref. 91). Trophoblast cells are covered with an amorphous layer of mucoprotein, much like that in the hamster cheek pouch, between 0.1 and 2.0 μ in thickness (92). This is described as a sialomucin of high negative charge, which repels the negatively charged lymphocytes (91). However, maternal antibody against paternal antigens may be present, and also serves to protect the fetus against the cytotoxic activity of the maternal lymphocytes (93). Greene (94) used continued growth of xenogeneic tumor transplants in the anterior chamber (e.g., human tumors in the rabbit eye) as a test of the tumor's metastatic potential, or simply its growth potential. This highly important observation requires confirmation and reinvestigation by contemporary techniques of lymphocyte biology.

The use of diffusion chambers constructed with micropore filters (4) was introduced in the midfifties by Algire, Weaver, and Prehn (5,6). In general, grafts within the chambers were protected against the cytotoxicity of lymphoid cells, even in highly immunized hosts (90). Normal lymphocytes placed in such chambers were not cytotoxic, whereas sensitized lymphocytes were highly so (91), even in normal hosts. On the other hand, tumors sensitive to humoral antibody, such as L cells or heterografts, were readily destroyed within the chambers. The use of chambers, being more cumbersome than the use of completely *in vitro* methods, has recently been largely supplanted by the latter.

Tolerance and Antigenic Competition

McCullagh (95,96) has shown that competent rat lymphocytes transferred to tolerant recipients are unable to respond to antigen though retaining their reactivity for 3 days or more in the recipient. Conversely, a tiny dose of intrathymic antigen in normal adult rats suffices to render them systemically tolerant for some immune responses within a few days (97). Repeated massive doses of sheep erythrocytes can render B lymphocytes completely and specifically tolerant only in the presence of T lymphocytes (98). Asherson has shown that tolerance to contact sensitization of mice by picryl chloride can be conferred on normal animals by transfer of tolerant cells (98a). These observations all suggest the production of an immunosuppressive effect exerted by reacting cells, possible T cells, upon their immediate neighbors. There are good arguments (and evidence), however, to show that some forms of tolerance may be mediated by "enhancing" humoral antibody (99) while others are entirely cellular (100). Allison and his colleagues have offered a general theory of regulation, i.e., tolerance to self-antigens, based on T cells (100a).

Competition between two types of erythrocytes given in succession to irradiated mice reconstituted with spleen cells is greater with increasing doses of the latter (101), suggesting inhibition of the response to the second antigen by a humoral factor produced in response to the first. Gershon and Kondo (102) and Möller and Sjöberg (103,104) have shown that this phenomenon requires T cells and appears to be exerted on B cells. It is inhibited by actinomycin D given with the first (competing) antigen (105) and thus may depend on production and release of inhibiting protein mediators. In some systems, in fact, an immune response elicited in lymph nodes draining one footpad competes effectively with the immune response in the contralateral nodes to a different antigen injected in the corresponding footpad (106). This implies that an inhibitory mediator (or cells producing such a mediator) may circulate. The response to the protein carrier of a conjugate, in animals preimmunized against the carrier, is inhibitory to the primary response against the hapten (107). In a particularly interesting series of papers, Liacopoulos and his coworkers (108–110) have found that the induction of tolerance by repeated massive doses of protein antigen has the effect of inhibiting immune responsiveness to other antigens as well. This effect is seen both with antibody formation of the usual type (108), with delayed sensitization (109), and with graft-versus-host competence (110), i.e., cell-mediated types of response.

Kantor and his colleagues (111) have shown that when guinea pigs with existing delayed sensitivity to multiple antigens are desensitized, by moderate doses of one or more of these, reactivity to the remaining antigens is likewise diminished. This inhibitory phenomenon could be duplicated *in vitro*. The authors infer that the effect described must be mediated by a soluble factor, which they name "feedback inhibition factor" (FIF). They suggest that a similar mechanism may account for the serum factor shown to accompany reduced delayed reactivity in lepromatous leprosy and the "anticutins" associated with anergy in sarcoidosis. Okumura and Tada in an entirely different system, have shown that the γE-antibody (reagin) response to DNP-ascaria conjugates in rats is of short duration but may be greatly prolonged by adult thymectomy or splenectomy, in the absence of any change in the γM or γG responses (112), yet is easily suppressed by transferred thymoctes or spleen cells sensitized against the carrier (112a).

All these phenomena strongly suggest immunosuppressive effects mediated by T cells reacting to antigen. The inhibited functions involve T cells in some instances (e.g., the delayed reactions studied by Kantor) and different kinds of B cells in others (γM, γG, and γE-antibody responses). They are clearly reminiscent of the immunosuppression that accompanies the systemic GVH reaction, and may be produced by soluble mediators. Whether they are the consequence of activation of a particular T cell subpopulation (113) remains to be established. The possibility that B cell stimulation by antigen may sometimes interfere with immune responses to unrelated antigens (114) has been inadequately investigated.

Allotype Suppression

In certain mouse strain combinations, e.g., hybrids of SJL males with BALB/c females, immunization of the latter against paternal histocompatibility antigens produces in the offspring a durable suppression of immunoglobulin synthesis of the paternal allotype (114a). This suppression continues even after transfer of normal syngeneic lymphocytes to the suppressed animals. Conversely, the suppression is transferrable with spleen cells and is therefore dependent on an active lymphocytic process. The cells involved are found in both thymus and spleen of 6-month mice, are $\Theta+$, and must be regarded as T lymphocytes.

Allogeneic Inhibition

The phenomenon of "hybrid resistance" or "syngeneic preference" was first described as a relative resistance of F_1 hybrid animals to grafts of parental tissues such as marrow (115). It can be readily duplicated in cell transfer systems, e.g., of tumor cells mixed with lymphocytes, and in culture (reviews in refs. 116 and 117). It requires a genetic difference between the two participating cells and is now generally referred to as "allogeneic inhibition." The reacting participant need not be capable of *immunologic* reaction in the test system. Thus hybrid cells will react against parental cells, and immunologically incompetent lymphoma cells are active. The effect is undiminished in thymectomized, irradiated hosts, incapable of expressing cell-mediated immunity (118), but is inhibited by injecting the host with antibody against as yet unidentified histocompatibility antigens (not H-2) (118a). Heavy irradiation (4000 to 10,000 R), chloroquine, or steroid treatment of the lymphocytic partner or sonication of these cells does not diminish the allogeneic effect. The phenomenon is enhanced by treatment of a cell mixture with a blastogenic agent such as PHA *in vitro* prior to injection into a suitable host (119). The mechanism is quite unknown but appears to require "recognition" of foreign histocompatibility antigen and the stimulation of synthetic processes.

IN VITRO OBSERVATIONS

Several distinct types of lymphocyte-mediated cytotoxicity phenomena have been recognized *in vitro* (9,120,121). Immune lymphocytes are *directly cytotoxic* to target cells bearing the specific antigen, whether this is an intrinsic component of the cell surface or a soluble antigen adsorbed or chemically conjugated to the cell. Immune lymphocytes reacting with antigen in solution may be cytotoxic to "innocent bystander" cells by *release of toxic soluble mediators*. Nonsensitized lymphocytes may produce cytotoxic effects on suitable target cells by a number of mechanisms. *Allogeneic inhibition* has already been mentioned. *Cells coated with specific antibody* may be lysed by normal lymphocytes, as may cells in contact with *lymphocytes activated by mitogens* such as phytohemagglutinin (PHA). *Complement lysis* is mediated by normal lymphocytes as well. Cytotoxic lymphocytes may be formed as a result of *in vitro immunization*. Many of the phenomena produced by cytotoxic lymphocytes are mimicked by *macrophages bearing cytophilic antibody* or in some instances by *macrophages activated by mediators* released *from stimulated lymphocytes*. These cells, in turn, may act directly to damage target cells or may release soluble cytotoxic factors. Unfortunately none of these phenomena has yet been analyzed in sufficient depth to permit its complete definition at all levels; gross, morphological, and biochemical. Detailed reviews are found in refs. 9, 11, and 12, and entire books devoted to the *in vitro* correlates of cell-mediated immunity have recently appeared (14,15). We deal here only with some aspects of more recent work (approximately since 1960).

Direct Cytotoxicity

The first demonstrations of the cytotoxic activity of immune lymphocytes for target cells of donor type were those of Govaerts (122) and Rosenau and Moon (123,124), and similar studies soon followed from many laboratories (125–129) (for complete listing, see Table I in ref. 9). The essential findings were similar with cells from various species, immunized by grafting of tumors or normal tissues, and tested on target cells of donor type. Adherence of the sensitized lymphocytes to the target cells, "contactual agglutination," occurred within the first hour, and was followed by morphologic evidence of target cell damage beginning as early as 3 to 6 hours and well expressed by 18 to 22 hours. Target cells showed an initial loss of cloning efficiency and permeability changes, followed by rounding up, vacuolation, and nuclear pyknosis, and finally death of over half the cells by 48 hours. The lymphocytes were reported to be damaged themselves in this process (123,124) but there is strong evidence against this (125). Indeed, after reacting with specific target cells, the lymphocytes retain the ability to kill a new lot of target cells added to the system (130,131)

The adherence of lymphocytes is an immunologically specific event, while the subsequent target cell effects are regarded as nonspecific (132,133). Free antibody and complement play no role in this process; in fact, the whole reaction can be carried out in the absence of serum (123). The initial reaction of antibody-like receptors on the lymphocyte surface with target cell antigen triggers the subsequent killing of the target cell. The responsible antigen may be a natural component of the cell (see ref. 134) or artificially attached antigen (135). For the special case of transplantation antigens, Brondz (136) and subsequently Brunner and his colleagues (130,131) have shown that all or most of the specificities of the H-2 antigenic complex in mice are involved in the reaction. The reaction requires close contact of lymphocyte and target cell and is prevented by any barrier, such as a micropore filter (132,133). Indeed antibody directed against the lymphocyte (131,137,138), against the immunoglobulin receptor on the lymphocyte (139,140), or against specific antigens of the target cell (131,137,140–144) inhibits the entire reaction. Similarly, trypsin treatment, which removes lymphocyte receptors, inactivates the cells for a period of 1 to 3 hours, and reactivity is not regained if synthesis of new immunoglobulin is prevented by cycloheximide (131). The inhibition of cytotoxicity by antibody to target cell antigens has been shown to represent an important component in the growth and spread of malignant tumors in a variety of natural and experimental situations in intact animals and, indeed, in man (19,144,145). Concanavalin A, which acts at the cell surface, is also a powerful inhibitor of lymphocyte-mediated cytotoxicity (146,147; Resch and Perlmann in ref. 148).

The production of cytotoxicity by lymphocytes sensitized against soluble protein antigen, when they are activated by exposure to specific antigen (149–151), appears to be mediated by the release from the lymphocytes of soluble "lymphotoxins" and is discussed in a separate section below.

The use of mitogens such as PHA to stimulate lymphocytes, which then exert a cytopathic effect on other cells in the system, was shown first by Holm et al (152) and confirmed in a number of subsequent studies with PHA, pokeweed mitogen, concanavalin A, ALS, streptolysin O, and staphylococcal filtrate (151,153–155a). This effect can be elicited in completely syngeneic systems and therefore does not involve any initial antigen-antibody reaction. However, it also requires close contact of lymphocyte and target cell, being prevented by interposition of a micropore filter (152), by antibody against surface components of the lymphocyte (137,156), by antibody that coats the target cell (137), or by other coating substances such as heparin (157). As in the case involving sensitized lymphocytes and target cells bearing specific antigen, cytotoxic effects are observed within 4 to 8 hours.

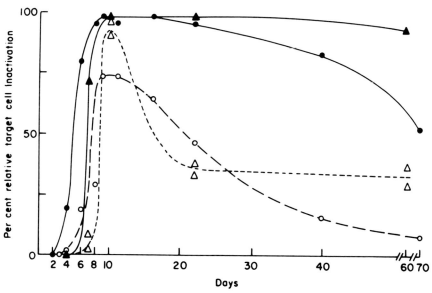

Figure 1. Appearance of cytotoxic lymphocytes in peripheral blood (▲ and △) and spleen (● and o) of C57B1 mice following immunization with 3×10^7 DBA/2 mastocytoma cells. Cell survival at 48 hours in mastocytoma cultures incubated with lymphocytes at ratios of 100:1 (▲ and ●) and 10:1 (△ and o). From ref. 130.

The lymphocytes responsible for direct cytotoxic effects *in vitro* are T cells. Their appearance in the blood and spleen is shown in Figure 1. These are found in the lymph nodes draining a graft site by 6 to 7 days (in rats and mice) and in the thoracic duct 2 to 3 days later (125), in agreement with the findings in local or systemic transfer discussed earlier. They appear to be enriched in peritoneal exudates (157a). They are described as small-medium, nonadherent, intensely pyroninophilic cells. Cerottini and his coworkers (158,159) have shown that the cytotoxic activity of C57B1/6 or C3H spleen cells, immunized by injection into lethally irradiated DBA/2 recipients and tested 4 days later on ^{51}Cr-labeled DBA/2 mastocytoma cells, is completely inhibited by anti-Θ but is not affected by anti-μ or anti-Fab. Conversely, cells capable of producing plaques of lysis with the aid of complement were inhibited by the latter reagents and unaffected by anti-Θ. The cytotoxic lymphocytes also differ from those forming plaques in density, and can be separated from them on albumin density gradients (160). These findings have been duplicated in several other laboratories (160a; Golstein and Sabbadini in ref. 148). The cytotoxic lymphocytes can be enriched specifically by allowing them to adhere to monolayers of the specific target cells. By this criterion each cell possesses receptors of only a single specificity, synthesized by the cell itself and not adsorbed (Golstein). These receptors, while not affected by antiimmunoglobulin sera, are effectively inhibited by Ramseier-type antisera directed against idiotypic determinants of the combining site itself (Sabbadini).

The killing of target cells by lymphocytes stimulated by antigen or mitogens does not require blast transformation (147,155). It apparently is not mediated by released cytotoxic factors, since labeled third-party cells present in the mixture of lymphocytes and specific target cells are not killed (140,161) and since the supernatant fluids show no cytotoxicity after tenfold concentration (140). It should be noted, however, that mitogens such as PHA and concanavalin A also cause release of "lymphotoxin(s)" (see below), and Granger and his colleagues feel that a single subpopulation of lymphocytes is responsible for both direct cytotoxicity and release of mediators (147). It does not require mediation by humoral antibody or complement (123,125,128,140,162). The ability of a given number of lymphocytes to kill a larger number of target cells has been related to the fact that they may adhere to several target cells at once or may move from one to another (140; Wunderlich in ref. 148). Wilson (132) has described a linear relation between the number of lymphocytes used and the log percentage of survival (see Figure 2); this implies a 1-hit phenomenon, 1 lymphocyte to 1 target cell. No more than 1 to 2% of the lymphocytes are active. Accordingly peak cytotoxic activity

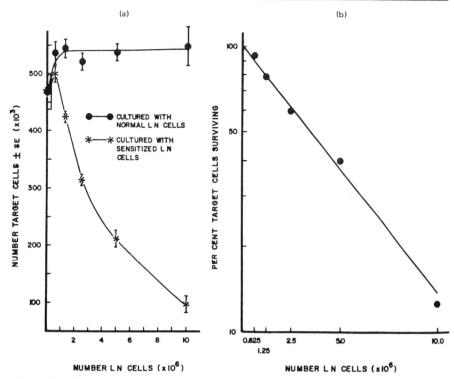

Figure 2.   (a) Relationship between number of cytotoxic lymphocytes (lymph node cells of DA rats immunized against Lewis histocompatibility antigen) and number of surviving target cells (Lewis tumor cells) after 48 hours in culture. In (b), the surviving cells in cultures with sensitized lymphocytes expressed as a percentage of those surviving in cultures with normal lymphocytes are plotted against the absolute number of lymph node cells used. From ref. 132.

is observed with lymphocyte—target cell ratios near 100:1 (130,131,142). Other workers have found the degree of lysis simply proportional to the absolute number of lymphocytes (128,163). However, this finding is characteristic of systems involving release of soluble lymphotoxic mediators, and lysis of third-party target cells was in fact observed in Sabbadini's experiments (163). The lymphocytes must be living, and their metabolic activity is essential to cytotoxicity, which is not seen at low temperatures (164) or in the presence of antimycin A (165) or inhibitors of RNA and protein synthesis (133,142). The cytotoxic effect is also inhibited by cytochalasin B, a fungal product affecting transport of simple molecules and microfilament function (165a), and by organophosphorus serine esterase inhibitors (165b). While cytotoxicity may be correlated with DNA synthesis, as in the dose-dependent response to PHA (151), it reaches a maximum when the latter is just starting, i.e., is independent of it (147,155), and indeed is not affected by inhibitors of DNA synthesis such as FUDR (131). Berke and his colleagues (165c) have distinguished an attachment phase, an intermediate phase, and a highly temperature-dependent lytic phase. The effector lymphocytes are not themselves lysed but can enter a new lytic cycle with additional target cells. Henney (165d) distinguishes a first phase sensitive to cytochalasin B and prostaglandins affecting intracellular cAMP levels but not by extracellular cation concentrations, and a second phase unaffected by cytochalasin B and PGE$_2$ but requiring extracellular calcium and therefore inhibitable by EDTA.

A variety of cells have been used as targets in direct cytotoxicity systems, as well as in studies of lymphotoxin and of antibody-mediated lymphotoxicity described later in this chapter. Tumor cells and established cell lines have been very widely employed, on the simple ground of convenience; among them are mouse L cells (125,126,166–170), mouse mastocytoma (129–131), sarcoma I (90,128,162,163,171), B16 melanoma (163), polyoma virus-induced tumors (132), Moloney sarcomas (145), mouse mamary carcinoma (145), methylcholanthrene sarcomas (172–174), HeLa cells (166,167,170), Chang cells (175), human lymphocyte lines (176), human colon and lung adenocarcinomas (145), human neuroblastoma (144), BMK cells (166,167), guinea pig hepatomas (177,27), ascitic forms of lymphoid tumors (140), and Shope rabbit papilloma (145). Normal rat or mouse embryo fibroblasts (130,132,133,-149,150,178,179), macrophages (128), various types of kidney cells (122,125,152), heart (170), muscle (180), thyroid (181), colonic epithelium (182,183), glial cells (184), and myelin (185–187) have been extensively used (see Figures 3a and b). Finally, erythrocytes of several species have been used in studies of lymphocyte cytotoxicity mediated by antibody in particular (135,188,189). In studies of contact allergy (190–192), red cells with dinitrofluorobenzene coupled to the surface have served as satisfactory target cells. The cytopathic effects noted have varied with the identity of the cell line employed, the degree of cell or tumor passage, as well as the conditions of culture (9,12,130,131,193). Thus Bruener et al (130,131) showed marked differences in susceptibility of mouse embryo fibroblasts, DBA/2 mastocytoma, and lymphoma to the same immunized C57B1 lymphocytes. There is little general support, however, for Holm's suggestion (148) that the cytotoxicity of antigen-stimulated lymphocytes is manifested preferentially against target cells having the same species of origin.

The nature of the pathologic change in affected target cells remains poorly understood. While there have been suggestions that the effect

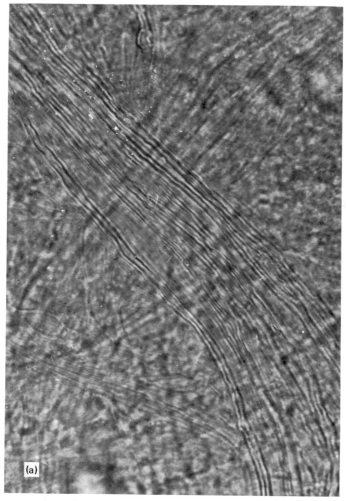

Figure 3.   (a) Myelinated peripheral nerve fibers in cultures of fetal rat trigeminal ganglion.

is simply an inhibition of DNA synthesis (177), actual counts have shown that a true killing of target cells may take place (132,133). There is general agreement that cells such as fibroblasts which become detached from the glass or plastic surface of the culture flask are dead (see ref. 9). Counting and metabolic studies thus far have been largely limited to the cells that remain attached. The techniques used for detecting or measuring cytotoxicity shed some light on the target cell events. These include simple morphologic observation (122,124–129), counting of surviving cells or nuclei (124,125,132,133,149,150), production of plaques

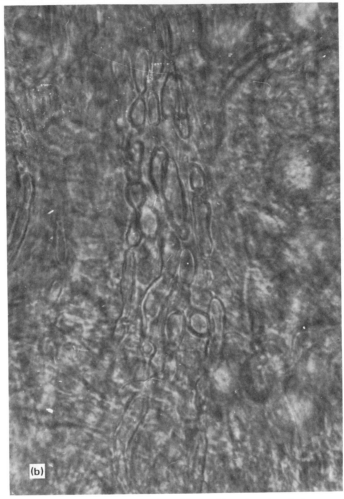

Figure 3.   (b) Myelin destruction 48 hours after addition of lymph node cells from syngeneic rats sensitized 10 days earlier with rabbit nerve in Freund's adjuvant. Phase contrast, × 640. From ref. 276.

of cell lysis (24,97,194), use of trypan blue to estimate percentages of dead cells (126,128,169), inhibition of cloning or colony formation (19,129,144,145,170), inhibition of the sheep cell plaque-forming cell response of spleen cells used as target (195), release of ^{51}Cr (130,140,-163,168,171,196), release of nucleic acids labeled with ^{3}H or ^{14}C-thymidine (127,152), or of cytoplasmic protein labeled with ^{14}C-amino acids (152,182,183,197), or of ^{32}P (152,183), and loss of ability to synthesize DNA (174) or protein (147,153,198,199). Changes in cloning efficiency and release of ^{51}Cr or of cell contents are detectable within

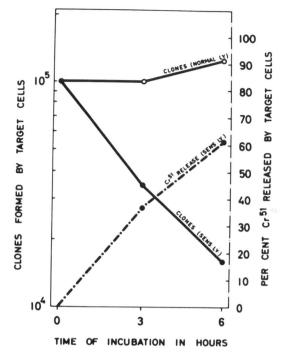

Figure 4. Cytotoxic effect of sensitized C57B1 mouse spleen cells on DBA/2 mastocytoma cells in culture. Comparison between assays of ⁵¹Cr release (corrected for spontaneous ⁵¹Cr release) and cloning efficiency of target cells. From ref. 143.

a half-hour (see Figure 4), morphologic damage is clear-cut only at 12 to 20 hours, while massive cell destruction and the formation of plaques is best seen at 48 to 72 hours (199a). The advantages and disadvantages of these various methods are discussed by Perlmann and Holm (9).

Electron-microscopic studies, both in cases involving sensitized lymphocytes (162,171,200) and in those with mitogen-stimulated unsensitized cells (200a), establish that the lymphocytes first attach to the Golgi pole of the target cells by their uropods. They infiltrate under the target cells, loosen, and finally detach them. The detached cells show cytopathic changes without any preceding marked change. Attached cells, even if covered with lymphocytes, show little effect, although a few may degenerate to spindle form. The claim is made, based on autoradiographic evidence (201,202), that DNA and RNA pass from donor to target cell via the uropod, with resultant hybridization of the latter and an undefined lethal effect. Lymphocytes transformed into blasts, on the other hand, achieve close contact with their targets over extensive areas, with interdigitating, spikelike projections, followed by the appearance of swelling and vacuolation in the target cells. The authors (200) suggest that the effect is primarily on cell membranes. Agents that increase cyclic AMP levels in the lymphocytes inhibit cytotoxicity effects (203). Antimetabolites such as imuran prevent cytotoxicity (133,137,204) while steroids do not affect the attachment phase of the response but inhibit target cell destruction (205). For further details see refs. 4 and 9.

In Vitro Immunization and Production of Cytotoxic Lymphocytes

Ginsburg and Sachs (206,207) showed in 1965 that normal rat lymphocytes plated on mouse fibroblasts in monolayer culture would undergo blast transformation within 2 to 3 days and produce lysis of the target fibroblasts by 5 to 6 days. This work was extended by the same group of authors (208–210; see ref. 211), and the cumbersome morphologic evaluation of lysis was simplified by the technique of measuring ^{51}Cr release (212). Lysis is highly specific; when immunized rat cells are transferred to various fresh monolayers, they can distinguish mouse fibroblasts which differ in H-2, killing only cells corresponding to those used for immunization. On the other hand, while the sensitization phase of this process is specific, the killing as such is nonspecific in that labeled third-party cells, mixed with unlabeled specific cells in the test monolayer, are also destroyed (213). The sensitization phase is said to require cooperation of T and B lymphocytes, both partners participating in the recognition of antigen (214,215,215a,b), as well as macrophages (215c).

There are interesting variations on this theme, which may depend on as yet unrecognized heterogeneity in the lymphocytes undergoing sensitization. Rat lymphocytes placed on allogeneic rat fibroblasts undergo blast transformation but may fail to lyse the target cells (216). Similarly, mouse lymphocytes, plated on allogeneic mouse fibroblasts, undergo transformation and acquire the ability when transferred to cause rejection of tumors that correspond in antigenic specificity to the original monolayer; yet these cells also do not produce lysis of target fibroblasts in the culture system (217). However, other workers have reported that mouse lymph node cells or thymocytes enriched in competent cells by cortisone treatment, when exposed to mitomycin C-treated allogeneic lymphocytes, undergo transformation (the mixed lymphocyte reaction) and become cytotoxic for fibroblasts of the corresponding H-2 locus (218,219,219a,b). The competent cells are Θ+ and are not found in the spleens of nude (athymic) mice (219b,c). Therefore they are clearly T lymphocytes. Antigenic microsomal lipoprotein is effective in producing transformation and acquisition of cytotoxic potential for specific target (tumor) cells (220; see also ref. 221). Similarly, human lymphocytes are activated and become specifically cytotoxic when exposed to cells of established lymphoid cell lines (176). Brunner et al, in their work with the mouse mastocytoma system (130,131), noted an acceleration in target cell destruction when fresh mastocytoma cells were added to an existing cytotoxic preparation. Both rat or mouse lymphocytes appear to be sensitized by syngeneic fibroblasts and acquire the ability to produce "graft-versus-host" reactions when injected into newborn syngeneic hosts (222). The authors explain this phenomenon as due to loss of reversible self-tolerance normally maintained *in vivo* by continuing antigen excess.

Ginsburg and his colleagues have shown that cells, induced to undergo blast transformation in the presence of PHA, concanavalin A, or poke-weed mitogen and a fibroblast monolayer, remain large and produce lysis as long as the mitogen remains present in the culture (179,223,224). Thymocytes will not undergo this change, but can be activated by con-canavalin A if they are first purified and sensitized on xenogeneic fibro-blasts (155a). Coulter counting provides a simple method for evaluating the number and size of blasts. However, if transferred to a fresh feeder layer without mitogen, the cells revert to small, "secondary" lymphocytes, which differ from primary lymphocytes by possession of a distinct nu-cleolus. These cells remain viable for as long as a month, and can be reactivated by any of the three mitogens, with transformation to blasts and renewal of the capability to lyse fibroblasts. However, pokeweed mitogen appears to act specifically, in that cells stimulated initially with this substance produce much greater lysis when reexposed to the *same* mitogen than is the case with any other combination of stimulants. The finding is interpreted as showing that pokeweed mitogen acts as a speci-fic "transplantation antigen" and leads to lysis of cells coated with it by immune lymphocytes (179). The cells responding have been shown to be T lymphocytes by the use of anti-Θ sera (224a). Stejskal et al (discussion in ref. 48) have succeeded in producing specific *in vitro* im-munization of human blood lymphocytes incubated with chicken red cells coated with rabbit antibody. The cells, in approximately 5 days, acquire the ability to lyse chicken but not duck erythrocytes. In this case the effective immunogen appears to be the antigen-antibody com-plex, since the erythrocytes alone do not immunize.

Cytotoxicity of Soluble Mediators Released from Lymphocytes

This topic is covered in Chapter 2, and therefore is discussed here only briefly (see also refs. 10, 12, 13, 147, and 167).

The production of cytotoxic mediators by sensitized rat lymphocytes reacting with specific antigen was first described by Ruddle (149,150, 225,226). A typical experiment is shown in Figures 5 and 6. The Granger and his coworkers (227,228), showed the release of similar factors by normal mouse and human lymphocytes reacting against histocompatibility antigens or stimulated with PHA, concanavalin A, or ALS and later extended this finding to sensitized cells and antigen (147,229). These authors introduced the term "lymphotoxin" (LT), and, as stated in Chapter 3, another term "lymphokines" has been suggested to embrace all soluble lymphocytic mediators (230).

The antigen-cell reaction is specific, occurring within a half-hour (226). Similarly, stimulation by PHA occurs within 15 minutes and is maximal by 1 hour (231). The release of LT, however, can usually not be detected before 2 to 6 hours and continues over long periods of time (231). Its formation requires energy and protein synthesis but not synthesis of DNA (147,231). Killed cells and cells incubated in the absence of antigen or mitogen do not of course produce LT. Irradiated cells, on the other hand, do (147,231). Cells of a variety of experimental animal species produce lymphotoxin, among them rat, mouse, guinea pig, hamster, cat, and man (149,167,227,229,232). Many types of peripheral lymphocyte preparations, including those of human adenoids (147), have been used. The cells releasing LT are T lymphocytes, since PHA and concanavalin A act exclusively on T cells. Thymocytes do not release cytotoxic substances (147,227). However, if the immunocompetent subpopulation of thymocytes is enriched by cortisone treatment, these can now serve as killer cells (219). Granger et al have shown continuous release of LT by cells of 26 established human cell lines among 39 lines tested (233), and other "lymphokines" are similarly formed by these cells (233; Wallace in ref. 148). It has yet to be shown that LT is always the same, when release is triggered by antigen and different nonspecific agencies, since it is conceivable that these may stimulate different subpopulations of lymphocytes.

LT production by sensitized cells in response to antigen requires the presence of macrophages (233a). Its production can be inhibited by cytochalasin B added to cultures as late as 6 hours after exposure to antigen and after release of LT has actually begun. However, in the presence of preformed macrophage lymphocyte-activating factor, cytochalasin B is inhibitory only if added at the start of the culture. In all these details LT action differs sharply from direct cytotoxicity.

Early studies established that LT was active on a variety of normal and neoplastic target cells (149,167,232,234). The techniques for measuring cytotoxicity are those described in the preceding section. The degree of target cell destruction is determined by the absolute number of immune lymphocytes in the experimental system rather than by the

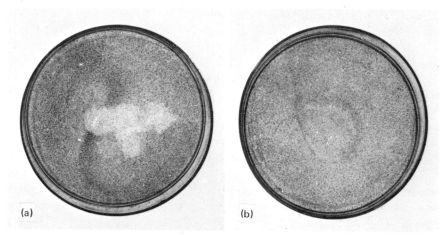

Figure 5.   (a) Plaque of lysis produced on Lewis rat fibroblast monolayer 72 hours after adding 150 × 10⁵ tuberculin-sensitive syngeneic lymph node cells plus PPD 12.5 μ g/ml. (b) Similar monolayer exposed to the same cells in the absence of antigen. Giemsa. From ref. 150.

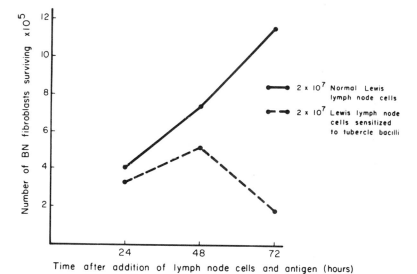

Figure 6.   Time course of cell death in rat fibroblast monolayer exposed to tuberculin-sensitized lymph node cells plus PPD compared with monolayer exposed to nonimmune cells plus PPD. Coulter counts of surviving cells in trypsinized preparation. From ref. 149.

ratio of lymphocytes to target cells, as in the case of direct cytotoxicity (163). In some instances, involving tumor cells such as SaI or B16 melanoma, the demonstration that a soluble mediator is active in cytotoxicity is accomplished by showing that lysis (^{51}Cr release) of labeled cells syngeneic with the immune lymphocytes accompanies the reaction of the latter with unlabeled specific target cells (163).

The LT molecule is protein. Human and mouse lymphotoxins are said to be antigenically distinct (228). The former, on G150 Sephadex, is found to have a molecular weight of 80,000 to 90,000. It has the mobility of a slow β-globulin, and is stable at 56° C but not at 100° C and in the pH range of 5 to 8. It resists DNAse, RNase, and trypsin. The mouse molecule is described (234,235) as having a molecular weight between 90,000 and 150,000 and being stable at 100° C and pH 2 to 12. Guinea pig LT, on Sephadex G100, elutes as a fraction smaller than albumin, which also contains other mediators such as MIF (168,236). It can be separated from the latter on cesium chloride gradients (237). Not all laboratories, however, are in agreement with this description (169).

Lymphotoxin appears to act on the plasma membrane of target cells (Granger in ref. 10), and its action may be blocked by polyanions such as DNA, RNA, and PVP (234), as well as by specific antibody against LT (147). While target cell effects are seen as early as 12 hours, the LT effect is said to be reversible up to 25 hours (234). In high concentrations, LT gives killing of most types of target cells. With dilution there is a spectrum of cell sensitivities, and at low concentration it stimulates biosynthesis and cell division in some types of cells (147). Acid phosphatase increases in target cells by 24 hours (226,238). The cytotoxic effect is enhanced in the presence of 2,4-dinitrophenol, puromycin, or cycloheximide and is inhibited by low temperature (234). The morphologic changes that have been described (bipolar and perinuclear vacuolation, rounding up, detachment from glass or plastic) are relatively nonspecific. Electron-microscopic study (Granger in refs. 10 and 239) has revealed only cell clumping and increased surface membrane activity of the target cells. There is extensive blebbing of the surface, with small partial discontinuities in the cytoplasmic membrane which appear to leak bleb contents into the medium.

Other "lymphokines" have been described which exert a cytotoxic effect on target cells by inhibiting proliferation. "Cloning inhibition factor" is described as a nondialyzable, heat-labile (56° C, 30 minutes) substance released by tuberculin-sensitized human lymphocytes incubated with PPD, which arrests division in HeLa cells reversibly (240; Valentine in ref. 148). "Proliferation inhibiting factor" (241), produced by human lymphocytes after stimulation either with antigen (PPD) or PHA, is a heat-stable (85° C, 30 minutes), nondialyzable protein that produces similar effects on a variety of human cells, among them HeLa, Hep-2, KB, and amnion cells, but not on chick or mouse fibroblasts. In high concentration, this agent kills target cells. An "inhibitor of DNA synthesis" is described in supernatants of mixed lymphocyte reactions, of mouse spleen cells treated with PHA, and of established human lymphocytic cell lines which acts on a variety of human or mouse lymphocytes responding to stimulation with PHA, antigen, or lipopolysaccharide endotoxin, as well as on L cells (242; Smith in ref. 11). This substance is labile at 56° C and at pH outside the range 6 to 8, and is active in very low concentration (1:50,000). There may be additional cytotoxic mediators, such as the substance extracted from human (243,244) or mouse (245) lymphocytes which acts on allogeneic fibroblasts to produce hyperploidy—and broken or abnormal chromosomes. The possible relationships of these factors to each other and to the remainder of the 16 or more mediators that have been described are still to be explored.

Tolerance and Antigenic Competition

Several newly described *in vitro* phenomena appear to correspond to the mechanisms given these names *in vivo*. Many investigators have found difficulty in producing tolerance by simply incubating spleen or lymph node cell suspensions with protein antigens. Yet injection of bovine γ-globulin into the intact spleen readily gives subsequent unresponsiveness of these cells (246). This finding implies the need for cell interaction in shutting off reactivity of one or more of the concerned cell types.

Spleen cells of F_1 mice, injected a week earlier with parental spleen and thus undergoing a graft-versus-host reaction, show a marked decrease in ability to make a primary response to sheep erythrocytes in tissue culture (247). If mixed with normal syngeneic spleen cells, these cells inhibit markedly the primary response of the latter. These cells also show inhibition of the conventional response to PHA in culture (247a). This suggests that competition is produced by secretion of factors or direct contact of the normal cells with "active" cells of the GVH response. An entirely similar effect is seen with the spleen cells of mice injected several days earlier with *Corynebacterium parvum* (247b,c). The suppression of the PHA response in culture can be duplicated simply by excessive stimulation with PHA and by cell crowding (247d). The primary response in culture is inhibited if mixtures of normal spleen cells are employed from mice differing at the H-2 locus. In this case a mixed lymphocyte reaction and activation of T cells presumably occur (248). In a closely similar instance, the secondary response of rabbit spleen cells in culture to DNP-BSA, introduction of PHA into the system gave increased thymidine incorporation and decreased antibody formation (248a). Finally, Kantor et al (111) found that when peritoneal cells of two guinea pigs sensitized to different antigens were exposed *in vitro* to one of these antigens, the ability to respond to the other with migration inhibition was lost, though the cells were still inhibitable by preformed MIF.

Cytotoxicity Produced by Antibody and Normal Lymphocytes

Perlmann and Perlmann have studied, with their colleagues, a type of lymphocyte-mediated cytotoxicity produced when cells coated with an antibody directed against cell surface antigens are incubated with normal lymphocytes (137,188). This is illustrated in Figure 7. In these and similar studies, when chicken or burro erythrocytes (or, for that matter, other nucleated cells) are incubated with rabbit or guinea pig sera and subsequently with human, rabbit, mouse, or guinea pig lymphocytes, there is aggregation of lymphocytes on the target cells. By 1 to 2 hours ^{51}Cr release is seen and this increases to a peak at 24 hours. The same type of lysis is produced when cells are coated first with various antigens and then incubated with specific antibody directed to the attached antigen plus lymphocytes. For this purpose, materials as diverse as PPD (135,249), thyroglobulin (249a), and an antigen extracted from rat colon (250) have been used. Other techniques have been employed to produce what is probably the same cytotoxicity phenomenon. Rabbit lymphocytes incubated with goat antiserum against rabbit immunoglobulin are lytic for chicken red cells (251). If the latter are coated with rabbit antibody against red cell antigens, the goat antiserum serves to link this immunoglobulin with immunoglobulin receptor molecules on the lymphocytes (Resch in ref. 148). Accordingly the serum is active at concentrations below that required to induce lymphocyte transformation and does not work with lymphocytes of other species, e.g., pig. Mitogens such as PHA and concanavalin A, since they act on a different class of lymphocytes (see below), do not induce the type of cytotoxicity discussed here and, in fact, inhibit it in many systems (Resch and Perlmann in ref. 148). Conversely, antilymphocyte serum inhibits the cytoxocity induced by PHA (138).

Antibody of the γM class does not act to produce normal lymphocyte cytotoxicity, but γG is effective (188,250). In systems involving guinea pig sera, γ_2 rather than γ_1 produces lysis (249a). As little as 1 ng of γG antibody will produce 50% lysis in a suitable system, an amount estimated

CYTOTOXIC EFFECTS OF LYMPHOID CELLS *in Vitro*

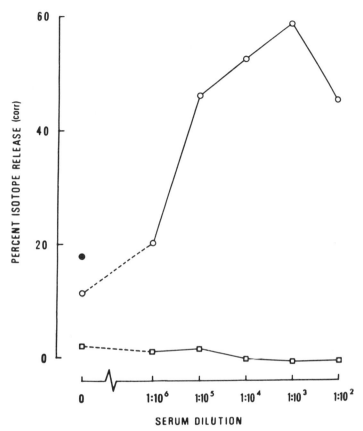

Figure 7. Cytotoxic effect (^{51}Cr release over 20 hours, corrected for spontaneous release) of normal human peripheral blood lymphocytes on Chang cells coated with rabbit antibody. Target cells washed after 30-minutes incubation with heat-inactivated antiserum and then incubated with 10% guinea pig complement □ or lymphocytes 25:1 plus 10% inactivated guinea pig serum ○. Addition of PHA ● did not enhance the lymphocyte effect. From ref. 137.

as equivalent to 80,000 antibody molecules/target cell (250). Complement is not involved, since cytotoxicity is seen with noncomplement-fixing types of antibody and with amounts of antibody too small to trigger complement-mediated lysis (9,137,188,252). The time course of the two types of lysis is also entirely different, requiring hours in the one case and minutes in the other.

The lytic phenomenon is not correlated with delayed sensitivity in the donor of either the antibody employed or the lymphocytes (135).

Lymphocytes from various sources (spleen, peripheral blood, thoracic duct lymph) appear to be equally effective. These are lytic even when highly purified (>99%), but aggregation and lysis both occur more rapidly with crude cell suspensions such as spleen which contain macrophages and/or polymorphs (249a). There seems to be little question that the effective cells are B lymphocytes (253,254,254a; Perlmann in ref. 148). The cells of thymectomized, irradiated, marrow-restored animals are fully competent or, indeed, show an increased capacity to lyse target cells. Spleen suspensions from which T lymphocytes have been removed with anti-Θ are active. Conversely, treatment of these suspensions with anti-κ and complement eliminates lytic activity. B lymphocytes have a receptor for the Fc moiety of antibody, IgG₁ especially (254b,c).

The kinetics of cytotoxicity in the systems under discussion and in those involving mitogens are quite different. Resch and Fischer (251), in comparing chicken erythrocyte lysis by rabbit lymphocytes activated with PHA and treated with goat antirabbit immunoglobulin, showed that the former started immediately and proceeded in a linear manner, while the latter started at 20 hours and was sigmoidal. A maximal rate of lysis was attained with lymphocyte—target cell ratios of 1:1 in the case of PHA and 5:1 with antiimmunoglobulin, presumably since T and B lymphocytes, respectively, are involved. The effects were synergistic; a greater degree of lysis was produced by the two agents acting in concert than the sum of activities produced by each alone. Like direct cytotoxicity, antibody-mediated lymphocyte cytotoxicity requires direct contact with the target cell. Third-party, uncoated cells are not lysed (254a), and the reaction is blocked by agents which keep the cells apart (ALS, concanavalin A) (see ref. 9). Living lymphocytes alone are active and their action requires energy, being inhibited by antimycin A. They are also inhibited by antimetabolites (137) and by cytochalasin B (165a), but not by puromycin (255).

Cytotoxicity Mediated by Complement and Normal Lymphocytes

Perlmann et al (121,256) have studied lysis of chicken red cells sensitized with 19S anti-Forssman antibody plus various portions of the human complement sequence by human peripheral mononuclear cells. Purified small lymphocytes would lyse cells on which C1–7 or C5,C6, and C7 had acted but not cells in the C4, C2, or C3 state (see Figure 8). Sonicates of the lymphocytes were equally lytic, and an active soluble factor was obtained intermediate in size between albumin and γG-globulin. C8 is present in sonicates, and the living lymphocytes may manufacture C9

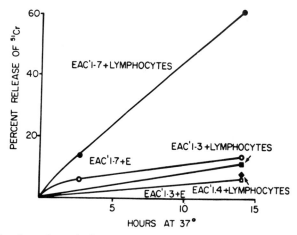

Figure 8. ⁵¹Cr release from chicken red blood cells treated with dilute rabbit 19S antibody, purified human complement components, and human blood lymphocytes at 80:1 ratio. Open symbols refer to data obtained with untreated chicken erythrocytes as substitute for lymphocytes. From ref. 9.

(Perlmann in ref. 148). Human monocytes were able to lyse cells in the C3 state, but not those that had reacted with components only up to C4 or C2 (121,256). There are many important differences between complement-mediated lysis and that involving the action of living B lymphocytes on antibody-coated target cells (9,188,252; Hobbs in ref. 148). Aside from the obvious difference in kinetics (20 minutes versus 20 hours) and in effective immunoglobulin (γM versus γG), the Fc fragment of the antibody can be altered enzymatically so that is loses the capacity to mediate the first of these mechanisms without losing its ability to fix complement and thereby mediate the second. Also, antibody is active as a mediator of lymphocyte cytotoxicity at concentrations 1000-fold less than that required for complement activation. Nevertheless, Perlmann and Holm report (9) preliminary experiments to show that antibody against C5 and C8 blocks lysis by human lymphocytes treated with antibody or PHA. They infer that activated C8 may have a more general role in cytotoxicity involving cell contact.

Allogeneic Inhibition

This topic is largely covered in our earlier discussion. The phenomena observed *in vivo* have been fully confirmed in *in vitro* studies (116,117).

It is clear that mouse or human lymphoid cells that are stimulated with mitogens in the presence of allo or xenogeneic cells are capable of producing plaques of target cell lysis (97) and release of radiolabeled cell constituents such as DNA (257). F_1 lymphocytes can kill cells of parental genotype (97), and tolerant lymphocytes kill cells of the tolerated specificity (258). The phenomenon does not require the use of aggregating agents to bring lymphocyte and target together, but is correlated with blast transformation (196). The latter can be brought about in all the usual ways, such as with PHA or staphylococcal filtrate or with PPD used on tuberculin-sensitized lymphocytes. However, DNA synthesis is not required, since heavily irradiated cells (4000 to 10,000 R) are perfectly effective. Allogeneic inhibition may be a special case of contact inhibition.

Macrophage Cytotoxicity

There is little doubt that macrophages coated with cytophilic antibody can duplicate many of the *in vitro* properties usually attributed to sensitized T lymphocytes, among them cytotoxicity, as shown particularly by Weiser and his colleagues (259). The early demonstration of tumor destruction by macrophages *in vivo* (90) was followed by the observation (24,25) that "macrophages" from sensitized animals would rapidly attach to target (tumor) cells in culture and damage them by 12 to 24 hours, with the production of plaques of lysis. This effect was mediated by cytophilic antibody and was highly specific; third-party target cells introduced into the system were not killed. Tumor cells placed on monolayers of immune macrophages failed to grow (260). This form of cytotoxicity may be analogous to the red cell damage produced by macrophages coated with cytophilic antibody (261). For more recent studies of this process, see refs. 261a to c.

Electron-microscopic study (262,263; see ref. 4) has shown an intimate contact between the plasma membranes of macrophage and target cell. One sees surface invaginations and there may be actual phagocytosis of the target cell, followed by shrinkage and digestion of its cell wall and cytoplasmic elements. Alternatively, by 5 hours, there is breakdown of the cell membranes in the zone of contact, vesiculation of the target cell cytoplasm, and degeneration of the nucleus. Pretreatment of the macrophages with sodium azide, DNP, or sodium flouride does not diminish their cytotoxic effectiveness (25). Actinomycin D and chloramphenicol, while not affecting their ability to adhere to target cells, diminished plaque formation. On the other hand, sodium flouride, if present during the first hour of interaction between macrophages and target cells, inhibited lysis without affecting protein synthesis, presumably by a membrane effect (264).

Macrophages also produce soluble cytotoxins: These cells, of course, contain a large variety of lysosomal hydrolases, some of which are readily released into the culture medium (reviews in refs. 265 and 266). Weiser and his collaborators have claimed that the soluble cytotoxin released by tuberculin-sensitized guinea pig macrophages exposed to antigen is indistinguishable from lymphotoxin by gel filtration, heat sensitivity, and various biological tests (267). Its relation to the cytotoxin released when macrophages from C57Bl/Ks mice immunized against SaI are tested on L cells (268) remains to be demonstrated. Pincus et al (170,269–271) have shown that guinea pig macrophages activated specifically by protein antigens or nonspecifically release substances cytotoxic for a variety of established cell lines. These have been identified as (1) a phospholipid, which acts on the target cell membrane and can be inhibited by N-acetylglucosamine or N-acetylgalactosamine, and (2) a similar substance, possibly attached to protein (272,273).

The possibility that cytotoxic effects observed *in vitro* and attributed to macrophages may in fact depend on lymphocytes, which contaminate all preparations of peritoneal exudate or alveolar cells, must be kept constantly in mind. This is all the more a matter of concern insofar as mediators released by lymphocytes result in marked macrophage activation (273a). Similarly, effects attributed to either of these cells may be produced by the presence of contaminating granulocytes (155,274,-275).

CLINICAL SIGNIFICANCE

The demonstration of specific lymphocyte cytotoxicity *in vitro* in a variety of experimental situations has inevitably been followed by attempts to show the same phenomenon in diseased human subjects and to make use of it for diagnostic or prognostic purposes. In general the relevant techniques are slightly more difficult than the commonly used measurement of blast transformation with specific antigen or with PHA, but not more difficult than the demonstration of macrophage migration inhibition (see refs. 14 and 15). Thus cytotoxicity seen in experimental autoallergic disease affecting the central nervous system (184–186), peripheral nervous system (276), muscle (180), and thyroid (181) is paralleled by cytotoxicity observations in multiple sclerosis (186), the Landry-Guillain-Barré form of acute polyneuritis (187), myositis, and acute ulcerative colitis (182,183). Conversely, lymphocyte-mediated cytotoxicity in standard test systems, such as toxicity for Chang cells in the presence of PHA, is diminished in lymphomatous diseases such as chronic lymphocytic leukemia and Hodgkin's disease (175).

The use of the colony-inhibition technique has demonstrated the presence of specifically cytotoxic lymphocytes in animals with a variety of spontaneous, carcinogen-induced or virus-induced tumors (19). These include mouse mammary carcinoma, methylcholanthrene-induced sarcoma, Shope rabbit papilloma, Moloney virus sarcoma in mice, and polyoma and Rous tumors in rats. In animals with long-standing, progressive, or metastatic disease the *in vitro* study has permitted the demonstration of circulating blocking ("enhancing") antibody that can prevent the cytotoxic effect by coating target cell sites. An exact parallel has been shown in man (see brief review in ref. 19). Almost every patient studied with neuroblastoma, lung, colon, or breast carcinoma, malignant melanoma, fibrosarcoma, osteogenic sarcoma, and retinoblastoma was found to have strong cytotoxic lymphocyte immunity. In almost every case with progressive or metastatic tumor growth, blocking antibody was also present.

Presumably lymphocyte cytotoxicity will find its place in the armamentarium of analytic and diagnostic tools used in medicine. It has already proved invaluable in the analysis of both experimental and human disease.

REFERENCES

1. Kidd, J. G., Toolan, H. W., *Am. J. Pathol.* **26,** 672 (1950).
2. Waksman, B. H., A comparative histopathologic study of delayed hypersensitive reactions, in *Ciba Foundation Symposium on Cellular Aspects of Immunity,* Churchill, London, 1960, p. 280.
3. Winn, H. J., The immune response and the homograft reaction, *Natl. Cancer Inst. Monogr.* **2,** 113 (1960).
4. Amos, D. B., The use of simplified systems as an aid to the interpretation of mechanisms of graft reject, *Prog. Allergy* **6,** 468 (1962).
5. Algire, G. H., Weaver, J. M., and Prehn, R. T., Growth of cells *in vivo* in diffusion chambers. I. Survival of homografts in immunized mice, *J. Natl. Cancer Inst.* **15,** 493 (1954).
6. Weaver, J. M., Algire, G. H., and Prehn, R. T., The growth of cells *in vivo* in diffusion chambers. II. The role of cells in the destruction of homografts in mice, *J. Natl. Cancer Inst.* **15,** 1737 (1955).
7. Wilson, D. B. and Billingham, R. E., Lymphocytes and transplantation immunity, *Adv. Immunol.* **7,** 189 (1967).
8. Hellström, K. E. and Hellström, I., Cellular immunity against tumor antigens, *Adv. Cancer Res.* **12,** 167 (1969).

REFERENCES   **167**

9. Perlmann, P. and Holm, G. Cytotoxic effects of lymphoid cells *in vitro*, *Adv. Immunol.* **11,** 117 (1969).

10. Lawrence, H. S. and Landy, M., Eds., *Mediators of Cellular Immunity*, Academic Press, New York, 1969.

11. Smith, R. T. and Landy, M., Eds., *Immune Surveillance*, Academic Press, New York, 1970.

12. David, J. R., Cellular hypersensitivity and immunity: Inhibition of macrophage migration and the lymphocyte mediators, *Prog. Allergy* **16,** 300–449 (1971).

13. Stetson, C. A., Ed., President's symposium on effectors of cellular immunity, *Am. J. Pathol.* **60,** 435 (1970).

14. Bloom, B. R. and Glade, P. R., Eds., *In Vitro Methods in Cell-Mediated Immunity*, Academic Press, New York, 1971, 604 pp.

15. Revillard, J. P., Ed., *Cell-Mediated Immunity: In Vitro Correlates*, University Park Press, Baltimore, 1971, 240 pp.

16. Hellström, K. E. and Möller, G.: Immunological and immunogenetic aspects of tumor transplantation, *Prog. Allergy* **9,** 158 (1969).

17. Mitchison, N. A., Passive transfer of transplantation immunity, *Proc. Roy. Soc., Ser. B* **142,** 72 (1954).

18. Bennett, B., Specific suppression of tumor growth by isolated peritoneal macrophages from immunized mice, *J. Immunol.* **95,** 656 (1965).

19. Hellström, K. E., and Hellström, I., Immunologic defenses against cancer in *Immunobiology* (R. A. Good and D. W. Fisher, Eds.), Sinauer Associates, Stamford, Connecticut, 1971, p. 209.

20. Mitchison, N. A., Studies on the immunologic response to foreign tumor transplants in the mouse. I. Role of lymph node cells in conferring immunity by adoptive transfer, *J. Exp. Med.* **102,** 157 (1955).

21. Mitchison, N. A. and Dube, O. L., Studies on the immunologic response to foreign tumor transplants in the mouse. II. The relation between hemagglutinating antibody and graft resistance in the normal mouse and mice pretreated with tissue preparations, *J. Exp. Med.* **102,** 179 (1955).

22. Andreini, P., Drasher, M. L., and Mitchison, N. A., Studies on the immunologic response to foreign tumor transplants in the mouse. III. Changes in the weight and content of nucleic acids and protein, of host-lymphoid tissues, *J. Exp. Med.* **102,** 199 (1955).

23. Gershon, R. K., Carter, R. L., and Lane, N. J., Studies on homotransplantable lymphomas in hamsters. IV. Observations on macrophages in the expression of tumor immunity, *Am. J. Pathol.* **51,** 1111 (1967).

24. Granger, G. A. and Weiser, R. S., Homograft target cells: Specific destruction *in vitro* by contact interaction with immune macrophages, *Science* **145,** 1427 (1964).

25. Granger, G. A. and Weiser, R. S., Homograft target cells: Contact destruction *in vitro* by immune macrophages, *Science* **151,** 97 (1966).

26. Gorer, P. A., Some recent work on tumor immunity, *Adv. Cancer Res.* **4,** 149 (1956).

27. Zbar, B., Wepsic, H. T., Borsos, T., and Rapp, H. J., Tumor-graft rejection in syngeneic guinea pigs: Evidence for a two-step mechanism, *J. Natl. Cancer Inst.* **44,** 473 (1970).

28. Wiener, J., Spiro, D., and Russell, P. S., An electron microscopic study of the homograft reaction, *Am. J. Pathol.* **44,** 319 (1964).

29. Wiener, J., Lattes, R. G., and Pearl, J. S., Vascular permeability and leukocyte emigration in allograft rejection, *Am. J. Pathol.* **55,** 295 (1969).

30. Simonsen, M., *Biological Incompatibility in Kidney Transplantation in Dogs,* Ejnar Munksgaard, Copenhagen, 1953, 86 pp.

31. Porter, K. A., Joseph, N. H., Rendall, J. M., Stolinski, C., Hoehn, R. J., and Calne, R. Y., The role of lymphocytes in the rejection of canine renal homotransplants, *Lab. Invest.* **13,** 1080 (1964).

32. Feldman, J. D. and Lee, S., Renal homotransplantation in rats. I. Allogeneic recipients, *J. Exp. Med.* **126,** 783 (1967).

33. Guttmann, R. D., Lindquist, R. R., Parker, R. M., Carpenter, C. B., and Merrill, J. P., Renal transplantation in the inbred rat. I. Morphologic, immunologic, and functional alterations during acute rejection, *Transplantation* **5,** 668 (1967).

34. Lindquist, R. R., Guttmann, R. D., and Merrill, J. P., Renal transplantation in the inbred rat. II. An immunohistochemical study of acute allograft rejection, *Am. J. Pathol.* **52,** 531 (1968).

35. Flax, M. H. and Barnes, B. A., The role of vascular injury in pulmonary allograft rejection, *Transplantation* **4,** 66 (1966).

36. Lee, S. and Edgington, T. S., Heterotopic liver transplantation utilizing inbred rat strains. I. Characterization of allogeneic graft rejection and the effects of biliary obstruction and portal vein circulation on liver regeneration, *Am. J. Pathol.* **52,** 649 (1968).

37. Flax, M. H. and Caulfield, J. B., Cellular and vascular components of allergic contact dermatitis. Light and electron microscopic observations, *Am. J. Pathol.* **43,** 1031 (1963).

38. Willms-Kretschmer, K., Flax, M. H., and Cotran, R. S., The fine structure of the vascular response in hapten-specific delayed hypersensitivity and contact dermatitis, *Lab. Invest.* **17,** 334 (1967).

39. Søndergaard, J. and Greaves, M. W., Recovery of a pharmacologically active fatty acid during the inflammatory reaction, invoked by patch testing in allergic dermatitis, *Int. Arch. Allergy* **39,** 56 (1970).

40. Gell, P. G. H. and Hinde, I. T., The histology of the tuberculin reaction and its modification by cortisone, *Brit. J. Exp. Pathol.* **32,** 516 (1951).

41. Gell, P. G. H., Cytologic events in hypersensitivity reactions, in *Cellular and Humoral Aspects of the Hypersensitive States* (H. S. Lawrence, Ed.), Hoeber-Harper, New York, 1959, p. 43.

42. Williams, R. M. and Waksman, B. H., Thymus-derived cells in early phase of tuberculin reaction, *J. Immunol.* **103,** 1435 (1969).

43. Lubaroff, D. M. and Waksman, B. H., Bone marrow as source of cells in reactions of cellular hypersensitivity. I. Passive transfer of tuberculin sensitivity in syngeneic systems, *J. Exp. Med.* **128,** 1425 (1968).

44. Lubaroff, D. M. and Waksman, B. H., Bone marrow as source of cells in reactions of cellular hypersensitivity. II. Identification of allogeneic or hybrid cells by immunofluorescence in passively transferred tuberculin reactions, *J. Exp. Med.* **128,** 1437 (1968).

45. Wiener, J., Lattes, R. G., and Spiro, D., An electron microscopic study of leukocyte emigration and vascular permeability in tuberculin sensitivity, *Am. J. Pathol.* **50,** 485 (1967).

46. Voisin, G. A. and Toullet, F., Modifications of vascular permeability in immunological reactions mediated through cells, in *Ciba Foundation Symposium on Cellular Aspects of Immunity* (G. E. W. Wolstenholme and M. O'Connor, Eds.), Churchill, London, 1960, p. 373.

47. Voisin, G. A., Toullet, F., and Voisin, J., Études sur l'hypersensibilité. III. Caractère géneral du phénomène d'augmentation de perméabilité vasculaire au niveau des réactions d'hypersensibilité de type retardé, *Ann. Inst. Pasteur* **106**, 353 (1964).

48. Goldberg, B., Kantor, F. S., and Benacerraf, B., An electron microscopic study of delayed sensitivity to ferritin in guinea pigs, *Brit. J. Exp. Pathol.* **43**, 621 (1962).

49. Dvorak, H. F., Simpson, B. A., Flax, M. H., and Leskowitz, S., The fate of antigen in delayed hypersensitivity skin reactions, *J. Immunol.* **104**, 718–727 (1970).

50. Nagaya, H. and Sieker, H. O., Histochemical study of aminopeptidase and acid and alkaline phosphatase in the tuberculin reaction, *Am. Rev. Resp. Dis.* **91**, 245 (1965).

51. Dannenberg, A. M., Jr., Cellular hypersensitivity and cellular immunity in the pathogenesis of tuberculosis: Specificity, systemic and local nature, and associated macrophage enzymes, *Bacterial. Rev.* **32**, 85 (1968).

52. Weiss, C. and Boyer-Manstein, M. L., On the mechanism of liquefaction of tubercles. I. The behavior of endocellular proteinases in tubercles developing in the lungs of rabbits, *Am. Rev. Tuberc.* **63**, 694 (1951).

53. Waksman, B. H. and Adams, R. D., A histologic study of the early lesion of experimental allergic encephalomyelitis in the guinea pig and rabbit, *Am. J. Pathol.* **41**, 135 (1962).

54. Lampert, P. W., Demyelination and remyelination in experimental autoallergic encephalomyelitis, *J. Neuropathol.* **24**, 371 (1965).

55. Lampert, P. W., Electron microscopic studies on ordinary and hyperacute experimental allergic encephalomyelitis, *Acta Neuropathol.* **9**, 99 (1967).

56. Åstromm, K. E., Webster, H. deF., and Arnason, B. G., The initial lesion in experimental allergic neuritis. A phase and electron microscopic study, *J. Exp. Med.* **128**, 469 (1968).

57. Flax, M. H., Experimental allergic thyroiditis in the guinea pig. II. Morphologic studies of development of disease, *Lab. Invest.* **12**, 199 (1963).

58. Billingham, R. E., Brent, L., and Medawar, P. B., Quantitative studies on tissue transplantation immunity. II. The origin, strength, and duration of actively and adoptively acquired immunity, *Proc. Roy. Soc. B* **143**, 58 (1954).

59. Billingham, R. E., Silvers, W. K., and Wilson, D. B., Further studies on adoptive transfer of sensitivity to skin homografts, *J. Exp. Med.* **118**, 397 (1963).

60. Perey, D. Y. E., Dupuy, J. M., and Good, R. A., Effector mechanisms of skin homograft rejection in agammaglobulinemic chickens, *Transplantation* **9**, 8 (1970).

61. Pearsall, N. W. and Weiser, R. S., The macrophage in allograft immunity. II. Passive transfer with immune macrophages, *J. Reticuloendothel. Soc.* **5**, 121 (1968).

62. Najarian, J. S. and Feldman, J. D., Passive transfer of transplantation immunity. IV. Transplantation antibody from extracts of sensitized lymphoid cells, *J. Exp. Med.* **118**, 759 (1963).

63. Powell, A. E., Ray, O., Hubay, C. A., and Holden, W. D., The induced rejection of guinea pig skin homografts by a partially purified transfer factor, *J. Immunol.* **92**, 73 (1964).

64. Lawrence, H. S., Transfer factor, *Adv. Immunol.* **11,** 196 (1969).

65. Simonsen, M., Graft-versus-host reactions. Their natural history, and applicability as tools of research, *Prog. Allergy* **6,** 349 (1962).

66. Nisbet, N. W. and Heslop, B. F., Runt disease, *Brit. Med. J.* **1,** 129 (1962).

67. Good, R. A., Dalmasso, A. P., Martinez, C., Archer, O. K., Pierce, J. C., and Papermaster, B. W., The role of the thymus in development of immunologic capacity in rabbits and mice, *J. Exp. Med.* **116,** 773 (1962).

68. Gorer, P. A. and Boyse, E. A., Pathological changes in F₁ hybrid mice following transplantation of spleen cells from donors of the parental strains, *Immunology* **2,** 182 (1959).

69. Aisenberg, A. C., Wilkes, B., and Waksman, B. H., The production of runt disease in rats thymectomized at birth, *J. Exp. Med.* **116,** 759 (1962).

70. Streilein, J. W., and Billingham, R. E., An analysis of graft-versus-host disease in Syrian hamsters. I. The epidermolytic syndrome: Description and studies on its procurement, *J. Exp. Med.* **132,** 163 (1970).

71. Schlesinger, M. and Essner, E., Histochemical and electron microscopic studies of the liver in runt disease, *Am. J. Pathol.* **47,** 371 (1965).

72. Jutila, J. W. and Weiser, R. S., Studies on homologous disease. I. Factors concerned in the production of homologous disease of mice, *J. Immunol.* **88,** 621 (1962).

73. Voisin, G. A., Protection against runting by specific treatment of new-born mice, followed by increased tolerance, *Ciba Foundation Symposium on Transplantation* (G. E. W. Wolstenholme and M. P. Cameron, Eds.), Little, Brown, Boston, Massachusetts, 1962, p. 286.

74. Streilein, J. W. and Billingham, R. E., An analysis of graft-versus-host disease in Syrian hamsters. II. The epidermolytic syndrome: studies of its pathogenesis, *J. Exp. Med.* **132,** 181 (1970).

75. Binhammer, R. T., Epstein, S., and Whitehouse, A., Development of parabiosis intoxication in rat parabionts, *Anat. Rec.* **145,** 503 (1963).

76. Cornelius, E. A., Clinical, hematologic, and pathologic changes following parabiosis of syngeneic tolerant and intolerant mice, *Lab. Invest.* **19,** 282 (1968).

77. Cornelius, E. A., Yunis, E. J., Martinez, C., and Good, R. A., Pathologic features of parabiosis intoxication, *Lab. Invest.* **19,** 324 (1968).

78. Howard, J. G. and Woodruff, M. F. A., Effect of the graft-versus-host reaction on the immunological responsiveness of the mouse, *Proc. Roy. Soc. B* **154,** 532 (1961).

79. Blaese, R. M., Martinez, C., and Good, R. A., Immunologic incompetence of immunologically runted animals, *J. Exp. Med.* **119,** 211 (1964).

80. Barnes, D. W. H., Loutit, J. F., and Micklem, H. S., "Secondary disease" of radiation chimeras: A syndrome due to lymphoid aplasia, *Ann. N. Y. Acad. Sci.* **99,** 374 (1962).

81. Barnes, D. W. H. and Mole, R. H., Aplastic anemia in sublethally irradiated mice given allogeneic lymph node cells, *Brit. J. Haematol.* **13,** 482 (1967).

82. Salomon, J. C. and Lecourt, J. C., Studies on homologous disease using germ-free mice, *Proc. Soc. Exp. Biol. Med.* **122,** 640 (1966).

82a. Gershon, R. K. and Kondo, K., Infectious immunological tolerance, *Immunology* **21,** 903–914 (1971).

82b. Gershon, R. K., Cohen, P., Hencin, R., and Liebhaber, S. A., Suppressor T cells, *J. Immunol.* **108**, 586–590 (1972).

83. Elkins, W. L., Cellular and pathologic aspects of graft-versus-host reactions, *Prog. Allergy* **15**, (1971), in press.

84. Dvorak, H. F., Kosunen, T. U., and Waksman, B. H., The "transfer reaction" in the rabbit. I. A histologic study, *Lab. Invest.* **12**, 58 (1963).

85. Elkins, W. L., Invasion and destruction of homologous kidney by locally inoculated lymphoid cells, *J. Exp. Med.* **120**, 329 (1964).

86. Elkins, W. L., The interaction of donor and host lymphoid cells in the pathogenesis of renal cortical destruction induced by a local graft-versus-host reaction, *J. Exp. Med.* **123**, 103 (1966).

87. Snell, G. D., Winn, H. J., and Kandutsch, A. A., A quantitative study of cellular immunity, *J. Immunol.* **87**, 1 (1961).

88. Bennett, B., Specific suppression of tumor growth by isolated peritoneal macrophages from immunized mice, *J. Immunol.* **95**, 656 (1965).

89. McKhann, C. F., Destruction of immune lymphoid cells in transplantation immunity, *J. Immunol.* **91**, 693 (1963).

90. Paker, B., Weiser, R. S., Jutila, J., Evans, C. A., and Blandau, R. J., Mechanisms of tumor homograft rejection: The behavior of sarcoma I ascites tumor in the A/Jax and the C57/Bl/6K mouse, *Ann. N. Y. Acad. Sci.* **101**, 46 (1962).

91. Currie, G. A. and Bagshawe, K. D., The masking of antigens on trophoblast and cancer cells, *Lancet* **1**, 708 (1967).

92. Kirby, D. R. S., Billington, W. D., Bradbury, S., and Goldstein, D. J., Antigen barrier of the mouse placenta, *Nature* **204**, 548 (1964).

93. Hellström, K. E., Hellström, I., and Brawn, J., Abrogation of cellular immunity to antigenically foreign mouse embryonic cells by a serum factor, *Nature* **224**, 914 (1969).

94. Greene, H. S. N., The significance of the heterologous transplantability of human cancer, *Cancer* **5**, 24 (1952).

95. McCullagh, P. J., The transfer of immunological competence to rats tolerant of sheep erythrocytes with lymphocytes from normal rats, *Aust. J. Exp. Biol. Med. Sci.* **48**, 351 (1970).

96. McCullagh, P. J., The immunological capacity of lymphocytes from normal donors after their transfer to rats tolerant of sheep erythrocytes, *Aust. J. Exp. Biol. Med. Sci.* **48**, 369 (1970).

97. Möller, G. and Möller, E., Plaque-formation by nonimmune and x-irradiated lymphoic cells on monolayers of mouse embryo cells, *Nature* **208**, 260 (1965).

98. Gershon, R. K. and Kondo, K., Cell interactions in the induction of tolerance: The role of thymic lymphocytes, *Immunology* **18**, 721 (1970).

98a. Asherson, G. L., Zembala, M., and Barnes, R. M. R., The mechanism of immunological unresponsiveness to picryl chloride and the possible role of antibody-mediated depression, *Clin. Exp. Immunol.* **9**, 111 (1971).

99. Hellström, K. E. and Hellström, I., Immunological enhancement as studied by cell culture techniques, *Ann. Rev. Microbiol.* **24**, 373 (1970).

100. Mitchison, N. A., Perspectives of immunological tolerance in transplantation, *Transplant. Proc.* **3**, 953 (1971).

100a. Allison, A. C., Denman, A. M., and Barnes, R. D., Cooperating and controlling functions of thymus-derived lymphocytes in relation to autoimmunity, *Lancet* **2**, 135 (1971).

101. Radovich, J. and Talmage, D. W., Antigenic competition: Cellular or humoral, *Science* **158**, 512 (1967).

102. Gershon, R. K. and Kondo, K., Antigenic competition between heterologous erythrocytes. I. Thymic dependency, *J. Immunol.* **106**, 1524 (1971).

103. Möller, G. and Sjöberg, O., Effect of antigenic competition on antigen-sensitive cells and on adoptively transferred immunocompetent cells, *Cell. Immunol.* **1**, 110 (1970).

104. Möller, G., Induction of antigenic competition with thymus-dependent antigens. Effect on DNA synthesis in spleen cells, *J. Immunol.* **106**, 1566 (1971).

105. Wust, C. J. and Hanna, M. G., Jr., The effect of actinomycin D on the immune response to two antigens given in sequence, *J. Reticuloendothel. Soc.* **3**, 415 (1966).

106. Fauci, A. S. and Johnson, J. S., Suppression of antibody synthesis. I. Evidence for a circulating inhibitor of antibody synthesis demonstrated at the cellular level, *J. Immunol.* **107**, 1052 (1971).

107. Fauci, A. S. and Johnson, J. S., Suppression of antibody synthesis. II. The effect of carrier-specific cells upon haptenic competition, *J. Immunol.* **107**, 1057 (1971).

108. Liacopoulos, P., Halpern, B. N., and Perramant, F., Unresponsiveness to unrelated antigens induced by paralyzing doses of bovine serum albumin, *Nature* **195**, 1112 (1962).

109. Neveu, T., Halpern, B. N., Liacopoulos, P., Biozzi, G., and Branellec, A., Repression of delayed hypersensitivity to conjugated serum albumin during immune paralysis induced in guinea pig by heterologous proteins, *Nature* **197**, 1023 (1963).

110. Liacopoulos, P., Merchant, B., and Harrell, B. E., Inhibition of the graft-versus-host reaction by pretreatment of donors with various antigens, *Transplantation* **5**, 1423 (1967).

111. Kantor, F. S., Hall, C. B., and Lipsmeyer, E. A., Regulatory mechanisms in delayed hypersensitivity, in *Cellular Interactions in the Immune Response* (S. Cohen, G. Cudkowicz, and R. T. McCluskey, Eds.), S. Karger, Basel, Switzerland 1971, p. 213.

112. Okumra, K. and Tada, T., Regulation of homocytotropic antibody formation in the rat. III. Effect of thymectomy and splenectomy, *J. Immunol.* **106**, 1019 (1971).

112a. Okumura, K. and Tada, T., Regulation of homocytotropic antibody formation in the rat. VI. Inhibitory effect of thymocytes on the homocytotropic antibody response, *J. Immunol.* **107**, 1682 (1971).

113. Raff, M. C. and Cantor, H. I., Subpopulations of thymus cells and thymus-derived lymphocytes in *Progress in Immunology* (D. B. Amos, Ed.), Academic Press, New York, 1971, p. 83.

114. Nakashima, I., Kobayashi, T., and Kato, N., Alterations in the antibody response to bovine serum albumin by capsular polysaccharide of Klebsiella pneumoniae, *J. Immunol.* **107**, 1112 (1971).

114a. Jacobson, E. B. and Hersenberg, L. A., Active suppression of immunoglobulin allotype synthesis. I. Chronic suppression after perinatal exposure to maternal antibody to paternal allotype in (SJL + BALB/c)F₁ mice, *J. Exp. Med.* **135**, 1151, 1972.

114b. Jacobson, E. B., Herzenberg, L. A., Riblet, R., and Herzenberg, L. A., Active suppression of immunoglobulin allotype synthesis. II. Transfer of suppressing factor with spleen cells, *J. Exp. Med.* **135,** 1163 (1972).

115. Cudkowicz, G. and Stimpfling, J. H., Hybrid resistance to parental marrow grafts: Association with the K region of H-2, *Science* **144,** 1339 (1964).

116. Möller, G. and Möller, E., Interactions between allogeneic cells in tissue transplantation, *Ann. N. Y. Acad. Sci.* **129,** 735 (1966).

117. Hellström, K. E. and Hellström, I., Allogeneic inhibition of transplanted tumor cells, *Prog. Exp. Tumor Res.* **9,** 41 (1967).

118. Lindholm, L., Lapp, W., and Möller, E., Allogeneic inhibition in thymectomized animals lacking homograft reactivity, *Nature* **228,** 1326 (1970).

118a. Gregory, C. J., McCulloch, E. A., and Till, J. E., Repressed growth of C57Bl marrow in hybrid hosts reversed by antisera directed against non-H2 alloantigens, *Transplantation* **13,** 138–141 (1972).

119. Hellström, K. E., Hellström, I., and Bergheden, C., Allogeneic inhibition of tumour cells by *in vitro* contact with cells containing foreign H-2 antigens, *Nature* **208,** 458 (1965).

120. Dutton, R. W. *In vitro* studies of immunological responses of lymphoid cells, *Adv. Immunol.* **6,** 253 (1967).

121. Müller-Eberhard, H. J., Perlmann, P., Perlmann, H., and Manni, J. A., Destruction of complement-target cell complexes by mononuclea leukocytes, *Bayer Symp. Curr. Probl. Immunol.* **1,** 5 (1969).

122. Govaerts, A., Cellular antibodies in kidney homotransplantation, *J. Immunol.* **85,** 516 (1960).

123. Rosenau, W. and Moon, H. D., Lysis of homologous cells by sensitized lymphocytes in tissue culture, *J. Natl. Cancer Inst.* **27,** 471 (1961).

124. Rosenau, W. and Moon, H. D., Effect of splenic homogenates on homologous cells *in vitro, Lab. Invest.* **11,** 1260 (1962).

125. Wilson, D. B., The reaction of immunologically activated lymphoid cells against homologous target tissue cells *in vitro, J. Cell Comp. Physiol.* **62,** 273 (1963).

126. Taylor, H. E. and Culling, C. F. A., Cytopathic effect *in vitro* of sensitized homologous and heterologous spleen cells on fibroblasts, *Lab. Invest.* **12,** 884 (1963).

127. Vainio, T., Koskimies, O., Perlmann, P., Perlmann, H., and Klein, G., *In vitro* cytotoxic effect of lymphoid cells from mice immunized with allogeneic tissue, *Nature* **204,** 453 (1964).

128. Brondz, B. D., Interaction of immune lymphocytes *in vitro* with normal and neoplastic tissue cells, *Folia Biol.* **10,** 164 (1964).

129. Brunner, K. T., Mauel, J., and Schindler, R., *In vitro* studies of cell-bound immunity; cloning assay of the cytotoxic action of sensitized lymphoid cells on allogeneic target cells, *Immunology* **11,** 499 (1966).

130. Brunner, K. T., Mauel, J., Rudolph, H., and Chapuis, B., Studies of allograft immunity in mice. I. Induction, development, and *in vitro* assay of cellular immunity, *Immunology* **18,** 501 (1970).

131. Mauel, J., Rudolph, H., Chapuis, B., and Brunner, K. T., Studies of allograft immunity in mice. II. Mechanism of target cell inactivation *in vitro* by sensitized lymphocytes, *Immunology* **18,** 517 (1970).

132. Wilson, D. B., Quantitative studies on the behavior of sensitized lymphocytes *in vitro.* I. Relationship of the degree of destruction of homologous target cells to

the number of lymphocytes and to the time of contact in culture and consideration of the effects of isoimmune serum, *J. Exp. Med.* **122,** 143 (1965).

133.   Wilson, D. B., Quantitative studies on the behavior of sensitized lymphocytes *in vitro*. II. Inhibitory influence of the immune suppressor, imuran, on the destructive reaction of sensitized lymphoid cells against homologous target cells, *J. Exp. Med.* **122,** 167 (1965).

134.   Dumonde, D. C., Tissue-specific antigens, *Adv. Immunol.* **5,** 245 (1966).

135.   Perlmann, P., Perlmann, H., Wasserman, J., and Packalen, T., Lysis of chicken erythrocytes sensitized with PPD by lymphoid cells from guinea pigs immunized with tubercle bacilli, *Int. Arch. Allergy* **38,** 204 (1970).

136.   Brondz, B. D., Complex specificity of immune lymphocytes in allogeneic cell cultures, *Folia Biol.* **14,** 115 (1968).

137.   Holm, G. and Perlmann, P., Cytotoxicity of lymphocytes and its suppression, *Antibiot. Chemother.* **15,** 295 (1969).

138.   Biberfeld, P., Holm, G., and Perlmann, P., Inhibition of lymphocyte peripolesis and cytotoxic action *in vitro* by antilymphocyte serum (ALS), *Exp. Cell Res.* **54,** 136 (1969).

139.   Winkler, G. F. and Arnason, B. G., Antiserum to immunoglobulin A: Inhibition of cell-mediated demyelination in tissue culture, *Science* **153,** 75 (1966).

140.   Canty, T. G. and Wunderlich, J. R., Quantitative *in vitro* assay of cytotoxic cellular immunity, *J. Natl. Cancer Inst.* **45,** 761 (1970).

141.   Möller, E., Antagonistic effects of humoral isoantibodies on the *in vitro* cytotoxicity of immune lymphoid cells, *J. Exp. Med.* **122,** 11 (1965).

142.   Brunner, K. T., Mauel, J., Cerottini, J.-C., and Chapuis, B., Quantitative assay of the lytic action of immune lymphoid cells on ^{51}Cr-labeled allogeneic target cells *in vitro;* inhibition by isoantibody and by drugs, *Immunology* **14,** 181 (1968).

143.   Brunner, K. T., Mauel, J., Cerottini, J.-C., Rudolph, H., and Chapuis, B., *In vitro* studies of cellular and humoral immunity induced by tumor allografts, in *Mechanisms of Inflammation Induced by Immune Reactions* (P. A. Miescher and P. Grabar, Eds.), Grune and Stratton, New York, 1968, p. 342.

144.   Hellström, I. E., Hellström, K. E., Pierce, G. E., and Bill, A. H., Demonstration of cell-bound and humoral immunity against neuroblastoma cells, *Proc. Natl. Acad. Sci.* **60,** 1231 (1968).

145.   Hellström, I., Hellström, K. E., Evans, C. A., Heppner, G. H., Pierce, G. E., and Yang, J. P. S., Serum-mediated protection of neoplastic cells from inhibition by lymphocytes immune to their tumor-specific antigens, *Proc. Natl. Acad. Sci.* **62,** 362 (1969).

146.   Perlmann, P., Nilsson, H., and Leon, M. A., Inhibition of cytotoxicity of lymphocytes by concanavalin A *in vitro, Science* **168,** 1112 (1970).

147.   Shacks, S. J. and Granger, G. A., Studies on *in vitro* models of cellular immunity, *J. Reticuloendothel. Soc.* **10,** 28 (1971).

148.   Amos, D. B., Ed., *Progress in Immunology,* Academic Press, New York, 1971.

149.   Ruddle, N. H. and Waksman, B. H., Cytotoxic effect of lymphocyte-antigen reaction in delayed hypersensitivity, *Science* **157,** 1060 (1967).

150.   Ruddle, N. H. and Waksman, B. H., Cytotoxicity mediated by soluble antigen and lymphocytes in delayed hypersensitivity. I. Characterization of the phenomenon, *J. Exp. Med.* **128,** 1237 (1968).

151. Holm, G. and Perlmann, P., Cytotoxic potential of stimulated human lymphocytes, *J. Exp. Med.* **125**, 721 (1967).

152. Holm, G., Perlmann, P., and Werner, B., Phytohaemagglutinin-induced cytotoxic action of normal lymphoid cells on cells in tissue culture, *Nature* **203**, 841 (1964).

153. Granger, G. A. and Williams, T. W., Lymphocyte cytotoxicity *in vitro:* Activation and release of a cytotoxic factor, *Nature* **218**, 1253 (1968).

154. Williams, T. W. and Granger, G. A., Lymphocyte *in vitro* cytotoxicity: correlation of derepression with release of lymphotoxin from human lymphocytes, *J. Immunol.* **103**, 170 (1969).

155. Lundgren, G. and Moller, G., Nonspecific induction of cytotoxicity in normal human lymphocytes *in vitro:* Studies of mechanism and specificity of the reaction, *Clin. Exp. Immunol.* **4**, 435 (1969).

155a. Stavy, L., Treves, A. J., and Feldman, M., Capacity of thymic cells to effect target cell lysis following treatment with concanavalin A., *Cell. Immunol.* **3**, 623–628 (1972).

156. Lundgren, G., Induction and suppression of the cytotoxic activity of human lymphocytes *in vitro* by heterologous antilymphocyte serum, *Clin. Exp. Immunol.* **5**, 381 (1969).

157. Taylor, H. E. and Culling, C. F. A., Cytopathic effect of sensitized spleen cells on fibroblasts. The protective effect of heparin, *Lab. Invest.* **15**, 1960 (1966).

157a. Berke, G., Sullivan, K. A., and Amos, B., Rejection of ascites tumor allografts. I. Isolation, characterization, and *in vitro* reactivity of peritoneal lymphoid effector cells from BALB/c mice immune to E14 leukosis, *J. Exp. Med.* **135**, 1334–1350 (1972).

158. Cerottini, J.-C., Nordin, A. A., and Brunner, K. T., Specific *in vitro* cytotoxicity of thymus-derived lymphocytes sensitized to alloantigens, *Nature* **228**, 1308 (1970).

159. Cerottini, J.-C., Nordin, A. A., and Brunner, K. T., Cellular and humoral response to transplantation antigens. I. Development of alloantibody-forming cells and cytotoxic lymphocytes in the graft-versus-host reaction, *J. Exp. Med.* **134**, 553 (1971).

160. Pelet, J., Brunner, K. T., Nordin, A. A., and Cerottini, J.-C., The relative distribution of cytotoxic lymphocytes and of alloantibody-forming cells in albumin density gradients, *Eur. J. Immunol.* **1**, 238 (1971).

160a. Golstein, P., Wigzell, H., Blomgren, H., and Svedmyr, E. A. J., Cells mediating specific *in vitro* cytotoxicity. II. Probable autonomy of thymus-processed lymphocytes (T cells) for the killing of allogeneic target cells, *J. Exp. Med.* **135**, 890–906 (1972).

161. Brunner, K. T., in *Immunopathology, Sixth International Symposium* (P. Miescher, Ed.), Grune and Stratton, New York, in press.

162. Hanaoka, M. and Notake, K., Quantitative studies on the cellular antibody *in vitro.* II. Comparative activities of humoral and cellular antibodies on SC1 cultured leukemic cells, *Ann. Rep. Inst. Virus Res., Kyoto Univ.* **6**, 119 (1963).

163. Sabbadini, E., Studies on the mechanism of target cell lysis induced by immune cells, *J. Reticuloendothel. Soc.* **7**, 551 (1970).

164. Wilson, D. B., Lymphocytes as mediators of cellular immunity: Destruction of homologous target cells in culture, *Transplantation* **5**, 986 (1967).

165. Perlmann, P., Perlmann, H., Wasserman, J., and Packalen, T., Lysis of chicken immunized with tubercle bacilli, *Int. Arch. Allergy* **38**, 204 (1970).

165a. Cerottini, J.-C. and Brunner, K. T., Reversible inhibition of lymphocyte-mediated cytotoxicity by cytochalasin B., *Nat. New Biol.* **237**, 272–273 (1972).

165b. Ferluga, J., Asherson, G. L., and Becker, E. L., The effect of organophosphorus inhibitors, *p*-nitrophenol, and cytochalasin B on cytotoxic killing of tumour cells by immune spleen cells, and the effect of shaking, *Immunology* **23**, 577–590 (1972).

165c. Berke, G., Sullivan, K. A., and Amos, B., Rejection of ascites tumor allografts. II. A pathway for cell-mediated tumor destruction *in vitro* by peritoneal exudate lymphoid cells, *J. Exp. Med.* **136**, 1594–1604 (1972).

165d. Henney, C. S. and Bubbers, J. E., Studies on the mechanism of lymphocyte-mediated cytolysis. I. The role of divalent cations in cytolysis by T lymphocytes, *J. Immunol.* **110**, 63 (1973).

166. Williams, T. W. and Granger, G. A., Lymphocyte *in vitro* cytotoxicity: Lymphotoxins of several mammalian species, *Nature* **219**, 1076 (1968).

167. Granger, G. A., Kolb, W. P., and Williams, T. W., *In vitro* studies of cell-associated transplantation immunity, in *Cellular Recognition* (R. T. Smith and R. A. Good, Eds.), Appleton-Century-Crofts, New York, 1969, p. 235.

168. Dumonde, D. C., Wolstencrofts, R. A., Panayi, G. S., Matthew, M., Morely, J., and Howson, W. T., "Lymphokines": Nonantibody mediators of cellular immunity generated by lymphocyte activation, *Nature* **224**, 38 (1969).

169. Heiser, E. R. and Weiser, R. S., Factors in delayed sensitivity: Lymphocyte and macrophage cytotoxins in the tuberculin reaction, *J. Immunol.* **103**, 570 (1969).

170. Pincus, W. B., Cell-free cytotoxic fluids from tuberculin-treated guinea pigs, *J. Reticuloendothel. Soc.* **4**, 140 (1967).

171. Hanaoka, M. and Notake, K., Quantitative studies on the cellular antibody *in vitro*. I. Inhibitory effect of sensitized homologous lymph node cells on strain SC1 of cultured leukemic cells, *Ann. Rep. Inst. Virus Res., Kyoto Univ.* **5**, 134 (1962).

172. Yoshida, T. O., Further evidence of immunologic reaction against methylcholanthrene-induced autochthonous tumors, *Jap. J. Exp. Med.* **35**, 115 (1965).

173. Rosenau, W. and Morton, D. L., Tumor-specific inhibition of growth of methylcholanthrene-induced sarcomas *in vivo* and *in vitro* by sensitized isologous lymphoid cells, *J. Natl. Cancer Inst.* **36**, 825 (1966).

174. Ming, S.-C., Klein, E., and Klein, G., Inhibition of DNA synthesis of target cells *in vitro* by sensitized lymphocytes, *Nature* **215**, 1390 (1967).

175. Holm, G., Perlmann, P., and Johansson, B., Impaired phytohaemagglutinin-induced cytotoxicity *in vitro* of lymphocytes from patients with Hodgkin's disease or chronic lymphatic leukaemia, *Clin. Exp. Immunol.* **2**, 351 (1967).

176. Hardy, D. A., Ling, N. R., Wallin, J., and Airet, T., Destruction of lymphoid cells by activated human lymphocytes, *Nature* **227**, 723 (1970).

177. Oppenheim, J. J., Zbar, B., and Rapp, H., Specific inhibition of tumor cell DNA synthesis *in vitro* by lymphocytes from peritoneal exudate of immunized syngeneic guinea pigs, *Proc. Natl. Acad. Sci.* **66**, 1119 (1970).

178. Ginsburg, H. and Sachs, L., Destruction of mouse and rat embryo cells in tissue culture by lymph node cells from unsensitized rats, *J. Cell Comp. Physiol.* **66**, 199 (1965).

179. Ginsburg, H., Hollander, N., and Feldman, M., The development of hypersensitive lymphocytes in cell culture, *J. Exp. Med.* **134**, 1062 (1971).

180. Kakulas, B. A., Destruction of differentiated muscle cultures by sensitized lymphoid cells, *J. Pathol. Bacterial* **91**, 495 (1966).

181. Rose, N. R., Kite, J. H., Jr., Doebbler, T. K., and Brown, R. C., *In vitro* reactions of lymphoid cells with thyroid tissue, in *Cell-Bound Antibodies* (B. Amos and H. Koprowski, Eds.), Wistar Institute Press, Philadelphia, 1963, p. 19.

182. Perlmann, P. and Broberger, O., The possible role of immune mechanisms in tissue damage in ulcerative colitis, in *Mechanism of Cell and Tissue Damage Produced by Immune Reactions* (P. Grabar and P. Miescher, Eds.), B. Schwabe, Basel and Stuttgart, 1962, p. 288.

183. Perlmann, P. and Broberger, O., *In vitro* studies of ulcerative colitis. II. Cytotoxic action of white blood cells from patients on human fetal colon cells, *J. Exp. Med.* **117,** 717 (1963).

184. Koprowski, H. and Fernandes, M. V., Autosensitization reaction *in vitro*—Contactual agglutination of sensitized lymph node cells in brain tissue culture accompanied by destruction of glial elements, *J. Exp. Med.* **116,** 467 (1962).

185. Berg, O. and Källén, B., White blood cells from animals with experimental allergic encephalomyelitis tested on glia cells in tissue culture, *Acta Pathol. Microbiol. Scand.* **58,** 33 (1963).

186. Berg, O. and Källén, B., Studies of experimental allergic encephalomyelitis and multiple sclerosis with aid of glia cell culture, *Acta Neurol. Scand.* **41,** Suppl. 13, 625 (1965).

187. Arnason, B. G. W., Winkler, G. F., and Hadler, N. M., Cell-mediated demyelination of peripheral nerve in tissue culture, *Lab. Invest.* **21,** 1 (1969).

188. Perlmann, P. and Perlmann, H., Contactual lysis of antibody-coated chicken erythrocytes by purified lymphocytes, *Cell. Immunol.* **1,** 300 (1970).

189. Williams, T. W. and Granger, G. A., Lymphocyte *in vitro* cytotoxicity: Mechanisms of lymphotoxin-induced target cell destruction, *J. Immunol.* **102,** 911 (1969).

190. Lubaroff, D. M. and Ritts, R. E., *In vitro* cytotoxicity in delayed-type hypersensitivity and immunologic tolerance, *Proc. Soc. Exp. Biol. Med.* **116,** 823 (1964).

191. Delescluse, J. and Turk, J. L., Lymphocyte cytotoxicity: A possible *in vitro* test for contact dermatitis, *Lancet* **2,** 75 (1970).

192. Milner, J. E. *In vitro* lymphocyte responses in contact hypersensitivity, *J. Inv. Dermatol.* **55,** 34 (1970).

193. Williams, T. W. and Granger, G. A., Comparisons of the sensitivities of various cell lines to human lymphotoxin, *Fed. Proc.* **29,** 306 abstr. (1970).

194. Lundgren, G. and Möller, G., Nonspecific induction of cytotoxicity in normal human lymphocytes *in vitro:* Studies of mechanism and specificity of the reaction, *Clin. Exp. Immunol.* **4,** 435 (1969).

195. Friedman, H., Inhibition of antibody plaque formation by sensitized lymphoid cells: Rapid indicator of transplantation immunity, *Science* **145,** 607 (1964).

196. Holm, G. and Perlmann, P., Cytotoxic potential of stimulated human lymphocytes, *J. Exp. Med.* **125,** 721 (1967).

197. Perlmann, P., Broberger, O., and Klein, E., Cytotoxic action of immune lymph node cells on mouse ascites tumor cells, *Fed. Proc.* **21,** 12 (1962).

198. Nathan, C. F., Karnovsky, M. L., and David, J. R., Alterations of macrophage function in MIF-rich supernatants, *Immunopathology: Sixth International Symposium* (P. Miescher, Ed.), Grune and Stratton, New York, in press.

199. Nathan, C. F., Rosenberg, S. A., Karnovsky, M. L., and David, J. R., Effects of MIF-rich supernatants on macrophages, in *Proceedings Fifth Leukocyte Culture Conference,* Ottawa, 1970, in press.

199a. Henney, C. S., Studies on the mechanism of lymphocyte-mediated cytolysis. II. The use of various target cell markers to study cytolytic events, *J. Immunol.* **110,** 73 (1973).

200.   Able, M. E., Lee, J. C., and Rosenau, W., Lymphocyte-target cell interaction *in vitro, Am. J. Pathol.* **60,** 421 (1970).

200a. Biberfeld, P., Cytotoxic interaction of phytohemagglutinin-stimulated blood lymphocytes with monolayer cells: A study by light and electron microscopy, *Cell. Immunol.* **2,** 54 (1971).

201.   Svet-Moldavskii, G. Ya. and Chernyakhovskaya, I. Yu., Interferon and reactions of allogeneic normal and immune lymphocytes with L cells, *Dokl. Akad. Nauk. USSR* **175,** 224 (1967).

202.   Sura, S. N., Chernyakhovskaya, I. Yu., Kagaghidze, Z. G., Fuks, B. B., and Svet-Moldavsky, G. J., Cytochemical study of interaction between lymphocytes and target cells in tissue culture, *Exp. Cell Res.* **24,** 656 (1968).

203.   Henney, C. S. and Lichtenstein, L. M., The role of cyclic AMP in the cytolytic activity of lymphocytes, *J. Immunol.* **107,** 610 (1971).

204.   Rubin, A. L., Stenzel, K. H., Hirschhorn, K., and Bach, F., Histocompatibility and immunologic competence in renal homotransplantation, *Science* **143,** 815 (1964).

205.   Rosenau, W. and Moon, H. D., The inhibitory effect of hydrocortisone on lysis of homologous cells by lymphocytes *in vitro, J. Immunol.* **89,** 422 (1962).

206.   Ginsburg, H. and Sachs, L., Destruction of mouse and rat embryo cells in tissue culture by lymph node cells from unsensitized rats, *J. Cell Comp. Physiol.* **66,** 199 (1965).

207.   Ginsburg, H., Growth and differentiation of cells of lymphoid origin on embryo cell monolayers, in *Methodological Approaches to the Study of Leukemias* (V. Defendi, Ed.), Wistar Institute Press Symposium Monograph, Philadelphia, 1965 Chapter 4, p. 21.

208.   Ginsburg, H., Graft-versus-host reaction in tissue culture. I. Lysis of monolayers of embryo mouse cells from strains differing in the H-2 histocompatibility locus by rat lymphocytes sensitized *in vitro, Immunology* **14,** 621 (1968).

209.   Berke, G., Ax, W., Ginsburg, H., and Feldman, M., Graft reaction in tissue culture. II. Quantification of the lytic action on mouse fibroblasts by rat lymphocytes sensitized on mouse embryo monolayers, *Immunology* **16,** 643 (1969).

210.   Berke, G., Ginsburg, H., Yagil, G., and Feldman, M., Graft reaction in cell culture, *Israel J. Med. Sci.* **5,** 135 (1969).

211.   Ginsburg, H., The function of the delayed sensitivity reaction as revealed in the graft reaction culture, *Adv. Cancer Res.* **13,** 63 (1970).

212.   Berke, G., Yagil, G., Ginsburg, H., and Feldman, M., Kinetic analysis of a graft reaction induced in cell culture, *Immunology* **17,** 721 (1969).

213.   Cohen, I. R. and Feldman, M., The lysis of fibroblasts by lymphocytes sensitized *in vitro:* Specific antigen activates a nonspecific effect, *Cell. Immunol.* **1,** 521 (1971).

214.   Lonai, P. and Feldman, M., Cooperation of lymphoid cells in an *in vitro* graft reaction system. The role of the thymus cell, *Transplantation* **10,** 372 (1970.

215.   Lonai, P. and Feldman, M., Cooperation of lymphoid cells in an *in vitro* graft reaction system. II. The "bone-marrow-derived" cell, *Transplantation* **11,** 446 (1971).

215a. Dyminski, J., and Argyris, B. F., *In vitro* sensitization to transplantation antigens. III. Thymus-bone marrow cooperation, *Transplantation* **13,** 234–238 (1972).

215b. Dyminski, J. and Argyris, B. F., *In vitro* sensitization to transplantation antigens. V. Suppression of T-cell and of B-cell function *in vitro*, *Cell. Immunol.* **5,** 561–569 (1972).

215c. Wagner, H., Feldmann, M., Boyle, W., and Schrader, J. W., Cell-mediated immune response *in vitro*. III. The requirement for macrophages in cytotoxic reactions against cell-bound and subcellular alloantigens, *J. Exp. Med.* **136,** 331–343 (1972).

216. Ginsburg, H. and Lagunoff, D., Aggregation and transformation of rat lymphocytes on rat embryo monolayers, *J. Cell. Biol.* **39,** 392 (1968).

217. Cohen, I. R., Globerson, A., and Feldman, M., Rejection of tumor allografts by mouse spleen cells sensitized *in vitro*, *J. Exp. Med.* **133,** 821 (1971).

218. Hodes, R. J. and Svedmyr, E. A. J., Specific cytotoxicity of H-2 incompatible mouse lymphocytes following mixed culture *in vitro*, *Transplantation* **9,** 470 (1970).

219. Svedmyr, E. A. and Hodes, R. J., On the specificity of cell-mediated cytotoxicity *in vitro*, *Cell. Immunol.* **1,** 644 (1970).

219a. Wagner, H. and Feldmann, M., Cell-mediated immune response *in vitro*. I. A new *in vitro* system for the generation of cell-mediated cytotoxic activity, *Cell. Immunol.* **3,** 405–420 (1972).

219b. Wagner, H., Harris, A. W., and Feldmann, M., Cell-mediated immune response *in vitro*. II. The role of thymus and thymus-derived lymphocytes, *Cell. Immunol.* **4,** 39–50 (1972).

219c. Wagner, H., The correlation between the proliferative and the cytotoxic responses of mouse lymphocytes to allogeneic cells *in vitro*, *J. Immunol.* **109,** 630–637 (1972).

220. Manson, L. A. and Simmons, T., An *in vitro* model for study of the development of the alloimmune response, in *Cellular Interactions in the Immune Response* (S. Cohen, G. Cudkowicz, and R. T. McCluskey, Eds.), S. Karger, Basel, Switzerland, 1971, p. 235.

221. Koldovsky, P., An attempt at *in vitro* sensitization of immunologically competent cells against tumour-specific antigen, *Folia Biol.* **12,** 238 (1966).

222. Cohen, I. R., Globerson, A., and Feldman, M., Autosensitization *in vitro*, *J. Exp. Med.* **133,** 834 (1971).

223. Ginsburg, H., Lysis of target cell monolayers by lymphocytes stimulated with pokeweed mitogen, *Transplantation* **11,** 408 (1971).

224. Ginsburg, H., Cycles of transformation and differentiation of lymphocytes *in vitro*, *Transplant. Proc.* **3,** 883 (1971).

224a. Ginsberg, H. and Hollander, N., Effect of anti-Θserum on target cell lysis produced by lymphocytes stimulated with pokeweed mitogen, *Transplantation* **15,** 257–259 (1973).

225. Ruddle, N. H., and Waksman, B. H., Cytotoxicity mediated by soluble antigen and lymphocytes in delayed hypersensitivity. II. Correlation of the *in vitro* response with skin reactivity, *J. Exp. Med.* **128,** 1255 (1968).

226. Ruddle, N. H. and Waksman, B. H., Cytotoxicity mediated by soluble antigen and lymphocytes in delayed hypersensitivity. III. Analysis of mechanism, *J. Exp. Med.* **128,** 1267 (1968).

227. Granger, G. A. and Williams, T. W., Lymphocyte cytotoxicity *in vitro:* Activation and release of a cytotoxic factor, *Nature* **218,** 1253 (1968).

228. Kolb, W. P. and Granger, G. A., Lymphocyte *in vitro* cytotoxicity: Characterization of human lymphotoxin, *Proc. Natl. Acad. Sci.* **61,** 1250 (1968).

229. Granger, G. A., Shacks, S. J., Williams, T. W., and Kolb, W. P., Lymphocyte *in*

vitro cytotoxicity: Specific release of lymphotoxin-like materials from tuberculin-sensitive lymphoid cells, *Nature* **221,** 1155 (1969).

230.   Dumonde, D. C., Wolstencroft, R. A., Panayi, G. S., Matthew, M., Morley, J., and Howson, W. T., "Lymphokines": Nonantibody mediators of cellular immunity generated by lymphocyte activation, *Nature* **224,** 38 (1969).

231.   Williams, T. W. and Granger, G. A., Lymphocyte *in vitro* cytotoxicity: Correlation of derepression with release of lymphotoxin from human lymphocytes, *J. Immunol.* **103,** 170 (1969).

232.   Williams, T. W. and Granger, G. A., Lymphocyte *in vitro* cytotoxicity: Lymphotoxins of several mammalian species, *Nature* **219,** 1076 (1968).

233.   Granger, G. A., Moore, G. E., White, J. G., Matzinger, P., Sundsmo, J. S., Shupe, S., Kolb, W. P., Kramer, J., and Glade, P. R., Production of lymphotoxin and migration inhibitory factor by established human lymphocytic cell lines, *J. Immunol.* **104,** 1476 (1970).

233a.   Yoshinaga, M. and Waksman, B. H., Regulation of lymphocyte responses *in vitro.* IV. Role of macrophages in rat lymphocyte responses and their inhibition by cytochalasin B, *Ann. Immunol.,* in press.

234.   Williams, T. W. and Granger, G. A., Lymphocyte *in vitro* cytotoxicity: Mechanism of lymphotoxin-induced target cwlfestruction, *J. Immunol.* **102,** 911 (1969).

235.   Kolb, W. P. and Granger, G. A., Lymphocyte *in vitro* cytotoxicity: Characterization of mouse lymphotoxin, *Cell. Immunol.* **1,** 122 (1970).

236.   Rosenberg, S. A., Henrichon, M., Coyne, J., Remold, H. G., and David, J. R., unpublished results.

237.   Coyne, J. A., Remold, H. G., and David, J. R., Guinea pig macrophage inhibitory factor and lymphotoxin: Are they different?, *Fed. Proc.* **30,** 647 abstr. (1971).

238.   Lyampert, I. M. and Toder, V. A., Acid phosphatase measurement in macrophages with the delayed type hypersensitivity, *Biull. Eksp. Biol. Med.* **69,** No. 2, 60 (1970).

239.   Smyth, A. C. and Weiss, L., Electron microscopic study of inhibition of macrophage migration in delayed hypersensitivity, *J. Immunol.* **105,** 1360 (1970).

240.   Lebowitz, A. and Lawrence, H. S., Target cell destruction by antigen-stimulated human lymphocytes, *Fed. Proc.* **28,** 630 abstr. (1969).

241.   Green, J. A., Cooperband, S. R., Rutstein, J. A., and Kibrick, S., Inhibition of target cell proliferation by supernatants from cultures of human peripheral lymphocytes, *J. Immunol.* **105,** 48 (1970).

242.   Smith, R. T., Bausher, J. A. C., and Adler, W. H., Studies of an inhibitor of DNA synthesis and a nonspecific mitogen elaborated by human lymphoblasts, *Am. J. Pathol.* **60,** 495 (1970).

243.   Fialkow, P. J., The induction of chromosomal aberrations *in vitro* by allogeneic lymphocyte extract, *Transplantation* **5,** 989 (1967).

244.   Fialkow, P. J. and Gartler, S. M., Hyperploidy effect of lymphocyte extract on fibroblasts *in vitro, Nature* **211,** 713 (1966).

245.   Fialkow, P. J., Hellström, I., and Hellström, K. E., Chromosomal abnormalities induced *in vitro* by extracts of mouse allogeneic lymphocytes, *Exp. Cell Res.* **49,** 223 (1968).

246.   Scott, D. W. and Waksman, B. H., Mechanism of immunological tolerance. I. Induction of tolerance to bovine -globulin by injection of antigen into intact organs *in vitro, J. Immunol.* **102,** 347 (1969).

247.   Sjöberg, O., Antigenic competition *in vitro* of spleen cells subjected to a graft-versus-host reaction, *Immunology* **21**, 351 (1971).

247a.   Sjöberg, O., Effect of allogeneic cell interaction on the primary immune response *in vitro*. Cell types involved in suppression and stimulation of antibody synthesis, *Clin. Exp. Immunol.* **12**, 365 (1972).

247b.   Scott, M. T., Biological effects of the adjuvant Corynebacterium parvum. I. Inhibition of PHA, mixed lymphocyte and GVH reactivity, *Cell. Immunol.* **5**, 459 (1972).

247c.   Scott, M. T., Biological effects of the adjuvant Corynebacterium parvum. II. Evidence for macrophage-T-cell interaction. *Cell. Immunol.* **5**, 469 (1972).

247d.   Folch, H. and Waksman, B. H., Regulation of lymphocyte response *in vitro*. V. Suppressor activity of adherent and nonadherent rat lymphoid cells, *Cell. Immunol.*, in press.

248.   Hirano, S. and Uyeki, E. M., A study of mixed cell interactions between sensitized and allogeneic mouse spleen cells *in vitro* using the hemolytic plaque assay, *J. Immunol.* **106**, 619 (1970).

248a.   Sulica, A., Tarrab, R., Haimovich, J., and Sela, M., Effect of phytohemagglutinin on thymidine incorporation and antibody production in the secondary response *in vitro* towards a defined hapten, *Eur. J. Immunol.* **1**, 236 (1971).

249.   Wasserman, J., Packalén, T., Perlmann, P., and Perlmann, H., Antibody-induced lysis of PPD-coated chicken erythrocytes by spleen cells of nonimmunized guinea pigs, *Int. Arch. Allergy* **40**, 905 (1971).

249a.   Wasserman, J., Packalén, T., and Perlmann, P., Antibody-induced lysis of thyroglobulin-coated chicken erythrocytes by lymphocytes of nonimmunized guinea pigs, *Int. Arch. Allergy* **41**, 910 (1971).

250.   Carlsson, H. E., Hammarström, S., Lanteli, M., and Perlmann, P., Antibody-induced destruction of colon antigen-coated chicken erythrocytes by normal human lymphocytes, *Eur. J. Immunol.* **1**, 281 (1971).

251.   Resch, K. and Fischer, H., Cell-mediated immune reactions *in vitro*: Cytotoxicity of lymphocytes activated by phytohemagglutinin and antiimmunoglobulin serum, *Eur. J. Immunol.* **1**, 271 (1971).

252.   MacLennan, I. C. M., Loewi, G., and Harding, B., The role of immunoglobulins in lymphocyte-mediated cell damage *in vitro*. I. Comparison of the effects of target cell specific antibody and normal serum factors on cellular damage by immune and nonimmune lymphocytes, *Immunology* **18**, 397 (1970).

253.   MacLennan, I. C. M. and Harding, B., Failure of certain cytotoxic lymphocytes to respond mitotically to phytohaemagglutinin, *Nature* **227**, 1246 (1970).

254.   van Boxel, J. A., Stobo, J. D., Paul, W. E., and Green, I., Antibody-dependent lymphoid cell-mediated cytotoxicity: No requirement for thymus-derived lymphocytes, *Science* **175**, 194 (1972).

254a.   Möller, G. and Svehag, S.-E., Specificity of lymphocyte-mediated cytotoxicity induced by *in vitro* antibody-coated target cells, *Cell. Immunol.* **4**, 1 (1972).

254b.   Basten, A., Miller, J. F. A. P., Sprent, J., and Pye, J., A receptor for antibody on B lymphocytes. I. Method of detection and functional significance, *J. Exp. Med.* **135**, 610 (1972).

254c.   Basten, A., Warner, N. L., and Mandel, T., A receptor for antibody on B-lymphocytes. II. Immunochemical and electron microscopy characteristics, *J. Exp. Med.* **135**, 627 (1972).

255. MacLennan, I. C. M. and Harding, B., The role of immunoglobulins in lymphocyte-mediated cell damage, *in vitro*. II. The mechanism of target cell damage by lymphoid cells from immunized rats, *Immunology* **18**, 405 (1970).

256. Perlmann, P., Perlmann, H., Müller-Eberhard, H. J., and Manni, J. A., Cytotoxic effects of leukocytes triggered by complement bound to target cells, *Science* **163**, 937 (1969).

257. Holm, G. and Perlmann, P., Phytohaemagglutinin-induced cytotoxic action of unsensitized tissue culture cells, *Nature* **207**, 818 (1965).

258. Möller, E. and Lapp, W., Cytotoxic effects *in vitro* by lymphoid cells from specifically tolerant animals, *Immunology* **16**, 561 (1969).

259. Pearsall, N. N. and Weiser, R. S., *The Macrophage,* Lca and Febiger, Philadelphia, 1970, p. 204.

260. Evans, R. and Alexander, P., Cooperation of immune lymphoid cells with macrophages in tumour immunity, *Nature* **228**, 620 (1970).

261. LoBuglio, A. F., Cotran, R. S., and Jandl, J. H., Red cells coated with immunoglobulin G: Binding and sphering by mononuclear cells in man, *Science* **158**, 1582 (1967).

261a. Evans, R. and Alexander, P., Role of macrophages in tumour immunity. I. Cooperation between macrophages and lymphoid cells in syngeneic tumour immunity, *Immunology* **23**, 615 (1972).

261b. Evans, R. and Alexander, P., Role of macrophages in tumour immunity. II. Involvement of a macrophage cytophilic factor during syngeneic tumour growth inhibition, *Immunology* **23**, 627 (1972).

261c. Lohmann-Matthes, M.-L., Schipper, H., and Fischer, H., Macrophage-mediated cytotoxicity against allogeneic target cells *in vitro, Eur. J. Immunol.* **2**, 45 (1972).

262. Journey, L. J. and Amos, D. B., An electron microscope study of histiocyte response to ascites tumor homografts, *Cancer Res.* **22**, 998 (1962).

263. Chambers, V. C. and Weiser, R. S., The ultrastructure of target cells and immune macrophages during their interaction *in vitro, Cancer Res.* **29**, 301 (1969).

264. McIvor, K. L. and Weiser, R. S., Mechanisms of target cell destruction by alloimmune peritoneal macrophages. I. The effect of treatment with sodium fluoride, *Immunology* **20**, 307 (1971).

265. Weissmann, G., The many-faceted lysosome, in *Immunobiology* (R. A. Good and D. W. Fisher, Eds.), Sinauer Associates Stamford, Connecticut, 1971, p. 37.

266. Weissmann, G., Lysosomes, *New England J. Med.* **273**, 1084, 1143 (1965).

267. Heise, E. R. and Weiser, R. S., Factors in delayed sensitivity: Lymphocyte and macrophage cytotoxins in the tuberculin reaction, *J. Immunol.* **103**, 570 (1969).

268. McIvor, K. L. and Weiser, R. S., Mechanisms of target cell destruction by alloimmune peritoneal macrophages. II. Release of a specific cytotoxin from interacting cells, *Immunology* **20**, 315 (1971).

269. Pincus, W. B., Sokolic, I. H., and Readler, B., The demonstration of a phenomenon *in vitro* applicable to the study of delayed hypersensitivity, *J. Allergy* **34**, 337 (1963).

270. Pincus, W. B., Formation of cytotoxic factor by macrophages from normal guinea pigs, *J. Reticuloendothel. Soc.* **4**, 122 (1967).

271. Pincus, W. B., Woods, W. W., and Pang, R. K., Immune-specific cytotoxic factor formation by small lymphocytes, *J. Reticuloendothel. Soc.* **7**, 220 (1970).

272. Sintek, D. E. and Pincus, W. P., Cytotoxic factor from peritoneal cells: Purification and characteristics, *J. Reticuloendothel. Soc.* **8,** 508 (1970).

273. Pincus, W. B., Spanis, C. W., and Sintek, D. E., Cytotoxic factor from peritoneal cells: Site of action, *J. Reticuloendothel. Soc.* **9,** 552 (1971).

273a. Nathan, C. F., Karnovksy, M. L., and David, J. R., Alterations of macrophage functions by mediators from lymphocytes, *J. Exp. Med.* **133,** 1356 (1971).

274. Lundgren, G., Zukoski, C. F., and Möller, G., Differential effects of human granulocytes and lymphocytes on human fibroblasts *in vitro, Clin. Exp. Immunol.* **3,** 817 (1968).

275. Falk, R. E., Falk, J. A., Möller, E., and Möller, G., Lymphocyte-activating factors released *in vitro* by sensitized and nonsensitized human lymphocytes, *Cell. Immunol.* **1,** 150 (1970).

276. Winkler, G. F., *In vitro* demyelination of peripheral nerve induced with sensitized cells, *Ann. N. Y. Acad. Sci.* **122,** 287 (1965).

Chapter Eight

Cell Mediated Immunity and The Response to Infection

ROBERT J. NORTH

Trudeau Institute, Sarranac Lake, New York 12983

Immunity to infection with those bacteria which can survive and multiply in host macrophages is not mediated by humoral antibodies. Neither treatment with killed vaccines which induce the production of high titers of circulating antibodies, nor the passive transfer of large volumes of immune serum can completely protect animals against systemic infection with pathogenic *Mycobacteria, Brucella, Salmonella* or *Listeria*. Immunity to these infections depends, instead, on the acquisition by the host of macrophages with increased antibacterial mechanisms. The development of this type of immunity is invariably accompanied by the development of a state of specific delayed hypersensitivity to antigens of the infecting organism. This knowledge, together with that which shows that delayed sensitivity also is not mediated by humoral antibody, forms the basis for the hypothesis that delayed sensitivity is causally related to the immunity it accompanies.

For many years most studies of cellular, or cell-mediated, immunity

This work was supported by Grant No. AI-10351-02 from the National Institute of Allergy and Infectious Diseases of the National Institutes of Health, Department of Health, Education, and Welfare.

to bacterial infection have concentrated on the properties of resistant macrophages. More recent studies, in contrast, have been directed at discovering the immunological basis for the production of resistant macrophages. As a result, it is now possible to hypothesize that the adaptive changes which enable host macrophage populations to express immunity are mediated by a population of immunologically committed lymphocytes produced in response to infection. Furthermore, it is becoming increasingly evident that immunity to infection with certain viruses, protozoa, and metazoa is mediated by similar cells.

The host response leading to cell-mediated immunity to bacterial infection may be divided into two separate components: a macrophage component that expresses immunity, and a lymphocyte component that mediates immunity. It is convenient to discuss the macrophage component first.

THE MACROPHAGE COMPONENT OF THE HOST RESPONSE

It has been argued since the extensive studies of Metchnikoff that macrophages play a key role in immunity to a number of infectious diseases. Indeed, it would seem reasonable to propose that the best way for a host to overcome those infectious agents which can initially survive and multiply inside its phagocytic cells would be for it to acquire phagocytes with an intracellular environment unfavorable to the survival of such agents. The importance of macrophages in the expression of acquired immunity to infection with intracellular parasites became increasingly evident from early histopathological studies of experimental tuberculosis where it was repeatedly observed that the tubercle bacillus in infected tissues almost exclusively is engaged by host macrophages. The prevalent view of the 1930s was summed up by Lurie (1) when he concluded that "the most significant factor in the mechanism of immunity to tuberculosis is the rapid mobilization of mononuclear phagocytes with an increased physiological capacity to destroy or inhibit the growth of tubercle bacilli." Evidence to support the proposition that macrophages are the effectors of acquired cell-mediated immunity to bacterial infection with a variety of intracellular parasites has accumulated over the past few years.

A number of adaptive changes occur in host macrophage populations during infection. These include a physiological activation of individual macrophages, and an augmentation of macrophage numbers in infected tissues through local division of tissue macrophages and an influx of macrophage precursors from blood.

Macrophage Activation

The proposition that acquired immunity to tuberculosis is expressed by macrophages with an increased capacity to restrict the intracellular multiplication of the tubercle bacillus received support from the experiments of Lurie (2) who compared the growth of virulent tubercle bacilli in macrophages from normal and BCG-vaccinated rabbits implanted in the anterior chamber of the eye. He showed that macrophages from vaccinated rabbits possessed a capacity to restrict intracellular multiplication of bacilli greatly when compared to normal macrophages which supported abundant intracellular growth. Since the parasite-macrophage interaction took place in the eyes of normal rabbits, Lurie concluded that the increased bacteriostatic properties observed were the result of intrinsic changes in the macrophages, and were not influenced by immune humoral factors; a conclusion supported by the additional observation that the ingestion of tubercle bacilli by macrophages in the presence of immune serum prior to implantation in the eye did not significantly modify the intracellular growth of the bacilli. Lurie's conclusions received support from experiments of Suter (3) and of Berthrong and Hamilton (4) who showed that macrophages from BCG-vaccinated guinea pigs possess properties that enable them to restrict the growth of virulent tubercle bacilli *in vitro*. It was concluded from the design of these experiments that immune serum played no part in the bacteriostatic properties of resistant macrophages. These results were essentially confirmed in turn by Maxwell and Marcus (5).

Acquired immunity to experimental *Brucella* infection is also expressed by macrophages with increased bacteriostatic properties. The experiments of Pomales-Lebrón and Stinebring (6), Elberg et al (7), and Holland and Pickett (8) provided convincing *in vitro* demonstrations of the enhanced bacteriostatic capacity of peritoneal macrophages from *Brucella*-infected guinea pigs, rats and mice. These workers showed, in addition, that immune serum does not modify the intracellular growth of brucellae. The results of *in vitro* experiments were in complete agreement, therefore, with the parallel demonstration *in vivo* that killed vaccines do not protect animals against infection, despite the ability of these vaccines to induce the production of high titers of circulating antibodies.

Acquired immunity to infection with *Listeria monocytogenes* has received a great deal of study over recent years. Killed vaccines and the passive transfer of immune serum provide no protection against infection with this organism (9,10). A living infection, in contrast, leaves the host resistant to intravenous challenge with enormous numbers of organisms (9). The role of resistant macrophages in the expression of anti-*Listeria* immunity was demonstrated by Mackaness (9) who employed an *in vitro* plaquing technique to compare the growth of *Listeria* in monolayers of peritoneal macrophages from normal and convalescing mice. The development of numerous discrete areas of necrosis in monolayers of normal macrophages indicated the location of infected cells and the spread of bacteria to neighboring cells. The virtual absence of such plaques in monolayers from convalescing mice clearly demonstrated that these macrophages were highly resistant to infection. These results have since been confirmed by Armstrong and Sword (10a).

Similar procedures have been employed to show that acquired immunity to *Salmonella* infection also relies for its full expression on the acquisition by the host of macrophages with an enhanced bactericidal capacity. The studies of Hobson (11), Mitsuhashi et al (12,13), Howard (14), and Sato et al (15) support the view that immunity to *Salmonella* infection is essentially cellular in nature. The role of resistant macrophages was clearly demonstrated by the *in vitro* experiments of Mitsuhashi et al (13), who showed that peritoneal macrophages from mice infected with *S. enteritidis* would not support the intracellular growth of this organism in contrast to normal macrophages in which it grew unrestrictedly. They showed, in addition, that immune serum had no inhibitory effect on the intracellular growth of *S. enteritidis*. The proposition that immunity to salmonellosis is essentially cellular in nature has received recent support from a convincing series of studies by Mackaness and his collaborators (16–18).

There is convincing evidence, therefore, that the expression of immunity to infection with those bacterial parasites which have the capacity to survive and multiply within macrophages relies on the acquisition by the host of macrophages with intrinsically enhanced bactericidal properties. It should be noted, however, that not all host macrophages may acquire this property during infection, and that a proportion of macrophages from uninfected animals may already possess mechanisms which enable them to inactivate certain facultative intracellular parasites. This fact was stressed by Holland and Pickett (8) in relation to the *in vitro* expression of immunity to brucellosis. They suggest the possibility that there is selection for more resistant macrophages during infection. This subject has also been discussed by Blanden (19) who showed that the heterogeneity in the killing capacity of peritoneal macrophages of normal mice for *Salmonella typhimurium* is not due to differences in the capacity of individual bacteria to resist intracellular destruction, because the survivors of an initial encounter with macrophages were shown to be killed in the same proportion during a second encounter with fresh macrophages. This observation explains why opsonic antibody can modify the course of a *Salmonella* infection by ensuring that all bacteria are phagocytosed, and that a certain proportion are thereby killed by natively resistant macrophages. The failure of antibody alone to protect against a moderate intravenous challenge is due to multiplication of bacteria in a large proportion of susceptible macrophages and their subsequent liberation into the blood in overwhelming numbers (16). In the same way, the organisms that give rise to a *Listeria* infection are those that survive and multiply in susceptible macrophages during the first few hours of infection.

The changes that take place in macrophage populations during infection are now collectively referred to as *macrophage activation*. This is a useful term in view of the knowledge that an increased ability to destroy bacteria is not the only property displayed by these cells. For instance, infection with *Mycobacteria* may result in macrophages which display increased metabolic activity (20), increased amounts of lysosomal enzymes (21–23), and increased numbers of lysosomes (24). Macrophages with increased numbers of lysosomes also appear during infection with other intracellular parasites (19). Perhaps one of the most striking properties of activated macrophages, however, can be their enormously increased ability to spread on glass *in vitro*. Thus, whereas peritoneal macrophages from normal mice may take several hours to spread maximally on glass *in vitro*, peritoneal macrophages from mice infected intravenously with *Mycobacteria, Listeria,* or *Salmonella* spread maximally and to a greater extent within 20 to 30 minutes (19,24,25). The difference between the spreading capacities of normal and activated macrophages is shown in Figure 1. Although the significance of increased spreading has yet to be firmly established, it seems almost certain that it indicates an increased potential for phagocytosis. This is evidenced by the results of a recent study of the requirements for the spreading of guinea pig macrophages *in vitro* (26). It was found that those compounds which either stimulate or suppress phagocytosis also either stimulate or suppress spreading. For instance, it was shown that both the rate and extent of spreading are greatly increased by surfaces that have been coated with an antigen-antibody complex (26,27). This means that spreading, like phagocytosis, is triggered by a reaction between opsonic antibody and a receptor on the macrophage plasma membrane which binds to the Fc portion of the antibody molecule (28). It has been hypothesized, therefore, that cellular spreading on a planar surface represents an attempt to phagocytose a sphere of very large diameter (26). It is not surprising, therefore, that activated macrophages also display an enhanced capacity for phagocytosis. The peritoneal macrophages of mice infected with either *Mycobacteria* or *Listeria* show a greatly increased ca-

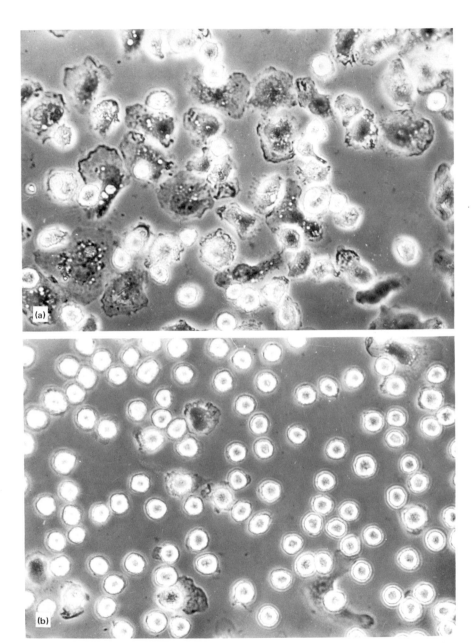

Figure 1. The spreading of macrophages from a *Listeria*-infected (a) and a normal mouse (b). The macrophages were harvested from the peritoneal cavity and incubated for 20 minutes at 37°C. The peritoneal macrophages from infected mice spread much more rapidly than the control macrophages. It can be seen, however, that a small percentage of the macrophages from the normal mouse show a large capacity for spreading. This is not usually seen. Phase contrast X 704.

190

pacity to phagocytose inert particles *in vitro* in the presence of either heterologous serum or no serum at all (25). There is little doubt, therefore, that an increased potential for spreading and phagocytosis is an intrinsic property of the activated cells, and is not dependent on the presence of immune humoral factors. Furthermore, because phagocytosis (29) and spreading (26) are dependent on the expenditure of metabolic energy, it follows that activated macrophages have an increased potential for energy metabolism. These changes are of obvious survival value during infection.

Nonspecific Properties of Activated Macrophages

It is now established that the increased microbicidal activity of activated macrophages is nonspecific in the sense that it is effective against a range of heterologous bacteria. The nonspecific nature of acquired cellular resistance was demonstrated *in vivo* by Pullinger (30) who showed that guinea pigs infected with *Mycobacteria* developed increased resistance to *Brucella* infection. Nyka (31) demonstrated the converse by showing that mice infected with *Brucella* have increased resistance to tuberculosis. It has also been demonstrated that mice infected with BCG show increased resistance to infection with *Salmonella* (32) and *Listeria* (24,33). That increased nonspecific resistance *in vivo* is the result of the presence of activated macrophages was demonstrated by Elberg et al (33a), who showed that macrophages obtained from rabbits immunized with either *Mycobacteria* or *Brucella* have an increased capacity to suppress the multiplication of one or the other parasite *in vitro*. Again, the high level of resistance to *Listeria* challenge developed by *Brucella*-infected mice is associated with a greatly increased capacity on the part of their peritoneal macrophages to inactivate *Listeria in vitro* (33). Likewise, cross-resistance between *Salmonella*- and *Listeria*-infected mice is associated with the presence of macrophages that can inactivate either parasite *in vitro* (17,19).

While there is no doubt, therefore, that activated macrophages display enhanced nonspecific microbicidal properties, it should nevertheless be realized that the degree of protection that this affords the host against infection with heterologous organisms is only relative, and never absolute. Among other things, the degree of protection will depend on the organism responsible for the primary infection and the organism chosen for challenge. Some parasites are more resistant to intracellular inactivation than others and these tend to produce resistance against a larger spectrum of parasites. Thus, while infection with *Mycobacteria* in mice results both in acquired specific resistance and a high level of nonspecific resistance against challenge with *Listeria* (17) and *Salmonella* (32), the converse is not true (34). It seems, therefore, that the degree of macrophage activation achieved during infection with *Mycobacteria* is greater than that achieved during infection with *Listeria* and *Salmonella*.

The Bactericidal Mechanisms of Activated Macrophages

It can be stated that the mechanisms responsible for the intracellular inactivation of facultative intracellular parasites are not known. Early investigations of this problem consisted of attempts to extract antibacterial material from infected tissues, but the results of such studies are of doubtful significance (35). More recently, attention has been directed at the mechanisms responsible for intracellular inactivation of a range of extracellular parasites by polymorphonuclear leukocytes where it is apparent that the metabolic liberation of hydrogen peroxide is of central importance (36,37). Polymorphs, however, appear to be of little use in defense against intracellular parasites. It is probable, therefore, that a different mechanism operates in activated macrophages.

There is also doubt about the significance of lysosomal enzymes in the bactericidal activity of activated macrophages. The possible importance of increased amounts of lysosomal enzymes in the inactivation of tubercle bacilli has been stressed by Dannenberg (38) and Kanai (39) but direct evidence that these enzymes contribute to the bactericidal mechanisms of macrophages is lacking.

Augmentation of Macrophage Numbers in Infected Tissues

The foregoing discussion provides ample evidence that the expression of cell-mediated immunity to bacterial infection rests with the capacity of the host to acquire macrophages with properties which enable them to inactivate the infecting organism. The effectiveness of this arm of the host's antibacterial assault can be greatly amplified, however, by an increase in the size of macrophage populations in infected tissues. This can occur as the result of two separate processes: by an increase in the proliferation of resident tissue macrophages, and by an influx of macrophage precursors from blood.

(A) THE DIVISION OF TISSUE MACROPHAGES

It has been known for some time that infection can result in a general hyperplasia of the reticuloendothelial system as evidenced mainly by the appearance of increased numbers of macrophages in the sinusoids of the liver (40). It has been proposed that this hyperplasia is a result of an increase in the division of tissue macrophages. This proposition is based on the assumption, however, that the liver and other organs do not receive macrophages from the blood. That tissue macrophages divide in increased numbers in response to infection was not revealed until tritiated thymidine was employed for the specific purpose of labeling macrophages replicating *in situ*. Thus, North has demonstrated (41) that intravenous infection with *Listeria monocytogenes* results in a striking increase in the replication of macrophages in liver sinusoids. Whereas a single pulse of tritiated thymidine labels about 1% of sinusoid cells in normal liver, a similar pulse labels 18% or more on days 2 and 3 of *Listeria* infection. Since the major portion of a pulse of tritiated thymidine is available *in vivo* for only about 15 minutes, and as the livers in these experiments were processed for radioautography within 30 minutes, it can be assumed that the cells which labeled were present in liver sinusoids at the time thymidine was injected. Furthermore, because the labeled cells were elongated and closely opposed to the walls of sinusoids, it was concluded that they were resident macrophages. This conclusion received further support from experiments in which liver macrophages were physiologically marked by allowing them to ingest colloidal carbon *in vivo* 2 weeks before infection. It was found that the majority of cells that subsequently incorporated tritiated thymidine on the 2nd day of infection also contained conspicuous amounts of carbon that must have been ingested prior to infection. Even so, it has been shown (42,43a) that two distinct types of cells populate liver sinusoids: endothelial cells and macrophages. Endothelial cells are responsible for providing the continuous lining of sinusoids. They are flatter and more elongated in section than macrophages, and are characterized by the presence of numerous holes or fenestrae in their peripheral cytoplasm. Since these differences can only be seen with the electron microscope, and because both types of cells have the capacity to ingest colloids (42) it is obvious that the true identity of the sinusoid cells that divide in response to infection can only be established by an examination of their ultrastructure. For this reason the cells that divide in liver sinusoids in response to *Listeria* infection were studied by radioautography at the electron-microscope level (43). It was found (Figure 2) that the cells which incorporate tritiated thymidine are indeed macrophages, and that of the 100-odd labeled cells so far examined none had the ultrastructure of endothelial cells. Similar techniques have been employed to show that infection in mice with *Mycobacteria* and *Brucella* (43) also results in a large increase in the proliferation of liver macrophages. In these infec-

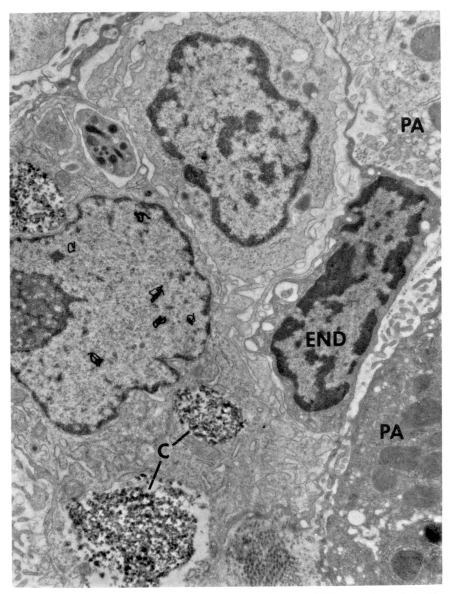

Figure 2. Radioautograph of Kupffer cell (liver macrophage) in DNA synthesis labeled with tritiated thymidine on day 2 of a *Listeria* infection. The labeled cell (silver grains on euchromatin of nucleus) was allowed to ingest colloidal carbon (C) 2 weeks before infection. Note the difference in structure between the labeled Kupffer cell and the endothelial lining cell (END) closely apposed to the underlying parenchyma (PA). Electron micrograph X 10,824.

tions, however, macrophage proliferation occurs at a later stage of infection, as do other parameters of the host response (44). It is anticipated that similar techniques will be employed to establish the true identity of dividing cells in other tissues during infection.

The augmentation of macrophage numbers resulting from local division should not be underestimated. Considering the size of the liver, and the evidence that as many as 38% of its cells can be littoral cells (45), it is obvious that an 18-fold increase in the percentage of replicating macrophages, even for a short time, must result in a very large increase in the total number of macrophages in this organ. This is of obvious survival value because in systemic infections the liver is the most severely infected organ. Thus the sudden increase in macrophage proliferation between the 1st and 2nd day of a *Listeria* infection coincides with an increase in the capacity of the liver to inactivate a challenge dose of *Salmonella typhimurium* (41). Similarly, a progressive increase in liver macrophage division between the 6th and 12th day of a systemic infection with *Mycobacteria* is coincident with a progressive increase in the capacity of the liver to inactivate a standard challenge infection with *Listeria* (67). These findings clearly indicate that the increased number of liver macrophages resulting from local division contributes significantly to the increased capacity of the livers of infected animals to inactivate a challenge infection with heterologous bacteria. Part of the increased bactericidal activity of the liver must result, however, from macrophage activation. Obviously, the presence of an expanded population of activated macrophages is responsible for the increased capacity of the reticuloendothelial system of infected animals to clear colloids and bacteria from the blood (40).

Liver macrophages are not the only macrophages that show increased proliferative activity during systemic infection. Peritoneal macrophages also divide in increased numbers during intravenous infection with *Listeria*, *Brucella* (46), and *Mycobacteria* (25). The identity of these cells was investigated by techniques similar to those used to identify the cells that divide in liver sinusoids (41). Peritoneal macrophages were allowed to ingest polystyrene latex spheres *in vivo* 2 weeks before intravenous infection with either *Listeria* or *Mycobacteria*. Pulse labeling with tritiated thymidine on the days of peak cell division in the peritoneal cavity showed that the majority of cells that incorporated thymidine also contained polystyrene spheres. Thus the macrophages that labeled with tritiated thymidine must have been present in the peritoneal cavity before infection. Electron microscopy of radioautographs showed the labeled cells to have the ultrastructure of mature resident macrophages (Figure 3).

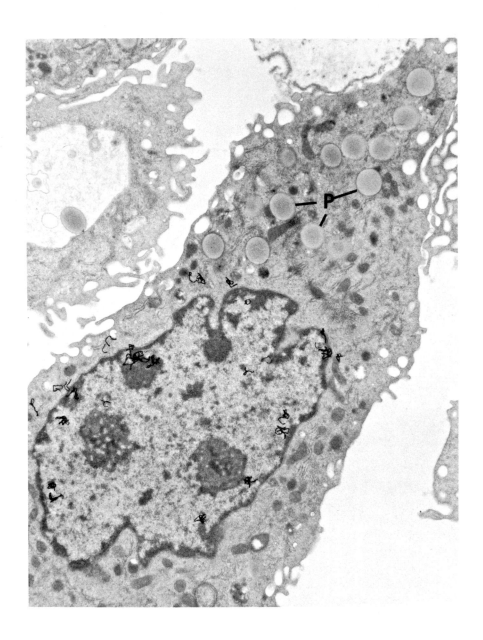

Figure 3. Radioautograph of a replicating peritoneal macrophage labeled with tritiated thymidine on day 2 of a *Listeria* infection. This cell was allowed to ingest polystyrene spheres (P) 2 weeks before infection. Electron micrograph X 7,920.

Because peak division of peritoneal macrophages coincides with peak division of liver macrophages and can occur in the absence of infection in the peritoneal cavity, it is possible that increased macrophage division is triggered systemically by a humoral factor. Though the significance of increased peritoneal macrophage division to the host's defense against infection outside the peritoneal cavity is not known, it is possible that newly formed macrophages may leave the peritoneal cavity and contribute to macrophage populations in infected tissues. This seems a likely possibility in view of the knowledge (47) that labeled peritoneal macrophages when injected into the peritoneal cavity of recipient mice migrate to draining lymph nodes via afferent lymphatics, and apparently can be found at sites of inflammation elicited in the skin (48).

In view of the finding that infection with *Listeria* and other parasites results in the coincident division of macrophages in the liver and peritoneal cavity, it might be expected that macrophages in other tissues should show increased proliferative activity at the same time. This possibility appears not to have been investigated. It may be mentioned, however, that radioautography at the light and electron-microscope levels (43) has so far failed to reveal any large increase in the division of macrophage-like cells in the spleen. This could indicate that the so-called phagocytic reticulum cells which comprise a large proportion of splenic phagocytes are not true macrophages.

(B) CONTRIBUTION OF BLOOD MONOCYTES TO INFECTED TISSUES

Systemic infection with bacterial parasites characteristically results in the formation of numerous foci of infection throughout the reticuloendothelial system. These represent sites of bacterial implantation in susceptible macrophages where the parasites can multiply extensively and spread to infect neighboring cells. If the host fails to contain the bacteria at these sites, they are free to escape into the body fluids and to create additional foci of infection, and eventually a fatal bacteremia. Since most parasites are present at infective foci during the initial stages of infection, it is obvious that it must be at these sites that cell-mediated immunity is expressed. Recent evidence indicates that blood monocytes play a major role in this event.

It is now well established that blood monocytes are the progeny of a rapidly dividing population of precursor cells in bone marrow (49,50), and that they are constantly released into blood where they circulate with a half-time of about 42 hours in the rat (51) and 22 hours in the mouse (52). It is also established that blood monocytes represent a constant supply of mobile macrophage precursors, and are the major source of macrophages that populate sites of inflammation (49,50,53).

It is obvious, therefore, that blood monocytes are the most likely source of macrophages that accumulate at infective foci. The contribution of blood monocytes to the cellular composition of infective foci in the liver during *Listeria* infection, therefore, was recently investigated by North (54,55). Mice were pulsed with tritiated thymidine 1 to 2 hours before infection in order to label the dividing precursors of monocytes in bone marrow. Since it is known that this procedure is followed for several days (52,56) by a continuous release of labeled monocytes from bone marrow into blood, it was anticipated that there should be a progressive accumulation of labeled macrophages at infective foci over the first few days of infection. It was shown by radiometry that there was a progressive increase between the 2nd and 4th day of infection in the amount of labeled DNA in infected livers. Radioautography of liver sections showed that the progressive increase in radioactivity corresponded to a progressive accumulation of labeled macrophages at infective foci and also in the liver sinusoids at large. It was possible to conclude, therefore, that most of the macrophages that accumulate at infective foci are derived from blood monocytes. A similar procedure was employed to study the origin of macrophages that form tubercles in mice infected with *Mycobacterium tuberculosis*. In this case macrophages do not begin to accumulate in large numbers at sites of bacterial implantation until about the 5th or 6th day of infection (67). If a pulse of tritiated thymidine is given on the 6th day of infection, there is a subsequent and progressive accumulation of labeled macrophages in developing tubercles in the liver and spleen (43), as illustrated in Figures 4 and 5. Since it is known that macrophages which are already in tubercles do not divide (67), it follows that the labeled macrophages in tubercles were directly derived from labeled monocytes in blood.

The importance of macrophage accumulation at infective foci to the expression of acquired immunity is indicated by the finding that it is coincident with the onset of bacterial elimination from infected organs (54,55,57,67). Its importance is further indicated by the knowledge that treatment with vinblastine (55) cortisone acetate (58), or X-irradiation, all of which are known to suppress the immune response to *Listeria* infection, causes a paucity or complete absence of macrophages at infective foci. Under these conditions the parasite is able to multiply unrestrictedly to kill the host.

THE LYMPHOCYTE COMPONENT OF THE HOST RESPONSE

The proposition that acquired cell-mediated immunity to bacterial infection is dependent on the development of a specific immunological response is indicated by the knowledge that this type of immunity is almost invariably associated temporarily with the development of a state of specific delayed sensitivity to antigens of the infecting organism. This knowledge and the fact that neither immunity nor delayed sensitivity is mediated by circulating antibody suggest that both are functionally dependent on a common underlying mechanism. This type of evidence, however, is circumstantial at best, and may be criticized superficially on the grounds that the immunity generated is nonspecific in its expression.

Sensitized Lymphocytes as Mediators of Immunity

Evidence that cell-mediated antimicrobial immunity is dependent on the development of an immunological component of the host response was presented by Mackaness (33), who showed that although infection in the mouse with one organism results in the generation of both specific and nonspecific immunity, an accelerated recall of both types of immunity can only be achieved by reinfecting the host with the homologous organism. This indicates that primary infection results in the development of a state of immunologic memory, and that the expression of nonspecific as well as specific immunity is dependent on a specific immunological response. A direct role for sensitized lymphocytes was clear-

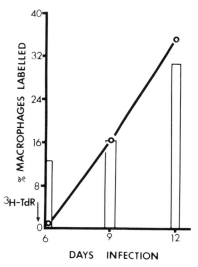

Figure 4.   The accumulation of thymidine-labeled macrophages in tubercles in the liver of mice infected intravenously with *M. tuberculosis*. Mice were pulsed with tritiated thymidine on day 5 of infection. Radioautographs of livers showed that there was a subsequent progressive increase in the percent labeled macrophages in tubercles. The histogram shows that the total number of macrophages in cross sections of tubercles increased during the same time. Means of 5 mice per time point.

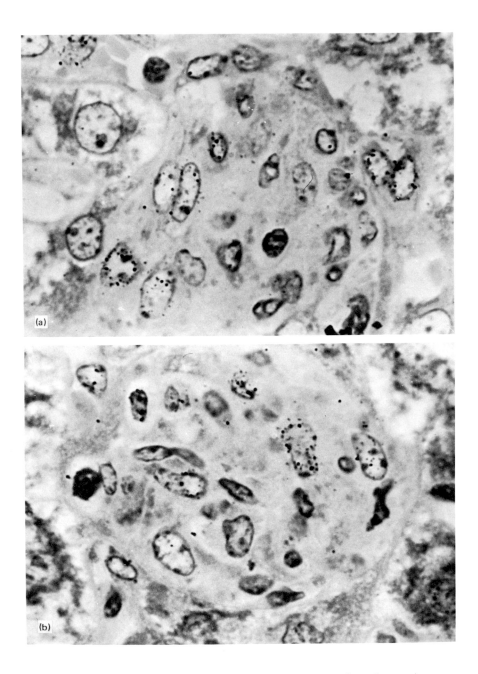

Figure 5. Radioautograph of tubercles containing labeled monocyte-derived macrophages on day 9 of infection with *M. tuberculosis* as described for Figure 4. X 1,620.

ly shown by cell transfer experiments (59) in which normal recipient mice were infused intravenously with splenic lymphoid cells from *Listeria*-infected donors. It was found that the recipients of lymphoid cells acquired high levels of systemic anti-*Listeria* immunity against lethal challenge. The adoptive immunity was fully operational in the livers and spleens of recipients within 24 hours of cell transfer. This means that the infused lymphocytes were capable of rapidly activating recipient macrophages.

A possible criticism of the evidence just mentioned is that the lymphoid cell suspensions used to transfer immunity, although filtered through cotton wool to remove macrophages, nevertheless may have contained macrophage precursors. That transferred macrophages contributed to the immunity is unlikely, however, in view of the results of further experiments (60) which showed that the cells responsible for the transfer of immunity are susceptible *in vitro* to the action of heterologous antilymphocyte globulin. The role of sensitized lymphocytes as mediators of anti-*Listeria* immunity was even more firmly established by a series of experiments in rats (61–63) in which the purity of the lymphoid cell populations used for transfer was assured by employing lymphocytes from thoracic duct lymph. It was demonstrated that high levels of systemic anti-*Listeria* immunity could be transferred to normal rats with thoracic duct lymphocytes from subcutaneously infected donors. As in the mouse, the adoptive immunity was effective against lethal challenge, and was quickly established in the liver and spleen. It was further demonstrated that the lymphocytes responsible for mediating anti-Listeria immunity in rats are part of a population of rapidly dividing cells that, when injected into an intermediate recipient, do not recirculate from blood back to lymph for at least 48 hours. They are different, therefore, from the majority of small lymphocytes that are known to divide only infrequently and to recirculate rapidly blood to lymph (64). Another important observation was that the mediator lymphocytes show a predilection to enter sites of inflammation and can be concentrated in inflammatory peritoneal exudates to the exclusion of long-lived recirculating lymphocytes. This may represent a mechanism by which the host is able to concentrate immunologically reactive cells at infective foci in the tissues. This finding should be viewed in the light of the knowledge that peritoneal exudates are the best source of lymphocytes for the cellular transfer of delayed sensitivity (65).

Antituberculous immunity in the rat can also be transferred to normal recipients with thoracic duct lymphocytes from infected donors (66). The physiological properties of the mediators of antituberculous immunity, however, have yet to be discovered.

Lymphoid Cell Proliferation

Increased division of lymphocytes is a characteristic of all immune responses. It should not be surprising to find, therefore, that it occurs during the development of cell-mediated antimicrobial immunity. It has been shown that the development of immunity to intravenous *Listeria* and *Mycobacteria* infections in the mouse is associated with intense lymphoid cell proliferation in the spleen. Pulse labeling studies with tritiated thymidine (44,58) have revealed that intravenous infection with *Listeria* results in a striking and progressive increase in lymphoid cell proliferation in the spleen over the first 6 days of infection. At peak proliferation the spleens of infected mice incorporate 4 to 5 times more thymidine than control spleens. Proliferation then progressively declines to reach control values by the 14th day. The significance of increased proliferation of lymphoid cells is indicated by the finding that it exactly parallels the development of delayed sensitivity to *Listeria* antigens (44). More important, maximum transfer of adoptive anti-*Listeria* immunity to normal mice is achieved with lymphoid cells harvested from donor spleen at the time of peak cellular proliferation. A progressive decay of cellular proliferation, on the other hand, is accompanied by a progressive loss from the spleen of cells capable of transferring immunity. It seems certain, therefore, that the observed proliferation represents in part the production of *Listeria*-committed lymphocytes, and it is apparent that the same cells are responsible for mediating delayed sensitivity reactions.

Similar techniques have been employed to study the proliferation of lymphoid cells during infection with *Mycobacteria tuberculosis* (67). In this infection a large and progressive increase in cell division occurs in the spleen between the 6th and 12th day of infections initiated by intravenous inoculation. Delayed skin reactivity to PPD increases and peaks at the same times. Furthermore, the levels of delayed sensitivity which can be transferred to normal recipients with spleen cells from infected donors are proportional to the levels of delayed sensitivity and lymphoid cell proliferation in the donors. These findings, together with those which show that peak spleen cell proliferation is coincident with the onset of active bacterial elimination from the tissues, indicate that lymphoid cell proliferation represents the production of committed lymphocytes. Practically no lymphoid cell proliferation occurs in the spleens of mice injected intravenously with large numbers of dead organisms, which also fail to generate hypersensitivity or immunity (67).

Autoradiography of sections of spleen (44,67) shows that in both *Listeria* and tuberculous infections most of the dividing cells are medium-sized, pyroninophilic cells located mainly in the red pulp. The white pulp, in contrast, appears to be only minimally involved in the cellular response to *Listeria* and *Mycobacteria* infection, though it seems likely that the process is initiated in the periarteriolar lymphatic sheaths.

The Role of Thymus-Dependent Lymphocytes

It has been demonstrated that cell-mediated immune reactions in mammals are thymus dependent. The development of allograft immunity, graft-against-host reactions, and delayed sensitivity is severely depressed in animals thymectomized at birth, and in adult animals thymectomized, lethally irradiated, and protected with bone marrow (68). This cannot serve to distinguish cell-mediated immunity from humoral immunity, however, because many antibody responses are also thymus dependent. If a basis for distinction exists, it will almost certainly be explained in terms of the participation of two recently discovered subpopulations of lymphocytes called T cells and B cells. The discovery of these two types of lymphocytes arose from the observation that restoration of the capacity of lethally irradiated mice to mount an antibody response against heterologous red cells could not be achieved by an infusion of either bone marrow cells or thymus cells alone, but could be achieved if both types of cells were infused together (69,70). Cooperation between these two types of cells is also required for antibody responses to certain protein antigens (71). The responsible cells in the thymus were called T cells and those in bone marrow, B cells (72). It was later shown that B cells are the precursors of antibody-forming cells, and that T cells probably serve in some way either to prepare or arrange the antigen for presentation to B cells (see ref. 73). Both types of cells originate in bone marrow, but T cells require the presence of the thymus for their differentiation. Animals that are either thymectomized at birth, or thymectomized, irradiated, and bone marrow protected as adults, are virtually devoid of T cell function, but this function can be restored by infusions of thymus lymphocytes or thoracic duct cells. The majority of T cells in mice can be detected by the use of an alloantibody directed against the theta (θ) alloantigen found only on thymus lymphocytes and thymus-dependent lymphocytes. It has been shown with anti-θ serum that the majority of cells in thoracic duct lymph are T cells, and that T cells constitute 70 to 80% of the lymphocytes in lymph nodes and 30 to 50% of the lymphocytes in the spleen, the remaining lymphocytes being B cells. When administered to intact animals, heterologous antilymphocyte serum acts mainly on T cells which disappear from the so-called thymus-dependent areas of lymphoid tissue. B cells, on the other hand, are characterized by a high density of surface immunoglobulin determinants, have surface receptors for antigen-antibody complexes, and are susceptible to an anti-B cell antiserum (73a). The properties just described may be used to separate either T or B cells from lymphoid cell suspension *in vitro.*

There is direct evidence that T cells are both the initiators and effectors of allograft immunity. It has been shown in the mouse, for instance, that an infusion of spleen cells into lethally irradiated allogeneic hosts results in the formation of lymphocytes that are cytotoxic for host strain target cells *in vitro,* and also in the formation of cells producing antibody to H2 antigens of the host strain (74). If thymus cells are infused instead, only cytotoxic lymphocytes are produced, indicating their derivation from T cells, and that alloantibody-producing cells are B cells. It was further shown that cytotoxic lymphocytes and their precursors carry the Θ alloantigen (75). More recently it was shown (76) that an infusion of thymus cells into irradiated allogeneic hosts results in the appearance of rapidly dividing blast cells in the spleen, and a subsequent appearance of dividing T cells (as detected by specific antisera) in thoracic duct lymph. These cells were called activated T cells because they have an enhanced capacity to initiate allograft rejection and to destroy target cells *in vitro.* They are specifically activated against the H2 antigens that trigger their formation. B cells, apparently, do not participate in these examples of allograft immunity.

This degree of experimental sophistication has not yet been applied to infection models of cell-mediated immunity. It is possible, nevertheless, to give some idea of the possible importance of T and B cells. It is now known, for instance, that the development of antituberculous immunity in the mouse is thymus dependent. It has been shown (77) that neonatally thymectomized mice fail to express normal levels of immunity to infection with *Mycobacteria tuberculosis* and *M. bovis* in their livers and spleens. Likewise, adult mice that have been thymectomized, irradiated, and bone marrow protected show little evidence of developing immunity to systemic infection with *M. tuberculosis* (43). In normal mice this organism grows log linearly in the liver and spleen for 6 days, and then shows a reduced rate of growth between days 6 and 12. After the 12th day there is active bacterial elimination from both organs. In adult thymectomized mice, however, a phase of bacterial elimination does not occur (Figure 6), and the organism may continue to multiply unrestrictedly until the mice die. When the proliferation of splenic lymphoid cells was studied in these animals it was found that both the rate and extent of lymphoid cell proliferation in thymectomized mice were about one-third the rate and extent of proliferation in normal infected

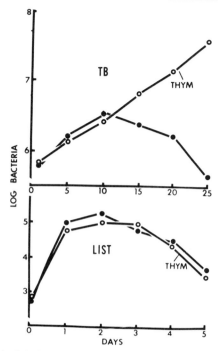

Figure 6.   The effect of adult thymectomy on the development of cell-mediated immunity to intravenous infection with *M. tuberculosis* (top graph) and *Listeria*. Experimental mice were thymectomized, irradiated with 900 rad, and protected with 10^6 bone marrow cells 4 weeks before infection. The graphs show the growth of bacteria in the livers. Thymectomy prevents the development of immunity to infection with *M. tuberculosis*, but does not effect immunity to *Listeria* infection. Means of 5 mice per time point.

mice. Macrophage accumulation at infective foci and the division of macrophages in the liver were similarly reduced, as was the capacity to develop delayed hypersensitivity to tuberculoprotein. That these reductions in the parameters of the antituberculous response were caused by a deficiency in immunocompetent T cells was indicated by the finding that they could be restored by infusing the host with normal thymocytes immediately before infection (43).

Thymectomy also greatly reduces the capacity of mice to retard the growth of *Mycobacterium leprae* in their tissues. Inoculation of the footpads of mice with *M. leprae* results in local slow growth of this organism for several months followed by a cessation of growth when bacterial numbers reach about 10^6 per footpad. In mice that have been thymectomized, irradiated, and bone marrow protected, in contrast, multiplication continues for many more months until at the end of the period of observation their footpads may contain 100 to 1000 times more bacteria than do the footpads of control mice (78,79). Neonatally thymectomized rats are also unable to control the growth of the human leprosy bacillus (80).

The immune response of mice to *Mycobacterial* infection can also be suppressed by treatment with heterologous antilymphocyte serum which acts *in vivo* mainly only on T cells. It was shown by Gaugas and Rees (81) that subcutaneous injections of antilymphocyte serum into mice on days 1, 4, 7, and 10 of a lethal intravenous infection with *M. tuberculosis* result in a much shorter survival time. Similar treatment with antilymphocyte serum reduces the capacity of mice and rats to control the growth of *M. leprae* in their tissues (80). It seems fairly certain, therefore, that immunity to *Mycobacterial* infection is T cell dependent.

Immunity to *Listeria* infection at first sight appears to be different because the growth of this organism in the livers and spleens of thymectomized, irradiated, and bone-marrow-protected mice (43) and rats (82) is identical to its growth in the livers and spleens of normal animals (Figure 6). This could be taken as evidence that anti-*Listeria* immunity is T cell independent. In contradiction to this evidence, however, is the demonstration that those spleen cells from *Listeria*-infected donor mice capable of transferring immunity to normal recipients are destroyed *in vitro* by conventionally prepared antitheta serum and complement (82a), and with anti-Θ serum prepared with congenic mice (43). There is little doubt, therefore, that the mediators of anti-*Listeria* immunity are T cells. The apparent contradiction can be explained by assuming that mice made T cell deficient by thymectomy and irradiation, and protected with bone marrow contain a residual population of competent T cells which is large enough to generate anti-*Listeria* immunity, but not antituberculous immunity. That this is so is shown by the findings (43) that spleen cells from *Listeria*-infected T-cell-deficient mice can transfer immunity to normal recipients provided the number of cells infused is equivalent to the number of cells in the spleen of a normal infected mouse. In fact, it takes 3 spleen equivalents of cells from infected T-cell-deficient mice to equal the immunity transferred with 1 spleen equivalent of cells from normal infected mice. This fits with the additional findings that at the peak of the anti-*Listeria* response, T-cell-deficient mice show one-third as much infection-induced spleen cell proliferation as infected controls, and contain one-third as many spleen cells. It has yet to be determined nevertheless, whether the mediators of anti-*Listeria* immunity in T-cell-deficient mice are T cells. It is still possible that other types of lymphocytes are also involved in the mediation of this immunity.

Another property of the mediators of anti-*Listeria* immunity is that a large proportion of them are eliminated from the spleen following a 2.5-mg injection of cortisone acetate (44). This loss of mediator cells, furthermore, is associated with a massive loss of replicating pyroninophilic cells from the splenic red pulp, but not from the periarteriolar sheaths of the white pulp. These findings should be considered in the light of evidence (83) that the same dose of cortisone acetate does not eliminate from the spleen and other lymphoid organs those immunocompetent T cells responsible for initiating graft-versus-host reactions. It is probable, therefore, that there is a physiological difference between competent and committed T cells.

The reason why thymectomized, irradiated, and bone-marrow-protected mice can develop anti-*Listeria* immunity, but cannot develop normal levels of antituberculous immunity, is probably a reflection of the degree of macrophage activation required to destroy each parasite. It is known that the tubercle bacillus is much more resistant to inactivation by macrophages than is *Listeria*. Consequently, the host may need to develop a much higher level of macrophage activation to express antituberculous immunity than to express anti-*Listeria* immunity, and this may require the production of a larger number of committed T cells—a number that cannot be realized in T-cell-deficient mice.

Mediation of Macrophage Activation

The knowledge that acquired immunity to *Listeria* infection is expressed by macrophages, and that an infusion of *Listeria*-committed lymphocytes can confer high levels of adoptive immunity on normal recipients, means that committed lymphocytes must mediate the activation of recipient macrophages. The need for recipient macrophages in the expression of adoptive immunity is indicated by the results of experiments in which prospective recipients of committed lymphocytes were treated with agents that are known to suppress the production of blood monocytes. It was found that an infusion of *Listeria*-committed lymphocytes fails to confer protection on recipients that have been pretreated with X-rays, vinblastine (84), or cyclophosphamide (85).Direct evidence that committed lymphocytes can mediate functional changes in recipient macrophage populations is shown by the finding (86) that an infusion of *Listeria*-committed lymphocytes and *Listeria* into normal recipients causes a rapid increase in the proliferation of macrophages in the recipients' livers as detected by pulse labeling with tritiated thymidine (Figure 7). This proliferation is much faster and much more intense than the proliferation which occurs in the livers of recipients that are given normal

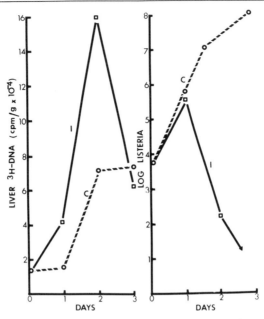

Figure 7. The accelerated division of liver macrophages in normal mice (left-hand graph) caused by an infusion of splenic lymphoid cells from *Listeria*-infected donors. Macrophage division was assessed by pulse labeling with tritiated thymidine at the times indicated. An infusion of immune lymphoid cells (I) caused a much earlier and much more intense incorporation of thymidine into liver DNA than did an infusion of normal lymphoid cells (C). The right-hand graph shows the corresponding levels of adoptive immunity in the livers expressed against a lethal challenge with *Listeria*. A high level of adoptive immunity is transferred with immune spleen cells (I), but not with normal spleen cells (C). Means of 5 mice per time point.

lymphocytes and *Listeria,* and in mice combating a primary infection. The identity of the dividing cells in sinusoids was established by pre-marking them *in vivo* with colloidal carbon. It was further shown that macrophage proliferation does not occur in recipients that have been X-irradiated prior to cell transfer. It seems highly likely, in view of these results, that macrophage division during primary infection is mediated by committed lymphocytes. This does not mean, however, that the recipients' blood monocytes are not the prime expressors of adoptive immunity. On the contrary, it has been shown (86) in normal recipients prelabeled with tritiated thymidine that an infusion of committed lymphocytes causes a much faster than normal accumulation of labeled monocytes at infective foci in the liver. It was also shown that this accumulation of monocytes at infective foci can be completely prevented by X-irradiating the recipients prior to cell transfer, a procedure that prevents the recipients from expressing adoptive immunity. It is apparent, therefore, that the accumulation of effector macrophages at sites of bacterial implantation is under the direction of committed lymphocytes.

There is evidence that macrophage activation can be mediated by committed lymphocytes *in vitro*. It has been demonstrated (87) that lymphocytes obtained from peritoneal exudates of guinea pigs with delayed sensitivity when incubated with specific antigen produce soluble factors which can activate macrophages *in vitro* as measured by increased capacities for spreading, phagocytosis, and energy metabolism. The procedure used to purify these factors dismisses the possibility that antibodies are involved in this example of macrophage activation. Similar experiments were performed by Simon and Sheagren (88) who used *in vitro* killing of *Listeria* as a measure of macrophage activation. Again, Godal and coworkers (89) have shown that rabbit lymphocytes in a mixed leukocyte culture produce soluble factors which can activate macrophages *in vitro* as evidenced by increased division and changes in morphology. More important, macrophages activated in this way have an increased capacity to suppress the intracellular growth of *M. lepraemurium*. It would be of interest to know whether these soluble factors can also trigger macrophage division *in vivo*.

That lymphocytes cooperate with macrophages in cell-mediated antibacterial immunity is further suggested by the knowledge that both types of cells are invariably seen together at foci of infection where immunity is mainly expressed. Lymphocytes are constant companions of macrophages in developing tubercles of tuberculous animals (90), and at allergic granulomas in general, including delayed sensitivity reactions in the skin (90a,b). In a recent study of tubercle formation in the livers of mice infected with *M. tuberculosis* (67), it was shown by pulse labeling with tritiated thymidine that developing tubercles are constantly surrounded by a population of dividing pyroninophilic lymphocytes. Electron microscopy of radioautographs (43) confirmed that the replicating cells were lymphocytes and showed that many of them had the ultrastructure of blast cells, as evidenced by their large content of polyribosomes (Figure 8). Electron microscopy showed, in addition, that the lymphocytes were in close proximity to macrophages and that many of them were squeezed between macrophages at the periphery of tubercles. Similar types of cells have been observed at infective foci of *Listeria*-infected mice (43). Thus, if macrophage activation is mediated by soluble factors released from committed lymphocytes, there is ample opportunity for it to be achieved at infective foci where both types of cells are in close proximity and where antigen is present in large concentrations. The presence of committed lymphocytes at these sites could also serve

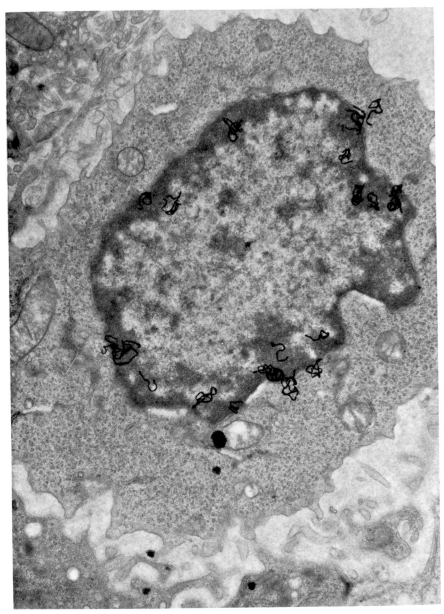

Figure 8. Radioautograph of dividing blast cell at edge of a tubercle in the liver of a mouse on day 9 of infection with *M. tuberculosis*. This cell was labeled by a single pulse of tritiated thymidine. The presence of replicating blast cells is a constant feature of developing tubercles. Electron micrograph X 15,400.

to speed up macrophage accumulation as a result of a release of migration inhibitory factor or a chemotactic factor, as discussed in Chapter 3 (see also ref. 91).

It is apparent from the foregoing discussion that macrophage activation, macrophage division, and the mobilization of macrophages at infective foci are all under the direction of committed lymphocytes.

The Role of Delayed Sensitivity

The evidence that delayed sensitivity is functionally related to cell-mediated immunity to infection has recently been reviewed (92,93). The evidence overwhelmingly favors a functional connection: The striking temporal relationship between the development of sensitivity and the development of immunity; the fact that both can be transferred to normal animals with living lymphoid cells but not with serum; and the knowledge that animals with delayed sensitivity are capable of displaying an accelerated immune response to reinfection with the homologous organism, even when delayed sensitivity is induced by injecting dead organisms in oil (94), are all reasons for hypothesizing a functional association. The knowledge that the cells which accumulate at a delayed skin reaction are of the same morphological types as those which accumulate at a focus of infection is further evidence that a common mechanism is involved, and serves to explain why animals with delayed sensitivity are able to mobilize macrophages rapidly at a site of infection. Ultimate proof of a cause and effect relationship between delayed sensitivity and immunity will only be achieved, however, when it is demonstrated that both are mediated by the *same* lymphocytes.

CELL-MEDIATED IMMUNITY TO NONBACTERIAL INFECTIONS

Cell-Mediated Immunity to Viral Infection

Preoccupation with the importance of neutralizing antibody and interferon has resulted in a relatively small literature on the subject of cell-mediated immunity to viral infection. This is surprising, because it has been known for some time that the increased susceptibility to viral infections of individuals with immune deficiency diseases is associated with deficiencies affecting cellular immunity rather than immunoglobulin production (95). Von Pirquet (96) first drew attention to the similarities between a normal vaccination reaction and a cutaneous delayed sensitivity reaction. Established examples of the development of delayed sensitivity during viral infections have been documented by Allison (97), and Mims (98) has pointed out that delayed sensitivity can be found to develop during most viral infections when an effort is made to detect it. The host response to many viral infections must therefore be thought to include a cell-mediated component. Furthermore, there is evidence that in certain cases this component of the immune response appears to represent the basic mechanism of recovery from primary viral infections.

The finding that immunity to infections with certain viruses can be suppressed by treating the host with antilymphocyte globulin has been taken as evidence that the immunity is cell mediated (99). It has been shown, for instance, that treatment of mice with antilymphocyte globulin suppresses immunity to infection with vaccinia and herpes simplex viruses, and to certain oncogenic viruses such as polyoma, Moloney leukemia, and adenovirus (100). Similar treatment, however, does not suppress immunity to infection with influenza and yellow fever viruses. It was concluded, therefore, that immunity to the first group is cell mediated while immunity to the latter is antibody mediated. It is doubtful, however, whether suppression by antilymphocyte globulin by itself is acceptable evidence for cell-mediated immunity, because it is known that some humoral antibody responses can also be suppressed by this agent (101). The proposition that antiviral immunity can be cell-mediated rests more firmly, however, on evidence that replication of virus can proceed in target organs in spite of high titers of circulating antibody, that recovery from infection can proceed in the absence of detectable circulating antibody, and that immunity can be transferred to normal animals with sensitized lymphoid cells at a time when immune serum is still ineffective.

Thus it has been shown (102) that progressive vaccinia infection can occur in some humans despite the production of high titers of circulating antibody. Moreover, immunity to vaccinia infection in mice was shown by Hirsch and Murphy (100) to be suppressed by antilymphocyte globulin without concomitant suppression of antibody production. Similarly, Volkert and Lundstedt (103) have shown that treatment with antilymphocyte globulin can induce latent infection with lymphocytic choriomeningitis virus in mice despite the continued presence of high titers of circulating antibodies; and Blanden (104) has demonstrated that antilymphocyte globulin can completely suppress immunity to sublethal infection with ectromelia virus without altering the capacity of mice to produce neutralizing antibody and interferon.

That sensitized lymphocytes are responsible for mediating nonhumoral antiviral immunity is indicated by the demonstration (105) that immunity to tumors caused by infection with polyoma virus can be transferred to immunosuppressed mice with spleen cells from polyoma-infected donors, but not with spleen cells from normal donors. Antibodies appear to play no part in this experimental model. The most thorough study of the cellular transfer of cell-mediated immunity to viral infection, however, has been carried out by Blanden (104,106,107). The following findings are important: The onset of recovery from infection with ectromelia infection in mice is coincident with the development of delayed sensitivity, and is evident before antibodies can be detected in circulation. Immunity and delayed sensitivity can be transferred to normal mice with splenic lymphoid cells, but not with serum from donor mice infected 6 days prior to transfer with avirulent virus. Adoptive immunity is operational in cell recipients despite an absence of either detectable antibody or circulating interferon. That the lymphocytes which mediate this immunity are T cells is indicated by the findings that the capacity of splenic lymphoid cells from infected mice to immunize normal recipients adoptively can be abrogated by incubating the spleen cells with heterologous antilymphocyte serum, antilight-chain serum, or antitheta serum.

The mechanism by which the immune host effects the destruction of virus is not known. Blanden demonstrated by immunofluorescence (107) that the rapid destruction of virus protein in the infective foci of adoptively immunized mice is associated with an accelerated accumulation of mononuclear cells at these sites. That monocytes may be responsible for virus destruction in this infection was indicated by the finding that sensitized lymphoid cells cannot confer much protection on recipients which have been irradiated prior to cell transfer (100), a procedure that is known to block monocyte production in bone marrow. There is additional evidence that macrophages may play a role in the expression of antiviral immunity. It has been shown by Tompkins and collaborators (108), for example, that purified peritoneal macrophages from rabbits infected with vaccinia virus show greatly enhanced antiviral activity *in vitro* in the absence of antibody. It is possible, therefore, that cell-mediated immunity to viral infection may be similar to cell-mediated immunity to bacterial infection in that it requires the activation and mobilization of host macrophages by immunologically committed lymphocytes. It is possible, however, that activated lymphocytes by themselves may be capable of achieving virus inactivation at infective foci as a result of their known capacity for producing interferon (109).

Cell-Mediated Immunity to Infection with Protozoa and Metazoa

There is evidence that immunity to certain protozoa and metazoa is also cell-mediated. Two examples will suffice to illustrate this point. A possible example of cell-mediated immunity to a protozoal infection is that generated in rats against *Plasmodium bergei,* the causative agent of rodent malaria. The rat is able to develop a solid immunity to reinfection with the blood form of this parasite. Many workers have failed to show a protective role for humoral antibodies (110), but there is ample evidence to the contrary (111–113). The possibility that cell-mediated immunity also plays a role in acquired resistance is indicated by the findings that treatment of rats with heterologous antilymphocyte serum suppresses the development of immunity without apparently suppressing antibody production (114). In addition, the development of immunity can be suppressed by neonatal thymectomy (115) without any effect on the production of humoral antibodies (116). Again, normal rats can be protected by an infusion of lymphoid cells from convalescing donors (116–118), although immune serum can also transfer some immunity.

Perhaps a more convincing model of cell-mediated immunity to *Plasmodium bergei* infection is that developed by Nussenzweig and her collaborators (119) for studying immunity developed against the sporozoite stage of this parasite in mice. It has been shown that an injection of irradiated sporozoites results in the generation of a high level of immunity to sporozoite infection. The immunity is operational well before circulating antibodies can be detected, and infusions of immune serum confer practically no protection.

A possible example of cell-mediated immunity to infection with metazoa is that generated against the helminth, *Trichostrongylus colubriformis,* which parasitizes the gut of guinea pigs. It has been shown that infusions of large volumes of antiserum fail to confer protection on normal animals (120). In contrast, high levels of protection can be adoptively transferred with lymphocytes from resistant animals (121). It seems significant, moreover, that the infused lymphocytes tend to "home" into the infected gut (122). The exact way in which this example of cell-mediated immunity is accomplished has yet to be determined.

CONCLUSION

An attempt has been made to show that acquired immunity to certain facultative intracellular bacterial parasites is mediated by immunologically committed lymphocytes, but is expressed by activated macrophages. Evidence was presented to show that the adaptive changes which occur in host macrophages during infection include an increase in their numbers in infected tissues, and an increase in their phagocytic and bactericidal capacities. The fact that these changes enable the host to inactivate a range of unrelated bacteria can no longer be used as evidence that this form of acquired antibacterial resistance does not have an immunological basis. On the contrary, it has been shown that these changes in macrophages can be mediated by committed lymphocytes both *in vivo* and *in vitro*. The fact that macrophage populations so activated can protect the host against a range of pathogens is of obvious survival value.

The knowledge that antibacterial immunity is or is not dependent on T cells cannot yet be used by itself to decide whether this immunity is cell mediated, although there is little doubt that T cells play a central role in the examples studied. The fact that immunity is not mediated by free antibody is still the best evidence for hypothesizing the existence of a cell-mediated mechanism. The large amount of evidence that shows that this immunity is expressed by macrophages which acquired intracellular antimicrobial mechanisms is completely consistent with such a hypothesis. Without such macrophages opsonic antibodies could do no more than promote an infectious process caused by bacteria with a capacity to multiply intracellularly.

The state of delayed sensitivity that accompanies cell-mediated antibacterial immunity almost certainly enables the host to accumulate effector macrophages at infective foci at an accelerated rate. It could be argued that macrophages accumulate around any foreign matter in the tissues, including substances that do not give rise to an immunological response. It has been convincingly demonstrated by Warren and coworkers, however, that there is a fundamental difference between formation of allergic granulomas and foreign body granulomas (123). The formation of allergic granulomas is greatly retarded in animals which have been immunosuppressed by a variety of procedures. The same procedures, in contrast, need not affect the rate of formation of foreign body granulomas. The formation of allergic granulomas, therefore, is under the direction of immunological mediators. These must be committed lymphocytes.

REFERENCES

1. Lurie, M. B., *J. Exp. Med.* **69**, 579 (1939).
2. Lurie, M. B., *J. Exp. Med.* **75**, 247 (1942).
3. Suter, E., *J. Exp. Med.* **97**, 235 (1953).
4. Berthrong, M. and Hamilton, M. A., *Am. Rev. Tuberc.* **79**, 221 (1959).
5. Maxwell, K. W. and Marcus, S., *J. Immunol.* **101**, 176 (1968).

6. Pomales-Lebron, A. and Stinebring, W. R., *Proc. Soc. Exp. Biol. Med.* **94,** 78 (1956).

7. Elberg, S. S., Schneider, P., and Fong, J., *J. Exp. Med.* **106,** 545 (1957).

8. Holland, J. J. and Pickett, M. J., *J. Exp. Med.* **108,** 343 (1958).

9. Mackaness, G. B., *J. Exp. Med.* **116,** 381 (1962).

10. Miki, K. and Mackaness, G. B., *J. Exp. Med.* **120,** 93 (1964).

10a. Armstrong, A. S. and Sword, C. P., *J. Infect. Dis.* **114,** 258 (1964).

11. Hobson, D., *J. Hyg.* **55,** 334 (1957).

12. Mitsuhashi, S., Kawakami, M., Yamaguchi, Y., and Nagal, M., *Jap. J. Exp. Med.* **28,** 249 (1958).

13. Mitsuhashi, S., Sato, I., and Tanaka, T., *J. Bacteriol.* **81,** 863 (1961).

14. Howard, J. G., *Nature (London)* **191,** 87 (1961).

15. Sato, I., Tanaka, T., Salto, K., and Mitsuhashi, S., *Proc. Jap. Acad. Sci.* **37,** 261 (1961).

16. Mackaness, G. B., Blanden, R. V., and Collins, F. M., *J. Exp. Med.* **124,** 573 (1966).

17. Blanden, R. V., Mackaness, G. B., and Collins, F. M., *J. Exp. Med.* **124,** 585 (1966).

18. Collins, F. M., Mackaness, G. B., and Blanden, R. V., *J. Exp. Med.* **124,** 601 (1966).

19. Blanden, R. V., *J. Reticuloendothel. Soc.* **5,** 179 (1968).

20. Stahelin, H., Karnovsky, M. L., Farnahm, A. E., and Suter, E., *J. Exp. Med.* **105,** 265 (1957).

21. Suter, E. and Hulliger, L., *Ann. N. Y. Acad. Sci.* **88,** 1237 (1960).

22. Thorbecke, G. J., Old, L. J., Benacerraf, B., and Clarke, D. A., *J. Histochem. Cytochem.* **9,** 392 (1961).

23. Salto, K. and Suter, E., *J. Exp. Med.* **121,** 727 (1965).

24. Blanden, R. V., Lefford, M. J., and Mackaness, G. B., *J. Exp. Med.* **129,** 1079 (1969).

25. North, R. J., *J. Exp. Med.* **130,** 299 (1969).

26. North, R. J., *J. Reticuloendothel. Soc.* **5,** 203 (1968).

27. North, R. J., *Exp. Cell Res.* **54,** 267 (1968).

28. Rabinovitch, M., Phagocytic recognition in *Mononuclear Phagocytes* (R. van Furth, Ed.), Blackwell Scientific Publications, Oxford and Edinborough, 1970, p. 229.

29. Karnovsky, M. L., *Physiol. Rev.* **42,** 143 (1962).

30. Pullinger, E. J., *J. Hyg.* **36,** 4560 (1936).

31. Nyka, W., *Am. Rev. Tuberc.* **73,** 251 (1957).

32. Howard, J. G., Biozzi, G., Halpern, B. N., Stiffel, C., and Mouton, D., *Brit. J. Exp. Pathol.,* **40,** 281 (1959).

33. Mackaness, G. B., *J. Exp. Med.* **120,** 105 (1964).

33a. Elberg, S. S., Schneider, P., and Fong, J., *J. Exp. Med.* **106,** 545 (1957).

34. Mackeness, G. B., personal communication.

35. Hirsch, J. G., *Ciba Symposium on Experimental Tuberculosis* (G. E. W. Wolstenholme and M. P. Cameron, Eds.), Little, Brown, Boston, Massachusetts, 1955, p. 115.

36. Klebanoff, S. J., *Science* **169,** 1095 (1970).

37. Strauss, R. R., Paul, B. B., Jacobs, A. A., and Sbarra, A. J., *Infect. Immunity,* **3,** 595 (1971).

38. Dannenberg, A. M., *Bacteriol. Rev.* **32,** 85 (1968).

39. Kanal, K., *Jap. J. Med. Sci. Biol.* **21,** 405 (1968).

40. Thorbecke, G. J. and Benacerraf, B., *Prog. Allergy* **6,** 559 (1962).

41. North, R. J., *J. Exp. Med.* **130,** 315 (1969b).

42. Wisse, E., *J. Ultrastruct. Res.* **31,** 125 (1970).

43. North, R. J. in preparation.

43a. Wildman, J., Cotran, R. S., and Fahimi, H. D., *J. Cell Biol.* **52,** 159 (1972).

44. North, R. J., *Cell. Immunol.* **3,** 501 (1972).

45. Jandl, J. H., Files, N. M., Barnett, S. B., and MacDonald, R. A., *J. Exp. Med.* **122,** 299 (1965).

46. Khoo, K. K. and Mackaness, G. B., *Aust. J. Exp. Biol. Med. Sci.* **42,** 707 (1964).

47. Roser, B., *J. Reticuloendothel. Soc.* **8,** 139 (1970).

48. Vernon-Roberts, B., *Nature (London)* **222,** 1286 (1969).

49. Volkman, A. *Ser. Haematol.* **3,** 62 (1970).

50. van Furth, R., *Sem. Hematol.* **7,** 125 (1970).

51. Volkman, A., *Haematol. Lat. (Milano)* **10,** 61 (1967).

52. van Furth, R. and Cohn, Z. A., *J. Exp. Med.* **128,** 415 (1968).

53. Spector, W. G. and Ryan, G. B., The mononuclear phagocyte in inflammation, in *Mononuclear Phagocytes* (R. van Furth, Ed.), Blackwell Scientific Publications, Oxford and Edinborough, 1970, p. 219.

54. North, R. J., *J. Exp. Med.* **132,** 521 (1970).

55. North, R. J., *J. Exp. Med.* **132,** 535 (1970).

56. Volkman, A. and Gowans, J. L., *Brit. J. Exp. Pathol.* **46,** 62 (1965).

57. Truitt, G. L. and Mackaness, G. B., *Am. Rev. Resp. Dis.* **104,** 829 (1971).

58. North, R. J., *J. Exp. Med.* **134,** 1485 (1971).

59. Mackaness, G. B., *J. Exp. Med.* **129,** 973 (1969).

60. Mackaness, G. B. and Hill, W. C., *J. Exp. Med.* **129,** 993 (1969).

61. McGregor, D. D., Koster, F. T., and Mackaness, G. B., *J. Exp. Med.* **133,** 389 (1971).

62. Koster, F. T. and McGregor, D. D., *J. Exp. Med.* **133,** 864 (1971).

63. Koster, F. T., McGregor, D. D., and Mackaness, G. B., *J. Exp. Med.* **133,** 400 (1971).

64. Gowans, J. L. and McGregor, D. D., *Prog. Allergy* **9,** 1 (1965).

65. Kirchheimer, W. F. and Weiser, R. S., *Proc. Soc. Exp. Biol. Med.* **66,** 166 (1947).

66. Lefford, M. J., McGregor, D. D., and Mackaness, G. B., in preparation.

67. North, R. J., Mackaness, G. B., and Elliott, R. W., *Cell. Immunol.* **3,** 680 (1972).

68. Miller, J. F. A. P. and Osoba, D., *Physiol. Rev.* **47,** 437 (1967).

69. Claman, H. N. and Chaperon, E. A., *Transplant. Rev.* **1,** 92 (1969).

70. Claman, H. N., Chaperon, E. A., and Triplett, R. F., *Proc. Soc. Exp. Biol. Med.* **112,** 1167 (1966).

71. Taylor, R. B., *Transplant. Rev.* **1,** 114 (1969).

72. Roitt, I. M., Greaves, M. F., Torrigiani, G., and Brostoff, J., *Lancet* **2,** 367 (1969).

73. Miller, J. F. A. P., Basten, A., Sprent, J., and Cheers, C., *Cell. Immunol.* **2,** 469 (1971).

73a. Raff, M. C., *Am. J. Pathol.* **65,** 467 (1971).

74. Cerottini, J.-C., Nordin, A. A., and Brunner, K. T., *Nature (London)* **227,** 1308 (1970).

75. Cerottini, J.-C., Nordin, A. A., and Brunner, K. T., *Nature (London)* **228,** 72 (1970).

76. Sprent, J. and Miller, J. F. A. P., *Nature (London)* **234**, 195 (1971).

77. Takeya, K., Mori, R., Nomoto, K., and Nakayama, H., *Am. Rev. Resp. Dis.* **96**, 469 (1967).

78. Rees, R. J. W., *Nature (London)* **211**, 657 (1966).

79. Gaugas, J. M., *Nature (London)* **220**, 1248 (1968).

80. Fieldsteel, A. H. and McIntosh, A. H., *Proc. Soc. Exp. Biol. Med.* **138**, 408 (1971).

81. Gaugas, J. M. and Rees, R. J. W., *Nature (London)* **219**, 408 (1968).

82. McGregor, D. D., in preparation.

82a. Lane, F. C. and Unanue, E. R., *J. Exp. Med.* **135**, 1104 (1972).

83. Cohen, J. J., Fischbach, M., and Claman, H. N., *J. Immunol.* **105**, 1146 (1970).

84. Tripathy, S. P. and Mackaness, G. B., *J. Exp. Med.* **130**, 17 (1969).

85. McGregor, D. D. and Koster, F. T., *Cell. Immunol.* **2**, 317 (1971).

86. North, R. J. and Mackaness, G. B., in preparation.

87. Nathan, C. F., Karnovsky, M. L., and David, J. R., *J. Exp. Med.* **133**, 1356 (1971).

88. Simon, H. B. and Sheagren, J. N., *J. Exp. Med.* **133**, 1377 (1971).

89. Godal, T., Rees, R. J. W., and Lamvik, J. O., *Clin. Exp. Immunol.* **8**, 625 (1971).

90. Lurie, M. B., *Resistance to Tuberculosis,* Harvard University Press, Cambridge, Massachusetts, 1964.

90a. Uhr, J. W., *Physiol. Rev.* **46**, 359 (1966).

90b. Turk, J. L., *Delayed Hypersensitivity,* North-Holland Publishing, Amsterdam, John Wiley and Sons, New York, 1967.

91. Ward, P. A., Remold, H. G., and David, J. R., *Cell. Immunol.* **1**, 162 (1970).

92. Kanai, K., *Jap. J. Med. Sci. Biol.* **20**, 20 (1967).

93. Collins, F. M., *Adv. Tuberc. Res.* **18**, 1 (1972).

94. Collins, F. M. and Mackaness, G. B., *Cell. Immunol.* **1**, 266 (1970).

95. Merigan, T. C. and Stevens, D. A., *Fed. Proc.* **30**, 1858 (1971).

96. Von Pirquet, C. E., *Arch. Int. Med.* **7**, 259 (1911).

97. Allison, A. C., *Brit. Med. Bull.* **23**, 60 (1967).

98. Mims, C. A., *Bacteriol. Rev.* **30**, 739 (1966).

99. Hirsch, M. S., *Fed. Proc.* **29**, 169 (1970).

100. Hirsch, M. S. and Murphy, F. A., *Lancet* **2**, 37 (1968).

101. James, K., *Fed. Proc.* **29**, 160 (1970).

102. O'Connel, C. J., Karzon, D. T., Barron, A. L., Plaut, M. E., and Ali, V. M., *Ann. Int. Med.* **60**, 282 (1964).

103. Volkert, M. and Lundstedt, G., *J. Exp. Med.* **127**, 327 (1968).

104. Blanden, R. V., *J. Exp. Med.* **132**, 1035 (1970).

105. Allison, A. C., *Proc. Roy. Soc. Med.* **63**, 1077 (1970).

106. Blanden, R. V., *J. Exp. Med.* **133**, 1074 (1971).

107. Blanden, R. V., *J. Exp. Med.* **133**, 1090 (1971).

108. Tompkins, W. A. F., Zarling, J. M., and Rawls, W. E., *Infect. Immunity* **2**, 783 (1970).

109. Green, J. A., Cooperband, S. R., and Kibrik, S., *Science* **164**, 1415 (1969).

110. Zuckerman, A. and Ristic, M., *Infectious Blood Diseases of Man and Animals,* Vol. I (D. Weinman and M. Ristic, Eds.), Academic Press, New York, 1968.

111. Fabiani, G. and Fulchiron, G., *C. R. Soc. Biol. (Paris)* **147,** 99 (1953).

112. Bruce-Chwatt, L. J. and Gibson, F. D., *Trans. Roy. Soc. Trop. Med. Hyg.* **50,** 47 (1956).

113. Briggs, N. T., Wellde, B. T., and Sadun, E. H., *Mil. Med.* **131** (Suppl.), 1243 (1966).

114. Spira, D. T., Silverman, P. H., and Gaines, C., *Immunology* **19,** 759 (1970).

115. Brown, I. N., Allison, A. C., and Taylor, R. B., *Nature (London)* **219,** 292 (1968).

116. Stechschulte, D. J., *Proc. Soc. Exp. Biol. Med.* **131,** 748 (1969).

117. Stechschulte, D. J., *Mil. Med.* **134,** 1147 (1969).

118. Phillips, R. S., *Exp. Parasit.* **27,** 479 (1970).

119. Nussenzweig, R. S., Vanderberg, J., Spitalny, G., Rivera, I., Orton, C., and Most, H., *J. Trop. Med. Hyg.,* **21,** 722 (1972).

120. Wagland, B. M. and Dineen, J. K., *Aust. J. Exp. Biol. Med. Sci.* **43,** 429 (1965).

121. Dineen, J. K. and Wagland, B. M., *Immunology* **11,** 47 (1966).

122. Dineen, J. K., Ronai, P. M., and Wagland, B. M., *Immunology* **15,** 671 (1968).

123. Kellermeyer, R. W. and Warren, K. S., *J. Exp. Med.* **131,** 21 (1970).

Chapter Nine

Cellular Aspects of Tumor Immunity

IRA GREEN, M.D. AND ETHAN M. SHEVACH, M.D.

Laboratory of Immunology, National Institute of Allergy and Infectious Diseases, National Institutes of Health, Bethesda, Maryland

A few years ago, Borrel remarked that the recognition by natural immunity represented the key to the problem of carcinoma. This is also my opinion, but I am convinced that natural immunity does not depend on the presence of antibodies but is only conditioned by purely cellular forces. . . . But gentlemen, we do not want to look into the future pessimistically. If we succeed in protecting the little experimental animals in simple and secure ways against the infection with tumor material of colossal virulence, thus there surely exists the possibility of achieving the same thing in a human being. The deeper we penetrate into the mechanism in animal experiments the greater will become the chances to later promote the therapy of the illness in a human. That was also the reason that I have taken up your attention today with the purely theoretical presentation of the state of experimental carcinoma research. For the medical art, the apt phrase applies, *Natura Artis Magistra.*

> From a lecture delivered by Paul Ehrlich at the University of Amsterdam, June 1, 1908. From *The Collected Papers of Paul Ehrlich* (F. Himmelweit, Ed. Pergamon Press, New York, 1957, p. 561.

It is not the purpose of this chapter to be all inclusive, rather we present an overview and try to discuss interpretatively what we feel are the currently important issues and problems in the field.

We start with a few generalizations. The immune response to tumors was investigated, and was part of the thinking of immunologists from almost the earliest beginnings of this discipline. There is really no tumor immunology as such; there is a general immunology and some parts of this immunology also apply to antigens that happen to be on or part of tumor cells. Thus, there is no evidence that there are special immunological situations that apply to tumors or tumor antigens which do not also apply to ordinary cells, tissues, or antigens. Although the general focus of tumor immunology has been to develop methods of using immunological forces for therapeutic or diagnostic use, another aspect of immunology which should not be overlooked is that the general insights into problems of cell differentiation obtained by studying the workings of the immune system may help to understand the nature of the disordered differentiation that is a part of malignant transformations.

Tumor immunology, and more particularly, the study of the precise manner by which lymphocytes and monocytes interact with tumor cells, is handicapped by the lack of fundamental immunological knowledge concerning the nature of recognition of ordinary antigens by cells. What happens in any particular host-tumor cell interaction, whether *in vivo* or *in vitro*, depends on the simultaneous interaction of several forces, often opposing. These forces may operate differently at different stages of tumor growth and differently depending on which site in the host the tumor is growing and perhaps even differently in different parts of the same tumor.

The idea that lymphocytes and mononuclear cells have a role to play in the rejection and destruction of tumors is not a new idea—it was stated clearly by Russell (1) and Ehrlich (2) in 1908, and by Dafano (3) and Woglom (4) in 1912 [using *in vitro* techniques, some of these authors (1912) looked unsuccessfully for toxic factors produced by lymphocytes]. Similar observations were made by other investigators during the early part of the twentieth century. *In vivo* studies demonstrated that almost any combination of cellular infiltrates, ranging from almost pure plasma cell infiltrate, to pure lymphocyte infiltrates, to mixtures of lymphocytes, monocytes, and plasma cells could be observed (5,6). These observations were made by both light and electron microscopy. Morphological observations alone, however, were and are not sufficient to define the mechanism by which these various cell types perform their roles. It is now known that destruction of tumor cell types *in vivo* or *in vitro* can be accomplished either by antibody and complement, by lymphoid cells, or by lymphoid cells and antibody. Under other circumstances antibody can inhibit or block the destruction of tumors by lymphoid cells. The word lymphoid cells is used as a general term here because, as we discuss below, different types of lymphoid cells can now be subdivided into bone-marrow-derived lymphocytes (B cells), thymus-derived lymphocytes (T cells), and macrophages, and each of these cell types may have its own and separate role to play in tumor cell damage. Of all these interactions, only the mechanism of destruction of tumor cells by antibody and complement is understood with any degree of sophistication.

Early in the 1960s a series of technical and conceptual advances allowed a concerted attack to be made on these problems. The main technical advances consisted of the development of *in vitro* models that allowed an identification and quantitation of tumor target cell-lymphocyte or antigen-lymphocyte interactions leading to the destruction of target cells or to the elaboration of "lymphokines" as well as to lymphocyte proliferation (7). Techniques were also developed to investigate receptors and antigens on the surface of lymphoid cells as well as on tumor cells. Conceptual advances were the identification of, and knowledge of interactions between, two classes of lymphocytes, B lymphocytes and T lymphocytes, and the identification of different receptors, immunoglobulins, and differentiation antigens on the surfaces of these different types of lymphocytes as well as on tumor cells. Finally, the nature of the interactions between lymphocytes, lymphokines, monocytes, and antibodies leading to immunological protection against infectious bacterial disease suggested that similar types of interactions could be expected between the immunological system and tumor cells (8).

Having made these generalizations, we now try to pinpoint the state of knowledge certain aspects of cellular immunity have currently reached, as well as the critical problems and areas for future study.

IMMUNE SURVEILLANCE

First we discuss evidence which suggests that immune forces are of importance in the defense against malignant growth, as was first suggested by Ehrlich and a number of other investigators in the first half of the twentieth century. These ideas were stimulated anew in 1959 when Thomas (9) suggested that it was unlikely that the mechanism of allograft rejection existed solely to protect the body against foreign skin grafts, but rather is probably the primary mechanism for natural defense against neoplasia. This concept was then championed by Burnet (10) who felt that inheritable genetic changes must occur commonly in somatic cells, and some of these genetic changes will, in turn, lead to new surface antigens as well as to malignancy. According to Burnet's postulate, it is an evolutionary necessity that there be some mechanism for inactivating or eliminating these dangerous malignant cells, and it is highly likely that this mechanism is immunological in nature. The concept of immune surveillance has proved difficult to submit to direct experimental proof, but has served as the stimulus for the rebirth of tumor immunology over the past decade.

Evidence for the surveillance function of cell-mediated immunity comes from a variety of clinical as well as experimental observations. A series of predictions based on this premise can be made. First, an increased incidence of malignant diseases should be seen at ages when the immunological function of the body is relatively inactive. Second, conditions associated with depression of cell-mediated immunity should be associated with an increased likelihood of neoplasia. Third, when a malignancy appears the process of surveillance has therefore failed, yet there should be occasions when tumors spontaneously regress owing to late activity of the surveillance mechanism, or alternatively, augmentation of cell-mediated immunity should lead to regression of malignancy. Evidence for the first two predictions is reviewed in this section. The role of augmentation of cell-mediated immunity for tumor immunotherapy is discussed separately.

It is of note that the role of the thymus in leukemogenesis in mice was discovered first (11), and indeed thymectomy of newborn mice for purposes of investigating viral leukemogenesis led to the discovery of the role of the thymus in cell-mediated immunity. A great number of studies have been performed to illustrate the effect of neonatal thymectomy on the subsequent development of malignancy. The role of the thymus in polyoma virus tumor induction was explored by Miller (11) and Ting and Law (12). C3H mice are ordinarily susceptible to the development of tumors following polyoma virus inoculation immediately after birth. C57 mice are quite resistant to tumor development under these conditions, while F_1 (C3H × C57) show about a 50% incidence of tumors. Following thymectomy at 3 days of age both C57 and F_1 mice are rendered susceptible to the effects of the oncogenic virus given 2 to 4 weeks after birth. The immunologic defect seen in these animals following thymectomy can be prevented by a variety of methods: (a) grafting of newborn thymus; (b) the intravenous injection of adult lymphoid cells from syngeneic donors; (c) the intraperitoneal installation of cell-tight micropore diffusion chambers containing neonatal thymus tissues. The explanation offered for the defect in cell-mediated immunity induced by thymectomy is that the newly acquired antigen on the tumor tissue does not evoke an effective immunologic response on the part of the host due to lack of the appropriate thymus-derived lymphocytes. On the other hand, it should be noted, that although a defect in cell-mediated immunity is implied by these studies, little or no lymphocyte depletion is seen in these animals. They are quite capable of rejecting allogeneic skin grafts. Their antibody response to sheep erythrocyte or to polyoma virus is normal. The effects of thymectomy also lead to an increased incidence of chemical carcinogen-induced neoplasms. Miller found that repeated painting of the skin with benzopyrene was more effective in producing multiple papillomata and skin carcinoma in neonatally thymectomized mice (13).

Immunosuppression by heterologous antilymphocyte serum also leads to an increased incidence of leukemias secondary to Moloney virus in BALB/c mice that are normally resistant to the leukemogenic effects of this virus (14).

In the experiments described to this point, the carcinogenic agent, whether it be oncogenic virus or chemical carcinogen, is introduced in the animals following thymectomy. However, the role of thymectomy or chronic administration of ALS in causing an increased incidence of spontaneous neoplasms in experimental animals is by no means clear; in some systems augmentation of malignancy is seen, while in others no increase in malignancy is seen. In other situations, such as tumor induction by the mammary tumor virus, prior administration of ALS or neonatal thymectomy leads to decreased frequency of tumors (15).

The human analogy to the neonatally thymectomized mice is the large group of patients, usually children, with inborn errors of the immune system. From the studies of Good and associates (16), data have been accumulated which show that malignancy occurs in this group of patients at a much higher frequency than age-matched controls. In patients with ataxia telangiectasia, a defect of both cell-mediated and humoral immunity, 36/300 have developed tumors which include leukemias, lymphosarcoma, Hodgkins disease, reticulum cell sarcoma, medulloblastomas, and epithelial tumors. Also of patients with the Wiskott-Aldrich syndrome 12/92 have developed malignancy usually of the lymphoreticular type. Of 50 patients with sex-linked agammaglobulinemia, 5 patients have developed leukemia, with 2 of these originating in the thymus. It should be noted that this group of patients has no demonstrable defects of cell-mediated immunity. Perhaps B lymphocytes also play a role in surveillance. On the other hand, the disordered architecture of the lymphoid organs of these patients may predispose them to malignant degeneration in these organs just as the disordered architecture of bone and colon in patients with Paget's disease and ulcerative colitis leads to increased frequency of bone and colonic neoplasms in these patients.

Although the increased incidence of malignancy in these experiments of nature with depressed cell-mediated immunity is indeed impressive, it is difficult to demonstrate that there is evidence of defective cell-mediated immunity in the ordinary adult with malignancy. A large number of studies have demonstrated that patients with widely disseminated malignancies have a significant impairment of their ability to manifest delayed cutaneous hypersensitivity to a variety of commonly encountered antigens as well as prolongation of skin graft survival (17,18). Most of the patients in these studies had far-advanced disease, and the abnormal test results are probably secondary to the advanced state of the disease rather than its cause. However, a recent study by Eilber and Morton of patients with localized nonlymphoreticular neoplasms has shown some impairment in the ability to develop delayed cutaneous hypersensitivity to 2,4-dinitrochlorobenzene (DNCB) (19). These authors demonstrated that 95% of normal people, but only 60% of patients with potentially resectable neoplasms, exhibited delayed cutaneous skin reactions to DNCB. Furthermore, a positive correlation was seen between the inability to react to DNCB and the incidence of either inoperability, local recurrence, or distant metastases 6 months postoperatively. If these studies are confirmed with a large series of patients with a wide variety of malignancies, it would suggest that an abnormality in cell-mediated immunity is present in many patients with localized malignancy and the presence or absence of DNCB sensitization may have important prognostic significance. Whether this inability to demonstrate contact sensitivity to DNCB is a specific manifestation of some disorder of lymphocyte function or whether it reflects an inability to mobilize macrophages is uncertain. The recent demonstration that many patients with malignancy have both abnormal croton oil responses as well as failure to sensitize with DNCB suggests that abnormalities of general inflammatory responses may also play a role in inability to contain tumor growth (20).

One of the other factors that may be responsible for the increased incidence of neoplasms in the aged is the possibility that the cell-mediated immune system may decline with age. This aspect of immunological function has not been investigated thoroughly. On the other hand, many of the childhood cancers (neuroblastoma, Wilm's tumor, acute leukemia, retinoblastoma, Burkitt's lymphoma) probably are initiated at birth or in utero when thymic function may not have been fully developed.

One group of patients which has received wide attention and careful monitoring for the development of malignancy is the growing number of recipients of allografts who are under long-term immunosuppressive therapy. Here again, the incidence of malignancy is indeed impressive (21,22). Of the more than 5000 renal and cardiac allograft recipients 52 have developed cancer which could not be attributed to malignant cells in the graft. Twenty-eight of these tumors were of epithelial origin and 24 were mesenchymal, predominantly lymphomas. Eight patients have also been observed who have supported transplants of malignant cells from donors bearing an epithelial malignancy. In one well-studied case, a metastatic carcinoma from the bronchus did not appear until 18 months after the renal allograft was placed (23). When immunosuppressive therapy was discontinued the previously functioning kidney was promptly rejected, whereas tumor growth was not altered. However, when the rejected kidney was removed along with the bulk of the tumor tissue and adjacent lymph nodes, disappearance of the residual cancer was seen. From the studies cited above, it would appear that the surveillance function of cell-mediated immunity is indeed compromised in patients on long-term immunosuppression.

As pointed out by Schwartz, depression of cell-mediated immunity may not be the only explanation for the development of malignancies in allograft recipients (24). In his view, organ transplantation provides persistent antigenic stimulation to the lymphoid system of the recipient. Some of the lymphoid hyperplasia then progresses to malignancy. A number of experimental situations offer some support to this view. Animals that have indolent chronic graft-versus-host reactions have a high incidence of malignancy (25). Burkitt lymphoma only occurs in areas where malaria is endemic; perhaps the prolonged stimulation of the lymphoid system by this parasite is a prerequisite for the development of lymphoma (26). A number of patients with systemic lupus erythematosus, ulcerative colitis, regional enteritis, or autoimmune hemolytic anemia are now being treated with immunosuppressive agents. Although an increased incidence of malignancy has not been reported in this now large group of patients, many more years of careful observation are needed before it can be concluded that these patients will not be subject to the high incidence of malignancy seen in allograft recipients.

Although this discussion has focused on the importance of the role of cell-mediated immunity in immune surveillance, we do not wish to conclude that defective surveillance is the *sine qua non* for the development of malignancy. A number of arguments have been offered against the surveillance concepts and have been reviewed by Prehn (27). In his view, the immune surveillance hypothesis requires that all tumors be antigenic and immunogenic, but not all tumors in experimental situations can be shown to bear tumor-specific antigens. It follows from the immunosurveillance argument that tumors that have escaped the surveillance mechanism should be nonantigenic or at least only weakly antigenic, yet many of these tumors bear easily detectable antigens. If a tumor develops in an environment where surveillance functions are absent (i.e. *in vitro* in a tissue culture system), it should be strongly antigenic, yet most of these tumors are not.

Nature and Immunogenicity of Tumor-Associated Antigens

The prime assumption of the immune surveillance concept is that tumor cells contain antigens that are not found on normal cells. When the surveillance mechanism is functioning normally, these antigens are recognized as immunogens, and an immune response is mounted against the antigen and the malignant cell which bears it. There is no reason to believe that what is known of the normal immune response to structurally well-defined protein molecules does not apply to the more complex antigens of the malignant cell. In order to more fully understand and interpret the large body of experimental evidence concerning tumor antigens, we briefly review at this time the nature of these antigens and their mode of recognition.

Most antigens are composed of haptenic portions and carrier portions. The immune system interacts with the antigen by a complex series of events in which macrophages, T cells, B cells all play a role. As is discussed in detail elsewhere in this volume (for example, in Chapters 1 and 4), the T cells are thought to interact with the carrier portions and the B cells produce antibody to the haptenic portions of the antigens. These interrelationships can be seen, for example, in the immune response to a single antigen such as bovine glucagon composed of 29 amino acids (28). Tryptic digestion of glucagon yields two polypeptides, NM and C. Antibody from immune animals is directed against only the NM peptide and shows no binding to C. Only the intact molecule and the C fragment stimulate lymphoid cells from animals immunized with glucagon to synthesize DNA *in vitro*. Thus, in the case of glucagon, the major immunogenic determinant is the C peptide and it plays the role of carrier; the NM peptide takes the role of hapten. However, both NM and C elicit delayed hypersensitivity and inhibit the migration of peritoneal macrophages from immune animals. This lack of correlation between *in vitro* stimulation of DNA synthesis and skin reactivity has been reported for a number of antigens including tobacco mosaic virus (29) and a carbohydrate fraction isolated from tuberculin (30). These findings probably indicate a further complexity in the mechanism of binding of antigen by the T lymphocyte.

The immune response to tumor antigens can also be viewed in terms of a hapten-carrier relationship. In this manner, certain tumor antigens would provoke both delayed hypersensitivity and antibody production. The specificity of the antibody could be directed to the hapten determinant portion of the antigen, whereas the forces of delayed hypersensitivity would be directed against the carrier portions of the tumor antigen. On the other hand, since it has been shown that it is relatively easy to immunize an animal artificially to produce just delayed hypersensitivity without detectable antibody production (31), it is conceivable that the *in vivo* immune response to some tumor antigens might invoke only delayed hypersensitivity (DH). As is seen with glucagon peptides, a tumor antigen might provoke one arm of the cell-mediated immune system, i.e., those lymphocytes which release migration inhibition factor, but might not induce those lymphocytes which mediate other functions, i.e., proliferation of lymphocytes or lymphocyte-mediated cytotoxicity.

Although one might argue that cell-associated antigens might behave differently from simple protein molecules, an examination of the immune response to human blood group mucopolysaccharide antigens demonstrates that these systems may behave in similar fashions (32). When guinea pigs are immunized with either human blood group A or Le^a substance, circulating antibody is produced with specificity for the immunizing antigen; no cross-reactive antibody is produced. Yet when the delayed skin reactions are examined in these animals, a marked degree of cross-reactivity is seen between these substances. Thus, animals immunized with A substance showed delayed hypersensitivity not only to A but also to Le^a. B, and H substances, despite the distinct antibody specificities of these mucopolysaccharides. This antibody specificity has been shown to be directed against the polysaccharide moiety of the macromolecule. The cross-reactivity of the delayed response is attributed to a shared integral component of the blood group substance molecules which is probably in the polypeptide portion of the molecule. Thus, in terms of at least one class of cell-associated antigen, the blood group antigens, the immune response resembles that observed to hapten-protein conjugates; a dissociation between the specificity of the antihapten antibody response and the delayed skin reaction is present.

Another aspect of the immune response to tumor antigens which may be of importance is that the genetic makeup of the host plays an important role in the recognition of immunogenicity. Genetic control of the immune response has been demonstrated to a large variety of antigens, both simple synthetic polyα-amino acid antigens and complex protein antigens (33). These genetic influences on the immune response can operate on at least two levels. First, at the level of the sequence of nucleotides in the DNA which encode for the sequence of amino acids in the variable portions of the light and heavy chain of the immunoglobulin molecule which in turn determine the configuration of the antibody-combining site. Second, genetic influences operate by as yet poorly understood mechanisms at the level of the recognition of immunogenicity of the carrier portion of the antigen; here the cell involved is thought to be the thymus-derived lymphocyte. Extensive analysis of several immune response genes (Ir genes) of the guinea pig has demonstrated that the presence of these genes is associated with delayed hypersensitivity and *in vitro* manifestations of cellular immunity, whereas in the absence of the gene, no evidence for cellular immunity can be elicited (34). However, when animals lacking the gene are immunized with these antigens electrostatically complexed to foreign protein antigen, antibody can be produced. Thus, in these animals the structural information for antibody synthesis appears to be intact.

A similar analysis of several mouse Ir genes has led to a similar conclusion. That is, the defect is in the thymus-derived cell and recognition of carrier function is lacking in nonresponder animals. Another remarkable feature of these immune systems is that there is often a linkage between the Ir gene and the major histocompatibility antigen of the species (35). This association has been most extensively studied in the mouse and guinea pig. The precise functional meaning of this association has aroused considerable speculation, but definitive answers are not yet apparent.

In early 1960s, shortly before these developments in immunology, a series of investigations clearly demonstrated that there was a variety of associations between the H-2 type of mouse and *in vivo* susceptibility to murine viral oncogenesis (36). These two series of facts rapidly led to the conclusion that there may be an important relationship between histocompatibility-linked Ir genes and problems of oncognesis and immune response to tumor antigens. During the past 2 years, positive correlations have been made between the presence of certain HLA types and the frequency of certain types of malignancy and autoimmune disease (37,38).

These associations may be based on at least 4 theoretical mechanisms. In the first, histocompatibility antigens may provide a receptor site on the cell membrane for causational virus. Second, the H-2 type is a major determinant of the ability of the virus-induced antigen to integrate into the cell membrane—this hypothesis also assumes that the malignant transformation requires the presence of this new antigen. Third, histo-compatibility antigens may closely resemble antigens present on viruses, thus tolerance to the virus would be present, thereby limiting an effective immune response. Fourth, the presence or absence of specific Ir genes would determine specific immune responses, either cellular or humoral, to antigenic components of the virus or antigens of malignant cells. The ability of Ir genes to determine the immune response to complex tissue antigens has been amply demonstrated by the effect of the genes on the rejection of male skin grafts in mice (39) and rejection of parental bone marrow by F_1 mice (40). No definitive evidence in favor of any of these mechanisms is available however, and no evidence was found for the first and second hypotheses (36). Aoki et al observed that those mice resistant to Gross virus leukemogenesis of the $H\text{-}2^b$ or $H\text{-}2^b/H^k$ type had a higher level of natural antibody to Gross tumor-specific anti-gen. This suggests that histocompatibility-linked Ir genes may be respon-sible for specific antibody production to such tumor antigens and thus the resistance observed in certain strains to Gross virus leukemogenesis (41).

The extreme complexity and large areas of uncertainty in the manner in which mouse leukemia viruses interact with the proper murine host to induce leukemia makes an analysis of mechanisms of the H-2-linked effects very difficult (42). In view of the fact that the meaning and mechanism of action of histocompatibility-linked Ir genes also remain a mystery, definitive answers as to the nature of the relationships in human disease would appear to be in the more distant future and will certainly require identification of Ir genes in humans. Thus, although it is apparent that histocompatibility-linked Ir genes may play several important roles in human and animal tumor immunology, each particu-lar case of association between HLA type and disease will require inten-sive study and it may well be that different specific associations may depend on different mechanisms or constellations of mechanisms. Final-ly, an analysis of the immune response to, and mechanism of recognition of, very simple synthetic antigens may lead to an understanding of the general mechanisms involved in immune recognition of more complex antigens, such as tumor antigens. More work in this area is therefore warranted.

It should be recalled that the early studies on tumor immunology were hampered by the lack of knowledge of the allograft response and that it was only with the development of inbred strains of animals that immunity to tumor-specific antigens could be studied in the absence of immunity to histocompatibility antigens (43). Over the past 15 years experimental tumor immunology has concentrated on two classes of tumors—those induced by oncogenic viruses and those induced by carcinogens. The tumor-associated antigens of these two classes of tumors differ markedly in their properties, and these differences are briefly reviewed. Most of the impetus for these experimental studies on animal tumors is based on the hope that the observations will be applicable to the neoplasms of man, and may lead to the development of a rational immunotherapeutic approach to human malignancy. However, as is discussed below, the application of this experimental approach to the species *Homo sapiens,* which consists predominantly of noninbred strains, is fraught with difficulty.

The earliest studies demonstrating tumor-specific antigens were performed on carcinogen-induced tumors of inbred mice by Gross (44), Foley (45), and Prehn and Main (46). These investigators demonstrated that if methylcholantharene (MCA)-induced sarcomas were allowed to grow in mice and then later surgically removed, then upon subsequent challenge with the tumor, marked inhibition of tumor growth was seen. These and later studies demonstrated that carcinogen-induced tumors bear specific antigens that are unique to each tumor. Even when multiple tumors are induced in one animal, each tumor has distinctive antigenicity. The transplantation technique for the demonstration of tumor-associated antigens is an *in vivo* procedure using either a small tumor inoculum, amputation of a growing tumor, irradiated tumor cells, or the *in vitro* admixture of immune cells or serum with the tumor, followed by inoculation into a susceptible host. The subsequent rejection of a challenge dose of tumor cells by the immune animal resembles the allograft rejection. A tumor-specific transplantation antigen was then assumed to be present on the tumor cell when such a maneuver could be performed.

Whether these antigens are unique to malignant cells or whether each individual normal cell has its own unique antigen has not been resolved. According to the latter argument when a cell becomes malignant and multiplies its unique antigen greatly increases in quantity and then appears as a specific tumor transplantation antigen. A precedent for this thought is the fact that each normal plasma cell makes a unique immunoglobulin. When plasma cells become malignant a large amount of this protein is produced. Finally, it has been shown that a protein from such a malignant plasma cell can act as a tumor-specific antigen because when syngeneic normal mice are immunized with this particular myeloma protein, such mice are then protected against inoculation with the myeloma cells producing the specific myeloma protein (47,48).

In contrast to the antigens induced by carcinogens, animal tumors induced by one of the RNA or DNA viruses demonstrate a different pattern of tumor-associated antigenicity (49). All tumors induced by the same virus share tumor-specific antigens; thus, an animal immunized against one polyoma-induced tumor is immune to the growth of any polyoma tumor induced in the same species. Those tumors induced by the DNA viruses also bear an intranuclear neoantigen, the "T" or transformation antigen (50). T antigens can be demonstrated by the immunofluorescent technique or by complement fixation tests. Although this latter group of antigens is not found on the cell surface and hence does not lead to the rejection of growing tumor, they are useful in the detection of viral infection of the cell.

Studies of the precise chemical composition of both carcinogen-induced antigens and viral-associated transplantation antigens are in their infancy. When more information concerning the chemical structures is known, then perhaps a decision can be made as to which portions of the antigen serve as carrier and haptenic determinants.

Attempts to Demonstrate Humoral and Cellular Immunity to Tumors in Humans

The distinctive patterns of tumor-associated antigenicity of the two major classes of animal neoplasms, the chemical carcinogen-induced and the viral-induced, offer an approach to the analysis of tumor-associated antigenicity in man. The early observation that lymphoid infiltration of tumors is roughly correlated with a good prognosis suggested that host resistance to cancer in man may be of an immunologic nature (51), although mononuclear infiltrates by themselves do not guarantee an underlying immunologic mechanism (see Chapter 3). One of the earliest and most direct approaches to the demonstration of tumor-specific antigens was to show that tumor cell explants are rejected in the tumor's own host. These studies by Southam (52) demonstrated that tumor cell explants were rejected in the autologous host if small numbers of tumor cells were used. Large cell inocula (greater than 10^8 cells) resulted in tumor takes in the majority of instances. Solid tumor implants would more readily take than implants of dissociated cells. These studies suggested that there was some resistance to the implantation growth of human cancer, but offered little proof that this resistance was immunological in nature. Unfortunately, most cancer autotransplantation studies were performed in patients with incurable disease because of the fear that in a curable patient an autotransplant might develop into a focus of malignancy. Thus, experimental autotransplantation is limited to those patients who have shown little or no resistance to their own cancer.

If oncogenic *viruses* play an etiologic role in the genesis of human malignancy, it might be possible to detect antibodies to viral-induced antigens in the sera of patients with certain classes of malignancy. A number of studies offer some evidence that this may be the case. Klein (53) used the indirect immunofluorescent technique and demonstrated that cells from fresh biopsies of Burkitt lymphomas and from cell lines propagated in culture possess antigens that can be detected by incubation of the tumor cells with scrum from the Burkitt patients. However, these studies did not establish whether the antigens so detected were viral in origin. Those patients that responded well to chemotherapy were more prone to have antibodies against their tumors than those patients in whom therapy had little effect. Most sera demonstrated reactivity with allogeneic tumor cells as well as with autologous tissue; quite a few positive reactions were also seen with the sera from patients with diseases other than the Burkitt lymphoma. These studies suggested that a common antigen, perhaps of viral origin, is present on Burkitt lymphoma cells. Antibodies to this antigen are present in the sera of a high proportion of patients, and also in the sera of other individuals who might have been exposed to this single etiologic agent. Similar results have been reported by Morton's group in the study of patients with malignant melanoma (54). The immunofluorescent technique demonstrates prominent cytoplasmic and perinuclear fluorescence of autologous or allogeneic tumor cells when the sera of patients with melanoma are examined. Patients with localized melanoma were found to have significantly higher antibody levels than patients with widespread disease. About 20% of healthy blood donors demonstrated a positive staining pattern, while 85% of relatives of patients had positive tests. Here again, exposure to a common environmental antigen (possibly oncogenic virus) is postulated as the cause of positive sera from normal individuals and relatives. Similar results have been obtained by this group of investigators in the study of osteogenic sarcoma (55).

A number of questions can be raised about the nature of the antibody detected in these studies. In Klein's study the antibody was not cytotoxic for the tumor *in vitro,* yet the presence of this antibody was a good prognostic sign. In Morton's study of sarcomas, a rising titer of antibody was usually seen following resection of the tumor. This was interpreted as decreased absorption of antibody by large tumor mass (54). Do these antibodies possess cytotoxic properties *in vivo?* If so, then the responses to these classes of solid tumors would be atypical in that tumor immunity would be primarily humoral in nature.

Although the presence of serum antibodies to tumor-associated antigens may have important diagnostic and perhaps prognostic significance, the great majority of studies in animals demonstrate that tumor immunity is cellular rather than humoral in nature.

In order to avoid the limitations of the autotransplantation technique of living tumor cells a number of studies have been performed using delayed skin reactivity to tumor cell extracts as a measure of cell-mediated immunity or *in vitro* assessment of cellular immunity. One of the early studies by Hughes and Lytton (56) demonstrated positive DH skin reactivity in 25% of patients to crude extracts of carcinomas (breast, stomach, colon, lung); no correlation was seen between reactivity to the tumor cell sonicate and the clinical state. Studies of Burkitt lymphoma patients by skin testing with membrane extracts of autologous tumor cells revealed a marked correlation between the clinical condition of the patient and skin reactivity (57,58). When a patient in remission with a positive skin test relapsed, the positive skin reaction rapidly converted to negative. It should also be noted that some DH responses could be observed when extracts of normal tissues were used. Of interest is that in this study very little skin reactivity could be demonstrated to extracts of allogeneic Burkitt tumors; this is in marked contrast to cross-reactivity of serum antibody to allogeneic Burkitt tumor tissue demonstrated by Klein using the immunofluorescent technique.

Although the DH skin reaction might prove to be a simple direct measure of cell-mediated immunity to tumor antigens, a number of problems arise in the interpretation of these studies. First, a recent study of skin test reactivity of African patients with malignant melanoma (59), although again demonstrating a high incidence of positive DH skin test to autologous tumor, showed that a significant percentage of these patients also reacted to an extract of normal skin. This suggests that some of the immunity was tissue specific rather than tumor specific, and/or that nonspecific irritation by these extracts was also present. Second, most of these studies suggest a positive correlation between the magnitude of skin reactivity and the favorable clinical state of the patient. It is therefore implied that a strong antitumor response is reflected in the skin test. Again, nonimmunological inflammation may also be depressed in ill patients.

The *in vitro* assay of cell-mediated immunity to tumor-associated antigens in humans has been performed by three techniques: the stimulation of lymphocytes to undergo blast transformation when incubated with autologous tumor cells; the inhibition of macrophage migration by soluble tumor extracts; and *in vitro* assays of lymphocyte-mediated cytotoxicity. Stjernsward (60) has found reactivity against Burkitt lymphoma cells, sarcomas, and carcinomas of the kidney, lung, and testis by *in vitro* stimulation of proliferation of lymphocytes by these tumor cells. In his studies no correlation was seen between lymphocyte stimulation and the clinical state of the patient. Only in the case of renal cell carcinoma were normal kidney cells used as control. Jehn et al (61) have shown that the lymphocytes from patients with malignant melanoma could be markedly stimulated *in vitro* by material extracted from autologous tumors. In this study, material extracted from one of the tumors stimulated the lymphocytes of all the other patients, but did not stimulate the lymphocytes of normal individuals. This suggests that each patient became sensitized to a common antigen, perhaps viral, present in malignant melanoma.

A number of studies of patients with acute leukemia have shown stimulation of remission to normal lymphocytes by autologous viable blast cells which had been stored in the frozen state (62,63). However, other investigators studying identical twins, one of whom had leukemia, did not demonstrate that the leukemia cells from the patient could stimulate the cells of the normal twin; the cells from the normal twin never stimulated the cells from the leukemia patient (64). In inbred guinea pigs (65), the macrophage migration technique was used to demonstrate cellular immunity to soluble antigens of a chemically induced tumor. Recently, Anderson (66) has shown that extracts of breast cancer can also inhibit the migration of autologous leukocytes in a significant number of patients; these tumor cell extracts do not inhibit the migration of normal leukocytes.

A number of *in vitro* techniques have recently been developed to assay the cytotoxic activity of lymphocytes from patients against tissue culture cells derived from the appropriate tumors. The Hellströms (67) have used the *in vitro* inhibition by sensitized lymphocytes of colony formation (CI) with tissue culture cells derived from neuroblastomas, carcinomas of the colon, nasopharynx, bladder, breast, lung, kidney, testis, and a variety of other tumors. In their system, allogeneic lymphocytes from patients with the same histological type of tumor give positive reactions, suggesting that a common antigen of each tumor type is detected by this technique. Patients' lymphocytes give negative reactions when reacted against tissue culture cells derived from different histological types of tumors. However, the reaction of patients' lymphocytes against tissue culture cells derived from normal cells has concomitantly been examined in only some cases, and the possibility exists that the reaction detected by the CI assays may be organ specific rather than tumor specific. The *in vitro* release assay using ^{51}Cr-labeled target cells is another way to study tumor immunity (68). This technique should prove useful in the study of human tumors such as the leukemias or lymphomas which can be readily chromium labeled.

In summary, the majority of both the *in vitro* and *in vivo* studies of tumor immunity in man suggest that there is some activity of the cell-mediated immune system toward tumor-associated antigens. However, at present, few conclusions can be drawn from the large number of studies that have been performed. Only after a large number of patients with different malignant diseases have been studied simultaneously by a number of standardized techniques will it be possible to correlate the presence of a DH skin reaction, the presence or absence of humoral immunity, and/or the presence of *in vitro* blast transformation to tumor antigens with the clinical course and prognosis.

MECHANISMS OF TUMOR CELL DESTRUCTION

In this section we wish to examine in more detail what is known about how lymphocytes exert their cytotoxic effects and how antibodies modify lymphocyte-mediated cytotoxicity. For this purpose the following *in vitro* models have been employed (69): (1) lymphoid cells from animals sensitized to target cells. This sensitization can also be accomplished *in vitro*. It has been demonstrated that at least in some of these models, the lymphocytes involved are thymus derived. Cells from animals sensitized to protein antigens can also damage innocent bystander red blood cells coated with the antigen (70,71); (2) lymphoid cells from normal animals stimulated with PHA (72), or lymphoid cells from normal animals in the presence of antibody to target cells can also mediate damage (73–75). These lymphocytes may prove to be bone marrow derived (75). In a variant of this latter experiment, target red blood cells can be coated with antibody and various complement components (76); (3) populations of macrophages can also be employed in attacking cells (77); (4) very recently there has been a suggestion of T cell or B cell cooperation in damage to tumor cells (8). Finally, there are models in which soluble supernatant factors produced by lymphoid cells *in vitro* can damage various types of target cells (78).

Many of the early *in vitro* studies were performed using whole spleen cells or lymph node cell populations as attacking cells before all these facets of the problem were understood. It is now apparent under such circumstances in these seemingly simple *in vitro* situations that several different types of destructive processes may be going on simultaneously. For example, one type of destructive process involves thymus-derived lymphocytes (79), another type may involve interactions between normal lymphocytes, perhaps bone marrow derived and small amounts of antibody to target cells produced *in vitro* by plasma cells. At the same time, this antibody may inhibit the cytotoxic effect of T lymphocytes (80). Also some complement components may be produced *in vitro* and may participate. Nonspecific T cells in the population may also become activated by antigen-antibody complexes so that they may also become cytotoxic. Lymphocytes may also produce various "lymphokines" which may directly damage target cells; in addition certain lymphokines activate macrophages so that these cells become cytotoxic for tumor cells and/or surrounding normal tissues. In addition, any polymorphonuclear leukocytes present can also damage target cells (81). Thus, the *in vitro* interactions can almost be as complicated as *in vivo* interactions. The present goal therefore is to identify and then take each of these separate types of destructive interactions and study them in detail. There are currently available a number of *in vitro* procedures that allow collection of populations of one or another type of cell. Selective destruction of certain classes of lymphoid cells can be employed; for example, anti-Θ and complement can be used for destruction of mouse T cells, anti-κ and complement for destruction of mouse B cells. Recently, a heterologous antiguinea pig T cell antibody has also become available (82). Alternatively, B cells and macrophages have receptors for either immunoglobulin or immunoglobulin-antigen-complement complexes which allow properly sensitized erythrocytes to form rosettes with either B cells or macrophages (83). These rosettes can be separated by sedimentation and then collected. The adherent red blood cells can be removed and pure B cells obtained. The remaining unsedimented cells are enriched in T cells. *In vivo* maneuvers involving irradiation of animals followed by either bone marrow or thymus cell reconstitution can also provide almost pure populations of either B or T cells. Also, combination of *in vitro* depletion of specific cell types followed by *in vivo* infusion of remaining cells into irradiated recipients results in pure populations of either B or T cells. Only by the use of such separately obtained pure cell populations to study cytotoxic effects will further progress be made. Yet appearing on the near horizon are further difficulties. For example, there may be subsets of different T cells that may collaborate with each other and, alternatively, that may have different functions (84). Also, B cells have on their surface different subclasses of immunoglobulin; each subclass-bearing cell may have a different biological property. Since the "death" of target cells may in itself be a complex event, attempts should also be made to simplify the target—perhaps lipid membranes in the form of liposomes in which protein antigens have been incorporated could be used (85). Here, electron microscopy, electrobiophysical measurements, as well as release of materials from within the liposome, could be studied. Another fruitful area for future investigation should be electron-microscopic examination, by negative staining techniques, of target erythrocytes undergoing destruction by various types of lymphocyte-mediated cytotoxic reactions. The presence or absence of 80- to 100-Å holes in the erythrocyte membrane, similar to those observed after the action of antibody and complement, might provide an important clue as to what is happening (86). Preliminary attempts in our laboratory to visualize such holes in target erythrocyte membranes have been unsuccessful. Previous electron-microscopic studies of either *in vivo* or *in vitro* lymphocyte-target cell interactions have been interesting and have demonstrated, among other things, fusion of the membranes between lymphocytes and target cells, and involvement of the uropod of the lymphocytes. However, these studies have not provided definitive insights as to the mechanism of killing (87,88).

The question of the specificity of these *in vitro* reactions can be briefly summarized as follows: At the present time the majority of the *in vitro* models studied suggest that the destructive effects of lymphoid cells are highly specific—adjacent nonspecific target cells remain intact (89). Also, close contact between attacking and target cell is necessary. However, some studies demonstrate innocent bystander effects; it should be noted that the bystanders may not be completely innocent—in some cases antigen may be absorbed on their surface.

The precise chemical nature of the antigen on the surface of tumor cells which is required to first sensitize and activate, for example, T cells, and the nature of the antigen on the surface of the target cell which is necessary for the subsequent cytotoxic reaction by that T cell are unknown. Also unknown is whether the cell that is the first recognizing cell is also the executor cell. We would guess, however, that the material recognized as foreign may well be the carrier portion of the antigen, possibly protein in nature, since a variety of evidence suggests that T cells appear to recognize the carrier portion of the antigen in other cellular immune phenomena such as delayed hypersensitivity and the T–B cell interaction that leads to augmented antibody production (90,91). Studies of Brondz (92,93) amd Brunner (94) suggest that an entire array of antigens must be displayed on the target cell before lymphocytes can exert their "cytotoxic" effects.

Quantitative studies of the behavior of killer lymphocytes *in vitro* suggest that a single lymphocyte is capable of adversely affecting a single target cell. As many as 2% of cells in a population may have this property (95).

Whether the "killer" properties of T lymphocytes are clonally distributed or whether a lymphocyte is polyvalent in its ability to kill target cells has also not been definitely settled. The recent studies of Golstein (96), Berke (97), and their coworkers, however, strongly suggest that the "killer" property is clonally distributed.

The ultimate aim of all these *in vitro* models is to use the information gained in the model studies to try to reconstruct and manipulate the many events that are involved in the *in vivo* recognition and attack upon the tumor antigens by the immune mechanisms of the animal or human host. Considering that in most cases the *in vitro* events are only beginning to be understood and sorted out, the exact reconstruction of *in vivo* events would appear to be a more distant goal.

The next subject that we wish to discuss is the role of enhancement or blocking antibodies in tumor immunology. This subject is far from new, and yet new concepts, techniques, and clinical hopes have given a fresh impetus for studies in this area. In 1960 Peter Gorer remarked at the 4th Tissue Homotransplantation Conference (98), "many of us have unburdened ourselves of theories of enhancement. I plead guilty; Medawar has done it; Snell has done it; and Kaliss has done it. I think I can speak for all of us if I say that none of us is really very devoted to any of the theories we have put forward, but all of us, I think, would agree on one thing: that somehow humoral antibody can interfere with the proper function of the host cells." This unburdening process has continued until the present time—and 12 years later a definite answer is not available. The reason for this is probably that here again enhancement of tumor growth, either *in vivo* or *in vitro,* is merely a description of a phenomenon—there are probably many different types of enhancement, each working by its own separate mechanism. In any one *in vivo* or *in vitro* situation, several types of enhancement may be occurring simultaneously. The three favorite mechanisms of enhancement that have been postulated are in the broadest terms: (1) afferent block—antigen is prevented from sensitizing, (2) efferent block—antibody covers sites on target cell which are subject to attack, and (3) central—antibody or antigen-antibody complexes directly prevent function of lymphocytes.

During the past few years a considerable amount of interest has been generated by several studies which demonstrated that in animals or humans bearing growing tumors, lymphoid cells are present in the host which are capable of damaging these same tumor cells *in vitro*. Addition of serum from the host "blocks" or "enhances" this *in vitro* cytotoxicity (99,100). These studies therefore suggest that these tumors first of all have TSTA*; furthermore, some of these antigens are shared in common by tumors of the same type from different individuals; and finally, the continued *in vivo* growth of these tumors is postulated to be due to enhancement (101).

Recently, the "tolerance" seen in allophenic mice has been claimed by some (102) but not all authors (103) to be on this same basis, as has the classical "Nobel prize tolerance" of Medawar and his associates, which was induced by injecting lymphoid cells into newborn mice (104,105). The major mechanism currently proposed for these observations is that antibody is invariably present in the tolerant animal and that antibody-antigen complexes centrally inhibit the *in vivo* functioning of attacker lymphocytes (106). The ultimate interpretation of these findings is rendered difficult because the subject of enhancement and tolerance to tissue grafts has in a sense been examined and considered rather separately from "tolerance" to ordinary protein antigens. Here again tolerance is only the description of a phenomenon. In each field a large and complex literature has arisen (107,108). It would be desirable if some type of combined thinking concerning these two different types of tolerance would be undertaken. It is immediately obvious that an analysis of tolerance to tissues (which is defined as the duration or survival of such grafts) is exceedingly more complex than an analysis of tolerance to a simple protein antigen. The survival of tissue grafts undoubtedly depends on the simultaneous interaction of many forces, both humoral and cellular. At the present time it is exceedingly difficult to measure and quantitate these humoral and cellular factors independently of measuring the survival of the graft in either *in vivo* or *in vitro* systems. Tolerance to a tissue may thus be the end result of increased antibody production of certain classes, decreased antibody production of other classes, and the decrease in function of more than one type of lymphocyte-mediated cytotoxicity. In contrast, in tolerance to simple protein antigens either *in vivo* or *in vitro*, precise measurements of the degree of impairment of antibody production, the fine specificity and affinity of the antibody can all be measured (109). The impairment of cellular immune functions, after tolerance induction by protein antigens, can be measured by *in vivo* delayed sensitivity and by the degree of

---

*Tumor-specific transplantation antigen.

in vitro stimulation of proliferation or by production of MIF.

Recently it has been shown that tolerance to protein antigens can exist both at the B cell level and at the T cell level (110). The time requirements, ease, and the nature of the antigenic determinant necessary to induce tolerance in B cells and T cells also appear to be different. Also, B cells can be made tolerant with haptens alone, whereas the production of T cell tolerance may require the presence of the immunogenic carrier (111).

Clearly, the evaluation of the cellular sites of tolerance to tissues, tumors, and other grafts cannot as yet be made with the same degree of precision as is the case with tolerance to protein antigens. Again, this should be a future goal for investigators interested in tolerance to tissues.

Now that we have made these rather general comments, we wish to deal with the current problem of whether all inhibition of cytotoxic T cell function can be ascribed to the presence of blocking antibody, or whether T cells can be rendered tolerant or removed or killed without the intervention of antibody but rather by some direct interaction with antigen. It is clear that in certain aspects of T cell function, notably helper effects in which T cell–B cell interaction leads to increased antibody production, that T cell function can be removed directly or inactivated by physical means such as absorption of T cells by antigen affinity columns (112), or by exposure of T cells to highly radioactive antigens (113). Furthermore, transferred thymus cells from mice made tolerant *in vivo* to human gamma globulin cannot cooperate with normal bone marrow in radiated recipients to allow antibody production (110). Here again it is difficult to imagine how antibody could be inhibiting the functions of these washed, tolerant T cells in the recipient animal. In an *in vitro* system in which one directly evaluates a presumably T-cell-mediated cytotoxicity it has been recently demonstrated that specific T cells can be specifically removed by absorption to target cells. The remaining supernatant cells were unable to mediate cytotoxicity and are therefore "tolerant," and again antibody cannot easily be implicated in this tolerance (96,97). The ability of modest numbers of injected lymphocytes, either normal or immune, to abolish tolerance of a long-standing skin graft easily (114) or to cause rejection of a tumor (115) again suggests that enhancing antibody may not be the entire explanation for the inactivity of T-cell-mediated cytotoxicity *in vitro* or *in vivo*.

Considering that even in *in vitro* models of lymphocyte-mediated cytotoxicity, of which colony inhibition is an example, several different lymphocyte cytotoxic phenomena may be going on at the same time, and since both polymorphonuclear leukocytes and monocytes, which may also be present in the attacker populations, are also capable of causing target cell death, great caution must be exercised in the interpretation of findings in these systems. Our overall opinion is that although antibody-enhancing mechanisms play a role *in vivo* in preventing lymphocyte-mediated cytotoxicity, other mechanisms involving direct antigen inactivation of cytotoxic lymphocyte function may also play important roles. It can be noted here parenthetically that blocking or enhancing antibody has been suggested as one of the mechanisms preventing autoimmune aggression by lymphocytes against normal self-antigens in normal individuals. According to this hypothesis, the reason that patients with hypogammaglobulinemia have an increased incidence of autoimmune disease is that they have lost their enhancing or blocking antibody to normal self-antigens (116).

IMMUNOTHERAPY OF CANCER

The ultimate purpose of understanding the immunological forces involved in the immunity to tumors is to develop rational immunotherapeutic techniques. If the development of malignancy signifies a defective surveillance function of the cell-mediated immune system, one approach to tumor therapy would be to augment the cell-mediated immune responses of the tumor-bearing host. A number of different experimental approaches have been used to achieve this purpose. The observation by Old et al (117) that an inoculum of a small number of tumor cells containing TSTA may develop into tumors, while an inoculum consisting of a large number of cells is rejected, suggests that in certain instances an actively growing tumor may not induce the maximum possible antigenic stimulus. One approach to tumor immunotherapy is the injection of tumor cells into a tumor-bearing host in order to increase the effective antigenic challenge. Tumor "vaccines" have been produced using (1) subthreshold doses of living tumor cells, (2) irradiated tumor cells, (3) living cells inoculated intradermally, a site known to promote growth followed by regression, (4) cells emulsified in an adjuvant, or (5) cell-free extracts. Nadler and Moore (118,119) treated 73 patients with advanced cancer with homologous vaccines consisting of irradiated or nonirradiated cultured tumor cells; one patient in this large series may have shown a response. Czajkowski et al (120), in an attempt to increase the antigenicity of a nonantigenic substance, treated 14 patients with far-advanced malignant tumors with autologous tumor cells chemically coupled to a highly antigenic foreign protein such as rabbit gamma globulin. Although 13/14 patients demonstrated antitumor antibody following immunization and 14/14 had positive titers to rabbit gamma globulin, no beneficial antitumor response was seen. Kronman et al (121) have recently reported the successful treatment of a solid tumor in the guinea pig by repeated intradermal injection of living tumor cells. In these experiments, living tumor cells were injected intramuscularly; 5 days later the first of 3 weekly intradermal inoculations with live tumor cells was initiated. The effect of intradermal immunizations was dependent on the challenging dose of the tumor cells inoculated intramuscularly. At the two lower doses used, 4/12 animals were free of tumor and survived for more than 1 year. Success or failure of immunotherapy in this and other systems is dependent on the number of cells in the challenge inoculum.

Another approach to tumor immunotherapy is the so-called passive transfer of cell-mediated immunity by immunocompetent cells. In animal experiments, Klein and Sjogren (122) demonstrated that if syngeneic lymphocytes obtained from animals immune to the tumor were mixed with tumor cells *in vitro* and then inoculated into a susceptible syngeneic host, inhibition of tumor growth can be seen. Immune cells are also capable of suppressing tumor growth when transferred a number of days after tumor challenge; however, in this situation, the size of the tumor at the time of immune cell transfer is critically important. Tumors larger than 2.5 cm in diameter rarely show any response.

A number of experimental studies have also been performed involving the transfusion of immune or nonimmune allogeneic or xenogeneic lymphocytes into tumor-bearing animals or patients. The subject has been reviewed recently by Alexander (123). Although it would initially appear likely that the mechanisms of action of sensitized allogeneic lymphocytes would be to destroy the tumor cells which bear the specific tumor transplantation antigens, a number of experimental observations suggest that this possibility is rather unlikely. In animal studies the infused cells are not found at the site of the tumor, but rather the majority are found in the spleen; the antitumor action of the immune lymphocytes was abolished if the tumor-bearing animals had been splenectomized; and finally blockade of the host's reticuloendothelial system with colloidal carbon, which might be expected to facilitate preventing their destruction in the RE system, reduces the antitumor effect. Alexander has suggested that the allogeneic immunocompetent cells release RNA which stimulates the production of cytotoxic immunocytes by the tumor-bearing animal. In his experiments he was able to achieve results, similar to those obtained by the infusion of immune lymphocytes, by using RNA extracted from thoracic duct lymphocytes obtained from specifically immunized donors. No effect on tumor growth was seen with RNA isolated from the lymphocytes of animals that had not been immunized or by RNA from animals immunized with another tumor. These results have been confirmed in a similar tumor model by Pilch and his associates (124). In their studies, immunity to tumor isografts in inbred mice can be mediated by syngeneic spleen cells preincubated with RNA extracted from the lymphoid organs of guinea pigs immunized with the specific tumor that is to be treated. Normal nonimmune spleen cells are then converted to specific, immunoreactive status during this brief *in vitro* incubation with immune RNA. The response is specific for the particular tumor used to immunize the guinea pig from whose lymphoid organs the immune RNA was prepared.

The exact mechanism of transfer of immunologic competence with RNA is not known. It has been suggested that highly immunogenic complexes of a unique species of RNA with antigen or certain antigenic determinants (the "superantigen"), or perhaps the presence of true informational RNA moieties that are incorporated by normal lymphoid cells and then code for a specific immune response are responsible. The concept of an immunologically active RNA that can be extracted from sensitized lymphoid cells of another species and then confer tumor immunity on the lymphoid cells of tumor-bearing animals is indeed attractive. However, a number of studies have demonstrated that RNA extracted from the lymphoid cells of an immunized animal is unable to transfer immune competence to the lymphoid cells of a nonimmunized animal. For example, Bluestein et al (125) extracted RNA from the lymph node cells of responder (strain 2) guinea pigs immunized with DNP-PLL, and then added this RNA *in vitro* to the lymph node cells from normal nonresponder (strain 13) guinea pigs; the strain 13 lymphoid cells exposed to the RNA did not respond to the antigen DNP-PLL. Before immune RNA is used therapeutically for patients with a malignancy, more confirmatory experiments, as well as information on the mechanism of these transfers of immunocompetence, should be obtained by working with the transfer of immunological competence to simple protein antigens in animal systems.

Although sensitized allogeneic or xenogeneic cells may play a role in tumor immunotherapy, a large number of studies have been performed using nonsensitized normal allogeneic lymphocytes; in these studies a beneficial antitumor effect has also been observed. Thus, Woodruff and Nolan (126) used unsensitized spleen cells instead of sensitized spleen cells to treat 8 patients with terminal malignancy. After transfer of between 5×10^9 and 48×10^9 cells/patient, temperature elevations, hyperemia, and necrotic reactions were seen at the site of tumor nodules. In this situation when allogeneic or xenogeneic cells are injected they should be quickly rejected by the immunocompetent host. Therefore, in most animal studies the recipients are either lethally or sublethally irradiated prior to the injection of the allogeneic cells. This procedure in turn leads to an acute graft-versus-host (GVH) reaction. In the experiments of Boranic (127) where the acute graft-versus-host reaction was modified by cytotoxic drug therapy and the life span of the radiation chimeras was prolonged, no recurrence of an experimental leukemia was seen. Thus, it appears that the induction of a GVH reaction by transfer of allogeneic cells can have a significantly beneficial antitumor effect.

The presumed mechanisms of action of this beneficial effect of GVH reaction is through augmentation of the host's cellular immune responses. Recent studies by Katz, Ellman, et al (128,129) have attempted to analyze which cell type in the host is activated by the GVH reaction. In the experimental model employed in these studies, strain 13 guinea pig lymphoid cells were transferred into normal nonirradiated strain 2 recipients prior to challenge with the syngeneic leukemia L2C. Highly significant protection was seen in those guinea pigs given allogeneic lymphoid cells 1, 3, or 6 days prior to lethal leukemic challenge; allogeneic cells transferred 21 days prior to leukemia challenge were completely ineffective in prolonging survival times. Lymphoid cells obtained from F_1 (2×13) donors were ineffective in this system, indicating that a graft-versus-host reaction is required for an antileukemic effect. One population of cells that could be activated by the GVH reaction consifts of the primary cells of the reticuloendothelial system, the macrophages. Indeed, in the mouse, following the induction of GVH in nonirradiated F_1 recipients of parental donor cells, there is a significant increase in the host's resistance to bacterial infection, which is attributed to activation of the host's macrophage populations (130). Activated macrophages could be responsible for the antileukemic effect in the guinea pig system; however, in the guinea pig, the allogeneic effect is maximal 6 days prior to leukemic challenge, while in the mouse the increased resistance to bacterial infection is seen 3 weeks after allogeneic cell transfer. Another possibility is that the host's lymphocytes could be stimulated to produce nonspecific cytotoxic factors as a result of immunological attack of grafted donor cells against host tissue. Such cytotoxic factors produced by host cells following induction of the GVH reaction have been demonstrated to destroy tumor cells (131). The third possibility is that the

GVH reaction initiates or augments a specific cell-mediated antitumor immune response. In the guinea pig experiments described above, a large proportion of those animals that had a prolonged survival were later able to reject a second lethal challenge of leukemia cells. This finding indicates that lasting cell-mediated immunity presumably due to specifically sensitized lymphocytes had developed during the course of the GVH reaction.

The role of the reticuloendothelial system in the host's resistance to neoplasia has been actively explored over the past decade. A number of studies have demonstrated that prior treatment with certain agents including endotoxin, zymosan, and infection with Bacillus Calmette-Guerin (BCG) (132) and recently toxoplasmosis (133) alters favorably the host's response to bacterial or viral infection or to challenge with ionizing radiation. These agents also enhance the capacity of the host to form antibody, and heightened phagocytic and increased bactericidal capacity of the macrophages can be demonstrated. Initial studies showed that prior infection with BCG markedly increased an animal's resistance to subsequent challenge with a tumor. While much smaller doses of BCG were able to increase resistance to bacterial challenge, relatively large doses of BCG were required to obtain tumor protection. With carcinogen-induced tumors occasional enhancement of tumor growth was seen. It has also been shown recently that a methanol-insoluble residue (MER) of phenol-killed BCG is also effective when given before tumor challenge (134). The advantage of this preparation is that it is nonliving and is chemically and physically stable; it is also well tolerated by tissues locally and induces only a low degree of tuberculin sensitivity. The effects of MER are considerably less when it is given simultaneously with tumor cells or after tumor implantation. Thus, BCG and its extracts can presumably enhance the activity of the RE system and thereby inhibit tumor growth. However, the effect of BCG infection is minimal once the tumor has been established. In one experiment, where BCG was injected 2 weeks prior to carcinogen injection, it did not alter the rate of tumor appearance or final incidence (132). Alternatively, when the injection of BCG was initiated 80 days following carcinogen injection, a definite delay in the appearance of the tumors was observed, although the final cumulative incidence of tumors was eventually similar to that seen in the control group.

More recent studies have demonstrated that the injection of BCG directly into a tumor nodule may have a significant immunotherapeutic effect. Thus, Morton et al (135) showed a complete regression in 90% of 184 melanoma nodules that were directly injected with BCG, in 5 patients who became tuberculin positive. A fourfold rise in melanoma-specific antibody was also seen in these patients. It is likely that a large portion of the antitumor effect was nonspecific and resulted from a delayed hypersensitivity reaction occurring within the melanoma nodules. However, in 3 of the patients, lymphocytic infiltration and rejection of uninjected nodules were seen. The response to BCG injection was clearly related to the status of the cell-mediated immune system in the patient. All patients who could be sensitized to DNCB, or who developed tuberculin hypersensitivity, or who developed a fourfold rise in antibody titer, had some response to immunotherapy; anergic patients had no response.

The mechanism of antitumor action of locally injected BCG has been carefully evaluated in the guinea pig by Zbar et al (136). They demonstrated that the growth of an intradermally transplanted syngeneic tumor in guinea pigs is markedly suppressed by the presence of BCG. Optimal suppression of tumor requires living BCG, close contact between tumor cells and BCG, and a cell-mediated immune response on the part of the host. Injection of living BCG alone at one site and tumor alone at another site does not lead to suppression of tumor growth. It is not clear whether tumor cells are killed at the site of BCG injection entirely as a consequence of a delayed hypersensitivity reaction to BCG, or whether there is a contribution of specific tumor immunity. It is felt by these investigators that specific tumor immunity is of minor importance in the rejection of tumor cells at the site of BCG injection. These investigators were also able to demonstrate that living tumor cells could be killed at the site of a delayed hypersensitivity reaction against antigenically unrelated tumor cells (137). In the latter instance, it should be recognized that much more than just the tumor cells are being destroyed. A large amount of damage to normal tissue (although perhaps clinically unimportant) may be going on. The fact that such nonspecific damage to normal tissue must occur is not at all surprising since necrosis of normal skin, as a part of ordinary tuberculin reactions, has been known for 60 to 70 years! Here the damage to normal tissues may occur because of the very intimate association between tubercle proteins and normal skin components—the Lawrence "self + X" hypothesis (138). On the other hand, there are a number of studies that clearly indicate that a small number of nonspecific tumor cells or normal cells, for example parental skin melanocytes, can be in the immediate environment of the rejection of a large number of specific F_1 target cells and yet survive (139).

All that can be said about these contradictory observations is that the result of each particular experimental design must be considered separately and that under some circumstances the reaction is specific and in others it is not. This, of course, is not very reassuring to those who are planning to extrapolate from animal experiments optimal conditions for the treatment of human cancer.

One popular example given in support of the concept of the specificity of damage to tumors involves basal cell carcinoma (140). The discovery that superficial basal cell carcinoma can be treated successfully by topical sensitization with reactive haptens such as dinitrofluorobenzene (DNFB) has been greeted with much glee from tumor immunologists. However, here the rather specific damage to the basal cell carcinoma may have very little to do with the fact that what is being damaged is a tumor. What probably happens is that the normal epidermal barrier to penetration of materials is absent over the tumor, and therefore the dose of DNFB received by the tumor is significantly greater than that received by normal skin. The same authors have demonstrated that basal cell tumors of the skin can also respond well to nonimmunological topical therapy—for example, with 5-fluorouracil—and probably for the same reason (140). At this point it can be added parenthetically that there are other good theoretical justifications for the use of chemically reactive haptens as immunotherapeutic agents. The reactive hapten after conjugation with selfproteins makes a configuration to which the animal is not tolerant. Thus rabbit thyroglobulin conjugated with a reactive hapten becomes immunogenic for rabbits (141). The cells that become sensitized to this conjugate, however, may also cross-react with unmodified thyroglobulin. There is evidence that this indeed occurs, and that a form of autoimmune thyroiditis ensues.

By the same reasoning, a tumor antigen can be coupled to a reactive hapten, and hopefully the specificity of the sensitized immune cells may encompass the unmodified tumor antigen. Thus, in a sense an autoimmune disease to a tumor may hopefully be induced. This maneuver has also been recently reported to be successful in a murine tumor system (142). However, if the tumor antigen load is excessively large, this maneuver would not be likely to succeed. Thus, in rabbits immunized with hapten conjugates of rabbit serum albumin (RSA), no "autoimmune disease" involving normal albumin could be demonstrated—the half-life of unmodified albumin was unchanged in animals immunized with hapten conjugates of RSA (143).

FINAL COMMENTS

At the beginning of this chapter, it was stated that there is really no tumor immunology—just immunology, some of which also applies to antigens on tumor cells. Nevertheless, tumors do have certain specific properties that influence their interaction with the immunological systems of the host. For example, as demonstrated by the penetration of dyes, there are regions of large tumors which may have very poor blood supply and yet contain living tumor cells (144). Since both cells and various humoral components such as antibodies and complement may not easily reach tumor cells in these regions (145,146), these are, in a sense, immunologically privileged sites. Another special aspect of tumor cells is that they may have unusual surface structures, increases in glycolipids and glycoproteins, and rearrangement or uncovering of cryptic sites (147). Also, certain tumors may release large quantities of antigens which circulate; these antigens may have complex and widespread effects on the immunological systems of the host. The understanding and manipulation of these surface features of tumor cells may allow methods (for example, neuraminidase treatment) that will enhance the immune response to such tumor cells (148). Finally, recent studies have demonstrated the feasibility of studying intercellular communications between various populations of immunocompetent cells (149) and between agressor lymphoid cells and target cells (150). We believe that future investigation in these areas may prove highly rewarding.

To conclude, tumor immunology is an exceedingly complicated field. There are an array of poorly understood immunological forces and a heterogeneous group of human tumors, *in vitro* models, and clinical situations. Each particular combination of tumor and immunological response, either *in vivo* or *in vitro*, in animals or in man, appears to be different. Although a detailed and ultimately complete knowledge of the many individual mechanisms involved in cellular host defenses would be most desirable for the treatment of human malignant disease, this knowledge does not appear to be immediately forthcoming. Therefore, a continued combination of basic research in immunological mechanisms together with the somewhat empirical experimentation in human disease is indicated. With luck, empirically successful methods for human cancer immunotherapy may be developed before all is known at the most basic levels.

REFERENCES

1. Russell, B. R. G., Third Scientific Report of the Imperial Research Fund, 1908, p. 341.
2. *The Collected Papers of Paul Ehrlich* (F. Himmelweit, Ed.), Pergamon Press, New York, 1957.

3. Defano, C. Fifth Scientific Report of the Imperial Cancer Research Fund, 1912, p. 57.

4. Woglom, W. H., Fifth Scientific Report of the Imperial Cancer Research Fund, 1912, p. 43.

5. Gorer, P. A., *Ann. N. Y. Acad. Sci.* **73,** 707 (1958).

6. Baruah, B. D., *Cancer Res.* **201,** 1184 (1960).

7. *Mediators of Cellular Immunity* (H. S. Lawrence and M. Landy, Eds.), Academic Press, New York, 1969.

8. Grant, C. K., Currie, G. A., and Alexander, P., *J. Exp. Med.* **135,** 150 (1972).

9. Thomas, L., in *Cellular and Humoral Aspects of the Hypersensitive States* (H. Sherwood Lawrence, Ed.), Hoeber-Harper, New York, 1959, p. 529.

10. Burnet, F. M., *Prog. Exp. Tumor Res.* **13,** 1 (1970).

11. Miller, J. F. A. P., *Adv. Cancer Res.* **6,** 292 (1961).

12. Ting, R. C. and Law, L. W., *Prog. Exp. Tumor Res.* **9,** 165 (1967).

13. Miller, J. F. A. P., Grant, G. A., and Roe, F. J. C., *Nature* **199,** 920 (1963).

14. Law, L. W., *Fed. Proc.* **29,** 171 (1970).

15. Heppner, G. H., Wood, P. C., and Weiss, D. W., *Israel J. Med. Sci.* **4,** 1195 (1968).

16. Good, R. A., in *Immune Surveillance* (R. T. Smith and M. Landy, Eds.), Academic Press, New York, 1970, p. 442.

17. Aisenberg, A. C., *Cancer Res.* **26,** 1152 (1966).

18. Solowey, A. G., and Rapaport, F. T., *Surg. Gynecol. Obstet.* **14,** 756 (1965).

19. Eilber, F. R. and Morton, D. L., *Cancer* **25,** 362 (1970).

20. Johnson, M. W., Maibach, H. I., and Salmon, S. E., *New England J. Med.* **284,** 1255 (1971).

21. McKhann, C. F., *Transplantation* **8,** 209 (1969).

22. Schneck, S. A. and Penn, I., *Lancet* **1,** 983 (1971).

23. Wilson, R. E., Hager, E. B., Hampers, C. L., et al *New England J. Med.* **278,** 479 (1968).

24. Leibowitz, S. and Schwartz, R. S., *Adv. Int. Med.* **17,** 95 (1971).

25. Schwartz, R. S. and Beldotti, L., *Science* **149,** 1151 (1965).

26. O'Connor, G. T., *Am. J. Med.* **48,** 279 (1970).

27. Prehn, R. T., *Prog. Exp. Tumor Res.* **14,** 1, (1971).

28. Senyk, G., Williams, E. B., Nitecki, D. E., and Goodman, J. W., *J. Exp. Med.* **133,** 1294 (1971).

29. Spitler, L., Benjamini, E., Young, J. D., Kaplan, H., and Fudenberg, H. H., *J. Exp. Med.* **131,** 133 (1970).

30. Chaparas, S. D., Thor, D., Godfrey, H. P., Baer, H., and Hedrick, S. R., *Science* **170,** 637 (1970).

31. Uhr, J. W., Salvin, S. B., and Pappenheimer, A. M., Jr., *J. Exp. Med.* **105,** 11 (1957).

32. Holborow, E. J. and Loewi, G., *Immunology* **5,** 278 (1962).

33. McDevitt, H. O. and Benacerraf, B. B., *Adv. Immunol.* **11,** 31 (1969).

34. Green, I., Ellman, L., Martin, W. J., and Benacerraf, B. B., in *Cellular Interactions in the Immune Response* (S. Cohen, G. Cudkowicz, and R. T. McCluskey, Eds.), S. Karger, Basel, Switzerland, 1971, p. 76.

35. Benacerraf, B. B. and McDevitt, H. O., *Science* **175,** 273 (1972).

36. Lilly, F., in *Cellular Interactions in the Immune Response* (S. Cohen, G. Cudkowicz, and R. T. McCluskey, Eds.), S. Karger, Basel, Switzerland, 1971, p. 103.

37. McDevitt, H. O. and Bodmer, W. F., *Am. J. Med.* **52,** 1 (1972).

38. Ellman, L., Green, I., and Martin, W. J., *Lancet* **1,** 1104 (1970).

39. Stimpfling, J. H. and Reichert, A. E., *Transplantation* **12,** 527 (1971).

40. Cudkowicz, G. and Stimpfling, J. H., *Immunology* **7,** 291 (1964).

41. Aoki, T., Boyse, E. A., and Old, L. J., *Cancer Res.* **26,** 1415 (1966).

42. Kaplan, H. S., *Cancer Res.* **27,** 1325 (1967).

43. Woglom, W. H., *Cancer Rev.* **4,** 129 (1929).

44. Gross, L., *Cancer Res.* **3,** 326 (1943).

45. Foley, E. J., *Cancer Res.* **13,** 578 (1953).

46. Prehn, R. T. and Main, J. M., *J. Natl. Cancer Inst.* **18,** 769 (1957).

47. Sirisinha, S. and Eisen, H. N., *Proc. Natl. Acad. Sci.* **68,** 3130 (1971).

48. Shearer, W. T., Graff, R. J., and Eisen, H., *Transplantation* **13,** 345 (1972).

49. Allen, D. W. and Cole, P. *New England J. Med.* **286,** 70 (1972).

50. Habel, K., Malignant transformation of viruses, in *Recent Results in Cancer Research,* (H. Kirsten, Ed.), Springer-Verlag, New York, 1966, p. 60.

51. Black, M. M. and Speer, F. D. *Surg. Gynecol. Obstet.* **109,** 105 (1959).

52. Southam, C., *Prog. Exp. Tumor Res.* **9,** 1 (1967).

53. Klein, G., Clifford, P., Klein, E., and Stjernsward, J., *Proc. Natl. Acad. Sci.* **55,** 1628 (1966).

54. Morton, D. L., Eilber, F. R., and Malmgren, R. A., *Prog. Exp. Tumor Res.* **14,** 25 (1971).

55. Eilber, F. R. and Morton, D. L., *J. Natl. Cancer Inst.* **44,** 651, (1970).

56. Hughes, L. E. and Lytton, B., *Brit. Med. J.* **1,** 209 (1964).

57. Fass, L., Herberman, R. B., and Ziegler, J., *New England J. Med.* **282,** 776 (1970).

58. Bluming, A. Z., Ziegler, J. L., Fass, L., and Herberman, R. B., *Clin. Exp. Immunol.,* **9,** 713 (1971).

59. Bluming, A. Z., Vogel, C. L., Ziegler, J. L., and Kiryabwire, W. M., *J. Natl. Cancer Inst.* **48,** 17 (1972).

60. Stjernsward, J., Almgard, L. E., Franzen, S., von Schreeb, T., and Wadstrom, L. B., *Clin. Exp. Immunol.* **6,** 963 (1970).

61. Jehn, V., Nathenson, L., Schwartz, R. S., and Skinner, M., *New England J. Med.* **283,** 329 (1970).

62. Friedman, W. H. and Kourilsky, F. M., *Nature* **224,** 277 (1969).

63. Leventhal, B. G., Halterman, R., Rosenberg, E. B., and Herberman, R. B., *Cancer Res.,* **32,** 1820 (1972).

64. Rudolph, R. H., Mickelson, E., and Thomas, E. D., *J. Clin. Invest.* **49,** 2271 (1970).

65. Bloom, B. R., Bennett, B., Oettgen, H. F., McLean, E. P., and Old, L. J., *Proc. Natl. Acad. Sci.* **64,** 1176 (1969).

66. Anderson, V., Bendixen, G., Schiolt, T., and Dissing, I., *Int. J. Cancer* **5,** 557 (1970).

67. Hellström, K. E. and Hellström, I., *Adv. Cancer Res.* **12,** 167 (1969).

68. Canty, T. G. and Wunderlich, J. R., *J. Natl. Cancer Inst.* **45,** 761 (1970).

69. Perlmann, P. and Holm, G., *Adv. Immunol.* **11,** 117 (1969).

70. Perlmann, P., Perlmann, H., Wasserman, J., and Packalen, A., *Int. Arch. Allergy* **38,** 204 (1970).

71. Chapuis, B. and Brunner, K. T., *Int. Arch. Allergy* **40,** 321 (1971).

72. Holm, G., Perlmann, P., Werner, B., *Nature* **203,** 884 (1964).

73. Bubenik, J., Perlmann, P., and Hasek, M., *Transplantation* **10,** 290 (1970).

74. MacLennan, I. C. M. and Harding, B., *Nature* **227,** 1246 (1970).

75. van Boxel, J. A., Stobo, J. D., Paul, W. E., and Green, I., *Science* **175,** 194 (1972).

76. Perlmann, P., Perlmann, H., Müller-Eberhard, H. J., and Manni, J. A., *Science* **163,** 937 (1969).

77. Granger, G. A. and Weiser, R. S., *Science* **151,** 97 (1966).

78. Ruddle, N. and Waksman, B., *J. Exp. Med.* **128,** 1260 (1968).

79. Lonai, P., Clark, W. R., and Feldman, M., *Nature* **229,** 566 (1971).

80. Moller, E. *J. Exp. Med.* **122,** 11 (1965).

81. Pickaven, A. H., Ratcliffe, N. A., Williams, A. E., and Smith, H., *Nat. New Biol.* **235,** 186 (1972).

82. Shevach, E. M., Green, I., Ellman, L., and Maillard, J., *Nat. New Biol.* **235,** 19 (1972).

83. Bianco, C., Patrick, R., and Nussenzweig, V., *J. Exp. Med.* **132,** 702 (1970).

84. Cantor, H. and Asofsky, R., *J. Exp. Med.* **131,** 235 (1970).

85. Sessa, G. and Weissman, G., *J. Lipid Res.* **9,** 310 (1968).

86. Humphrey, J. H. and Dourmashkin, R., *Adv. Immunol.* **11,** 75 (1969).

87. Journey, L. J. and Amos, D. B., *Cancer Res.* **22,** 998 (1962).

88. Weiss, L. and Smyth, P., *J. Immunol.* **105,** 1375 (1970).

89. *Immune Surveillance* (R. T. Smith and M. Landy, Eds.), Academic Press, New York, 1970, p. 181.

90. Raff, M. C., *Nature* **226,** 1257 (1970).

91. Mitchison, N. A., *Eur. J. Immunol.* **1,** 8 (1971).

92. Brondz, B. D., *Folia Biol. (Prague)* **14,** 115 (1968).

93. Brondz, B. D. and Golberg, N., *Folia Biol. (Prague)* **16,** 20 (1970).

94. Mauel, J., Rudolf, H., Chapuis, B., and Brunner, K. T., *Immunology* **18,** 517 (1970).

95. Wilson, D. B., *J. Exp. Med.* **122,** 143 (1965).

96. Golstein, A., Svedmyr, E. A. J., and Wigzell, H., *J. Exp. Med.* **134,** 1305 (1971).

97. Berke, G. and Levey, R. H., *J. Exp. Med.* **135,** 972 (1972).

98. *Ann. N. Y. Acad. Sci.* **87,** 291 (1960).

99. Hellström, I., Hellström, K. E., and Sjogren, H. O., *Cell. Immunol.* **1,** 18 (1970).

100. Hellström, I. and Hellström, K. E., *J. Reticuloendothel. Soc.* **10,** 131 (1971).

101. Hellström, K. E., Hellström, I., Sjogren, H. O., and Warner, G. A., in *Progress in Immunology* (B. Amos, Ed.), Academic Press, New York, 1971, p. 940.

102. Wegman, T. G., Hellström, I., and Hellström, K. E., *Proc. Natl. Acad. Sci.* **68,** 1644 (1971).

103. Ceppellini, R., in *Progress in Immunology* (B. Amos, Ed.), Academic Press, New York, 1971, p. 973.

104. Billingham, R. E., Brent, M., and Medawar, P. B., *Nature* **172,** 603 (1953).

105.   Hellström, I., Hellström, K. E., and Allison, A. C., *Nature* **230**, 49 (1971).

106.   Sjogren, H. O., Hellström, I., Bansal, S. C., and Hellström, K. E., *Proc. Natl. Acad. Sci. U.S.A.* **68**, 1372 (1971).

107.   Dresser, D. N. and Mitchison, N. A. *Adv. Immunol.* **8**, 129 (1968).

108.   Voisin, G. A., *Cell. Immunol.* **2**, 670 (1971).

109.   Paul, W. E., Siskind, G. W., and Benacerraf, B., *Immunology* **13**, 147 (1967).

110.   Chiller, J. M., Habicht, G. S., and Weigle, W. O., *Science* **171**, 813 (1971).

111.   Green, I., Paul, W. E., and Benacerraf, B., *J. Exp. Med.* **127**, 43 (1968).

112.   Davie, J. M. and Paul, W. E., *Cell. Immunol.* **1**, 404 (1970).

113.   Basten, A., Miller, J. F. A. P., Warner, N. L., and Pye, J., *Nat. New Biol.* **231**, 104 (1971).

114.   Billingham, R. E. and Brent, L., *Philos. Trans. Roy. Soc. London (Ser. B)* **242**, 439 (1959).

115.   Mitchison, N. A., *J. Exp. Med.* **102**, 157 (1955).

116.   Green, I. and Sperber, R. J., *N. Y. State J. Med.* **62**, 1679 (1962).

117.   Old, L. J., Boyse, E. A., Clarke, D. A., and Carswell, E. A., *Ann. N. Y. Acad. Sci.* **101**, 80 (1962).

118.   Nadler, S. H. and Moore, G. E., *Ann. Surg.* **164**, 482 (1966).

119.   Nadler, S. H. and Moore, G. E., *Arch. Surg.* **100**, 244 (1970).

120.   Czajkowski, N. P., Rosenblatt, M., Wolf, P. L., and Vasquez, J. *Lancet* **2**, 905 (1967).

121.   Kronman, B. S., Wepsic, H. T., Churchill, W. H., Zbar, B. et al *Science* **168**, 257 (1970).

122.   Klein, E. and Sjogren, H. O., *Cancer Res.* **20**, 452 (1962).

123.   Alexander, P., *Prog. Exp. Tumor Res.* **10**, 23 (1968).

124.   Pilch, Y. H., Ramming, K. P., and Deckers, P. J., *Israel J. Med. Sci.* **7**, 246 (1971).

125.   Bluestein, H. G., Green, I., and Benacerraf, B., *Proc. Soc. Exp. Biol. Med.* **135**, 146 (1970).

126.   Woodruff, M. F. A. and Nolan, B., *Lancet* **2**, 426 (1963).

127.   Boranic, M., *J. Natl. Cancer Inst.* **41**, 421 (1968).

128.   Katz, D. H., Ellman, L., Paul, W. E., Green, I., and Benacerraf, B., *Cancer Res.* **32**, 133 (1972).

129.   Ellman, L., Katz, D. H., Green, I., Paul, W. E., and Benacerraf, B., *Cancer Res.* **32**, 141 (1972).

130.   Howard, J. G., *Brit. J. Exp. Pathol.* **42**, 72 (1961).

131.   Singh, J. N., Sabadini, E., and Sehon, A. H., *Transplantation* **11**, 475 (1971).

132.   Old, L. J., Benacerraf, B., Clarke, D. A., Carswell, E. A., and Stockert, E., *Cancer Res.* **21**, 1281 (1961).

133.   Hibbs, J. B., Lambert, L. H., and Remington, J. S., *J. Infect. Dis.* **124**, 587 (1971).

134.   Weiss, D. W., Bonhag, R. S., and Leslie, P., *J. Exp. Med.* **124**, 1039 (1966).

135.   Morton, D., Eilber, F. R., Malmgren, R. A., et al, *Surgery* **68**, 158 (1970).

136.   Zbar, B., Bernstein, I. D., and Rapp, H. J., *J. Natl. Cancer Inst.* **46**, 831 (1971).

137.   Zbar, B., Wepsic, H. T., Borsos, T., and Rapp, H. J., *Natl. Cancer Inst.* **44**, 473 (1970).

138.   Lawrence, H. S., *Physiol. Rev.* **39**, 811 (1959).

139. Mintz, B. and Silvers, W. K., *Transplantation* **9,** 497 (1970).

140. Williams, A. C. and Klein, E., *Cancer* **25,** 450 (1970).

141. Weigle, W. O., and Nakamura, R. M., *J. Immunol.* **99,** 223 (1967).

142. Martin, W. J., Wunderlich, J. R., Fletcher, F., and Inman, J. K., *Proc. Natl. Acad. Sci.* **68,** 469 (1971).

143. Nachtigal, D. and Feldman, M., *Immunology* **7,** 616 (1964).

144. Goldacre, R. J. and Sylven, B., *Brit. J. Cancer* **16,** 306 (1962).

145. *Molecular Biology of Human Proteins*, Vol. 1 (H. E. Shultze and J. F. Heremans, Eds.), Elsevier, New York, 1966.

146. Carpenter, C. B., Ruddy, S., Shehadeh, I. H., Müller-Eberhard, H. J., et al, *J. Clin. Invest.* **48,** 1465 (1969).

147. Singer, S. J. and Nicolson, G. L., *Science* **175,** 720 (1972).

148. Simmons, R. L. and Rios, A., *Science* **174,** 591 (1971).

149. Hülsen, D. F. and Peters, J. H., *Eur. J. Immunol.* **1,** 494 (1971).

150. Sellen, D., Wallach, F. H., and Fischer, H., *Eur. J. Immunol.* **1,** 453 (1971).

Chapter Ten

Cellular Aspects of Transplantation Immunity

RAPHAEL H. LEVEY. M. D.

Department of Surgery, The Children's Hospital Medical Center and the Department of Surgery, Harvard Medical School, Boston, Massachusetts

The study of the cellular dynamics of the rejection of experimental and clinical allografts has led to the conclusion that the homograft reaction is a manifestation of a hypersensitivity of the delayed type, although the exact mechanisms by which it goes into effect are not yet fully understood. It is probable that conventional grafting methods will not answer this question regarding the final common pathway of the effector mechanism. However, workers in the field of transplantation biology have accumulated an impressive amount of fundamental knowledge of lymphoid cell kinetics and insights into immunological reactions generally. This chapter attempts to summarize some of this material selectively, to deal with studies that show the involvement of lymphocytes in the response of animals to allografts, and to justify the case for classifying the homograft reaction among the cellular immunities.

Supported by American Cancer Society Grant No. IC-48 and by U.S. Public Health Service Grant No. AM 16392-01.

HISTORICAL REVIEW

As early as 1596, Gaspare Tagliacozzi (1), a Renaissance Bolognese surgeon and anatomist, despaired of the idea of transplanting tissue from one individual to another because of the "force and power of individuality," although he owned a great reputation in restoring lost noses by means of a flap of tissue from the upper arm. In 1804, Baronio (2) demonstrated the survival of free skin autografts in sheep, and in 1823, Bunger (3) used free skin grafts from the thigh to reconstruct part of a patient's own nose. Paul Bert (4), a pupil of Claude Bernard, studied the fate of skin grafts between animals of the same and different species and concluded that there was a difference in the behavior of grafts depending on how closely the donor and recipient were related.

Gardeners and aborculturists have known for centuries that plants of one species could be grafted on to another one without in any way affecting the essential characters of either. Seventy-five years ago Joest (5) showed that a permanent union could be achieved between segments of two worms, *Lumbricus rubellus* and *Allolobophora terrestris*, and noted that each of the segments retained its individual characteristics. Similar observations were extended to tadpoles by Morgan (6) and Harrison (7). In 1897 Born (8) performed a more sophisticated study and attempted to unite two different amphibian grafts into one organism and found that such grafts failed within 14 to 16 days, while grafts between members of different orders of amphibia lasted only 1 or 2 days.

Six years later in 1903 Jensen (9) showed that certain spontaneous mammary tumors in mice could be transplanted within the same species, but would be rejected by members of other species. He also found that a second transplant of the same tumor would be rejected in an accelerated fashion and so established for the first time the importance of immunization in the transplantation of homologous tissue. Within a few years much was added to the knowledge of underlying tissue grafting in warm-blooded animals through the study of transplantable tumors. Rous (10) showed the strictness of the newly understood laws of tissue specificity by demonstrating that a certain chicken sarcoma failed to grow in any other than blood-related animals during its first few transfers, that later it would grow only in pure stock animals of the same variety, and lastly, would not grow in chickens of another variety until the malignancy had become greatly enhanced.

In 1910 DeFano (11) performed extensive histologic studies of the reaction about the cancer graft in immune animals. He showed that there was a marked increase in lymphocyte and plasma cell numbers about the graft at least during the first inoculation of the carcinoma into resistant animals but only in very small numbers at the time of the second inoculation, unless the first immunizing dose was weak, e.g., mouse embryo skin, in which a strong cellular reaction attended the second tumor graft. This description was the first which differentiated the histopathological response in virgin and immunized animals.

The first attempt at a genetic analysis of transplantation was made by Little and Tyzzer (12) followed by a whole series of papers by Fleisher, Little, Strong, Cloudman, and Bittner (13–18). These early reports recognized the presence of lymphocytes in rejected tumor and cartilage grafts, but it was Murphy who first clearly appreciated the fact that it was the lymphocyte which was the cell responsible for the development of transplantation immunity. In a series of remarkable and incisive papers in the 10 years from 1912 to 1922, Murphy (19–25) not only showed that the resistance to "heteroplastic" tissue grafts depended on the activity of the lymphocyte but also touched on many areas of research in transplantation biology that were to be elaborated in years to come in classic reports by other workers. He demonstrated among other things the immunological incompetence of the embryo, the coincident acquisition of competence and development of the lymphoid apparatus, the ability to equip the embryo with the power to reject tumor grafts by the transfer of small bits of adult lymphoid tissue to it, and the efficacy of X-irradiation in causing immune suppression by destruction of the lymphocyte. That Murphy recognized the causal relationship between immunity and lymphocyte function is clearly beyond doubt. He also stated that the natural and acquired resistance to tissue transplantation was an immunological phenomenon; however, at no time did he consider that these cells might be just one factor in a more encompassing series of immunological events as shown by his papers on local irradiation and heat application (26) as a method of increasing or decreasing the cellular response in limited areas that were then resistant or susceptible to grafts.

After Murphy, many reports showed that resistance to homologous tumor grafting could be abrogated by irradiation of the host (28–31). Mottram and Russ (32) demonstrated that rats immune to Jensen sarcoma could be rendered susceptible by such treatment.

Much of the early work on tissue transplantation was carried out using malignant tumors. However, the nature of the immunity reactions that determined the fate of transplanted neoplasms remained in dispute. Woglom (33) reviewed the subject in 1929 and concluded that immunity to transplanted tumors was unrelated to other forms of immunity. The unitary character of such reactions by lymphocytes, connective tissue, and humoral factors was stressed by Loeb (34) in his theory of organismal differentials. Little and Strong (35) had earlier formulated a more general genetic theory of tumor transplantation in the following terms: "The fate of the implanted tumor tissue when placed in a given individual (host) is brought about by a reaction between the host, determined to a large extent by its genetic constitution, and the transplanted tumor cell, controlled to some extent by its genetic constitution." Gorer (36) extended this hypothesis by rewording it as follows: "Normal and neoplastic tissues contain isoantigenic factors which are genetically determined. Isoantigenic factors present in the grafted tissue and absent in the host are capable of eliciting a response which results in destruction of the graft." He showed that the stimulus for graft destruction was immunological and that neither normal nor neoplastic tissue could be successfully transplanted into individuals drawn from genetically heterogeneous populations. Further studies by Gorer (37) demonstrated that isoantiserum directed against the transplantable mouse leukemic cells would inhibit the growth of that tumor.

At the same time Medawar (38–41) described the rejection of skin homografts in man and in rabbits and formulated the general rule that transplantation immunity was the outcome of a systemic and not a local reaction. Gibson and Medawar (38) observed the more rapid breakdown of a second skin homograft taken from the same donor and concluded that this reaction was due to the recipient being immunized by the graft itself. Medawar also suggested that the presence of a lymphatic drainage system is necessary for immunity to be called into being and that penetration by blood vessels must occur before it can come into effect. In his classic study of the fate of skin grafts in rabbits Medawar (39) conclusively demonstrated that graft destruction was accompanied by a heavy lymphocyte infiltration into the homograft.

A causal relationship between the morphologic alterations observed and the functional changes noted was first demonstrated in 1938 by Potter et al (42), who transferred immunity to a transplantable leukemia to mice by means of spleen cells.

A series of important experiments by Mitchison (43,44) and by Billingham, et al (45) demonstrated that transplantation immunity could be conferred on "virgin" animals by activated lymphoid cells just as Landsteiner and Chase (46) had shown that contact sensitivity in guinea pigs could be transferred to nonimmune hosts by suspensions by viable peritoneal exudate cells. Voisin and Maurer (47) repeated similar experiments and showed that living lymphocytes were required to transfer immunity to skin homografts.

In this atmosphere of new and rediscovered understanding Gorer (48) was able to conclude that several immunological mechanisms underlie the rejection of foreign grafts, depending on the various model systems involved. He recognized at least three types: (1) a graft of a solid tumor with a fibrovascular stroma into which infiltrate primarily lymphocytes; (2) a graft which proliferates without a stroma, such as an ascites tumor growing freely in the abdominal cavity and in which few lymphoid or plasma cells are present; (3) a leukotic graft in which cellular infiltrate is minimal and graft destruction is completed without the collusion of even histiocytes.

It soon became apparent that the histological rejection pattern of kidney allografts in the unsensitized recipient conformed to a pattern which generally resembled that observed with solid tumors.

Alexis Carrel (49) was the true pioneer both of vascular surgery and kidney transplantation, although in 1902 Ullmann (50) reported technical successes with both autologous and homologous renal transplants in dogs. The earliest long-term functioning of an autograft was described by Zaaijer (51) in 1908. In 1923 Williamson (52) noted the lymphocytic infiltration in renal homografts and recognized that the variation in survival times was probably the result of varying genetic relationships between donor and recipient. In the next 30 years sporadic reports (53–55) appeared which demonstrated the functional capabilities of renal homografts and the fact that cessation of function often occurred in the presence of histologically normal glomeruli and interstitial edema and round cell infiltration. However, the significance of these findings was not appreciated until the later and classic studies of Simonsen (56), Dempster (57–59), Hume (60), and their coworkers. It was at this time that the functional capacities of the small lymphocyte were being elegantly described by Gowans; and just as Harvey's insights regarding the circulation of the blood would have been impossible without the concurrent understandings of the mechanisms of actions of pumps in general, so immunologists and transplanters were able to join together to show that the lymphocyte was the agent and effector of transplantation immunity.

HISTOLOGY OF GRAFT REJECTION

In 1924 Emile Holman (61) reported two cases of repeated skin grafting in children in which the same donor was used. He found that while the second graft was more rapidly rejected than the first, skin from another donor remained intact. He concluded that a specific sensitization had occurred. Twenty years later, Medawar was still able to point out that the plastic surgeon had in the past relied upon the laboratory worker neither for "inspiration, principle nor technical aid." This was certainly true of early investigators who made no distinction between the fate of native and foreign skin. The fact that the histological picture of allograft destruction may represent a different immunological mechanism than that of conventional antigen-antibody reactions was first appreciated by Medawar.

In his classic reports to the War Wounds Committee of the Medical Research Council concerning the behavior and fate of skin autografts and homografts in rabbits, Medawar (39,40) described the cycle of events that lead to homograft destruction and emphasized the characteristic infiltration of lymphocytes in the dermis and perivascular spaces of the graft. He also saw large lymphocytes with an abnormally large investment of basophilic cytoplasm, cells most likely analogous to the large pyroninophilic cells of Gowans. This "atypical inflammation"—in view of the role of the lymphocyte—was associated in a dynamic fashion with the functional events that occurred: Namely, graft breakdown was anticipated by the specific lymphoid cell aggregations. The behavior of "second set" grafts was also described and he showed that the graft generated a systemic immune state which was specific in that it did not extend with equal vigor to skin from a graft donor other than the original one, that local immunity added little to the phenomenon, and lastly that ready-made antibodies did not seem to intervene in the reaction.

Primary canine renal allografts will maintain a dog in good health for some days before disintegration occurs. Microscopically the outstanding feature of this destruction is a cellular infiltration. Some authors felt that this cellular aggregation reflected an infection which terminated the natural life of the allografted organ (62,63) which then ended in parenchymal liquefaction of the rejected kidney.

Simonsen (56) and Dempster (57–59,64,65) were the first workers to take seriously the cells infiltrating the kidney and not to attribute the death of the graft to some typical or variant form of nephritis. Simonsen found the essential changes in a primary transplant to consist of focal interstitial infiltrations, localized in the periglomerular and perivascular spaces, and consisting almost exclusively of mononuclear cells, half of which were small lymphocytes and the remainder of which were larger cells of highly varying forms, which, as a common feature, showed pyronin staining of the cytoplasm. The necrotic areas displayed a more pronounced infiltration with polymorphonuclear leukocytes.

Dempster also noted a cellular infiltration which started in the cortex, usually between 2 and 3 days after transplantation, and which always remained more advanced there. He described cells that he called immature plasma cells, followed by mature plasma cells and polymorphs. There was no evidence of lymphocytes developing into plasma cells.

Simonsen and Dempster both were convinced that these cells were autochthonous in origin and that they developed from the reticulum cells and histocytes of the transplanted kidney, corresponding to those initially described by Bjorneboe and Gormsen in 1943 (66) in kidneys of hyperimmunized rabbits. Simonsen interpreted the pyroninophilic reaction as a defense of the kidney against host antibody. Dempster even dismissed the relevance of these cells in the rejection process and put forward the suggestion that the renal tubular cells themselves were reacting against unknown factors.

However, Porter and Calne (67) questioned the origin of this pyroninophilic cellular infiltration. These authors labeled the prospective host dog with tritiated thymidine 3 hours prior to transplanting a kidney to it and found heavily labeled host cells in the 3 dogs studied. Other studies in homograft systems (68,69) and in delayed hypersensitivity reactions (70,71) have shown that there may not be a selective, preferential accumulation of specifically immunized lymphoid cells either in the graft or at the place of the reaction, in spite of the fact that an immune reaction takes place which results in graft destruction and tissue injury. Foker et al (72) have recently reported that the mechanism for cellular infiltration into dog kidney allograft involves at least 2 different processes and it is possible to invoke these mechanisms in an attempt to explain this apparent discrepancy.

The histopathological changes in kidney allografts in other species have also implicated the lymphocyte in the operational destruction of the graft, although in the rabbit alterations in autograft cellular and vascular constituents resemble those seen in autografts, suggesting that the reaction may be in part nonimmunological in nature. Certainly, the insult which triggers the immigration of neutrophils into areas of tissue necrosis requires no invocation of immunological parameters in the strict sense. Semb et al (73) and Lund and Jensen (74,75) found that lymphocytes were trapped in greater numbers in allografted kidneys than in autografted kidneys, both *in vivo* and *in vitro*. The trapping of lymphocytes took place in the intertubular capillaries and venules of the juxtaglomerular cortical zone. Lymphocytes were occasionally seen traversing the venule wall in support of the observation of Feldmann and Lee (76) that in the rat, the large postcapillary venule was the main route of lymphocyte extravasation.

In the rabbit, the dominant cell changed from the small to the large lymphocyte 4 to 5 days after transplantation. In the studies of Lund (74,75) the occurrence of these larger cells was often associated with an acceleration of the rate of proliferative vascular and exudative changes in vessels and glomeruli. In a quantitative study of differences in the degree of mononuclear cell proliferation in rat renal allografts

Gutmann et al (77) observed increasing cellular proliferation as the genetic disparity between donor and host was widened. In rabbits, the cessation of kidney function and the cellular infiltrate are clearly associated, as are the other histopathological findings of endothelial cell proliferation, endarteritis, and exudative glomerulitis. Lund also reported a patchy cortical necrosis which was closely associated with the lymphocytic infiltration and suggested that the necrosis was caused by these changes.

Porter (78) has presented a comprehensive review of the morphological aspects of renal allograft rejection, both in untreated and in modified recipients. The two major changes he stressed were rupture of the peritubular capillaries and venules in which infiltrating cells were conspicuously present, and arteriolar and arterial lesions in which such cells were usually absent. Kountz et al (79) reported the establishment of cytoplasmic continuity between host and graft cells, especially those lining the small peritubular vessels. A sequence of biochemical and structural abnormalities ensued which led to inadequacy of tubular perfusion and eventual disruption. In these studies the cellular infiltrate was clearly indicted as the villain of allograft destruction.

In summary, Medawar (80) put forward 6 propositions which he developed from observations of the behavior of skin allografts, and which were sufficient in themselves to establish the immunological character of the homograft reaction.

1. There is a latent period before its inception.
2. The intensity of the reaction is a function of the dosage of tissue used to provoke it, although in quantitative terms this relationship is rather feeble.
3. The rejection of a graft specifically sensitizes the recipient as shown by the "second set" phenomenon which records the existence of a prevailing state of immunity, rather than being illustrative of a serological anamnestic response.
4. There is no local immunological reflex associated with allograft immunity, rather the sensitivity is systemic.
5. The state of sensitivity is specific vis-à-vis the donor.
6. The state of sensitivity is not tissue or organ specific.

CHANGES IN REGIONAL LYMPHOID TISSUE

A further clue that the lymphoid apparatus is the seat of responsiveness to tissue allografts can be found in the cellular changes that occur in the nodes and spleen following grafting. It was initially believed that the morphologic response to allografts was localized mainly to the lymph nodes draining the site of the foreign tissue, but Andre et al (81) demonstrated that while the initial reaction began in the contiguous nodes, it gradually spread to involve distant lymph nodes and the spleen.

Gallone and coworkers (82) reported that following skin homografting, there occurred an increase in pyronin-staining elements in the regional lymph node and concluded that the response is similar to that following injection of certain antigens. These authors did not analyze in any detail the cellular character of the response nor did they discuss morphologic changes in the spleen or distant nodes.

Scothorne and McGregor (83) studied cellular changes in the nodes and spleen following skin homografting in the rabbit. It was evident in their experiments that the maximal response of the lymphatic tissue occurred in the node regional to the graft site. They felt that a "homograft factor" reached the regional node principally by way of the lymphatics, for if it had been blood-borne, they expected greater or equal weight gain in the spleen and contralateral node. This problem of the route of graft sensitization is discussed at length in a subsequent section.

The histological findings revealed a characteristic large lymphoid cell in the paracortical regions of the node, an area which has since been recognized as being thymus dependent and thus further involving the small thymus-derived lymphocyte in allograft rejection. The response is fully developed by 4 days. They did not find these cells in the spleen and concluded that this organ was little affected by orthotopic skin homografts.

Homburger and Savard (84,85) found that the protein nitrogen of the lymph nodes increased after the implantation of tumors in mice, and Kidd and Toolan (86) reported histological changes in lymph nodes of nonsusceptible mice implanted with tumors. Andreini and coworkers (87) made a study of variation in weight of the host lymph nodes, spleen, and thymus after implantation of transplantable tumors in susceptible and nonsusceptible hosts and demonstrated increases in the nitrogen DNA and RNA contents of regional nodes draining heterografts in nonsusceptible animals. Radici and Piredda (88) and Masse et al (89) also found hypertrophic draining lymph nodes containing large pyroninophilic lymphoid cells. Craigmyle (90) found weight gain changes in the regional nodes following implantation of foreign cartilage in the guinea pig. Burwell and Gowland (91) noted a marked increase in the numbers of large and medium lymphoid cells in the cortex of contiguous nodes, probably out in the germinal centers, in rabbits grafted with cancellous bone.

In a far more detailed study Andre and Schwartz (81) demonstrated that following skin homografting in the rabbits, "hemocytoblasts" or strongly pyroninophilic large (12 to 15 μ in diameter) cells appeared in the adjacent lymphoid tissue with subsequent effacement of normal architecture and a barely perceptible plasmocytic response. Later these changes were also found in distant lymph nodes and in the spleen.

In summary, the histopathological changes in rejected allografts strongly suggest that the small lymphocyte is the effector of transplantation immunity. The findings in regional nodes strengthen this argument but neither group of experiments directly convicts the small lymphocyte as the agent of graft destruction.

LYMPHOCYTE TRAFFIC AND THE ALLOGRAFT REACTION

The evidence for the complicity of the lymphocyte in the processes that lead to allograft rejection has been based in large measure on histological studies of transplanted tissue. These morphological studies have not, however, unraveled the functional heterogeneity of the observed cellular infiltrates. While it seems certain that the small lymphocyte is the chief actor in the local and systemic drama of tissue destruction its role may well not be either singular or magical. It may be mentioned parenthetically that other cells have certainly been implicated in immunological responses, and even the so-called classic histological changes are not pictures of uniformity but rather a display of cellular heterogeneity involving cells of different sizes and classes such as macrophages and plasma cells (92,93). Weiner et al (94) described a group of 5 to 7.5 μ"graft rejection cells" in the dermis and epidermis which by electron microscopy bore somewhat of a resemblance to large pyroninophilic cells. They possessed a large nucleus, prominent nucleoli, and an electron-dense banding adjacent to the nuclear membrane. There appeared to be a direct relationship between the appearance of these cells and epidermal death and it was suggested that they arose in the regional nodes as the progeny of the large pyroninophilic cells of Gowans as apparently occurs in graft-versus-host reactions.

Because of this complexity it is mandatory to consider other classes of evidence before prejudging the case in favor of the small lymphocyte. In addition to the static studies involving the morphologic aberrations occurring in rejecting tissue allografts are those investigations which examine directly the cell types in active transit from such grafts. Pedersen and Morris (95) have shown that remarkable changes occur in the lymph draining from a sheep renal allograft, with an extensively increased migration of lymphocytes within the first 18 hours, indicating that the stimulus to the host's lymphoid cells to migrate was transmitted early in the inductive phase of the rejection process. By 24 hours, many of these cells were already undergoing transformation to blast cell types. The differentiation and proliferation of these cells continued *in vitro*. Much of the early cellular transformation occurred at the interface of the graft blood vessels and host lymphocytes. When the afferent lymph was allowed to reach the regional node the sequence of events in the graft and in the node paralleled one another, and the reaction in the node never preceded that in the graft. Diversion of the lymph did not alter the fate of the graft, indicating that the lymph nodes functioned to amplify the homograft response rather to initiate it, just as Smith et al (96) have shown in immune responses to conventional antigens. In a shrewd experiment, Pedersen and Morris (95) showed that the transfer of lymph-borne cells to a remote lymph node initiated blast cell and humoral antibody production in those ectopic locales. These authors also found antibody production in the regional nodes as early as 48 to 60 hours after grafting and suggested that its absence in the blood was probably due to its being bound by the tissues of the graft.

There is evidence which suggests that solid organ grafts which are immediately vascularized and have a high flow of blood through them are rejected in a different way from skin grafts. For skin grafts, it seems certain that in order for the crucial sensitization of the host to occur an intact lymphocyte drainage from the graft is crucial. Barker and Billingham (97) have shown that for the all-important act of "recognition" of foreign antigen in a skin graft to take place an intact lymphatic drainage system had to be present. Other experiments had shown that temporary disruption of the lymphatic drainage from skin homografts prolonged their survival.

For reasons of brevity I will not consider in detail the question of survival of grafts placed in immunologically privileged sites. These are locations with adequate blood supply but lacking a lymphatic drainage such as the brain (98), anterior chamber (99), and hamster cheek pouch (100). For purposes of the argument here it is sufficient to note that grafts placed in these sites enjoy a prolonged but not necessarily indefinite survival. This prolongation has been attributed to the absence of normal lymphatic connections in these sites.

At variance with this concept are the experiments of Hall in which he monitored the lymph that drained from areas bearing skin homografts throughout the life of the graft (101). He showed that the efferent lymph contained large amounts of cellular debris having the staining characteristics of nuclear material but relatively few leukocytes. There was no change in the cellular response in the regional lymph node until late in the life of the graft, when the rejection process was already well advanced. This finding is in accord with the proposition that sensitization of the host against donor antigens occurred peripherally within the graft itself. However, this thesis loses some of its conclusiveness because the small size of the graft would generate but minute amounts of lymph, small changes.in which may proceed undetected.

Wesolowski and Fennessey (102) and Hume and Egdahl (103) studied the progressive destruction of canine heart and renal allografts that had been enclosed in plastic bags in order to preclude the regeneration of lymphatic continuity and found that rejection proceeded in the normal manner. These observations have been confirmed by others (104,105). Ballantyne and Nathan (106) found that exposure of rats to *ex vivo* renal allografts provoked a detectable level of sensitivity even after 30 minutes of contact.

These findings all bear out the original concept of Medawar (107) that the distinguishing feature of hypersensitivities of the delayed type was the fact that sensitization occurred peripherally, that is, at the interface of foreign tissue-lymphocyte contact, be it the vascular frontier of the kidney allograft or in the microcirculation of an orthotopic skin transplant. Such an hypothesis can be supported by both circumstantial and direct evidence. For example, a small skin homograft in a cow will produce a reaction as violent and as rapid as a graft of the same magnitude will provoke in a mouse, both explicable by the assumption that the same number of lymphocytes have percolated through each. Billingham and coworkers (108) demonstrated that the excision of the regional lymph nodes had very little effect on the survival time of skin homografts, suggesting that both the activation and effector stages take place in graft itself. That this is possible in principle was demonstrated by Elkins (109) who showed that the injection of parental-strain thoracic duct lymphocytes into the parenchyma of an F_1 hybrid kidney caused a local graft-versus-host reaction and extensive destruction of the organ.

The experiments of Strober and Gowans (110) provide further coherence to this reasoning. They perfused thoracic duct lymphocytes from rats of strain A through an isolated kidney of strain B which were then returned to other rats of strain A. Skin grafts from strain B placed on the recipients of the perfused lymphocytes were rejected in an accelerated fashion. In these studies the possibility that donor strain leukocytes were unavoidably transferred with the perfusate cannot be excluded despite efforts to flush out the kidneys prior to commencing perfusion. Billingham et al (111) have demonstrated that as few as 2000 splenocytes inoculated intraperitoneally in mice will elicit a detectable level of sensitization, indicating that such hazards are not only apparent but real. Ballantyne and Nathan (106) found that a saline perfusate of a rat kidney could be immunogenic, an observation at variance with those of Strober and Gowans.

The sophisticated technology of Hall, Morris, and their colleagues (101,112–121) has made possible in the most elegant fashion studies on lymphocyte traffic in response to antigenic stimulation. The results show that changes in efferent lymph follow the same pattern regardless of the nature of the provocation. Broadly similar results are observed after bacteria, viruses, heterologous serum proteins on red cells, skin-sensitizing chemicals, or normal and neoplastic allografts. After an initial phase of markedly diminished lymphocyte output, the recirculation of cells rapidly increases at a rate that may be double or treble that of the prestimulation figure. Between 80 and 120 hours after stimulation the large pyroninophilic immunoblasts reach a peak of up to 40% of all the cells in the lymph. Once these immunoblasts gain entry into the bloodstream they are able to enter homografts, and when recovered they may exert a specific and powerful cytotoxic action *in vitro*. The lymph-borne immunoblasts also play an important role in humoral immunity.

The successive steps of lymphocyte sensitization and transformation were shown to take place *in vivo* after a human kidney allograft by Hamburger and his coworkers (122,123). On days 5 and 6 following transplantation a sudden appearance of immunoblasts occurred. These cells were analogous to the transformed cells of the mixed lymphocyte reaction and were metabolically active as judged by their incorporation of tritiated thymidine. These findings support the concept of peripheral sensitization and transformation.

A series of events could then be proposed to occur which starts with lymphocyte-graft interactions, proceeding to immunoblast formation, vascular compromise, and tissue destruction. The passage of antigen and immunoblasts to nodes and blood leads to amplification of the response, but is not the sine qua non of either its initiation or of its fruition.

THE LYMPHOCYTE AS THE EFFECTOR

Adoptive Transfer of Immunity

If the small lymphocyte does in fact initiate the reaction to allografts, the injection of such cells would be expected to transfer this capacity to nonimmune animals and lead either to sensitization of the new recipient or to the breakdown of well-established grafts in tolerant hosts. These expectations were borne out in a series of classic experiments on the adoptive transfer of immunity.

In 1954 Mitchison (43) showed that transplantation immunity to tumor grafts could be passively transferred by cells from the contiguous lymph nodes, although cells from distant nodes and the spleen failed to do so. Billingham, et al (45) found that animals rendered tolerant by perinatal exposure to transplantation antigens could be immunologically reequipped and tolerance to skin grafts abolished by transplantation into them of lymph node cells from normal histoidentical donors. This landmark observation pinpointed the deficiency in tolerant animals in the lymphoid apparatus. These observations were extended and confirmed by Billingham, Gowans, and their coworkers. Billingham (124) showed that immunologically activated cells were present in the peripheral blood of animals sensitized by the application of skin allografts beginning on the 6th day after transplantation and remaining demonstrable for up to 1 year as evidenced by their capacity to destroy skin grafts in tolerant mice. This interval of 2 days between the appearance of histological changes in the node and emergence of activated cells is in accord with the findings of Gowans (125,126) that large pyroninophilic cells do divide and with the data of Hall (117) on lymphocyte traffic from activated nodes.

These experiments did not identify the exact nature of the cell that was affected. Gowans (127–129) confirmed that the responsible cell was the small lymphocyte by showing that homogeneous populations of these small cells harvested from the thoracic duct of normal rats would destroy long-standing skin grafts in 9 of 12 recipients when injected intravenously at a dose of 50×10^6 cells/recipient. These cells also mounted a graft-versus-host assault on the tolerance-conferring cellular residue in the new recipients, since large pyroninophilic cells derived from the injected small lymphocytes were also found in the spleen and in widely separated lymph nodes without any predilection for the regional node. Billingham and Gowans have both speculated that the tempo of breakdown of the tolerant graft would be influenced in a quantitative fashion by the volume of the chimeric tissue present, although there are no experiments to show whether the relationship is direct or inverse. Billingham speculated that some chimeric tissue would be of benefit in that it was a ready and good source of stimulating antigen. On the other hand, an excess might serve as an antigenic sponge to soak up the energy of the adoptively transferred cells. Silvers and Billingham (130) have recently shown that the facility with which tolerance can be abolished by transfer of isologous cells is a function of the dosage of the inoculum used to induce tolerance.

An objection to the view that specific nonreactivity or tolerance is due solely to a deletion of a subpopulation of lymphocytes is the failure to find adoptively transferred labeled cells at the site of homograft destruction *(vide infra)*. Aside from the technological considerations concerning loss and/or reutilization of label and timing of the injection of isotope, it should be noted that (a) a very small number of donor cells can probably trigger destruction, and (b) a small number of activated cells may trigger entire populations to behave as if sensitized as in the experiments of David et al (131) in which the addition of 2.5% of PPD-"sensitized" lymphocytes inhibited the migration of the whole assemblage of mononuclear cells.

Gowans (132) demonstrated that newly formed cells do selectively accumulate in skin allografts in rats given repeated systemic doses of ^{3}H-thymidine. Prendergast (133) confirmed and extended this observation and showed that up to 11% of labeled cells would involve a homograft of skin on the ear of the rabbit at a time when only 0.2% of mononuclear cells in the peripheral blood was labeled. His experiments were designed in such a way that it was the cells from the regional node which showed an immunologically nonspecific predilection for homografts irrespective of origin and he concluded that such cells would participate in graft destruction.

It is clear then that for lymphocytes to perform properly *in vivo* they may need other cells or agents to promote their activation but must be brought to the right place, at the right time, and in the right number. In the case of organ allografts, once recognition has occurred a succession of events is set in motion which leads to cellular differentiation which may take place in a variety of settings and will terminate in graft destruction. The demonstration by Barker and Billingham (134) that restoration of lymphatic continuity between isolated skin flaps in the guinea pig or skin homografts sequestered in ectopic cheek pouch skin tissue on the sides of hamsters' chests shows that this cycle may be triggered at any time and that the sensitizing power of an allograft, since sensitization occurs peripherally, is in no way a transient phenomenon and is not confined to the period of ischemic necrosis and the liberation of large amounts of cellular debris. The upshot of the experiments cited in this section is that the requirements for graft destruction are fairly limited: namely, immunologically competent cells in the host, the opportunity for those cells to gain contact with the foreign tissue, and a chance for the committed cells to divide.

By piecing together evidence which at times is circumstantial a picture of a total cellular immune response *in vivo* can be drawn. A more self-contained and very illuminating story of cell-mediated responses as they bear on the allograft problem can be written about graft-versus-host reactions, including the normal and immune lymphocyte transfer tests.

Graft-versus-Host Reactions

The graft-versus-host reaction (GVH) can be considered an analog of graft rejection, the similitude resting on the fact that in each case lymphocytes mount an assault in immunologically underprivileged tissue. Simonsen (135) and Billingham and Brent (136) have clearly made the case for implicating the donor lymphoid tissue as the attacking agent, but just as the final mediator in allograft destruction is not delineated, so the pathogenesis of GVH disease is unknown. In his classic experiments Gowans and his coworkers (125,126,137) identified the small lymphocyte as the most deadly cell type and documented the changes that it undergoes in the course of its contact with foreign antigens. These observations strengthen the argument for equating the two processes in which the roles of donor and host are reversed and make it logical to infer that the same cell type initiates both reactions.

It has been shown that the antigens against which small lymphocytes react in GVH reactions are the same as those which induce tolerance on behalf of an allograft of skin (138). Furthermore, the large pyroninophilic cell generated during GVH reactions is morphologically indistinguishable from cells arising in regional nodes and efferent lymph during graft destruction and with those observed when lymphocytes from allogeneic donor/recipient pairs are incubated together. Neither GVH disease nor cellular transformation occurs when cells from tolerant donors are injected into otherwise susceptible recipients.

A variety of sources can provide cells which can mount GVH reactions. The cell fractionation experiments of Terasaki (139) showed that it was the number of small lymphocytes and not the number of monocytes which determined the degree of splenomegaly in embryo chicks. Studies with purified suspensions of small lymphocytes derived from the peripheral blood of mice (140) and from the thoracic duct of rats also placed responsibility for GVH reactions on the small lymphocyte.

Lymphocyte Transfer Reaction

Another manifestation of a delayed-type hypersensitivity reaction analogous to those observed both in transplantation systems and in GVH reactions is the transfer reaction evoked in guinea pigs following the intradermal injection of normal or immune lymphoid cells, as described by Brent and Medawar (141,142). The amplitude of the response, as measured by induration, is a function of the strength of the preimmunizing stimulus to the transferred cells. The evolution of both the normal lymphocyte transfer and immune lymphocyte transfer responses is similar, and in all cases these responses are biphasic, the first peak representing the period of antigenic recognition by clonally precommitted subpopulations of competent cells, followed by a fadeout, which is then succeeded on the 5th to 6th day by a high-pitched flare up to levels of greater intensity resulting from multiplication of the population of effector cells.

This test lends itself ideally to the measurement of the degree of immunological competence of lymphoid cells of various origins. In the meritocracy of aggressiveness blood lymphocytes were found to be 2 to 5 times more virulent than lymph node lymphocytes, while thymocytes were only 1/20th as powerful.

The reactions are magnified when the immunological competence of the host is suppressed by preirradiation with 600 R. In contrast, conventional immunosuppressive agents prevent multiplication of cells and thus depress the second peak of the response while the first one is untouched. On the other hand, antilymphocyte sera can abolish both the recognition and later peaks (143), and are evidence for the action of such sera on peripheral small lymphocytes.

Specific "Homing" of Lymphocytes

A major objection to the hypothesis that the lymphocyte is the mediator of transplantation immunity has been the failure to recover specifically sensitized lymphocytes from rejecting allografts. The negative reports of Najarian and Feldman (68,69) and Hall (101), and those of Prendergast (133), McCluskey et al (70), and Turk and Cort (71), which failed to show the strict preferential localization of sensitized cells in reaction sites, have been countered, at least in part, by the studies of Dineen and coworkers (144) in which the fate of lymphocytes from guinea pigs infected with an intestinal parasite was followed, and those of Emeson and Thursh (145) in which the localization of lymphocytes in nodes contiguous to skin allografts was studied. In the latter report "small but definite" differences in specifically sensitized cells were observed and attributed to specific attraction of such cells to depot antigen which had accumulated in the draining node. Zatz and Lance (146) have found, however, that such "trapping" is an immunologically nonspecific event.

In a more convincing study, Lance and Cooper (147) have shown the specific localization of ^{125}I UDR-labeled small lymphocytes in CBA mice that were grafted with A or C57B1/6 tail skin. These authors followed the accumulation of ^{125}I-labeled cells, recovered both from regional nodes and more widely distributed sites, and concluded that a specific subpopulation of cells arises in both the draining node and spleen during the sensitization phase of skin allograft rejection, and that these cells will home selectively to a skin graft of appropriate specificity.

LYMPHOCYTE DEPLETION

Algire (148) was the first to demonstrate that various normal and malignant cells can thrive and flourish in diffusion chambers which effectively prevent host cell access to the foreign tissue.

A further operational proof of the causative role played by the small lymphocyte in allograft rejection has been provided by the prolongation of graft survival achieved after initiation of those strategies which lead to lymphocyte depletion. In general, it may be expected that any maneuver or event which leads to the reduction in numbers or elimination of the thymus-derived T lymphocyte will result in abrogation of cell-mediated immune responses. This expectation has been borne out.

Neonatal Thymectomy

Adult mice, rats, hamsters, and rabbits thymectomized at birth will show impaired cell-mediated immunological reactions such as those in transplantation systems and in humoral responses to antigens in which the cooperation of thymus-derived cells is required (149–156). This depression of responsiveness is manifest in the decreased capacity to reject skin allografts and to mount GVH reactions after inoculation into appropriate recipients (157,158,161). It has been convincingly demonstrated that the cellular basis of the immunological defects in thymectomized mice is the decrease in the size of the pool of circulating small lymphocytes (159). To these studies may be added the histological studies of Parrott et al (160) which show the absence of such cells in neonatally thymectomized animals.

Thoracic Duct Drainage

Chronic thoracic duct drainage has been associated with depressed immunological responsiveness in rats (161) and in mice (162) and has been attributed to a specific depletion of small lymphocytes. Thoracic duct fistulae have been used to prolong the life of renal allografts in calves

(163) and, in conjunction with other immunosuppressive agents, as an adjunctive measure in decreasing rejection crises in patients receiving renal allografts (164).

Prolonged drainage of the thoracic duct depletes the thymus-dependent subcortical areas of lymph nodes, while the bursa-dependent regions and germinal centers are spared (165,166). Thoracic duct lymph has been shown to contain at least two discrete populations of lymphocytes, one the small recirculating cell (161) active in allograft rejection and another larger lymphoid cell with a shorter life expectancy (167). Caffrey, Everett, and Rieke (168,169) have demonstrated that in rats the cells with a slow turnover constitute 90% of the formed elements in thoracic duct lymph and possessed the tinctorial and morphological characteristics of the classical small lymphocyte. These observations have been confirmed by Cronkite and his coworkers (170–172).

Antilymphocyte Serum

There is extensive evidence that heterologous antilymphocyte serum (ALS) acts by depleting the long-lived, small recirculating lymphocyte. This preferential affinity for these cells is the result of the physiological action of ALS on peripheral cells, and is not due to a biochemical specificity for receptors on these cells. That ALS does exert its effect primarily at the periphery of the lymphoid apparatus was first appreciated by Levey and Medawar (173,174). These observations were extended by Denman et al (175–177), using labeling studies, by Taub (178), who showed that the residual populations of lymphocytes in ALS-treated animals were predominantly of the short-lived variety, and by the experiments of Martin and Miller (179) and of Leuchars et al (180) which demonstrated the selective effect of ALS on antigen-sensitive cells.

Parallel assays of cell-mediated and humoral immunological responses have clearly established the differential effect of ALS on the two modalities of responses, with the former being far more susceptible to suppression (181). While there is not universal agreement on this point (182,183) it does seem certain that humoral immunity is resistant to ALS, at least in a relative sense, when compared to cellular immunity (184–186).

This preferential action has also been confirmed by the selective morphological changes that occur after ALS administration (187–189), namely, depletion of the paracortical regions of nodes and periarteriolar regions of the spleen. There is thus a good correlation between functional and morphological findings.

The rationale for combining various modalities of cellular depletion is based on the ability of various strategies to remove unwanted lymphocytes in the first instance and to prevent their regeneration in the second. The classic experiments of Woodruff and Anderson (190,191) on thoracic duct drainage and ALS administration in rats to prolong skin allograft survival illustrate the first goal, while the work of Monaco and his coworkers (192) on the immunosuppressive efficacy of adult thymectomy and ALS in mice bears on the second goal. In general, a combination of the two therapies led to far longer graft survival than either one alone.

Action of Conventional Immunosuppressive Agents

Among all the immunosuppressive agents ALS is therefore unique in its preferential action on cell-mediated immunity. Conventional agents such as radiation, DNA base analogs, alkylating agents, and folic acid antagonists are nonspecific in the effects they produce, for they act either by randomly depleting the animal of immunologically competent cells or by producing some widespread tissue damage. It is beyond the scope of this chapter to review the vast literature on chemical immunosuppression. It is important to note, however, that drugs such as azathioprine and prednisone can prolong, apparently indefinitely in some cases, the life of renal allografts in man, although the degree of immunosuppression achieved is not easily quantifiable, and excellent function may be maintained in the face of significant cellular infiltration. Whether some form of adaptation of the graft to its new host has occurred or whether or not the organ is enhanced or the host tolerant remains at issue. Based on the foregoing evidence it is generally assumed that some specific modification of immunological responsiveness has occurred and that this change is the result of alteration of either the host's lymphoid apparatus or the donor organ.

TOLERANCE AND ENHANCEMENT

Any specific change in the small lymphocyte toward nonreactivity or any specific removal of a clone of lymphocytes can be regarded as immunological tolerance. The means by which such changes are brought about are unknown, and because of this ignorance a controversy has brewed between those who suggest that specific antibody is the mediator of tolerance, just as it is of enhancement, and those who maintain that in fact the two phenomena are entirely different. Any review of the cellular aspects of transplantation must consider this argument. According to Burnet's clonal hypothesis (193) it can be postulated that the loss of a clone of lymphoid cells of appropriate specificity accounts for natural and acquired tolerance. However, scientific reduction methodology (194) necessitates that at least one other hypothesis be formulated to explain how such a clone is lost or inactivated in an effort to answer the difficult question first raised by Woodruff (195) as to whether tolerance represents the absence of reactive cells or the presence of nonreactive cells.

To provide either theoretical arguments or evidential data which propose or illustrate that these phenomena can be accounted for by some form of antibody or antigen-antibody complexes acting at a cellular level in no way repudiates the case of Medawar and his colleagues (196) that tolerance represents a "central" as opposed to peripheral failure of the immunological apparatus. Furthermore, the fact that the tolerant animal can be restored by normal lymphoid cells does not negate or validate the claims of proponents or antagonists of such theories, partly because it may be extremely difficult to demonstrate such mediators of tolerance which are rapidly and efficiently removed from the circulation. However, not all forms of tolerance can be abolished by normal lymphoid cells alone (197,198) as is the case in the model of Silvers et al (199,200) which shows that tolerance to male mouse skin can be broken only by the coinjection of immunogenic adult male lymphocytes.

During the past 3 years a controversy has raged between those who hold that serum blocking factors are responsible for tolerance and those who maintain that they are not. The Hellströms (201–205) have shown in a variety of experimental allograft models that such factors can be demonstrated, and that their presence seems to be correlated with the maintenance of the tolerant state. On the other hand, Brent and his colleagues (206) failed to find such factors in tolerant, chimeric mice— the "authentically tolerant" mice of Medawar—and that serum from such mice did not interfere with the GVH activity of otherwise competent lymphoid cells. Atkins and Ford (207) showed that thoracic duct lymphocytes from tolerant rats were incapable of mounting a GVH reaction. Beverley et al (208) reported that lymph node cells from tolerant mice were not cytotoxic to donor strain target cells, and could not be stimulated in one-way mixed leukocyte culture (MLC) by donor cells although they responded to third-party cells. Rouse and Warner (209) demonstrated that bursectomized chicks could be made tolerant, even though they fail to produce alloantibody, and there are reports (210–213) from many centers of the successful establishment of cellular chimerism in patients suffering from the severe-combined-immunodeficiency syndrome. However, at least on a theoretical level there is nothing to preclude the notion that such grafts in man and in fowl produce tolerance on their own behalf through some humoral or cellular mechanism yet to be described, such as T cell repressor function (214). Thus, the complexity of the mechanisms of induction and maintenance of the tolerant state have been enhanced by the observations of Gershon and his co-workers on the nature of the adoptive transfer of tolerance to a nontolerant cell population (215,216). This transfer was mediated by educated thymocytes and was interpreted as being dependent on a suppressor T cell population. Tolerance becomes an active process in which either specific suppressor cells or immunospecific suppressor molecules are generated. The data of Weissman (217) involving the transfer of tolerance to male-specific antigen are in support of this concept, although other interpretations cannot be excluded.

Cozenza and Kohler (218) have demonstrated that antiidiotypic antibodies directed against a specific antigen can act as "antireceptor" antibodies and specifically prevent the induction of the primary response only to that antigen. These antibodies seemed to be specifically directed against the binding-site region of receptor molecules on antigen-sensitive cells. The combining-site region of the receptor for the antigen, regardless of its class of heavy and light chains, must have been similar to the combining site of the IgM antibody synthesized in the primary response to the antigen. The general implication is that antibodies and antigen receptors belonging to different immunoglobulin classes but having specificity for the same antigen may share similar binding-site regions encoded by identical variable genes. The results further imply that in an individual there are clones of cells bearing restricted specificity for an antigen. Also, it is proposed that, in an individual, cells having receptors for the combining-site region of antibody produced by other cells in the same individual may have the capacity to synthesize "antireceptor" antibody against those cells and so further regulate the immune response. Such speculation of antibody acting as antigen carried a bit further could lead to a theory of self-tolerance as well as to an explanation of successful bone marrow transplantation in agammaglobulinemic individuals.

In support of such an idea are the observations of Manning and Jutila (219) in which specific, profound humoral immunosuppression was achieved in neonatal or adult young mice with heterologous antisera against specific heavy chains.

These findings are in accord with the experimental data which show that B cells have immunoglobulin-like molecules on their surfaces (220–224) and that stimulation of B cells results from the interaction of antigen with this immunoglobulin (225–229). Therefore, the specificity of humoral antibody production is inherent in the antigen-receptor interaction (230–232).

The situation regarding cells mediating delayed-type hypersensitivity responses, including GVH reactions and transplantation immunity, is less clear, for the nature of the T cell receptor has not been established. However, there are data which indicate that antiimmunoglobulin can modulate T-cell-mediated responses (233,234). Graft-versus-host reactivity in mice has been modified by antiimmunoglobulin, and Theis and Thorbecke (235) have reported the inhibition of delayed hypersensitivity in agammaglobulinemic, bursectomized chickens by injection of rabbit antichick Ig antisera. The presence of circulating high titers of this antisera was essential for complete inhibition. There are several possible explanations for this phenomenon, including interaction between anti-L chain antibody and an Ig receptor on appropriate T lymphocytes, steric interference with antigen binding, or the blocking of a soluble factor released by activated T cells. The conflicting data on T cell receptors (236–239) may be due to a low concentration of Ig on the cell surface, to its configuration (240,241), or to differences in the specificity of the various anti-Ig antisera (242). In any case, the data indicate that T cell blocking is an active process and may be antibody mediated.

The ease of induction of tolerance and its relative persistence in neonatal animals stand in marked contrast to the difficulties encountered in tolerizing adults, especially to allografts and transplantation antigens. This age-specific effect is not exclusive since mature animals can be made tolerant. Nevertheless, it does represent a difference, in an operational sense, between tolerance and enhancement, for there is no evidence that it is easier to raise enhancing antibody in neonatal individuals than in adults, other than the observations of Zimmerman and Feldman (243) that skin allograft life in the rat could be most consistently extended with antiserum specific for graft antigens in 10- to 12-day-old recipients. Bearing on these points—age specificity and tolerance versus enhancement—are two recent papers by Terman and his associates (244,245) which show that neonatal tolerance to BSA cannot be broken by the administration of normal immunocytes, and that this tolerance can be transferred both adoptively with splenocytes and passively with antiserum into normal immunocompetent syngeneic recipients. Their findings suggest that tolerance is an actively maintained state in which antibody plays an important role and which is quantitatively more difficult to abrogate in neonates than in X-irradiated adults. The authors were able to elute antibody from tolerant spleen cells and postulate that tolerizing antibody may be cytophilic, perhaps for macrophages, an idea put forth initially by Ryder and Schwartz (246).

It is therefore clear that all the biochemical, physiological, and immunological factors that control the induction and maintenance of tolerance are not known. A recent review of the models of tolerance and enhancement (247) suggests that there may well be no disparity between the two phenomena and that one may be a variety of the other. Nonetheless, certain fundamental questions remain to be answered, especially in regard to transplantation systems. As Medawar points out (248), the last word has not yet been said concerning these matters, and the definitive experiment showing that antibody can induce specific unresponsiveness in a single fully competent lymphoid cell remains to be done.

SUMMARY

Morphological, physiological, and functional studies indicate that the circulating small, long-lived lymphocyte is the mediator of transplantation immunity. This cell can not only adoptively transfer cell-mediated responses but can also procure specific nonreactivity to transplantation antigen in appropriate recipients. In both situations the final means by which such activities take place are unknown, but current research suggests that these thymus-derived lymphocytes have receptors on their surfaces which can passively and actively participate in the two types of reactions—namely, graft destruction and tolerance procurement. Of special theoretical and practical importance is the fact that the lymphocyte in its role as tolerogen is affecting cell subpopulations of its own functional clique.

REFERENCES

1. Tagliacozzi, G., De Curtorum Chirugia per Insitionem, Venice (1597), translated by M. T. Gnudi and J. P. Webster, in *The Life and Times of Gaspare Tagliacozzi*, Reichner, New York, 1950, p. 185.
2. Baronio, G., *Degli Innesti Animali*, Stampere e Jonderia del Genio, Milan, 1804.
3. Bunger, C., *J. Chir. Augenheil* **4**, 569 (1823).
4. Bert, P., *These pour le doctorat en Medecine "de la greffe Animale"*, Paris, 1863.
5. Joest, E., *Arch. J. Entwicklungsmech. Organ.* **5**, 419 (1897).
6. Morgan, T. H., *Biol. Bull.* **1**, 7 (1899).
7. Harrison, R. G., *Arch. J. Entwicklungsmech. Organ.* **7**, 430 (1898).

8. Born, G., *Arch. J. Entwicklungsmech. Organ.* **4,** 349 (1897).

9. Jensen, C. O., *Zentralbl. Bakt.* **34,** 28 (1903).

10. Rous, P., *J. Exp. Med.* **13,** 397 (1911).

11. DeFano, C., *Z. Immunitaetsforsch. Orig.* **5,** 1 (1910).

12. Little, C. C. and Tyzzer, E. E., *J. Med. Res.* **33,** 393 (1915).

13. Fleisher, M. S., *J. Med. Res.* **38,** 191 (1918).

14. Little, C. C. and Johnson, B. W., *Proc. Soc. Exp. Biol. Med.* **19,** 163 (1921).

15. Loeb, L. and Wright, S., *Am. J. Pathol.* **3** 251 (1927).

16. Strong, L. C., *J. Cancer Res.* **13,** 103 (1929).

17. Cloudman, A. M., *Am. J. Cancer* **16,** 568 (1932).

18. Bittner, J. J., *J. Genet.* **31,** 471 (1935).

19. Murphy, J. B., *J. Am. Med. Assoc.* **59,** 874 (1912).

20. Murphy, J. B., *J. Exp. Med.* **17,** 482 (1913).

21. Murphy, J. B., *J. Exp. Med.* **19,** 513 (1914).

22. Murphy, J. B. and Morton, J. J., *Proc. Natl. Acad. Sci. U.S.A.* **1,** 435 (1915).

23. Murphy, J. B. and Morton, J. J., *J. Exp. Med.* **22,** 204 (1915).

24. Murphy, J. B. and Taylor, H. D., *J. Exp. Med.* **28,** 1 (1918).

25. Murphy, J. B., Monograph 21, Rockefeller Institute (1926).

26. Murphy, J. B., Hussey, R., Nakahara, W., and Sturm, E., *J. Exp. Med.* **33,** 299 (1921).

27. Murphy, J. B. and Sturm, E., *J. Exp. Med.* **29,** 25 (1919).

28. Chambers, H., Scott, G., and Rus. S., *J. Pathol. Bacteriol.* **23,** 384 (1920).

29. Wagner, A., *Acta Radiol.* **10,** 539 (1929).

30. Krebs, E., Rask-Nielsen, H. and Wagner, A., *Acta Radiol. (Suppl.)* **10,** 1 (1930).

31. Furth, J., Siebold, H., and Rathbone, R., *Am. J. Cancer* **19,** 521 (1933).

32. Mottram, J. C. and Russ, S., *Proc. Roy. Soc. London (Ser. B)* **90,** 1 (1917–19).

33. Woglom, W. H., *Cancer Rev.* **4,** 129 (1929).

34. Loeb, L., *Physiol. Rev.* **10,** 547 (1930).

35. Little, C. C. and Strong, L. C., *J. Exp. Zool.* **41,** 93 (1924–1925).

36. Gorer, P. A., *J. Pathol. Bacteriol.* **47,** 231 (1938).

37. Gorer, P. A., *J. Pathol. Bacteriol.* **54,** 51 (1942).

38. Gibson, T. and Medawar, P. B., *J. Anat.* **77,** 299 (1943).

39. Medawar, P. B., *J. Anat.* **78,** 176 (1944).

40. Medawar, P. B., *J. Anat.* **79,** 157 (1945).

41. Medawar, P. B., *Brit. J. Exp. Pathol.,* **27,** 9 (1946).

42. Potter, J. S., Taylor, M. I., and MacDowell, E. C., *Proc. Soc. Exp. Biol. Med.* **37,** 655 (1938).

43. Mitchision, N. A., *Proc. Roy. Soc. London (Ser. B)* **142,** 72 (1954).

44. Mitchison, N. A., *J. Exp. Med.* **102,** 157 (1955).

45. Billingham, R. E., Brent, L. and Medawar, P. B., *Phil. Trans. Roy. Soc. London, (Ser. B),* **239,** 357 (1956).

46. Landsteiner, K. and Chase, M. W., *Proc. Soc. Exp. Biol. Med.* **49,** 688 (1942).

47. Voisin, G. A. and Maurer, P., *Ann. N. Y. Acad. Sci.* **64,** 1053 (1957).

48. Gorer, P. A., *Adv. Cancer Res.* **4,** 159 (1956).

49. Carrel, A., *Lyon Med.* **98,** 859 (1902).

50. Ullmann, E., *Wein. Klin. Wochr.* **15,** 281 (1902).

51. Zaaijer, J. H., *Dtsch. Med, Wochenschr.* **34,** 1777 (1908).

52. Williamson, C. S., *J. Urol.* **10,** 275 (1923).

53. Ibuka, K., *Am. J. Med. Sci.* **171,** 420 (1926).

54. Wu, P. P. T. and Mann, F. C., *Arch. Surg.* **28,** 889 (1934).

55. Lefebvre, L., *Arch. Int. Physiol.* **57,** 110 (1949).

56. Simonsen, M., Buemann, A., Gammeltaft, F., Jensen, F., and Jorgensen, K., *Acta Pathol. Microbiol. Scand.* **32,** 1 (1953).

57. Dempster, W. J., *Brit. J. Surg.* **40,** 447 (1953).

58. Dempster, W. J., *Brit. J. Urol.* **27,** 66 (1955).

59. Dempster, W. J., Harrison, C. V., and Shackman, R., *Brit. Med. J.* **2,** 969 (1964).

60. Hume, D. M., Merrill, J. P., Miller, B. F., and Thorn, G. W., *J. Clin. Invest.* **34,** 327 (1955).

61. Holman, E., *Surg. Gynecol. Obstet.* **38,** 100 (1924).

62. Williamson, C. S., *J. Urol.* **16,** 231 (1926).

63. Smadel, J. E., *J. Exp. Med.* **64,** 921 (1936).

64. Dempster, W. J. and Williams, M. A., *Brit. Med. J.* **1,** 18 (1963).

65. Williams, M. A., Morton, M., Tyler, H. M., and Dempster, W. J., *Brit. J. Exp. Pathol.* **45,** 22 (1964).

66. Bjorneboe, M. and Gormsen, H., *Acta Pathol. Microbiol. Scand.* **20,** 649 (1943).

67. Porter, K. A. and Calne, R. Y., *Transplant. Bull.* **26,** 458 (1960).

68. Najarian, J. S. and Feldman, J. D., *J. Exp. Med.* **115,** 1083 (1962).

69. Najarian, J. S. and Feldman, J. D., *J. Exp. Med.* **117,** 449 (1963).

70. McCluskey, R. T., Benacerraf, B., and McCluskey, J. W., *J. Immunol.* **90,** 466 (1963).

71. Turk, J. L. and Oort, J., *Immunology* **6,** 140 (1963).

72. Foker, J. E., Clark, D. S., Pickering, R. J., Good, R. A., and Varco, R. L., *Surgery* **66,** 42 (1969).

73. Semb, B. K. H., Williams, C. M., and Hume, D., *Transplantation* **6,** 977 (1968).

74. Lund, B., and Myhre Jensen, O., *Acta Pathol. Microbiol. Scand.* **78,** Sect. A, 701 (1970).

75. Lund, B. and Myhre Jensen, O., *Acta Pathol. Microbiol. Scand.* **78,** Sect. A, 713 (1970).

76. Feldmann, J. D. and Lee, S., *J. Exp. Med.* **126,** 783 (1967).

77. Gutmann, R. D., Lindquist, R. R., Parker, R. M., Carpenter, C. B., and Merrill, J. P., *Transplantation* **5,** 668 (1967).

78. Porter, K. A., *Brit. Med. Bull.* **21,** 171 (1965).

79. Kountz, S. L., Williams, M. A., Williams, P. L., Kapros, C., and Dempster, W. J., *Nature* **199,** 257 (1963).

80. Medawar, P. B., *Proc. Roy. Soc. London, (Ser. B)* **148,** 145 (1958).

81. Andre, J. A., Schwartz, R. S., Mitus, W. J., and Damashek, W., *Blood* **19,** 313 (1962).

82. Gallone, L., Radici, G., and Riquier, G., *Arch. Ital. Chir.* **2,** 329 (1952).

83.   Scothorne R. J. and MacGregor, I. A., *J. Anat.* **89,** 283 (1955).

84.   Homburger, F., *Science* **107,** 648 (1948).

85.   Savard, K. and Homburger, F., *Proc. Soc. Exp. Biol. Med.* **70,** 68 (1949).

86.   Kidd, J. G. and Toolan, H. W., *Fed. Proc.* **9,** 385 (1950).

87.   Andreini, P., Drasher, M. L., and Mitchison, N. A., *J. Exp. Med.* **102,** 199 (1955).

88.   Radici, G. and Piredda, A., *Gior. Ital. Dermatol. Sij.* **1,** 49 (1957).

89.   Masse, C., Chassaigne, J. P., and Kermarec, C., *Bordeaux Chir.* **2,** 70 (1960).

90.   Craigmyle, M. B., *J. Anat.* **92,** 74 (1958).

91.   Burwell, R. G. and Gowland, G., *Nature (London)* **188,** 159 (1960).

92.   Waksman, B. H., in *Ciba Foundation Symposium on Cellular Aspects of Immunity* (G. E. W. Wolstenholm and M. O'Connor Eds.), Churchill, London, 1960 p. 280.

93.   Waksman, B. H., *Lab. Invest.* **12,** 46 (1963).

94.   Weiner, J., Spiro, D., and Russell, P. S., *Am. J. Pathol.* **44,** 319 (1964).

95.   Pedersen, N. C. and Morris, B., *J. Exp. Med.* **131,** 936 (1970).

96.   Smith, J. B., Cunningham, A. J., Lafferty, K. J. and Morris, B., *Aust. J. Exp. Biol. Med. Sci.* **48,** 57 (1970).

97.   Barker, C. R. and Billingham, R. E., *J. Exp. Med.* **128,** 197 (1968).

98.   Medawar, P. B., *Brit. J. Exp. Pathol.* **29,** 58 (1948).

99.   Woodruff, M. F. A. and Woodruff, H. G., *Philos. Trans. Roy. Soc. London (Ser. B), Biol. Sci.* **234,** 559 (1950).

100. Billingham, R. E. and Silvers, W. K., *Proc. Roy. Soc. London (Ser. B)* **161,** 168 (1964).

101. Hall, J. G., *J. Exp. Med.* **125,** 737 (1967).

102. Wesolowski, S. A. and Fennessey, J. F., *Circulation* **8,** 750 (1953).

103. Hume, D. M. and Egdahl, R. H., *Surgery* **38,** 194 (1955).

104. Vetto, R. M. and Lawson, R. K., *Transplantation* **5,** 1537 (1967).

105. Nathan, P., *Ann. N. Y. Acad. Sci.* **120,** 459 (1964).

106. Ballantyne, D. L. and Nathan, P., *Transplantation* **6,** 342 (1968).

107. Medawar, P. B., *Brit. Med. Bull.* **21,** 97 (1965).

108. Billingham, R. E., Brent, L., and Medawar, P. B., *Proc. Roy. Soc. B* **143,** 58 (1954).

109. Elkins, W. L., *J. Exp. Med.* **120,** 329 (1964).

110. Strober, S. and Gowans, J. L., *J. Exp. Med.* **122,** 347 (1965).

111. Billingham, R. E., Brent, L., and Mitchison, N. A., *Brit. J. Exp. Pathol.* **38,** 467 (1957).

112. Hall, J. G. and Morris, B., *Quant. J. Exp. Physiol.* **47,** 360 (1962).

113. Hall, J. G. and Morris, B., *Quant. J. Exp. Physiol.* **48,** 235 (1963).

114. Hall, J. G. and Morris, B., *J. Exp. Med.* **121,** 901 (1965).

115. Hall, J. G. and Morris, B., *Brit. J. Exp. Pathol.* **46,** 450 (1965).

116. Hall, J. G., Morris, B., and Woolley, G., *J. Physiol. London* **180,** 336 (1967).

117. Hall, J. G., *Quant. J. Exp. Physiol.* **52,** 200 (1967).

118. Morris, B., *Nouv. Rev. Fr. d'Hematol.* **8,** 525 (1968).

119. Hall, J. G., *Lancet* **1,** 25 (1969).

120. Hall, J. G. and Smith, M. E., *Nature (London)* **226,** 262 (1970).

121. Hall, J. G., Smith, M. E., Edwards, P. A., and Shooter, K. V., *Immunology* **16,** 773 (1969).

122.   Hamburger, J., Dimitriu, A., Bankir, L., Debray-Sacho, M., and Auvert, J., *Nature (London)* **232,** 633 (1971).

123.   Hamburger, J., *Transplant. Proc.* **4,** 669 (1972).

124.   Billingham, R. E., Silvers, W. K., and Wilson, D. B., *J. Exp. Med.* **118,** 397 (1963).

125.   Gowans, J. L., McGregor, D. D., and Cowen, D. M., *The Immunologically Competent Cell, Ciba Foundation Study Group No. 16,* Churchill, London, 1963, p. 20

126.   Gowans, J. L., McGregor, D. D., Cowen, D. M., and Ford, C. E., *Nature (London)* **196,** 651 (1962).

127.   Gowans, J. L., Gesner, B. M., and McGregor, D. D., in *Biological Activity of the Leukocyte, Ciba Foundation Study Group No. 10,* Churchill, London 1961, p. 32.

128.   Gowans, J. L. and McGregor, D. D., *Prog. Allergy* **9,** 1 (1965).

129.   Gowans, J. L. and Knight, E. J., *Proc. Roy. Soc. London (Ser. B)* **159,** 257 (1964).

130.   Silvers, W. K. and Billingham, R. E., *Transplantation* **8,** 167 (1969).

131.   David, J. R., Lawrence, H. S., and Thomas, L., *J. Immunol.* **93,** 274 (1964).

132.   Gowans, J. L., *Brit. Med. Bull.* **21,** 106 (1965).

133.   Prendergast, R. A., *J. Exp. Med.* **119,** 377 (1964).

134.   Barker, C. F. and Billingham, R. E., *J. Exp. Med.* **133,** 620 (1971).

135.   Simonsen, M., *Prog. Allergy* **6,** 349 (1962).

136.   Billingham, R. E. and Brent, L., *Proc. Roy. Soc. London (Ser. B)* **242,** 439 (1959).

137.   Gowans, J. L., *Harvey Lect.* **64,** 87 (1968–69).

138.   Billingham, R. E. and Silvers, W. K., *J. Exp. Zool.* **146,** 113 (1961).

139.   Terasaki, P. I., *J. Embryol. Exp. Morphol.* **7,** 394 (1959).

140.   Hildemann, W. H., *Transplantation* **2,** 38 (1964).

141.   Brent, L. and Medawar, P. B., *Brit. Med. J.* **2,** 269 (1963).

142.   Brent, L. and Medawar, P. B., *Brit. Med. Bull.* **23,** 55 (1967).

143.   Levey, R. H. and Medawar, P. B., *Proc. Natl. Acad. Sci. U.S.A.* **58,** 470 (1967).

144.   Dineen, J. K., Ronai, P. M., and Wagland, B. M., *Immunology* **15,** 671 (1968).

145.   Emeson, E. E. and Thursh, D. R., *J. Immunol.* **106,** 635 (1971).

146.   Zatz, M. and Lance, E. M., *Cell. Immunol.* **1,** 3 (1970).

147.   Lance, E. M. and Cooper, S., *Cell. Immunol.* **5,** 66 (1972).

148.   Algire, G. H., *J. Natl. Cancer Inst.* **15,** 493 (1954).

149.   Miller, J. F. A. P., *Lancet* **2,** 748 (1961).

150.   Good, R. A., Dalmasso, A. P., Martinez, C., Archer, O. K., Pierce, J. C., and Papermaster, B. W., *J. Exp. Med.* **116,** 773 (1962).

151.   Arnason, B. G., Jankovic, B. D., and Waksman, B. H., *Nature (London)* **194,** 99 (1962).

152.   Miller, J. F. A. P., *Proc. Rmy. Soc. London (Ser. B)* **156,** 415 (1962).

153.   Miller, J. F. A. P., in *Tolerance Acquise et Tolerance Naturelle a l'egard de Substance Antigeniques Definies,* Paris Colloq. Intern. Centre Rech. Sci., 1963, p. 47.

154.   Humphrey, J. H., Parrott, D. M. V., and East, J., *Immunology* **7,** 419 (1964).

155.   Fahey, J. L., Barth, W. F., and Law, L. W., *J. Natl. Cancer Inst.* **35,** 663 (1965).

156.   Arnason, B. G., deVaux St. Cyr, C., and Shaffner, J. B., *J. Immunol.* **93,** 915 (1964).

157.   Dalmasso, A. P. C., Martinez, C., and Good, R. A., *Proc. Soc. Exp. Biol. Med.* **110,** 205 (1962).

158. Miller, J. F. A. P., Marshall, A. H. E., and White, R. G., *Adv. Immunol.* **2,** 111 (1962).

159. Miller, J. F. A. P. and Mitchell, G. F., *Nature (London)* **216,** 659 (1967).

160. Parrott, D. M. V., deSousa, M. A. B., and East, J., *J. Exp. Med.* **123,** 191 (1966).

161. McGregor, D. D. and Gowans, J. L., *J. Exp. Med.* **117,** 303 (1963).

162. Mitchell, G. F. and Miller, J. F. A. P., *J. Exp. Med.* **128,** 821 (1968).

163. Townsend, C. M., Fish, J. C., Vyvial, T., Kiamar, M., and Ritzmann, S. E., *Transplantation* **10,** 284 (1970).

164. Tilney, N. L., Atkinson, J. C., and Murray, J. E., *Ann. Int. Med.* **72,** 59 (1970).

165. Fish, J. C., Mattingly, A. T., Ritzmann, S. E., Sarles, H. E., and Remmers, A. R., *Arch. Surg.* **99** 664 (1969).

166. Fish, J. C., Beathard, G. A., Sarles, H. E., Remmers, A. P., and Ritzmann, S. E., *Surgery* **67,** 658 (1970).

167. Robinson, S., Brecher, G., Lowrie, I. S., and Haley, J. E., *Blood* **26,** 281 (1965).

168. Caffrey, R. W., Riecke, W. O., and Everett, N. B., *Acta Haematol. Scand.* **28,** 145 (1962).

169. Everett, N. B., Caffrey, R. W., and Rieke, W. O., *Ann. N. Y. Acad. Sci.* **113,** 887 (1964).

170. Sipe, C. R., Chenanve, A. D., Cronkite, E. P., Joel, D. D., and Schaffer, L. M., *Proc. Soc. Exp. Biol. Med.* **123,** 158 (1966).

171. Sajier, S., Cottier, H., Cronkite, E. P., Jansen, C. R., and Kanti, R. R., *Blood* **30,** 301 (1967).

172. Wagner, H. P., Cottier, H., Cronkite, E. P., Cunningham, L., Jansen, C. R., and Kanti, R. R., *Exp. Cell Res.* **46,** 441 (1967).

173. Levey, R. H. and Medawar, P. B., *Proc. Natl. Acad. Sci. U.S.A.* **56,** 1130 (1966).

174. Levey, R. H. and Medawar, P. B., in *Ciba Foundation Symposium on Antilymphocytic Serum* (G. E. W. Wolstenholme and M. O'Connor, Eds.), Churchill, London, 1967, p. 72.

175. Denman, A. M. and Frenkel, E. P., *Immunology* **14,** 115 (1968).

176. Denman, A. M., Denman, E. J., and Ernbling, P. H., *Lancet* **1,** 321 (1968).

177. Denman, A. M., Denman, E. J., and Holoborow, E. J., *Nature (London)* **217,** 177 (1968).

178. Taub, R. N., in The immune response and its suppression, *Antibiot. Chemother., Basel,* **15,** 520 (1969).

179. Martin, W. J. and Miller, J. F. A. P., *J. Exp. Med.* **128,** 855 (1968).

180. Leuchars, S. E., Wallis, V. J., and Davies, A. J., *Nature (London)* **219,** 1325 (1968).

181. Lance, E. M. and Batchelor, R., *Transplantation* **6,** 490 (1968).

182. James, K. and Anderson, N. F., *Clin. Exp. Immunol.* **3,** 227 (1968).

183. Monaco, A. P. and Franco, D. J., *Transplant. Proc.* **1,** 474 (1969).

184. Gray, J. G., Monaco, A. P., and Russell, P. S., *Surg. Forum* **15,** 142 (1964).

185. Monaco, J. G., Wood, M. L., Gray, J. G., and Russell, P. S., *J. Immunol.* **96,** 229 (1966).

186. Lance, E. M., in *International Symposium on Pharmacological treatment in Organ and Tissue Transplantation* (A. Bertelli and A. P. Monaco, Eds.), Exerpta Medical Foundation, Milan, 1969, p. 242.

187.   Turk, J. L. and Willoughby, D. A., *Lancet* **1,** 249 (1967).

188.   Parrott, D. M. V., *J. Clin. Pathol. Suppl.* **20,** 456 (1967).

189.   Taub, R. N. and Lance, E. M., *J. Exp. Med.* **128,** 1281 (1968).

190.   Woodruff, M. F. A. and Anderson, N. F., *Nature (London)* **200,** 702 (1963).

191.   Woodruff, M. F. A. and Anderson, N. F., *Ann. N. Y. Acad. Sci.* **120,** 119 (1964).

192.   Monaco, A. P., Wood, M. L., and Russell, P. S., *Science* **149,** 432 (1965).

193.   Burnet, F. M., *The Clonal Selection Theory of Acquired Immunity,* Cambridge University Press, Cambridge, Massachusetts, 1959.

194.   Hempel, C. G., *Aspects of Scientific Explanation,* Free Press, New York, 1965.

195.   Woodruff, M. F. A., in *Biological Problems of Grafting* (F. Albert and J. Leujeurs-Ledant, Eds.), Blackwell Scientific Publications, Oxford and Edinborough, 1959, p. 258.

196.   Billingham, R. E., Brent, L., and Medawar, P. B., *Philos. Trans. Roy. Soc. B* **239,** 357 (1956).

197.   Smith, R. T. and Bridges, R. A., *J. Exp. Med.* **108,** 227 (1958).

198.   Shellam, G. R., *Int. Arch. Allergy* **40,** 507 (1971).

199.   Silvers, W. K., *J. Exp. Med.* **128,** 69 (1968).

200.   Wachtel, S. S. and Silvers, W. K., *J. Exp. Med.* **135,** 388 (1972).

201.   Hellström, K. E. and Hellström, I., *Am. Rev. Microbiol.* **24,** 373 (1970).

202.   Hellström, K. E., Hellström, I., and Brown, J., *Nature (London)* **244,** 914 (1969).

203.   Hellström, I., Hellström, K. E., Storb, R., and Thomas, E. D., *Proc. Natl. Acad. Sci. U.S.A.* **66,** 65 (1970).

204.   Hellström, I., Hellström, K. E., and Allison, A. C., *Nature (London)* **230,** 49 (1971).

205.   Pierce, G. E., Quadracci, L. J., Tremann, J. A., Moe, R. E., Striker, G. E., Hellström, I., Hellström, K. E., and Marchiaro, T. L., *Ann. Surg.* **174,** 609 (1971).

206.   Brent, L., Brooks, C., Lubling, N., and Thomas, A. V., *Transplantation* **15,** 000 (1973). In press.

207.   Atkins, R. C. and Ford, W. L., *Transplantation* **13,** 442 (1972).

208.   Beverley, P. C. L., Brent, L., Brooks, C., Medawar, P. B., and Simpson, E., *Transplant. Proc.* **5,** 679 (1973).

209.   Rouse, B. T. and Warner, R. L., *Eur. J. Immunol.* **2,** 102 (1972).

210.   Catti, R. A., Meuwissen, H. J., Allen, H. D., et al, *Lancet* **2,** 1366 (1968).

211.   de Konnig, J., van Bekkum, D. W., Dicke, K. A., et al, *Lancet* **2,** 571 (1969).

212.   Levey, R. H., Klemperer, M. R., and Gelfand, E. W., *Lancet* **2,** 571 (1971).

213.   Stilhm, E. R., Lawlor, G. J., Kaplan, M. S., et al, *New England J. Med.* **286,** 797 (1972).

214.   Mitchison, N. A., *Transplant. Proc.* **3,** 953 (1971).

215.   Gershon, R. K. and Kondo, K., *Immunology* **21,** 903 (1971).

216.   Gershon, R. K., Cohen, P., Hencin, R., and Liebhaber, S. A., *J. Immunol.* **108,** 586 (1972).

217.   Weissman, I., *Transplantation* **15,** 265 (1973).

218.   Cozenza, H. and Kohler, H., *Proc. Natl. Acad. Sci. U.S.A.* **69,** 2701 (1972).

219.   Manning, D. D. and Jutila, J. W., *J. Exp. Med.* **135,** 1392 (1972).

220.   Wigzell, H. and Makela, O., *J. Exp. Med.* **132,** 110 (1970).

221.   Rajf, M. C., Sternberg, M., and Taylor, R. B., *Nature (London)* **225,** 553 (1970).

222.   Unanue, E. R., Grey, H. M., Rabellino, E., Campbell, P., and Schmidtke, J., *J. Exp. Med.* **133,** 1188 (1971).

223.   Pernis, B., Forni, L., and Amante, L., *J. Exp. Med.* **132,** 1001 (1970).

224.   Unanue, E. R., *J. Immunol.* **107,** 1168 (1971).

225.   Sell, S. and Gell, P. G., *J. Exp. Med.* **122,** 428 (1965).

226.   Siskind, G. W. and Benacerraf, B., *Adv. Immunol.* **10,** 1 (1969).

227.   Lesley, J. and Dutton, R. W., *Science* **169,** 487 (1970).

228.   Makela, O. and Cross, A. M., *Prog. Allergy* **14,** 146 (1970).

229.   Baur, S., Vitetta, E. S., Sherr, C. J., Schenkein, I., and Uhr, J. W., *J. Immunol,* **106,** 1133 (1971).

230.   Makela, O., *Transplant. Rev.* **5,** 3 (1970).

231.   Hart, D. A., Want, A. L., Pawlak, L. L., and Nisonojf, A., *J. Exp. Med.* **135,** 1292 (1972).

232.   Makela, O., *Cold Spring Harbor Symp. Quant. Biol.* **32,** 423 (1967).

233.   Mason, S. and Warner, N. L., *J. Immunol.* **104,** 762 (1970).

234.   Riethmuller, G., Rieber, E. P., and Seeger, I., *Nat. New Biol.* **230,** 248 (1971).

235.   Theis, G. A. and Thorbecke, J., *J. Immunol.* **110,** 91 (1973).

236.   Jones, G., Torrigiani, G., and Roitt, I. M., *J. Immunol.* **106,** 1425 (1971).

237.   Basten, A. Miller, J. F. A. P., Warner, N. L., and Pye, J., *Nat. New Biol.* **231,** 104 (1971).

238.   Marchalonis, J. J., Cone, R. E., and Atwell, J. L., *J. Exp. Med.* **135,** 956 (1972).

239.   Gonatas, N. K., Antoine, J. C., Stieber, A., and Avrameas, S., *Lab. Invest.* **26,** 253.

240.   Bankhurst, A. D., Warner, N. L., and Sprent, J., *J. Exp. Med.* **134,** 1005 (1971).

241.   Nossal, G. J. V., Warner, N. L., Lewis, H., and Sprent, J., *J. Exp. Med.* **135,** 405 (1972).

242.   Warner, N. L., *Transplant. Proc.* **3,** 848 (1972).

243.   Zimmerman, B. and Feldman, J. D., *J. Immunol.* **103,** 383 (1969).

244.   Terman, D. S., Minden, P., and Crowle, A. J., *Cell. Immunol.* **6,** 273 (1973).

245.   Terman, D. S., Minden, P., and Crowle, A. J., *Cell. Immunol.* **6,** 284 (1973).

246.   Ryder, R. J. W. and Schwartz, R. S., *J. Immunol.* **103,** 971 (1969).

247.   Levey, R. H., *Transplant. Proc.* **4,** 543 (1972).

248.   Medawar, P. B., *Transplant. Proc.* **5,** 7 (1973).

Chapter Eleven

Transfer Factor: Initiation and Augmentation of Cell-Mediated Immunity

H. SHERWOOD LAWRENCE

Infectious Disease and Immunology Division
Department of Medicine
New York University School of Medicine

A major advance in our understanding of the origins and consequences of delayed-type hypersensitivity (DTH) and cell-mediated immunity was achieved by the discovery of cellular transfer of delayed-type hypersensitivity in the guinea pig by Landsteiner and Chase (1). This experimental approach separated that category of immune responses initiated by cells from those mediated by humoral antibodies. Moreover, this finding provided clues to the cellular immunologic reagents responsible for the transaction, and thereby permitted the undertaking of an analysis of the mechanism of the response. Thus it was initially observed that only intact and viable cells of the lymphoid series were able to transfer sensitivity in the experimental animal (2).

Work from the author's laboratories has been supported by the USPHS Research Grant A1-01254-17 and Training Grant 5-T01-00005-15 and in part by the Streptococcal and Staphylococcal Commission of the Armed Forces Epidemiological Board.

The study of transfer factor (TF) in human subjects began with the use of viable buffy coat leukocytes as vehicles of TF to transfer tuberculin and later streptococcal sensitivities (3,4). The system in man proved similar in some respects to that described in the guinea pig, particularly with regard to the stringent, dual quantitative requirements for successful transfer to occur, namely: (1) the critical necessity to select TF donors with marked degrees of cutaneous reactivity to the antigen under study, and (2) the obligatory use of adequate numbers of leukocytes. However, with careful attention to such quantitative details, it soon became apparent that humans were much more responsive to cellular transfer than animal species (5–7). This heightened capacity of humans to respond took two forms: (1) much fewer donor cells per kilogram of recipient were required, and (2) the transferred sensitivity endured in man from months to 1 to 2 years compared to a 5 to 7 day duration in allogeneic animals. The cause of the short duration of transferred sensitivity in animals has been clarified by subsequent studies which have shown that allogeneic cells are rejected in recipient animals via a homograft response and that the sensitivity endowed by the transferred cells is thus terminated (8,9). In man, however, the active moiety, transfer factor, is readily dissociable from the HLA antigens of its cellular vehicle, and although the cells bearing it are rejected, transfer factor itself is not rejected (10).

The most striking difference detected in the human system, however, was the unexpected finding that extracts of leukocytes are as effective as viable cells in the transfer of DTH and cellular immunity (11). This observation allowed efforts to isolate, identify, and characterize the active subcellular moiety to begin. We have termed the active moiety transfer factor (TF) as a convenient shorthand with the full appreciation that more than one factor may be involved. Early attempts to pinpoint this activity employed water-lysed leukocyte extracts incubated at 37°C for 4 to 6 hours. The cell contents under these conditions are subjected to digestion by a battery of endogenous nucleases as well as lysosomal hydrolases and proteases that are released and activated by this disruptive procedure (12). This treatment had no adverse effect on the capacity to transfer tuberculin or streptococcal sensitivity.

Moreover the addition of exogenous enzymes such as DNAse, RNAse, and DNAse plus tryspin was also without effect on the capacity of frozen and thawed leukocyte extracts to transfer tuberculin sensitivity. From these results it was concluded that transfer factor activity did not depend on polymerized macromolecules of DNA or RNA, or such proteins that are susceptible to tryptic digestion (12).

Slavin and Garvin (13) subsequently showed that nonadherent blood mononuclear cells alone, comprised of 94 to 98% lymphocytes, are sufficient to effect the transfer of DTH in humans, and granulocytes or glass-adherent cells are not obligatory for this activity. This finding was also confirmed by Hattler and Amos (14), who transferred DTH to a panel of antigens (tuberculin, Histoplasmin, Candida, Trichophytin, mumps) in humans using 90 to 98% pure blood lymphocytes prepared by a nylon column technique. They also found, as we (15) and others (16–19) had, that the pattern of multiple antigenic specificities of DTH transferred to recipients was concordant with, and dictated by, the particular specificities expressed by the donor as well as their intensity. Most of the recent clinical studies employing TF for immunotherapy have used dialyzable TF (TFᴅ) prepared from enriched lymphocyte preparations purified by Ficoll-hypaque gradient techniques. These preparations consist of 98% lymphocytes and 2% monocytes.

A further insight into the mechanism of transfer was afforded by the successful serial passage of DTH using blood leukocyte extracts from natively sensitive donor A to negative recipient B and thence to negative recipient C (12). In this fashion streptococcal DTH was transferred from a sensitive donor A to a primary recipient B using an extract prepared from 425×10^6 lysed leukocytes. On day 3 posttransfer, an extract of 425×10^6 lysed leukocytes prepared from B was used to transfer streptococcal DTH to a secondary recipient C. Similarly, tuberculin DTH was transferred from another sensitive donor A to a primary recipient B using a frozen and thawed extract prepared from 170×10^6 leukocytes. After week 3 of posttransfer, a frozen and thawed extract of 425×10^6 leukocytes prepared from B transferred tuberculin DTH to a secondary recipient C. This type of result, considered in relation to the minute quantities of the material initially employed for transfer, and the dilutional aspects of passaging a molecular species from individual A to B to C. tended to weaken the notion that a "superantigen" is responsible for transfer of DTH. Moreover, any possible contribution of a unique and perhaps yet undiscovered type of immunoglobulin to the effects observed was excluded.

This early observation on serial transfer of DTH has become understandable and more acceptable in the light of recent evidence, documented by ourselves as well as a number of other investigators, showing that TF, in addition to conferring cutaneous DTH and cell-mediated immunity on normal or diseased recipients, causes a new population of antigen-responsive lymphocytes to appear in the recipient's circulation (39,56). Following transfer, the recipient's lymphocytes can be shown to transform and proliferate and/or elaborate such lymphokines as migration inhibitory factor (MIF) and lymphotoxin (LT) when exposed to the specific antigens to which the TF donor is sensitive. Thus, TF clearly endows the recipient with cutaneous DTH reactivities and results in the induction of a new population of circulating lymphocytes that interact with antigen in a specificity pattern dictated by that donor. Following interaction with antigen such cells then undertake most of the *in vivo* and *in vitro* responses usually only detected in natively sensitive individuals.

The basic details of the efficacy of leukocyte extracts compared with viable cells in the transfer of DTH response in humans have been amply confirmed and extended (17,20–22). For example, Maurer showed that the DTH transferred by leukocyte extracts was not due to the elevation of a latent sensitivity or to screening tests with antigen by employing neoantigen, ethylene oxide-treated human serum proteins (22). We had reached essentially the same conclusion following the transfer of cocci-diodin sensitivity to residents on the Eastern seaboard who had not been exposed to that antigen because of the geographic distribution of that pathogen (23). This conclusion was subsequently reinforced by our demonstration of the transfer of skin allograft rejection with specifically sensitized leukocyte extracts—a system where prior exposure or prior testing of TF recipients with antigen is reasonably excluded and the *de novo* production of a new specific TF was documented in the donors (24).

The adaptation of TF to the study of mechanisms of transplant rejection in man also yielded further evidence for: (1) the *de novo* generation of TF in a host undergoing sensitization to a new antigen mosaic, and (2) the specificity of the TF raised for the constellation of HL-A antigens. This study thus documented the appearance of a histocompatibility TF following specific, appropriate sensitization with skin allografts. Moreover, the new TF was not present in the host after 1 skin graft exposure, and it became barely detectable after sequential exposure to 2 skin grafts. The specific TF raised and assayed in this fashion reached levels quantitatively sufficient to transfer enduring systemic sensitivity only after sequential exposure of the TF donor to an antigenic stimulus supplied by 4 successive skin grafts from the same donor (25). Moreover, the specificity of the TF raised was directed against the tissues of the individual used to sensitize the TF donor and not directed against tissues of other individuals. In this setting TF induced against individual A and injected into individual B caused accelerated rejection of skin allografts obtained from A but not those obtained from C or D simultaneously in residence on individual B. This system proved a most discriminating test of the specificity of TF and eliminated any possible contributions of prior screening tests with antigen. It also excluded elevation of latent sensitivity as a mechanism of TF activity, a possibility that ear-

Table 1   Cutaneous DTH or CMI Conferred by TF from Immune Donors [a]

Microbial antigens:

Bacterial	Fungal	Viral	Parasitic
Tuberculin	Coccidioidin	Vaccinia	Schistosomal
Streptococcal	Histoplasmin	Herpres	(monkey)
Diphtheria toxoid	Candidin	Rubeola	Coccidiodes
Lepromin	Trichophyton	Mumps	(rat)
Tularin	T. rubrum		
	Blastomycin		

<u>Neoantigens</u>   Ethylene oxide human serum protein; KLH

<u>Histocompatibility antigens:</u>   HLA skin allocraft specificities

<u>Tumor antigens:</u>   Melanoma
                        Sarcoma

<u>Other antigens:</u>   Kveim
                        "Cat-scratch"

<u>Comment:</u>   Recipients express pure DTH or CMI in absence of Ab to same determinants.

[a] Reprinted with permission, Lawrence, H. S., *Harvey Lecture Series 68, 1972–73*, Academic Press, New York, in press.

lier studies on the transfer of sensitivity to ubiquitous microbial antigens had raised. Parenthetically, in those patients with renal transplants, it is the few lymphocytes bearing the specific TF directed against the particular constellation of HL-A antigens borne by the kidney which should be the proper target of immunosuppression. The converse situation is illustrated by the tumor-bearing patient where serum "blocking factors" constitute nature's own immunosuppressive device to allow the survival of that allograft by abrogating the activity of host lymphocytes bearing the specific TF versus alien tumor-specific antigens.

The scope of the general capacity of TF obtained from specifically immune donors to transfer cutaneous DTH or cell-mediated immunity to diverse groups of antigens is outlined in Table 1.

The search for the identity and biochemical nature of TF was greatly facilitated by our finding that it passes through a Visking cellophane dialysis sac (26). With this one simple maneuver all of the macromolecules of the leukocyte extracts, assorted passenger virions, and histocompatibility antigens are separated from TF and left behind in the sac. The dialyzate containing TF is then concentrated, and may be stored as a lyophilized powder that is stable for as long as 5 years at ordinary refrigerator temperatures ($-4°C$) without loss of potency (15).

Further studies revealed dialyzable TF to be held up in passage through Sephadex G-25 and emerge under a broad peak in the region of molecules that are less than 10,000 molecular weight. TF is not antigenic and does not raise detectable neutralizing antibody to itself when administered in massive doses over long periods in humans nor when injected in Freund's adjuvant into rabbits (15). No protein is detectable in the dialyzate upon addition of 10% trichloroacetic acid. It is not an immunoglobulin or light chain, and Bence-Jones protein or papain-digested gamma globulin fragments added to the inside of the bag as markers are not detected in the dialyzate using sensitive immunologic tests. Materials in the dialyzate give orcinol and biuret positive tests.

The dialyzable nature, the polypeptide-polynucleotide composition, the adsorption spectra peaks prepared following passage of dialyzate on Sephadex G-25, as well as the low molecular weight (<10,000 MW) of TF have all been repeatedly confirmed in precise detail in several laboratories both in this country and abroad (27–30). Curiously, heating the dialyzate to 56 or 100°C for 30 minutes followed by rapid cooling has resulted in inactivating its capacity to transfer *local* tuberculin sensitivity in sarcoid patients (31). Moreover, treatment of the dialyzate with pancreatic RNAse has no effect on the capacity to transfer, although known species of control RNA added to the dialyzate are readily attacked by this enzyme, excluding the presence of an inhibitor of RNAse activity as a cause of this result (26,32).

Since the polypeptides and polynucleotides are the only materials other than carbohydrate in the dialyzate that are candidates for the biological activities of TF, thermal inactivation of this type coupled with resistance to treatment with pancreatic RNAse may have special meaning. Such properties are characteristic of double-stranded RNA polynucleotides. Nevertheless, we remain aware of the potential biological activity of other oligonucleotides as well as low molecular weight peptides and carbohydrate moieties that are also present in the dialyzate. Thus, TF may be proved either a polynucleotide, a polypeptide, or a peptide-nucleotide complex. Experiments designed to determine which chemical species comprise the active moiety are under way in a number of laboratories. In any event the availability, potency, and partial purification of TF in lyophilized dialyzates have virtually assured the successful conclusion of the long search into the biochemical composition and molecular structure of that substance.

Baram and his associates, in their biochemical analyses of dialyzates, have concluded that TF_D is an RNA polynucleotide lacking guanidine (27). They also find a nondialyzable moiety with TF activity that may represent the parent molecular species from which the dialyzable fraction is dislocated by the disruptive treatment of the cells that bear it or may, we believe, represent residual, TFᴅ that has diffused back following equilibrium with the dialyzate.

Earlier experiments performed with Pappenheimer revealed a type of TF that is specifically released from sensitive cell populations within 30 minutes following incubation with antigen (33,34). This antigen-liberated, monospecific TF, like TFᴅ prepared from WBC extracts and possessing multiple specificities, exhibits all of the potency and activity of the cells from which it is prepared. Recent successful application of TF to the immunotherapy of coccidiodomycosis has revealed that such monospecific antigen-liberated TF is dialyzable, and exhibits comparable potency to the TF prepared from extracts (35). These experiments showing prompt liberation of TF as well as the preparation of TF from leukocyte extracts emphasize the presence of TF in cells as a preexistent moiety rather than a product of cells such as the mediator lymphokines, since the latter require antigen stimulation, lymphocyte activation, and a variable latent period for their synthesis to begin.

There remains much to be done before any final answer is in. Happily, the materials and techniques have been provided to make this quest, in Medawar's felicitous phrase, the "art of the soluble."

BIOLOGICAL PROPERTIES OF TF

In considering the biological functions of TF, it is important to emphasize at the outset that the responses initiated in the recipient of TF also occur in the donor upon his exposure to the appropriate antigens. Thus most of the *cellular* immune memories possessed by the donor, providing that they are of sufficient intensity, are conferred on and expressed by the recipient only following exposure to the specific antigens. In addition to those specific responses that the battery of antigens currently available can reveal, there probably exists an unknown number of specific TF's congruent with other antigenic determinants that have yet to be appreciated or studied systematically. These may include specific TF's induced during prior successful encounters with known viruses (e.g., Epstein-Barr (EB) virus; AU antigen); or mycoplasma species; or directed toward an array of TSTA of mutant neoplastic cells that have arisen and have been rejected as allogeneic cells via the mechanism of immunologic surveillance; or perhaps various neoantigens of cell membrane constituents in autoimmune states arising from prolonged and intimate intracellular microbial or viral parasitism resulting in alterations of HL-A antigens via a self + X mechanism we had proposed some years ago (36), and which is discussed further in a subsequent section.

Of further interest is the fact that the natively sensitive donor of TF expresses DTH responses and cell-mediated immune responses with a variable contribution of humoral antibody directed against the same antigenic determinants. In direct contrast, the recipient of TF can express only DTH and cellular immunity following transfer, since TF prepared from *blood* leukocytes has been shown incapable of transferring the capacity for antibody synthesis to the corresponding antigenic determinants for DTH to normal (33) or to agammaglobulinemic subjects (37). Thus the responses of recipients of TF are examples of "pure" DTH reactions mounted without the intercession of humoral antibody and none of the donor's immunological memories for circulating immunoglobulin production is transferred.

This is not to say, however, that induction of cellular immunity with TF may not have a role in facilitating T and B cell interaction and thereby indirectly contribute to immunoglobulin production. Nevertheless, up until the present a careful search has failed to detect antibody with antigenic specificity concordant with that of the cellular immunity transferred. These studies included the sensitive *in vivo* rabbit skin neutralization test for diphtheria antitoxin that detects less than 0.01 mg/ml antibody in normal recipients with transferred DTH to diphtheria toxoid (33) as well as additional attempts to detect antibody in agammaglobulinemic recipients of TF (37).

A further clue to the relationships cellular and humoral immunity have may be found in the results achieved when sensitive and primed lymph node slices were transplanted to an agammaglobulinemic recipient (38). In these experiments the viable lymph node slices transferred simultaneously both tuberculin DTH and the capacity to make a secondary immunoglobulin response to other antigens. The transferred Ig production lasted only 110 days and was brought to an end by the rejection of the transplanted lymph node slices by the recipient. In sharp contrast, however, the transferred tuberculin sensitivity persisted for as long as it was tested (>300 days), long after the transferred cells were rejected. This type of result suggests that: (1) cell populations that inhabit lymph nodes, unlike circulating leucocytes, can transfer the capacity for antibody synthesis in humans, and (2) such transfer of antibody formation requires functioning viable cells in the recipient and is quite unlike the transfer of DTH responses. In view of the current interest in T and B cell interactions for certain types of humoral immunity, this result may provide clues for the interpretation of certain animal transfer experiments.

The chief *in vivo* function of TF in recipients is the initiation of cell-mediated immune responses that eventuate in (a) delayed cutaneous

Table 2   Some Properties of Dialyzable Transfer Factor [a]

Biological	Biochemical	Immunological
Properties of WBC extract:	Soluble, dialyzable, lyophilizable	Not immunoglobulin
Prompt onset (hours)	< 10,000 MW	Not immunogenic
Long duration (>1 year) Equal intensity	No Protein, albumin, or -globulin	Immunologically specific
Dissociable from transplantation antigens	Orcinol positive	Converts normal lymphocytes *in vitro* and *in vivo* to antigen-responsive state
	Polypeptide/polynucleotide composition	Transformation and clonal proliferation of converted lymphocytes exposed to antigen
Small quantities → magnified effects	Inactivated 56°C-30 minutes	
	Resists pancreatic RNAse	Informational molecule/depressor/receptor site?
	Retains potency — 5 years	

[a] Reprinted with permission, Lawrence, H. S., *Advances in Immunology*, Academic Press, New York, 1969, Volume 11, p. 195.

reactivity to a variety of bacterial, viral, fungal, and artificial protein antigens; (b) allograft rejection; (c) recovery from intracellular viral and fungal infections such as disseminated vaccinia, coccidiodomycosis, tuberculosis, and candidiasis; (d) reconstitution of congenital (Wiskott-Aldrich, Swiss-type agammaglobulinemia) as well as acquired (sarcoid, leprosy, neoplasia) cellular immune deficiency syndromes; (e) rejection of malignant melanoma as an allograft. In all of these diverse functions the specificity of the cellular immune responses expressed by the recipient is usually concordant with the pattern of specific DTH's or cellular immunities that are possessed by the donor of TF. We have indicated above how this may come about and have discussed elsewhere the occasional exceptions detected (39).

We discuss below evidence that the essential targets of TF are foreign histocompatibility antigens and how this interpretation serves to unify the apparently diverse functions of TF listed above. Some of the salient biological, biochemical, and immunological properties of TF insofar as they are currently known are listed in Table 2 and Figure 1.

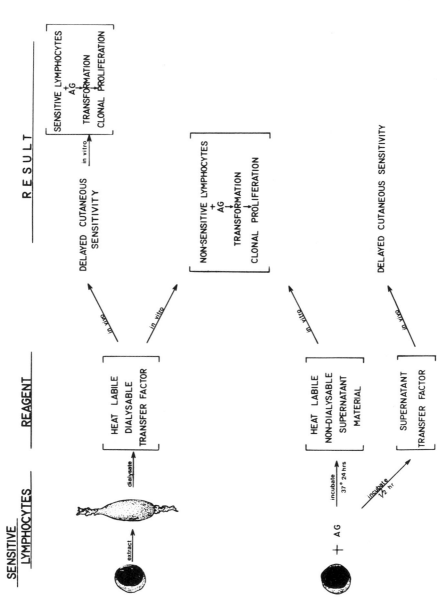

Figure 1. Summary of the salient biological, biochemical, and immunological properties of transfer factor. From H. S. Lawrence, *Adv. Immunol.* **11**, 195 (1969). Reprinted with permission from Academic Press.

TF AND THE MEDIATORS OF CELLULAR IMMUNITY

In Chapter 2 Remold and David describe the form and functions of the products of lymphocyte activation. These activities generated by lymphocytes following perturbation of their membranes, by antigen or plant mitogens, comprise a family of molecules that were collectively designated "mediators" or "effectors" of cell-mediated immunity immediately following their discovery and early description (39) and subsequently by the more scholarly designation of "lymphokines" (40). By whatever name, this rapidly growing list of activities detected in supernatants of activated lymphocytes is apparently limited only by the conception and scope of the design of *in vitro* targets contrived to reveal their presence (41,42). It is worth reemphasis to indicate that all of the mediators appear in the same supernatant after a similar latent period of several hours (i.e., 6 hours or longer) following lymphocyte activation and are present in varying concentrations depending on the number of lymphocytes engaged in their production (e.g., ca. 70% lymphocytes "nonspecifically" activated by PHA versus <2% lymphocytes specifically activated by antigen). The pressing questions that work on the mediators has raised are as follows: (1) How many of the activities detected are properties of distinctive molecules, and how many the properties of the same molecule in differing concentrations? (2) Which of the activities detected are antigen dependent and why? (3) Which lymphocyte population actually produces the mediators and what are the *in vivo* inhibitors of these activities? (4) Do the mediators have an *in vivo* function, and if so, is the scope of such activities limited to a microenvironment or are there systemic reflections of molecules with such demonstrable *in vitro* potency? These topics are covered in detail in Chapters 2, 3, and 12.

In any event, work on the discovery of the mediators occurred at a propitious time, when *in vivo* transfer studies of cellular immunity had just demonstrated that a paucity of labeled, sensitized donor cells converged at the site of cutaneous DTH reactions in the recipient (43). These findings raised questions as to the nature of the mechanisms that allowed the amplification of full-blown cellular immune responses from so disappointingly few progenitor cells.

Work from our laboratory employing time-lapse cinematography of antigen-stimulated human lymphocytes has shown that less than 2% of circulating lymphocytes are antigen responsive and the larger number of lymphoblasts (ca. 30 to 40%) detected by 7 to 8 days following culture with antigen could be satisfactorily explained by repeated cell division and clonal proliferation of the original small number of antigen-reactive lymphocytes initially present (44). We approached this study fully prepared to detect evidence of recruitment since we had previously isolated products of sensitive lymphocytes and demonstrated their capacity to cause nonsensitive lymphocytes to respond to antigen, namely transfer factor (TF) *in vivo* and lymphocyte transforming factor (LTF) *in vitro* (15,45–47). Since our cine observations began 48 to 72 hours after the lymphocytes had been activated by antigen, we have not excluded the possibility of recruitment occurring in the critical latent period from 0 to 72 hours.

Although the mediators are triggered into production following lymphocyte activation with specific antigen, they are nonimmunoglobulin moieties, and are nonspecific in their effects. They appear to serve as an amplification system for cell-mediated immune responses in several ways: activating more lymphocytes (LTF); attracting (MCF), agglutinating, and impeding macrophages (MIF); metabolically activating macrophages for enhanced phagocytosis (MAF), production of interferon, and attraction of other leukocytes. In general, the few lymphocytes activated appear to be signaling for help from the diverse cellular participants in the DTH inflammatory and cellular immune response. This aspect of cell cooperation is discussed more fully in Chapter 12. In this sense the mediators of cellular immunity function much like the concatenations of the complement system in its cascading amplification of humoral immune responses.

What then is the relationship of transfer factor to the mediators of cellular immunity? The answer to this question is a very direct one: Transfer factor functions as an initiator of cellular immunity by converting a select population of lymphocytes to a specific antigen-responsive state (48–50). This event is not detectable until the recipient or his circulating lymphocytes are exposed to the corresponding specific antigens. Following such exposure of recipients to antigen *in vivo*, delayed reactivity is detected in the skin, and *in vitro* the TF recipient's lymphocytes either transform to lymphoblasts, undergo clonal proliferation, and/or produce such mediators as MIF and LT. Thus TF initiates cell-mediated immunity with specificities dictated by the donor and prepares the lymphocytes it has converted to interact with antigen, following which they produce the mediators in consequence of this recognition event.

Another distinctive difference results from the detection of TF as a preexistent moiety that can leak out of damaged cells upon standing or be rapidly extracted from cells that bear it by freezing and thawing. Moreover, incubation of sensitive human blood cell populations with specific antigen causes the selective, liberation of the corresponding specific TF within 15 to 30 minutes, thereby desensitizing the cells that bear it (33). If such populations are selected to contain cells of 2 specificities (e.g., tuberculin sensitive, toxoid sensitive), only the tuberculin TF will be liberated upon incubation with PPD whereas the toxoid TF remains in the cell pellet (34). This property of TF as a preexistent moiety differs from the mediators which have not been detected until after lymphocyte activation by antigen and then only after a variable latent period between activation and their detection that extends anywhere from 6 to 24 hours or longer. The mediators also require active protein synthesis, and their production is inhibited by puromycin and actinomycin (51,52).

Other important differences include chemical composition and immunological specificity. TF is a dialyzable moiety of less than 10,000 molecular weight which is comprised of polypeptides and polynucleotides, whereas the mediators are nondialyzable macromolecules ranging from 12,000 to 80,000 molecular weight. In its immunological properties TF exhibits specificity, whereas the effects of the mediators are nonspecific.

Some of the contrasts between TF and the mediators are summarized in Table 3.

IMMUNOTHERAPY WITH TRANSFER FACTOR

Interest in the nature and immunologic significance of TF has been rekindled recently by a growing literature documenting the remarkable effectiveness of this specific immunologic reagent in the initiation or restoration of cellular immunity to patients with a wide range of congenital and acquired cellular immunodeficiency diseases, tumors, and intracellular infections. This turn of events is an outgrowth of the gradual general acceptance of TF as a real entity, and with this acceptance the sudden realization that TF and the cell-mediated immunity it conveys may have impact on so many of the distressing *in vivo* states which we define as disease (53,55). In addition to providing effective therapy of diseases for which other measures have proved merely palliative or ineffective, TF is providing a clearer understanding of the precise immunopathology involved as well as delineating the scope of the homeostatic functions it serves in normal individuals. Earlier approaches to this form of immunologic intervention employed viable buffy coat leukocytes or lymphocyte suspensions. More recent approaches designed either to confer or elevate cell-mediated immunity selectively have employed TF_D.

The putative advantages of transferring living lymphocytes are (a) the possible contribution of a graft-versus-host reaction and its consequences including macrophage activation, and (b) the possible release of lymphokines from such cells. However, such advantages may be short-

Table 3   Comparison of Transfer Factor with Effector Molecules

	Transfer Factor	Effector Molecules
Activity	Initiator of cellular immunity; converts lymphocytes to Ag-responsive state	Effectors of cellular immunity produced by Ag-stimulated lymphocytes
Latency	Preexistent "memory" moiety liberated promptly from sensitive cells by Ag or by extraction	Latent period required for production after contact of sensitive cells with Ag
Specificity	Immunologically specific	Nonspecific effects
Properties	Dialyzable; < 10,000 MW	Nondialyzable; ca. 80,000 MW (except interferon)
Composition	Polynucleotides and/or polypeptides	Non immunoglobulins, migrate with albumin
In vivo function	Delayed cutaneous reactivity; homograft rejection; reconstitution of cellular immune deficiency disease; recovery from disseminated intracellular infection.	Cutaneous reactivity of delayed type (MIF; SRF)—others to be determined

[a]Reprinted with permission, Lawrence, H. S. *Proceedings, V Leukocyte Culture Conference,* Academic Press, New York, 1970.

lived, and terminate with the rejection and disposal of the transfused lymphocytes. When viable allogeneic cells are employed in this fashion, the immunologically competent host will reject them and prepare his own TFd *in vivo,* while the incompetent host may experience a graft-versus-host reaction, with its possible grave consequences. The use of preformed TFd, rather than intact cells, avoids such reactions and results in the conversion of the recipients own lymphocytes to an antigen-reactive state so that they are capable of responding to antigen with a variety of cell-mediated immune responses. Moreover, TF is easy to prepare, and when concentrated by lyophilization, much higher dosages can be administered repeatedly with safety. This approach has much to recommend it since this small, nonantigenic molecule possesses all of the potency of the parent leukocyte or leukocyte extract from which it is prepared, and since quantitative considerations such as dosage and repetitive administration of TF have been shown to determine the outcome of such immunotherapy. The latter is particularly germane to the eradication of infectious disease; few physicians would expect to cure pneumococcal pneumonia or pulmonary tuberculosis with an inadequate dose of an antibiotic merely given on only one occasion.

RESTORATION OF DTH IN ACQUIRED CELLULAR IMMUNODEFICIENCY

In this section we do not go into any great clinical detail, but rather indicate the general nature and extent of the undertaking (56). In Table 4 are summarized the results of the restoration of cellular immunity by TF to microbial antigens (PPD, SK-SP) in a variety of diseases associated with deficient cell-mediated immunity. It may be noted that patients with sarcoidosis, lymphomatous disease, leukemia, and all of the other varieties of metastatic carcinoma studied respond to TF with the development of cutaneous DTH responses to microbial antigens possessed by the donor. This was also demonstrable in malnourished children suffering from Kwashiokor or marasmus.

All told, 61 of 68, or 89% of the patients that received various preparations of TF responded with development of cutaneous DTH. The notable exception is Hodgkins disease where none of 42 patients responded to TF compared to 41 of 43 normal controls which did respond.

This type of experience has much to tell us about the origins and reversibility of the anergy encountered in acquired immunodeficiency disease. It is also clear that tumor-bearing patients, even those with extensive metastatic disease, still retain a functioning cell population that is responsive to the restorative properties of TF. How this information may be applied to the specific immunotherapy of neoplastic disease is discussed below.

TF IMMUNOTHERAPY OF INFECTIOUS DISEASES

TF has been shown to confer cell-mediated immunity on, and favorably affect the course of, patients suffering from infections where the microbe is a preferential or obligatory intracellular parasite. Whole viable buffy coat leukocytes or lymphocytes or TF$_D$ have been used in such patients. Most recent studies have employed TF$_D$ for the reasons discussed above.

Table 4 Transfer Factor—Reconstitution of Acquired Cellular Immune Deficiency States

Disease	Author	TF Preparation	Number of Patients	Specific DTH Transferred		Number Reconstituted per Number treated
				Local	Systemic	
Sarcoid	Urbach	WBC	6	6 (+++)	0	11/13
	Lawrence	TF$_D$	7	5 (+++)	2 (+)	
Lymphoma	Muftuoglu	WBC				
Acute leukemia			4		3 (+)	8/10
Chronic leukemia			2		2 (+)	
Lymphosarcoma			4		3 (+)	
Carcinoma	Hattler	Lymphs	18	17 (+++)	0	30/33
	Solowey	TF$_D$	10	10 (+++)	10 (+)	
	Oettgen	TF$_D$	5		3 (++++)	
Kwashiorkor, marasmus	Brown	TF$_{ext}$	12		12	12/12

Total patients reconstituted/total treated = 61/68 or 89%

Hodgkins	Fazio	WBC	7	O	0	
	Good	WBC	13	ND	0	
	Muftuoglu	WBC	22	ND	0	0/42

Total Hodgkins reconstituted/total treated = 0/42 versus 41/43 transfers to normal controls

WBC = buffy coat leukocytes
Lymphs = circulating lymphocytes
TF$_{ext}$ = transfer factor WBC extracts
TF$_D$ = transfer factor dialzsate

Urbach et al, *New England J. Med.* **47**, 794 (1952).
Lawrence and Zweiman, *Trans. Assoc. Am. Phys.* **81**, 240 (1968).
Muftuoglu and Balkuv, *New England J. Med.* **277**, 126 (1967).
Hattler and Amos. *J. Natl. Cancer Inst.* **35**, 927 (1965).
Solowey et al, in *Histocompatibility Testing*, S. Karger, Basel, Switzerland, 1967, p. 75.
Oettgen et al, *J. Clin. Invest.* **50**, 71a (1971).
Brown and Katz, *J. Pediatr.* **70**, 126 (1967).
Fazio and Calciati, *Pan. Minerva Med.* **4**, 164 (1962).
Good et al, *Prog. Allergy* **6**, 187 (1962).

[a] Reprinted with permission from Lawrence, H. S., in *Immunologic Intervention* (J. Uhr and M. Landy, Eds.), Academic Press, New York, 1971.

Viral Infections

Early experience using viable leukocytes as vehicles of TF demonstrated the prompt eradication of disseminated vaccinia in 3 patients treated with leukocytes from vaccinia-positive donors (57–59). There has been no trial of TFᴅ as yet in this viral disease. However, this experience would suggest that TFᴅ would be effective in initiating cell-mediated immunity to the vaccinia virus.

Moulias et al (68) have treated 2 children suffering from measles "giant cell" pneumonia with measles-positive TFᴅ. Both children responded promptly, with marked improvement of their pulmonary lesions and their overall clinical course. This favorable clinical response coincided with conversion of the leukocyte migration test from negative to positive in the presence of measles viral antigen in each child.

Moulias et al (68) have also reported the clinical and immunological responses in 7 children suffering from subacute sclerosing panencephalitis (SSPE) following treatment with measles-positive TFᴅ. Two of the 7 patients experienced improvement in clinical and electroencephalographic parameters, as well as a return of cerebrospinal fluid composition toward normal, following TFᴅ therapy. This was associated with conversion of their leukocyte migration tests from negative to positive with respect to measles viral antigen. Another 3 patients showed conversion of this test, but without clinical improvement of their disease.

Moulias et al (68) have treated a newborn child suffering from congenital herpes with TFᴅ. The herpetic lesions disappeared shortly thereafter. No leukocyte migration tests were performed.

Mycobacterial Infections

The conversion of 11 of 22 patients with lepromatous leprosy to positive lepromin and tuberculin reactivity following administration of TF (69,70) holds promise for successful immunotherapy of this disease. The carefully studied patients of Bullock et al (70) responded equally well to lepromin-positive viable lymphocytes or equal aliquots of TFᴅ, supporting our earlier claim that TFᴅ exhibits potency equivalent to the cells from which it is prepared (26). Although the long-term course of the disease remained unchanged, Bullock's patients exhibited recall flare of DTH reactions in the cutaneous depots of previously tolerated leprabacilli concomitant with the acquisition of lepromin sensitivity and cell-mediated immunity. This inflammatory response could be inhibited by small doses of prednisone. It is very likely that the single dose of TF administered to these patients with defective cell-mediated immunity was insufficient to alter the chronic course of such disseminated disease. The successful eradication of disseminated candidiasis in the patients studied by Schulkind et al (61) and by Pabst and Swanson (62) would suggest that repeated doses of TF are necessary not only to initiate but also to sustain the cell-mediated immunity necessary to place the host in a quantitatively favorable position to eradicate the myriads of microbes that have parasitized his tissues (71,72).

In an analogous disseminated mycobacterial infection, Whitcomb and Rocklin (73) have recently produced a sustained remission in a patient with miliary tuberculosis following therapy with TF from tuberculin-positive donors. Although this patient's tubercle bacillus was sensitive to the antibiotics that were used, her disease failed to respond until TF was given and cell-mediated immunity restored. In this instance, as was the case in the report of successful treatment of candidiasis by TF, the patient received multiple (6) doses of TF over a 3-month period.

Fungal Infections

The use of TF in the treatment of amphotericin-resistant, disseminated mucocutaneous candidiasis has been particularly successful, with restoration of cutaneous DTH to candida in 21 of 25 patients. Clinical improvement or cure was noted in 14 of the 25. Lymphocytes from 12 of the patients treated with transfer factor made MIF in the presence of candida antigen. Lymphocytes from 4 of the patients were made capable of a blastogenic response following therapy (60–67). This dissociation of lymphocyte proliferation and MIF production in patients treated with TF$_D$ could arise either as a consequence of the underlying disease or could be an expression of quantitative factors such as the dose given and the duration of therapy.

Graybill et al (35) have shown that 2 of 3 patients suffering from amphotericin-resistant disseminated coccidiodomycosis of several years' duration have experienced prolonged clinical remissions following several doses of TF$_D$ from coccidiodin-positive donors. The ability to produce MIF was conferred to each of the 3 anergic patients. Skin tests became positive in 2, and blast transformation was induced in only 1. The TF$_D$ used in this study was prepared by the usual method of dialysis of leukocyte extracts (26), or by incubating cells with specific antigen (33,34). This latter procedure yields a monospecific TF, with obvious advantages for immunotherapy.

The results of TF$_D$ therapy in the various categories of infectious disease are summarized in Table 5.

Table 5 TFD Immunotherapy—Infectious Disease [a]

Disease	TF$_D$ Source	Responders	Immune Conversion DTH	MIF	LYMPH	Clinical Improvement	Reference
Viral							
Measles	Rubeola +	2/2		+	0	2/2	Moulias
SSPE	Rubeola +	5/7		+	0	3/7	Moulias
Cong. herpes	Herpes +	1/1				1/1	Moulias
		10/12				8/12	
Mycobacterial							
Leprosy	Lep +	6/9	+		0	6/9 Reversal	Bullock
Tuberculosis	Tub +	1/1	+	+	+	1/1	Whitcomb
Fungal							
Coccidiodomycosis	Cocci +	3/3	+	+	+	2/3	Graybill

	Candidiasis	Candida +			Candida +		Author
		+	1/2			0/2	Rocklin
	+	+	1/1			1/1	Schulkind
	+	+	1/1			1/1	Pabst
	+	+	4/5		+	2/5	Kirkpatrick
	+	+	5/7		+	1/7	Spitler
	+	+	1/1		+	1/1	Vladimarsson
	+	+	5/5		0	5/5	Hitzig
	+		1/1		+	1/1	Griscelli
	+		2/2			2/2	Bläker
			21/25			14/25	
Total			40/49 (80%)			26/50 (50%)	

Bläker et al, *Dtsch. Med. Wschr.* **98**, 415 (1973).
Bullock et al, *New England J. Med.* **287**, 1053 (1972).
Graybill et al, *Cell. Immunol.* **8**, 120 (1973).
Griscelli et al, *Biomedicine* **18**, 120 (1973).
Hitzig et al, *Schw. Med. Wschr.* **102**, 1237 (1972).
Kirkpatrick et al, *Clin. Exp. Immunol.* **6**, 375 (1970).
Kirkpatrick et al, *J. Clin. Invest.* **51**, 2948 (1972).
Moulias et al, *Nouv. Presse Med.* **2**, (20), 1374 (1973).

Pabst and Swanson, *Brit. Med. J.* **2**, 442 (1972).
Rocklin et al, *Cell. Immunol.* 1, 290 (1970)
Schulkind et al, *Cell. Immunol.* **4**, 606 (1972).
Spitler et al, *Clin. Res.* **20**, 519 (1972).
Vladimarsson et al, *Clin. Exp. Immunol.* **11**, 151 (1972).
Whitcomb and Rocklin, *Ann. Int. Med.* **79**, 161 (1973).

[a] Reprinted with permission, Lawrence, H. S., *Harvey Lecture Series 68, 1972–73*, Academic Press, New York, in press.

IMMUNOTHERAPY OF CELLULAR IMMUNODEFICIENCY DISEASE

Wiskott-Aldrich Syndrome

The use of TF therapy in the Wiskott-Aldrich syndrome by Levin et al (74) and Spitler et al (75) has proved to be an exciting advance in the treatment of this disease. The syndrome is characterized by deficient cell-mediated immunity in the face of relatively normal immunoglobulin responses to all antigens tested except polysaccharides. The children suffer repeated respiratory and nasopharyngeal infections, eczematous lesions, splenomegaly, abnormal bleeding due to low platelet levels, and leukopenia. They usually die at an early age either from repeated infection, hemorrhage, or hematologic neoplasia. Seven of 12 patients treated with 1 dose of TF acquired the pattern of DTH reactions concordant with the donor, and their blood lymphocytes produced MIF when cultured with appropriate antigens. Clinical improvement was also noted after TF therapy in 7 of the 12 patients so treated. Six of 10 patients experienced recovery from their infections and regression of splenomegaly, 5 of 11 showed clearing of eczema, and 3 of 10 showed a diminution of their bleeding tendency. The dose of TFᴅ was that obtained from the leukocyte content of 250 cc of blood.

The course of one of these patients is illustrative. His initial response to TFᴅ therapy included DTH reactivity, MIF production, clearing of eczema, regression of splenomegaly, and subsidence of infections. This remission lasted 6 months, and the patient relapsed. Both DTH reactivity and MIF production were lost at that time. A second dose of TFᴅ produced another 6 month remission. Similar patterns of relapse and remission have occurred through a total of 5 doses of TFᴅ (75).

The careful documentation of a relapse-recovery cycle correlating closely with therapy suggests that TFᴅ is indeed causally related to the improvement seen. It is clearly a replacement rather than a curative therapy. The clone of reactive lymphocytes induced by TFᴅ in this T-cell-deficiency state appears to have a limited life span; they appear to be exhausted after a 6-month period. This is in contrast to the situation where TFᴅ is given to normal individuals where induced cutaneous reactivity may remain for longer than 2 years. Fortunately, since TFᴅ is not antigenic in man, it can be given in large doses and on repeated occasions to such patients (15).

Swiss-Type Agammaglobulinemia

Two of 3 patients with this disease have responded to TF$_D$ with conversion of cutaneous reactivity in both, and induction of MIF in one (66). One patient showed clearing of concomitant candidiasis in addition to general clinical improvement (66).

Ataxia-Telangiectasia

Griscelli et al (67) have treated 5 patients suffering from this disease. Four of these patients treated with TF$_D$ developed cutaneous reactivity, and 3 developed blast transforming ability (2 to specific antigen and 1 to phytohemagglutinin). Three of these 5 patients showed clinical improvement.

Combined Immunodeficiency

Four patients with combined immunodeficiency syndromes have been treated with TF$_D$. Two showed clinical improvement and restoration of immunologic reactivity (DTH, MIF, blast transformation). Of 3 patients with a probable Nezelof syndrome, none has responded to TF$_D$ therapy. Neither of 2 patients with a variable hypogammaglobulinemia syndrome has shown clinical improvement following administration of TF$_D$, although both developed DTH and blast transforming ability to antigens to which the TF$_D$ donors were sensitive.

The immunologic conversions and clinical responses of the patients with these various immunodeficiency syndromes are outlined in Table 6. It should be noted that 66% of such patients, formerly anergic, have undergone conversion to DTH reactivity and/or MIF production and-/or blast transformation to corresponding antigens or PHA following TF$_D$ therapy. Clinical improvement was noted in 44% of patients so treated.

Immunotherapy of these congenital deficiency states has enlarged the range of application of transfer factor therapy and helped to elucidate its functions in a manner not possible with either normal subjects (as in our earlier studies) or patients with anergy secondary to an acquired disease process. Thus administration of TF$_D$ to individuals with null reactivity has highlighted the nonspecific contribution of any normal subset of TF's that accompany the *de novo* endowment of a pattern of specific

Table 6[a] TF$_D$ Immunotherapy of Congenital Immunodeficiency Disease[b]

Disease	Responders	Immune Conversion[c] DTH	MIF	Lymph	Clinical Improvement	Reference
Wiskott-Aldrich	7/12	+	+	–	7/12	Levin-Spitler
	4/4	+	ND	+ (1/4)	2/4	Griscelli
	2/2	+	ND	+	0/2	Gotoff[d]
Swiss-type agamma	2/3	+	+	ND	1/3	Hitzig
		+	ND	ND		Pirofsky[d]
		–	ND	ND		Stiehm[d]
Ataxia-telangiectasia	4/5	+	ND	+	3/5	Griscelli
Combined deficiency	1/1	+	–	+	2/4	Montgomery
	1/1	+	+	–		Mogerman
	0/2	–	ND	–		Griscelli
Dysgamma	1/1	+			1/1	Levin
Nezelof	0/3	–	–	–	0/3	Lawlor
Variable hypogamma	2/2	+	ND	+	0/2	Griscelli
Total	24/36 (66%)				16/36 (44%)	

Griscelli et al, *Biomedicine* **18**, 220 (1973).
Hitzig et al, *Schw. Med. Wschr.* **102**, 1237 (1972).
Lawlor et al, *Clin. Res.* **21**, 306 (1973).
Levin et al, *Proc. Natl. Acad. Sci.* **67**, 821 (1970); *J. Clin. Invest.* **50**, 59a (1971).

Mogerman et al, *Clin. Res.* **21**, 310 (1973).
Montgomery et al, *Clin. Res.* **21**, 118 (1973).
Spiter et al, *J. Clin. Invest.* **51**, 3216 (1972).

[a] Reprinted with permission, Lawrence, H. S., *Harvey Lecture Series 68, 1972–73*, Academic Press, New York, in press.
[b] TF$_D$ = Dialyzable TF from normal donors; DTH = delayed skin reactivity; Lymph. = lymphocyte transformation.
[c] Multiple specificities transferred (DTH, MIF, or transformation) were generally concordant with TF donor pattern of cutaneous reactions
[d] Unpublished observations.

DTH and other cell-mediated immune responses *in vivo* and *in vitro*. Where it has been studied carefully, the pattern of antigen-specific cutaneous DTH, MIF production, and lymphocyte transformation expressed by the recipient is usually concordant with that expressed by the donor of TF$_D$. Nevertheless, there also occurs a general elevation and/or *de novo* endowment of cell-mediated immunity "across the board" which includes acquisition of lymphocyte receptor sites for PHA (67), for sheep erythrocytes (98), and for the mixed leukocyte culture (MLC) response to histocompatibility antigens (99). Additionally, following TF$_D$ administration, immunodeficient children acquire the capacity to respond to active sensitization to DNCB *in vivo* (67).

TF AND TUMOR IMMUNOTHERAPY

The application of TF$_D$ as a mode of tumor immunotherapy has as its rational basis the suggestion of Thomas (76), subsequently extended by Burnet (77), that cell-mediated immunity evolved for the purpose of immunologic surveillance and the rejection of mutant neoplastic cells. Our understanding of the plight of the tumor-bearing patient has been extended by the extensive studies of the Hellströms (78) which have documented the presence of cell-mediated immunity to the specific tumor antigens in most human and animal tumor-bearing hosts. Unfortunately, such cell-mediated immunity is negated by "blocking factors" found in the sera of tumor patients. These blocking factors have been shown to coat the target tumor cells, and in addition to coat the host's circulating immune lymphocytes and block their response to tumor-specific transplantation antigens.

As we have indicated previously in Table 4, patients with a wide variety of metastatic neoplastic disease, although themselves anergic, can respond to TF specific for microbial antigens (e.g., PPD, SK-SD) with the acquisition of cutaneous DTH reactions. These findings suggest that should a TF with specificity directed against the patient's tumor antigens be administered, even those anergic patients with metastatic disease might respond immunologically.

As is outlined on Table 7, the potential of TF$_D$ immunotherapy of cancer has just begun to be appreciated. Earlier studies of malignant melanoma are instructive, in that cross-sensitization of patients with each others' tumors followed by cross-transfusion of specifically sensitized lymphocytes produced temporary clinical improvement in some patients (79). More recently, antimelanoma TF prepared from leukocyte extracts of a patient sensitized in this fashion caused a recipient to respond vigor-

Table 7 TFD Immunotherapy of Cancer [a]

Disease	TF$_D$ Source	Responders	Immune Conversion	Clinical Response	Reference
Breast cancer	Pooled "nonspecific"	3/5	+ DTH to PPD, SK-SD	Remission 1/5.	Oettgen
Melanoma	Sens. donor specific WBC-ext.	1/1	N.D.	Reject. metastatic nodules 1/1	Brandes
	Family specific	2/9	+ Lymph. to TSTA	Regress. lesions 2/9	Spitler
	Sens. donor specific	4/10	N.D.	Regress. lesions 4/10	Morse
Sarcoma					
Alveolar	Twin specific	1/1	+ MIF to TSTA	0/1	Neidhardt
Osteogenic	Family specific	1/1	+ RFC	0/1	Levin
Nasopharyngeal arcinoma	Infectious mononucleosis patients	2/2	Fall AB titer to EB-viral AG	Regression 2/2	Goldenberg
Total		14/29 (48%)		10/29 (34%)	

Brandes et al, *Lancet* **1**, 293 (1971).
Goldenberg and Brandes, *Clin. Res.* **20**, 947 (1972).
Levin et al, *Clin. Res.* **20**, 568 (1972).
Oettgen et al, *J. Clin. Invest.* **50**, 71a (1971).

Lo Buglio et al, *Cell. Immunol.* **7**, 159 (1973).
Morse et al, *Clin. Res.* **21**, 71 (1973).
Neidhardt et al, *Clin. Res.* **20**, 748 (1972).
Spitler et al, *J. Clin. Invest.* **51**, 92a (1972).
Spitler et al, *J. Clin. Res.* **21**, 221 (1973).

TF$_D$ = dialyzable TF; DTH = delayed skin test; Lymph. = lymphocyte transformation.
[a] reprinted with permission, Lawrence, H. S., *Harvey Lecture Series 68, 1972–73*, Academic Press, New York, in press.

ously to his tumor and reject the tumor nodules in his skin. Refinements of this approach have led to the use of TFᴅ prepared from lymphocytes of family contacts of melanoma patients who exhibit lymphocyte reactivity to the patient's tumor. TFᴅ from such sources was administered to 4 melanoma patients, with no response in 3 of them. One developed lymphocyte transforming ability when challenged with tumor antigen *in vitro;* this was associated with regression of metastatic skin lesions. He remains free of new lesions for a total of 7 months of continuing therapy (81).

Similar results have been obtained for patients with other tumors. In osteogenic sarcoma (82), a significant increase in rosette-forming cells (RFC) was noted following several injections of TFᴅ. This appeared to correlate with clinical improvement. In alveolar sarcoma (83), TFᴅ therapy conferred on the patient's lymphocytes the ability to produce MIF when exposed to his tumor antigens.

The question of whether a specific TFᴅ directed against host tumor antigens is either necessary or more desirable than nonspecific TF's for effective tumor immunotherapy is unresolved. Our own experience relating to this question involved a trial of immunotherapy of advanced breast cancer using batches of pooled TFᴅ obtained from *healthy* women over 45 years of age (84). Of 5 patients treated with this material 2 to 3 times a week for 9 months, 1 patient sustained tumor regression with a 6-month remission followed by relapse. The choice of donors was based on the assumption that many healthy women over 45 might have met and successfully responded to breast tumor antigens in the course of their own immune surveillance. Thus, specific TFᴅ might have been involved and therefore, the question of specificity is unresolved, since the donors were not screened with the highly sensitive *in vitro* assays for tumor immunity currently available. These were used to screen the prospective TF donors for specific lymphocyte reactivity in the more recent studies outlined above (81–83).

Of great interest are the findings of Goldenberg and Brandes (96) that TFᴅ prepared from healthy young adults who had recovered from infectious mononucleosis, when administered to 2 patients with nasopharyngeal carcinoma, caused regression of the tumor in each. In one patient, regression was associated with lymphocytic infiltration of the tumor, conversion to cutaneous reactivity to PPD, and fall in antibody titers to viral capsid antigen of the Epstein-Barr virus. These results forge another link in the tenuous chain connecting EB virus infections, mononucleosis, and nasopharyngeal carcinoma. The results also raise the possibility that mononucleosis TFᴅ might be of use in the therapy of Burkitts lymphoma.

SPECIFICITY OF TF IN RELATION TO IMMUNOTHERAPY

The notion that a specific TF is required for effective immunotherapy of infectious diseases and tumors has arisen from the large numbers of studies carried out in *normal* individuals. This body of data, secured in many laboratories, and using a variety of preparations of TF (cf. ref. 15), has with few exceptions (12,17,23) repeatedly confirmed the specific effects of TF as well as the need for two stringent requirements for successful transfer to occur: (1) a donor with intense cutaneous DTH to the antigen or antigens under study, and (2) use of an adequate number of leukocytes bearing TF of that specificity.

When either the degree of donor sensitivity is minimal or the dosage of leukocytes is reduced, transfer of cutaneous DTH may fail to occur, even in normal individuals. It should be noted that donor and recipient in all such studies were screened only by skin test procedures. With the advent of more sensitive *in vitro* screening techniques for cell-mediated immunity, it is now possible to detect minimal degrees of sensitivity in both the donor and the recipient of TF which can be present in the face of negative skin tests.

These precise requirements for specificity have been shown also to operate in controlled experimental situations where the *de novo* appearance of a new TF of known specificity has occurred and been detected in the prospective donor deliberately. Two cogent examples of this are afforded by studies of *de novo* sensitization of nonimmune TF donors with neoantigens prepared from ethylene oxide-treated human serum proteins (22) and various individual sets of HL-A antigens in skin allografts (24). In each of these instances, a new TF is raised in the nonimmune host, who, following immunization, acquires the capacity to transfer the specific cutaneous DTH or reject the specific allograft used to sensitize.

This is not to say that nonspecific consequences of the transferred cell-mediated responses (e.g., facilitation of T–B interactions, macrophage activation, etc.) were not engendered in such recipients in addition to the transfer of reactivity to the specific antigens. Indeed, such nonspecific responses very likely do occur in most recipients following the administration of TF$_D$, but have yet to be measured in either normal or diseased recipients of TF. In this regard, the cumulative experience in TF immunotherapy of a variety of congenital immunodeficiency diseases is germane. In most instances in the Wiskott-Aldrich syndrome, for example, the recipient acquires the cutaneous DTH pattern and his lymphocytes acquire the capacity to produce MIF corresponding to the antigens to which the donor expresses cutaneous DTH. In addition, a general state of cell-mediated immunity ensues; PHA responsiveness, RFC formation, MLC responsiveness, DNCB reactivity, and resistance to infections are all restored for about 6 months following 1 dose of TF. It is of interest that specificity of TF is not a requisite for this effect, and any normal individual's subset of specific TF's appears sufficient to initiate and sustain a general state of cell-mediated immunity in these T-cell-deficient patients.

As Bloom (87) has indicated, the whole question of whether a specific TF is obligatory for successful immunotherapy of infectious or neoplastic disease takes on more than theoretical interest in the elucidation of the mechanism by which such a small molecule confers immunologic specificity on recipient lymphocytes. With the increasing success of TF immunotherapy in ameliorating or curing certain infectious diseases and the early suggestions that TF elevates specific tumor immunity in patients with neoplasia, resolution of this issue becomes a very practical matter. It would be, of course, most desirable if one had a "universal" TF effective for all categories of infectious or neoplastic disease—or if a nonimmune donor's TF proved to be as beneficial to the patient as that prepared from a specifically immune donor. For these reasons, a controlled and double-blind protocol has been recently drawn up for testing the effects of lepromin-postive versus lepromin-negative TF on the clinical and immunological responses of leprosy patients by a World Health Organization panel (88).

Thus, TFD conveys both specific and nonspecific immune reactivity. These effects are summarized in Table 8.

MECHANISM OF ACTION OF TF

The precise mechanism of action of TF is still unknown, as is the precise subpopulation of cells acted upon, and the precise biochemical moiety involved in the transaction. Any consideration of mechanism therefore remains operational and descriptive.

With these limitations in mind, it may be stated that TF confers on normal individuals most of the memories of cell-mediated immunity possessed by the donor, and yet only in proportion to the intensity of the donor's remembrance of things past. Fading memories, as evidenced by weak or minimal cutaneous reactivities expressed by the donor, are usually not amenable to transfer. It has been evident for some time that TF causes the normal recipient to respond promptly and for prolonged periods to microbial, fungal, viral, protein neoantigens, and histocompatibility antigens with concordant cell-mediated immune re-

Table 8   Specific Activities and Nonspecific Consequences of TF[a]

Specific Activities	Nonspecific Consequences
1. Cutaneous DTH and CMI	1. General stimulus CMI
2. Homograft rejection	2. Transfer PHA response
3. Lymphocyte transformation	3. Transfer RFC response
4. Mediator production	4. Transfer capacity for DNCB
5. New TF's raised *de novo*	5. Transfer polychemotaxis

Macrophage activation—probable

T B cell facilitation—possible

Are nonspecific consequences of TF sufficient for effective immunotherapy?

or

What additional beneficial increment conferred by TF's specific for related infection or tumor?

[a] Reprinted with permission, Lawrence, H. S., *Harvey Lecture Series 68, 1972–73,* Academic Press, New York, in press.

sponses (5,15). The serial transfer studies described in an earlier section of this chapter exclude passage of a unique immunoglobulin as an explanation of the transfer factor effect and also tend to lessen the possibility that TF is functioning as a "superantigen" or "superimmunogen." Nevertheless, the notion of "superantigen" effect remains the most appealing explanation for most immunologists, because of the immunological specificity of TF observed in normal subjects. This explanation also eliminates the conceptual difficulties involved in understanding how such a small molecule as TF_D can transmit the requisite information and still remain true to the current "central dogma" of the macromolecular world. The truth may be best served by keeping an open mind and not attempting to force interpretation one way or the other. My own feeling is that TF is trying to tell us of a new function of cells that we are not yet fully prepared to understand.

The cumulative data provided by earlier, as well as current *in vivo* and *in vitro* studies, suggest that TF acts operationally as though it either uncovers or causes the *de novo* appearance of specific receptor sites on the recipient's lymphocytes, resulting in the generation of a new clone of antigen-reactive cells, or that it activates a clone of cells already programmed to respond to a given antigen. In addition to antigen-specific receptor sites, recent evidence resulting from TF_D therapy of immunodeficient children suggests that TF_D alters the behavior of lymphocytes by uncovering or causing the appearance of receptor sites with other recognition units. Some of these are considered to be "nonspecific," such as receptor sites that permit interaction with PHA and result in PHA responsiveness (67), and receptor sites that permit interaction with sheep erythrocytes and result in rosette formation (98). Other receptor sites appear that permit interaction with histocompatibility antigens on the lymphocytes of another individual in the mixed leukocyte culture (MLC) response (99). It is of interest that all of these expressions of cell-mediated immunity occurring in the immune TFᴅ donor or in the previously nonimmune recipient of such TFᴅ are thought but not yet proved to be T cell functions.

To summarize, the small molecular weight TFᴅ appears to confer or uncover specific antigen-receptor sites on the recipient's circulating lymphocytes. Upon contact with antigen, these cells proliferate to form new clones with the particular specificities. These cells can produce soluble mediators. Why the clones induced following TF administration are short-lived in patients with T-cell-deficiency diseases such as the Wiskott-Aldrich syndrome, and long-lived in normal individuals is not fully understood. Nevertheless, the initiation of a new population of circulating lymphocytes with appropriate antigen-receptor sites appears to be a fact that is documentable at will. The mystery that remains concerns exactly how this feat is accomplished by TF. Happily, there is no shortage of investigators currently addressing themselves to this challenging problem. Our understanding of the mechanisms involved will be hastened by a precise definition of the biochemical moiety responsible for this activity, and by the perfection of a reproducible *in vitro* assay system. Required also are the discovery and exploitation of experimental animal models.

ANIMAL MODELS FOR STUDIES OF TF

The work on TF in man has stimulated new approaches in two major areas, namely: (1) the search for TF in experimental animals, and (2) the subcellular transfer of immune responses using a variety of RNA preparations both *in vivo* (89) and *in vitro* (90). The latter studies have progressed to the point where they became the topic of an entire symposium (91) and need not be reconsidered here. Suffice it to say that such immunogenic or "informational" RNA preparations differ from TF in size and molecular weight (they are nondialyzable), as well as in their susceptibility to inactivation by pancreatic RNASE. The relationship, if any, of TF to such macromolecules remains to be elucidated.

The search for a transfer factor capable of inducing cutaneous DTH responses in the guinea pig is a related undertaking, and one that has experienced its own share of vicissitudes. These have been summarized and critically reviewed *in extenso* (2), and newer approaches continue to appear (92,93). Nevertheless, there are several recent developments in monkeys and rats that give promise of reviving this whole area of investigation.

Maddison et al (94) have recently shown that monkeys *(Macaca mulatta)* infected with either *Schistosoma mansoni* or a variety of mycobacterial strains develop classical DTH reactions to PPD or to an extract of *S. mansoni* adult worms, respectively, as determined by skin biopsy. They compared dialyzable and nondialyzable TF prepared from blood leukocytes of animals sensitive to mycobacteria and found that TF$_D$ transferred skin reactivity in 1 of 2 animals, while the nondialyzable residue was capable of transfer in 2 of 2 animals. In this group of 4 monkeys, none became sensitive to schistosomal antigens. When TF was prepared from blood leukocytes of animals sensitive to *Schistosoma mansoni,* TF$_D$ transferred schistosomal reactivity to 4 of 4 monkeys, and the nondialyzable residue transferred reactivity to 2 of 2 additional monkeys. In this group of 6 animals, none became sensitive to tuberculin. In 2 monkeys that had become skin-test positive following injection of TF from schistosome-infected donors, this state was associated with *in vitro* reactivity of the recipient's lymphocytes, as evidenced by blast transformation on exposure to schistosomal antigen.

Monkeys that were not artificially infected or sensitized were used to prepare TF$_D$, which transferred tuberculin DTH to 3 of 3 animals. The nondialyzable TF induced transfer in 1 of 2 animals. None of the animals in this group developed DTH to schistosomal antigens.

These investigators also transferred cutaneous tuberculin sensitivity to monkeys using TF$_D$ from tuberculin-positive but schistosomal antigen-negative human donors. The monkey recipients of human TF$_D$ acquired biopsy positive cutaneous sensitivity to PPD but not to schistosomal antigen. Their lymphocytes responded to PPD with transformation and proliferation. These *in vivo* and *in vitro* effects are similar to those obtained in human-to-human transfers.

Similar successful human-to-monkey transfers of cutaneous DTH with TF$_D$ have been achieved by Zanelli, Wu, Adler, Lance, and Medawar (personal communication), and by Kirkpatrick and Gallin (Proc. Nat. Acad. Sci. in press, 1974). Zanelli et al utilized a two-antigen system (PPD and hemocyanin) and found that the transferred reactivity was immunologically specific. In spite of successful transfer of cutaneous reactions, they could not demonstrate *in vitro* thymidine incorporation upon stimulation of the recipient's lymphocytes with specific antigen.

Another animal model for TF studies has been described recently by Liburd et al (95). They transferred immunity against an intracellular protozoan intestinal parasite *(Eimeria neishulzi)* with TF prepared from lymph nodes and spleens of immune rats. The number of oocytes excreted in the stool was used as a measure of immunity. The rats given immune TF 48 hours before primary infection were noted to have a sevenfold reduction of oocyte excretion (ca. 5×10^6) when compared either to untreated controls (ca. 35×10^6) or controls injected with TF prepared from unimmunized donors (ca. 38×10^6). The animals treated with immune TF before the primary challenge were completely immune to a second challenge of the parasite. The rat model, like the monkey model, thus may offer a promising system not only for the study of TF but also for the study of mechanisms of cell-mediated immunity in experimentally induced intracellular infections.

In any event, it begins to appear that transfer of reactivity is possible with TF in animals, and that man is not so unique after all. There is irony in the fact that if TF had been discovered in the guinea pig and brought to its present stage of development, we would just about be ready for exploring its therapeutic possibilities in man. Instead, the reverse has occurred—but then one cannot quarrel with nature.

Some of the new findings in animals are summarized in Table 9.

IN VITRO PROPERTIES OF TF

The chief impediment to the precise biochemical identification of transfer factor and its mechanism of action has been the lack of a reproducible *in vitro* assay (29,39,50). We have recently reported (97) a method by which TFD of proven *in vivo* potency can convert nonimmune lymphocytes to immune responsiveness *in vitro* as reflected by antigen-triggered lymphocyte proliferation. TFD prepared by dialysis against water, as it is usually done for *in vivo* studies, exhibits diminished activity *in vitro* and is frequently toxic against lymphocyte cultures. Thus, for these studies, TF is dialyzed against tissue culture medium. Such media-dialyzed transfer factor (TFDM) causes nonimmune lymphocytes to respond to antigen with an increment of thymidine incorporation which ranges from 2 to 25 times that of such cells cultured with antigen alone. When TFDM alone is added to lymphocyte cultures, no stimulation occurs. This increase of proliferative response following conversion of lymphocytes to immune reactivity by TFDM is generally observed only in the presence of those antigens to which the donor had expressed delayed cutaneous reactivity. It appears to be related in magnitude to the degree of donor

Table 9 New Animal Models for TF$_D$[a]

| | | | | | Immune Responses to TF | | |
Author	Species	TF Source	TF Prep	DTH Skin Conversion	Lymphocyte Transformation	MIF	Other
Madison	Monkey to monkey	Blood WBC	TF$_D$	PPD or schistomal Ag	Pos	ND	—
	Human to monkey	Blood lymphs	TF$_D$	PPD, not schistomal Ag	Pos	ND	—
Liburd	Rat to rat		TF$_D$	ND	ND	—	Resistance to infection + excretion coccidia

[a]For older attempts and recent experience with guinea pig model for TF$_D$ see Bloom and Chase (2) and Burger et al (92,93).

322

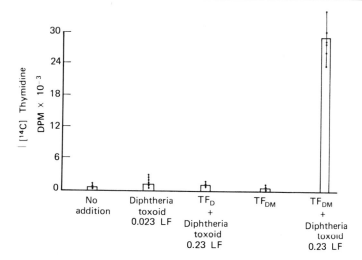

Figure 2.   Transfer factor *in vitro:* TF$_{DM}$, but not TF$_{D}$' is active. Each aliquot of TF was obtained from 6×10^6 lymphocytes from a toxoid-sensitive donor. Recipient lymphocytes were from a toxoid-negative individual. In this and all figures, bars represent means and dots (·) individual replicate points. From M. S. Ascher et al, *Proc. Natl. Acad. Sci.,* in press (1974). Reprinted with permission.

sensitivity. The activity of this preparation of transfer factor is distinguishable from nonspecific adjuvant effects in that TF$_{DM}$ fails to enhance PHA stimulation of lymphocytes, it is active at optimal antigen concentrations, and its effects are not duplicated by endotoxin. This *in vitro* assay holds promise for the elucidation of the molecular identity and mechanism of action of the active moiety in dialyzates containing transfer factor. Examples of the results achieved are shown in Figures 2 and 3.

TF AND IMMUNOLOGIC HOMEOSTASIS

The common targets of TF which appear to unify its diverse functions are foreign histocompatibility antigens. As we have discussed elsewhere (53), foreign histocompatibility antigens are usually thought of as being introduced from without in the form of tissue or organ transplants. Some years ago, in the "self + X" hypothesis, we suggested that subtle alterations of self-histocompatibility antigens could arise following the prolonged intracellular residence of microbes and virions (93). The existence of this type of self + X alteration has been subsequently proved with the discovery of new T antigens or membrane antigens arising in

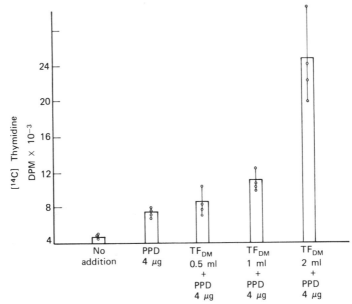

Figure 3.   Dose response of lymphocytes from tuberculin-negative individuals to tuberculin-positive TF DM in the presence of a constant concentration of PPD. One milliliter of TF DM is that obtained from 6×10^6 lymphocytes. From M. S. Ascher et al, *Proc. Natl. Acad. Sci.*, in press (1974). Reprinted with permission.

cells infected with either oncogenic or nononcogenic viruses. Similar alterations of histocompatibility antigens may be the basis for the existence of autoantibodies in patients with lepromatous leprosy, although this remains a speculation at the present time. In any event, in the self + X hypothesis, all DTH responses were virtually identified as allograft responses. In this view, the consequences of such prolonged and amicable intracellular microbial and viral parasitism are regarded as an invitation to autoimmunity (55). Another source of foreign histocompatibility antigens arising from within the host is the neoantigens of embryonal or oncogenic origin detected in the mutant cells that become neoplastic and comprise the tumors of man and animals.

We have discussed in a previous section the evidence demonstrating that an individual can generate a new TF to correspond to each new set of HL-A antigens following his exposure to skin allografts. Similarly, the TF induced by the tubercle bacillus can be involved in the pathogenesis of caseous, cavitary pneumonitis in tuberculosis; in attempting to reject that bacillus, the patient may be misguided into rejecting part of his lung as if it were an allograft, via a self + X mechanism. Thus an affliction that was initiated as an infection could be construed as an autoimmune disease. An even stronger case can be made in lepromatous leprosy with its associated classical autoantibodies such as rheumatoid factor, and antinuclear, Wasserman, and antithyroid antibodies. Happily, both tuberculosis and leprosy have escaped classification as "autoimmune" diseases since the mycobacteria involved are readily visualized, and Koch's postulates have been fulfilled. However, the analogies with the autoimmune state in these diseases provide good evidence for the working of a self + X sequence of alterations.

We would also postulate that those individuals that remain cancer free by virtue of adequate immunologic surveillance mechanisms do so by virtue of a repertoire of specific TF's directed against the various mutant neoplastic cells that have been recognized and rejected in the course of a lifetime.

In view of these considerations, it should come as no surprise that TF therapy has been effective against those microbes or viruses that are preferential or obligatory intracellular parasites that take refuge in cells either by covering themselves with bits and pieces of the host's histocompatibility antigens, or by incorporating themselves into his genome.

Figure 4 presents, in abbreviated and oversimplified form, a concept of the manner in which circulating lymphocytes, which may be T cells,

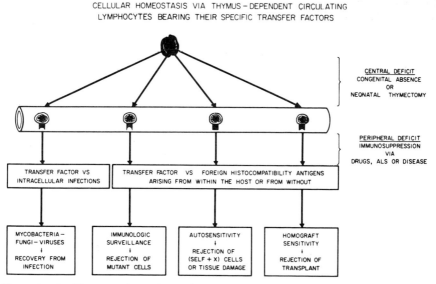

Figure 4. Predilection and specificity of transfer factor for foreign histocompatibility antigens arising from within or without the host. From H. S. Lawrence, *N. Engl. J. Med.* **283,** (1970). Reprinted with permission.

undertake their various homeostatic functions. We propose that it is the specific TF induced in a particular lymphocyte subpopulation that equips such cells to seek out, recognize, and interact with other tissue cells bearing the congruent antigenic configuration. The scope of the immunologic origins and consequences of such interaction, in this view, is represented by the subject matter of this entire volume.

REFERENCES

1. Landsteiner, K. and Chase, M. W., *J. Exp. Med.* **71,** 237 (1940).
2. Bloom, B. R. and Chase, M. W., *Prog. Allergy* **10,** 151 (1967).
3. Lawrence, H. S., *Proc. Soc. Exp. Biol. Med.* **71,** 516 (1949).
4. Lawrence, H. S., *J. Immunol.* **68,** 159 (1952).
5. Lawrence, H. S. in *Cellular and Humoral Aspects of the Hypersensitive States* (H. S. Lawrence, Ed.), Hoeber-Harper, New York, 1959, p. 279.
6. Lawrence, H. S. *Ciba Foundation Symposium on Cellular Aspects of Immunity* (G. E. W. Wolstenholme and M. O'Connor, Eds.), Churchill, London, 1960, p. 243.
7. Lawrence, H. S., in *Mechanisms of Hypersensitivity* (J. H. Shaffer, G. A. LoGrippo, and M. W. Chase, Eds.), Little, Brown, Boston, Massachusetts, 1959, p. 453.
8. Harris, T. N. and Harris, S., *Ann. N. Y. Acad. Sci.* **87,** 156 (1960).
9. Warwick, W. J., Archer, D. K., and Good, R. A., *Ann. N. Y. Acad. Sci.* **99,** 620 (1962).
10. Rapaport, F. T., Dausset, J., Converse, J. M., and Lawrence, H. S., *Transplantation* **3,** 490 (1965).
11. Lawrence, H. S., *J. Clin. Invest.* **33,** 951 (1954).
12. Lawrence, H. S., *J. Clin. Invest.* **34,** 219 (1955).
13. Slavin, R. G. and Garvin, J. E., *Science* **145,** 52 (1964).
14. Hattler, B. G. and Amos, D. B., *J. Natl. Cancer Inst.* **35,** 927 (1965).
15. Lawrence, H. S., *Adv. Immunol.* **11,** 195 (1969).
16. Warwick, W. J., Good, R. A., and Smith, R. T., *J. Lab. Clin. Med.* **56,** 139 (1960).
17. Jensen, K., Patnode, R. A., Townsley, H. C., and Cummings, M. M, *Am. Rev. Resp. Dis.* **85,** 373 (1962).
18. Kirkpatrick, C. H., Wilson, W. E. C., and Talmage, D. W., *J. Exp. Med.* **119,** 727 (1964).
19. Kirkpatrick, C. H., Rich, R. R., and Smith, T. K., *J. Clin. Invest.* **51,** 2948 (1972).
20. Baram, P. and Mosko, M. M., *J. Allergy* **33,** 498 (1962).
21. Brown, R. E. and Katz, M., *J. Pediatr.* **70,** 126 (1967).
22. Maurer, P. H., *J. Exp. Med.* **113,** 1029 (1961).
23. Rapaport, F. T., Lawrence, H. S., Millar, J. W., Pappagianis, D., and Smith, C. E., *J. Immunol.* **358,** 84 (1960).
24. Lawrence, H. S., Rapaport, F. T., Converse, J. M., and Tillett, W. S., *J. Clin. Invest.* **39,** 185 (1960).

25. Lawrence, H. S., Rapaport, F. T., Converse, J. M., and Tillett, W. S., *Ciba Foundation Symposium Transplantation* (G. E. W. Wolstenholme and M. P. Cameron, Eds.), Churchill, London, 1962, p. 271.

26. Lawrence, H. S., Al-Askari, S., David, J. R, Franklin, E. C., and Zweiman, B., *Trans. Assoc. Am. Phys.* **76,** 84 (1963).

27. Baram, P., Yuan, L., and Mosko, M. M., *J. Immunol.* **97,** 407 (1966).

28. Arala-Chaves, M. P., Lebacq, E. G., and Heremans, J. F., *Int. Arch. Allergy Appl. Immunol.* **31,** 353 (1967).

29. Fireman, P., Boesman, M., Haddad, Z. H., and Gitlin, D., *Science* **155,** 337 (1967).

30. Brandriss, M. W., *J. Clin. Invest.* **47,** 2152 (1968).

31. Lawrence, H. S. and Zweiman, B., *Trans. Assoc. Am. Phys.* **81,** 240 (1968).

32. David, J. R. and Lawrence, H. S., unpublished observations.

33. Lawrence, H. S. and Pappenheimer, A. M., Jr., *J. Exp. Med.* **104,** 321 (1956).

34. Lawrence, H. S. and Pappenheimer, A. M., Jr., *J. Clin. Invest.* **36,** 908 (1957).

35. Graybill, J. R., Silva, J., Alford, R. H., and Thor, D. E., *Cell. Immunol.* **8,** 120 (1973).

36. Lawrence, H. S., *Physiol. Rev.* **39,** 811 (1959).

37. Good, R. A., Varco, R. L., Aust, J. B., and Zak, S. J., *Ann. N. Y. Acad. Sci.* **64,** 882 (1957).

38. Martin, C. M., Waite, J. B., and McCullogh, N. B., *J. Clin, Invest.* **36,** 405 (1957).

39. Lawrence, H. S., in *Mediators of Cellular Immunity* (H. S. Lawrence and M. Landy, Eds.), Academic Press, New York, 1969, pp. 145–175.

40. Maini, R. N., Bryceson, A. D., Wolstenholme, R. A., and Dumonde, D. C., *Nature* **222,** 43 (1969).

41. Lawrence, H. S., Introductory remarks, intersociety symposium on *in vitro* correlates of delayed hypersensitivity, *Fed. Proc.* **27,** 3 (1968).

42. Bloom, B. R. and Glade, P. R., Eds., *"In Vitro Methods of Cell-Mediated Immunity,* Academic Press, New York, 1971.

43. McCluskey, R. T., Benacerraf, B., and McCluskey, J. W., *J. Immunol.* **90,** 466 (1963).

44. Marshall, W. H., Valentine, F. T., and Lawrence, H. S., *J. Exp. Med.* **130,** 327 (1969).

45. Valentine, F. T. and Lawrence, H. S., *J. Clin. Invest.* **47,** 98a (1968).

46. Valentine, F. T. and Lawrence, H. S., *Science* **165,** 1014 (1969).

47. Spitler, L. E. and Lawrence, H. S., *J. Immunol.* **103,** 1072 (1969).

48. Lawrence, H. S., in *Proceedings of the Fifth Leukocyte Culture Conference* (J. E. Harris, Ed.), Academic Press, New York, 1970, p. 551.

49. Lawrence, H. S. and Valentine, F. T., *Am. J. Pathol.* **60,** 437 (1970).

50. Lawrence, H. S. and Valentine, F. T., *Ann. N. Y. Acad. Sci.* **169,** 269 (1970).

51. Bloom, B. R., *Adv. Immunol.* **13,** 101 (1971).

52. David, J. R. and David, R., *Prog. Allergy* **16,** 300 (1972).

53. Lawrence, H. S., *New England J. Med.* **283,** 411 (1970).

54. Lawrence, H. S., in *Immunologic Intervention* (J. Uhr and M. Landy, Eds.), Academic Press, New York 1971, p. 20.

55. Lawrence, H. S., *Clin. Immunobiol.* **1,** 47 (1972).

56. Lawrence, H. S., *Clin. Immunobiol.* **2,** (1973).

57. Hathaway, W. E., Githens, J. W., Blackburn, W. R., Fulginiti, V., and Kempe, C. H., *New England J. Med.* **273,** 953 (1965).

58. Kempe, C. H., *Pediatrics* **26,** 176 (1960).

59. O'Connell, C. J., Karzon, D. T., Barron, A. L., Plaut, M. E., and Ali, V. M., *Ann. Int. Med.* **60,** 282 (1964).

60. Rocklin, R. E., Chilgren, R. A., Hong, R., and David, J. R., *Cell. Immunol.* **3,** 606 (1972).

61. Schulkind, M. L., Adler, W. H., Altemeir, W. A., and Ayoub, E. M., *Cell. Immunol.* **3,** 606 (1972).

62. Pabst, H. F. and Swanson, R., *Brit. Med. J.* **2,** 442 (1972).

63. Vladimarsson, H., Wood, C. B. S., Hobbs, J. R., and Holt, P. J. L., *Clin. Exp. Immunol.* **11,** 151 (1972).

64. Kirkpatrick, C. H., Rich, R. R., and Smith, T. K., *J. Clin. Invest.* **51,** 2498 (1972).

65. Spitler, L. E., Levin, A. S., Fudenberg, H. H., Pirofsky, B., Hitzig, W., and Feigin, R., *Clin. Res.* **20,** 519 (1972).

66. Hitzig, W. H., Fontanellaz, H. P., Muneener, U., Paul, S., Spitler, L. E., and Fudenberg, H. H., *Schweitz. Med. Wochenschr.* **102,** 123 (1972).

67. Griscelli, C., Revillard, J. P., Betuel, H., Herzog, C., and Touraine, J. L., *Biomedicine* **18,** 120 (1973).

68. Moulias, R., Goust, J. M., Reinert, P., Fournel, J. J., Deville-Charrole, A., Duong, N., Muller-Berat, C. N., and Berthaux, P., *Nouv. Presse Med.* **2,** 1341 (1973).

69. Paradisi, E. R., De Bonaparte, Y. P., and Morgenfeld, M. C., *New England J. Med.* **280,** 859 (1969).

70. Bullock, W. E., Fields, J. P., and Brandriss, M., *New England J. Med.* **287,** 1053 (1972).

71. Editorial, Transfer factor and leprosy, *New England J. Med.* **278,** 333 (1968).

72. Lawrence, H. S., Editorial *New England J. Med.* **287,** 1092 (1972).

73. Whitcomb, M. E. and Rocklin, R. E., *Ann. Int. Med.* **79,** 161 (1973).

74. Levin, A. S., Spitler, L. E., Stites, D. P., and Fudenberg, H. H., *Proc. Natl. Acad. Sci.* **67,** 821 (1970).

75. Spitler, L. E., Levin, A. S., Stites, D. P., Fudenberg, H. H., Pirofky, B., August, C. S., Steihm, E. R., Hitzig, W. H., and Gatti, R. A., *J. Clin. Invest.* **51,** 3216 (1972).

76. Thomas, L., in *Cellular and Humoral Aspects of the Hypersensitive States* (H. S. Lawrence, Ed.), Hoeber-Harper, New York, 1959, p. 529.

77. Burnett, F. M., *Lancet* **1,** 1171 (1967).

78. Hellström, K. E. and Hellström, I., *Ann. Rev. Microbiol.* **24,** 373 (1970).

79. Nadler, S. H. and Moore, G. E., *Arch. Surg.* **99,** 376 (1969).

80. Brandes, L., Galton, D. A. G., and Wiltshaw, E., *Lancet* **2,** 293 (1971).

81. Spitler, L. E., Levin, A. S., Blois, M. S., Epstein, W., Fudenberg, H. H., Helleström, I., and Hellström, K. E., *J. Clin. Invest.* **51,** 92a (1972).

82. Levin, A. S., Spitler, L. E., Wybran, J., Fundenberg, H. H., Hellström, I., and Hellström, K. E., *Clin. Res.* **20,** 568 (1972).

83. Neidhardt, J., Hilberg, R., Allen, E., Metz, E., Balcerzak, S., and LoBuglio, A., *Clin. Res.* **20,** 748 (1972).

84. Oettgen, H. F., Old, L. J., Farrow, J. H., Valentine, F. T., Lawrence, H. S., and Thomas, L. T., *J. Clin. Invest.* **50,** 71a (1971).

85. Porter, H., *Am. J. Dis. Child.* **90,** 617 (1955).
86. Good, R. A., in *Cellular and Humoral Aspects of the Hypersensitive States* (H. S. Lawrence, Ed.), Hoeber-Harper, New York, 1959, p. 437.
87. Bloom, B. R., Editorial, *New England J. Med.* **288,** 908 (1973).
88. W.H.O. Expert Panel, Immunology of leprosy, *Bull. W.H.O.,* in press (1973).
89. Deckers, P. J. and Pilch. Y. H., *Nature (London)* **231,** 181 (1971).
90. Paque, R. E., Dray, S., Kniskern, P., and Baram, P., *Cell. Immunol.* **6,** 368 (1973).
91. Friedman, H. and Adler, F., et al, RNA in the immune response, *Ann. N. Y. Acad. Sci.,* in press (1973).
92. Burger, D. R. and Jeter, W. S., *Infection and Immunity* **000,** 575 (1972).
93. Burger, D. R., Vetto, R. M., and Malley, A., *Science* **175,** 1473 (1972).
94. Maddison, S. E., Hicklin, M. D., Conway, B. P., and Kazan, I. G., *Science* **178,** 757 (1972).
95. Liburd, E. M., Pabst, H. F., and Armstrong, W. D., *Cell. Immunol.* **5,** 487 (1972).
96. Goldenberg, G. and Brandes, L., *Clin. Res.* **20,** 947 (1972).
97. Ascher, M. S., Schneider, W. J., Valentine, F. T. and Lawrence, H. S., *Fed. Proc.* **32,** 955 abstr. (1973), *Proc. Natl. Acad. Sci.* in press (1974).
98. Wybran, J., Levin, A. S., Spitler, L. E., and Fudenberg, H. H., *New England, J. Med.* **288,** 710 (1973).
99. Ballow, M., Dupont, B., and Good, R. A., *J. Pediatrics* **83,** 772 (1973).

Chapter Twelve

Cell Cooperation in Cell-Mediated Immunity

STANLEY COHEN, PETER A. WARD,
AND PIERLUIGI E. BIGAZZI

Departments of Pathology and Microbiology, State University of New York at Buffalo and the Department of Pathology, University of Connecticut Medical Center, Storrs, Connecticut

As indicated in the preface to this volume, manifestations of cell-mediated immunity are now recognized in a large variety of *in vitro* and *in vivo* biological systems. This was not always the case; for many years, the only system available for exploring cell-mediated immunity was the "tuberculin" reaction, a skin lesion which evolved slowly at the intradermal site of antigen administration in a suitably immunized subject. This "delayed hypersensitivity" reaction, which was shown to be mediated by sensitized cells rather than antibody, was the focus of most of the studies aiming toward the elucidation of the mechanisms involved in this class of immunologic phenomena. The subsequent discovery of a variety of assay systems that represented *in vitro* correlates of delayed hypersensitivity markedly extended the range of possible experimental designs, and directly and indirectly led to much of our understanding in this field.

Some of the work reported here was supported by U.S.P.H.S. Grants AI-09114 and CA-02357.

331

One can approach the subject of cell-mediated immunity in a variety of ways, and indeed this variety is, in part, the theme of this book. However, if we think of cell-mediated immunity as a series of interacting systems, and make, as a slight oversimplification, the starting assumption that it consists of all reactions mediated by T cells, then these interactions can be approached in terms of the ways in which T cells modify the behavior of, and are in turn modified by, the other cells with which they come in contact. In this regard, it is widely assumed that many of the reactions of cell-mediated immunity are dependent on the activity of one or more lymphokines. Interestingly, there has been little evidence that any of the various lymphokines, which are the putative mediators of such T-cell-dependent reactions, are in fact produced by T cells. One study which approached this problem directly involved the macrophage disappearance reaction (MDR). As stated in Chapter 3, this reaction was shown to be mediated by T cells across a cell-impermeable micropore barrier, and by supernatants from antigen-stimulated cultures of such cells (1). Recently, we have reexplored this question with respect to MIF production by guinea pig lymphocytes (2). It was found that when pure soluble protein or hapten-protein antigens were used, MIF production was a property of the sensitized T cells in the suspensions. When PPD was used to stimulate cells from animals immunized with these antigens in complete Freund's adjuvant, the B cells as well as the T cells made MIF. This was thought to be related to the fact that PPD is a B cell mitogen (2,3). In support of this contention was the observation that B cells from unimmunized guinea pigs, but not T cells from those animals, could also be stimulated by PPD to make MIF. Also, endotoxin lipopolysaccharide, another known B cell mitogen (4), could induce B cells from unimmunized animals to make MIF. These results were all confirmed in an *in vivo* system involving the MDR.

The conclusion that emerges from these and other studies in progress, is that activation of lymphocytes for lymphokine production by specific antigen is a property of T cells. However, B cells, as well as T cells, may be so activated by agents that act nonspecifically. These observations may have implications for the general problem of T – B interaction, as is discussed in a subsequent section.

In this chapter, we focus on two main categories: (1) the interactions between T cells and other lymphocytes, and (2) interactions between T cells and other, nonlymphoid inflammatory cells. We discuss in detail a relatively small number of relevant observations bearing on these points, rather than attempt an encyclopedic survey of the available literature. Moreover, we specifically exclude from consideration those interactions that involve effects on cells which are the ultimate targets or victims of T cell attack, as that subject has been definitively explored in Chapter 7.

LYMPHOCYTES

Perhaps the most extensively studied manifestation of cell cooperation involving T cells in the current literature is that relating to their effects on other lymphocytes. The activity which is best defined involves enhancement of B cell function by T cells, the so-called helper effect. In addition, it is known that under appropriate conditions, T cells can inhibit or interfere with B cell function. This is the "suppressor" effect. Finally, there is some evidence that certain T cells can regulate the behavior of other T cells. All these interactions may properly be considered manifestations of cellular immunity in the broad sense because they involve T cells, and as we shall see, they may relate more directly to those reactions which we usually think of as comprising the cell-mediated immune response.

Helper Function

A large body of evidence has accumulated on the cooperation between T and B cells for antibody production. This has been discussed extensively in recent reviews (5–7) and only a relatively brief summary of some of the points relevant to the present discussion is presented here.

Cooperation between T and B cells has been demonstrated in the induction of antibody production to many antigens, such as heterologous erythrocytes (8–11), serum proteins (12,13), and hapten-protein conjugates (14–17). Both cell types can respond to specific antigenic stimulation (18,19), but actual secretion of detectable amounts of antibody appears to be limited to B cells. T cells have therefore been described as "helper" cells.

Even though the mechanism of T–B cell cooperation is not yet well defined, several hypotheses have been advanced to explain it. One possibility is that a signal in the form of genetic information may be transmitted from T to B cells (20). Experiments based on the use of immunoglobulin allotype markers and/or studies of the affinity of antihapten antibodies seem to exclude this hypothesis (21,22).

Another possibility is that antigen is recognized and bound by T cells, and then carried and presented in appropriate concentrations to B cells. This "matrix" or "antigen focusing" theory has been proposed by Mitchison, and postulates a somewhat passive role for the T cell (23). The presentation of antigen may be accomplished by formation of an antigen bridge between T and B cells, possibly endowed with receptors specific for different determinants of the same antigen, or through intermediary cells such as macrophages. This theory can explain many aspects of T and B cell interactions, but it is difficult to imagine appropriate mechanisms for bringing the "correct" T and B cells for a given antigen together *in vivo,* since for any single antigen those cells constitute a minute fraction of the total lymphoid cell mass. Moreover, since the T cell is presumed to play a passive role, it should be possible to substitute for them other cell types coated with antigen, or even antigen-coated inert particles. Experiments using antigen-coated macrophages (24), antigen-coated polyacrylic resin particles (7), and nonreactive T or B lymphocytes artificially coated with antigen (25) have all failed to support this hypothesis, and suggest that T cells interact with B cells not in a passive, but in an active, more complex fashion.

A third possibility, namely that a mediator released from specifically stimulated T cells acts on the antibody-forming B cells, was first suggested by Davies et al (26). A number of soluble factors effective in T–B cell cooperation have been reported. Kennedy et al (27) observed that a supernatant obtained from peritoneal exudate lymphocytes caused B cells to produce antiburro erythrocyte antibodies, upon adoptive transfer to irradiated recipient mice. Parenthetically, it should be noted that this, as well as other lymphocyte-derived soluble factors which have been reported, represent, by definition, lymphokine activities. They have not been defined explicitly in this manner because of a lack of interaction between investigators studying T–B interactions and those studying cell-mediated immunity. Haskill et al (28) found that thymus cells or the heavy fraction of mouse spleen cells separated by density gradient centrifugation could stimulate an *in vitro* antisheep erythrocyte response when added to the light density fraction. This response could take place even when the cells of the different fractions were separated by a dialysis or micropore membrane. Doria et al (29) described a factor released from thymocytes cultured with or without antigen, capable of restoring the immune response to sheep erythrocytes by T-cell-depleted spleen cells. A similar factor was described by Gorczynski et al (30), but that factor was released only when the lymphocytes were incubated with antigen. Rubin and Coons (31) have demonstrated that specifically activated T cells release a nonspecific chemical mediator which triggers B cells that have already bound antigen through interaction with receptors on their surface membranes. This factor, termed "enhancing factor" (EF), was released into the supernatants of cultures of sensitized spleen cells or thymocytes primed with antigen. Once released, it enhanced the immune response to another, unrelated antigen. The activity of this mediator was nondialyzable, and unaffected by mild heat or treatment with DNAse or RNAse. It was, however, inactivated by protease. Feldmann and Basten (32) have reported that carrier-primed T cells, stimulated with a specific hapten-carrier complex, could collaborate with similarly stimulated B cells to produce a response to the hapten, even though the two populations of lymphocytes were physically separated by a cell-impermeable membrane. B cells were unable to respond in this system, if carrier-stimulated T cells were not present. The soluble factor involved selectively enhanced the response of B cells only to specific determinants linked to the specificities recognized by T cells, and is therefore probably distinct from the enhancing factor of Rubin and Coons. It was therefore defined as "antigen-specific factor" (SF). In subsequent investigations (33), evidence was presented that SF might act on B cells indirectly via macrophages. When macrophages were incubated in the bottom compartment of double-chamber cultures (separated by a cell-impermeable membrane) together with specifically activated thymus cells and antigen in the upper compartment, they were then capable of immunizing B cells. Trypsinization studies provided evidence that SF was localized on the surface of the macrophages. A variety of evidence was provided in support of the following model: Activated T cells release monomeric IgM receptors (IgX, or IgT) complexed with antigen. This complex binds to the surface of macrophages, where it forms a lattice of antigenic determinants. This lattice or matrix provides the functional immunogen for B cells of appropriate specificity. This model is attractive, but does not account for recent information on the "allogeneic effect." This is a phenomenon in which specific B cells become activated by antigen in the absence of antigen-specific T cells by virtue of a direct interaction with histoincompatible T cells recognizing surface antigen differences on these B cells (34–37). Soluble factors factors produced by T cells in allogeneic cell mixtures have been reported to act on B cells (38–41). By using cell-free supernatants and the most stringent conditions to demonstrate the absence of T cells, Schimpl and Wecker (42) have shown that a factor is produced by T cells on contact with foreign histocompatibility antigens, capable, if added in sufficient amounts, of replacing T cells in a system requiring T–B interaction for an *in vitro* response to unrelated antigens. This substance was named "T cell replacing factor" (TRF). This factor can stimulate both IgM and IgG responses (42). The evidence obtained by investigations of the allogeneic effect has been interpreted by Feldmann (33) as consistent with the possiblity that activated T cells can produce two distinct factors, both with the effect of enhancing antibody formation. The large molecular weight SF might be a complex of T cell monomeric IgM and antigen, while a smaller "allogeneic factor" (AF), not antigen specific, might be produced as a consequence of stimulation of T cells by histoincompatible cells. The former factor is postulated to act early in the response, initiating antibody production through the intervention of macrophages, and the latter factor is presumed to function later in the response. This hybrid hypothesis, however, is further challenged by recent observations by Katz et al (43). They found good cooperation between T and B lymphocyte populations derived from syngeneic donors, while no "physiologic" T–B cooperation could occur across a major histocompatibility barrier. Feldmann's model would allow for effective cooperation between allogeneic cells. Katz et al (43) have suggested that a site on the B cell membrane, closely related to the histocompatibility specificity, is critically involved in T–B interactions. They postulate an "acceptor" molecule on the B cell surface which represents a binding site either for a T cell factor or the T cell itself. The antigen-activated T cell, in close proximity to the appropriate B cell, either engages in direct contact at the acceptor site and/or releases one or more effector products which bind to that site. These surface phenomena are then followed by the actual triggering of the B cell.

The above-mentioned observations, which represent only a small sampling of the available literature, are difficult to reconcile into a "unified field theory" of the immune response. In exact analogy with the situation for cell-mediated immunity, there is now a multiplicity of soluble effector substances with awesome acronyms, some of which may not be distinct entities. Some broad generalizations do emerge. First, there are mediator substances that act nonspecifically, and others that act specifically. The former are produced as a consequence of activation of specifically sensitized T cells by the specific antigen, but, once formed, can enhance the B cell response to unrelated antigens. The latter, produced also as a consequence of the specific activation of T cells, show specificity for that antigen in the subsequent B cell-enhancing step. This situation is further complicated by the fact that mitogens may activate T cells to produce enhancing factors: in this situation the factors obviously act nonspecifically on the subsequent immune response. The specificity requirements of some of the mediator substances require that at least a portion of their molecular configuration be either antibody-like or represent an antigenic fragment or determinant. This situation is exactly analogous to that involving one of the lymphokines which plays a role in certain reactions of cell-mediated immunity, namely the eosinophil chemotactic factor (ECF) (44,45). The mechanisms involved in ECF generation are discussed in a subsequent section of this chapter. Another requirement, which represents the second generalization, is that at least some of the enhancing factors may be capable of histocompatibility recognition. There is not yet sufficient experimental data to specify precisely the range of mechanisms whereby this could occur.

The various theories described above do not take into account the specific nature of the helper phenomenon. If one invokes a soluble mediator substance in this reaction, then, as stated previously, one is dealing with a lymphokine. It is tempting to speculate that the mechanisms involved in helper function may not be dissimilar to those which are involved in some aspects of cell-mediated immunity. Recent observations which suggest that the same subpopulation of cells may mediate both phenomena (46) are consistent with this notion. Two lymphokines which affect lymphocytes have been described. One is a mitogenic factor, described in Chapter 2. The second is a factor that is chemotactic for lymphocytes (47,48). One way in which such factors could play a role in helper function is developed in the remainder of this section.

In experiments in which the *in vitro* stimulation of DNA synthesis in lymphoid cells from immunized donors by specific antigen was studied, removal of T cells by lysis with an appropriate antiserum largely abolished the capacity of the cell population to manifest this response (49), whereas enrichment of T cells by glass bead column chromatography enhanced the response (50). Thus, this system behaves identically to that involving MIF production insofar as that specific antigen activates T rather than B cells. The situation with respect to nonantigenic activation is quite different. Nonspecific agents may function as B cell mitogens, inducing blast transformation and DNA synthesis. These include not only PPD and endotoxin lipopolysaccharide (2–4) but also agents previously considered to be only T cell mitogens, such as pokeweed mitogen, phytohemagglutinin, and concanavalin A (4). Again, this is analogous to the situation for MIF production.

In vivo, antigen must somehow lead to a wave of proliferative activity in an appropriate subpopulation of the B cell series, in order to account for the observed kinetics of antibody formation in both the primary and secondary response. As noted, specific antigen-induced activation of B cells for proliferation has not been observed *in vitro* in the absence of T cells. Since there is abundant evidence that lymphocytes which play a role in cell-mediated immunity may produce lymphokines with mitogenic activity (see Chapter 2), it is possible that at least some of these agents might act selectively on B cells. In other words, T cells might function *in vivo* in a manner similar to that of endotoxin lipopolysaccharide or PPD *in vitro*. Thus, endotoxin lipopolysaccharide can alter thymic-deficient mice so that they can respond to thymic-dependent antigens (51). Endotoxin can induce an immune response in mice to a hapten coupled to a "nonimmunogenic" carrier (52). Humoral factors produced by thymocytes may potentiate the ability of concanavalin A to activate B cells (53). Activated lymphocyte cultures have a small but definite mitogenic effect on spleen cells from nude mice, which lack T cells (54). Although a lymphokine specifically mitogenic for B cells has not yet been described, such an endogenous mitogen might provide one mechanism by which the helper function of T cells expresses itself. Once B cell activation by such a substance occurs, production of lymphokines by the B cells themselves would provide for further amplification of the immune response. The role of an accessory chemotactic factor in this sequence of events is clear; it would help to accumulate cells in regions where antigen is present and thus promote the various necessary interactions. Investigations in progress in our laboratories are concerned with the existence of such mitogenic and chemotactic factors, and with the possibility that they may be associated with antigenic fragments, in analogy with the situation for eosinophil chemotactic factor.

T Cell–T Cell Interactions

The graft-versus-host reaction (GVH) first described by Simonsen (55) is generally accepted as representing a cell-mediated immune response. The reaction can be elicited by grafting lymphoid cells from an adult animal of parental strain to a neonatal F_1 hybrid recipient. The recipients are subject to a wasting disease. Since splenomegaly is a rather consistent finding in GVH, indices expressing increases in splenic weight have been used to quantitate the reaction. Using this assay, Cantor and Asofsky have shown (56) that appropriate mixtures of lymphoid cells from certain tissues of mice interacted synergistically in the induction of GVH reactions. Studies involving neonatal thymectomy and the use of heterologous antithymocyte serum (57) led to the conclusion that two different subpopulations of cells were involved, and that both were T cells. The T cell present in excess in the thymus and spleen (T1), and which recirculated slowly, if at all, was the precursor of the cell that inflicted immunologic injury. That activity was amplified by a rapidly recirculating T cell (T2) present in excess in the peripheral blood and lymph nodes. These studies were subsequently extended to include a mortality assay system for GVH (58) so as to exclude complications in interpretation of splenomegaly, which is known to be produced, in large part, by immunologically nonspecific proliferation of host cells (59–61).

Suppressive Effects of T Cells on
B Cell Function

In certain circumstances T cells appear to inhibit or suppress rather than enhance B cell activity. Indirect evidence for this comes from a number of studies in which the *in vivo* administration of antilymphocyte serum (ALS) caused enhanced antibody responses to subsequent immunization with antigen (62,63). This is opposite to the usual effect of ALS. There are two possible interpretations which do not require the existence of suppressor T cells. First, it has been suggested (7) that appropriate doses of ALS may exert a stimulatory effect on T cells. Second, it is possible that destruction of large numbers of T cells that do not participate in the specific immune response under study creates a favorable "lebensraum," and possibly gives rise to stimulatory factors released during cell breakdown. These two effects might favorably influence the environment of B cells responding to the test antigen. It may be that in some experimental designs, this effect outweighs the negative effect produced by what is probably a partial loss of the appropriate T cells directly involved in the response.

More direct evidence in favor of true suppressor T cell function came from studies of Baker et al (64), who showed that passively transferred lymphocytes could suppress an antitype III pneumococcal polysaccharide response. Similarly, Armstrong et al (65) have found that addition of thymic lymphocytes to thymic-deprived mice depressed the antibody responses of such mice to a "thymus-independent" antigen.

Recently, Rich and Pierce (66) have identified a subpopulation of T cells which, upon activation by concanavalin A, suppresses the development of plaque-forming cell responses in mouse spleen cell cultures. It could not be determined whether the suppressor cells formed a subpopulation distinct from that containing "helper" cells. Although many of these and other experiments (67–69) have been interpreted as being consistent with the release of an inhibitory lymphokine-like substance by certain T cells, no direct evidence on this point is presently available.

It seems reasonable to conclude that in both suppressive and enhancing T–B interactions, and possibly in T–T interactions as well, lymphocyte-derived mediator substances play an important role. This role may represent the unrecognized framework upon which most of the early associations and relationships between delayed hypersentitivity and antibody formation were based (reviewed in ref. 70). It would be interesting to review those studies in the light of our modern concepts of cell-mediated immunity.

MACROPHAGES

To a large extent, studies of the classic delayed hypersensitivity reaction in the skin of suitably sensitized subjects, and many of the *in vitro* correlates of this reaction, respresent studies of lymphocyte-macrophage interactions. These subjects have been covered in detail in Chapters 1 and 2. Similarly, in studies that have been designed to explore the *in vivo* activity of lymphokines, the macrophage or its circulating precursor, the monocyte, plays an important role. This is perhaps best illustrated in the MDR (see Chapter 3) in which the interaction between sensitized T cell and specific antigen leads to a reduction in the macrophage content of a nonspecifically induced inflammatory infiltrate in the peritoneal cavity. In Chapter 8, the role of the macrophage in cell-mediated immunity to certain infectious agents is discussed at length. Many of the other chapters of this volume are concerned with subjects that involve, at least in part, lymphocyte-macrophage interactions. In this section, we therefore focus specifically on the process of activation of macrophages by lymphocytes or lymphocyte products, with apologies for some unavoidable repetition.

Mooney and Waksman (71) and Nathan et al (72) have studied various changes in macrophages produced by lymphocyte culture supernatants. These investigations can be summarized by stating that enhancing effects were noted on the following functions of macrophages: surface spreading, amoeboid motility, phagocytosis, glucose oxidation, and protein synthesis. In general, these effects fall into two categories, stimulation of metabolism and alteration of surface properties. Dvorak et al (73) have noted that macrophages whose migration from capillary tubes is inhibited by sensitized lymphocytes and specific antigen lose the layer of cell coat material normally adherent to the outer leaflet of the trilaminar unit membrane. Macrophages in such cultures aggregate to form clumps, and this phenomenon may be related to the surface alterations observed. These results prompted Hammond and Dvorak (74) to study the incorporation of glucosamine by guinea pig exudate macrophages, since that amino sugar is known to be a precursor of the macromolecular polysaccharides found at the cell periphery. They observed that incorporation of glucosamine into macromolecular material was a general property of guinea pig macrophages, but was increased up to 17-fold in the presence of specific antigen and sensitized lymphocytes.

These various studies suggest that activated lymphocytes, either directly, or more likely through the elaboration of effector lymphokines, induce profound alteration of macrophage membranes. In theory, such alterations should be detectable by virtue of secondary changes in the biophysical properties of such membranes. Indeed, Caspary (75) found that the interaction of antigen with sensitized lymphocytes resulted in the elaboration of a protein substance capable of reducing the electrophoretic mobility of peritoneal macrophages. On the basis of indirect evidence, Caspary suggested the possibility, but could not prove, that this substance was related to MIF.

On the basis of this information, we postulated that lymphocyte-induced macrophage membrane changes should be measurable in terms of alterations in the interfacial tension of those membranes. This property, which is often referred to as "surface tension," is influenced by the chemical composition of the membrane, the molecular configuration of its constituents, and the nature and extent of any coating layers about it. It has no direct relationship to surface charge. The studies to explore this point were performed using the contact-angle technique, which is illustrated schematically in Figure 1. In brief, this method involves the

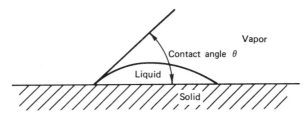

Figure 1. Diagrammatic sketch illustrating the contact angle between a liquid droplet and a solid surface. In the experiments described in the text, the solid surface consists of a macrophage monolayer.

measurement of the angle a drop of saline placed on a cell monolayer makes with that monolayer. In most cases, a liquid placed on a solid surface remains there as a drop having a definite angle of contact between the liquid and solid phases. This angle can be altered by changing the composition of a surface, a hydrophobic surface causing a higher angle than a hydrophilic one. We measured the contact angle made between 10 μl sessile drops of phosphate-buffered saline and macrophage cell monolayers. These angles, which remain stable for approximately 12 seconds after application of the drop, are determined by use of a telescope with cross-hairs attached to a goniometer (76). Typically, alveolar and peritoneal macrophages have similar contact angles under these conditions. The incubation of macrophages of either source with supernatant fluids from cultures of sensitized lymphocytes incubated with specific antigen for as little as 1 hour at 37°C results in a significant reduction of that contact angle (77). This effect reflects a reduction in the interfacial energy of the cell surface. It is carrier specific, and is not due to antibody or antigen in the cell culture fluids. The responsible lymphokine appears concomitantly with MIF activity, but seems to be distinct from it. It is of interest that we could demonstrate enhanced phagocytosis in association with the lowered macrophage surface tension produced by the activated supernatants, since it has been suggested in studies of other systems (76) that these properties are causally related.

Much of the early work on the effects of lymphokines on macrophages has been related to the factors influencing the migration and distribution of these cells. However, as we have seen in this section, many investigators are now addressing themselves to the broader question of how lymphocytes and lymphocyte products alter macrophages, and how these alterations affect macrophage function.

EOSINOPHILS

Eosinophils are conspicuous components of inflammatory infiltrates at sites of various kinds of immunologic reactions. They are found in the nasopharynx and bronchi of patients with allergic conditions such as hay fever or asthma, and in the intestinal tract as a consequence of parasitic infestations. In experimental situations, they are present in peritoneal exudates following multiple injections of foreign protein (78), in lymph nodes draining sites of antigen administration (78–80), in skin following injection of antigen-antibody complexes into normal animals (81), and in skin of delayed hypersensitive animals following multiple injections of antigen at the same site (82). In addition, eosinophils may be found in certain autoimmune lesions which involve cell-mediated immune responses, such as experimental autoimmune thyroiditis (83). All these observations show a relationship between the eosinophil and the immune system, and the last two findings cited suggest that this relationship, in part, involves cell-mediated immunologic reactions. Further support for this association comes from the work of Basten et al (84,85) who showed that the ability of rats to respond to parasitic infestation with peripheral eosinophilia was dependent on the presence of recirculating lymphocytes. They found also that this ability could be transferred adoptively by intact lymphoid cells in diffusion chambers, suggesting the role of a diffusible material.

The various experimental findings described above led us to the suspicion that a lymphokine with chemotactic activity for eosinophils exists. Preliminary studies of MIF-rich supernatant fluids from antigen-stimulated lymphocyte cultures failed to detect such a factor. We soon discovered (44,45), however, that these supernatants contained an inactive precursor substance (ECFp) which could be activated by reaction with preformed immune complexes *in vitro* to generate a potent eosinophil chemotactic factor (ECF). Although complement is not involved in this reaction, there is a requirement for Y2, but not Y1 antibody in the complex. This factor appears to be biologically unique, since previously described chemotactic factors for the various inflammatory cell types require for their generation either immune complexes or lymphokine-like substances released into lymphocyte culture, but not both. Moreover, in the case of ECF, the interaction between the substance elaborated by the lymphocytes and the immune complexes appears to be specific in that the immune complexes must contain the same antigen as that used to activate the lymphocyte cultures. In addition, this interaction shows an apparent species specificity; if supernatant fluids are obtained from cultures of guinea pig lymphocytes, then immune complexes containing guinea pig antibody are effective in generating eosinophil chemotactic activity, but complexes containing rabbit antibody are not.

There are two possible explanations for the apparent immunologic specificity of ECF activation. First, it is possible that ECFp is antibody-like, and recognizes a joint antigenic determinant composed of part of the original antigen and the adjacent portion of the antibody molecule in the immune complex. If this possibility is correct, it also provides an explanation of the species specificity observed. If ECFp can recognize a determinant that is part immunoglobulin, then it must have obtained this ability during the course of immunization of the animals from which the ECFp-producing lymphocytes were taken. Since this involved active immunization of guinea pigs, the only such antibody available for recognition was guinea pig antibody. Another explanation for the species specificity may be found in the subclass restriction to Y2 which was referred to above. This immunoglobulin restriction may hint at a requirement for a specific kind of antibody needed, which is simply not present in the rabbit preparations that have been studied. In this latter view, ECFp shows specious species specificity.

Fluids containing ECFp activity are heat stable, and the substances responsible for activity sediment in the ultracentrifuge in a biphasic manner, with peaks near BSA and IGG markers. Sephadex G-100 gel filtration identifies, in addition to a peak near the BSA marker, a smaller one near the cytochrome marker. These correspond to the locations of MIF activity. ECFp and MIF activity are not separable when these fractions are each subjected to a second separation procedure, agarose block electrophoresis. The physicochemical characterization of ECFp shows that if ECFp is antibody-like, it cannot be conventional antibody.

The second interpretation of the data is that ECFp is antigen-like rather than antibody-like, i.e.., that it contains an antigenic fragment. If so, it could combine with the immune complex during the activation step by simple coprecipitation.

One way in which an attempt has been made to distinguish between these two possibilities is by the use of immunoadsorption techniques (45). Sepharose was conjugated to either antigen or antibody, and columns prepared. Passage of supernatant fluids from lymphocyte cultures stimulated with bovine gamma globulin (BGG) through a BGG-conjugated column did not result in loss of ECFp activity, whereas ECFp was entirely adsorbed to columns conjugated with anti-BGG antibody. No loss of MIF activity occurred under these conditions, demonstrating that these activities are distinct, even though they were not separable by physicochemical techniques.

It is of interest that the antibody-conjugated column, while capable of removing ECFp, cannot activate it to ECF. This is analogous to the inability of antibody alone to activate ECFp and suggests that changes in the configuration of antibody within an immune complex are important to this conversion process. This has obvious parallels to the situation for activation of complement by immune complexes, although as stated above, complement is not involved in the generation of ECF.

Although the antibody-conjugated column can remove ECFp from supernatant fluids passed through it, it is not capable of absorbing preformed ECF. These observations, and a variety of other experimental findings (45), have led to the model for activation which is shown in Figure 2. In this model, ECFp combines with a free antibody site in the immune complex by virtue of its own "piece" of antigen. As a consequence of this interaction, a modified, active, antigen-free substance (ECF) is then released. It should be noted that the antigen component of ECFp must be quite small, as this substance behaves physicochemically in a manner similar to MIF's which have been shown to lack antigen by immunoadsorption studies (86).

Although most of the studies of ECF have depended on *in vitro* assays based on the Boyden double-chamber system, ECF was demonstrated to be biologically effective *in vivo* by simply injecting it into guinea pig skin (44). At this site, ECF produces an inflammatory infiltrate in which the predominant cell type is the eosinophil. Clinically, eosinophilia is seen in two situations: It may be present in association with allergic states that are clearly related to immediate hypersensitivity such as asthma and nasal allergies. Also, eosinophilia may be present in autoimmune diseases which appear to have a component of cell-mediated immunity, for example, some of the so-called collagen diseases. It is very likely

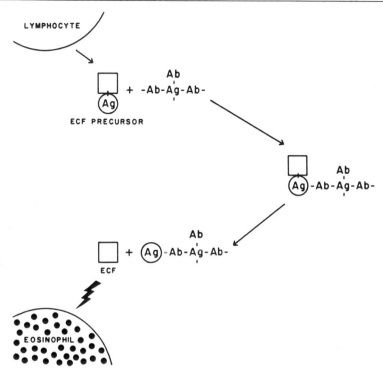

Figure 2.   Diagrammatic representation of the proposed interaction between ECFp and immune complexes to generate ECF activity. From ref. 45.

that factors for eosinophils dependent only on antibody, such as those described by Kay (87,88), play an important role in immediate hypersensitivity reactions, whereas ECF is involved in cell-mediated reactions. Experiments involving experimental autoimmune thyroiditis have provided indirect support for this latter mechanism (83). Guinea pigs immunized with thyroid extract in complete Freund's adjuvant develop thyroid lesions, consisting, for the most part, of mononuclear cell infiltrates. The nature of the inflammatory infiltrate in this disease suggests that cell-mediated immune responses play a major role in its pathogenesis, and indeed, a variety of experimental observations support this contention (89,90). Under the experimental conditions chosen in the experiments described here, small amounts of circulating antithyroid antibodies were present in many, but not all of the experimental animals. When examined by appropriate histologic techniques, eosinophils were found only in the thyroids of those animals with both thyroid lesions and circulating antibody. When present, they were located in close proximity to small blood vessels, and in large numbers in the fibrofatty tissue surrounding the gland. Only rarely were they seen in the lymphoid infiltrates themselves. The injection of immune sera from these animals did not lead to the appearance of eosinophils in the thyroids of normal guinea pigs, but increased the incidence of eosinophil infiltration in the glands of animals with minimal thyroid mononuclear infiltrates and no detectable circulating antibody of their own. The requirement for both mononuclear infiltration and circulating antibody, and the distribution of eosinophils in what appeared to be interface regions between sites of access of antibody formed systemically and sites where lymphokine production could occur locally, suggested that ECF might be involved in the mechanism of eosinophil accumulation in this model of thyroiditis (83). Further work is necessary to confirm this possibility, as well as to study the mechanisms whereby ECF exerts its effects on eosinophils both *in vitro* and *in vivo*.

BASOPHILS

Basophils may be found in a variety of lymphocyte-mediated delayed hypersensitivity reactions in animals and man (91). As is the case for eosinophils, basophils are not well visualized by ordinary histologic methods. Their detection in tissue requires procedures of fixation and processing which are modifications of those used for electron microscopy.

Basophils were first noted by Dvorak and his associates (92) in skin reactions induced in guinea pigs with "Jones-Mote" hypersensitivity, a form of cell-mediated immunity that is seen following immunization with antigen in incomplete Freund's adjuvant. These skin reactions can only be elicited in the first few weeks following such sensitization, and tend to be erythematous rather than indurated. In the past, they have been considered to represent a mild form of the typical delayed, or "tuberculin-type" skin reaction. When these reactions were studied in appropriately prepared histologic sections, approximately one-third of the infiltrating cells were found to be mature basophils (92,93).

These reactions have properties similar to those of classic delayed hypersensitivity. They may be transferred passively with sensitized lymphoid cells, but not with immune serum, and they are inhibitable with antilymphocyte serum (92,94). Induction of this form of immunologic reactivity is associated with hyperplasia of the thymus-dependent paracortical zones of draining lymph nodes (95).

Immunization of guinea pigs with protein antigens as immune complexes formed in antibody excess also leads to a state of delayed reactivity in which basophils comprise a considerable percentage of the infiltrating inflammatory cells (94). In contrast, the typical, intense delayed reactions that follow immunization with antigen in complete Freund's adjuvant contain only small numbers of basophils. Interestingly, even in this situation, if skin tests are performed early after immunization, then basophils may be found in abundance (94). Basophils can also be observed in delayed reactions in human subjects, when the skin window technique is employed (96). Thus, it seems likely that basophils may be found in all delayed hypersensitivity reactions, and that their numbers may be a function of the nature of the immunization procedure, the time following immunization, the intensity of the reaction, and a host of other nonspecific factors. Indeed, in many of the published studies on this subject, one is struck by the inverse relationship between the intensity of mononuclear cell infiltration and the number of basophils present. It is tempting to speculate that, in addition to the basophil chemotactic factors that are described below, certain populations of lymphocytes may produce inhibitory factors which suppress basophil infiltration. This possibility has not yet been experimentally explored.

It has been discovered that basophil infiltration is a prominent feature of other manifestations of cell-mediated immunity in addition to the various kinds of skin reactions described above. These include skin allograft and tumor rejection, viral immunity, and contact allergy in man. Dvorak demonstrated the presence of basophils in guinea pig allografts in place 6 days or longer, but not in autografts (97). Similar observations were made in a system involving inoculation of syngeneic tumor (98). Guinea pigs immunized with ascites variants of hepatomas develop specific resistance to tumor growth, associated with delayed-type skin reactions to subsequent injections of those tumors. The local skin reactions show substantial infiltration with basophils, and associations have been reported between basophils and dying tumor cells. Lymphocytes, macrophages, and neutrophils infiltrated sites of tumor injection in unsensitized animals, but basophils were infrequent.

Another situation in which basophils are present in immunologically induced inflammatory infiltrates is the response to vaccinia infection. Adult guinea pigs infected with an intradermal inoculum of vaccinia virus develop a long-lasting state of hypersensitivity associated with blast transformation in the draining lymphoid tissue, and characterized by delayed-type skin reactions rich in basophils. These reactions are erythematous and nonindurated. If the animals are sensitized with the same dose of virus in complete Freund's adjuvant, the reactions are more intense, indurated, and contain much fewer basophils (99).

Like the situation for eosinophils, a variety of chemotactic agents for basophils exist. These include 2 complement-derived agents, plasma kallikrein, diffusates from lung fragments challenged with pollen antigen, and supernatants from cultures of sensitized lymphocytes challenged with specific antigen *in vitro* (100). The latter, by definition, represent lymphokine activity. These studies were based on *in vitro* assay systems using human peripheral blood basophils from 2 patients with chronic myelogenous leukemia. A recent report has described a lymphokine chemotactic for basophils obtained from the peripheral blood of normal human subjects (101). It is not stated in these reports whether the donor lymphocytes were obtained from animals immunized in complete or incomplete Freund's adjuvant. The basophil chemotactic factor in supernatants of lymphocyte cultures, unlike the case for the eosinophil chemotactic factor, does not require activation by immune complexes. It has not yet been further characterized.

A final word is in order concerning the mast cell. The morphology, granule content, and immunologic properties of mast cells closely resemble those of basophils (102). There is a well-known inverse relationship between basophil and mast cell frequency in various species. Mast cell hyperplasia is associated with lymphocytic infiltration in chronic inflammation, parasitic infestation, and neoplasia in many species (102). These facts suggest, as has been pointed out by the Dvoraks (98), that basophils and mast cells are complementary cells with similar functions. It is a well-known observation that mast cells may be seen in lymph nodes obtained from human biopsy material, and we have noted that this relationship is more likely when the hyperplasia involves thymus-dependent rather than thymus-independent areas of the gland (unpublished observations). Similarly, mast cells have been shown to proliferate in rat lymph nodes following antigenic stimulation (103). It is quite possible that lymphocytes exert a regulatory role over mast cells by virtue of the production of one or more lymphokines with specific affinity for those cells.

NEUTROPHILS

In all delayed hypersensitivity reactions, neutrophils are present to some extent, and are generally found in moderate numbers (104). In severe lesions with necrosis, intense neutrophil infiltration may be seen. In the mouse, the delayed cutaneous response to the intradermal injection of antigen is characterized by an infiltrate that is predominantly neutrophilic (105–107) and for this reason, the question of whether it is possible to produce delayed hypersensitivity skin reactions in that animal remains controversial (105–111). It is possible to elicit a macrophage disappearance reaction (MDR) in the mouse, and in unpublished observations we have noted that species of mice that are good responders in this regard develop erythematous, nonindurated delayed-onset skin reactions upon intradermal challenge with antigen. These reactions contain mainly neutrophils, but substantial numbers of mononuclear cells are present as well. There is no evidence of vasculitis, gross hemorrhage, or microscopic extravasation of erythrocytes, suggesting that these lesions are not due to Arthus reactions. Thus, our preliminary results suggest that although the histologic appearance of delayed skin reactions in the mouse differs from that of the guinea pig, such reactions can be readily induced if appropriate strains are used.

Ward et al (112) have described a lymphokine that is chemotactic for neutrophils. This factor was separable from both MIF and a factor chemotactic for monocytes by polyacrilamide gel electrophoresis. It was considerably less potent than the monocyte chemotactic factor in the Boyden double-chamber assay, in spite of the fact that this system is more favorable to neutrophils than monocytes, since the former cells migrate through micropore filters more readily. Both neutrophil and monocyte chemotactic factors were obtained from antigen-stimulated guinea pig lymphocyte cultures. In the light of the difference in the inflammatory response in delayed skin lesions of the guinea pig and mouse, it would be of interest to study lymphokines obtained from cultures of mouse lymphocytes. One would predict that in this situation, neutrophil chemotactic activity might be higher than that observed for monocytes.

These observations all suggest that the neutrophil, like the other inflammatory cells discussed above, accumulates at sites of cell-mediated reactions in response to specific lymphocyte signals, as well as in response to the factors that are liberated at sites of tissue injury in general.

THE CLOTTING SYSTEM

A variety of studies have suggested an association between the coagulation system and certain aspects of cell-mediated immunity. Wood and Bick (113) observed the suppression by heparin of the ocular reaction to tuberculin in sensitized rabbits. Subsequently, Nelson and North (114,115) described the partial inhibition of the tuberculin reaction in guinea pigs. This experiment was suggested by the observation by Nelson that heparin could inhibit the MDR. Cohen et al (116) confirmed those studies, and extended the observations to contact reactions induced by a skin-sensitizing chemical. These lesions represented pure manifestations of delayed hypersensitivity without an Arthus component. Both heparin and coumadin, agents which act at different steps in the clotting sequence, were shown to be effective in suppressing these reactions. The ability of animals treated with anticoagulants to serve as cell donors in transfer of delayed hypersensitivity to normal recipients, and also their ability to produce antibody in response to antigenic challenge, were shown to be unaffected. This indicated that the anticoagulants were not interfering with the process of sensitization, but rather were acting at some critical step in the formation of the inflammatory infiltrate. It was also shown that the action of anticoagulants was short-lived, with subsequent full recovery of reactivity, and that the suppressive effect could not be ascribed to anticomplementary properties of the compounds used, or to nonspecific physicochemical factors relating to their charge and configuration. These latter points are of importance, since a recently described pharmacologic inhibitor of delayed hypersensitivity reactions, fumaropimaric acid, has both anticoagulant and anticomplementary activity (117), although it is unrelated chemically to either heparin or coumadin.

These initial observations were difficult to interpret, since the clotting mechanism had not been implicated in delayed hypersensitivity reactions, and the histologic features of the reactions do not include intravascular clotting or thrombosis. A clue to the understanding of the anticoagulant effect came from observations by Dvorak and Mihm (118), who discovered the accumulation of substantial amounts of a fibrin-like material in the dermis in lesions of allergic contact dermatitis in man, in the course of an investigation into the role of basophils in that response. The presence of such material had not been previously reported, and its detection seemed related to the specific techniques of fixation and tissue processing used by those investigators. This observation prompted a series of experiments by Colvin et al (119) utilizing immunofluorescence techniques. Using appropriate fluorescein-conjugated antisera, they were able to demonstrate fibrin deposition in both allergic contact dermatitis and classic delayed hypersensitivity skin reactions in man. This material was found mainly in the intervascular portions of the reticular dermis, with sparing of vessels and their associated cuffs of mononuclear cells. It was found in vessel walls in only 2 of 94 biopsies studied. With only one exception, deposition of immunoglobulins and complement was not observed. This pattern is quite distinct from that observed in antibody-mediated lesions in animals or man.

The pathogenesis and significance of fibrin deposition in delayed reactions are not clear. The bulk of the evidence, as stated, is that the coagulation system is involved in the second, nonspecific step of the reaction, which involves the development of a nonspecific inflammatory infiltrate in response to the first step of specific interaction between antigen and sensitized lymphocyte. This sequence of events is associated with changes in vascular permeability which may favor the accumulation of circulating fibrinogen. Polymerization of extravascular fibrinogen could be triggered by dermal elements such as collagen, or by a product of the sensitized lymphocytes. This latter possibility is most intriguing, but as yet, no lymphokine with such properties has been described.

One of the anticoagulants described above, heparin, has been shown to affect other systems involving cell-mediated immunity. Thus, both the induction and the expression of experimental allergic encephalomyelitis have been inhibited by heparin given either during the latent period after immunization or just before the onset of disease (120). Heparin may also have *in vitro* activity as well. Currie (121) observed a significant depression in the percentage of blast cells observed in stained smears of mixed human peripheral blood lymphocytes after 3 days of culture by as little as 0.1 units/ml heparin. Taylor and Culling (122) reported that heparin partially inhibited the cell-mediated killing of allogeneic fibroblasts by immunized lymphoid cells. Martz and Benacerraf (123) have demonstrated that heparin retarded the cell-mediated lysis of mouse ascitic tumor cells or normal spleen cells by effector spleen cells from alloimmunized mice. The retardation was reversible by removal of the heparin. Heparin reduced the rate of cell lysis without preventing the eventual complete destruction of the target cell population. In distinction to the results of Currie, these investigators found that heparin did not inhibit incorporation of tritiated thymidine in mixed lymphocyte cultures, and thus was not nonspecifically toxic for lymphocytes in their test system. In contrast to the results obtained in studies of delayed skin reactions, where nonanticoagulant sulfated polymers are without suppressive effect, such polyanions could affect the rate of cell lysis *in vitro* in a manner comparable to that of heparin (123).

These various studies all implicate clotting factors in at least some of the effector stages in cell-mediated reactions. As stated above, there is no direct information relating to a specific role of the lymphocyte in triggering the coagulation system. However, sensitized lymphocytes have been implicated in reactions involving interactions with platelets. Barbaro and Zvaiffler (124) demonstrated that a well-washed mixture of platelets and leukocytes from rabbits immunized with dinitrophenylated bovine serum albumin in complete Freund's adjuvant released histamine on the addition of specific antigen. This mode of allergic histamine release differed from those described previously in that it did not require added antibody and plasma factors. Further studies by Schoenbechler and Barbaro (125) demonstrated that the reaction could not be ascribed to the presence of adsorbed homocytotropic antibody. In addition, by using various leukocyte fractions, they showed that the cell responsible for triggering the platelet for histamine release was the lymphocyte. Other workers have challenged this latter conclusion. Henson (126) considered that the lymphocyte was the cell that induced platelet histamine release, but then concluded that the monocyte was responsible (127). Siraganian and Osler (128,129) present data which implicate the basophil. In the light of our previous discussion, it is entirely possible that the lymphocyte-platelet interaction might be mediated, in part, indirectly with lymphocyte-monocyte or lymphocyte-basophil interactions resulting in secondary platelet effects. In any case, there is direct morphologic evidence for reactions involving only lymphocytes and platelets. Aikawa et al (130) studied suspensions of platelets and sensitized leukocytes. In control suspensions not activated by antigen, no physical interactions were observed. In combinations of platelets of sensitized leukocytes activated with antigen, changes in physical and morphologic relationships were identified by electron microscopy. Many aggregates of platelets surrounded small lymphocytes and occasional monocytes. Many of the platelets were irregular in shape, with pseudopods extending toward the lymphocytes. Often, the pseudopods were in close contact with lymphocytes, and their tips were inserted into the cytoplasm of these cells, forming an anastomosis. The platelets appeared to be vacuolated, and some had lost granular inclusions. Although these results are suggestive, a definitive link between cell-mediated immunity and platelet function awaits the use of purified (T cell) subpopulations of lymphocytes.

The diverse experimental findings summarized in this section all point to multiple interrelationships between the coagulation system and the cellular immune system. As can be seen, however, a great deal of further work is necessary to pinpoint the exact loci at which such relationships occur, and to understand their biologic significance.

SUMMARY AND CONCLUSIONS

In this chapter, we have focused on interactions between lymphocytes and other cells which occur in a variety of cell-mediated immunologic reactions. One example of cell-cell interaction which was singled out for extensive discussion was that between lymphocyte and lymphocyte.

Lymphocyte-lymphocyte interactions have been found to underlie all immunologic phenomena. T–B cell cooperation is involved in the antibody response to many antigens, and such cooperation has implications for tolerance and immunologic memory as well. Reactions between T and B cells can also lead to suppression as well as enhancement. This may have implications for the phenomenon of antigenic competition. Recent studies have shown that in addition to T–B interactions, T–T cooperative effects may occur *in vitro* and *in vivo*.

To the extent that these diverse reactions involve T cells, they may be said to be manifestations of cell-mediated immunity. This relationship between the class of immunologic phenomena known as cell-mediated immunity and the whole area concerned with cell interactions in the immune response is more than a semantic trick. Although we do not yet know whether the same T cells participate in each, we do know that soluble mediator substances elaborated by lymphocytes are involved in both cases. We have speculated that some of the effector substances that play a role in the "helper" effect may be related to lymphokines which participate in cell-mediated reactions, and have outlined ways in which this might occur.

Cell-mediated immunity plays yet another role which has been discussed in detail in this chapter. It is one of the major links between the immune system and the inflammatory system. This is shown diagrammatically in Figure 3. A noxious agent may function *in vivo* as

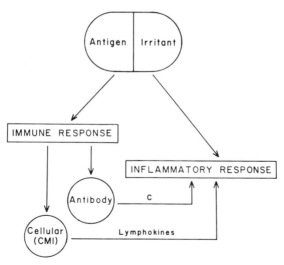

Figure 3.   Schematic representation of relationships between the immune and inflammatory responses.

both irritant and antigen. As irritant, it can directly trigger an inflammatory response, by nonimmunologic mechanisms that are beyond the scope of this book. In addition, as antigen, it can trigger a humoral and cellular immune response. Antibody-antigen complexes can activate the complement system, and various products of such activation have profound effects on vascular permeability and inflammatory cells. Cell-mediated immunity also plays a crucial role in initiating and maintaining an inflammatory response. Sensitized lymphocytes can release substances which affect vascular permeability (131,132). In addition, as we have seen here, they affect all of the inflammatory cell types of the body. They lead to accumulation, retention, and activation of such cells via mechanisms that are dependent, in most cases, on lymphokine production.

A final comment is in order regarding the significance of lymphokine production in the overall biologic scheme of things. In this chapter, we noted that although activation of lymphocytes for lymphokine production by specific antigen is a property of T cells, B cells may be so activated nonspecifically by certain mitogens (2). Moreover, it has been shown that MIF, or substances with similar biologic and physicochemical properties, may be found in certain replicating cultures of nonlymphoid cells (133,134). Also, we have recently shown that migration inhibitory activity (135,136), as well as certain other lymphokine-like activities such as macrophage and lymphocyte chemotaxis (137), may appear following the *in vitro* or *in vivo* infection of nonlymphoid as well as lymphoid cells by certain viruses. These results all suggest that lymphokine production, rather than "merely" representing an effector mechanism for cell-mediated immunity and for certain kinds of helper functions in antibody synthesis, represents a general biologic phenomenon which may play a role in various aspects of host defense. Thus, such mediator substances should be more properly called "cytokines." Lymphokines represent a restricted set of cytokines made by one class of cells (lymphocytes) activated in certain unique ways. In this view, the lymphocyte has acquired some specialized means for triggering such production, not available to other cells.

REFERENCES

1.   Sonozaki, H. and Cohen, S., *Cell. Immunol.* **3,** 644 (1972).
2.   Yoshida, T., Sonozaki, H., and Cohen, S., *J. Exp. Med.*, **138,** 784 (1973).
3.   Sultzer, B. M. and Nilsson, B. S., *Nat. New Biol.* **240,** 198 (1973).
4.   Elfenbein, E. J. and Green, I., *Fed. Proc.* **32,** 877 abstr. (1973).
5.   Claman, H. N. and Mosier, D. E., *Prog. Allergy* **16,** 40 (1972).

6. Feldmann, M. and Nossal, G. J. V., *Quart. Rev. Biol.* **47,** 269 (1972).

7. Katz, D. H. and Benacerraf, B., *Adv. Immunol.* **15,** 1 (1972).

8. Miller, J. F. A. P. and Mitchell, G. F., *Transplant. Rev.* **1,** 3 (1969).

9. Davies, A. J. S., *Transplant. Rev.* **1,** 43 (1969).

10. Claman, H. N. and Chaperon, E. A., *Transplant. Rev.* **1,** 92 (1969).

11. McArthur, W. P., Gilmour, D. E. and Thorbecke, G. J., *Cell. Immunol.* **8,** 103 (1973).

12. Taylor, R. B., *Transplant. Rev.* **1,** 114 (1969).

13. Miller, J. F. A. P., in *Cell Interactions and Receptor Antibodies in Immune Responses* (O. Makelä, A. Cross, and T. V. Kosunen, Eds.), Academic Press, 1971, p. 293.

14. Katz, D. H., Paul, W. E., Goidl, E. A., and Benacerraf, B. *J. Exp. Med.* **132,** 261 (1970).

15. Paul, W. E., Katz, D. H., Goidl, E. A., and Benacerraf, *J. Exp. Med.* **132,** 283 (1970).

16. Rajewski, K., Schirrmacher, V., Nase, S., and Jerne, N. K., *J. Exp. Med.* **129,** 1131 (1969).

17. Mitchison, N. A., *Eur. J. Immunol.* **1,** 10 (1971).

18. Basten, A., Miller, J. F. A. P., Warner, N. L., and Pye, J., *Nat. New Biol.* **231,** 104 (1971).

19. Miller, J. F. A. P., Basten, A., Sprent, J., and Cheers, C., *Cell. Immunol.* **2,** 469 (1971).

20. Mitchell, G. F. and Miller, J. F. A. P., *Proc. Natl. Acad. Sci. U.S.A.* **59,** 296 (1968).

21. Mitchison, N. A., *Eur. J. Immunol.* **1,** 18 (1971).

22. Katz, D. H., Paul, W. E., Goidl, E. A., and Benacerraf, B., *J. Exp. Med.* **132,** 261 (1970).

23. Mitchison, N. A., in *Immunological Tolerance* (M. Landy and W. Braun, Eds.), Academic Press, New York, 1969, p. 149.

24. Unanue, E. R., *J. Immunol.* **105,** 1339 (1970).

25. Miller, J. F. A. P., Sprent, J., Basten, A., Warner, N. L., Breitner, J. C. S., Med. **134,** 1266 (1971).

26. Davies, A. J. S., Leuchar, E., Wallis, V., Marchant, R., and Ellis, E. V., *Transplantation* **5,** 222 (1967).

27. Kennedy, J. C., Treadwill, P. E., and Lennox, E. S. *J. Exp. Med.* **132,** 353 (1970).

28. Haskill, J. S., Byrt, P., and Marbrook, J., *J. Exp. Med.* **131,** 57 (1970).

29. Doria, G., Agarossi, G., and DiPietro, S., *J. Immunol.* **108,** 268 (1972).

30. Gorczynski, R. M., Miller, R. G., and Phillips, R. A., *J. Immunol.* **108,** 547 (1972).

31. Rubin, A. S. and Coons, A. H.., *J. Exp. Med.* **136,** 1501 (1972).

32. Feldmann, M. and Basten, A., *Nat. New Biol.* **237,** 13 (1972).

33. Feldmann, M., *J. Exp. Med.* **136,** 737 (1972).

34. Katz, D. H., Goidl, E. A., Paul, W. E., and Benacerraf, B., *J. Exp. Med.* **133,** 169 (1971).

35. Osborne, D. P. and Katz, D. H., *J. Exp. Med.* **136,** 439 (1972).

36. Katz, D. H. and Osborne, D. P., *J. Exp. Med.* 445 (1972).

37. Osborne, D. H. and Katz, D. H., *J. Exp. Med.* **137,** 991 (1973).

38. Schimpl, A. and Wecker, E., *Nat. New Biol.* **237,** 15 (1972).

39. Dutton, R. W., Falkoff, R., Hirst, J. A., Hoffmann, M., Keppler, J. W., Kettman,

J. R., Lesley, J. F., and Vann, D., in *Progress in Immunology* (B. Amos, Ed.), Academic Press, New York, 1971, p. 355.

40. Ekpaha-Mensah, A. and Kennedy, J. C., *Nat. New Biol.* **233,** 174 (1971).

41. Britton, S., *Scand. J. Immunol.* **1,** 89 (1972).

42. Schimpl, A. and Wecker, E., *J. Exp. Med.* **137,** 547 (1973).

43. Katz, D. H., Hamaska, T., and Benacerraf, B., *J. Exp. Med.* **137,** 1405 (1973).

44. Cohen, S. and Ward, P. A., *J. Exp. Med.* **133,** 133 (1971).

45. Torisu, M., Yoshida, T., Ward, P. A., and Cohen, S., *J. Immunol.,* **111,** 1450 (1973).

46. Kettman, J., *Immunol. Comm.* **1,** 289 (1973).

47. Ward, P. A., Montgomery, J. R., and Offen, C. D., *Fed. Proc.* **30,** 1721 (1971).

48. Cohen, S., Ward, P. A., Yoshida, T., and Burek, L., *Cell. Immunol.* **9,** 363 (1973).

49. Shevach, E., Green, I., Ellman, L., and Maillard, J., *Nat. New Biol.* **235,** 19 (1972).

50. Rosenthal, A. S., Davie, J. M., Rosenstreich, D. L., and Blake, J. T., *J. Immunol.* **108,** 279 (1972).

51. Moran, E., Andersson, J., and Sjoberg, O., *Cell. Immunol.* **4,** 416 (1972).

52. Schmidtke, J. R. and Dixon, F. J., *J. Exp. Med.* **136,** 392 (1972).

53. Andersson, J., Moller, G., and Sjoberg, O., *Eur. J. Immunol.* **2,** 99 (1972).

54. Vischer, T. L., *J. Immunol.* **109,** 401 (1972).

55. Simonsen, M. *Prog. Allergy* **6,** 349 (1962).

56. Cantor, H. and Asofsky, R., *J. Exp. Med.* **131,** 235 (1970).

57. Cantor, H. and Asofsky, R., *J. Exp. Med.* **135,** 764 (1972).

58. Tigelaar, R. E. and Asofsky, R., *J. Exp. Med.* **135,** 1059 (1972).

59. Howard, J. G., Michie, D., and Simonsen, M., *Brit. J. Exp. Pathol.* **42,** 478 (1961).

60. Zeiss, I. M. and Fox, M. *Nature* **197,** 673 (1963).

61. Elkins, W. L., *Transplantation* **9,** 273 (1970).

62. Baum, J., Lieberman, G., and Frenkel, E. P., *J. Immunol.* **103,** 1342 (1969).

63. Baker, P. J., Barth, R. F., Stashak, P. W., and Amsbaugh, D. F., *J. Immunol.* **104,** 1313 (1970).

64. Baker, P. J., Stashak, P. W., Amsbaugh, D. F., Prescott, B., and Barth, R., *J. Immunol.* **105,** 1581 (1970).

65. Armstrong, W. D., Diener, E., and Shellam, G. R., *J. Exp. Med.* **129,** 393 (1969).

66. Rich, R. R. and Pierce, C. W., *J. Exp. Med.* **137,** 649 (1973).

67. Radovich, J. and Talmage, D. W., *Science* **158,** 512 (1967).

68. Gershon, R. K. and Kondo, K., *J. Immunol.* **106,** 1524 (1971).

69. Gershon, R. K. and Kondo, K., **106,** 1531 (1971).

70. Pappenheimer, A. M., Jr., Scharff, M., and Uhr, J. W., in *Mechanisms of Hypersensitivity* (J. H. Shaffer, G. A. LoGrippo, and M. W. Chase, Eds.), Little, Brown, Boston, Massachusetts, 1959, p. 417.

71. Mooney, J. J. and Waksman, B. H., *J. Immunol.* **105,** 1138 (1970).

72. Nathan, C. F., Karnovsky, M. L., and David, J. R., *J. Exp. Med.* **133,** 1356 (1971).

73. Dvorak, A. M., Hammond, M. E., Dvorak, H. F., and Karnovsky, M. J., *Lab. Invest.,* in press.

74. Hammond, M. E. and Dvorak, H. F., *J. Exp. Med.* **136,** 1518 (1972).

75. Caspary, E. A., *Clin. Exp. Immunol.* **11,** 305 (1972).

76. van Oss, C. J. and Gillman, C. G., *J. Reticuloendothel. Soc.* **12,** 283 (1972).

77. Thrasher, S. G., Yoshida, T., van Oss, C. J., Cohen, S., and Rose, N. R., *J. Immunol.* **110,** 321 (1973).

78. Litt, M., *Ann. N. Y. Acad. Sci.* **116,** 964 (1964).

79. Cohen, S. G., Sapp. T. M., and Gallia, A. R., *Proc. Soc. Exp. Biol. Med.* **113,** 29 (1963).

80. Cohen, S., Vassalli, P., Benacerraf, B., and McCluskey, R. T., *Lab. Invest.* **15,** 1143 (1966).

81. Cohen, S. G. and Sapp, T. M., *J. Allergy* **36,** 415 (1965).

82. Arnason, B. G. and Waksman, B. H., *Lab. Invest.* **12,** 737 (1963).

83. Cohen, S., Rose, N. R., and Brown, R. C., *Clin. Immunol. and Immunopath* (in press.)

84. Basten, A., Boyer, M. H., and Beeson, P. B., *J. Exp. Med.* **131,** 1271 (1970).

85. Basten, A. and Beeson, P. B., *J. Exp. Med.* **131,** 1288 (1970).

86. Yoshida, T., Janeway, C. A., Jr., and Paul, W. E., *J. Immunol.* **108,** 201 (1972).

87. Kay, A. B., *Clin. Exp. Immunol.* **6,** 75 (1970).

88. Kay, A. B., *Clin. Exp. Immunol.* **7,** 723 (1971).

89. Rose, N. R. and Kite, J. H., Jr., in *International Convocation on Immunology* (N. R. Rose and F. Milgrom, Eds.), S. Karger, Basel, Switzerland, 1969, p. 247.

90. Flax, M. H., in *Cellular Interactions in the Immune Response* (S. Cohen, G. Cudkowicz, and R. T. McCluskey, Eds.), S. Karger, Basel, Switzerland, 1971, p. 282.

91. Dvorak, H. F. and Dvorak, A. M., *Human Pathol.* **3,** 454 (1972).

92. Richerson, H. B., Dvorak, H. F., and Leskowitz, S., *J. Exp. Med.* **132,** 546 (1970).

93. Dvorak, H. F., Dvorak, A. M., Simpson, B. A., Richerson, H. B., Leskowitz, S., and Karnovsky, M. J., *J. Exp. Med.* **132,** 558 (1970).

94. Dvorak, H. F., Simpson, B. A., Bast, R. C., Jr., and Leskowitz, S., *J. Immunol.* **107,** 138 (1971).

95. Dvorak, A. M., Bast, R. C., Jr., and Dvorak, H. F., *J. Immunol.* **107,** 422 (1971).

96. Wolf-Jügensen, P., *Basophil Leukocytes in Delayed Hypersensitivity,* Munksgaard, Copenhagen, 1966.

97. Dvorak, H. F., *J. Immunol.* **106,** 279 (1971).

98. Dvorak, H. F. and Dvorak, A. M., in *Microenvironmental Aspects of Immunity* (B. D. Jankovic and K. Isokovic, Eds.), Plenum, New York, 1972, p. 573.

99. Dvorak, H. F. and Hirsch, M. S., *J. Immunol.* **107,** 1576 (1971).

100. Kay, A. B. and Austen, K. F., *Clin. Exp. Immunol.* **11,** 557 (1972).

101. Boetcher, D. A. and Leonard, E. L., *Immunol. Comm.* **2,** in press.

102. Pedawar, J., *Ann. N. Y. Acad. Sci.* **103,** 1 (1967).

103. Miller, J. J. and Cole, L. J., *Nature* **217,** 263 (1968).

104. Cohen, S. and McCluskey, R. T., in *Principles of Immunology* (N. R. Rose, F. Milgrom, and C. J. van Oss, Eds.), MacMillan, New York, 1973.

105. Freund, J. and Stone, S. H., *J. Immunol.* **76,** 138 (1956).

106. McCamish, J. and Benedict, A. A., *J. Immunol.* **91,** 651 (1963).

107. Vredevoe, D. L., *J. Immunol.* **92,** 717 (1964).

108. Crowle, A. J., *Science* **130,** 159 (1959).

109.   Crowle, A. J., *J. Allergy* **33,** 458 (1962).

110.   Crowle, A. J. and Hu, C. C., *Fed. Proc.* **25,** 550 (1966).

111.   Munoz, J., *J. Immunol.* **98,** 638 (1967).

112.   Ward, P. A., Remold, H. G., and David, J. R., *Cell. Immunol.* **1,** 162 (1970).

113.   Wood, R. M. and Bick, M. W., *A.M.A. Arch. Ophthalmol.* **61,** 709 (1959).

114.   Nelson, D. S., *Immunology* **9,** 219 (1965).

115.   Nelson, D. S. and North, R. J., *Lab. Invest.* **14,** 89 (1965).

116.   Cohen, S., Benacerraf, B., McCluskey, R. T., and Ovary, Z., *J. Immunol.* **98,** 351 (1967).

117.   Feinman, L., Cohen, S., and Becker, E. L., *J. Immunol.* **104,** 1401 (1970).

118.   Dvorak, H. F. and Mihm, M. C., Jr., *J. Exp. Med.* **135,** 275 (1972).

119.   Colvin, R. B., Johnson, R. A., Mihm, M. C., Jr., and Dvorak, H. F., *J. Exp. Med.,* **138,** 686 (1973).

120.   Chelmicka-Szorc, E. and Arnason, B. G. W., *Arch. Neurol.* **27,** 153 (1972).

121.   Currie, G. A., *Nature* **215,** 164 (1967).

122.   Taylor, H. E. and Culling, C. F. A., *Lab. Invest.* **15,** 1960 (1966).

123.   Martz, E. and Benacerraf, B., *Clin. Immunol. Immunopathol.,* in press.

124.   Barbaro, J. F. and Zvaiffler, N. J., *Proc. Soc. Exp. Biol. Med.* **122,** 1245 (1966).

125.   Schoenbechler, M. J. and Barbaro, J. F., *Proc. Natl. Acad. Sci.* **60,** 1247 (1968).

126.   Henson, P. M., *Fed. Proc.* **28,** 1721 (1969).

127.   Henson, P. M., *J. Exp. Med.* **131,** 287 (1970).

128.   Siraganian, R. P. and Osler, A. G., *J. Immunol.* **106,** 1244 (1971).

129.   Siraganian, R. P. and Osler, A. G., *J. Immunol.* **106,** 1252 (1971).

130.   Aikawa, M., Schoenbechler, M. J., Barbaro, J. F., and Sadun, E. H., *Am. J. Pathol.* **63,** 85 (1971).

131.   Willoughby, D. A. and Spector, W. B., *J. Pathol. Bacteriol.* **87,** 353 (1964).

132.   Willoughby, D. A. and Spector, W. B., *J. Pathol. Bacteriol.* **88,** 557 (1964).

133.   Tubergen, D. G., Feldman, J. D., Pollack, E. M., and Lerner, R. A., *J. Exp. Med.* **135,** 255 (1972).

134.   Papageogious, P. S., Henley, W. L., and Glade, P. R., *J. Immunol.* **108,** 494 (1972).

135.   Flanagan, T. D., Yoshida, T., Genco, R. J., and Cohen, S., *Clin. Immunol. and Immunopath.* in press.

136.   Flanagan, T. D., Yoshida, T., and Cohen, S., *Infect. Immun.* **8,** 145, 1973.

137.   Ward, P. A., Cohen, S., and Flanagan, T. D., *J. Exp. Med.* **135,** 1095 (1972).

Appendix One

Preparation of Labeled Cells for Transfer Studies

PAUL D. LEBER AND ROBERT T. MCCLUSKEY

Department of Pathology, Harvard Medical School and the Children's Hospital Medical Center, Boston, Massachusetts

The identity of the participants in cell-mediated immune reactions has been most successfully studied *in vivo* in passive transfer experiments employing labeled cells. While the steps involved are relatively few, the procedures employed vary in detail from one laboratory to another. The reasons for these variations often appear to be based less on theoretical considerations than on the personal preferences and experience of the individual investigators. Accordingly, we do not attempt a review of the literature on methods used in cell transfer studies, but instead describe several methods that have proved particularly useful in our own studies of cell-mediated reactions.

In the ideal experiment, a pure population of cells would be isolated and labeled in a manner that does not alter cell function and then administered intravenously to a syngeneic recipient in which the lesion of interest would be studied. Moreover, the cells should be of a kind that could be expected to enter the circulation. These conditions are difficult to satisfy.

Some of the studies described here were supported by USPHS AI 10700.

Completely pure cell populations cannot be obtained. Instead, populations that have been selectively enriched in one or more cell types by relatively nonspecific physical techniques are commonly obtained. While these may seem relatively homogeneous as judged by certain criteria such as size and morphologic features, they may prove heterogeneous when judged by other standards. In view of this, the possibility that a minority component in a cell transfer inoculum is responsible for the observed results must be considered. Other methods of purification involve depletion of cells bearing certain surface markers by treatment with specific antisera (such as antitheta) plus complement.

The preparations obtained by disruption of lymphoid organs (lymph nodes, thymus, or spleen), which are often employed in the transfer experiments, contain cells that would not be expected to enter the circulation under ordinary circumstances. Such cells include immature members of types destined to circulate, as well as cells that never do (i.e., connective tissue and supporting elements, and certain kinds of lymphocytes). There is evidence that many such cells are rapidly removed from the circulation by the liver (1). However, some immature lymphocytes may home to lymph nodes or possibly enter sites of cell-mediated reactions. In large part, this problem may be circumvented by the use of *in situ* labeling of lymph node cells (see below). The surest way to avoid the problem, however, is to begin with a source of cells which contains only mature and appropriate types, such as the lymph or blood. However, even here, damage to cells may occur during the collection or purification process. Further, as discussed subsequently, these sources are not available in all species, or suffer from other limitations such as low yield.

The radiolabeling of cells for transfer studies presents few difficulties. Nonetheless, certain precautions must be borne in mind.

Generally speaking, the incorporation of ^{14}C- or ^{3}H-labeled nucleotides into cell DNA or RNA does not alter cell function unless the isotopes are administered in very high concentrations or specific activities. As a rule, one should employ the lowest dose and specific activity that renders sufficient numbers of cells detectable in the system under study. As a check of the functional integrity of the labeled cells, the pattern of "homing" of cells after transfer to normal animals may be studied. The labeling of cells is never homogeneous and in some circumstances may show marked variations among cells of different classes or degrees of maturity. For example, in the rat, small B lymphocytes fail to incorporate the RNA precursor uridine as efficiently or avidly as do small T lymphocytes. In fact, this difference is so marked that it has been used to distinguish between the two cell classes (2).

The choice of label requires discussion. For studies in which the cells are to be traced by counts of radioactivity, ^{51}Cr is generally the label of choice (3,4). As far as is known, labeling with ^{51}Cr does not disturb lymphocyte migration pathways *in vivo* (3,4). For autoradiographic studies, a tritium label is preferable. ^{3}H-Thymidine offers the advantage of being a stable label, which, once incorporated, remains with the cell until death or division. However, since ^{3}H-thymidine is incorporated only by cells engaged in DNA synthesis, only a small percentage of cells will be labeled *in vitro* and small lymphocytes will not become labeled at all. A higher percentage of cells can be labeled by repeated injections of ^{3}H-thymidine *in vivo,* and this will also include labeled small lymphocytes, but this is expensive and time-consuming.

In spite of these problems, cell transfer has been and continues to be an extremely useful tool for the study of cell-mediated immune phenomena.

The most useful source of lymphocytes obtainable without disruption of tissue is the thoracic duct lymph. However, in order to obtain thoracic duct lymph in significant quantity, drainage for several hours, or even days, is required. Moreover, this procedure can be performed reliably only by a skilled operator, and among experimental animals, is feasible only in rats and (with even greater difficulty) in mice. Although the method of thoracic duct cannulation has been described in the literature (5), the technique is best learned in a laboratory where it is routinely employed. Hence, we do not describe it here.

The blood is another source of cells that can be obtained without disruption of tissues. Its major disadvantages lie in the heterogeneity of the cells obtained and their small numbers. Considering that in most transfer studies a minimum of 100 to 200 million lymphocytes is administered to each recipient, one would have to obtain more than 25 cc of donor blood for each recipient. When working with small animals, this proves burdensome and expensive in comparison with other techniques. For example, one may obtain over 100 million lymph node cells from a single immunized donor rat. Thus, techniques involving disruption of tissue make up somewhat in the way of economy and convenience for what they lack in other respects.

All methods involving collection of cells by disruption of lymphoid tissue are basically of the same design. Their aim is to dissociate the cells from the parent structure with a minimum of trauma and to deliver them to a life-supporting medium as swiftly as possible. For illustrative purposes, the collection of lymph node cells from the rat is described.

Prospective donor animals are immunized in 4 footpads with the appropriate antigen, commonly in complete Freund's adjuvant, often with concomitant injection of B pertussis. The day of harvest varies from one system to another, but is commonly between 5 and 12 days. In some models, the day of transfer is critical, as for example in autoimmune adrenalitis or encephalitis in rats. The animals are anesthetized and the popliteal, inguinal, axillary, and periaortic nodes removed, taking care to keep the capsules of the node intact. The nodes are then placed in chilled medium 199 supplemented with 10% fetal calf serum (FCS) and containing heparin 10 units/ml (Panheparin*). Here, the excess fat and perinodal connective tissue are trimmed away. The cleaned, but intact nodes are next transferred to a petri dish containing fresh medium and are diced by repetitive cuts using a fine iris scissors. As cells accumulate, the fluid becomes grossly turbid. This fluid is transferred to a chilled receiving flask after first being passed through a loose filter made of surgical gauze to remove large debris. The cells are next spun in a refrigerated centrifuge at 500 to 1000 rpm; higher forces may damage the cells. They are then resuspended in medium 199 containing FCS but free of heparin.† The resuspended cells are allowed to stand for 10 minutes. During this time agglutinated cells settle out or sediment toward the bottom of the tube. At the end of this period the upper half to two-thirds of the fluid should consist largely of a single cell suspension; this may be checked by direct examination in a counting chamber. The cells may now be washed by three cycles of centrifugation and resuspension in heparin-free media containing 10% FCS. After the final wash, the cell button may be suspended and an aliquot taken for counting. At this point cells may be labeled (vide infra) or processed further to remove one cell population or another. For the final suspension of cells for transfer we prefer to supplement the basic medium with 10% normal serum of the species being employed. Finally, aloquots of the final suspensions are taken for counting, preparation of smears,‡ and viability testing. The methods used for separation of cell classes or subtypes are not described here.

As mentioned earlier, the inclusion in a transfer inoculum of labeled cells not normally destined to enter the circulation produces certain arti-

---

*Panheparin is a preservative-free preparation. When heparin containing preservatives is used, untoward effects on cell behavior and/or viability may be observed.

†The removal of heparin is advised, for this highly negatively charged molecule, in addition to its known anticoagulant activity, may bind to and hence potentially modify certain functions of lymphocytes (6).

‡We have routinely employed a Shandon cytofuge for the making of smears for differential counts and radioautography. For a single slide, we usually spin 0.2 cc of suspension of cells at 1×10^6/ml in 50% normal serum-supplemented media at 500 rpm for 5 minutes.

facts in tracer studies. In an effort to circumvent this problem, Werdelin and associates developed a method of *in situ* labeling of cells from a single node (7). The advantage of the method is that while various classes of cells are labeled, only those normally destined to enter the circulation actually do so. To some extent, the trauma of intranodal injection might dislodge some inappropriate or immature cells into the circulation, but the numbers involved are probably trivial. The technique is as follows. The anesthetized rat is placed prone with extremities extended on an operating board. A tourniquet consisting of a rubber band and a hemostat is positioned around the right hind limb proximal to the popliteal space, but left loosely fitting for the moment. The skin over the popliteal node (which is obvious in the immunized animal) is identified by palpation. An incision (i.e., 5 to 6 mm) is made in the facia and muscle overlying the node. Then with gentle pressure the node is forced toward the surface.

The proximal tourniquet is now secured and after a minute 50 μl containing 20 to 30 μCi of tritiated thymidine are injected through a 27 gauge needle into the node using a 250-μl Hamilton syringe. The surface of the node is blotted with saline-dampened gauze and the incision closed. At this point, while the tourniquet is still secure, an injection of cold thymidine is given via the tail vein. The dose administered is generally 20,000 times greater on a weight basis than the radioactive material given. For example, approximately 0.4 cc of thymidine solution containing 40 mg/cc water is used in a rat given approximately 700 ng of radioactive material. The tourniquet is now released and the procedure completed.

The technique results in intense labeling of many cells in the injected node, whereas cells in other tissues are not labeled to an extent that is detectable by ordinary autoradiographic techniques. This is most easily checked by examination of intestinal epithelium (7). Labeled lymphocytes are found outside the injected node (in other lymphoid tissue and in certain inflammatory infiltrates) within several hours, showing migration from the injected node.

Until recently, morphology alone was used to establish the identity of cell types in the population to be transferred. However, it is now possible to classify the cells by additional criteria. For example, the availability of antisera directed against cell surface antigens (i.e., theta or others in the mouse) or against immunoglobulin determinants (most species) has permitted the identification of T and B lymphocytes, respectively, by immunofluorescence (8).

To illustrate this approach we describe the method we employ to identify in suspension Ig-bearing lymphocytes (B lymphocytes) in the rat.

Rabbits are immunized with rat gamma globulin isolated by ammonium sulfate fractionation, thus producing a broad spectrum antiglobulin reagent. In our hands, the direct immunofluorescence technique has proved superior to the indirect method. We have found it preferable to use late antisera (presumably because of its higher affinity) and to conjugate to higher fluorescein protein molar ratios (i.e., 5:7) than generally used in tissue immunofluorescence. While the latter would lead to nonspecific staining in tissue preparations, it is of little concern when studying cell suspensions.

The number of B cells are estimated as follows. Between 5×10^6 and $\times 10^7$ cells are washed in 3 or 4 ml of media at 4°C by three cycles of centrifugation (1000 rpm) and resuspension. After the final wash, the cell button is not resuspended. The tube is placed in an ice water bath and 50 μl of cold fluoresceinated, recently filtered antisera is added to the tube and mixed. After 30 minutes, cold medium is added and 3 poststaining washing cycles are performed. Care must be taken to keep the cells cold through the entire washing procedure. After the final wash the cells may be suspended in 0.5 cc of medium or PBS. A drop or two is placed on a slide and coverslipped. The margins of the coverslip are sealed using a good grade of vacuum grease. The final dilution of cells can be adjusted for ease of counting. It is convenient to count both the total cells in a field and the number demonstrating a surface fluorescence. Several distinct patterns of granular staining produced by antibody reacting with antigens distributed on the cell surface are recognized (8). When stained for Ig, discrete small beadlike granules may be found uniformly distributed over the entire surface of the cell membrane. Other cells can display irregularly distributed patches of aggregated granules. Still others may show cap formation with congregation and apparent fusion of aggregates at one pole of the cell. It is thought that the patterns described represent progressive steps in the membrane flow of surface immunoglobulin receptors triggered by their combination with the fluorescent antibody. Eventually the cap of immunoglobulin is internalized, but under the conditions given above, this is not a problem. With time, however, particularly after the suspension has been mounted and maintained at room temperature, more capping may occur. For this reason, it is advisable to keep the stained cells in an ice water bath until they are ready to be viewed. Alternatively, some workers prefer to add a metabolic inhibitor to their preparations (e.g., sodium azide). It is important to distinguish these patterns of staining from those produced by uptake of antibody in phagocytic vacuoles. This may usually be accomplished by carefully focusing from one surface of the cell to another. While true surface fluorescence is restricted to the cell membrane, phagocytic vacuoles may be detected at all levels within the cell sap. Dead cells are recognized by their diffuse cytoplasmic staining brought about by the failure of devitalized cell membrane to exclude labeled antibody.

We have found it most convenient to enumerate cells using dark field fluorescence with a transmitted light source. The scope used is equipped with red suppressing and interference filters on the excitation side (i.e., BG38 and KP490). A set of barrier filters in the 510- to 530-nM range may be used. The number of specifically fluorescent cells in a field may be counted with the red suppressing filter in place. Under these conditions only positive staining cells are easily seen. Then, the red suppressing filter is removed and the total number of cells in the field are counted.* Under these conditions negative cells refract the red light entering the specimen obliquely from the dark-field condenser, rendering them visible to the microscopist. The final result is expressed as the number of positive cells per total number of cells present.

The final step of the transfer study is to remove and evaluate the lesion. In our laboratory this is most often accomplished using light microscopy and autoradiography. For a detailed discussion of autoradiography one should consult a standard text like that of Rogers (9).

REFERENCES

1. Gesner, B., Woodruff, J., and McCluskey, R. T., *Am. J. Pathol.* **57**, 215 (1969).
2. Howard, J., Hunt, S., and Gowans, J., *J. Exp. Med.* **135**, 200 (1972).
3. Woodruff, J. and Gesner, B. M., *Science* **161**, 176 (1968).
4. Woodruff, J. and Gesner, B. M., *J. Exp. Med.* **129**, 551 (1969).
5. Bollman, J., Cain, J., and Grindlay, J., *J. Lab. Clin. Med.* **33**, 1349 (1948).
6. Martz, E. and Benacerraf, B., *Clin. Immunol. Immunopathol.*, in press.
7. Werdelin. O., McCluskey, R. T., and Witebsky, E., *Lab. Invest.* **23**, 144 (1970).
8. Rabellino, E., Colon, S., Grey, H., and Unanue, E., *J. Exp. Med.* **133**, 156 (1971).
9. Rogers, A. W., *Techniques of Autoradiography*, Elsevier, Amsterdam, 1969.

---

*We are indebted to Dr. Emil R. Unanue of Harvard Medical School for calling our attention to this means of enumerating nonfluorescent cells under dark-field illumination.

Appendix Two

Reactions of Macrophages to Lymphocyte Products

HEINZ G. REMOLD, JOHN R. DAVID,
PETER A. WARD, AND STANLEY COHEN

Departments of Medicine and Biological Chemistry, Robert B. Brigham Hospital and Harvard Medical School, Boston Massachusetts, and Departments of Pathology, University of Connecticut and State University of New York at Buffalo

The mediator substances released by activated lymphocytes have many different effects on a variety of cell types. Perhaps the best studied are those which modify the behavior of macrophages. In this appendix, we describe procedures for three assays which are based on lymphocyte-macrophage interactions mediated by soluble lymphocyte products. These are (1) the macrophage migration inhibition reaction, (2) macrophage chemotaxis, and (3) the macrophage disappearance reaction.

INHIBITION OF MACROPHAGE MIGRATION

This method for detecting delayed-type hypersensitivity *in vitro* by measuring inhibition of peritoneal exudate (PE) cell migration from capillary tubes was first described by George and Vaughan (1), and further developed by David and his colleagues (2). It can be used to detect the presence of sensitive lymphocytes or antigen, to detect the presence of a soluble mediator substance (MIF), or to evaluate macrophage response to either sensitized lymphocytes or MIF. Only an outline of the procedure is presented here, as a more elaborate treatment is available in a recent volume on methodology by Bloom and Glade (3).

Harvesting Guinea Pig PE Cells

Thirty milliliters of sterile light mineral oil (Marcol 52, Humble Oil and Refining Company) is injected intraperitoneally approximately 72 hours before the peritoneal exudate cells are to be harvested. The animals are exsanguinated by cardiac puncture under ether anesthesia. Then the shaved abdomens of the animals are wiped with alcohol and a skin incision along the linea alba is made. One hundred fifty milliliters of cold Hank's BSS (GIBCO Labs) is injected intraperitoneally into each animal. The animal is agitated vigorously and a Duke cannulated trocar (Sklar, #215-15) and sheath are introduced. The trocar is next removed and replaced by the cannula which is attached to polyethylene tubing. The peritoneal fluid, containing oil and exudate, is then drained out into a separatory funnel. The peritoneal wash is poured into a centrifuge bottle, leaving the oil behind. The aqueous peritoneal wash is centrifuged at 450 × g for 15 minutes, and the centrifuged cells are washed twice in Hank's BSS. After the final wash, the cell suspension is adjusted to 10% by volume in minimal essential medium (MEM) containing 100 units of penicillin and streptomycin/ml and 15% guinea pig serum.

Preparation of Capillaries and Migration Chambers

The cell suspension is mixed and drawn up in capillary tubes. One end of each tube is plugged with warm wax. As the capillaries are filled, they are put into a test tube and centrifuged at 250 × g for 5 minutes at room temperature. After centrifugation, the capillaries are placed on ice. They are next wiped with a sterile alcohol pad, and then a dry pad, and then cut with an ampoule file about 0.5 mm into the cells, below the cell-fluid interface. With a thumb forceps, the capillaries are picked up and placed into a chamber (Berton Plastics, Hackensack, N.J.) which was sealed underneath earlier with a coverslip and liquid wax. The capillaries are anchored to the lower coverslip by dabs of silicone grease. The top coverslip is then placed on the chamber and sealed with wax. The chamber is filled with test medium and the inlet hole sealed with wax. These chambers are incubated for 8 to 24 hours at

37°C in a dry incubator. The migration area made by the cells as they travel out of the capillary tube is traced on white paper by means of a projection microscope. The migration areas are then calculated with the use of a standard planimeter. The ratio of the migration areas of the experimental groups to those of the controls is taken as a measure of the inhibition of migration produced by the test substance.

CHEMOTAXIS OF MACROPHAGES

Chemotaxis of mononuclear cells can be measured by the micropore filter technique. This involves the use of a modified Boyden chamber containing a micropore filter with a pore size of 5 to 8 μ(4). The cell suspension is placed on one side of the filter, the chemoattractant on the other, and after a suitable period of incubation, the filter is removed, stained, and examined by light microscopy. In addition to the usual controls, it is important to include chambers in which the same concentration of chemoattractant is present on both sides of the filter. This abolishes a chemical gradient, and thus rules out the possibility that increased migration of cells through the filter is simply due to a nonspecific increase in motility produced by the test substance. It is important also to include chambers containing a known source of chemotactic factor as a positive control, in order to be certain that the indicator cells are active and capable of responding to any chemotactic stimulus in the experimental chambers.

Preparation of Indicator Cells

In this section we describe the procedure for the study of the chemotaxis of peritoneal exudate macrophages. Studies involving macrophages from other sources, blood monocytes, or lymphocytes are performed in a similar manner. We obtain macrophages 4 days after a mineral oil (50 ml) induced peritoneal exudate is produced in New Zealand rabbits of either sex (5). The 4-day interval is important. At 3 days, a relatively large proportion of neutrophils is present. These will interfere with macrophage chemotaxis. At 5 days, many of the macrophages in the exudate are dead or dying. Thus, 4 days appears to be an optimal interval. The cells obtained at this time are gently centrifuged and then resuspended in 10% homologous rabbit serum diluted in medium 199, adjusting the cell concentration to 2.5×10^6 /ml. One milliliter of this suspension is used for each chamber. As mentioned above, human blood monocytes can be studied for chemotactic responsiveness, but this involves complex fractionation procedures in gradients, and the resultant cell yields preclude more than a few chambers in a given assay (6).

Micropore Filters

As indicated above, micropore filters made from mixed esters of cellulose are the basis of the chemotaxis assay. Pore sizes of 5 or 8 μ are usually used. These filters may be obtained from the Millipore Corporation (New Bedford, Mass.) or Schleicher and Schuell (Keene, N.H.). A different type of filter, Nucleopore, from Wallabs (San Rafael, Calif.), which consists of polycarbonate, has also been used (6,9), but most of the published studies of monocyte chemotaxis involve the former type of filter.

Chemotactic Factors

The two most active factors for macrophages appear to be a fragment of the fifth component (C5) of human complement (8), and the soluble product released by antigen or mitogen-stimulated lymphocytes (6,9,10). The first factor can be produced by activation of fresh human serum with zymosan or immune complexes, or by trypsin treatment of purified C5. The lymphocyte-derived chemotactic factor is released into culture supernatant fluids after a 48-hour period of incubation of lymphoid cells cultured in the presence of either specific antigen or nonspecific mitogens such as concanavalin A or phytohemagglutinin (6,9). Guinea pig lymphocytes are particularly good sources of this factor. Also, as mentioned above, the C5 factor is derived from human material. The indicator macrophages are obtained from rabbits. Thus, there does not appear to be species specificity in this reaction.

Boyden Chambers

The chambers used for this assay are the modified Boyden chambers obtainable from Schleicher and Schuell (Keene, N.H.), or from Bellco Glass Company (Vineland, N.J.). Others have used plastic chambers; they are similar in construction, and can be obtained from the Nucleoprobe Corporation (Bethesda, Md.) (6). Their advantage is that filters of smaller diameter can be used, along with a cell volume of only 0.3 ml (instead of 1.0 ml). The disadvantage of these plastic chambers is that they are difficult to wash thoroughly after use.

Incubation of Chambers

Once the indicator cells and appropriate test substances and controls are added to the chambers, they are incubated at 37°C for 5 hours in a conventional incubator. Because of the short duration of incubation, special gas mixtures are not required, and CO_2 is not added to the environment. It should be noted, however, that the tissue culture medium used for the cell suspensions and dilution of chemoattractants must be well buffered in order to stabilize the pH during the period of incubation. We use 0.025 M TRIS chloride at pH 7.4.

Staining of Filters

The technique first described by Boyden (4) is used in our laboratory, except that propanol is substituted for the fixing and the dehydrating agents (instead of methanol and ethanol). Millipore filters tend to dissolve in methanol, while Schleicher and Schuell filters dissolve in ethanol. The use of propanol solves these minor difficulties.

Measurement of Cell Migration

The chemotactic value is defined as the count of the number of migrated cells in the filter, examining five high-power fields by light microscopy (approximately 400×). There are two methods for obtaining this number: either counting all the cells migrating into channels of the filter, or counting only those cells that have migrated completely through (the cells which appear as a monolayer on the filter surface opposite to the side on which the cell suspension had been added). It is not difficult to determine which surface of the filter represents the original or upper surface (the starting surface for cell migration), since over 60% of the cells will have not responded. Additionally, there are invariably a few cell clumps that can be used to mark the original monolayer of cells. In actual practice, relatively few of the macrophages migrate completely through the channels of the filter, in marked contrast to the behavior of neutrophils. Accordingly, counts of *all* migrating cells seem to be the more productive technique for assessment of macrophage chemotaxis. In a typical experiment, the blank control should not give a value of greater than 45 (based on five high-power fields), whereas the positive control should be approximately 200 to 250. The test substance will usually fall within this range, and the value obtained will be a function of the concentration of the chemoattractant. Antigen-stimulated lymphocyte culture fluids (see ref. 9 for details of culture procedure) can be diluted 1:5 and still retain detectable chemotactic activity, although at this dilution no MIF activity can be detected using the capillary tube migration inhibition assay system. The chemotactic fragment of C5 shows good chemotactic activity for macrophages at a dose of approximately 5μ g.

MACROPHAGE DISAPPEARANCE REACTION

Aside from the injection of "skin reactive factor" into the skin of a test animal, the macrophage disappearance reaction (MDR) represents the only *in vivo* assay system for lymphokine activity. It is thought to represent the *in vivo* analog of the capillary tube migration inhibition reaction described above.

Nelson and Boyden (11,12) observed that the intraperitoneal injection of tuberculin into BCG-vaccinated guinea pigs caused the virtual disappearance of macrophages from peritoneal exudates which had been induced by the prior administration of glycogen. This observation has been confirmed using other antigens and other animal species (13,14). The MDR is observed whether the antigen is injected intravenously, subcutaneously, or intraperitoneally, but the intraperitoneal route requires smaller amounts of antigen and is effective in a shorter time. The reaction is sensitive, specific, and parallels skin reactions of delayed hypersensitivity. It has been demonstrated that the MDR may be passively transferred to unimmunized recipients by sensitized lymphocytes enclosed in micropore chambers, or by a soluble, lymphocyte-derived factor (lymphokine) (15,16).

Active MDR (Immunized Animals)

In a typical experiment, guinea pigs are injected with a soluble protein such as egg albumin emulsified in complete Freund's adjuvant. The material is administered intradermally into each footpad in a dose appropriate for the induction of good delayed hypersensitivity. The animals are skin tested 1 week prior to use, both to check their state of reactivity and to boost that reactivity. The animals are injected intraperitoneally with 10 ml of a sterile solution of shellfish glycogen (0.04 mg/ml). The peritoneal exudate is allowed to develop for 4 days. The animals are then given an intraperitoneal injection of a suitable dose of the test antigen (approximately 20 μg in the case of egg albumin or similar antigens) in 1 ml of phosphate-buffered saline (PBS). Each control animal receives only 1 ml of PBS. Five hours later, at the time of a peak MDR, the peritoneal exudates are collected using a total volume of 40 ml of PBS containing 10 units of heparin/ml. Total cell counts are then performed in the same manner as routine blood counts, using a hemocytometer. Giemsa-stained smears of the exudate are examined to obtain a differential count of lymphocytes, macrophages, and granulocytes according to the usual criteria. The total number of macrophages in the exudates from each guinea pig is obtained from the total cell count and the percentage of macrophages present. The percentage of macrophage loss is then calculated from the difference between the average count for that cell type in the exudates of the control animals and in the exudates of the animals that had received antigen. Typically, one may demonstrate up to a 95% loss in peritoneal macrophages in animals challenged with antigen, as compared to the PBS controls.

Passive MDR (Unimmunized Animals)

To perform a typical passive transfer experiment, sensitized lymphocytes are obtained from teased lymph nodes or peritoneal exudates from donors immunized as described above. Results are most clear-cut when purified populations of lymphocytes are used for transfer, to avoid introducing additional macrophages into the peritoneal exudates of the recipient animals. Purification of the donor cells may be accomplished by a variety of techniques; we favor passage through glass bead columns at 37°C in the presence of homologous serum (15). This leads to populations of cells consisting of over 99% lymphocytes, and of these, approximately 95% are small lymphocytes.

Unimmunized guinea pigs that will serve as recipients are treated with glycogen as described above. Four days later, they receive an intraperitoneal injection of approximately 1×10^6 lymphocytes obtained from sensitized donors and an appropriate amount of antigen (usually about 20 μg) in medium 199. The controls receive an identical aliquot of cells, but no antigen. Exudates are collected and examined as described above. This procedure will give rise to good MDR reactions, with macrophage losses of approximately 60 to 70%. To achieve a 95% reduction similar to that obtained in an active MDR, it is necessary to double or triple the doses of transferred cells and antigen mentioned above.

Detection of Lymphokine Activity

To demonstrate lymphokine activity, the transferred cells may be enclosed in micropore chambers prior to insertion into the peritoneal cavities of the unimmunized recipients (for details, see ref. 16). In these experiments, in contrast to those described for macrophage chemotaxis, filters are used with pore sizes sufficiently small to exclude the passage of cells during the time period of the assay. Alternatively, one may substitute lymphocyte culture supernatant fluids for the combination of sensitized lymphocytes and antigen. The conditions for obtaining active supernatant fluids and their controls are identical to those described for MIF production.

REFERENCES

1. George, M. and Vaughan, J. H., *Proc. Soc. Exp. Biol. Med.* **111,** 154 (1962).
2. David, J. R., Al-Askari, S., Lawrence, H. S., and Thomas, L., *J. Immunol.* **93,** 264 (1964).
3. David, J. R. and David, R. A., *in Vitro Methods in Cell-Mediated Immunity,* (B. R. Bloom and P. R. Glade, Eds.), Academic Press, New York, 1971, p. 249.
4. Boyden, S., *J. Exp. Med.* **115;** 453 1962.
5. Ward, P. A., *J. Exp. Med.* **128;** 1201 (1968).
6. Snyderman, R., Altman, L. C., Hausman, M. S., and Mergenhagen, S. E., *J. Immunol.* **108,** 857 (1972).
7. Horwitz, D. A. and Garrett, M. A., *J. Immunol.* **106,** 649 (1971).
8. Ward, P. A. and Newman, L. J., *J. Immunol.* **102,** 93 (1969).
9. Ward, P. A., Remold, H. G., and David, J. R., *Science* **163,** 1079 (1969).
10. Ward, P. A., Remold, H. G., and David, J. R., *Cell. Immunol.* **1,** 162 (1970).
11. Nelson, D. S. and Boyden, S. V., *Med. Res.* **1,** 20 (1961).
12. Nelson, D. S. and Boyden, S. V., *Immunology* **6,** 26 (1963).
13. Nelson, D. S., *Macrophages and Immunity,* John Wiley and Sons, New York, 1969.
14. Bultmann, B., Bigazzi, P. L., Heymer, B., and Haferkamp, O., *Z. Immun.-Forsch.* **142,** 267 (1971).
15. Sonozaki, H. and Cohen, S., *J. Immunol.* **106,** 1404 (1971).
16. Sonozaki, H. and Cohen, S., *Cell. Immunol.* **2,** 341 (1971).

Appendix Three

Specific Adsorption and Affinity Chromatography of Cells

JOHN K. INMAN

Laboratory of Immunology, National Institute of Allergy and Infectious Diseases, National Institutes of Health, Bethesda, Maryland

There are many important applications in experimental immunology for methods that permit the specific elimination or isolation of highly specialized lymphoid cells from the complex populations occurring in tissue samples. Many of the methods used for separating cells exploit differences in general properties such as size, density, morphology, adhesiveness to a foreign surface, electrical charge, partition coefficient, etc. Such methods often fail to be adequately selective for populations of cells possessing recognized properties of interest. Separations based on properties more directly related to biological function should prove far more useful for studies of the specialized roles of recognized cell types in interacting cell systems.

The ability of some lymphocytes to secrete (or to give rise to other cells that secrete) specific antibodies correlates with the presence of antibody-like receptors of the same specificity which are situated on the outer cell membranes (1–7). Antigenic determinants on cell surfaces are associated with genetic factors, differentiative history, various specialized functions, or the identity of clones (of tumors). The accessibility of surface membrane structures makes possible some elegantly specific methods of cell separation based on interactions of cell surfaces with substances (or analogs) used for recognition of receptors or determinants. It is possible to bind substances functioning as antigens or antibodies to insoluble, solid structures and to separate cells by differential adsorption to these materials in a fashion at least roughly analogous to affinity chromatography or immunoadsorption. The feasibility of such an approach has been amply demonstrated in the past several years by a number of investigators whose experimental techniques are summarized below. Interesting findings have emerged from these studies bearing on the nature of cell receptors and the clonal selection theory. The use of insoluble carrier-bound reagents has allowed the recovery of specifically depleted or enriched cell populations that are viable, functional, and uncontaminated by special reagents.

SPECIFIC CELL DEPLETION BY USE OF ANTIGEN-COATED GLASS OR PLASTIC BEADS

Glass bead columns have been used by a number of investigators for functional separations as, for example, the nonspecific depletion of plaque-forming and other larger lymphoid cells from spleen cell suspensions (8). However, techniques for the separation of cells based mainly on the specificity of their receptors were developed and used extensively by Wigzell, Andersson, and coworkers (1,9–11). Nonporous beads of glass or polymethylmethacrylate plastic (Degalan) were coated with an antigen and employed in column-type adsorptive filtrations of free cell suspensions. The beads, averaging 200 to 250 μ in diameter, were first cleaned and allowed to stand in a solution of a protein antigen or protein-hapten conjugate at 45° for 1 hour, or at 4° overnight (9). A protein concentration of about 5 mg/ml resulted in maximal uptake by either glass or plastic. The unbound antigen was removed by thorough washing with saline and medium. The uptake of antigen per unit surface area was about 25 times higher for plastic than for glass beads. Further treatment of the beads with 10% normal mouse or rabbit serum was found to decrease substantially the number of cells that were nonspecifically retained by the columns (9).

Wigzell et al (9–11) passed suspensions of up to 3×10^8 lymph node, spleen, or marrow cells through 1.5 × 80–150 cm columns of antigen-coated beads at rates of 1 to 3 ml/minute. Cell suspensions were prepared in Eagle's medium in Earle's solution or Eagle's Minimal Essential Medium, and separations were carried out at 4°C. Eluted cells were effectively depleted of immunocompetent cells having the specificity of the bound antigen, and were not depleted of cells immunocompetent for other antigens. Many cells (approximately 50% applied to all columns) were retained nonspecifically by the beads. Some of the retained cells could be eluted without serious loss of viability by carefully shaking the beads in a glass vessel (10). Attempts to specifically elute antihapten memory cells from columns with a solution of a monovalent hapten analog were not successful, although pretreatment of the cells with the analog prevented subsequent specific depletion by the columns. The binding of cells to these beads thus appears to be chemically irreversible. It was proposed (9) that specific, reversible interactions involving simultaneous contacts of a single cell with perhaps as many as 10^2 to 10^4 antigen molecules occur initially which result in retarded passage of the specific cells. The greater period of time in contact with the beads then allows a nonspecific, irreversible binding to take place which can only be broken by mechanical forces. The slower, irreversible binding also would be responsible for the considerable nonspecific retention of cells as indicated by the importance of maintaining high flow rates in order to minimize this problem.

The binding of antigen to glass beads was effected by physical adsorption. Some denaturation of protein usually occurs during such a process, and therefore new determinants may be introduced. Although little or no leakage of antigen occurs with passage of medium through coated glass bead columns (9), Richter (12) found that eluted cells contained some ^{125}I-labeled antigen and that more antigen was removed by mechanical elution (shaking).

Other studies with coated glass bead columns, according to the methods of Wigzell et al, have been reported (12,13). Recently, coated polymethylmethacrylate (Delagan) beads were employed for the selective depletion of B from T lymphocytes by virtue of the former's putative receptors for antigen-antibody complexes (14).

SPECIFIC CELL DEPLETION BY USE OF AGAROSE BEAD DERIVATIVES

Agarose beads have been employed to a limited extent as a support medium for cellular immunoadsorption (15–18,31). Antigens, antibodies, haptens, or other substances possessing primary amino groups are readily linked by covalent bonds to agarose beads following treatment of the latter with aqueous cyanogen bromide at pH 11 (19,20). The problem of antigen leakage may not be solved entirely, because of slight instability in the support and attachment structures. However, this problem should be less serious than with glass or Degalan beads. A much wider range of derivative structures can be used, and denaturation of bound protein should be minimal.

Attempts to separate cells by passage through agarose bead columns have usually failed (15,21) because of excessive holdup of cells in the support structure. The fragile beads have many fragments and irregularities resulting from preparative procedures which can cause mechanical entrapment, although nonspecific "stickiness" may be the principal reason for nonrecovery. The use of agarose in cell fractionation has therefore been restricted to batch-type operations except for a few column experiments recently reported by Edelman et al (31).

Experiments involving the specific depletion of cells from lymph node suspensions by Davie and Paul (16) were carried out with hapten-protein conjugates and DNP-lysine bound to agarose beads (Sepharose 2B, Pharmacia Fine Chemicals). One milliliter of conjugated beads was gently agitated at 4° for 1 hour with 300×10^6 to 800×10^6 lymphoid cells in 5 ml of tissue culture medium containing 10% serum. Cells not retained were filtered off. The average recovery of nonretained cells was about 30%. The losses were not related to the bound antigen. Similar nonspecific losses were encountered with glass and plastic bead columns (10). For this reason, enrichment factors for any specific cells eluted from these supports are not likely to be greater than several-fold. However, from agarose adsorbent depletion studies alone, a number of interesting conclusions could be drawn with regard to differences in the specificities of cells mediating cellular and humoral immune responses (16–18).

ENRICHMENT OF SPECIFIC CELL POPULATIONS BY ELUTION FROM DERIVATIZED POLYACRYLAMIDE BEADS

One of the most promising approaches to specific cell fractionation to be reported thus far involves the use of small columns packed with chemically derivatized beads of cross-linked polyacrylamide gel. In studies reported by Wofsy and coworkers (22–24) affinity columns prepared with these beads allowed binding of cells with antihapten antibody specificities, while permitting free passage and essentially complete recovery of other cells. Nonspecific, irreversible binding or "sticking" of cells to polyacrylamide surfaces occurred to a very much smaller extent than with glass, plastic, or agarose supports. The specific and reversible nature of the binding of cells to functional groups on polyacrylamide was demonstrated by Wofsy et al (23,24) through their success in eluting and recovering adherent cells with the aid of free hapten. Eluted cells were found to be 80 to 90% viable by trypan blue exclusion. These cells, mostly small lymphocytes, were enriched many-fold with hapten-specific plaque formers in relation to the unfractionated cells. The latter were obtained from spleens of immunized mice (23). Similar enrichment was obtained with respect to specific precursor cells from the spleens of unimmunized animals (24).

For the purpose of preparing adsorbents with desired specificities, one may bind any of a large variety of substances, including proteins, to preformed polyacrylamide beads. Convenient methods for binding substances to intact beads through stable, covalent bonds were described by Inman and Dintzis (25). Starting with these methods, Truffa-Bachi and Wofsy (22) prepared a histamine derivative of spherical beads (Bio-Gel P-6, from Bio-Rad Laboratories) to which they then coupled diazotized aminophenyl glycosides. Large beads (over 0.6 mm diameter or 16 to 25 mesh) were used in order to minimize mechanical entrapment and allow rapid flow rates through the support channels.

Wofsy et al (23) immunized mice with hemocyanin-azophenyl β- lactoside. Spleen cell suspensions from these animals (10^8 cells in 20 ml of medium) were passed through 2-ml beds of polyacrylamide beads that had been coupled with the homologous hapten. The columns were washed with buffer (pH 7.2 Tris-Eagle's medium) at 5°C until essentially free of nonadherent cells, then equilibrated (room temperature) with $1.5 \times 10^{-5}M$ p-aminophenyl β-lactoside (Lac) hapten in buffer; adherent cells were eluted by passage of the hapten solution at 5°C. Thirty percent of the original number of anti-Lac plaque-forming cells were recovered in an eluate fraction that was enriched almost 500 times with respect to other cells.

In preliminary experiments with larger azophenyl lactoside columns Truffa-Bachi and Wofsy (22) were able to recover 95 to 100% of the cells introduced while retaining about 82% of the specific plaque formers. In these experiments subsequent hapten elution was not carried out. If cells were introduced and eluted with buffer containing $10^{-5}M$ Lac hapten, all anti-Lac plaque formers passed through. Cells secreting antibody against sheep red cells or azophenyl β-glucoside passed readily through Lac columns. Anti-Lac cells also passed through columns of beads bearing glucoside, di-, or trinitrophenyl groups. The elution of anti-Lac cells with hapten was best demonstrated on the small columns (2 or 2.5 ml) because of the technical difficulty in removing eluting hapten from relatively small numbers of cells. It was feasible to dilute small volumes of eluate to reduce hapten concentrations below the level that would interfere with plaque assays.

Hapten-specific precursor cells from spleens of unimmunized Balb/c mice were isolated by Henry et al (24) by elution from Lac-coupled polyacrylamide bead columns by essentially the same technique as described above. These cells were recognized by their ability to permit a primary antibody response to Lac hapten when transferred with immunogen to primed, irradiated recipients. The number of cells recovered by hapten elution ranged from 1000 to $4000/10^8$ cells, whereas 50,000 to $200,000/10^8$ were recovered from spleens of mice primed only once with antigen 2 to 6 weeks earlier. A few thousand specifically purified cells from unimmunized mice permitted an antihapten response equivalent to that produced by about 10^7 unfractionated normal spleen cells.

It should be possible to separate lymphoid cells by the interaction of surface membrane antigens with corresponding antibodies bound to polyacrylamide beads. Elution could be effected with soluble, cross-reacting analogs of the antigenic determinants, with unbound antibody, or by suitable mechanical agitation. Sell and An (26) employed the latter approach to elute rabbit peripheral blood lymphocytes retained on polyacrylamide beads to which had been coupled IgG from either antiimmunoglobulin, antilymphocyte, or antiallotype sera. The first two adsorbents allowed separations of lymphocytes from erythrocytes, and the latter permitted separations of lymphocytes on the basis of surface allotypic determinants. Separations were partial but significant. Cells were easily eluted by slight agitation (shaking) of the beads. These results suggest that rather weak interactions occurred. Better separations might be expected with this type of approach if specifically purified antibody were bound to the columns instead of whole IgG. The importance of this point was discussed by Wigzell and Andersson (see ref. 27, p. 300), who judged that, on the basis of results with antigen-coated columns, a minimum of 10^3 specific binding sites/μ^2 bead area would be required for selective retention of cells, a density of sites in a monolayer achieved only with highly purified antibodies.

A similar type of separation was described by Stobo et al (28) who coupled the carbohydrate-binding protein, concanavalin A, to a carboxylate derivative (25) of large polyacrylamide beads by means of a water-soluble carbodiimide. Murine spleen cells (0.3 to 3×10^8), filtered through columns of these beads (2.5 $\times$ 40 cm), were fractionated according to their capacity to bind radioiodinated concanavalin A. The nonadherent fraction of cells was diminished 2.4-fold in binding capacity over the initial population. Cells that were specifically eluted with 0.3 M α-methyl D-glucopyranoside, a low molecular weight inhibitor of concanavalin A, were enriched 5.2-fold in binding capacity.

FRACTIONATION OF CELLS ON OPEN-PORE POLYESTER-POLYURETHANE FOAMS

Reticulated (open-pore) polyester-polyurethane foam was found to be a suitable matrix for specific immunoadsorptive separations of erythrocytes or lymphocytes (29,30). Studies by Evans, Mage, and Peterson showed that nonspecific adsorption of cells to clean foam surfaces could be greatly minimized by first coating the foam with polyanions, such as gum arabic, or with proteins. The latter were held firmly to the foam surface by adsorptive forces and possibly also by covalent bonds. Specific immunoadsorbents were thereby prepared by precoating with protein or gum arabic solutions containing purified antibodies. Since much of the surface consisted of concavities, serious entrapment of cells would occur in normal column filtrations. The workers above solved this problem by the ingenious expedient of operating the foam columns in a horizontal position and maintaining a slow rotation about the long (horizontal) axis of the column. Nonadherent cells escaped from pores by simple gravity sedimentation and were transported horizontally through the column by a slow buffer flow.

Mage et al (29,30) were able to specifically bind and elute erythrocytes with haptens bound on their surfaces by employing foams coated with antibodies against these haptens. Elution was effected by removing the foam in precut sections or discs and gently squeezing them in buffer. The shearing forces of this treatment were just adequate to dislodge adherent cells. In other experiments (30) plaque-forming cells against sheep erythrocytes were enriched four to six-fold by passage through a foam column coated successively with antisheep erythrocyte antibody and sheep erythrocytes. No enrichment was obtained with a human erythrocyte-coated column. The coated, reticulated foam techniques may be well suited for studies where soluble inhibitors are not available for specific elution and where very gentle mechanical recovery of cells is required.

FIBER FRACTIONATION OF CELLS

Recently, a very interesting technique for cell separation was described by Edelman and coworkers (31). Cells were allowed to interact with chemically derivatized fibers having bound to them molecules such as antigens, antibodies, or lectins. Cells specifically adsorbed to taut segments of fiber were removed either by treatment with soluble inhibitors, or by the simple expedient of plucking the fibers. The latter mechanical method of cell recovery (as with the foam method discussed above) is especially advantageous in situations where interacting surface components are either unknown or are unavailable in soluble form.

Nylon fibers (size 50 sewing nylon) were partially hydrolyzed in dilute acid and coupled with specific proteins by means of a water-soluble carbodiimide (31). The treated fibers were mounted on polyethylene frames which were fitted into petri dishes and rocked with cell suspensions. Mouse thymocytes and erythrocytes were bound and eluted from fibers coated with concanavalin A. Immunocytes from unimmunized and specifically immunized mice and rabbits were bound according to their membrane specificity to dinitrophenyl or tosyl groups which were bound to fibers via a bovine serum albumin carrier (31). The number of specifically bound cells increased after immunization, and binding was specifically inhibited by soluble antigen or antiimmunoglobulin (32). A number of possible applications of these techniques, including adsorption to flat surfaces, for the manipulation of cells in culture, and for quantitative characterization of immune cell populations, are discussed by these authors (31,32).

CONCLUDING REMARKS

Selective adsorption and affinity chromatography of cells represents one of several approaches to the separation of cells based on highly specific interactions or properties of selected membrane structures. Reports on cell separation methods that depend on membrane properties have been reviewed recently by Wigzell and Andersson (27).

It is possible that the specificity of separations employing liquid-liquid phase partitioning, electrophoresis, or differential sedimentation can be markedly altered or controlled; appropriate chemical reagents can be designed in such a way as to bind selectively to membrane structures and at the same time alter more general membrane properties (e.g., electrical charge, sedimentation rates, etc.). Several examples suggesting this approach may be worth mentioning: Rhie and Sehon (33) demonstrated the feasibility of altering the electrophoretic mobility of cells possessing antidinitrophenyl (DNP) receptors by treatment of cell suspensions with DNP conjugates of strongly charged, synthetic polyanions or polycations. Brooks and his coworkers (34) established that surface charge, or a charge-associated property, is an important factor in determining the partition behavior of cells in two-polymer, aqueous-phase systems; thus, liquid-liquid phase partitioning of cells also could be specifically controlled by the kind of reagent just mentioned.

These methods leave an investigator with the problem of removing special reagents bound to cell surfaces after separations have been completed. Such a task may not be easy when one deals with polymers or polyelectrolytes. Cell chromatography with stable adsorbents does not present this problem. Specific adsorptions and desorptions, furthermore, can be carried out rapidly in media best suited for maintaining viability and function. Other separation methods usually require more time, and the systems place more demands and limitations on the composition of the medium.

Cell affinity chromatography and selective adsorption methods are still at an early stage of development. Many variations remain to be tried which involve (1) support materials and their geometry, (2) the spacing and surface density of functional groups, (3) the nature of functional groups and specificities used, and (4) the techniques of adsorption and elution. Results to date make it appear likely that specific, solid-phase reagents will soon find many important uses in research in cellular immunology.

REFERENCES

1. Wigzell, H., *Transplant. Rev.* **5**, 76 (1970).
2. Naor, D. and Sulitzeanu, D., *Nature (London)* **214**, 687 (1967).
3. Byrt, P. and Ada, G. L., *Immunology* **17**, 503 (1969).
4. Dutton, R. W. and Eady, J. D., *Immunology* **7**, 40 (1964).
5. Mitchison, N. A., *Cold Spring Harbor Symp. Quant. Biol.* **32**, 431 (1967).
6. Paul, W. E., Siskind, G. W., and Benacerraf, B., *J. Exp. Med.* **127**, 25 (1968).
7. Davie, J. M., Rosenthal, A. S., and Paul, W. E., *J. Exp. Med.* **134**, 517 (1971).
8. Plotz, P. H. and Talal, N., *J. Immunol.* **99**, 1236 (1967).
9. Wigzell, H. and Andersson, B., *J. Exp. Med.* **129**, 23 (1969).
10. Wigzell, H. and Mäkela, O., *J. Exp. Med.* **132**, 110 (1970).
11. Walters, C. S. and Wigzell, H., *J. Exp. Med.* **132**, 1233 (1970).
12. Richter, M., *J. Immunol.* **105**, 259 (1970).
13. Abdou, N. I. and Richter, M., *J. Exp. Med.* **130**, 141 (1969).
14. Basten, A., Sprent, J., and Miller, J. F. A. P., *Nat. New Biol.* **235**, 178 (1972).
15. Wofsy, L., Truffa-Bachi, P., and Lampson, L., in *Developmental Aspects of Antibody Formation and Structure* (J. Sterzl and H. Riha, Eds.), Proceedings Symposium Czechoslovakian Academy of Science, Prague, Academic Press, New York, 1970–71.
16. Davie, J. M. and Paul, W. E., *Cell. Immunol.* **1**, 404 (1970).

17. Davie, J. M. and Paul, W. E., *J. Exp. Med.* **134,** 495 (1971).

18. Davie, J. M., Rosenthal, A. S., and Paul, W. E., *J. Exp. Med.* **134,** 517 (1971).

19. Porath, J., Axen, R., and Ernbach, S., *Nature (London)* **214,** 1302; **215,** 1491 (1967).

20. Cuatrecasas, P., *J. Biol. Chem.* **245,** 3059 (1970).

21. Davie, J. M., personal communication.

22. Truffa-Bachi, P. and Wofsy, L., *Proc. Natl. Acad. Sci. U.S.A.* **66,** 685 (1970).

23. Wofsy, L., Kimura, J., and Truffa-Bachi, P., *J. Immunol.* **107,** 725 (1971).

24. Henry, C., Kimura, J., and Wofsy, L., *Proc. Natl. Acad. Sci. U.S.A.* **69,** 34 (1972).

25. Inman, J. K. and Dintzis, H. M., *Biochemistry* **8,** 4074 (1969).

26. Sell, S. and An, T., *J. Immunol.* **107,** 1302 (1971).

27. Wigzell, H. and Andersson, B., *Ann. Rev. Microbiol.* **25,** 291 (1971).

28. Stobo, J. D., Rosenthal, A. S., and Paul, W. E., *J. Immunol.* **108,** 1 (1972).

29. Evans, W. H., Mage, M. F., and Peterson, E. A., *J. Immunol.* **102,** 899 (1969).

30. Mage, M. G., Evans, W. H., and Peterson, E. A., *J. Immunol.* **102,** 908 (1969).

31. Edelman, G., Rutishauser, U., and Millette, C. F., *Proc. Natl. Acad. Sci. U.S.A.* **68,** 2153 (1971).

32. Rutishauser, U., Millette, C. F., and Edelman, G., *Fed. Proc.* **31,** 735 (1972).

33. Rhie, J. O. and Sehon, A. H., *Nat. New Biol.* **235,** 156 (1972).

34. Brooks, D. E., Seaman, G. V. F., and Walter, H., *Nat. New Biol.* **234,** 61 (1971).

Appendix Four

Methods in Lymphocyte Transformation Studies

ROCHELLE HIRSCHHORN, KURT HIRSCHHORN,
AND WILLIAM I. WAITHE

Assistant Professor of Medicine, New York University School of Medicine,
Arthur J. and Nellie Z. Cohen Professor of Genetics and Pediatrics, Mt. Sinai School of Medicine
of the City University of New York,
Assistant Professor of Medicine, Le Centre Hospitalier de l'Universite, Laval, Quebec.

The methods for culturing lymphocytes and measuring their response to different agents which are described here were originally developed for use with human peripheral blood lymphocytes.

With some minor modifications, the basic methodology has also been used successfully for the culturing of lymphocytes from other lymphoid tissues and species. Essentially these modifications consist of variations in cell concentration, media, source of serum, and mitogen dose.

However, the interaction of lymphocytes in culture and the kinetics

The original work reported was supported in part by U.S.P.H.S. Grants HD 02552 and A1 10343 and Genetics Center Grant GM 19443. Rochelle Hirschhorn is the recipient of an N.I.H. Research Career Development Award A1 70254, Kurt Hirschhorn is a Career Scientist of the New York City Health Research Council (I-513), and William I. Waithe is a Scholar of the Medical Research Council of Canada.

and thermodynamics of the reaction of activators with lymphocyte membranes are complex and poorly understood. Many other variables such as the area of the culture surface, the concentration of activator, and the ratio of activator molecules to cells affect the kinetics and intensity of the response (1,2). The time of peak response, or of detectable response, varies not only with cell type but also with the particular activator, as discussed in Chapter 6. Therefore the exact conditions for optimal responses of these cells should ideally be verified experimentally by the individual researcher in his own laboratory.

PREPARATION OF CELL SUSPENSIONS

If purified lymphocyte suspensions are not essential, unit gravity sedimentation provides a simple procedure for obtaining lymphocytes for culture. Blood is drawn into a sterile syringe containing sufficient heparin* to give a final concentration of 50 to 100 units/ml. The syringe is gently inverted several times to ensure mixing of the anticoagulant and then clamped at a 45° angle (with the needle pointing upward) at room temperature or preferably in a 37°C incubator. The red blood cells are allowed to sediment for 1 to 2 hours, and a new disposable needle (18 gauge) is placed on the syringe and bent at a 45° angle with the aid of the plastic sheath. The supernatant plasma and white blood cells are then delivered into a sterile tube by upward displacement of the syringe plunger. The extent of granulocyte contamination can be reduced either by taking only the top two-thirds of the supernatant or by prolonging the time of sedimentation to 4 hours.

The rate of red blood cell sedimentation and thus the yield of lymphocytes can be increased by the addition of 1 volume of a dextran solution (molecular weight 250,000 6% w/v in normal saline) to 9 volumes of blood, or of 1 to 2 volumes of Plasmagel to 3 volumes of blood. However, contamination with red blood cells and granulocytes is increased by these procedures and may well be a factor to be considered depending on the particular experimental requirements.

In certain types of experiments, the presence of nonlymphoid cells may be undesirable. In such cases, suspensions of purified lymphocytes can be obtained by several different methods. These can be divided into two groups, those that depend on the phagocytic or adhesive properties of the nonlymphoid white cells, and those that utilize differences in cell density or size.

---

*Materials used are listed and described at the end of this appendix.

Separation of Lymphocytes Utilizing Adhesion of Macrophages and Granulocytes

Suspensions of cells of which 95% or more are lymphocytes can be obtained by filtering the white-cell-rich plasma through columns of cotton or nylon wool (3,4).

The supernatant obtained after red blood cell sedimentation is pipetted into a 20- to 50-ml syringe containing sterile (autoclaved) loosely packed cotton. The plunger is replaced (taking care not to compress the cotton or force out the fluid) and the unit is incubated for 15 to 20 minutes, at 37°C. After incubation, the nonadherent cells and the plasma are squeezed out of the syringe by compression of the plunger. The amount of cotton to be used should be sufficient to retain just the volume of supernatant to be purified. A 50-ml syringe is convenient for approximately 10- to 25-ml volumes of supernatant plasma.

Alternatively, nylon fibers can also be used. The nylon wool (Fenwal) is washed in several changes of distilled water, dried, fluffed, and packed loosely into the barrel of a syringe or 60-ml separatory funnel and the unit is plugged, autoclaved, and stored at 37°C. Approximately 8 g of nylon wool in the funnel is sufficient for the plasma from 500 ml of blood. A syringe barrel may also be utilized as for cotton wool. The supernatant plasma is placed on the column and allowed to incubate for 15 to 30 minutes, at 37°C. If a syringe is used, a three-way disposable stopcock is attached to the syringe and used to adjust the rate of flow to 1 to 2 ml/minute. One to two volumes of warm (37°C) medium (c.g., MEM, Eagles BSS, etc.) is used to elute the remaining cells. Platelets can be partially removed by the addition of adenosine diphosphate (5 to 15 mcg/ml) to the white-cell-rich plasma. The plasma is decanted from the aggregated platelets and is then passed through the column as described.

Glass bead columns utilizing the methodology developed by Rabinowitz (5) have also been extensively used. In addition, methods based on the phagocytosis of ferromagnetic particles have been used to eliminate macrophages and polymorphonuclear leukocytes (6). Different classes of lymphocytes can also be selectively purified based on specific binding to insolubilized mitogens or antigens as well as to antigen-antibody complement complexes (7,8).

Separation of Lymphocytes based on Physical Properties

A relatively simple, reliable, and rapid procedure with a high yield of cells and relatively reasonably good purity utilizes a mixture of Ficoll

serum or plasma from the donor of the responding cell population or human AB serum. The final culture tube will contain a total of 2×10^6 lymphocytes in 0.2 ml of which, in the mixtures, one-half of the lymphocytes (10^5) are from each donor. The following combinations should be included (A = responder, Am = responder cells treated with Mitomycin C, Bm = stimulating cells treated with Mitomycin C):

Combination	Measures
A + Bm	Stimulation of donor A by donor B
A + Am	Background or nonspecific activity of A
Am + Bm	Efficacy of Mitomycin C inhibition
A + PHA	Ability of donor A's cells to respond

Whole Blood

In studying the response of some small mammals such as mice (14,15) it may be more practical to utilize whole blood for certain types of experiments. Although this cannot be recommended without reservations as a generally applicable method, a very high mitotic index can be obtained in cultures of whole human peripheral blood, and this is now standard methodology for preparing karyotypes. Essentially 1 to 2 drops of blood is obtained by finger puncture and added to 4 ml of cultured media. Care must be taken to wipe the skin prior to puncture with a rapidly evaporating antiseptic such as acetone. This method is suitable for morphologic evaluation but has also been utilized for biochemical evaluation. One part of whole blood is diluted in 5 parts of McCoys medium containing 10% FCS. Cultures are performed in 1.2-ml aliquots. Such cultures may be labeled for measurement of DNA synthesis and treated as described below, but the hemoglobin must be removed prior to counting of radioactivity. This may be achieved by washing the cells twice in 2% acetic acid (15,16).

MEASUREMENT OF THE MAGNITUDE OF RESPONSE

The changes in morphology and in macromolecular synthesis in stimulated lymphocytes have been discussed in detail in Chapter 6. These alterations provide the basis for practically all of the assays of the *in vitro* response in general use.

Morphology

Morphologic alterations were historically the first response to be measured and still provide a surprisingly reliable, reproducible, and inexpensive although tedious means of measurement (17,18). Essentially, cultured cells are processed as if for karyotypic analysis, thus staining nuclei specifically. Stimulated lymphocytes are identified by the reticular, pale, euchromatic appearance of the nucleus, the presence of the nucleoli, and the increased size of the nucleus.

Either an aliquot of a culture or a separate culture tube is centrifuged at 600 RPM, the media removed, and the cells gently suspended in 1 to 2 ml of a prewarmed 1% solution of sodium citrate. The first few drops of sodium citrate should be added slowly with gentle agitation between drops to disperse any clumps of cells. The suspension is immediately centrifuged at 35 to 40 $\times$ g for 8 minutes, the sodium citrate removed, and the cells dispersed again with agitation and drop-by-drop addition of 1 to 2 ml of freshly prepared fixative (absolute methanol-glacial acetic acid, 3:1). After standing for 10 minutes, the tubes are centrifuged (35 to 40 g $\times$ 8 minutes) and the fixative is removed, leaving about 1 to 2 drops over the cell pellet. The cells are then suspended in this residual fluid, drawn up into a fine-tipped Pasteur pipet, and placed dropwise in tiny drops onto an alcohol-cleaned slide so that they air-dry almost instantaneously. To decrease the sampling error resulting from nonrandom distribution of the larger stimulated cells on the slide, the cell suspension should be placed on the slide in overlapping droplets so that a given area on the slide will contain cells which tend to settle at the periphery of a drop. The slides are stained by immersion in 1% aceto-orcein for 30 minutes, followed by a rinse in 45% acetic acid, two successive 15-second immersions in tertiary butyl alcohol, 1 minute in tertiary butyl alcohol-xylene (1:1), and two successive 1-minute immersions in xylene. Coverslips are affixed to the slide using Permount. By this staining method early stimulated lymphocytes may be recognized by the euchromatic appearance of the DNA, which occurs before the appearance of visible nucleoli or appreciable change in cell size. Determination of the percentage of stimulated cells may also be performed on tetrachrome or Giemsa stained slides, but requires great care in evaluation.

Macromolecular Response

In using the rate of macromolecular synthesis as a measure of the degree of activation it must be remembered that the measured event is temporally and physiologically far removed from the event of activation of initially responsive lymphocytes in the culture. In cultures incubated for more than 2 days, cell death and simultaneous cell division also complicate the analysis of the response.

In addition to these theoretical and unavoidable variables, good precision is dependent on accurate pipetting of the cell suspensions with adequate mixing, proper technique to ensure sterility, and careful addition of labeled isotopes. Cells should not be damaged by excessive centrifugal forces or by too vigorous mixing during preparation of the cell suspension. Cell pellets should be suspended by gentle agitation of the tube or by gentle trituration with a wide-bore pipet.

A. PROTEIN SYNTHESIS—LABELING

The method that we have developed (19) for measuring protein synthesis provides a relatively early measure of the lymphocyte response (within 16 hours after the addition of PHA) and should also prove useful as an adjunct to other assays.

In the case of PHA-like activators that give an "early response," the increased rate of protein synthesis may be assayed as early as 10 to 16 hours after addition of the activator. The radioactive isotope (uniformly labeled ^{3}H-L-leucine, specific activity ca. 50 Ci/mM, or ^{14}C-L-leucine, specific activity ca. 300 mCi/mM) is added at the start of the incubation period. The label can be added to the portion of the suspension to be used for the determination of the rate of protein synthesis before distribution of the suspension into the culture tubes. The final concentration of label should be 1.0 μCi/ml. After 10 to 24 hours of incubation at 37°C, the cultures are terminated and the radioactivity of the protein is determined as described below.

For cultures requiring more than 24 hours of incubation the labeled leucine is added 4 hours prior to termination of the cultures. For cultures of 0.2-ml volume, the label is added as follows: The stock label solution is diluted in medium to a concentration of 3 μCi/ml. After warming this solution to 37°C, 0.1 ml is added to each tube (giving a final concentration of 1.0 μCi/ml), the cells are gently mixed, and the incubation is continued for 4 hours. The tubes should be kept at 37°C during addition of the label. When adding the label, care should be taken that it is added close to the fluid level in the tube so that it can be mixed with the cell suspension by gentle tapping of the tube. Loss of cell clumps by their adherence to the side of the tube above the level of medium during mixing will result in loss of precision. This is especially the case when a strongly leukoagglutinating activator such as PHA is being used. We have found that the use of a purified PHA (such as MR-68 of Burroughs Wellcome), which is less agglutinating, eliminates this problem.

Controls for the labeling of protein should include 2 tubes to which the PBSA (see below) is added before addition of the label. This control ("0 hour control") will serve as an indication of the degree of contamination of the isolated protein by unincorporated labeled amino acid. It is also advisable, especially for the initial tests of the method, to check the efficacy of the isotope isolation procedure by including culture tubes to which 20 to 30 mcg/ml of puromycin has been added 30 minutes before addition of the label. The radioactivity of these tubes should be 5% or less of that of comparable untreated cultures. In this assay, if labeled leucine of the specific activities mentioned above is used, it is not necessary, nor is it advisable, to use leucine-free medium.

B. DNA SYNTHESIS—LABELING

Measurement of the rate of DNA synthesis is the basis for the majority of assay systems commonly used in the quantitation of the lymphocyte response to activators. Two pathways exist in lymphocytes for the utilization of thymidine: The "salvage" pathway utilizes exogenous or preformed thymidine, while the *"de novo"* pathway provides thymidine by synthesis from formate and serine (20). Thus, the possibility must be kept in mind that the incorporation of exogenous labeled thymidine may vary with different conditions and may be different in various lymphoid cell types. In adapting a DNA assay, therefore, it may be wise to ascertain its validity by the simultaneous use of another measure of the culture's activity such as morphology or protein synthesis.

Additionally, there is evidence that the amount of exogenous thymidine present in most culture systems is inadequate to maintain sufficient intracellular pool levels for more than 4 to 6 hours. In some assays, relatively long labeling periods (up to 24 hours) have been used to overcome the objection of asynchrony of the DNA synthetic period in lymphocyte cultures. To maintain "saturating levels" of thymidine for more than 4 hours while using sufficient labeled isotope may require a specific activity of labeled thymidine high enough to cause radiation damage and reduction of the rate of DNA synthesis.

However, in practice, several different methods (21,22) appear to provide a relatively reproducible measure of DNA synthesis which correlates well with other parameters of stimulation.

The rate of synthesis of DNA is determined by measuring the incorporation of ^{3}H- or ^{14}C-thymidine into TCA precipitable material. Stimulating agents which give an early response may be assayed after 2 to 3 days of incubation, while the response of antigen stimulated and mixed lymphocyte cultures can be assayed at days 5 to 7. The cultures are labeled by adding 0.1 ml of medium containing 10 to 20 μCi/ml ^{3}H-thymidine (specific activity ca. 400 mCi/mM) 4 to 6 hours before termination. The same precautions discussed above in the terminal labeling procedure for protein synthesis apply here. Cultures that are terminated by addition of the PBSA before labeling should also be included as a control of the isotope isolation procedure. Alternatively, 0.15 μCi ^{14}C-thymidine 1 ml culture (specific activity ca. 54 mCi/mM) can be added for periods of 6 to 24 hours prior to harvesting, with reproducible results for certain types of experiments.

C. DOUBLE LABELING

Simultaneous determination of the rate of protein and DNA synthesis in the same culture tube can be accomplished by the addition of 0.1 ml of medium containing both isotypes (^{14}C-L-leucine and ^{3}H-thymidine), each at the concentration given above) 4 hours before termination of the cultures. If double labeling is to be performed, isolation of the labeled material should be carried out by a solubilization method (see below) to permit adequate separation of both isotopes in the scintillation counter.

D. RNA SYNTHESIS—LABELING

The increase in RNA synthesis is an early event in lymphocyte stimulation, and with the use of large numbers of cells, increases can be demonstrated within 4 hours of addition of early activators. Some of this increase is apparently due to enhanced uptake and phosphorylation of the labeled precursor uridine as well as to increased synthesis. Accurate measurement of RNA synthesis requires a tedious process of separation and measurement of RNA (23). However, the increase in RNA synthesis as measured by these more sophisticated measures correlates well with cruder measures. Thus 0.25 μCi of ^{14}C-uridine is added per milliliter of culture (specific activity ca. 54 mCi/mM) for the last 3 or 4 hours of culture and the cells harvested as for determination of DNA synthesis.

Termination of Labeling and Measurement of Radioactivity

Two procedures are presented for the isolation and determination of the radioactivity of the labeled protein or nucleoprotein: a filter method and a solubilization method. The choice of procedure will depend on the needs and preference of the investigator. The filter method permits scintillation counting in a simple toluene-based fluid and requires less processing time. However, certain characteristics of the filter method must be taken into account. Because of self-absorption by radioactive material on filters, the resultant energy spectra do not permit proper separation of the isotopes in the counter. This precludes the use of filters in double-labeled experiments (e.g., simultaneous determination of the rates of protein and DNA synthesis). In addition, the heterogeneous nature of the system prevents the use of external standards for the determination of counting efficiency. It should also be realized that the capacity of filters to retain a protein precipitate quantitatively is limited. Therefore the accuracy of the method for the specific experimental conditions should ideally be verified by determining the recovery of increasing amounts of labeled material in the range to be encountered and by determining the linearity of increasing amounts of labeled material in the presence of a constant amount of protein on the filter.

The solubilization method, although requiring more time from termination of the cultures to counting, can accommodate larger numbers of cells per sample (several milligrams of protein can be dissolved in 0.2 ml of Hyamine without significant loss of counting efficiency) and, with the use of automatic dispensers for the addition of reagents, is actually quite convenient for the handling of large numbers of samples. Determination of counting efficiency with external standards is possible and the ability to separate energy spectra permits the simultaneous determination of protein and DNA synthesis in the same culture tube.

Other and, in some cases, shorter methods have been published for the isolation and counting of labeled macromolecules from lymphocyte cultures. From our experience with other methods and with the development of those given here, we feel that the latter represent the best possible compromise between speed of assay and accuracy while retaining convenience for handling large numbers of samples. If other methods are to be used, it is important that they be verified as to accuracy and specificity before they are adopted for use.

Termination of Cultures

1.   Suspend the cells in the culture medium and add 2 ml of cold (4°C) PBS or PBSA to each tube. Centrifuge (400 × g, 10 minutes, preferably at 4°C) and remove the supernatant fluid by suction. To avoid possible loss of cells, leave a small amount of fluid above the cell pellet.
2.   Suspend the cells in the residual fluid and add cold PBS (2 ml for micro- and 5 ml for macrocultures) and wash them by repeating the procedure above. At this point, the cells may be stored frozen for determination of protein synthesis.

3.   Add 0.1 ml 1 N NaOH and heat (50 to 60°C) to dissolve the cells (requires about 10 minutes). Proceed with steps 4 to 6 for the filter method or steps 4 to 9a for the solubilization method. For evaluation of DNA and RNA using macromethods, this step can be omitted and a second wash substituted in cold isotonic saline.

A. FILTER METHOD

4.   Add 2.0 ml of cold TCA, mix, and allow to stand for 15 minutes at 4°C. The tubes can be kept overnight in the cold at this point for protein.

5.   Suspend the precipitate by vigorous agitation (the use of a vortex mixer or similar device is convenient for mixing) and collect the precipitate on a 0.45-μ Millipore filter by carefully pouring the sample into the funnel on a Millipore filter assembly or similar device for radiochemical analysis. Rinse the culture tube twice with 1-ml portions of TCA, adding these rinses to the funnel. Apply suction to the filter and rinse it with an additional 10 ml of TCA.

6.   Place the filters in scintillation vials, dry them (75°C for 30 to 60 minutes), and add 10 ml of toluene-based scintillation fluid. (If properly dried, the filters will become transparent upon addition of the scintillation fluid.)

B. SOLUBILIZATION METHOD

(1)   For Protein   4a.   Add 0.1 ml of a solution containing about 2.5 mg/ml of carrier protein (serum albumin or whole serum diluted in saline) and precipitate with TCA as in step 4 above.

5a.   Centrifuge at 1000 to 2000 × g for 10 minutes and remove the supernatant TCA.

6a.   Add 0.1 ml 1 N NaOH, mix, and dissolve the precipitate by heating (50 to 60°C) with occasional mixing (takes about 10 minutes). This step may be omitted for determination of DNA synthesis.

7a.   Repeat the TCA precipitation as in step 4 of the filter method and remove the TCA as in step 5a.

8a.   Add 0.2 ml hydroxide of Hyamine and heat (50 to 60°C) until the precipitate is dissolved. Occasional agitation of the tubes will facilitate solution of the precipitate.

9a.   Add 0.5 ml of methanol, mix vigorously, and transfer the sample to a scintillation vial by pouring. Rinse the tube with an additional 0.5 ml of methanol and add this to the vial. Add 10 ml of modified Bray's solution and mix.

(2) For Nucleic Acid   4a.   For determination of RNA and DNA synthesis the solubilization in NaOH may be omitted but a third precipitation in TCA is added.

4b.   Add 5 ml of cold TCA to washed cell pellet.

5b.   Centrifuge at 1000 to 2000 × g for 15 minutes, remove the supernatant TCA.

6b.   Vortex the precipitate and resuspend in 5 ml (for macroculture) ice cold TCA. Centrifuge as in 5b.

7b.   Repeat the TCA precipitation as in 6b. The tube may be carefully and briefly inverted at this point onto tissue paper to drain.

8b.   Add 0.2 ml hydroxide of Hyamine and proceed as in 8a.

9b.   The solution may be transferred with methanol to Bray's solution as in 9a. Alternatively, it may be transferred directly to counting vials using toluene, PPO, POPOP, 15 to 20 ml (e.g., Permafluor).

MATERIALS

The following is a list of the supplies used in the assay procedures described in this appendix.

1.   *Heparin.*   Lyophilized heparin without preservative is available from Connaught Medical Research Laboratories, Toronto, Canada. Heparin preserved with benzoyl alcohol (i.e., Liquaemin sodium 50, Organon Inc., West Orange, N.J.) is also satisfactory, but phenol- or cresol-preserved heparin should not be used.

2.   *Medium.*   RPMI 1640 or Eagle's minimum essential medium (MEM) is supplemented with 10 to 20% (v/v) serum (fetal calf, homologous or autologous), 100 units/ml penicillin, and 100 mcg/ml streptomycin. Although the media already contain glutamine, unless they are purchased and stored frozen, fresh glutamine should be added. One milliliter of a stock solution of 200 mM glutamine (stored frozen) is added to 100 ml of medium before use. Sterile stock solutions of antibiotics and glutamine suitable for tissue culture are available commercially (i.e., Grand Island Biological Company, Grand Island, N.Y.).

3.   *Phosphate-buffered saline.*

	g/l
NaCl	8.0
$Na_2HPO_4 \cdot 7H_2O$	2.17
KH_2PO_4	0.2
KCL	0.2

(The pH is adjusted to 7.4.)

Phosphate-buffered saline with sodium azide (PBSA). Use 7.1 NaCl and 1.0 NaN$_3$ in the formula above. Phosphate-buffered saline is also available commercially.

4.   Plasmagel is obtained from Labatoire Roger Bellon, Neuilly, France.

5.   Dextran, molecular weight 250,000, can be obtained from Pharmacia Upsala, Sweden.

6.   Nylon wool is obtained as "scrubbed nylon fiber," catalog No. FT-242 from Fenwal Laboratories, Morton Grove, Illinois.

7.   Adenosine Diphosphate—1.5 mg/ml of medium is filter sterilized, divided into 1- to 2- ml aliquots and stored frozen. Solution can be kept frozen for 1 to 2 months but should not be refrozen.

8.   Hypaque (brand of sodium diatrizoate, U.S.P.) is obtained from Winthrop Laboratories, New York City, as a 50% sterile solution.

9.   Ficoll is obtained from Pharmacia Fine Chemicals, Upsala, Sweden.

10.   Culturing tubes, if plastic, *must* be specifically of tissue culture quality. Glass reusable tubes should be washed in a nontoxic detergent such as 7-X (Linbro Chemicals, New Haven, Conn.) and extensively rinsed in distilled H$_2$O. Disposable tubes (either glass or plastic) are highly recommended if feasible. Liners of screw-top caps should be of nontoxic material.

11.   *Trichloroacetic acid (TCA).*   6% (w/v) (Containing 65 mg/l leucine, if protein synthesis is measured.) The amount of unlabeled ("carrier") material is approximately 1000-fold the concentration of radioactive forms of the precursors present in the cultures.

12.   *Scintillation fluid: Toluene-based fluid.*   Five grams of 2,5-diphenyloxazole (PPO) and 0.5 g of *p*-bis(-2-(5-phenyloxazolyl))-benzene/liter of toluene. Toluene-based fluid is also available commercially prepared (i.e., Permafluor from Packard, Warrenville, Downers Grove, ill.).

Bray's solution (modified by omission of ethanol).

	g/l
Naphthalene	60.0
PPO	4.0
Dimethyl POPOP	0.2
Ethylene glycol	20.0 ml
p-Dioxane	q.s. 1.0 liter

13.   *Aceto-orcein stain.*   (Available from Grand Island Biological Co., Grand Island, N. Y..) Dissolve 1.0 g of orcein completely prepared in 45 ml of glacial acetic acid by boiling for 30 minutes. (Use a flask fitted

with a reflux condenser.) Add 55 ml of distilled water and continue to boil for 30 minutes. Filter the stain after it has been standing for about 24 hours.

REFERENCES

1. Leventhal, B. and Oppenheim, J. J., in *Proceedings of the Third Annual Leukocyte Culture Conference* (W. D. Rieke, Ed.), Appleton-Century-Crofts, New York, 1967, pp. 13–29.
2. Moorhead, J. F., Connolly, J. J., and McFarland, W., *J. Immunol.* **99**, 413 (1967).
3. Ling, N. R., Ed., in *Lymphocyte Stimulation,* North-Holland Publishing, Amsterdam, 1968, pp. 55–61.
4. Greenwalt, T. J., Gajewski, M., and McKenna, J. L., *Transfusion,* **2**, 221 (1962).
5. Rabinowitz, Y., *Blood* **23**, 811 (1964).
6. Lichtenstein, B., Paseltiner, L., Weingard, R., and Widmark, R., Technicon Bulletin.
7. Allan, D., Auger, J., and Crumpton, M. J., *Nature* **236**, 23 (1972).
8. Bianco, C. and Nussenzweig, V., *Science* **173**, 154 (1971).
9. Boyum, A., *Scand. J. Clin. Lab. Invest.,* Suppl. 97.
10. Shortman, K., *Aust. J. Exp. Biol. Med. Sci.* **46**, 375 (1968).
11. Noble, P. B. and Cutts, J. H., *J. Lab. Clin. Med.* **72**, 533 (1968).
12. Oettgen, H. F., Silber, R., Miescher, P. A., and Hirschhorn, K., *Clin. Exp. Immunol.* **1**, 771 (1966).
13. Bach, F. and Voynow, N. K., *Science* **153**, 545 (1966).
14. Park, B. H. and Good, R. A., *Proc. Natl. Acad. Sci.* **69**, 371 (1972).
15. Junge, U., Hoekstra, J., Wolfe, L., and Deinhardt, F., *Clin. Exp. Immunol.* **7**, 431 (1970).
16. Quagliata, F., personal communication.
17. Nowell, P. C., *Cancer Res.* **20**, 562 (1960).
18. Hastings, J., Freedman, S., Rendon, O., Cooper, H. L., and Hirschhorn, K., *Nature* **192**, 1214 (1961).
19. Waithe, W., Hathaway, P., and Hirschhorn, K., *Clin. Exp. Immunol.* **9**, 903 (1971).
20. Wolberg, W. H., *Clin. Exp. Immunol.* **8**, 177 (1971).
21. Schellekens, P. and Eijsvoogel, V. P., *Clin. Exp. Immunol.* **3**, 571 (1968).
22. Sample, W. F. and Chretien, P. B., *Clin. Exp. Immunol.* **9**, 419 (1971).
23. Cooper, H. L. and Rubin, A. D., *Blood* **25**, 1014 (1968).

Appendix Five

Cytotoxicity Reactions Mediated by Antigen-Activated Rat and Mouse Lymphocytes

NANCY H. RUDDLE

Department of Microbiology, Yale University School of Medicine, New Haven, Connecticut.

Sensitized lymphocytes kill innocent bystander cells in the presence of specific antigen (1–3). This cytotoxic reaction is an *in vitro* manifestation of delayed hypersensitivity in the rat as proved by its correlation with positive delayed skin reactions, carrier specificity, time course, and apparent absence of a requirement for complement components (2). Although the criteria that have been applied to the rat have not been applied as rigidly to all other species, cytotoxicity is also considered an *in vitro* correlate of delayed hypersensitivity in mice (4,5), guinea pigs, and humans (5) and is mediated by thymus-derived lymphocytes (6).

Antigens that have been used in lymphocytotoxicty tests have included those that are an integral part of the target cell such as transplantation antigens (7), tumor-specific antigens (8), and organ-specific antigens (9), and those that are added to the culture as soluble antigens, such as purified protein derivative and egg albumin (1,2), viruses such as mumps (10), and organ-specific antigens such as basic protein (11).

The mechanism of the cytotoxic reaction has been studied. It is due at least in part to a soluble mediator, called lymphotoxin by Granger (12), produced by sensitized lymphocytes in response to specific antigen. The final killing of fibroblasts is the result of at least three reactions: The first is a specific interaction of antigen with sensitized lymphocytes which can occur within an hour; lymphotoxin becomes detectable in the supernatant after approximately 8 hours (3,13); gross evidence of target cell death is seen by 24 hours. Toxicity can be assessed by adding sensitized lymphocytes and antigen directly to target cells or by harvesting supernatants after interaction of lymphocytes and antigen and then adding such supernatants to target cells.

Methods for assessing target cell death have been reviewed recently (14) and include ^{51}Cr release, clonal inhibition, inhibition of target cell DNA synthesis, inhibition of target cell protein synthesis, plaques in the target cell monolayer, and enumeration of surviving target cells with a hemocytometer or by Coulter counter. Both the Coulter counter method and isotope release methods measure direct lysis of target cells. However, the Coulter counter method of evaluating unirradiated target cells as described in the accompanying procedure is also a way of assessing inhibition of target cell proliferation.

The use of an appropriate target cell is important for successful evaluation of lymphocytotoxicity. Many cell types have been used with tremendous differences in sensitivity. For example, it has been noted that embryonic fibroblasts are less sensitive after many passages (11), and A9 cells are more sensitive than primary fibroblasts. The size of the target cell is important, as it must be large enough to be distinguished from the lymphocyte by the Coulter counter. Methods outlined below use syngeneic or allogeneic rat embryo fibroblasts or A9 cells with rat lymphocytes, and syngeneic or allogeneic mouse embryo fibroblasts or A9 cells with mouse lymphocytes.

Coulter counter assessment of target cell death after lymphocyte attack has some advantages over other methods. The most important one is the absence of background cytotoxicity (which is not the case with ^{51}Cr release). Because the machine distinguishes between cells on the basis of size differences, both lymphocytes and target cells can be present throughout the incubation period. Other advantages include economy, reproducibility, and applicability to any antigen which can be used to induce delayed hypersensitivity. The only limitation is that the antigen cannot be toxic (or stimulatory) to tissue culture cells. The major drawbacks of the method, as outlined below, are the incubation period (48 hours) and the number of lymphocytes (1×10^7). Micromethods have been developed (15) but they are tedious to evaluate and not as reproducible as the method described here. One should be aware of inherent toxicity of certain unsensitized cell populations [such as polymorphonuclear leukocytes and some peritoneal exudate cells (16)], and therefore include proper controls. These controls should also rule out the possibility that the antigen itself is toxic.

PROCEDURE FOR COULTER COUNTER EVALUATION OF LYMPHOCYTOTOXICITY

Procedures for sensitization of mouse and rat lymph node cells with egg albumin in complete Freund's adjuvant are included here, though many other antigens have and can be used. Target cells include syngeneic and allogeneic mouse and rat embryo fibroblasts and A9 cells.

In these studies, we used Lewis and DA rats obtained from Microbiological Associates, Bethesda, Maryland, and C57Bl/6, CAF₁ (Balb/c × A/J), and CDF₁ (Balb/c × DBA/2) mice obtained from Jackson Laboratory, Bar Harbor, Maine. Tubercle bacilli of the C, Dt, and PN strains are obtained from The Ministry of Agriculture, Fisheries and Food, Central Veterinary Laboratory, Weybridge, Surrey, England. Purified protein derivative (PPD) is also obtained through the Central Veterinary Laboratory. Egg albumin, 5x crystallized, is obtained from Nutritional Biochemicals Corporation, Cleveland, Ohio. Complete Freund's adjuvant consists of 6 mg/ml tubercle bacilli in 85% Bayol F (Humble Oil and Refining Company, Pearl River, N.J.), 15% Arlacel A (Atlas Chemical Company, Wilmington, Delaware).

Rats are injected in the right rear footpad with 0.1 ml of 100-µg egg albumin in complete Freund's adjuvant or 300 µg tubercle bacilli in Bayol F. Mice are injected subcutaneously in the tail with 0.04 ml 3-mg/ml tubercle bacilli in oil (120 µg) or 200-µg egg albumin in complete Freund's adjuvant.

Culture Media and Diluents

All media and additives used in our laboratory are obtained from Grand Island Biological Company, Grand Island, New York. Rat fibroblasts are maintained in complete medium, which consists of Minimum Essential Medium (Eagle's) with Earle's base, with 10% fetal calf serum (heat inactivated, 56°C, 30 minutes), 2 mM L-glutamine, 0.5% lactalbumin hydrolysate, and antibiotic-antimycotic solution (100 units penicillin, 100 µg streptomycin, 0.25 µg fungizione/ml). Medium for mouse fibroblasts and A9-L cells consists of Minimum Essential Medium (Eagle's) with Earle's base, 10% fetal calf serum, 2 mM L-glutamine, 50 units/ml penicillin, and 50 μg/ml streptomycin. Viokase solution is prepared by adding 10 ml 2.5% Viokase to 90 ml Madin-Darby solution. Madin-Darby contains 8 g NaCl, 0.4 g KCl, 0.58 g NaHCO₃, 1.0 g dextrose, and 0.2 g versene in 1000 ml distilled H₂O.

Preparation of Primary Rat Fibroblasts

A rat embryo (15 days gestation) is removed from a pregnant female and placed in a petri dish containing 37°C complete medium. Membranes are removed, and the embryo is rinsed twice with warm medium and cut into small pieces with scissors. The pieces are placed in a 125-ml Erlenmeyer flask containing 60 ml prewarmed (37°C) Viokase solution. A stirring bar is inserted in the flask and the pieces are stirred on a magnetic stirrer in a 37°C incubator. After 10 minutes, 20 ml of the solution (which contains many red cells) is removed and discarded. Twenty milliliters of fresh Viokase solution is added and the flask placed on the magnistirrer for 20 minutes. Forty milliliters of the supernatant which contains cells is removed and placed in a centrifuge with 4 ml fetal calf serum on ice. Forty milliliters of fresh Viokase is added to the flask and stirred for 20 minutes. This is repeated twice, so that there are 3 tubes which contain cells. The tubes are spun at 600 g for 10 minutes. The supernatant is discarded and the cells pooled and suspended in 12 ml complete medium. One milliliter of cells is added to a 75-cm² Falcon flask that has been gassed with 95% air, 5% CO₂ and contains 20 ml medium. The flasks are incubated at 37°C. The medium is changed at 24 and 48 hours and every 48 hours thereafter. The cells are transferred at confluency.

Preparation of Primary Mouse Fibroblasts

Essentially the same procedure for preparing rat fibroblasts as above is followed. However, because the mouse embryos are considerably smaller, more embryos (4) are removed from the pregnant female. The Erlenmeyer flask is 60 ml and only 20 ml Viokase solution is added to it. The first 10 ml is removed and discarded, 20 ml fresh Viokase is added, and the stirring is continued. After 15 minutes, 20 ml Viokase and cells is removed and saved. This step is repeated twice. The rest of the procedure is the same as that with rat cells.

A9 Cells

A subline of mouse L cells was obtained as a gift from Dr. Frank Ruddle.

Transfer of Cell Lines

All target cells are transferred once a week for routine maintenance. Medium is removed with a pipet. The cell sheet is rinsed once with 10 ml warm (37°C) Viokase solution. The Viokase is removed and discarded. Fifteen milliliters of fresh Viokase solution is added and the cells are incubated at 37°C for 10 to 15 minutes. The cell suspension is removed and placed in a centrifuge tube. The flask is rinsed once with fresh medium which is added to the tube. The cells are spun at $600 \times g$ for 10 minutes, resuspended in fresh medium, and counted; 2 $\times 10^6$ cells are added to 20 ml fresh medium in gassed 75-cm^2 Falcon flasks. For experimental use, target cells are seeded (2 $\times 10^5$ mouse or rat fibroblasts or 1.5 $\times 10^5$ A9 cells) in 4 ml medium in 35-cm^2 plastic flasks in an atmosphere of 95% air, 5% CO_2.

Preparation of Lymph Node Cells

Rats are killed with ether; mice are killed by cervical dislocation. All nodes are removed from normal animals. Only draining inguinal nodes are removed from sensitized animals. The nodes are trimmed of fat and placed in 37°C HBSS. The nodes are placed in fresh HBSS in a glass petri dish at room temperature and the cells teased out with rakes. The cell suspension is pipetted into 15-ml centrifuge tubes, and spun at $250 \times g$ for 10 minutes. The supernatant is discarded. Fresh HBSS is added. The cells are spun again at $250 \times g$ for 10 minutes. The supernatant is discarded, the cells resuspended in complete medium, and counted in a hemocytometer with trypan blue (0.2%) to determine viability.

Addition of Lymph Node Cells and Antigen to Target Cells

Lymph node cells (5×10^6 to 2×10^7) are added to target cells in 35-cm^2 flasks that were prepared 2 days previously. Antigen is added at the same time, usually at a concentration of 25 μg/ml. Each culture is set up in duplicate with proper controls. The latter include target cells in the presence and absence of antigen, target cells and normal lymphocytes in the presence and absence of antigen, and target cells with sensitized lymphocytes in the presence and absence of antigen.

Preparation of Cytotoxic Factor and Addition to Target Cells

Sensitized or normal lymph node cells (3×10^7 to 4×10^7) are placed in 4 ml medium in a 60×15-mm Falcon plastic tissue culture dish. Antigen ($25 \mu g/ml$) dissolved in complete medium is swinny-filtered and added to the cultures which are then incubated for 24 hours in a moist atmosphere of 95% air, 5% CO_2. The supernatants are harvested and spun 3 times at $600 \times g$ to remove all cells. Medium is removed from target fibroblasts prepared 2 days before, and cytotoxic factor, diluted with fresh complete medium, is added to the fibroblasts.

Evaluation of Fibroblast Survival with the Coulter Counter

Cell size distribution curves are determined for target cells (rat fibroblasts, mouse fibroblasts, A9-L cells) and lymphocyte populations individually. Following these determinations, known mixtures of target cells and lymph node cells are counted. The target cells can be counted at a lower aperture current setting than the lymphocytes due to their greater volume. The threshold can be set to exclude lymphocytes. The machine we used (Model A, 100μ pore) is set at aperture current 2 and threshold 25 for rat and mouse fibroblasts, threshold 15 for A9-L cells.

Target cell survival is determined in experimental and control flasks 3 days after addition of lymph node cells and antigen (or lymphotoxin). The medium is poured from each flask. The flask is rinsed twice with prewarmed HBSS, which removes most of the lymphocytes and floating debris; 2.5 ml prewarmed (37°C) Viokase solution is added to each flask. After 15 minutes at 37°C the flasks are rocked gently to dislodge cells. If the cells do not come off, the flasks are incubated an additional 10 minutes. The cells are pipetted approximately 15 times with a plastic disposable pipet to dislodge any that might remain attached to the surface and to ensure a single-cell suspension. One milliliter of cell suspension is added to 19 ml counting fluid (Isoton, Scientific Products). Each suspension is counted 3 times at that setting which includes target cells and excludes lymphocytes. Cytotoxicity (%) is calculated as 100 - ($A/B \times 100$), where A is the number of fibroblasts that survive in the presence of sensitized lymph node cells and antigen, and B is the number of fibroblasts that survive in the presence of normal lymph node cells and antigen.

REFERENCES

1. Ruddle, N. H. and Waksman, B. H., Cytotoxicity mediated by antigen and lymphocytes in delayed hypersensitivity. I. Characterization of the phenomenon, *J. Exp. Med.* **128**, 1237 (1968).

2. Ruddle, N. H. and Waksman, B. H., Cytotoxicity mediated by antigen and lymphocytes in delayed hypersensitivity. II. Correlation of the *in vitro* response with skin reactivity, *J. Exp. Med.* **128**, 1255 (1968).

3. Ruddle, N. H. and Waksman, B. H., Cytotoxicity mediated by soluble antigen and lymphocytes in delayed hypersensitivity. III. Analysis of mechanism, *J. Exp. Med.* **128**, 1267 (1968).

4. Ruddle, N. H., Cellular immunity in the mouse, *Fed. Proc.* **32**, 1039 (1973).

5. Granger, G. A. Schaks, S. J., Williams, T. W., and Kolb, W. P., Lymphocyte *in vitro* cytotoxicity: Specific release of lymphotoxin-like materials from tuberculin-sensitive lymphoid cells, *Nature (London)* **221**, 1155 (1969).

6. Cerottini, J. C., Nordin, A. A., and Brunner, K. T., *In vitro* cytotoxic activity of thymus cells sensitized to alloantigens, *Nature (London)* **227**, 72 (1970).

7. Wilson, D. B., Quantitative studies on the behavior of sensitized lymphocytes *in vitro*. I. Relationship of the degree of destruction of homologous target cells to the number of lymphocytes and to the contact in culture and consideration of the effects of isoimmune serum, *J. Exp. Med.* **122**, 143 (1965).

8. Vailler, D., Donner, M., Vailler, J., and Burg, C., Release of lymphotoxins by spleen cells sensitized against mouse tumor-associated antigens, *Cell. Immunol.* **6,** 466 (1973).

9. Winkler, G. F., *In vitro* demyelination of peripheral nerve induced with sensitized cells, *Ann. N. Y. Acad. Sci.* **122**, 287 (1965).

10. Speel, L. F., Osborn, J. E., and Walker, D. L., An immunocytopathogenic interaction between sensitized leukocytes and epithelial cells carrying a persistent-noncytocidal myxovirus infection, *J. Immunol.* **101**, 409 (1968).

11. Ellison, G. W., Waksman, B. H., and Ruddle, N. H., Experimental autoallergic encephalomyelitis and cellular hypersensitivity *in vitro*, *Neurology* **21**, 778 (1971).

12. Granger, G. A. and Williams, T. W., Lymphocyte cytotoxicity *in vitro*: activation and release of a cytotoxic factor, *Nature (London)* **218**, 1253 (1968).

13. Yoshinaga, M., Waksman, B. H., and Malawista, S. E., Cytochalasin B inhibits lymphotoxin production by antigen-stimulated lymphocytes, *Science* **176**, 1147 (1972).

14. Ruddle, N. H., Approaches to the quantitative analysis of delayed hypersensitivity, *Curr. Top. Microbiol. Immunol.* **57**, 75 (1972).

15. Takasugi, M. and Klein, E., A microassay for cell-mediated immunity, *Transplantation* **9**, 219 (1970).

16. McLaughlin, J. F., Ruddle, N. H., and Waksman, B. H., Relationship between activation of peritoneal cells and their cytopathogenicity, *J. Reticuloend. Soc.* **12**, 293 (1972).

Index